Linguistic Semantics

Linguistic Semantics

William Frawley
University of Delaware

LEA

LAWRENCE ERLBAUM ASSOCIATES, PUBLISHERS

1992   Hillsdale, New Jersey   Hove and London

Lawrence Erlbaum Associates, Inc., Publishers
365 Broadway
Hillsdale, New Jersey 07642

Library of Congress Cataloging-in-Publication Data
Frawley, William, 1953–
    Linguistic semantics / William Frawley.
      p. cm.
    Includes bibliographical references and index.
    ISBN 0-8058-1074-9 (c). — ISBN 0-8058-1075-7 (p)
    1. Semantics. I. Title.
P325.F67 1991
401'.43—dc20   91-36624
                         CIP

Printed in the United States of America
10 9 8 7 6 5

To the Memory of My Father
William J. Frawley

Contents

Introduction

Linguistic Semantics got its real start some 30 years ago, when I used to take a break from baseball practice and puzzle over the warning on a sign bolted to the nearby school building: "Anyone caught damaging this property shall be called a disorderly person." "Well," I thought, "that's not much of a punishment, is it? If that's all they mean . . . " Who is *anyone*? Is a policeman, or a dog, *anyone*? Must you be *caught* in the act? If I spit on the building, has *damaging* occurred? What is *this property*, the building, or the sign itself? If I am far away from *this property*, and it is then no longer *this* property, but *that* property, does the issue change? When is *shall*, and who does this name-calling? And, of course, what is a *disorderly person*, and what does it matter to be called something like this? I never did anything to the building, but I did wonder about what all this could possibly signify.

In large measure, this anecdote typifies what this book is all about: linguistic meaning. What do expressions represent? Does the meaning depend on who says the expressions and the context in which they are said? Why does meaning take certain forms? Could it all have been said otherwise?

The importance of linguistic meaning is its connection to comprehension. The gist of my puzzlement with the warning sign is that I was trying to *understand* it. I wanted to match my model of the world with the model of the world that was somehow "behind" the expressions written on the sign. This predicament is one of the basic human paradoxes: How can we ever make sense of another person's words when they reflect experiences we never, nor can ever, have? Conversely, how can we presume to talk to another person when what we say is merely symptomatic of our private worlds? How can anyone else get the meaning of our expressions and understand us? These problems are compounded by the fact that other languages have different systems of giving form to meaning and these differences obviously affect what can be understood and expressed at all.

We might just throw up our hands here and shuffle off into existential heaven if there were not indisputable universals of language—predictable regularities in sounds (phonology), surface form (syntax and morphology), and meaning (semantics) (and thus, by implication, in comprehension). These universals come from the fact that language is ultimately a product of our mental systems, and at the level of the necessary mental structures for expression and understanding, *we are all the same*. This is not to say that there is no human variation, but only that humans are at least as much exactly alike as they are different. In fact, the similarities are so fundamental and so critical to language that even differences across languages are highly constrained and quite predictable.

So, we should not throw up our hands in desperation because there are many things that we can predict about meaning in *any language*. This book is a manual of these predictions. Just as it would be a disaster to go into battle unarmed, it would be senseless to look into linguistic meaning without reliable expectations about what we will find. There are no bare facts in the universe; all pursuits, scientific or otherwise, require certain predispositions. *Linguistic Semantics* is a handbook of, I hope, the correct predispositions to have about linguistic meaning.

I have written *Linguistic Semantics* because, in my view, there is currently no introduction to linguistic meaning that is comprehensive, up-to-date, and readable. Lyons's *Semantics I & II* (1977), an admirable mainstay in the field, is heavily philosophical, and not always students' favorite reading material; it is also out-of-date in many places. Palmer's *Semantics: A New Outline* (1976) is extremely cogent, but it is true to its title and always needs to be supplemented. One of the most recent surveys, Allan's two-volume *Linguistic Meaning* (1986), is quite readable, but concentrates mostly on pragmatic meaning and thus often does not address what I take to be the seminal issues in semantics.

There is also no shortage of recent texts on formal semantics. Bach's *Informal Lectures on Formal Semantics* (1989) (which is required reading in my semantics course) and Chierchia and McConnell-Ginet's *Meaning and Grammar* (1990) are exceptional works. But the problem I have with formal semantics, as I explain in chapter 2, is that I do not think that logical form is the only, or even the required, place to look for linguistic meaning. This is not to say that formal semantics is wrong. On the contrary, formal semantics teaches us to look for the necessary features of meaning and to follow a rigorous method in doing so. It just turns out that, as Philip Johnson-Laird demonstrates in his excellent *Mental Models* (1983), formal logic is not mental logic, and we have decided to pursue universals of meaning because we are all the same in the relevant *mental structures*. In any case, if I understand some of the recent formal literature, then even formal semanticists are becoming increasingly partial to the doctrine of mental logic. At the end of his book, Bach (1989) suggests a linking of cognitive and formal approaches to meaning; in theoretical circles, I gather there is now talk of how logical form interacts with so-called "real world semantics."

Linguistic Semantics is more about mental logic and "real world semantics" than logical form, though logical matters are given their due in many places. It is also designed to be thorough, true to the data of natural languages, current, and accessible—in a single volume.

In writing this book, I have tried not to do two things. First, I wanted to avoid the trap of writing a textbook from other textbooks. A convenient way to survey a field is to read all the other surveys and then write your own. Usually, this results in some grand restatement of the same old theories with the same old data recycled as illustrations. I have read all the textbooks, but some time ago, and I have tried not to consult them too much here. I have written *Linguistic Semantics* in what I think are my own words, and I have sought out new and different data for examples.

Second, I have tried not to advocate any single theory of semantics or of language in general. My obvious partiality to cognitive explanations should not be taken as adherence to the new movement, Cognitive Linguistics. Linguistics itself is a cognitive science, and so my cognitivism is more of a requirement than a choice. Unfortunately, linguistics is also a rather belligerent discipline. In this corner, we have formal linguistics, with its deductive method, fierce pretenses to intellectual superiority, and often remarkable blindness. In the other corner, we have typological linguistics, with its hierarchies, implications, data from far-flung languages, pretenses to empirical superiority, occasional looseness, and substitution of description for explanation. I have tried to provide a lot of both sides in this book. Formal linguistics and typological linguistics are two scientific ideologies. Although the knee-jerk reaction to the word *ideology* is that it stands for something false and misleading, I prefer the advice of the educational theorist Michael Apple, who reminds us that an ideology is neither good nor bad, but simply a way to talk about a collection of truths. So, in fairness, I hope that I have represented some of the truths of each side.

The need to walk this middle ground in semantics is underscored by the fact that researchers in each camp have often said the same things, but either do not know of or do not admit to knowing the other side. For instance, the current formal theory of discourse anaphora (see chapter 8) is awfully close to what Givón proposed many years earlier (cf. the idea of a discourse file); I see little difference between the ontological claims made by Langacker and Givón and those required by Carlson's and Chierchia's formal theories: and I also see that neither camp cites the other. In many places in *Linguistic Semantics,* I have attempted to unify the formal and typological work in the interests of progress. I apologize in advance to the respective partisans who I am sure will complain that I have misunderstood or shortchanged them.

Linguistic Semantics concerns the relation between semantic structure and overt linguistic form. More technically, it is about grammaticalization patterns, or how languages carve up and express universal semantic space in grammatical form. This approach brings to light not only the traditional semantic issues, such as reference and naming, but also "hot issues," like how much of semantics motivates syntax and whether semantics and pragmatics can be separated. It also pushes the study of semantics into a concern for data proper.

How does *Linguistic Semantics* reach these goals? Chapters 1 and 2 define the domain of linguistic semantics and the tools needed to do semantic analysis: for example, the difference between semantics and pragmatics and the relation of meaning to form. There is an overriding concern that philosophical issues, such as the varieties of reference and the reduction of meaning to ontology (objects of reference) or context, are subservient to the fact that linguistic forms point to mental models, our *view of* the world, not the world itself. The goal of linguistic semantics is to identify the properties that "configure" our mental models and surface in the grammar of a language. Chapters 1 and 2 show how semantic properties are discovered, defined, and realized in languages. The rest of the book puts these tools and assumptions to use in eight areas.

First, we must consider the basic objects in a model of the world: things, actions, and the relation of things to actions. Chapters 3 and 4 address, respectively, the properties of entities and events; chapter 5 examines how entities and events are connected. Some of the traditional properties of entities, like animacy, gender, and countability, are covered in chapter 3; certain of these are considered in terms of their universal distribution, for example, hierarchies of animacy. The focus of chapter 4 is the kinds of events and states that languages lexicalize. There is particular attention to acts, states, motion, and causality; universal schemes for typing events are also presented. Chapter 5, on thematic roles, covers the relation of entities to events. Here the focus is on how arguments connect to predicates, with a typology of thematic roles and a synopsis of work on the relation of thematic roles to grammatical and morphological case.

Chapter 6 covers language and space. We look at two topics: location and deixis. Under the former, we describe the limited set of spatial positions that languages allow their speakers to encode. Under the latter, we consider how expressions can be contextually anchored in terms of a reference point, a located point, removal, and direction.

The next two chapters examine the internal structure of events—aspect—and the relative temporal ordering of events—tense. Chapter 7 presents a thorough picture of the aspectual structure of events, their boundedness, iteration, habituality, duration, rate, phase, and so on; it also looks at the development of aspect systems. Chapter 8 concerns event-time. Here, the relevant facts are the moment of speech, the moment of the event, how languages link the two (absolutely, with regard for the time of speech; relatively, without regard for the time of speech), and how they measure the distance between the two (in a simple line or in intervals).

How do languages constrain a speaker's epistemological stance? What are linguistic truth, linguistic falsity, linguistically justified knowledge, and linguistic commitment? To answer these questions, chapter 9 examines modality and negation. We first look at how languages mark real things versus unreal things, realis/irrealis, and consider modality as a form of deixis (in terms of the relation of the present world of reference to the actual world of expression). Thereafter we describe the various properties of negation: the domain of negation, the range of the effect of negation, and the distinction between denial and rejection. The predominant concern is to show what kinds of negation systems are allowed and how they are formed. We then look at epistemic modality, the nature of linguistic evidence (e.g., the priority of verbal and visual report), and the strength of a speaker's commitment to an assertion. We describe deontic modality: obligation and the likelihood of future action.

The book closes with a survey of modification, in chapter 10. We examine the range of qualities ascribable to entities: color, age, value, and so forth; we spend considerable effort on quantities, looking at logical quantifiers, scope, and numeral systems. We close the chapter with a theory of modifier order; this discussion typifies the approach of this book to bring together formal and typological accounts of meaning.

I am particularly happy with four features of *Linguistic Semantics*. First, I have written the book without ponderous language. When the choice is between *is* and *represents,* I say *is,* provided that nothing is lost thereby. When I say *we,* I intend that both you as the reader and me as the speaker work together through the description or problem; when I say *I,* I mean that the information that follows comes out of my head and only I am responsible for the view. I have assumed minimal knowledge of linguistics and explained each technical term at the point it is introduced. To be honest, I think there is real value in explaining this material in a very accessible way, and so if I have erred in simplicity, I have done so for the sake of the reader.

Second, the book is light on notation. Single quotes (' ') indicate meanings. Double quotes (" ") indicate direct quotation and shudders. Question marks prior to examples (??...) indicate anomalous expressions: Two marks stand for strong anomaly; one mark stands for mild anomaly. *Italics* indicate cited forms and emphasis. The arrowhead (>) indicates sequencing in a hierarchy (e.g., A > B > ...). Abbreviations are either self-explanatory or deducible from the text surrounding them: for example, *Subj* stands for *Subject*; *Irr* stands for *Irrealis,* which is explained in the immediate context. There is very little logical notation, and what is there is explained on the spot. If an instructor wants to use a lot of formalization, any book on linguistics and logic can be used in conjunction with *Linguistic Semantics* (Allwood, Anderson, and Dahl's *Logic in Linguistics* (1977) or McCawley's *Everything that Linguists Have Always Wanted to Know about Logic* (1981) are good companions; Chierchia and McConnell-Ginet's

Meaning and Grammar (1990) would also be a fine formal complement to the present book).

Third, the book has a lot of new data. Semantics books tend not to have data from languages other than English, and when there are illustrations from other languages, the same examples surface again and again. I have spent hours finding new examples. I think in many cases they are clearer than the traditional illustrations, and I know they do more justice to the world's languages at large. Semantics often seems more of an armchair conceptual discipline than one of data-analysis. I hope that the data in this book rectifies this situation.

Fourth, the chapters are consistently organized. Except for the first two chapters, which are introductory and have their own goals, all chapters have an introductory section, a descriptive section, and a theoretical section. In the introductory part, I define the phenomenon in question and explain some recent attempts at theorizing about it; in the descriptive part, I try to spell out the semantic and grammatical facts associated with the phenomenon under discussion; in the theoretical part, I try to simplify and unify the descriptive material, usually by reconciling formal and conceptual/typological views of an issue. Every chapter has many subdivisions with explicit titles: I have done this because the book is long and the reader will need a lot of guideposts along the way. I have also included numerous summaries: After an extended discussion, there is usually a summary, and there is a long summary at the end of every chapter. Finally, I have included three questions for discussion to close each chapter. These questions are in no way comprehensive, but are designed to reinforce significant conceptual matters in the chapters. They are the basis for broader discussion managed by the instructor and should show the reader that semantics is as much of a problem-oriented discipline as other areas of linguistics.

I hope that *Linguistics Semantics* is used not only by linguists, but also by others who have an interest in semantic structure. Besides linguistics courses, the book can be used in courses in English, foreign languages, communication, psychology, computer science, anthropology, and education. I asked a psychologist and a computer scientist to read the two introductory chapters, and the book has benefitted from the comments of these more-than-interested bystanders.

Many people have helped me with this book in one way or another. I have subjected 10 years of semantics students to these ideas, and I thank them here. I am grateful to the following people for discussing semantics with me and/or reading parts of the manuscript: Peter Cole, Robert DiPietro, Thomas Ernst, Roberta Golinkoff, Salikoko Mufwene, Ronald Schaefer, William Stanley, and Raoul Smith. A number of anonymous reviewers of the manuscript made helpful comments, and in many places I have borrowed their ideas. I hope this small acknowledgment is sufficient. I must thank Peter Cole again, this time for giving me a teaching schedule that let me work long uninterrupted hours on the book. Judith Amsel and Kathryn Scornavacca, from Lawrence Erlbaum Associates, made the publication of this book a very pleasurable experience. Finally, I must thank my wife for her constant help and support. In the time it took to write this book, there were four deaths in our family (not to mention the usual major illnesses and near-tragedies that make up a life). I don't know how she put up with my unforgivable moods, but without her, Pierre, Chloe, and, now, Christopher, I would have never finished this book. Thank you, Maria.

1 Semantics and Linguistic Semantics: Toward Grammatical Meaning

1.1. INTRODUCTION

In this chapter we define *linguistic semantics* as the study of literal, decontextualized, grammatical meaning. We begin with the difference between literal and implicational meaning and then illustrate meaning that has grammatical relevance. We contrast this view of meaning with that given by philosophical semantics, focusing on two basic questions: Is meaning possible? What kinds of meanings are possible? We show how linguistic semantics positions itself differently from philosophical semantics on such issues as the kinds of meaning that languages grammaticalize and the structural and empirical methods of semantic analysis. We close with a consideration of grammatical conditions on meaning and the relation of semantics to morphology.

1.2. GRAMMATICAL MEANING: AN INTRODUCTION AND ILLUSTRATION

Linguistic semantics is the study of literal meanings that are *grammaticalized* or *encoded* (i.e., reflected in how the grammar of a language structures its sentences). Defined as such, linguistic semantics is a branch of both *semiotics,* the study of meaning in general, and *semantics,* the study of linguistic meaning in particular. But linguistic semantics is narrower than either semiotics or semantics, focusing as it does on meanings that are actually reflected in overt form differences.

1

To see exactly what linguistic semantics admits and excludes, we begin with an example that illustrates grammatical meaning in contrast to other kinds of meaning. Thereafter, we examine the position of linguistic semantics in relation to semantics in general so that we can delimit more precisely the domain of linguistic semantics.

1.21.   Literal and Implicational Meaning

What does (1) mean?

1. Tom bought some rice.

We want to know what *state of affairs* or *situation in the world* the expression represents. This is its *literal* or *representational meaning*. The literal meaning of a linguistic form contrasts with its *implicational meaning,* or what the expression suggests about the speaker's intentions or the hearer's expected response to what has been said.

From the standpoint of literal meaning, (1) represents a situation with an event, 'buying,' and certain participants, 'Tom' and 'rice.' This state of affairs is uncontroversial and not open to dispute; it is decidable irrespective of the speaker or the circumstances. Certainly, (1) may be representationally false—there may have been no such state of affairs—but that does not affect its literal meaning, only the fidelity of the representation.

What does (1) say about the speaker's intentions or expectations of us in response, the implicational meaning? Unlike the literal meaning of (1), answers to this question are open to dispute. Perhaps the speaker wants to indicate something about Tom's life. Perhaps the speaker is lying, and is deliberately presenting us with a false representation, and perhaps we recognize this. For this implicational meaning, we must decide why something has been articulated or what has been suggested by the words. We can determine this only by *situating* the sentence, or putting it into a *real context* with a *real history* and a set of *real circumstances*.

These two views of the sense of (1) point up the clear difference between literal and implicational meaning. Literal meaning is determinable outside of context; it comes with its *own set of facts*. Literal meaning is thus said to be *decontextualized*. Implicational meaning is not so decidable; everything must be calculated by a hearer, working from the expression in relation to perceived intentions and circumstances. Implicational meaning is thus said to be *con-textualized*.

Linguistic semantics is concerned with literal, decontextualized meaning that, furthermore, is associated with the grammatical structure of language. Gram-matical structure, like literal meaning, exists outside of the contexts in which it is used. A speaker of German does not choose, on one day, to mark nouns in the dative case, and then choose on another day to mark the same nouns, in the same structure, in the accusative. The grammatical structure of German, like the linguistic meanings associated with that structure, is simply not negotiable. The intentions of a speaker of German, on the other hand, are not a matter of either grammatical structure or the literal meanings associated with grammatical structure. They *are* negotiable, and they are outside our purview.

1.22. Encoding and Grammatical Meaning

Now that we have a grasp of the nature of decontextualized meaning, let us look at how literal meaning is bound up with the mechanisms that language has for grammatical expression. Consider (1) again. This sentence gives overt form to both the event, 'buying,' and the participants, 'Tom' and 'rice,' by *grammaticalizing* them: They appear as structural categories, nouns and verbs, that are essential to the formation of sentences in English. By definition, the analysis and description of the event and its participants fall under the purview of linguistic semantics *because the event and its participants have grammatical relevance.*

What other literal information in (1) is given grammatically relevant form? In the situation described, we know that Tom *carried out* the event and *acted on* the rice. Moreover, we know this because of *the form of the sentence in English,* not because of the intentions of the speaker or anything connected with context and implication. The structure of English is such that the subject, which frequently (but not always) correlates with the actional doer, generally precedes the verb, which in turn usually precedes the object, which frequently (but not always) denotes the actional receiver. The participants in an event have some connection to the relative order of the forms that compose the expression as a whole. Obviously, in other languages, the formal facts differ, and order may matter less than explicit marking on the forms that represent the participants. But both the use of word order and explicit marking are reflexes, overt manifestations, of the grammatical status of literal meaning.

For comparison, let us now ask a different question: What is *not* grammaticalized in (1)? The form of (1) signals nothing about the social status of the speaker of the sentence or about the social status of the participants in the event. Is the speaker married or not? How much money does the speaker of the sentence make? To what social class does Tom belong? Is Tom educated? None of this is encoded. This is not to say that such information is irrelevant. Knowledge of the social status of the speaker and the participants in the event does bear on the overall comprehension of the sentence, its implications and its uses, but this information is not encoded in (1). Nor is structural encoding of the social status of speaker and participants necessarily ruled out in English or in any other language. In the many languages that have *honorifics* (Japanese, e.g., see chap. 3)—markers of the social position of speakers, hearers, and participants—this kind of information is clearly grammaticalized. But in (1), social status is not a grammatical fact because there is no structural reflex of it.

As a limiting case, consider a literal meaning that is never translated into syntactic form. There is no way in English to mark the eye color of the participants in (1). Certainly we could say *Blue-eyed Tom bought some rice,* but the phrase *blue-eyed* is not a grammatical reflex: It is not necessitated by the design of English as a system. There are no verbs in English, for example, that require that their subjects be blue-eyed. Nor does eye color appear to be grammatically necessitated by any other language. Linguistic semantics is about literal grammatical meanings, and for better or worse, eye color loses out in the enterprise.

This elementary discussion of grammatical meaning raises some general summary questions that drive our subsequent inquiry into linguistic semantics. If linguistic semantics is the study of grammaticalized meaning, then:

1. How do we decide what kind of information is within the purview of linguistic semantics?
2. How do we decide what is and is not grammatical meaning?
3. What can we expect to be grammaticalized in the world's languages?

The rest of this book is a tabulation of some of the received answers to these questions as well as a manual of procedures for finding solutions to problems that remain open. But before we consider the solutions in more detail, we turn to the idea of meaning in general—philosophical semantics—to set the stage for our more narrow pursuit of grammatical meaning.

1.3. PHILOSOPHICAL SEMANTICS
AND LINGUISTIC SEMANTICS

Traditionally, to make an inquiry along the lines of the questions raised at the end of the last section, we would turn first to the philosophical literature to ask about the nature of meaning itself. It is worthwhile to look into this work briefly to see how linguistic semantics falls out as a well-circumscribed subfield of semantics in general and takes such questions as its guide.

Philosophical semantics studies the following basic problems: (a) whether and how meaning is at all possible, and (b) the kinds of meanings that are in principle possible. The first problem concerns the logical underpinnings of linguistic meaning, that is, can we determine meaning at all and how? The second problem concerns what we should find, assuming that we have judged the pursuit in the first problem possible. These questions are clearly *ontological,* in the philosophical sense, in that they concern what *must be* the case. Philosophical semantics is primarily a deductive enterprise, devoted to an examination of what ought to be and from which the actual facts, what is, happily fall out. Linguistic semantics is primarily an *empirical discipline,* inductive, data-driven, and therefore involved first with what actually exists, not what in principle must be. This is not to say that the two are incompatible (or even that everyone would agree with this characterization) because in theory, what we actually run into in our investigations is a natural subset of what we must encounter. It turns out, however, that "in principle findings" frequently miss the mark when the "in practice necessities" of linguistic meaning arise. Often philosophical semantics has difficulty getting on to the actual meanings that languages produce. As we proceed, the pitfalls as well as the benefits of the deductive approach become apparent.

1.31.   Question 1: How Is Meaning Possible?

To say that something has meaning is to say that it is a *sign,* a composite unit consisting of a *relation* between an overt signal, called the *signifier,* and the information that this overt signal evokes, called the *signified.* The signifier, signified, and their relation make up the sign. Here we have the basic *semiotic definition* of meaning (see Barthes 1967; Saussure 1959), semiotics being the discipline that studies all meaningful signal exchange, from culture as rules for acceptable behavior to literature and art as conventionalized aesthetic meaning.

The semiotic characterization of meaning has always dominated philosophical semantics, as Katz (1986: 159–60) nicely articulates:

> We have had one attempt after another to treat meaning as something else. There have been attempts to reduce it to behavior-controlling stimuli, to images, methods of verification, stereotypes, truth conditions, extensions in possible worlds, use, illocutionary act potential, perlocutionary act potential of various sorts, and even physical inscriptions. Indeed, the history of philosophical semantics in this century might well be written as a succession of metaphysically inspired attempts to eliminate the ordinary notion of meaning or sense.

Katz's point, in semiotic terms, is that the history of philosophical semantics is largely a series of proposals to reduce meaning to an investigation of what the signifier (the overt mark) evokes: behavior, mental images, truth, and so forth. In philosophical semantics, meaning is possible because there is a *relation* between a signifier and the signified. The rest of the history of semantics is a series of attempts to delineate types of signifieds. But how do these things bear on grammatical meaning? How does this relational view of meaning in general shed light on meaning conveyed by the structure of language? What can we expect of particular languages?

If we look at the history of the study of the relation between signifier and signified, we find that philosophical semantics offers basically programmatic answers to questions about grammatical meaning. Approaches to meaning via the signifier/signified relation divide rather neatly into two camps: One sees a *direct relation* between linguistic signifiers and signifieds and the other an *indirect relation*.

1.311. The Direct View

The view that there is a direct, unmediated connection between the signifier and signified is most typically represented by Plato (see his dialogue *Cratylus*), who argued that the world we live in is populated by imperfect manifestations of a pure world of ideal forms. The imperfect forms reflect the pure forms, so every object in the present world is *motivated* to some extent as a reflex of the world of pure ideal forms. Words and their meanings also derive from ideal forms, so the word *table* reflects its primal connection with the ideal form of 'tableness' to which it refers. *Table* is therefore an *appropriate name* for the object because the ideal world of forms infused in the word legitimizes the name. In less ponderous phraseology, in a direct view like Plato's, language is *iconic*. There is a straightforward and necessary connection between the signifier and the signified. All things are appropriately named because all linguistic forms, words as signifiers, directly reflect their origin in pure being, their signifieds.

Centuries of science make this view a bit hard to swallow, unless one also accepts its metaphysical stance and believes in some other world of pure being. After all, where is this other world? In his defense, Plato (again in *Cratylus*) offered a number of etymologies that he said substantiate the iconic relation of signifier and signified. The god Pluto, for instance, is appropriately named because the name *Pluto* means 'wealth.' Wealth comes from under the ground (e.g., the wealth of natural resources), and Pluto is appropriately the god of the underworld.

Problems quickly surface with this account. If all signifiers iconically reflect pure being, then why are there different languages? Why are there different signifiers? Why is it *table* in English and *mesa* in Spanish?

In spite of these obvious problems, a number of versions of the direct view have been held through the years. The early Wittgenstein (1974/1918), for example, argued that propositions are logical pictures of the facts, by which he meant that the forms of propositions reflect what they depict. Truth and falsity are discoverable because of this infusion of the signified, the facts, in the signifier, the proposition. Katz (1981) takes a Platonic position on all aspects of language, arguing that actual linguistic forms derive from a world of pure linguistic forms. For Katz, meanings are abstract objects that exist independently of the minds that perceive them. Adherents of the *iconic theory of grammar,* for example Haiman (1980, 1983, 1985a, 1985b) and others like him theoretically, argue that linguistic categories—a kind of signifier—directly reflect ideal semantic forms: Nouns universally encode entities; verbs encode temporally dynamic relations (see also chaps. 3 and 4). All these views share the idea that, like all icons, the signifieds of language (entities, dynamic relations, appropriate names, facts) are recoverable from the signifiers (nouns, verbs, sentences). In short, meaning is a *transparent relation between signifier and signified.*

1.312.   The Indirect View

In contrast to the direct view, there is the indirect view: The connection between the linguistic signifier and the signified is mediated, noniconic, or opaque. This position in Western thought is usually traced back to Aristotle, who, in *On Interpretation,* claimed that the relation between words and their referents is *conventional,* that *social rules* determine how meanings are paired with overt forms. The connection between the signifier and signified is not necessary, but symbolic and unmotivated.

This position is intuitively more appealing. After all, languages do vary in their signifiers and signifieds over time. How else could there be semantic change unless the connection between the signifier and signified were nonnecessary? A more recent influential version of the indirect view of linguistic meaning is the *conceptualist position* proposed by Ogden and Richards (1923) in their comprehensive study of the definition of *meaning.* In that work, they characterize meaning as a *semiotic triangle,* a relation between a symbol (word) and referent (an object), *mediated by concepts:*

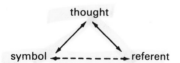

FIG. 1.1.   Ogden and Richards's semiotic triangle.

In the conceptualist view, meaning is an indirect association (as indicated by the broken line) between a signifier and signified, with thought playing the mediating role.

The conceptualist position has had numerous followers, though it is by no means the required or dominant view. Two of its contemporary adherents are Jackendoff (1983, 1988) and Lakoff (1987, 1988). Jackendoff claims that semantic analysis is exactly the same as conceptual analysis: "Meaning in natural language is an information structure that is mentally encoded by human beings" (1988: 81). Lakoff argues for a totally cognitive semantics, where meaning is coextensive with perceived experience, an "imaginative projection, using mechanisms of schematization, categorization, metaphor, and metonymy to move from what we experience in a structured way with our bodies to abstract cognitive models" (1988: 121).

Aristotle, Ogden and Richards, Jackendoff, and Lakoff may diverge on the details of the indirect connection between signifier and signified, but they all share the view that meaning itself is an indirect association between the linguistic signal and the information evoked by the signal.

1.313.   Grammatical Meaning and the Possibility of Meaning

The direct and indirect views of the first ontological question of philosophical semantics provide us with *metatheory:* claims about how we ought to proceed rather than analysis itself. Although all meaning is a relation between a signifier and a signified (whether or not this relation is direct), linguistic semantics is very particular about the content of the signifier: only those signifiers that have ramifications on the rest of the language as a formal system.

We are not obliged to hold either the direct or indirect view to do linguistic semantics, though we do see how a decision for one or the other can affect the units of analysis we propose (see chap. 2). A recent influential work in logical semantics, Dowty (1979), spends an entire chapter discussing whether the semantic units proposed in the book have any existence at all outside the system of analysis: And this discussion occurs *at the end* of the book, not as a prerequisite to the analysis! The principal task of linguistic semantics is to describe what languages *actually* deploy, not to worry about how meaning is possible, a worry that usually leads to talk *about* meaning instead of *elucidation and analysis of* meaning itself. Linguistic semantics is driven metatheoretically by what Lakoff (1988: 123) calls *basic realism:* The world exists, minds exist, other people exist, meaning exists, and our senses provide reliable reports of the status of the external world.

If the direct view of meaning is correct, for instance, and if the meaning of an expression is its underlying Platonic forms, then its linguistic semantic analysis is not seriously affected. Similarly, if the meaning of an expression is some set of conceptual mediations of the signifier and signified, the analysis still proceeds. The linguistic issues do not disappear because Plato's or Lakoff's metaphysics turns out to support the first question of meaning. We still have to confront the problem of actual meanings.

1.32.   Question 2:
What Kinds of Meanings Are Possible?

The lesson of the first question of philosophical semantics specifies that we have to accept a basic naive realism as a metatheoretical guidepost. Let us turn to the second question: What kinds of meanings are possible? Under the dictates of naive realism, this question becomes: What kinds of meanings do languages *actually express?* To answer this question, we examine the particular case of the philosophical dispute over the distinction between *natural kinds* and *nominal kinds*. As in the foregoing discussion of the very possibility of meaning, we find that the philosophical issues that have traditionally informed semantics sometimes raise procedure over analysis.

1.321. Natural and Nominal Kinds:
An Ontological Distinction

In philosophical semantics, it is generally understood that words, specifically, common nouns, denote classes of objects. The word *stallion,* like all common nouns, stands for a class of objects, in this case, members of the class defined by the conjunction of the properties of maleness and horseness. What does *horse* represent? Whereas the meaning of *stallion* can be seen as the conjunction of independent properties (like maleness and horseness), the meaning of *horse* cannot. For example, a horse is not uniquely a four-legged animal, and so *horse* does not refer to the class of animals that are differentiated by four leggedness. This is unlike *stallion,* which *does refer* to a class, horses, with a differentiating property, maleness. Nor can *horse* be defined as, say, 'equine animal.' Whereas the phrase *equine animal* always picks out a horse, it does so trivially: An equine is the *same thing as a horse,*and so this is tantamount to saying that *stallion* means 'stallion horse,' not a very informative proposition, to say the least.

These two common nouns denote their classes of objects in significantly different ways. *Stallion* denotes *compositionally* because the class that it selects is really derived from a conjunction of more fundamental properties. Thus, the class that *stallion* denotes is a class *in name only:* It is a *nominal kind.* In contrast, *horse* denotes *noncompositionally* because its meaning cannot be constructed out of more fundamental properties. It is *inherently a class,* a *natural kind,* a class that naturally occurs and is not derivable (see Churchland 1985; Cruse 1986; Kripke 1972; Putnam 1975; Schwartz 1979, 1980).

A little thought shows that the natural/nominal kind distinction cuts a wide path across the lexicon. Natural kind terms are *tiger, gold, hepatitis, heat, pain, red, grow.* Nominal kind terms are *car, wheel, succotash, coat, wedding, divorce,* and *president* (from Welsh 1988b; see also Welsh 1988a). But a little further thought shows that the distinction, although interesting philosophically, has little bearing on the grammatical structure of English. Items in the short list of natural kind terms have no unique structural properties. Welsh (1988b) shows that both natural and nominal kinds take articles (*the gold, the wedding*) and quantifiers (*some gold, many weddings*). English does not differentiate the two in terms of pluralization (*two tigers, two divorces*) or verb choice (*the tiger fell down, the coat fell down; pain annoys me, the president annoys me*).

The dispute over nominal and natural kinds is basically ontological, not linguistic. In fact, no language appears to differentiate natural from nominal kinds by any sort of formal device, precisely because, as Welsh (1988b) argues, the distinction can be captured by nongrammatical means, by their definitional structure. There is clearly a meaning difference between a natural kind and a nominal kind, but the distinction is not a question of grammatical structure at all.

The matter of distinguishing natural/nominal kinds highlights the importance of grammaticalization in linguistic semantics. The second fundamental question of philosophical semantics—what kinds of meaning are possible—contributes to the identification of a variety of potential meanings that language may encode. But only some of the results of an inquiry driven by this question are relevant. Not all possible meanings are grammaticalized; not all have empirical status. There may be an ontological distinction between natural kinds and nominal kinds, but that does not affect semantic analysis because languages do not signal the difference structurally.

1.322.   Natural and Nominal Kinds:
An Empirical Distinction

The ontological distinction between natural and nominal kinds has an interesting correlate in the empirical study of cognitive structure. In a series of experiments on how children develop conceptual categories, Keil (1979, 1986, 1988) demonstrates that children do not make the difference developmentally between natural kinds and nominal kinds, as defined in the philosophical literature. Instead, the distinction that is crucial to their development is that between *animate* and *inanimate* objects (*natural* and *artefactual,* in his terms).

Significantly, the linguistic evidence shows that in every language there appears to be some grammatical reflex of the difference between animate and inanimate objects (see chap. 3 for full discussion). In fact, in some languages, the degree of animacy—not the degree of "natural kindness"—determines subject–verb agreement, pronoun choice, and other structural phenomena (cf. English *I swim* and *the dog swims* but ?? *the pencil swims.*)

If the distinction between natural and nominal kinds is to have some effect on linguistic semantics, it is going to do so via the results of cognitive psychology, where the ontological distinction is "naturalized," in terms of animacy. What kinds of meanings are possible? Those that languages actually express.

1.33.   Linguistic Semantics as Linguistics

The distinction between natural and nominal kinds underscores the fundamental difference between philosophical semantics and linguistic semantics. The goals of the former are ontological and procedural. They are in-principle goals. As discussed in Chapter 2, much of the work in philosophical semantics is designed to spell out the necessary structure of meaning, especially in work on reference and logical form. The very possibility of meaning and the kinds of meaning expressible are somewhat removed from our concerns because they are meta-theoretical issues.

Our goals are empirical and structural. What kinds of meanings do languages actually have, and, whatever their referential status, how are they translated into grammatical form? In answering these questions, linguistic semantics turns out to be a branch of linguistics, not of philosophy.

1.4.   GRAMMATICAL MEANING REVISITED

In our discussion of both grammatical meaning and the relationship of linguistic semantics to philosophical semantics, we have often fallen back on *grammatical coding* as a crucial factor in arbitrating disputes. The notion has motivated the discussion of literal meaning, for example; it appears to be the leading cause of the differentiation of linguistic semantics from philosophical semantics and underlies the basic questions posed on p. 4. We now turn more specifically to grammatical coding.

1.41.   The Grammatical Constraint

Grammatically coded meaning is that information that bears on the structural design of the language as a formal system. Jackendoff (1983) considers this kind of meaning central to his theory of conceptual semantics, and makes meaning that has a structural effect a condition on the development of semantic theory itself. He calls this condition the *grammatical constraint*. Although in recent years linguistics has become increasingly interested in the fact that syntax and semantics are different, it should not be forgotten that the two link up in systematic ways: "This is not to say that every aspect of syntax should be explainable in semantic terms. . . . The point of the Grammatical Constraint is only to attempt to minimize the differences of syntactic and semantic structure" (Jackendoff 1983: 16; Jackendoff 1990, which has a fuller discussion).

All semantic information is, in a gross sense, background information, what the speaker and hearer bring to the task of talking and understanding; *only some* of it is directly mapped onto the form of an utterance. Only some properties are actually implemented into the rules of sentence formation. Meaning and form must be linked in the act of speaking and understanding. Consequently we should first examine those meanings that are directly involved in this relationship.

1.42. An Example of the Grammatical Constraint: Inchoatives and Middles

Let us consider an example of the linking of syntax and semantics via the Grammatical Constraint (this discussion is inspired by Bybee 1985: 17–9). The verb *kill entails*—truly and necessarily implies—the meaning 'cause someone to become dead.' That is, in all cases where X kills Y, it follows that X causes Y to become dead. This is not to say that *kill* means the same thing as, or is even adequately paraphrased by, 'cause to become dead' (see Wierzbicka 1980 and Fodor 1970 for the enormous discussion of this problem). It only means that *kill* involves at least three semantic notions: causing, becoming, and death.

In traditional analysis, these notions are called *components,* and the entailment test is the basis of *componential analysis,* or the analysis of the meaning of a form into its semantic components. To avoid overlap with this kind of project, we call the components *semantic properties:* They are the units that underlie our intuitions about literal meaning and are associated with the grammatical structure of a language.

Which of the three properties are conditioned by the Grammatical Constraint? Causing and becoming are; death is not. The rules that any language has for constructing sentences never make necessary reference to death. This is not even a remote possibility, and though languages may have a variety of verbs of dying, this is not a structural fact, but a fact about the world or the culture in which the language is spoken.

On the other hand, the property of causing *does have an effect* on the mechanisms for the construction of sentences in any language. In Chapter 4, we look at *causatives*—verbs that express 'causing'—in some detail, and we see that in a wide range of languages, it is possible to convert virtually any verb into a causative by the addition of a grammatical marking; the syntax of the language reflects the semantic distinction directly (see Comrie 1981).

Analogous facts hold for the property of becoming, technically known as *inchoative,* or 'change of state.' An inchoative verb denotes action constituted by two distinct states, one where some characteristic is present, and one where it is absent. The verb *kill* is inchoative because it requires that its object be alive at one point and not alive at another. This semantic property of inchoativeness has a number of ramifications on English syntax and thus can be shown to follow the Grammatical Constraint.

English has a construction known as the *middle,* whereby the subject of an intransitive verb is understood as the logical undergoer of the action, as in the following sentence:

2. Fish cooks quickly.

In (2), *fish* is the subject, but its logical structure is something like 'X cooks fish quickly,' where an unspecified agent, X, is understood and the grammatical subject, *fish,* is logically acted on by this agent. A number of linguists have pointed out that middles are constrained by the degree to which the grammatical subject is affected by the act (Keyser and Roeper 1984; Lebeaux 1988; Wilkins 1987; see also chap. 5). So, *Fish cooks easily* is possible, but not ?? *Oddities notice easily,* because the latter, though derivable from '*X* notices oddities easily,' does not have an affected subject: A fish is more affected by cooking than are oddities by noticing.

This semantic condition on the subjects of middles has a slight variation that brings home the spirit of the Grammatical Constraint. It is possible to have affected subjects, but no middle construction. For the middle, the *action itself must be inchoative,* as the following examples illustrate (thanks to Li May Sung and Lynn Messing for these observations):

3a. ?? The plate throws easily ('X throws the plate').
 b. ?? The bologna eats easily ('X eats the bologna').
 c. The plate flips easily ('X flips the plate').
 d. The bologna digests easily ('X digests the bologna').

Examples (3a) and (3b) certainly have subjects that are affected by the action, but *throw* and *eat* are not inchoative in that they do not denote a transition from the absence of a characteristic to its presence (or from its presence to its absence) during the action proper: No new state comes about for the plate or bologna while thrown or eaten. In contrast, (3c) and (3d) are inchoative. *Flip* denotes a change of positional state for the entity ('turning') in the act itself, and *digest* requires change of physical composition of an entity (from 'whole' to 'digested') as part of the action. Remarkably, middles are allowed only for the latter two, suggesting that English syntax is sensitive to the property of becoming, not just the affectedness of the object (see Chafe 1970 and Dowty 1979 for additional discussion; see also chap. 4).

The Grammatical Constraint reins in our semantic analysis by showing that the grammatical locus of the property of becoming is the *verb,* a clear structural constituent. With a detailed analysis of actual data, guided by the Grammatical Constraint, we can identify grammatically relevant semantic properties in systematic ways.

1.43.   The Form of Grammatical Meaning:
Morphology Versus Semantics

Now that we have reviewed the ideas of grammatical meaning in light of the Grammatical Constraint, we turn to the overt form the meaning may take, or how language grammatically encodes the relevant properties. Here we should be careful to distinguish linguistic semantics from morphology. Morphology studies the variety of actual forms that certain semantic properties may take; linguistic semantics limits its concerns to the fact that semantic properties *have a grammatical reflex,* whatever that reflex might be.

The form of grammaticalized meaning concerns us only very generally, and from this standpoint, there are just two choices: *explicit* or *implicit. Explicit encoding* is relatively easy to deal with. After all, if there is explicit form, the marker is there to be analyzed. So we do not make much of this, except to point out that explicit encoding can take the form of free or bound morphemes: words, affixes, clitics, or whatever.

The other option, *implicit encoding,* is less easy to understand. Essentially, implicit encoding means that grammatical meaning can be detected in how the combinations of forms that do appear are conditioned by the presence of a semantic property that is otherwise not given explicit form. More practically, how do we know something is there if it does not have a unique expression? We look at its effect on what *is* there. Implicit encoding of grammatically relevant meaning is revealed through *co-occurrence,* how forms select each other on the basis of covert properties.

Implicit coding may be seen in the following sentences:

4a. Tom punched Bob on Monday.
  b. Tom punched Bob for an hour.
  c. ?? Tom punched Bob in an hour.

These sentences show that the verb *punch* in English has the semantic property of punctuality. *Punch* encodes a momentary event and does not unfold over time or occupy any extended temporal space, 'inherently nonextended hitting with some force.' But how do we know this, without any overt marking of punctuality on the verb itself? The evidence lies in the choice of prepositional phrases.

Sentence (4a) is acceptable because the prepositional phrase, *on Monday,* simply fixes the event in time. The semantic content of the prepositional phrase is compatible with that of the verb: Simple location in time and punctuality do not contrast. Unlike this situation, (4b) is acceptable only if its interpretation is that the punching is repeated. Sentence (4b) means something like 'Tom did many separate acts of punching to Bob over the span of an hour.' This interpretation results from the interaction of the semantic content of the prepositional phrase—'extended location in time'—with the punctuality of the verb. For punctuality to be compatible with extension, the momentary event must be repeated. The same effect can be achieved by progressivizing the verb: *Tom was punching Bob (for an hour).* In contrast to both (4a) and (4b), (4c) is decidedly odd because the semantic content of the prepositional phrase forces the event to be viewed as expanding. The phrase *in an hour* signals that the time has extension, or that the event takes place in a "container of time." This is inherently incompatible with the punctuality of *punch,* which can be expanded only be repetition.

The point of (4) is that the punctuality *punch* is encoded, but only implicitly:

in the effect that this property has on the co-occurrence of the verb with other grammatically relevant phenomena. Thus, if we take a nonpunctual verb, it is compatible with all three structures already discussed, this time because of the *absence* of the semantic property:

5a. John ran on Monday.
  b. John ran for an hour.
  c. John ran in an hour.

Punctuality must thus bear on the semantic and syntactic structure of English. We can show its effect even when it is not overt. We just have to know what to look for and where and how to look.

SUMMARY OF CHAPTER

We can now summarize our view of linguistic semantics rather precisely. Linguistic semantics is the study of grammatical meaning—literal, decontextualized meaning that is reflected in the syntactic structure of language. We have seen how concentration on grammatical meaning differentiates linguistic semantics from traditional philosophical semantics by offering empirical answers to the ontological questions of the very possibility of meaning and the kinds of meaning allowable. Along the way, we have looked at a number of proposals and controversies regarding meaning in the philosophical literature: for example, the direct and indirect views of the relationship of the signifier to the signified and the distinction between natural kinds and nominal kinds. We have concluded the discussion of grammatical meaning with an examination of grammatical coding—the ways that grammatical meanings take structural form. Here we have seen several examples of the difference between meanings that are grammatically coded and those that are not; we have also looked at the difference between morphology and semantics—the latter concentrating on the form itself—and have made some observations about the form that grammatical meaning takes: explicit coding and implicit coding.

QUESTIONS FOR DISCUSSION

1. Turn back to (1), p. 2, and consider the form of the direct object, *some rice*. What semantic property might be involved in the meaning of this phrase? Is this semantic property an example of grammatical meaning? How do the following help in your answer?

  i. ?? Tom bought a rice.
  ii. ?? Tom bought seven rices.

2. Suppose that English had the word *blite*, meaning 'black and white together.' Is *blite* a natural kind term or a nominal kind term? No known language has a single term for 'black and white together'; instead, all languages have separate expressions for 'black' and 'white.' How does this affect your answer?

3. In Polish, direct objects are usually marked in the accusative case. However, direct objects denoting animate entities are marked in the genitive, as shown here:

> i. zakupi- łem   indyk- a.
>   buy/Perf 1Per/Past turkey Gen
>   I bought the turkey.

Is this evidence for animacy as a unit of grammatical meaning in Polish? Sentence (i) may also describe the buying of a dead turkey, say at the butcher shop. Does this mean that animacy is irrelevant?

2 Five Approaches to Meaning

2.1. INTRODUCTION

In Chapter 1, we presented the goals of linguistic semantics as the study of grammatical meaning. In the present chapter, we look at the nature and definition of *meaning* itself to get a sense of the fundamental issues in semantic analysis and to establish a backdrop against which to judge grammatically relevant meaning. Five views of meaning are considered: meaning as reference, meaning as logical form, meaning as context and use, meaning as culture, and meaning as conceptual structure. This five-part description is not designed to polarize the approaches, forcing all views of meaning into one of the categories. Rather, these are five general views of meaning, incommensurable with each other on some points, but compatible on others.

One way to think about grammatical meaning is in terms of how expressions with grammatical structure get interpretations. Linguistics is a discipline that analyzes, describes, and explains phenomena through *representations* or symbolic, rule-governed formulas. Given this, we might then ask: How are the syntactic representations of sentences paired with the semantic representations? This way of talking requires us to consider what grammatically relevant semantic representations *are*.

The five approaches to meaning that we survey in this chapter all provide different views of the content of semantic representations. We already know that semantic properties somehow comprise semantic representations, but now we need to make these notions more precise. Are semantic properties, as part of semantic representations, referential? Are they logical? Are they derived from the immediate context of use, or from the larger cultural context? Are semantic representations conceptual structures? From these five approaches to meaning, we develop a unified picture of semantic representations as involving reference to universal, gradient, inherent properties of a mentally projected world.

2.2.   APPROACH 1: MEANING AS REFERENCE

2.21.   Language and the World

If we ask someone the meaning of the word *dog,* we are very likely to be told that it is what the word *refers to,* or points out, *in the world:* either some discrete object or some set of observable features, like furriness, barking, faithfulness, and so on. In both cases, the meaning of the word is its constant reference in any context.

The view that meaning is reference to facts or objects *in the world* has a long history of discussion in semantics and a long history of unreliability. If the meaning of a linguistic form is what it refers to in the world, we are hard pressed to explain two things:

1. How can the reference be constant but the meaning vary?
2. How can the reference be indeterminate or nonexistent, yet there still be meaning?

The answers to each of these questions argue for the claim that reference takes place within a *mentally projected* world.

2.211.   Constant Reference but Variable Meaning: Extension, Intension, and Compositionality.

The first question at the end of section 2.21 is a classic problem in philosophical semantics. This predicament has its most famous articulation in the work of Gottlob Frege (1952), a 19th-century German logician, who noted that the following sentence is problematic for an account of meaning tied to reference in the world:

1. The Morning Star is the Evening Star.

Frege observed that at the strictly referential level, this sentence is meaningless because the phrases *Morning Star* and *Evening Star* pick out the same object, the planet Venus. From a strictly referential standpoint, (1) means 'Venus is Venus,' which is not exactly informative.

But for many people, (1) *does mean something* and *is informative.* Many people do not know that there is a Morning Star and an Evening Star, that the Morning Star is not even a star, but a planet, or that the Morning Star is Venus, much less that the Evening Star is Venus, too. How do we account for this kind of meaningfulness in spite of the referential redundancy?

Frege proposed that a distinction be drawn between two kinds of referential meaning. The first, what he called *reference,* is the actual object or real world entity picked out by a linguistic expression, in (1), the planet Venus. The second, what he called *sense,* is the meaning of an expression by virtue of how it is said, or the form of the proposition. The sense of (1) is all the other information evoked by how the expression itself is presented: that there is the Morning Star, that it is the same as Venus, and so on—all the information that makes the sentence meaningful to someone who may or may not know the referential facts.

Another way to think about this issue, and much less confusing in the long run, is to say that *reference* is the process by which a signifier relates to a signified. The object itself that is referred to is the *extension*; all the information other than the extension is the *intension.* So with (1) the extension may be constant, making the expression nonsensical at the extensional level. But this is different from the intension, which may vary in spite of constant extension and may make an otherwise nonsensical and redundant expression meaningful and informative.

Which is more important to meaning, extension or intension? From (1), we might argue that the intension *precedes and fixes the extension,* because (1) is meaningful to individuals who otherwise have no idea of the extension. Kripke (1972) made a similar point in claiming that the problem of reference centers on how expressions come to *rigidly designate:* that is, how they select the same objects and facts in spite of the variable contexts in which they appear. According to Kripke's solution, behind every term (in his theory, proper names and natural kind terms), there is a series of intensions that give every expression an effectively necessary, not ontologically necessary, name. A speaker's words refer because the speaker inherits a set of belief states from the community—intensions—that fix reference and thus effectively obligate the connection of a signifier to a signified. These intensions may be incorrect or inadequate to uniquely characterize the extension, but this is not the issue. Successful reference is more important than true reference, and rigid designation is accomplished from the inside out, as it were: from the world of information to the world of nameable facts (see, e.g., Kripke 1972: 309).

We can see Kripke's point in an examination of (2):

2. George Bush is George Bush.

In technical terms, (2) is a *tautology,* a statement that is always true. But (2) is a tautology only in terms of its extension, and we can eliminate the redundancy by changing *the way that the information is presented:*

   3a. I wonder if George Bush is George Bush.
    b. I doubt that George Bush is George Bush.
    c. George Bush is uncertain that George Bush is George Bush.

In each case, the redundancy is called into question because the tautology is put in the context of a *propositional attitude* verb (also known as a *belief context* or a *world creating predicate*): an expression that indicates something about the mental state or beliefs of the speaker (e.g., verbs like *know, deny, expect, think,* and the like). Propositional attitude verbs induce *referential opacity,* the clouding of the determination of the extension of an expression that is otherwise clear, straightforward, or self-evident; they do so because propositional attitudes are sensitive to descriptions of objects (intensions) not the objects themselves (extensions). In (3c), for example, the possibility that George Bush may not be George Bush is a consequence of the state of *uncertainty* that George Bush has about George Bush being George Bush. This extensional dilemma—the lack of a clear connection between two otherwise identical expressions (*George Bush* and *George Bush*)—is induced by the propositional attitude verb *be uncertain that.* The referential opacity is not the result of the facts of the world, because the extension is constant, but of how the world is represented, the intension.

These examples show that meaning cannot be strictly what an expression refers to *in the world.* What matters is *the way the world is presented,* the *projected world,* the world construed, not the bare facts, if, indeed, there even are such things as facts.

Let us reconsider the verb *punch,* which, as we know from Chapter 1, is punctual. Where is the punctuality? In the world, the extension, *punch* does not pick out a momentary event at all. Extensionally, *punch* refers to a set of events that do take up time: the folding of the fist, the movement of the arm, the contact of the fist with another object, and the subsequent recoil of the arm. In *actual fact,* the event of punching has duration, but in *linguistic fact,* it does not:

   4a. ?? It took five minutes to punch him.
    b. ?? I spent an hour punching him.

Example (4a) is disallowed because it attributes duration to the event; example (4b) is understandable only if it is seen as describing repeated actions of punching, not an extended single act. So, although we are agreed that one part of the meaning of *punch* is its punctuality, we must now also agree that this punctuality is not a part of its extension, but part of how it is presented in the language outside of the strict facts denoted.

If intension fixes extension, if reference occurs in a projected world, not in a real world, how does this work? The usual answer is *compositionally:* The meaning of an expression is a function of the meaning of its parts. Compositionality is a general condition on semantic representations; it derives from the work of Frege, who saw a principal goal of semantic theory to be to account for how expressions with arbitrary meaning, like words (which have unmotivated, conventionalized extension), are put in nonarbitrary meaningful combinations, or structures. Compositionality can hold either across an entire expression or within a single form. In the first case, the meaning of an entire expression is a function of the meaning of its component forms, as the interpretation of a sentence derives from the meanings of its words. In the second case, the semantic representation of a single form, say a word, is composed of semantic properties that in conjunction fix the reference of the form. We concentrate on this latter case, specifically on how intension fixes the reference of a form in a piecemeal manner, by selecting properties or components of a referent in a projected world.

The two words *tie* and *untie* are opposites because the latter expresses the reversal of the situation expressed by the former. But how does *untie* reverse the extensional facts expressed by *tie?* Again there is a mismatch between the extensional facts and the facts as represented by the language. If someone unties a shoe, that person does not perform the exact reversal of the events done in tying the shoe. Untying is not the extensional reversal of tying, just the projected reversal thereof. Furthermore, what counts for untying is only *a piece of the situation* represented. For untying to have acceptably occurred, the thing tied must only come to be untied; the exact process does not have to be duplicated. All that matters is that a portion or property of the projected world be selected. This is the *denotation,* the core information of the projected world that fixes reference. In the case of *tie* and *untie,* the *result* fixes reference.

The significance of these pieces or properties (vs. the entire act itself) in the projected world is the gist of compositionality, that the meaning of any expression is a function of its parts. The issue, of course, is what is meant by *parts.* For our purposes, the meaning of a linguistic expression is a function of semantic properties in a projected world. The verb *punch* refers to properties in a projected world, one of which is punctuality; the verb *untie* refers to the property of result, among other properties, in a projected world. Some of these properties are relevant to the structural rules of language. As it turns out, both punctuality and result have a grammatical reflex. Our concern is with identifying the range of *grammatically coded properties* in the projected, intensional world.

To summarize the argument thus far, we have seen that there is variation in meaning despite constancy of reference. This is because there is a split between extension and intension, with the latter fixing the former. Meaning variation in the face of constant extension is possible because meaning itself is the selection of properties, or pieces, of a projected world.

2.212. *Meaning Without Determinate Reference:*
Presupposition

Now let us consider the second question (p. 00), meaning with no determinate extension at all. This is the usual problem raised in discussions of reference. If meaning is what is referred to in the world, then how do words like *unicorn* and *devil* have meaning? There is a straightforward extensional answer to this: We have seen pictures of these things, or have heard reports about them, so they have meaning from those extensions in the pictures and reports.

It is hard to respond to this retort because there is always the picture/report counter in response. But consider the more ordinary linguistic world, apart from devils and unicorns. What about a word like *the?* What is the extension for *the?* By all counts *the* has a distinct reference: definite, specific, given, or knowable things. Significantly, *the* refers not to the things themselves, but to their definiteness, knowability, givenness, and specificity. It is one thing to say that some words have unusual extensions, like pictures, but it is quite another to say that words have extensions like knowability. Where is knowability? Where is definiteness? And what about other referentially indeterminate words, like *of, with, for,* and so on? These, along with *the,* are among the most frequently occurring linguistic forms, so their meaning cannot be relegated to a special case.

Issues like this are at the heart of the Russell/Strawson debate in philosophical semantics, a debate that once again illustrates the necessity of the projected world and its compositional properties independent of, and in fact prior to, the extensional world. We examine the debate briefly. It focuses on the following sentence:

5. The present king of France is bald.

Sentence (5) is meaningful in spite of the fact that it has no extension at all: There is no king of France.

Bertrand Russell (1905) argued that the sentence is meaningful because it is false. For Russell, (5) contains a hidden existential claim, an *assertion*—a statement offered for verification—that there *is* a king of France. In his view, (5) is a composite expression—'there is a king of France *and* he is bald.' By the rules of logic, an expression consisting of conjoined expressions is false as a whole if any of its conjuncts is false. So because the existential claim of (5) is false, (5) itself is false and thereby meaningful. Therefore for Russell, there really are extensions, just false ones in the case of (5), and with enough mental work, we can uncover the hidden extensions.

In contrast to this analysis, P. F. Strawson (1950) proposed that (5) does not assert the existence of a present king of France, but rather *presupposes* it in some possible universe of discourse. Strawson's notion of presupposition is slightly different from that currently employed in semantics (see the discussion of pragmatics, pp. 36–44), but we can appreciate the thrust of his claim. Example (5) is meaningful not by virtue of some verification test on a hidden existential assertion for which there is no extension. How can there be verification if there is nothing to verify? How do we know that there is no king of France?

For Strawson, the truth of 'there is a king of France' is secondary to its successful use in actual discourse (though see Russell's, 1957, terse reply). Example (5) has two components: its truth value and its informational value. The former is asserted, and the latter is presupposed, taken as background to the assertion. It is meaningful because of a world of presupposed information, not because of a world of verifiable extensions.

We are not going to settle the Russell/Strawson debate here, especially because it evokes the much larger dispute of the connection between semantics and pragmatics, which we consider in section 2.4. Rather, we point out that a clear solution to the problem of meaning without determinate extension relies on reference in a world of information, not a world of fact. Strawson showed that intensions can make expressions meaningful in the absence of extensions.

2.22.   What Language Is *About*

We have seen that the view of meaning as reference requires considerable refinement in terms of a distinction between extension and intension, assertion and presupposition, and acknowledgment that if expressions refer, then they do so with respect to a projected world. When we say that meaning is reference, we are actually making a claim regarding what linguistic expressions are *about*. We have come to see that the most reasonable way to understand *aboutness* is via intensions and a projected world. But where is this projected world? What is this world that linguistic expressions are about?

In several interesting papers on the nature of communication and the theoretical metaphors that drive our conceptions of information exchange, Michael Reddy (1973, 1979) points out the predominance of what he calls the *conduit metaphor,* the fallacious belief that when we talk, we talk about the world directly, and send our thoughts felicitously over to other individuals through the conduit of language. Linguistic communication is typically viewed as the cloaking of ideas *in words,* as if words as packages somehow contain reports on the world they represent.

Reddy observes that none of this really happens. When one person talks to another, words do not come out of the speaker's mouth as packages full of direct report on facts, which the hearer then opens up to discover the fully packed meaning inside. On the contrary, the speaker forces air out of the lungs and shapes the molecules with the vocal apparatus; these molecules vibrate on the hearer's eardrums, sending neurochemical impulses to the brain. The hearer then *constructs a model* of what the speaker is thought to have said. People understand each other and communicate not by direct conveyance at all, but by broadcasting signals, which themselves evoke mental models.

The apparent existential gloom this picture presents—that we are all trapped in our own mental models of the world—does not mean that we cannot have something like mutual knowledge or even speak about the same things. On the contrary, the conduit metaphor puts the discussion of reference itself in clear light. We do not speak *about* the extensional world, but *about the model of the world we make up in our heads.* Furthermore, our language is not about entities in the projected world as totalities, but, as we have demonstrated with regard to compositionality, about pieces or properties of the projected world.

There are two broad ways to think about meaning: (a) as a relation between language and the world, or in terms of truth; (b) as a relation between language and its users, or in terms of understanding (see Dowty 1979: 375–95, citing Putnam). Given the conduit metaphor and revisions of what language is about, truth (a) is subordinate to understanding (b). The relation of language to the world follows the relation of language to its users because the world, extension, is a property of its users and hence reference is confined to the phenomena that make up the projected world.

Under this view, the traditional philosophical notion that meaning is *true reference* via *verification,* or the procedure by which true or false reference is determined, must be understood in a different light. The meaning of a sentence or an expression is the conditions under which its saying is true, but verification has to be understood as the determination of truth by reference to a piece of a mentally projected world. Verification is a mental operation, not a mechanistic matching of linguistic signals to their object counterparts.

2.23. Reference and Grammatical Meaning

In this section, we have seen the necessity of the mentally projected world of information and how this world accommodates the priority of intension over extension, the need for compositionality, and the fixing of reference. We can apply this result straightforwardly to our project of the determination of grammatical meaning. The content of semantic representations is found in the components of the mentally projected world of reference. We are interested in those parts of the mentally projected world that are associated with the way a language constructs its sentences. That is, we are concerned with semantic representations constructed out of a subset of the intensions that fix linguistic reference: those that fix extensions in terms of grammatical structure. In this way, the property of being blue-eyed, as discussed in Chapter 1, may be part of the mentally projected world of reference, but so are causing and becoming, and these latter intensions are, as we know, more of our concern.

We now turn to a related formulation of meaning: The meaning of an expression is its logical structure. The view that meaning is logical form follows from considerations of reference because logical analysis is connected to truth.

2.3.   APPROACH 2: MEANING AS LOGICAL FORM

In this section, we examine how logical approaches to meaning shed light on the basic issues of the content of semantic representations and the nature of grammatically relevant semantic properties. The logical study of meaning has a long history, and here we can hope only to survey some of the results and present the spirit of logical analysis (clear accounts of logical semantics as a whole are given by Allwood et al. 1977; Bach 1989; Ladusaw 1988; and McCawley 1981). Consequently, we limit our exposition to the nature and requirements of formal semantics, to certain general problems that formal semantics poses for the description of grammatical meaning in empirical terms, and, in the end, to a consideration of how formal and nonformal semantics may be fruitfully brought together.

2.31.   Logic, Meaning, and Formal Semantics

Why should we want to consider the meaning of an expression its *logical form,* or its representation in the mechanisms and formulas of logical analysis? There are two reasons: (a) Logic is typically concerned with truth, inference, and the content of expressions; (b) logic has an explicit and rigorous means of representing the content of expressions.

2.311.   *Logical Analysis and Content*

There is an inherent connection between logic and meaning because logic is concerned with conditions under which statements may be *truly inferred* from other statements. Hence logic and the analysis of meaning involved therein are *truth conditional.* As a result of this goal, as McCawley (1981: 1) remarks, "Logic is of necessity concerned with semantic analysis," because semantic analysis reveals the content of the expressions connected by inference. Logical analysis directly affects our attempts to discover grammatically relevant semantic properties because we determine the presence or absence of such properties by making true inferences. Consider *Tom punched Bob* and *Tom made contact with Bob.* We know intuitively that *if* Tom punched Bob, *then* Tom hit Bob, but not vice versa and thus that *punch* implies 'contact.' How do we know this?

We first determine the content of each expression by differentiating their status as *statements* (forms conveying true or false information) from their status as *sentences* (forms with grammatical structure). We then analyze the relationship between the two expressions by making a series of inferences about their content: If Tom punched Bob, then there must have been contact between the two; hitting necessarily involves contact, and so it must also be true that if Tom punched Bob, then he also made contact with Bob. Our conclusion rests on our ability to make judgments about likeness and difference of meaning, two goals traditionally within the scope of logic. Such judgments are, moreover, the cornerstone of all logic systems, which is the discovery of all necessarily true inferences, or *entailments* (see p. 28 for fuller definition of this term).

Logic relies on semantic analysis of the content of expressions to determine necessarily true inferences. In this sense, semantics is a branch of logic. As such, it buys into the second goal of logical analysis: to represent statements in a precise and unambiguous language.

2.312. Formal Semantics and Semantic Representation

Though systems of logical analysis have different requirements, depending on their purposes and their assumptions about inference and semantic content, they all typically have two parts: a *formal syntax* and a *formal semantics*. Both contribute to the *logical form* of an expression.

The *formal syntax* of a logical system is a set of symbols, and rules for their proper combination, in which to represent the content of expressions. In propositional logic—a system for representing and analyzing entire sentences—there is a vocabulary to represent the content of the sentences themselves, the propositions (the symbols p, q, r), and connectives to express the combination of propositions ($\lor$ ('or'), $\sim$ ('not'), & ('and'), $\rightarrow$ ('if, then')). In predicate logic— a system for representing and analyzing the constituents of sentences—there is a vocabulary to express predicates, arguments, and quantifiers as well as the connectives of propositional logic.

The formal syntax is complemented by an *interpretation* or a *formal semantics*. This is a way to connect the syntax to referents, and, in doing so, to assign truth values to expressions in the formal syntax. The semantic interpretation that forms the basis of most current theories of logical form is a *model*, which is an abstract specification of the properties of a world to which expressions can in principle refer (whence the notion of *model-theoretic semantics*). Models generally consist of three sets of things (or four, if the third is divided in two: (a) individuals to which the logical vocabulary can refer: for example, entities, events, kinds, and so forth; (b) truth values: true or false, and in some models (trivalent logics) neither true nor false; (c) worlds and times in which truth values and individuals occur: for example, then, now, possibly then, and so forth. So when we say that the expression *Tom punched Bob* has a meaning, in formal terms, we are saying that its syntactic forms (e.g., its predicate and arguments, Punch [Tom, Bob]) can be assigned referents from the set of individuals (e.g., an event and two entities) and have truth values in a certain world at a certain time (e.g., true prior to the moment of speech).

To say that meaning is discovered by looking at logical form, then, is to say that we have to see how an expression bears a relation to a model. More particularly, the meaning of an expression determines how the individuals referred to by the forms can be assigned truth values in a world at a time (i.e., their *truth conditions*). In relating meaning to the formal notion of *truth in a model,* formal semantics provides us with an explicit account of the content of semantic representations: the content of the model itself. Indeed, formal semantics, as a theory of models, is often thought of by its adherents as equivalent to semantic theory in general (see Ladusaw 1988).

This view of meaning as interpretation via a model brings with it a number of advantages. First, the content of semantic representations is made exact and unambiguous. Certainly, one of the problems with an intuitive account of meaning, like that we have employed thus far, is the room it leaves for error and subjective judgment. What does it mean to say that an expression denotes 'punctuality'? For 'punctuality' to be part of a formal theory of meaning, the notion must be clearly specified somewhere in the model. The explication of meaning in terms of the logical forms of an expression is a *restrictive theory of meaning*: It builds meaning from the bottom up and relies on only what is known to be part of the model to begin with.

Second, this account of meaning is *formal,* in that it is independent of the content of what it represents and thus can be generally and mechanistically applied. The model is a mathematical object. Formal semantics spells out what is necessarily the case for the interpretation of an expression and investigates the constraints on the model as an idealized "denotational space" (see, e.g., van Bentham 1986). As Bach (1989: 109) says, "We want our semantic theories just to give us the general structure of meanings, not the specific content." This assumes that what languages actually do in assigning meanings to expressions is to appropriate and naturalize the ideal formal model. The overall advantage of the formal characteristic of meaning is that semantic representations, though restrictive, are also quite general.

Third, if meaning is formal, then we can use the rest of the apparatus of formal analysis to solve standard semantic problems. A traditional goal of semantics is to account for intuitions we have about semantic relations between and within expressions: semantic likeness, difference, and inclusion. Examples of these relations are given here:

A. Likeness of Meaning: Identity, Equivalence, or Repetition

  1. *Synonymy:* equivalence or identity of words; e.g., *couch* and *sofa.*

  2. *Paraphrase:* equivalence or identity of sentences; e.g., *Bill ate the pizza* and *the pizza was eaten by Bill.*

3. *Tautology:* invariant truth of an expression because of redundancy or repetition; e.g., *Bill's brother is a sibling* (*sibling* is redundant given the content of *brother*).

B. Difference of Meaning: Oppositeness, Exclusion, or Incompatibility

1. *Antonymy:* oppositeness of words; e.g., *alive* versus *dead* and *hot* versus *cold*.

2. *Contradiction:* invariant falsity of an expression because of exclusion; e.g., *Bill's brother is his sister* (the meaning of *brother* and *sister* exclude each other).

3. *Anomaly:* oddness of an expression because of incompatibility; e.g., *Bill's lawnmower murdered the flowers* (inanimate lawnmowers are incompatible with the action of murdering, which requires an animate subject).

C. Inclusion of Meaning:

1. *Hyponymy:* set membership of words; e.g., *couch* and *furniture* (a couch is included in the set of furniture).

2. *Entailment:* invariantly true implication of a sentence from another sentence because the first contains the second; e.g., *Bill ran* entails *Bill did something* (running includes the notion of action and so an expression with *run* necessarily implies an expression with *do something*).

Formal semantics can help us decide clearly about these semantic relations in terms of their truth conditions. For example, two sentences are *paraphrases* if they have the same truth conditions, or more technically, if they entail each other. Thus, if *Bill ate the pizza* is true, then *the pizza was eaten by Bill* is necessarily true, and vice versa. Synonyms are words that can be substituted for each other in an expression without affecting the truth value: *I bought a couch* has the same truth conditions as *I bought a sofa.*

Furthermore, we can refine this concern for truth conditions to determine more subtle types of likeness, difference, and inclusion of meaning. Lexical semanticists (those who study word meaning) typically identify two major kinds of antonymy—*ungradable* and *gradable* antonyms—determined by their truth conditions. *Ungradable antonyms* are words whose meanings mutually exclude each other, lexical contradictions, denotations with no middle ground. A standard test for such antonyms is as follows: the truth of one requires the falsity of the other ($X \rightarrow -Y$ and $Y \rightarrow -X$) and the falsity of one requires the truth of the other ($-X \rightarrow Y$ and $-Y \rightarrow X$). By this test, *alive* and *dead* are ungradable antonyms: If something is alive, it is not dead; if something is dead, it is not alive; if something is not alive, it is dead; if something is not dead, it is alive. Ungradable antonyms are sometimes called *complementaries* because they complete each other in excluding the middle ground.

If we slightly loosen the formal test for ungradable antonyms, we get *grada-*

ble antonyms (or *contraries*), those that have a middle ground. For gradables, only the first part of the formal test for ungradables holds: The truth of one requires the falsity of the other. *Hot* and *cold* meet this simpler test: If something is hot, it is not cold; if something is cold, it is not hot. Note, however, that if something is not hot, then it is not necessarily cold, but, perhaps, *warm*. Hence, *hot* and *cold* are antonyms with a middle ground, determined by the truth of the inferences that can be made from expressions containing them (see Cruse 1986 for fuller discussion).

This final example returns us to our original reason for doing formal semantics: We can enumerate the inferences that hold across statements through analysis of the content of the expressions those statements take. Semantic relations are all kinds of inference and are calculated on the basis of the semantic representations of the expressions involved: One expression entails another because the semantic representation of one is a necessary semantic consequence of the semantic representation of another. Formal semantics determines the nature of representations proper, so inferences are made with respect to a model for interpretation and can be defined in relation thereto.

2.32.   Two Problems with Formal Semantics

We have seen how a formal approach to meaning elucidates the nature and content of semantic representations. In particular, we have seen how the idea of a model as an abstract "denotational space" clarifies basic questions of meaning. In spite of this great advantage, there are certain problems inherent in formal semantics. To say that a system is formal is to say that it is *categorical* and *contentless*. It is these two features that ultimately force apart formal semantics and linguistic semantics.

Before we discuss these two features in relation to linguistic meaning, we should be aware of an important caveat. *Formal* does not mean 'formalism.' A popular method of debunking logic and of showing the divergence of formal and nonformal semantics is to point out that the *notation* of formal semantics is insensitive to distinctions made in ordinary language. For example, it is easy to show that in predicate logic, the notation for quantifiers excludes a variety of quantifiers that are otherwise found in ordinary language. Predicate logic has two quantifiers: the universal quantifier ('every/all'), and the existential quantifier ('at least one/some'). There is no way to represent the quantifiers *many, a couple, several,* and so on, quantifiers found commonly in everyday speech. It is sometimes thought that predicate logic and ordinary language are simply incompatible because of this absence. This is wrong. We could certainly develop a form of predicate logic that has symbols for these additional quantifiers. All we have to do is assign them a notation: M for *many*, S for *several*, and so on. The trick is not the notation. The formalism is arbitrary, and any phenomenon can be represented. The inadequacy of the notation of formal systems is a trivial objection. The heart of the matter lies in what makes the system formal, not in what makes the formalism.

2.321. *Categoricalness*

A formal system is *categorical:* The logical objects and operations that populate a formal system have discrete boundaries. There is no overlap, and one object categorically excludes another. For example, $\sim$, logical negation, categorically reverses the truth value of *whatever* it attaches to. There is no sense in propositional logic of more or less negation, or a gradience of falsity. The same may be said for the quantifiers in predicate logic. The universal quantifier $\forall$, for example, stands categorically for the totality of a set; the existential quantifier $\exists$ categorically defines 'some' or 'at least one.' There is no gradience of quantification in predicate logic, just as there is no gradience of truth value for the negative operator in propositional logic.

But if we look at ordinary language, we find that it is full of gradient phenomena, more technically known as *fuzziness* (see Lakoff 1972 for the classic study; see also Lakoff 1987, 1988; Jackendoff 1983: chap. 7). The insight behind fuzziness indicates that categories have vague boundaries and are internally organized from central focal values, the *prototype* (Rosch 1973, 1975), to less focal instances and fringe values. As the centrality of the category fades, and criteria for membership in the category are less decisively applied, and categories merge into each other. Therefore, a category may be said to have a *degree of inclusiveness* rather than strict criteria that ultimately draw a conceptual line between phenomena admitted and those excluded.

The need for gradience is especially pertinent in the case of *semantic categories,* in, for example, an account of natural language negation. Negation in formal semantics is categorical, but natural language requires *degrees of negation.*

Two reliable tests of the presence of negation in English are: (1) its co-occurrence with *any* as opposed to *some* and (2) the addition of a positive tag question (see Horn 1989; Klima 1964; J. Payne 1985; see also chap. 9). The following negative sentence takes both:

    6. The senator did not take any bribes, did she/he?

However, when we look at English in more detail, we see that a variety of phenomena trigger these same tests, though not all equally, and not all through explicit negation:

    7a. The senator seldom took any bribes, did/didn't she/he?
      b. The senator rarely took any bribes, did/didn't she/he?

Neither *seldom* nor *rarely* is overtly negative (there is no *not,* as in [6]), but they trigger *any* and so must have a negative in their semantic representations, something like 'not frequently.' Unfortunately for the negative analysis, they also trigger *both* kinds of tag questions. So, even though *seldom* and *rarely* are negative in some sense, they are not totally negative, at least not like *not.*

This picture is further complicated by the following:

8 a. Rather than take any bribes, the senator resigned.
   b. Before the senator took any bribes, he/she covered his/her tracks.
   c. Did the senator take any bribes?

These sentences allow *any,* but they are all clearly positive and so there is no obvious need for a negative in their semantic representations. It might be argued, however, that *rather* is an implicit negative, expressing something like 'so as not to.' *Before* might also be argued to be negative, 'unrealized action.' A similar explanation also accounts for the acceptability of *any* with questions. Information questions are designed to indicate 'uncertainty,' strictly speaking another form of negation.

Examples (6–8) illustrate the gradient status of negation. There is *focal negation,* or *denial,* signalled by *not,* which allows both reliable tests of negation. There are also markers of *attenuated negation,* like *seldom* and *rarely;* these take one of the tests clearly and arguably one of the others. There are, finally, markers of *uncertainty* and *unrealization,* a kind of a weak negation: not denial, but negation on the level of expectations. These also trigger a negative test.

It seems clear, then, that ordinary language admits negation by degree. In such a case, the categoricalness of negation in formal semantics is incompatible with the fuzziness of negation in language. In this case, the formal nature of logical analysis prevents accurate description, and linguistic semantics, because it must deal with all three forms of negation, has to be nonformal on this count.

2.322. *Contentlessness*

We have seen one problem with the formal nature of formal semantics, categoricalness. Linguistic semantics must admit scalar categories. Formal semantics is also associated with contentlessness. As Bach (1989) points out, semantic theories do not give specific content. But content clearly matters: Negation is possible in degree because of the *content of the negative expressions concerned.*

If specific content is excluded, as formal semantics has it, then two more particular problems arise:

1. formal semantics treats some phenomena alike that linguistic semantics treats differently;

2. formal semantics treats some phenomena differently that linguistic semantics treats alike.

As to the first problem, let us consider the quantifiers *each, every,* and *all*. In formal terms, they are all represented by the universal quantifier ∀, and are formally undifferentiated because they have the same effect on the truth of expressions in which they occur. But there are *clear content differences* across the three: *all* refers to the set it quantifies as a totality; *each* and *every* refer to the set by means of its individual members. *All* is thus said to be *collective; every* and *each* are said to be *distributive* (see chap. 10 for more discussion).

The difference between collective and distributive quantification may not make a difference formally, but it does make a difference empirically, as the following sentences indicate:

9a. All the boys lifted a truck.
  b. ?? Every boy lifted a truck.
  c. ?? Each boy lifted a truck.

Example (9a) is acceptable because the content of the quantifier interacts with the content of the verb *lift* and the content of the noun *truck*. This sentence can be understood only collectively, because trucks, if they are to be lifted at all, are preferably lifted by a group. Example (9b) is odd because it asserts that the activity is carried out distributively, a bizarre possibility because it suggests that the boys individually have superhuman strength; the same holds for (9c).

The anomalies in (9b) and (9c) disappear when the *semantic content* of the object changes:

10a. Every boy lifted a bag of top soil.
  b. Each boy lifted a bag of top soil.

The content of the new noun interacts with the distributive content of the quantifier. The semantic facts are then compatible, so the sentences are not anomalous. Interestingly enough, if the object is also changed for the collective quantifier, we now get ambiguity:

11. All the boys lifted a bag of top soil.

But it is important to note that the *semantic content* of the quantifiers and the nouns is a determining factor. From a formal standpoint, all three quantifiers are treated alike, but their content matters and so in practice, they must be treated differently.

Now, what about the second problem, that formal semantics treats some things differently that linguistic semantics treats alike? Previously it has been shown that negation is a gradient: from categorical denial to attenuated negation to uncertainty, respectively illustrated:

12a. Bob did not go. (denial)
  b. Bob rarely went. (attenuated)
  c. Did Bob go? (uncertainty)

In formal semantics, all three kinds of negation have a *different* treatment. Example (12a) is represented as logical negation; example (12b) is treated as a *positive* assertion; example (12c), if analyzable at all in formal terms, has to be accommodated by some logical system that can represent questions. Linguistically, however, (12a–c) have to be treated similarly at some level of analysis because they all encode negation. In fact, in many languages, the overt marking of negation and questions is the same: Proto-Indoeuropean, Latin, Quechua, and Turkish (Lehmann 1974: 153). In the case of negation, formal semantics may prevent the basic goal of linguistics—maximum generalization— from being achieved. It is difficult to see how these gradient facts can be accommodated by an approach that does not focus on exactly what makes one negative different in content from another.

2.33. Formal and Nonformal Semantics: Versus or Plus?

Though formal semantics has the virtue of exactitude about the content of semantic representations, it is often incompatible with the needs of linguistic semantics because the latter must address the content of the categories and objects it analyzes and allow for gradient category membership. This incompatibility is to a large extent the results of the fact that formal semantics, as Montague (1974) put it and as Partee (1979) so nicely explains, is really a branch of mathematics and is therefore not primarily an empirical discipline at all. Linguistic semantics, as pictured thus far, is what Montague (1974) called *lexicography,* the cataloguing of actual meanings. Lest this be taken as a slight, mathematics has no inherently larger claim to respectability than inductive, data-driven analysis. (The latter is arguably more important than the former if the history of ideas counts as support: Engineering gave rise to geometry, not the other way around!)

The goal of any formal system is to discover all the true entailments that the system allows. In a complete logical system, all the logically true expressions, the tautologies, are entailed by all the arbitrarily true ones. From a formal semantic viewpoint, *My brother's name is Bob,* which is arbitrarily true, entails *Whoever knows Spanish knows Spanish,* which is a tautology. Though this is a valid inference formally, it is simply not a real one. As Seuren (1985: 212) cogently remarks, we must distinguish "between those entailments that are natural" and those "that are mathematically valid." The latter typically "do not play any role either in cognition or in semantic processing" (Seuren 1985: 213), which makes them totally foreign to empirical semantics. How could they possible fit into a mentally projected world?

Formal semantics carves up the world differently from the way that linguistic semantics does. What formal semantics often holds as likeness, linguistic semantics hold as difference, and vice versa. This is why logicians find the results of linguistic semantics as puzzling as some semanticists find the results of formal semantics. Van Bentham (1986: 206–7) remarks that one of the problems with empirical generalizations making their way into formal semantics is not that the empirical generalizations are wrong, just that formal semanticists do not know how to evaluate such claims. Perhaps the reverse lesson is relevant too: How can categorical and contentless approaches be evaluated when semantic phenomena are fuzzy and when content matters?

In spite of these enormous differences, formal semantics and linguistic semantics appear to be converging. In the formal literature, there is now discussion of how the logical form of an expression links up with what is called *real world semantics,* or the actual models that are used to interpret formal expressions.

The same change of heart underlies recent attempts in model theoretic semantics to bring the model more in line with the requirements of natural language. One goal of formal semantics is to restrict the variety of objects to which expressions may refer and in so doing capture a wide range of denotations through a small set of individuals. For example, Carlson (1977, and in later works) attempts to reduce the set of referable entities to objects, kinds, and stages, roughly and respectively discrete individuals, classes and states, and events and actions (see Bach 1989: 96). The set of individuals in the model is thus severely limited so that reference is carried out from the simplest base. This is a decided advantage in formal terms, where simplicity is the ultimate criterion for an acceptable account.

It turns out, however, that real world semantics requires that the set of referable objects in formal theory be *increased* to accommodate the kinds of reference that actual expressions have. Bach (1989: 96) observes that the set of individuals in an adequate model for interpretation must contain such things as *eventualities,* roughly processes, and the only way to accommodate this "is just to 'put them in' as elements of the domain" (1989: 96). Ladusaw (1988: 100) calls this modification "adding structure to the ontology," and notes how doing so is necessary to capture one of the very problems of formal semantics raised earlier: the difference between distributive and collective quantifiers. The solution in formal semantics is to add them to the model, but this change follows from the requirements of real world interpretation.

As we need a more specific formal ontology, we end up doing something like conceptual semantics anyway by focusing on the content of the forms and letting truth follow from understanding. Formal semantics and linguistic semantics are not incompatible, but complementary. The former delineates the necessary restrictions on denotations in an ideal semantic space, a model. The latter spells out the requirements of actual semantic systems in real world languages.

Formal semantics is theory-driven and devoted to explanation over description, under the assumption that the descriptions are somehow a natural subset of the explanations. Linguistic semantics is data-driven and inductive, devoted to tabulations and empirical findings first. There is, of course, a well-known problem with the data-driven approach: In the mass of tabulated data, no explanation ever emerges and the pursuit reduces to a kind of elaborate linguistic accountancy.

It might be best to let the two work in tandem, provided that we understand that *real world semantics* is the ultimate goal of the analysis of meaning. Rather than seeing linguistic semantics as a kind of bad version of logical theory, we might do well to see formal semantics as an extreme version of empirical work. Categorical results are then the 100% applicability of a scale: Logical denial, for example, is just negation *in extremis*.

If we begin semantics with a categorical view, then we are forced to account for noncategorical findings as marginal or anomalous cases. But when the marginal cases turn out to be so productive—like the convergence of negation and questions—what are we to make of marginality? If we begin with empirical semantics, nothing is marginal. Categorical denial is certainly not marginal, nor is questioning a case of marginal negation. The real problem is: What are we to do with formal semantics when scalar phenomena do not suggest marginality?[1]

2.34.   Logical Form and Grammatical Meaning

In this section, we have seen the advantages and disadvantages of construing meaning as the logical form of an expression. What is the ultimate lesson of this inquiry for our project of identifying, tabulating, and explaining grammatical meaning? Formal semantics can help us discover the content of semantic representations by specifying the requirements of any denotation. If meaning is truth in a model, we must understand and be precise about how grammatically sensitive semantic properties are components of that model. Though model-theoretical semantics has come to see the need for real world semantics, we must not forget the opposite lesson: Without a theory-driven approach, we may never get to an explanation. So logical form and linguistic semantics must work together to account for grammatical meaning.

---

[1]One notable omission in the aforementioned discussion is the common argument that formal semantics is to be avoided because it is difficult to map formal structures onto syntax. Jackendoff (1983) makes this claim in invoking the Grammatical Constraint (see p. 11) and arguing for a close initial connection between syntax and semantics. For example, relative quantifier scope of the kind illustrated in the ambiguity of *All the boys lifted a bag of top soil* is typically captured in a formal structure by bracketing and serial position. The quantifier with the widest scope is put first. So, on one reading, where a single bag is lifted by many boys, the formal structure is roughly [a[all]], where *a* is to the left of *all,* deriving the one-to-many reading; conversely, the second reading, where many boys lift a single bag each, is roughly [all[a]], with the serial positions reversed, giving the many-to-one reading.

2.4. APPROACH 3:
MEANING AS CONTEXT AND USE

Thus far, we have seen two approaches to the content of semantic representations: the mentally projected world of reference and logical form. We now turn to another view of meaning, meaning as context and use, to see what this teaches us about how to proceed. Here we see that the properties to which linguistic expressions refer are relatively stable in any context because they are inherent in the expressions themselves. Just as extensional reference is subordinate to intensions, and logical form is best understood after the fact, so grammatically relevant meanings are not determined by use.

2.41. Context and the Selection of Meaning

To say that meaning is independent of context and use is certainly not a popular or even obvious position. It is common among the untrained to remark that the meaning of an expression is its context and its function in that context. Curiously, this is also a position held by some who apparently should know better, or who at least have heard arguments to the contrary.

Wittgenstein (1953), for example, is known to have changed his view of meaning from one where meaning is a logical picture of the facts—truth and reference inhering in an expression—to one where the meaning of an expression is a function of its use in a particular context—a *language game,* to use his words. A similar position is advanced by some who also take a formal approach to semantics. In the theory of Situation Semantics, for instance, meaning is viewed as a "relation between circumstances and content" (Barwise 1988: 29), or to use the phraseology of Situation Semantics, meaning is not reference to semantic properties, but the "articulation" of properties from the context. According to the adherents: "Most attention in semantics is paid to content" (Bar-

---

The problem with these formal structures is how to translate them into grammatical form. On the surface, *All the boys lifted a bag of top soil* has a single scope structure, [all[a]]. How does the first reading, [a[all]], surface in reverse? Seemingly arbitrary, and certainly overly complicated, rules appear to be required to match the semantics with the syntax.

In all fairness to formal semantics, I think these objections are without force. Nonformal semantics has the very same problems! Suppose that we say that *punch* is punctual. How does punctuality map onto syntax? Suppose there is a scale of negation? How does this scale map onto grammatical form? What motivates the relation other than descriptive findings: that is, that negatives do, in fact, look like questions in some languages? Linguists like Bybee (1985) and Talmy (1985) observe consistent meaning/form patterns, but the ultimate explanations seem just as arbitrary as those given for the mapping of formal structures onto syntax. How do we explain that the semantic property of desire is almost never coded by an affix, unlike mood, for example? Do we say that desire is more subjective than mood and subjective meanings tend to have free-standing forms? This seems more than a bit stretched to me, and it pushes aside the mapping question rather than explaining it, even if it pushes it aside imaginatively.

wise 1988: 29), but "the circumstances are crucial in getting from the sentence to its content" (Barwise 1988: 28).

The same position is often held by linguists who pursue discourse analysis. An extreme version of this position is that given by de Beaugrande (1985: 50): "The enterprise of stating all potential word classes and meanings—the ultimate step in abstract linguistics—is doomed precisely because the results of contextual determination cannot be foreseen. . . . A more auspicious enterprise would be to explore the processes of contextual determination."

Context and use—what is otherwise known as *pragmatics*—determine meaning. Linguistic semantics is therefore secondary to an examination of contexts and uses.

Why is this view appealing? For one thing, is appears to be self-evidently correct. In actual practice, context clearly matters in the selection of the particular meaning we use to understand a linguistic expression. Suppose that we are standing by a river, and I say: "I was near that bank yesterday." You certainly understand *bank* as 'river bank,' not 'financial institution.' Likewise, if we are on Wall Street, and I say "I was near that bank yesterday," you do not think I am referring to the edge of a river. Surely, then, the context *determines* the meaning.

This view that pragmatics exceeds or somehow precludes other approaches to meaning relies on the failure to distinguish—or the unwillingness to acknowledge the difference between—the selection of meaning from the meaning selected. Linguistic expressions come into a context of use with a set of possible meanings to be selected. Pragmatics involves the selection of the contextually relevant meaning, not the determination of what counts as the meaning itself.

There are a number of well-known characteristics that distinguish pragmatics from semantics. We concentrate on just a few of these to illustrate the differences further and to underscore that there are, in contrast to pragmatically selected meanings, grammatically relevant semantic properties that are relatively stable, inherent in linguistic forms, and independent of context and use.

2.42.   Truth-Conditionality, Context-Dependence, and Cancellability

Consider the following exchange:

A: I may win the lottery in Pennsylvania for $83 million.
B: There may be people on Mars, too.

How is this exchange meaningful? The implication of A's statement is not only that it is possible to win the lottery, but also that it is likely. In responding, speaker B denies the likelihood, not the possibility, of the future state of affairs implied by A's statement, but how so? B does this by presenting information that, on face value, is irrelevant to the situation and unlikely to be true. A's and

B's statements require inferences to be made for the exchange to be understood at all. A crucial part of this understanding is that the inferences that A triggers, that B denies, and that B suggests are not truth-conditional. *I may win the lottery* does not entail *I am likely to win the lottery.* Nor does it matter to the exchange whether or not there are people on Mars. In fact, even if there are people on Mars, what is critical to the exchange itself and the denial of the likelihood of A winning the lottery is the recognition by A and B that the existence of people on Mars is unlikely and that the content of B's statement is *ostensibly irrelevant.*

The inferences forced by statements like A's and B's are called *implicatures* (non-truth-conditional inferences). In pioneering work on pragmatics, Grice (1975, 1978; see also Levinson 1983) observed that in actual communicative practice, most exchanges have a great deal of information missing between what is actually said and what is understood to have been meant. Speakers and hearers fill in this information through implicatures, systematic inferences about what is intended built on the basis of what is actually said.

Implicatures, Grice noted, are not truth-conditional. In the earlier exchange between A and B, B's denial of the likelihood of A's winning the lottery is accomplished by B forcing the interlocutor to make an inference that focuses on the *acceptability* of the statement, its *communicative significance,* not its truth value. In contrast, let us compare implicatures, non-truth-conditional inferences, with truth-conditional inferences, *entailments* (see sec. 2.312). Entailment is a relation between two sentences such that if the first is true, then the second is necessarily true. One entailment of the sentence *I may win the lottery in Pennsylvania for $83 million* is *Pennsylvania is a place.* That is, the phrase *in Pennsylvania* indicates that Pennsylvania is a place, and this is true because of the semantic properties of the item *in,* which specifies locations in *all contexts.*

Note what happens to the original exchange if B denies an entailment:

A: I may win the lottery in Pennsylvania for $83 million.
B: Pennsylvania is not a place.

Here, B forces an inference about properties of the referents of the words themselves, rather than about the relevance of the intentions of the interlocutors. This exchange is very odd, precisely because B has denied an inherent property of the referent of *in,* namely that in all contexts *in* requires a place. B's statement here affects more seriously the information status of the exchange as a whole than does a denial through implicature.

Implicatures and entailments have a different range of effects and possibilities in actual linguistic exchange. The former are *context-dependent* and *non-truth-conditional;* the latter are *context-independent* and *truth-conditional.* Pragmatics studies, among other things, the forms that implicatures may take because implicatures are a function of how the pragmatic context intervenes in the selection of meaning. But in all cases, implicatures remain essentially different from entailments.

Grice identified two broad classes of implicatures: *conversational im-plicatures* and *conventional implicatures*. The former are non-truth-conditional inferences based on the principles of rational conversation. Grice noted that rational discourse proceeds according to four *maxims: quantity* (people do not say too much or too little), *quality* (people usually say the truth), *relevance* (people usually say things that are related to the topic), and *manner* (people say things reasonably expeditiously and in coherent order). If speakers violate or choose to flout any of these maxims, they trigger a conversational implicature by indicating to the hearer their intent about some piece of information unexpressed. Notice that the original exchange between A and B may be viewed as succeeding through the violation of one of two maxims. In one sense, speaker B cancels the implicature of likelihood by violating the maxim of relevance: What does Mars have to do with the lottery? In another sense, speaker B cancels the implicature by flouting the maxim of quality: We all know that there really are not people on Mars, so the assertion of a blatant falsity cancels the inference. Violations show that conversational implicatures are tied to the intentions of the speaker and the recognition of those intensions by the hearer. These characteristics do not hold for entailments. The meaning of the word *in,* for example, as 'location,' is not tied to the intentions of the speaker, nor is it a function of the hearer's decision to recognize it as meaning 'location.' *In* is *inherently* a locative, regardless of who says it, who hears it, or whatever context it occurs in.

In contrast to conversational implicatures, there are conventional im-plicatures. These are non-truth-conditional inferences triggered by words or phrases themselves, not by the violation of principles of exchange, and are said to be conventionally carried by the expressions. The word *even* is typically cited as a trigger of conventional implicature. *Even* implicates a contrast with prior information and has its force not by what it entails, but by what it says about the exchange of information. Consider the following exchange:

A: John had a party.
B: Even Fred showed up.

Here, *even* signals a contrast between the expectation that Fred does not come to parties and the fact that he violated that expectation. But note that this contrast is not part of the truth or falsity of the statement. The sentence *Even Fred showed up* is neither true nor false for that matter because of the word *even*. If *even* is eliminated, the sentence may have a truth value: *Fred showed up* is verifiable. Thus B's statement is accountable to its *interactional properties,* not its truth. Its appropriateness, furthermore, does not depend so much on the rules of conversa-tion as on the contrast it inherently signals.

Conventional implicature is therefore a kind of implicature, but it is *less context-dependent* than conversational implicature. Conventional implicatures are a property of the words and phrases that signal them, and thus are less negotiable. But they remain context-dependent in that they rely on the structure of the information exchange, as *even* requires a contrast with prior information. Hence on a scale of negotiability, conversational implicatures exceed conventional ones.

Pragmatic information, as implicatures, is non-truth-conditional and context-dependent; semantic information, as entailments, in contrast, is truth-conditional and context-independent. Pragmatic information is also *cancellable* (or *defeasible*); semantic information is not cancellable. Let us return for illustration to the implicatures discussed earlier.

Suppose that after hearing B's denial of the likelihood of his winning the lottery, A decides to reassert this likelihood, or to reject B's denial. The exchange might then continue:

A: I may win the lottery in Pennsylvania for $83 million.

B: There may be people on Mars, too.

A: What are you, some kind of astronomer?

A's retort calls into question B's authority for making that statement. In technical terms, A denies one of the *felicity conditions* on the exchange. These are the overall social conditions on speakers and hearers that allow them to utter things in contexts (authority to speak, sincerity in carrying out intentions, and so on: see Searle 1969). In denying B's authority, A *cancels the implicature* that B originally triggered.

Note what happens, however, if A tries to cancel the semantic information— the entailments:

A: I may win the lottery in Pennsylvania for $83 million.

B: There may be people on Mars, too.

A: Mars isn't a place.

This exchange is completely controverted by A's remark, which effectively cancels *all* the information, not just what is being exchanged. Thus, pragmatic information can be cancelled, but semantic information cannot be cancelled.

2.43. Scaling Pragmatics and Semantics: Implicature, Presupposition, and Entailment

All meaning—both pragmatics and semantics—is background information evoked by a linguistic signal. Given the discussion of the previous section, we can scale this information in terms of its context-dependence. Some depends on what speakers and hearers intend each other to infer about their words. Such information is typified by implicatures. Conversational implicatures depend wholly on the context of conversation; conventional implicatures are also context-dependent, but are more a function of what individual expressions bring to the exchange. If we thus set up these two on a scale of context-dependence or inherence, conversational implicatures are more dependent than conventional implicatures.

In maximum contrast to implicatures, there are entailments: *in* entails location; *punch* entails punctuality. Such information is independent of context. It does not rely on what the speakers and hearers believe about each other or what they intend to convey to each other by their words. Hence entailments are at the other end of the scale of context-dependence.

There is another kind of background information that rounds out this scale. Implicatures and entailment form the poles of this gradience. In between is *presupposition,* which is truth-functional and hence toward the inherent end of the scale, but may be cancelled and hence also like implicature.

2.431. Presupposition

We have already discussed presupposition informally in our account of Strawson's response to Russell (p. 22). According to the more technical definition, a *presupposition* is information that is true about a proposition whether or not the proposition is questioned or denied (see Fauconnier 1985; Kempson 1975; Levinson 1983; Oh and Dineen 1979). Classic examples of presupposition-bearing expressions are *factive verbs,* verbs that presuppose the truth of their syntactic complements (Kiparsky and Kiparsky 1970). One such verb is *regret:*

13. Tom regrets that Harry is here.

In the situation represented by (13), it is always true that Harry is here. This can be seen by subjecting the sentence to both question and denial:

14a. Does Tom regret that Harry is here?
   b. Tom doesn't regret that Harry is here.

In each case, it is again true that Harry is here. Therefore, *regret* presupposes its complement, *that Harry is here.*

Presuppositions, it should be noted, are different from entailments. Both a presupposition and an entailment are relations between antecedent and consequent sentences (or propositions, the content of sentences), but they have different truth conditions. For entailment, if X (the antecedent) is true then Y (the consequent) is necessarily true. But for presupposition, if X is true, Y is necessarily true and if X is false, Y is still true. Presupposition is, in a sense, independent because its truth holds regardless of the truth value of the antecedent (see Kempson 1975).

The relative independence of presupposition makes it difficult to put in a controverting context. Suppose that Tom is obsessed with Bob, hates Bob, and feels miserable whenever he and Bob are in the same place. The two happen to be at the same party when Harry comes up to Tom and convinces him that Bob is not such a bad guy. So now it is technically false that Tom regrets that Bob is at the party, but Bob is still at the party even though Tom no longer regrets it. In other words, the sentence *It's not true that Tom regrets that Bob is at the party* still presupposes that Bob is at the party. In spite of the falsity of the predicate, the presupposition holds.

Presupposition is relatively context-independent because it occurs in spite of the true-or-false context (for factives, in this case). This makes it like entailment, which is also independent of context. But unlike entailment, presupposition is cancellable, though under an extreme interpretation, as the following sentence shows:

15. Tom doesn't regret that Bob is at the party.

Sentence (15) is ambiguous. On one reading, (16) has the standard factive interpretation: 'It is false that Tom regrets that Bob is at the party, but in spite of this, Bob is still at the party.' But there is another reading where the presupposition itself may be cancelled: 'Tom doesn't regret that Bob is at the party because Bob isn't at the party! If Bob were at the party, then Tom would regret it.' Here, the presupposition can be cancelled, much like an implicature, even though presupposition is otherwise very much like entailment.

What are we to make of this? We can understand this situation if we accept that all meaning, as background information, may be context-dependent *to a varying degree*. There is noncancellable, context-independent information: entailment. There is information that is cancellable, but still context-independent: presupposition. There is information that is cancellable and context dependent, though it comes as a property of linguistic expressions and is not wholly derived from context: conventional implicature. There is information that is entirely context-dependent and cancellable: conversational implicature.

2.432. A Scale of Background Information

Figure 2.1 schematizes all the characteristics considered in terms of a scale of background information. Movement to the right on the scale increases semantic or representational meaning and truth-conditionality, and it decreases implicational meaning, context-dependence, relevance of speaker and hearer, and cancellability. Movement to the left reverses these characteristics.

Conversational   >   Conventional   >   Presupposition   >   Entailment
Implicature   Implicature

←——→

Pragmatics   Semantics
Non-truth-conditional   Truth-conditional
Context-dependent   Context-independent
Speaker/Hearer   No Speaker/Hearer
Cancellable   Noncancellable

FIG. 2.1.   Scale of background information.

2.44.   Meaning as Context Revisited

In light of a scale of information, as in Fig. 2.1, the view of meaning as context and use takes on a new understanding. When people say that meaning is use in context, they are really saying that some meaning is variable and selected by the situation at hand. This meaning is unlike the kind of information that is grammaticalized, which is a property of the expressions themselves and is relatively stable across any context.

The scalar relation between semantics and pragmatics also shows that it is not useful to force pragmatics and semantic apart. There is in fact a rather paradoxical relation between the two. Some semantic information is derived from pragmatic information. For example, many languages have ways of marking the social status of the speaker grammatically (by use of honorifics). This information obviously derives from extralinguistic facts like societal organization and hierarchies of authority. Social information about persons may become stabilized in a language and given consistent coding. But the pragmatic origins of some semantic information does not vitiate the distinction between semantics and pragmatics (see chap. 3, on social status).

Analogously, only some semantic information has pragmatic origins. In the case of color terms (see chap. 10), semantic distinctions are a function of the physiological apparatus that humans have for differentiating light waves. So here is some stable lexical information without a pragmatic source.

Thus, on one hand, some semantic information derives from pragmatics; on the other hand, in spite of the pragmatic origin of much semantic information, pragmatics requires semantics for its effect. Semantics cannot be eliminated just because of its origin in pragmatics. So in the earlier sample exchange when A says *I may win the lottery in Pennsylvania for $83 million,* likelihood is implicated, but not entailed. But this implicature is clearly related to the *semantic structure* of the sentence by being grounded in the semantic property of 'possibility.' In this case, contextual determination is driven by the semantic information inherent in the expression. The context must operate on the what semantics gives it, not the other way around, as a radical contextualist, like de Beaugrande (1985), might have it.

Higginbotham (1988: 29) remarks: "The rules of semantics . . . are independent of context; but they come alive only in use." This is because semantic properties are related to the design features of language, not the way that the design features are deployed. In fact, the design features themselves may constrain the way that meanings are deployed:

> Perhaps nothing at all that people say has its meaning wholly independently of context. It does not follow that semantic theory has little to say, or that it is in any way intrinsically incomplete. On the contrary, it is through only context-independent features that we know what aspects of a context to take as relevant in the first place to the interpretation of the utterances around us. (Higginbotham 1986: 1–2)

Here we see the ultimate lesson of the claim that meaning is context and use. Even if it is so, that does not deny literal stable, inherent meanings of linguistic expressions. If meaning is context and use, it may in the end turn out that context and use may be relevant *only because the linguistic expressions themselves bring semantic conditions with them into any context.*

2.45. Context, Use, and Grammatical Meaning

How does the essential independence of linguistic meaning from context and use relate to our goal of tabulating grammatically relevant semantic properties? Semantic representations, composed of a subset of intensions, supersede context and use. Structural meaning comes into a context of use immune to the contingencies of choice and belief that constitute the milieu of discourse. Hence even variation in grammatical meaning across languages and contexts must be constrained by some well-defined parameters of meaning and structure. No doubt this is because the structure of our mental representations in general, of which our semantic representations are a type, is the same for all humans. We see this possibility more closely in the following two sections, on culture and conceptual structure.

2.5. APPROACH 4: MEANING AS CULTURE

We have seen that context and use play a major role in the selection of meaning to be expressed, but a secondary role in the determination of the inherent meaning of a linguistic form. There is a position related to the contextualist view that also requires exploration. This is *cultural reductionism,* the often popular and popularized view that culture is the final arbiter of meaning, or that linguistic meaning is entirely determined by the cultural context in which the language occurs.

2.51.   Language, Culture, and Cultural Reductionism

It is fairly easy to see how *cultural reductionism* might take hold. *Culture* itself is defined as a people's system of beliefs and theories about the operation of the world—cosmology—passed down through generations through a symbolic tradition. Culture is the set of general meanings that a people uses to make order of its experience, to explain its origins, and to predict the future. Insofar as language is the principal means for transmitting information from one generation to the next and the principal means of representing information, it, too, must be a function of the cosmologies in which it is embedded and serves to propagate.

This view is as intuitively appealing as the position that meaning is pragmatically determined. Cultural reduction of meaning is essentially *variationist* in its sympathies, predicated on the observation that cultures and languages *differ* and the meanings that a language gives expression to *reflect the varying cultural context* in which the language occurs. Anecdotal evidence seems to support this view, moreover. Anyone who has ever spent some time in a culture other than one's own soon realizes that the world is organized a bit differently in the new culture. What counts for meaning in one place in one language does not always match up elsewhere.

Adherents of cultural reductionism like to trot out, in support, the example of Eskimos and their words for kinds of snow. The more that this anecdote is told, the more words the Eskimos seem to have for snow. In fact, Eskimos—Greenlandic Eskimos, to be precise—have about 49 words for snow and ice (Fortescue 1984: 366–7), a number that depends on two crucial assumptions: (a) we know what counts for a word in Eskimo, which is not an easy matter to say the least (see Mithun 1984 and Sadock 1986 for some heated discussion on this matter); and (b) we know that words actually have some bearing on thought and culture. These questions are never really addressed by those armed with stories about the ever-increasing snow vocabulary of Eskimos.

On close examination, these claims do not at all support the cultural reduction of meaning, but, to the contrary, beg the question. Skiers have a large number of words for snow, too, but it is unclear what this means for culture, language, or thought. American English has many words for killing, but does this mean that all Americans are seething with violence waiting to spill over? American English is also losing overt marking of the subjunctive mood. Few people say, "If this *be* the case. . . ," but instead express such an idea in the indicative mood: "If this *is* the case . . ." The subjunctive expresses possible worlds and contrary to fact situations, so does its loss indicate that Americans are likewise losing their abilities to think in such ways? The problem lies in our failure to decide what is to count as a culturally and cognitively significant linguistic form, much less for the connection between form and thought. Are words thoughts? Are sounds thoughts? Are inflections thoughts? Answers to these things have to be given *before* any discussion about cultural reduction can even begin.

2.52. The Sapir/Whorf Hypothesis and Linguistic Relativity

In spite of these fairly obvious objections, cultural reductionism has had many adherents. The most well-known version of cultural reductionism is the *Sapir/Whorf Hypothesis* (see Sapir 1921; Whorf 1956), which, in its strong form, goes roughly as follows. Language, culture, and thought are all mirrors of each other. It is possible to read thought off language, and language off culture, because linguistic distinctions reflect cultural distinctions, which in turn generate distinctions in thought. Thought itself differs across languages and culture because languages clearly differ from each other. Such variability can be traced by cataloguing the variation in linguistic forms proper: *From variations in linguistic forms,* one can see *variations in the culture* that determine these forms, and hence *variations in the thought* that the forms reflect.

How could such a simple way of reasoning be wrong? We begin with a methodological problem before going on to concerns that bear on the question of linguistic meaning. If the Sapir/Whorf Hypothesis is correct, then Whorf and Sapir themselves could not have known that it is correct. If language, culture, and thought are all bound up as they say, then Whorf and Sapir are forever trapped in their own language/culture/thought, and their hypothesis that language variation reflects cultural and conceptual variation is a figment of their own language, culture, and thought. In order for them to have observed that language, thought, and culture vary at all, they have to be able to compare, and thus see how another culture is put together. But this possibility is ruled out by the hypothesis itself because understanding is restricted to the language, culture, and thought in which the understanding occurs. So, the only way for the Sapir/Whorf Hypothesis to be correct is for it to be incorrect.

In all fairness to Whorf and Sapir, they did not hold so extreme a view as already presented, but this concession does not eliminate the methodological problem. If thought is tied to culture and language, and these vary and co-vary, how is it possible to know anything outside of culturally delimited information? Whorf himself argued for a weak version of the hypothesis: Language does not affect all thought, only that there is cultural determination of *habitual thought* though language. This is the essence of what has come to be known as *Linguistic Relativity*. Of course, it is not entirely clear what *habitual thought* means, and Whorf offered little on the matter. But even the weak version runs into the problems outlined earlier. Where is the point that habitual thought ceases to be linguistically influenced and becomes transcultural?

2.53. The Search for Invariants

Let us assume that the methodological paradox of linguistic relatively poses no problem for cultural reductionism and turn to some related semantic issues. Adherents of cultural reductionism often take a rather simpleminded view of language, culture, and thought. Anthropologists do not see culture as a monolithic construct, but made up of pieces, like institutions, roles, rituals and so on. Similarly, psychologists argue that thought is not unitary, but a composite of sensation, perception, memory, problem solving, metacognition, and so on. Analogously, linguists break language into its components, or *modules:* phonology, morphology, syntax, semantics, and pragmatics. Given the heterogenous structure of language, culture, and thought, the position that linguistic variations reflect variations in thought, because both are derivatives of culture, has little force. *What parts* of thought, language, and culture match up? Should we accept a clearly preposterous claim like phonological differences (language) reflect institutional differences (culture), and therefore bear on perception and memory (thought)? Nor does it do any good to engage in hand-waving here, as if we all really know what is meant by *culture, thought,* and *language.* The real issue is to get down to cataloguing the overlap. Cultural reductionists have the responsibility to make their claims precise.

One such precise claim holds that it is possible to read semantics off cosmology, and the distinctions found in this analysis reflect differences in conceptual categorization. To put it another way, semantic distinctions reflect cosmological distinctions made by the culture, and these distinctions are themselves reflected in mental categories. This is at least an arguable position, and it is clearly wrong. The usual cannon fodder in the counterargument is color vocabulary (Berlin and Kay 1969; see also chap. 10). Even a cursory look across languages shows wide variation in color vocabularies. The Dani, of New Guinea, have only 2 basic terms, one for 'dark' and one for 'light'; English has 11. Are these differences conceptual differences, forged as a result of two different world views, the Dani with a binary color scheme, and English with a more complex scheme?

Empirical work on color vocabulary shows that these linguistic differences turn out to be just that: *linguistic differences.* Rosch's (1973, 1975; Rosch and Mervis 1975) famous studies of color naming reveal that speakers of Dani and English organize their conceptual categories for color exactly the same way, in prototype structure from a focal point outward. Furthermore, the Dani, even though they have only two basic color terms, readily learn the English color terms, and when they do so, they again organize the terms in a prototype structure. An English speaker's focal green is the same as a Dani's, even though the latter has to be taught the linguistic form. The same results hold for spatial notions, such as shape and geometric form.

These findings imply that it is naive to try to read culture, semantics, and thought directly off each other. If Dani has only 2 basic color terms where English has 11, it is important to understand that in spite of this variation, the *same meanings are there* and the *same conceptual structure* exists. Thus, Kay and MacDaniel (1978) argue that the actual meaning for a color term is a *neurological invariant,* a product of the fixed cortical representation produced by sensory analyzers. Color terms have this conceptual and semantic invariance because of human neurophysiology. To use Kay and MacDaniel's (1978) phraseology, the meanings of color terms *are* the color terms. How languages decide to encode, relate, overlap, or separate the visual space is another matter, though the choices follow a pattern (as Berlin and Kay 1969 observed; see chap. 10); semantic structure and conceptual structure are invariant.

Cultural reductionists frequently advocate extreme variationism because they often *confuse significance with meaning.* Linguistic meanings are quite different from the impact that these meanings and their attendant formal distinctions may have for a member or an interpreter of culture. Perhaps the variety of basic color terms in English is *significant* in that it may imply that the people speaking the language have extensive technology to produce a variety of color referents. On the other hand, the variety does not necessarily signify anything: Maybe all the color terms have been borrowed from an invading culture! Again, this is not a claim about the linguistic meaning, and certainly not a claim about conceptual content. It is a claim about the import of these things to an observer, not what the words evoke in a user's projected world.

Culture and thought cannot be read directly off linguistic form because culture and thought always *exceed* language. Sperber and Wilson (1986), otherwise vehement adherents of the contextualist stance, articulate this view nicely: "There is a gap between semantic representations of sentences and the thoughts actually communicated by utterances. This gap is filled not by mere coding, but by inference" (1986: 9). Semantics is about the coding; pragmatics is about the inferences. Culture is more about the latter than the former.

The germ of problems with reductionist views of meaning as culture is, as we have noted, the tendency toward a *variationist account* of meaning. In contrast, *linguistic semantics is concerned with invariant meaning.* We want to examine the constancies in spite of the variation of contexts and see what is immune to cultural variation.

Good examples of the encoding of invariants can be found in an examination of pronoun systems. Pronouns in English are sensitive to the semantic property of animacy. *He* and *she,* for example, generally refer to animate, and often human, entities (with appropriate gender); *it,* on the other hand, generally refers to inanimate things. These conditions can be seen in the following examples, where the subscripts indicate coreference:

16.a.   Maria$_1$ rolled over and she$_1$ hit the wall.
　b.   ?? Maria$_1$ rolled over and it$_1$ hit the wall.
17.a.   The car$_1$ rolled over and it$_1$ hit the wall.
　b.   ?? The car$_1$ rolled over and she$_1$/he$_1$ hit the wall.

Notice, however, that the animate/inanimate distinction is a *gradient*. Animals sometimes take the animate pronouns and sometimes not:

18a.   The cow$_1$ rolled over and she$_1$/it$_1$ hit the wall.
　b.   The stallion$_1$ rolled over and he$_1$/it$_1$ hit the wall.

Similarly, newborn babies whose sex is indeterminate to the speaker are often referred to by the inanimate pronoun:

19.   Oh, what a cute baby$_1$! How old is it$_1$? (cf. ?? Oh, what a cute teenager$_1$! How old is it$_1$?)

Some people even personify their plants and choose the animate pronoun to refer to them:

20.   There's the cactus$_1$; he$_1$ needs some water.

The exact choice of form undoubtedly depends on the cultural context and the pragmatics of the moment, with farmers and plant buffs surely more likely to use the animate pronouns for animals and plants, respectively. But the choice itself is different from the possibilities of choice that are afforded by the semantic structure of the language outside of its contexts.

Animacy is an *invariant property* with a *gradient nature*. How this property is deployed in actual speech and context varies; but the property itself is constant. In Yagua, (D. Payne 1986), there are a variety of *noun classifiers,* forms that indicate the semantic class to which a noun belongs: for example, round objects, flat objects, long objects (see chap. 3). One such class is animate objects, but what Yagua selects as belonging to the animacy category seems a mish-mash to non-Yagua speakers. In Yagua, as in English, persons and animals are viewed as animate because of their internal dispositions and display of lifelike behavior. But also in the Yagua animate class are stars, months, rocks, and pineapples. An examination of the history of the culture shows the Yagua to be oriented toward the moon in cosmology and that rocks and pineapples are valued objects. Hence because of their *importance,* these things are classified as animate.

Does this difference between Yagua and English vitiate animacy as an invariant? Not at all. Yagua and English assign animacy to an object on the basis of the same features: internal disposition and importance. What each language then selects to include in the animate class then depends on how the culture uses the invariant criteria.

A variationist stance does not help at all. Are we to read different meanings off the Yagua classifier system in comparison to the English pronoun system? Are we to take the variation in form to reflect a variation in meaning and hence a variation in thought? If we do, we fail to see the constancy in the data. As with the discussion of the secondary status of pragmatics, arguments against cultural reductionism are not intended to demean cultural views of meaning. Surely, the influence of culture on linguistic meaning is a legitimate area of study, as long as it is done properly, with explicit assumptions. (The same is true for other contextualist views of meaning.) Without cultural information, for example, we are hard pressed to explain why Yagua classifies pineapples as animate. But it is more important to realize that both English and Yagua mark animacy with a grammatical reflex. This fact transcends culture.

2.54.   Culture and Grammatical Meaning

Much the same can be said for the connection between culture and grammatical meaning as has been said for the relation of context to grammatical meaning. Grammatically relevant semantic representations are invariant because they are constituted by relatively stable, decontextualized semantic properties. Culture may use the content of semantic representations, but culture does not determine this content. This is because culture itself is intensional, as becomes evident when we examine the relation between meaning and conceptual structure.

2.6.   APPROACH 5:
MEANING AS CONCEPTUAL STRUCTURE

From the previous approaches to meaning, we have learned that meaning is best understood in terms of reference to invariant, truth-functional properties of a projected world. Why are there invariant semantic properties? Why, in spite of the obvious variation in cultural organization and cultural preference, do the same properties recur? The answers to these questions bring us full circle, back to Approach 1, the nature of the projected world, and truth and reference within a mental model.

Semantic properties have the features they do because the form of all human minds is the same. Culture and context themselves are projected worlds, intensions, another way that we fix extensions. Semantic properties are invariant because the constituents of our mentally projected worlds of reference are cut from the same mental fabric and derived by the same mental processes.

2.61. Conceptual Semantics

One of the most articulate defenders of the position that mind projects the world of reference is Jackendoff (1983, 1988, 1990; see also Lakoff 1987, 1988), who argues that semantic structure is exactly the same as conceptual structure. In his account, semantic analysis is conceptual analysis because the structure of semantic and conceptual categories is the same. Here we look closely at Jackendoff's position to illustrate conceptual semantics.

Behind the argument that semantic structure is conceptual structure is the observation that language can report input from all sensory modalities. So, minimally, semantic information must be some kind of conceptual information— or the two must overlap somewhere—because no fact is excluded from expression. This is what Jackendoff calls the Cognitive Constraint: The best account of meaning allows linguistic and nonlinguistic information to converge in a central core of conceptual information. As Jackendoff (1988: 83) remarks: "People have things to talk about only by virtue of having represented them." The different sensory systems must deliver similar information for the reports to be so readily constructed.

We can take vision and visual reports as a case in point. Ultimately, there must be no mental distinction between the sorts of information that the visual system provides in analyzing visual input and the kind of information that we use to report on visual input linguistically because we are able to talk about what we see with no apparent difficulty. Furthermore, if we look at the kind of information that underlies visual experience, we find that it is basically the same kind of information that underlies *reports on* visual experience. The peripheral visual processors are designed to single out boundary conditions on objects based on changes in light intensity. From differential intensities, the visual mechanisms of the eye compute edges, corners, blobs, and surfaces. This information comprises the mental representations that are delivered by the peripheral visual system to central mental processing: all visual objects are built from this information (see Baron 1987; Marr 1982).

If we then look at the semantic information that is grammatically encoded in any language insofar as visual reports go, we find that the same boundary conditions recur. Noun classifier systems encode such properties as extension in one dimension (edges), two dimensions (surfaces), and three dimensions (blobs); curvature, boundedness, substantiality, containment are also encoded (see chap. 3 for fuller discussion). The most straightforward answer to this convergence of the information used to analyze input visually and used to report on visual input is to say that the information itself mentally converges.

2.611. Categorization

The coalescence of semantic and other conceptual information has additional support in the observation that both analysis of input and reports on input rely on *categorization,* or the construction of mental sets and ideal types. When the visual system analyzes input through the identification of edges and corners, the representation that the system delivers is categorial, requiring a decision that a certain object *belongs to* the category 'edge' or the category 'corner.' Similarly, when the visual receptors identify colors, the representation delivered to the brain is categorial, assigning input within a range of wave lengths to a certain class.

The same typing procedures operate in the assignment of semantic properties. To say that a verb has the property of punctuality is to say that the verb *belongs to the class* of punctual verbs; to say that a language is sensitive to animacy is to say that some entities meet the criteria for *inclusion in the set* of animate things.

The prevalence of categorization may seem to be an overly simple point, but it is worth repeating and carefully noting. Semantic properties and the properties of the representations constructed by the rest of the mental system (technically, the *mental predicates* of the language of thought) are constituted by categorization (pace Lakoff 1988, for whom mental image schemas play the same role). The mentally projected world is made up of *types*—semantic types, visual types, and so on—and these form the predicates of the code in which our mental representations are constructed, processed, validated, and developed.

2.612. Similarity and Difference

The argument that semantic information and other conceptual information converge because they both rely on categorization may seem rather shallow when all is said and done, amounting to little more than the claim that meaning and concepts, like most else in human minds, come in generalized groups. Is there any more detailed evidence for their unified treatment? Jackendoff argues that mental typing, whether visual, auditory, or semantic, is carried out by the same processes. Not only is categorization itself shared by semantics and conceptualization, but so are the procedures that derive the categories. At the heart of all typing are two mechanisms: the detection of *similarity* and the detection of *difference.* The extreme version of similarity is identity; the extreme version of difference is exclusion or nonidentity.

We can see these two mechanisms at work in visual categorization, where the very process of edge detection, the mechanism by which the individuation of objects in the visual field is accomplished, is constrained by how edges are detected through discontinuities in light intensity, regions of perceptual similarity and difference. Semantic analysis is analogously constrained by judgments of similarity and difference. The traditional goals of semantics have been the explanation of synonymy, paraphrase, antonymy, contradiction, taxonomy, entailment, inconsistency, and redundancy. Jackendoff (1983: 103–5) argues that all these standard goals are derived from the mechanisms of typing. Synonymy, paraphrase, redundancy, and entailment all result from judgments of likeness; antonymy, contradiction, and inconsistency derive from judgments of difference; taxonomy is category membership itself, which in turn is a result of judgments of both identity and difference.

Therefore, semantics has its traditional goals because semantic information *is* conceptual information and thus is built from the elemental principles of mental typing. The principles of linguistic inference are just a special case of the principles of all conceptual inference because all inference relies on the detection of identity and difference.

2.62. Problems with Conceptual Semantics

We have thus far painted a rosy and straightforward picture of the convergence of semantic and conceptual structure. However, a number of objections may be raised to viewing semantic structure as identical with conceptual structure. First, the evidence for the convergence is often of a very general sort, such as the claim that semantics and conceptualization overlap because they both rely on relative judgments of similarity and difference in the formation of categories. Under this argument, not only is semantic information identical to conceptual information, but so is *all other* linguistic information. Much of syntactic representation is also categorial. How then is syntactic information to be differentiated from semantic information if the general principles that allow semantics and conceptualization to converge also apply to grammatical structure? Even Jackendoff wants to differentiate syntax from semantics cognitively, but according to the criteria for conceptualization, phonological categories are conceptual. If no line can ultimately be drawn between conceptual information and any other information, what force does the identity of semantics and conceptual categories have?

A second objection to the ready convergence of semantics and concepts derives from the nature of concepts themselves. Conceptual categories are *fuzzy,* that is, their boundaries are vague and their internal structure is scalar. Certainly, some semantic categories are also fuzzy, but not all. Consider the concepts of, not the words for, life and death. We can conceive of intermediate states between life and death, but our language does not allow us to talk about these things meaningfully. Even expressions like *half dead* and *barely alive* do not refer to intermediate stages between life and death, unlike, for example, the words *tepid* and *warm,* which *do denote* midpoints on a temperature scale. *Half dead* and *barely alive* both refer to the "alive half" of the life–death dichotomy and are not referentially fuzzy at all.

Conceptual information is evidently scalar, whereas only some semantic information is such. It might be argued that there are fundamental mismatches between *what can be conceptualized* and *what can be semantically represented.* For instance, semantically, the word *hillock,* 'small hill,' denotes absolute height, but obviously height is a relative *concept.* Conceptual structure and semantic structure may overlap to a great extent, and the former may even give rise to the latter, but numerous examples can be marshalled to show that the two are not coterminous.

2.63. Saving Conceptual Semantics

The aforementioned objections, if taken as telling, may be sufficient to differentiate semantic structure from conceptual structure, but they nonetheless do not necessarily put semantics outside mental models.

First, even if conceptual structure and semantic structure are not indistinguishable, this does not mean that semantic information is not cognitive. Semantic categories may be best understood as a subset of conceptual categories: What we are able to denote is a function of what we can conceptualize. In plain terms, we are able to imagine much more than we can express, but everything that we can express is totally within the realm of the conceivable. From this standpoint, conceptual structure provides the backdrop for semantic structure, not its substitute.

Second, mismatches of semantic and conceptual structure do not deflect the kinds of ontological questions raised in Chapter 1: If semantic information is not conceptual, then what is it, and where is it? Dowty (1979) phrases the problem nicely by pointing out that even though intensions can be postulated with no necessary reference to psychological mechanisms, such a tack does seem to avoid the obvious question of the possible content of these intensional semantic representations. Linguistics as a whole relies heavily on cognitive psychology as the ultimate arbiter in theoretical disputes. As Culicover and Wexler (1980) point out in their discussion of the mathematical theory of language learnability, the final criterion that a proposed linguistic representation must meet is *feasibility,* practical learnability: that the representation is not only simple and correct, but also might actually be learned. Hence if intensions fix extensions, we are obliged to propose semantic representations that could actually be used and learned: Intensions have to be more than mathematical objects. This surely returns us to the empirical side of semantics and forces us to adhere to a believable ontology, not just the simplest one. As Jackendoff (1988: 87) says: "Once we see ontological claims as psychological questions [we must] investigate what evidence people take as relevant when they make judgments of identity or non-identity" in constructing semantic/conceptual categories.

2.64. Conceptual Structure and Grammatical Meaning

The critical words in Jackendoff's account, as well as in linguistic semantics more generally, are *what people take* rather than *what people should do*. What do languages actually do? What properties do languages actually provide for their users in referring to a mentally projected world?

Grammatical meaning is a subset of the intensions that comprise semantic representations, and this is in turn a subset of conceptual structure. This information is identifiable from how languages are actually put together and how speakers mentally project context, culture, and the world of reference.

The grounding of linguistic meaning in conceptual structure has a broader benefit than simply situating the ontology and naturalizing the content of semantic representations. It unifies all the major lessons of the four other approaches to meaning.

1. Linguistic expressions have their reference in terms of the components of the mentally projected world: for Jackendoff more explicitly, to concepts. Conceptual structure is intensional, so intensions may thus fix extensions, and truth is a mental projection.

2. Logical form is also a conceptual structure. If some semantic phenomena appear to be categorical, like tautology or contradiction, then this is a function of nearly total redundancy or anomaly of meaning: that is, the gradient categories of conceptual structure accommodate all the facts.

3. Context—pragmatic information—bears a scalar, not a deterministic, relation to linguistic meaning. Linguistic meaning *precedes* and *enters into* a context of use because speakers bring this meaning with them, in their heads, into the contexts of communication. Context and use are relevant to meaning only because speakers have a prior conceptual structure.

4. Cultural information may explain why languages vary, but we still have to account for the remarkable constancies across languages in terms of the meanings grammaticalized. Culture itself is a mental projection, so any bearing that culture may have on linguistic meaning must also be registered within conceptual structure.

2.7. POSTSCRIPT:
SOME NOTES ON DEFINITION

We have settled most of the preliminaries to linguistic semantics by looking at grammatical meaning and how the lessons of reference, logical form, context, culture, and conceptual structure contribute to the content of semantic representations. There is one remaining methodological concern. When we say that a verb like *punch* is punctual, we are making a claim about the *definition* of the word. What does it mean to define a linguistic form and how must the issues of definition be taken into account with regard to specifying grammatical meaning? The question of definition merits a book-length study of its own (see, e.g., Landau 1984), so we focus on only a few of the major problems.

2.71.   Criterial Definitions and Preference Rules

To define an expression in terms of semantic properties is *not* to provide a unique and exhaustive list of all and only the essential features of a projected referent so that it can be reliably selected in any context. Grammatically relevant semantic properties do not comprise necessary and sufficient—that is, reductive—definitions. Fodor, Garrett, Walker, and Parks (1980) have shown that necessary and sufficient definition is always inachievable. Take the word *bird,* for example. What properties always and only pick out a bird? Wings? Not always: A wingless bird is a bird. Feathers? Not always: There are plucked chickens. We can continue these examples ad nauseam, but that is the point. We will never arrive at a satisfactory final characterization of a bird in terms of a finite checklist of necessary and sufficient features. There is always some residue.

We can incorporate this result into our preliminaries by saying that semantic properties like animacy, negation, and punctuality are not necessary and sufficient features of the items they define, but *criteria* for fixing the reference in a projected world. They are not the only criteria, because pragmatics and semantics grade into each other and extralinguistic information is allowed in a full definition; nor are they absolute criteria, because the properties themselves may have prototype structure.

The status of semantic properties in definitions by criteria rather than by reduction can be seen in the by-now-familiar example of *punch.* When we note that the verb *punch* is punctual, we do so by its inability to co-occur with an adverbial of extended time, such as *all day:*

21.   ?? I punched Tom all day.

Example (21) is understandable only as a series of repeated punctual acts, just as the punctual verbs *wink* and *slide off:*

22a.   ?? I winked all day.
   b.   ?? I slid off the chair all day.

But *wink, punch,* and *slide off* are all punctual *to a different degree.* If a phrase that expresses extended time of the *action proper* is inserted, the judgments of punctuality change:

23a. ?? It took all day to wink.
   b. ? It took all day to punch Tom.
   c. It took all day to slide off the chair.

The unacceptability of (23a) shows that *wink* is undeniably momentary and prototypically punctual. Example (23b) shows that the action expressed by *punch* may be extended, but only with an unusual interpretation, for example that the puncher is continually interrupted. *Punch* is punctual, but to a lesser degree than *wink*. *Slide off* in (24c) is even less punctual. An expression of extended action can co-occur with this verb because its punctuality is restricted to the endpoint of the act—*slide off* means 'continuously come to the *point of* removal'—and so (23c) is acceptable with no unusual interpretation because the extension in time refers to the process leading up to the point of removal.

Does this variability mean that the three words are not punctual or they are not definable? Not at all. If punctuality is a matter of degree, there is no less punctuality because it is scalar. Temperature is scalar, but the gradience of temperature is never raised as a criterion for the rejection of temperature altogether.

With criterial definitions for these verbs, we are making no attempt to reduce them to punctuality. There is focal punctuality and less focal punctuality, and the denotations of the three verbs lie on the continuum of the property. They are defined *in relation to each other*, in terms of how they *relatively encode* punctuality (and whatever else fixes their reference). In Jackendoff's phraseology, there is *a preference rule* connecting these three items on a scale of punctuality (Jackendoff 1983; Lerdahl and Jackendoff 1983: 307–14). A preference rule is a statement in probabilistic form of the relative strength of two or more items for interpretation relative to some property or properties. To be interpreted punctually, *wink* is preferred over *punch*, which in turn is preferred over *slide off*, notationally, *wink* > *punch* > *slide off*.

A definition is not a reduction of the meaning of an item, but a statement about the *interpretation of an item in any context*. This can be done without pretenses to necessary and sufficient conditions. No lexicographer, for example, harbors any illusions that definitions absolutely define an entry word, or that an entry and its definitions can be read symmetrically. A lexicographic definition is also a preference rule: It fixes reference probabilistically as a statement of how to interpret an entry in any context.

The point here is much like that made by Wittgenstein (1953) in his functional theory of meaning. In arguing for meaning as the result of the use of an expression in well-defined, rule-governed contexts, language games, Wittgenstein observed that some phenomena are grouped alike not because they share a set of discrete, categorically specifiable properties that differentiate them uniquely from all other phenomena, but because they simply have a vague *family resemblance*. His famous example is the concept of a game. What makes baseball, checkers, and scrabble all games? They share no uniquely defining characteristic: not even the characteristic of being constituted by rules, because society, for instance, is also constituted by rules, and society is not a game. What makes a game a game is a preferential ordering of the properties of each game. Wittgenstein therefore proposed that definitions are organized by these family resemblances, nonnecessary, but criterial, constellations of properties.

Nothing is lost, and everything is gained, by having definitions organized in this manner. Preference rules, family resemblances, and prototypes do not introduce unrigorous or inexact characterization of meaning. Both *ambiguity* and *vagueness,* for example—two standard concerns of semantics—are still systematically identifiable even with gradient properties.

2.72. Ambiguity, Vagueness, and Exact Definitions

An expression that has two or more meanings may be either ambiguous or vague. It is *ambiguous* if there are at least *two distinct* semantic specifications underlying a single overt form. An expression is *vague* if it is *unspecified* for particular meanings and takes them from context. Consider (24):

24. I punched the paper.

Example (24) may have two meanings, either something like 'I hit the paper with my fist' or 'I pierced a hole in the paper, with some hole-punching machine.' Are these two interpretations the result of the fact that the *punch* has two different sets of properties, two different definitions ('hit with fist' and 'pierce'), and is thus ambiguous? If it is ambiguous, then there are really two different words here: $punch_1$ ('hit with fist') and $punch_2$ ('pierce'). Or is the dual interpretation the result of the fact that *punch* is just vague, unspecified for the kind of act that is carried out, just as long as there is contact? If so, there is only one word, and this word *inherits the rest of its definition from context.*

The usual test for ambiguity versus vagueness is as follows. If an expression is ambiguous, it is possible to assert it in both a positive and negative context simultaneously with no anomaly: If there is ambiguity, then the negative context will affect only one of the fully specified senses and leave the other untouched. Ambiguity is compatible with positive and negative assertion because there are in fact two different definitions.

This is not the case for vagueness. If an expression is vague, its simultaneous positive and negative assertion is anomalous, because the expression inherits meaning from context and thus inherits contradictory information.

By these tests, *punch* is ambiguous:

25. I punched the paper, but I didn't punch the paper.

Example (25) is acceptable because of the difference between mere contact and piercing. The sentence means either 'I hit the paper with my fist but didn't pierce a hole in it' or 'I pierced a hole in the paper but didn't hit it with my fist.'

The point to be made here is ultimately one about rigor and exactitude in the face of definitions as criteria. Note that the ambiguity of the *punch* obtains in spite of the gradience of punctuality. *Punch* as 'hit with fist' is *more punctual* than *punch* as 'pierce':

26a. ?? It took all afternoon to punch Tom.
  b. It took all afternoon to punch a hole in the metal.

The ambiguity has nothing to do with the scalar nature of punctuality, but with the fact that *punch* 'hit with fist' is *atelic,* or does not require a result (see chap. 6), whereas *punch* 'pierce' is *telic,* or necessarily resultative (see chaps. 3 and 6 for further discussion). The following paraphrases illustrate this difference:

27a. ?? Tom came out punched.
  b. The metal came out punched.

In both senses, *punch* is punctual, and so the ambiguity is not affected by the gradience of punctuality but by the presence of another semantic property, 'result.'

These examples show that ambiguity can still be rigorously identified in spite of the scalar nature of the properties that criterially define expressions. Rigor and exactitude are not lost or compromised by the fact that the properties that define expressions are scalar. Ambiguity and vagueness remain clearly identifiable. Necessary and sufficient definitions are not needed if definitions are understood as criterial, organized as preference rules for interpretation in any context.

SUMMARY OF CHAPTER

In Chapter 2, we have turned to the lessons of five traditional approaches to meaning. First, in looking at the proposal that meaning is reference, we have considered how meaning may be seen as reference in a mentally projected world and how a number of phenomena argue against a strictly referential view of meaning: for example, the priority of intension over extension, the relationship of propositional attitudes to referential opacity, the effect of presupposition, and the role of compositionality—meaning components—in determining reference. The fallacy of the conduit metaphor—that linguistic communication is (falsely) the sending and receiving of linguistic packages—has, in the end, been shown to be a more general principal to motivate reference in a mentally projected world and to temper an extensional view of meaning.

Second, we have examined meaning as logical form. Here we have looked at the requirements of formal analysis in general and the details of interpretation by a model. We have considered the difference between formal and nonformal approaches to meaning, arguing that the former runs into problems in its adherence to categoricalness and contentlessness. By looking at such things as quantifiers and negation, we have seen how an adequate description requires fuzzy categories and scales of meaning. Even traditionally logical phenomena, such as tautology and contradiction, are best understood in terms of the gradients of anomaly and redundancy that are part and parcel of a nonformal approach to meaning. We have in the end sought to unify formal and linguistic semantics in the search for real world meaning.

Third, we have considered meaning as context and use. We have argued that linguistic meaning is not reducible to context and use by showing how pragmatics differs from semantics on three counts: truth-conditionality, context-dependence, and cancellability. Pragmatics and semantics form a scale of background information, from implicature (heavily context-dependent) to presupposition (less context-dependent) to entailment (least context-dependent).

Meaning as culture has been our fourth approach. Here we have seen how the Sapir/Whorf Hypothesis and linguistic relativity—two historically influential views of the determinate relation between culture and meaning—are untenable because they propose simplistic views of language, culture, thought, and their interrelations. Cultural reductionists adhere to variationism, or the view that differences between languages and cultures are more important than similarities. But linguistic meaning has numerous invariants and thus is independent of—even if embedded in—culture.

Finally, we have considered meaning as conceptual structure, and we have seen how mental models account for categorization and likeness and difference of meaning. All the lessons of the previous four approaches converge on conceptual structure: the projected world, gradient categories, context-independence, and cultural-independence are all accommodated by locating meaning as a mental construct.

To conclude the chapter, we have made one methodological observation. Our goal is to provide definitions of linguistic expressions, and in doing so, we have not compromised either rigor or exactitude by seeking meaning in a mentally projected world. On the contrary, ambiguity and vagueness, for example, are both still precisely identifiable in spite of fuzzy and gradient categories. Definitions are preference rules—statements about the relative interpretation of expressions in terms of criterial attributes—not necessary, sufficient, and exhaustive reductions.

QUESTIONS FOR DISCUSSION

1. The following sentence has a number of interpretations:

i. I saw the point.

What are the interpretations? Are *saw* and *point* ambiguous or vague? Are the semantic properties that contribute to the different interpretations associated with grammatical meaning?

2. Is the adage *boys will be boys* a tautology? Does it trigger any implicatures, and if so, what kinds? Do you know of any similar adages in other languages, and do they have similar interpretations?

3. Recent work on children's acquisition of word meaning (Golinkoff et al. 1990) reveals that very young children first use words to refer to *entire objects* and thereafter to pieces or properties of those objects. For example, for young children, the word *hot* may mean 'stove' or 'cup,' and only later denotes a property of a stove or cup, like 'heat.' What does this finding say about the difference between extension and intension? Is this a conceptual fact that requires us to modify our claims? What does this finding say about the idea of a model for interpretation? What is the relationship between a child's model and the model of a formal semantic system?

3 Entities

3.1. INTRODUCTION

In this chapter, we consider the kinds of semantic properties that are typically encoded as nouns. We begin with a survey of definitions of *noun* as a syntactic, semantic, and discourse category and observe that, universally, temporally stable phenomena, entities, surface as nouns. We then look at the nature and encoding of eight kinds of semantic properties of nouns/entities: specificity, boundedness, animacy, kinship, social status, physical structure, and function. For each, we look at a number of subclasses (e.g., humans, animals, and inanimates under animacy) and their semantic and structural ramifications in a variety of languages. Thereafter, we consider the theoretical problem of unifying the semantic properties of entities internally (in relation to each other via neutralization) and externally (in relation to perceptual and cognitive structure).

3.11. Nouns and Entities: Formal and Notional Definitions

Any student reared in the Western grammatical tradition will say that a noun is the name of a person, place, or thing and thus define a noun by its semantic representation. Two observations conspire to weed this view out of our untutored beliefs about language. First, there are many things that are nouns but not exactly persons, places, or things. *Smoothness* is a noun, but it does not readily appear to represent a thing.

Second, a noun is not a *notional class,* something defined by its *conceptual content,* but a *form class,* something defined by its *structural* or *formal* properties (Lyons 1966, 1968). Formally, a noun is identifiable because of what other categories and forms *co-occur* with it. Under this view, a noun is something that can be a subject (that which controls agreement with a verb) or something that takes certain modifiers, like a definite article. By these criteria, *smoothness* is a noun, in spite of the variation in its notional content, because it co-occurs with the definite article: *the smoothness of the wood.*

The applicability of purely formal criteria for the identification of nouns is undeniable, even in languages where "nounhood" has to be more particularly defined: Russian and Chinese have no definite articles, for example, so the formal criteria have to be more carefully applied. But curiously, when the traditional notional definition ("a noun is the name of a person, place, or thing") is reversed, the definition turns out to be true. Nouns are not always persons, places, or things, but persons, places, and things *always turn out to be nouns!* (See the work by Givón 1979, 1984; Haiman 1985a, 1985b; Langacker 1987a, 1987b; Wierzbicka 1985).

Nouns *do have* purely formal properties because at the grammatical level they are contentlessly manipulated by syntax, just like any other category, but these formal properties are supported by overwhelmingly consistent semantic factors. Nouns incontrovertibly tend to encode *entities,* broadly construed.

This convergence of semantics and syntax is not meant to be reductionistic: Syntax cannot be read directly off semantics no more than semantics can be read directly off culture. To say that form classes are semantically motivated is to agree that the best semantic account is one that respects a close connection between form and meaning rather than one that severely separates—*modularizes*—the two. This is a position more in line with Jackendoff's Grammatical Constraint (see chap. 1), especially so because many morphosyntactic reflexes of nouns, such as number and gender, are correlated with, if not accountable to, the semantic properties underlying the formal category. Hence, semantics has a *direct effect* on the structural aspects of language, in this case *categoriality,* the status of form classes as classes. The traditional notional definition of *noun* thus resurfaces, if in modified form.

3.12. Three Accounts
of Categories and their Denotations

A number of recent studies of the universality of grammatical categories have come to conclusions similar to those on the semantic motivation of nouns as a formal category. Our brief examination of three accounts—one from discourse and two from conceptual linguistics—will show us the consistencies in semantic representations that underlie nouns as a category.

3.121.   Categories in Discourse

Hopper and Thompson (1984, 1985) have observed that the major lexical categories of noun and verb have a consistent discourse definition: Nominal and verbal categoriality is a matter of *degree and kind of information in discourse.* The goal of discourse is to report events happening to participants, with verbs encoding the *events* and nouns the *participants.* Form classes are a direct result of the informational requirements of verbal reports: The more individuated or discrete a discourse event, the more likely it is to be coded as a full verb; the more individuated the discourse participant, the more likely the form encoding the participant is to be a full noun.

With regard to nouns in particular, Hopper and Thompson (1984, 1985) show that languages have syntactic operations to decrease the categorial status of a noun as a function of the individuation and relative salience of the discourse participant that the noun encodes. Some verbs in English, for example, allow their semantically predictable direct objects to *incorporate,* or fuse, with a verb to form a new compound verb with the same meaning as the *separate* verb plus its individuated direct object: *fish for trout/trout fish, watch birds/bird watch, tend the bar/bartend.* Such incorporation has distinct *defocalizing effects* in discourse by reducing the informational status of the entity represented by the noun and reducing nominal categoriality. Nonincorporated forms, because they have full categoriality and are fully individuated in the discourse, may take subsequent pronouns, as illustrated in (1a); however, incorporated nouns do not take pronouns, as in (1b):

1a. Tom fished for trout$_1$. Bob fished for them$_1$, too.
  b. Tom trout$_1$ fished. ?? Bob fished for them$_1$, too.

Pronominalization is disallowed in (1b), even though there is an overt surface noun to serve as a potential antecedent, because incorporation *reduces the discourse role of the participants.* Low categoriality of the noun derives from low categoriality of the discourse referent, and because incorporation reduces the semantic individuation of the participant, pronominalization of the participant with reduced individuation is thereby constrained.

Hopper and Thompson propose that all languages follow a gradience of categoriality of nouns in discourse, from *presentative nouns* (those that introduce new, individuated participants and have *high categoriality*) to *anaphoric* and *contextually established* forms (those that refer to antecedents and have reduced forms and *intermediate categoriality*) to *nonreferring forms* and *zero anaphora* (those with limited surface expression, no individuation, and *low categoriality*). Although their proposal is not pursued any further here, we should note that their observations support the view that the form class *noun* can be seen as a matter of the *degree of the individuation of the entity encoded by the noun.* In Hopper and Thompson's theory, the category of *noun* is motivated by discourse referentiality.

3.122. Temporal Stability

Givón (1979, 1984) proposes an ontological foundation for linguistic categories and argues that the major grammatical form classes reflect *a scale of the perceived temporal stability of the phenomena they denote.* At one end of the scale of temporal stability are "experiences—or phenomenological clusters—which stay relatively *stable* over time, that is, those that over repeated scans appear to be roughly 'the same' " (1979: 51). At the other end are "experiential clusters denoting *rapid changes* in the state of the universe. These are prototypically *events* or actions" (1979: 52). In between are experiences of intermediate stability, sometimes stable, sometimes inchoative or changing. This scale directly manifests itself in grammatical classes: Nouns encode the most temporally stable, verbs the least temporally stable, and adjectives in between, as in Fig. 3.1 (after Givón 1984: 55):

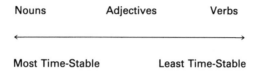

FIG. 3.1. Scale of temporal stability.

Givón observes that whereas all languages have both concrete and abstract nouns, the latter are *always* derived, most usually from verbs. This suggests that the basic noun in any language is that which encodes physically anchored, spatially bound entities; in contrast, verbs typically have "only existence in time" (1979:321). The temporal and nontemporal domains polarize experience and map respectively onto the major form class division in language: verb and noun.

Moreover, many languages do not have a productive class of adjectives, and in such languages, the burden of modification is taken up by nouns and verbs (Dixon 1982; Givón 1979, 1984; Schachter 1985; chap. 10). When this happens, the more temporally stable attributes are often encoded as nouns, and less temporally stable ones as verbs, thus splitting the burden along the scale itself.

In Toposa, the phenomenological attribute 'big' is encoded like a verb (with a prefixed pronoun) because size reflects ontological growth, and hence is temporally unstable (Givón 1984: 53):

2. à-pólōt.
    I big.
    I am big.
    More accurately: I am bigging.

But the attribution of location, a temporally stable phenomenon, is encoded more like a noun (see Givón 1984: 55 for analogous facts in the Bantu languages).

Adjectives are thus ontologically between nouns and verbs on the scale of temporal stability and their encoding properties split along these same lines in languages that must use other form classes to take up the slack for missing adjectives: More durable properties are encoded like nouns, and less durable properties are encoded like verbs, exactly what should be expected from an intermediate class.[1]

One problem with Givón's theory is its inconsistency when the analysis gets more fine-grained (Hopper and Thompson 1984: 705). Some nouns are less time-stable than others (compare *motion,* denoting a temporally unstable state, with *house*), and some verbs are more time-stable than others (compare *sits,* denoting a temporal constant, with *unfolds*). Givóns responds that the scale of temporal stability is a hologram, where a phenomenon is reflected everywhere in all parts: within the form classes, the scale also applies full force, so nouns, for example, are generally more time stable, but temporal stability also saturates the class, and some nouns are more time stable than others (Givón 1984: 55).

In Givón's defense, we should note that his generalization is really much less specific than what he claims or others attribute to him. Nouns do not encode temporally *stable* phenomena; rather, the phenomena that nouns encode are *not obliged to be temporally situated*. What makes an entity an entity is its *relative atemporality*. This characteristic contrasts with that of verbs, which *require* temporal fixing. So *time boundedness* seems to be the gist of Givón's time stability criterion for entities: "An entity x is identical to itself if it is identical only to itself but not to any other entity at time a and also at time b which directly follows time a" (Givón 1979: 320).

Crucial to individuated entities is their perceptual integrity, or constancy over time (see Jackendoff 1983: 42), unlike the notions encoded by verbs. Hence, for Givón, categoriality is a direct reflection of the temporal stability of entities: Their *relative atemporality* motivates their encoding as nouns.

3.123.   Cognitive Regions:
Interconnectedness and Density

The role of temporal priority that Givón stresses is at the heart of Langacker's (1987a, 1987b) characterization of the encoding of nouns. In his view, the mentally projected world that underlies reference is constituted by three kinds of objects: regions, temporal relations, and atemporal relations, respectively the

---

[1]Note also that in Spanish, relative temporal stability has a direct bearing on structure. As is well known to any student of Romance languages, Spanish has two verbs 'to be': *ser,* for temporal duration, and *estar,* for temporal change. Hence nouns and adjectives expressing temporally durable properties co-occur with *ser* but only temporary states and properties co-occur with *estar.*

denotations of nouns, verbs, and adjectives/adverbs. A noun designates a *region in conceptual space* (Langacker 1987b: 58); a *region* is defined by *interconnectedness* and *density*.[2]

The simplest way to think of a region is to imagine an array of points in "continuous extension along some parameter" (1987b: 198), a space of phenomenal continuity. The constituents that compose the space are *interconnected* and define the space by this interconnection. The word *book* has two meanings that correspond to two different regions. *Book* may refer to the physical object (an array of physical points along a surface) or to the informational content of the physical object (an array of points along the parameter of information). In both cases, *book* designates an inert, internally unified space.

A region also has *density, compactness* of the points in continuous extension. Density produces the prototype denotation for the category: The more compact the region, the more likely it is to instantiate the prototype. Langacker's example here is the difference between *archipelago* and *island*. The former denotes a discontinuous region, a series of small islands functioning semantically as a single unit, whereas the latter designates a continuous and dense region. Though each has the same semantic content, 'body of land surrounded by water,' *island* is more typical of the region expressed. Discontinuous and composite regions are less likely to surface as prototypes.

In Langacker's theory, the density and interconnectedness of regions in cognitive domains account for why nouns are remembered better, acquired earlier, translated more easily from language to language, less subject to encoding variability across languages, and more stable under paraphrase. Their internal stability, derived from their interconnectedness and density, allows them to be relatively immune to linguistic context and surface consistently in the form class *noun*.

3.13.   What Nouns Denote

We can summarize the convergence of these three accounts of categories and their denotations rather straightforwardly. The categoriality of a noun is a function of the relative stability of its typical denotation. For Hopper and Thompson, this is *informational stability,* individuated and salient discourse participants. For Givón, it is *temporal stability,* spatially anchored phenomena. For Langacker, it

---

[2]More particularly, for Langacker, "a noun . . . is a symbolic structure whose semantic pole instantiates the schema [THING]; or to phrase it more simply, a noun designates a thing" (1987b: 189). Virtually the same characterization is given by Jackendoff in his discussion of the elementary individuation of the mentally projected world: "One of the most obvious aspects of the projected world is that it is divided up into #things#—#entities# with a certain kind of spatial and temporal integrity" (Jackendoff 1983: 42; items in cross hatches represent projected world entities). Both of these characterizations have in common that nouns are viewed as encoding *atemporal bodies.*

is *cognitive stability,* a dense and interconnected region in conceptual space. These semantic features breathe new life into the notional definition of *noun.* Nouns may not always be persons, places, or things, but persons, places, and things almost always turn out to be nouns. *Entities,* relatively stable and atemporal discourse, ontological, and conceptual phenomena, motivate the form class.

3.2. EIGHT CLASSES
OF SEMANTIC PROPERTIES OF ENTITIES

We now have a sense of the basic issues involved in the semantics of nouns and entities. Here we turn to an enumeration of the properties that tend to be encoded as nouns. In section 3.1, we presented a picture of the broad content of the semantic representation of nouns: a relatively atemporal region in semantic or conceptual space. But languages often encode quite specific properties in their treatment of nouns, and so we must consider the more detailed content of their semantic representations. Our goal in this chapter is to take inventory of these components.

We examine eight classes of semantic properties: specificity, boundedness, animacy, gender, kinship, social status, physical structure, and function. All these have more specific subclasses and characteristic grammatical reflexes that deserve our attention.

The study of the semantic properties of entities and their grammatical manifestations is often carried out under the broader examination of *noun classes* and *classifiers:* particular morphological means to signal the semantic classes that nouns instantiate (Allan 1977; Denny 1976, 1986; Dixon 1982; Lakoff 1987). Elaborate classifier systems are found in a variety of genetically unrelated languages (Mandarin Chinese, American Sign Language, Chipewyan, and Swahili, e.g.); classifiers take a range of forms, from explicit coding in separate words to affixation by bound morphemes. Noun classifiers are clear instances of the encoding of specific semantic properties, and thus we resort to them as illustrations.

Classifiers either measure an entity by unit (*mensurals,* e.g., *yard of X*) or sort it by kind (*sortals,* e.g., *row of X*) (Lyons 1977: 463; Thomason 1972 is the seminal formal study). As Denny (1986) notes, classifiers, in combination with the entity, *compositionally determine* the meaning of the nouns they classify and so are good places to observe the requirements of semantic theory (see chap. 2). For example, in the phrase *wad of paper,* the sortal *wad* attributes a more specific property to the atemporal region denoted by *paper.* The semantic representation of the whole expression, 'irregular ensemble of paper,' is thus compositionally derived from the specific properties that make up its content. We want to account for the relatively few such specific properties that are actually instantiated in the vast range of possible properties that language could in principle encode.[3]

In many languages, classifiers mark grammatical agreement and concord. In other languages, they mark discourse participants and function much like pronouns (Downing 1986; Hopper 1986). So the semantic properties they encode have a direct effect on the structural design of language and fall in line with the Grammatical Constraint. We now turn to an examination of the semantic properties that languages tend to encode as or on nouns.

3.21. Specificity

3.211. Uniqueness
and the Specific/Nonspecific Distinction

An entity has been defined as an individuated, relatively atemporal region in conceptual space. Languages may also make reference to the *degree of individuation* of an entity. This is *specificity,* the uniqueness of the entity or, in more philosophical terms, the *relative singularity of the denotation.*

The effect of specificity can be seen in the possible interpretations of the following sentence:

3. I'm looking for a man who speaks French.

On one reading, *a man who speaks French* refers to a particular individual: 'I'm looking for a particular man who speaks French.' This is a specific reading. In another sense, however, *a man who speaks French* may refer to *any person whatsoever:* 'I'm looking for any old man who speaks French.' This is a nonspecific reading; the entity represented is any member of the class or kind so described, but no one member in particular.

The specific/nonspecific distinction has clear grammatical ramifications. The

---

[3]It should be pointed out here that this nonformal account also is compatible with more formal views. From a formal standpoint, nouns are considered predicates, because they represent nominal properties. So, a noun like *dog* is actually dog(x): 'dogness' is predicated of an entity, x (McCawley 1981, chap. 10; Montague 1974). Classifiers then are sorts that range over the predication of nouns. Denny (1986) proposes that classifiers be viewed as *restricted quantifiers* (quantifiers with a domain specified) ranging over the predicates. In this way, nouns denote properties, and classifiers denote the sort of those properties. None of this clashes with the view presented thus far; in fact, it is entirely in line with so nonformal a view as Langacker's. He argues (1987a: 183) that language consists of two kinds of predication: nominal and relational. The latter gives rise to all temporal and atemporal processes (verbs, adjectives, and adverbs); the former to things, or nouns. (Lehman 1979 attempts to reconcile formal and empirical accounts of classifiers.)

specific entity takes a personal pronoun in subsequent references while the non-specific entity takes the indefinite *one:*

4a. I'm looking for a particular man₁ who speaks French, and I'll find him₁/??one₁.
b. I'm looking for any old man₁ who speaks French, and I'll find one₁/??him₁.

The interpretations that we find in (3) are often formally differentiated in other languages. In Spanish, for instance, the difference between specific and non-specific entities is often signalled by the choice of *mood* (the grammatical device that signals the verifiability of a proposition: see chap. 9) for the verb in the clause modifying the noun in question. If the specific reading is intended, the indicative mood (for verifiable events) appears; if the nonspecific reading is intended, the subjunctive mood (for nonverifiable events) appears (Rivero 1975, 1977; Rojas 1977):[4]

5a. Busc-   o   a   un hombre que habl- a
    look for Pres/1Per Pers Obj a   man   who speak Indic
    francés
    French.
    I'm looking for a man who speaks French (Specific).
 b. Busc-   o   a   un hombre que habl- e
    look for Pres/1Per Pers Obj a   man   who speak Subjunc
    francés
    French.
    I'm looking for a man who may speak French (Nonspecific).

This mood difference has a certain logic. As Givón (1984: chap. 11) shows, referentiality (= specificity) correlates with *actual moods,* like the indicative, where information is represented as verifiable. Lack of referentiality correlates with *nonactual moods,* like the subjunctive, where information is represented as unreal or yet to be verified. Specificity implies uniquely determined reference, so it is connected with actual mood; nonspecificity, because it implies no uniquely determinable referent, is thus connected with nonactual mood.

What factors determine the relative specificity of an entity? This is an intricate philosophical and linguistic problem, with a lengthy and often fiercely argued

---

[4]Rojas argues against Rivero's original account—that the indicative is specific and the subjunctive nonspecific—saying instead that the subjunctive can support the specific reading as long as it is the *past subjunctive;* Rivero 1977 reaffirms her position. Both appear to be right. The past subjunctive supports specificity because of its association with *remoteness* and hence *individuation.* The examples in (5) use only the present subjunctive, which indisputably requires nonspecifics.

history. There is no space (or need, for that matter) to do justice to the number of proposals that have been handed down through the years. But before we embark on a more detailed survey of the issues, we should note that one factor *not* involved is *existence*. Specificity implies only that the referent can be *uniquely determined*. As Ioup (1977: 235) points out: "The ambiguities concerning specificity appear to be independent of ontological existence entailments." Thus we can induce the specific/nonspecific ambiguity even by asserting nonsense:

    6. I'm looking for a male sister.

There is no possible referent for *male sister,* but the specific/nonspecific ambiguity is preserved because (6) may mean either 'a particular male sister' or 'any old male sister.' It is important to note here, as elsewhere and elaborated in Chapter 2, that the uniqueness of the individual be *relative to some mentally projected universe.*

3.212.   Some Philosophical and Linguistic Accounts of Specificity

A number of factors other than existence have been postulated as the determinants of specificity. Proposals have come from both the philosophical and linguistic literature. We look at influential examples from each.

3.2121.   Philosophical Accounts: Russell, Donnellan, Kripke

In the philosophical literature, forms that *inherently induce specificity* are known as *singular terms.* They include such things as *proper names* (e.g., *George Bush*), *definite descriptions* (e.g., *the president of the United States*), *indefinite descriptions* (e.g., *a man in the White House who vacations in Kennebunkport, Maine*), and *indexicals* (forms that point to context: e.g., *that guy*) (see Fitch 1987; Schwarz 1979). How do these induce specificity?

Let us consider just the problem of proper names and related indexicals. Bertrand Russell, following suggestions by Frege, proposed that proper names have specific reference because they refer by an implicit definite description. The singular reference of *George Bush* is fixed by some definite description like *the current president of the United States.* All proper names are truncated definite descriptions, and definiteness induces specificity.

There are a number of widely discussed problems raised by this sort of analysis, notably the issue of empty proper names. *Bush George* is a proper name but has no reference and thus has no definite description. How then does this proper name refer? Donnellan (1966, 1972, 1978) argued that the definite description theory of singular reference is only partially correct. Definite descriptions have two different meanings: one is semantic, and functions to assign properties to an individual, that is, to denote. This function Donnellan calls *attributive*. The other function is more demonstrative and serves merely to pragmatically select a referent without attributing properties to that person. This function Donnellan calls *referential*.

We can see the two functions of definite descriptions in a simple example. Suppose I come upon a crowd of people listening to a person giving a speech. Someone next to me turns and says: "The leader of the Smoomies is some talker, isn't he?" On one interpretation, the definite description *the leader of the Smoomies* attributes properties to the individual talking; here, the speaker believes that I have a sense of the same denotation as he does. This is the *attributive function* of definite descriptions. But on another interpretation, I may have no idea of what *the leader of the Smoomies* singles out. On this interpretation, the definite description does not denote or attribute properties to an individual, but merely serves to indicate who is speaking: I still have to find out what this name means. This use is the *referential function*.

To Donnellan, Russell's theory accounts only for the attributive use. Singular terms and definite descriptions may also have a referential function. Furthermore, Russell failed to see that definite descriptions may still be definite without inducing singular reference. Consider the definite description *the big dog*, which may be nonspecific and thus refer to any member of the class of big dogs (*the big dog is an ugly dog*). Such expressions Donnellan confusingly labels *indefinite definite descriptions:* definite descriptions without singular reference. So Donnellan's critique of the definite description theory of proper names teaches us that *specificity cannot be simply traced to definiteness:* Not all definite descriptions attribute properties, and not all definite descriptions are specific.

A third view is held by Kripke (1972) and Kaplan (1978, though Kaplan is mainly concerned with indexicals). Kripke argues that singular reference of proper names is not a function of the definite description attached to expressions, but the result of the *causal connection* between the *use of a proper name* and *the context* that surrounds its original use to refer. In this view, definite descriptions may vary, or even be absent, as long as the proper name *rigidly designates*— persistently denotes through time. Hence, *George Bush* may be definitely described as *the current president of the United States, the man who succeeded Reagan,* or *the nicest guy in the White House.* All three rigidly designate the individual also represented by *George Bush,* but even more importantly, all three legitimately denote because of the contexts in which they have been connected to the referent. Under this view, proper names (and indexicals) have *direct reference:* Their meaning is not mediated by a definite description. What matters is the circumstances that give rise to the naming, not the definite description itself.

In dismissing the definite description theory, Kripke also dismisses Donnellan's modification thereon. Kripke (1979) says that in making a distinction between the attributive and referential functions, Donnellan fails to see that he is just distinguishing between meaning that resides in the language and meaning that resides in the speaker's choice of expression. Attributive meaning is what Kripke calls *semantic meaning*; referential meaning, what Kripke calls *speaker meaning*, is purely pragmatic and a question of how the speaker chooses to communicate in the situation at hand. So, for Kripke, Donnellan has just made the distinction between semantics and pragmatics, not one between two kinds of definite reference.

The point of this philosophical discussion can be stated fairly simply. Specificity, or singularity, is an independent semantic property. It is not necessarily an inherent property of singular terms and it is not wholly derivable from definiteness. As Seuren (1985: 471) notes: "Their [proper names'] referential behavior is not essentially different from ordinary descriptions. They do allow for variable reference." This brings philosophical accounts in line with the linguistic accounts of specificity, which detach specificity from existence, allowing it to be a semantic property *predicated of* things and to be a matter of degree.

3.2122.   Linguistic Accounts: Fodor and Givón

One of the earliest thorough linguistic accounts of specificity is Fodor's (1970). She argues that specificity is not a discrete property of a particular form but of the semantic representation of an expression as a whole, deriving from the interaction of a linguistic form with the rest of the linguistic context. Though Fodor is concerned more narrowly with the referential opacity of quantifiers (see chap. 2 for *referential opacity*), we can demonstrate her point with a different kind of example.

Consider the following sentence:

7. John bought the food.

Example (7) is unambiguous, with a specific reading for the direct object. However, note what happens when the tense of the verb changes from the past to the present habitual:

8. John buys the food.

Example (8) means either 'John habitually buys particular food' (Specific) or 'John habitually buys any old food' (Nonspecific). Arguably, the nonspecific reading is even the preferred interpretation, in spite of the definite article. What causes this change?

The most obvious explanation is the shift in tense. Habituality, like the nonactual moods in (5b), induces nonspecificity, unlike the past tense in (7), which is connected to actuality, verifiability, and hence the specific reading. In as much as specificity can be so derived, Fodor argues, it must not be an inherent property of the noun or determiner, but a function of the interaction of the semantic representation of the form having the specific interpretation, the noun, and the rest of the linguistic context. Otherwise, specificity should be constant in (7) and (8). In this way, specificity is independently predicated of an entity, as the philosophical accounts require (see also Jackendoff 1983: 97).

A slightly different account of specificity is given by Givón (1984), for whom specificity is a function of discourse structure and speaker's prior knowledge (see also Karttunen 1968 and Ioup 1977). The determinant of specificity is what he calls *referential accessibility* (Givón 1984: 399), the way entities can *assume* unique individuation, unique accessibility, in a mentally projected world. One way is for them to be part of the *permanent file,* the set of culturally or contextually accepted information that speakers take for granted at any moment of communication: proper names, indexicals, deducible parts of larger wholes, "such as body parts, kin relations or culturally-based possessions" (Givón 1984: 400). Or they may be part of the *active file,* information established as specific in the discourse at hand, such as prior mentions or discourse referents. In each case, specificity is a function of the referential accessibility of the entity.

Like Ioup (1977), Givón argues that specificity is not an existence claim, but a claim about the uniqueness, and hence accessibility, of an entity in a current discourse about a mentally projected world. Specificity may be independently predicated of an entity as long as the entity meets this requirement of uniqueness. Thus, an apparently nonspecific entity can be interpreted as specific, as in the case of past tense inducing specificity: *a boy played baseball*; conversely, an apparently specific entity can be nonspecific: *I wouldn't tolerate a New York City if you paid me. New York City*—normally with a unique reference—represents a type, so 'any old New York City' will do, even if it is Boston or Philadelphia.

3.2123.   The Unity of Each Account

In both the philosophical and linguistic explanations, we find that specificity is an independent semantic property, even if it can be functionally induced by tense, mood, definiteness, context of utterance or assumed knowledge base. Russell, Donnellan, and Kripke point out that specificity is the relative singularity of the denotation of a noun as a function of its associated description or inherited context of use. Fodor and Givón note that specificity is uniqueness as a function of linguistic and discourse context. All these views come together in Givón's broader position: Specificity is a matter of the degree of referential accessibility of an entity in a projected world.

3.213.   The Reflexes of Specificity

Now that we have seen some of the basic characteristics of specificity, let us look at some additional semantic and structural factors with respect to this property. Some languages, though relatively few, purely differentiate specifics from nonspecifics. Givón (1984) claims that Bemba does so through prefixation. VCV (vowel, consonant, vowel) prefixes indicate specificity; CV prefixes indicate nonspecificity (Givón 1984: 412):

9a. a- à-   fwaaya ici- tabo.
    he past want   Spec book
    He wanted the specific book.
 b. a- à   fwaaya ci-   tabo.
    he past want   Non-Spec book
    He wanted some (any old) book.

The VCV prefix *ici* signals specificity whereas the CV prefix *ci* signals nonspecificity; all else remains the same in the form of the expression, so Bemba appears to strictly differentiate the two semantic properties. (See also Dahl 1970 on Russian indefinites and Bickerton 1981 on creole languages.)

More commonly, however, specificity is bound up with other semantic and structural properties. We first consider the connection of specificity to definiteness; thereafter, we look at its relation to factivity, negation, and restrictive modification.

3.2131. Definiteness and Specificity

We might begin, as Russell did, by claiming that the specific/nonspecific distinction is mirrored by the definite/indefinite distinction in morphology. We immediately run into the problem that many languages do not productively differentiate definites from indefinites, but nonetheless retain the specific/nonspecific distinction. Nung is such a language (Saul 1980: 110–11):

10. hăhn cáh   slú' ọc ma.
    see   Class tiger out come
    He saw a/the tiger come out.

Example (10) has no formal distinction between *the tiger* and *a tiger*, each surfacing as *cáh slú'*, with a noun classifier and the noun for 'tiger.' These entities may or may not be specific, but this property is indiscernible from any marking for definiteness.

We cannot simply read specificity off definiteness because definiteness is conditioned by nonsemantic factors. On the one hand, there are *purely discourse conditions*: Definite nouns are associated with *given information,* what the speaker can assume to be in the consciousness of the hearer; indefinite nouns are associated with *new information,* what the speaker assumes is not in the consciousness of the hearer (Chafe 1974; Givón 1984). On the other hand, there appear to be some *purely syntactic characteristics* of the definite/indefinite distinction. A number of syntactic structures are sensitive to what has been called the *Definiteness Effect* (Reuland and ter Meulen 1987), a preference in certain constructions for either definite or indefinite nouns. Existential constructions (e.g., *there is . . .*) and predicate nominals tend to be indefinite; subjects tend to be definite (and are obligatorily so in some languages). These facts have led to explanations of the Definiteness Effect that are principally syntactic (Safir 1985; Heim 1982, 1987 incorporates given information into the syntactic account of definites, making it much more like Givón's 1984 "surfacey" typological account than formal theorists might actually desire).

Nonetheless, there is an *undeniable link between specificity and definiteness and nonspecificity and indefiniteness.* Milsark's (1974) original foray into the problem basically relies on a direct mapping from semantics onto syntax. Safir (1985), too, recognizes that the Definiteness Effect is at least *motivated by semantic factors*: "Indefinite NPs differ from definite NPs in that the former are 'less referential' " and "The DE [definiteness effect] . . . emerges as a formal syntactic property of a semantically definable class" (1985: 171). The unifying factor in all this is that definites tend to be *known,* and if they are known, they tend to be *referentially accessible*; if they are referentially accessible, they tend to be *specific*; if they are specific, they tend to be *definite.*

Seeing these meaning-form connections, Givón (1984) proposes a broad account of the coding of nouns with regard to their definiteness and specificity. There are three basic nominal codings:

1. *Definites,* which are overwhelmingly *specific,* and occur with definite determiners, numerals and quantities;
2. *Indefinites,* which, as we have seen, may be *specific* or *nonspecific*;
3. *Generics,* or types, which also may be either *specific* or *nonspecific* (cf. *those dinosaurs were a large beast,* definite generic, and *dinosaurs were a large beast,* indefinite generic).

These three categories determine the scale of coding shown in Fig. 3.2 (modified version of Givón 1984: 407). The possibility of definite encoding decreases from left to right, but the scale is to be read as a loop or helix. Generics, because they have either a specific or nonspecific reading, loop back to specific definites in encoding.

Givón claims that languages give a similar surface reflex to contiguous areas of the scale. Some languages encode the first two categories of the scale—specific definites and specific indefinites—alike because of their specificity, as in Nung (p. 75), which lacks a productive means of signalling definite versus indefinite. In such languages, often either the numeral 'one' or the demonstrative takes up the coding slack. These are entirely logical choices: If the numeral 'one' is chosen, the entity is itemized, counted, delimited, and specific; if the demonstrative is chosen, the entity is singled out contextually, again a specific reference. Interestingly enough, the demonstrative that tends to be selected for this

FIG. 3.2.   Scale of definiteness and specificity.

purpose is usually the *remote* or *obviative* demonstrative, the one that expresses a position *away from the speaker* (see chap. 6): in English, *that.* This choice is understandable because remote or distant entities are more likely to be perceived in their totality, and hence individuated and delimited, than objects up close.[5]

Nung, which we know lacks the definite/indefinite distinction, uses the numeral 'one' to indicate specific indefinite (Saul 1980: 59):

11. m'uhn sléng ọc ma   tú   lụhc n'uhng.
     she bear out come Class child one
     She gave birth to a child.

The situation expressed by (11) requires that entity be specific because birth does not involve 'any old child,' but the specific child that is born. Hence, even though (11) is indefinite, it *must be* specific in interpretation.

The second and third categories of the scale—specific and nonspecific indefinites—are coded similarly in many languages, like English, as the earlier discussion of the specific/nonspecific ambiguity of the indefinite article illustrates (pp. 69–71). There is no need to repeat the examples here.

English is also an example of a language that codes similarly the third and fourth categories of the scale, nonspecific indefinites and nonspecific generics:

12. I buy a tulip every day. —NONSPEC . INDEF or generic

In (12), *a tulip* denotes either a nonspecific indefinite ('any single tulip') or a generic ('a kind of tulip' or 'some tulip').

Finally, English illustrates the similar coding of both the fourth and fifth categories—nonspecific generics and specific generics—and the fifth and first—specific generics and definites. Consider the difference between the following:

13a. I buy tulips.
  b. I buy the tulip.

Example (13a) may be interpreted as either a specific ('those tulips') or nonspecific generic ('some tulips'), but in each case it is coded in the plural. Exam-

---

[5]Note how this use of remoteness is analogous to the use of the past tense—temporal remoteness—to mark specificity and override the subjunctive in Spanish: see the discussion on p. 70.

ple (13b) may refer to either a specific generic ('the tulip as a category of flora') or a specific definite ('the particular tulip'), but again the overt form remains the same.

These constancies bear out Givón's point nicely and support the broader connection of specificity and definiteness. Contiguous areas of the Scale of Definiteness and Specificity tend to be coded alike. This is because the definite/indefinite distinction in coding is symptomatic of, though not reducible to, the specific/nonspecific distinction, which turns on the relative accessibility of individuals in a mentally projected world.

3.2132. Factivity, Negation, and Restrictive Modification

Although specificity is very likely to trigger definiteness, there are a number of other surface manifestations of the specific/nonspecific distinction that deserve mention. As we know, specificity is related to actual moods, nonspecificity to nonactual moods. We ought then to expect specificity generally in expressions of verifiable information and nonspecificity in those conveying nonverifiable or contrary to fact information.

We can construct a test case for this hypothesis with the English indefinite because it is ambiguous between a specific or nonspecific reading. If our hypothesis is correct, then we ought to find only the specific reading in constructions in actual moods and the nonspecific reading in constructions in nonactual moods.

Factives and negation respectively characterize actual and nonactual moods. Factive verbs (see chap. 2) presuppose the truth of their complements, actual information, and thus ought to select the specific reading of the ambiguous indefinite in English. Consider the following:

14. I regretted reading a book.

In (14), the specific reading does appear to be the only one possible: 'I regretted reading a particular book.' It takes some doing to evoke the nonspecific reading, though this may be facilitated by inserting a marker of habituality: *I regretted ever reading a book*. Notably, the nonspecific reading is triggered by *ever*, a marker of habituality and hence nonactuality, not by the factive.

In contrast to factivity, a negative context selects the nonspecific reading of the indefinite:

15. I didn't read a book.

Here, the preferred interpretation is one that evokes the generic reading, an observation supported by the anomaly of overt specificity in the context of the negative:

16. ?? I didn't read a certain book.

The same distinction in the negative is found extensively in other languages. In Mandarin Chinese, for example, the indefinite specific is disallowed in negative (hence nonactual) contexts (example from Huang 1987: 249: tones deleted in original):

17. ?? wo meiyou kanjian yige   ren.
    I   not   see   Indef/Spec man
    I didn't see a certain man.

However, if the negation is deleted, the specific reading is allowed:

18. wo kanjian yige   ren.
    I   see   Indef/Spec man
    I saw a certain man.

Another structural correlate of specificity is *restrictive modification,* a syntactic device for attributing essential qualities to an entity. Clauses that restrictively modify tend to occur with nouns that represent nonspecific entities. We can see this condition with a proper name, which is more likely to be specific because of singular reference and is unlikely to be modified by a restrictive clause:

19. ?? New York that I visit is expensive.

But if the specificity of the proper name is decreased by making it representative of a class, then it can take a restrictive modifier:

20. The New York that I visit is expensive.

This effect occurs because restrictive modifiers limit the conceptual domain represented by the noun. But the domain is already inherently limited through singular reference and so further limitation by restrictive modification is precluded (as in 19). On the other hand, if the domain is nonspecific, then it can be naturally further limited by the restrictive modifier (as in 20).

In Lakhota, this interaction between specificity and restrictive modification is quite clear. Williamson (1987) remarks that all noun heads of relative clauses in Lakhota must be indefinite. Although it is unclear whether or not indefiniteness is the same thing as nonspecificity, Williamson's explanation is highly reminiscent of the discussion on pp. 75–78: "Why are definite NPs not possible heads? . . . A definite is familiar and presupposes the content of its predicate. I suggest that this property is at variance with the meaning of restrictive RCs, for if the head is already familiar to the hearer, further specification by the RC is, at best, unnecessary" (Williamson 1987: 187). Definite nouns are part of *the permanent file,* to use Givón's terminology, and are taken as specifics; indefinites must then be nonspecifics.

Lakhota has *internally headed relative clauses* (sometimes called *headless*), which means that the noun representing the entity to be modified by the relative clause (the *head noun*) is *inside the relative clause proper* (unlike English, e.g., where, for the most part, the noun is outside the relative clause). In Lakhota, the head noun must be nonspecific (Williamson 1987: 171):

21. Mary owiža wą   kaǧe ki he   ophewathų.
    Mary quilt Indef make the Dem I-buy
    I bought the quilt that Mary made.
    Lit. I bought the-Mary-made-a-quilt.

In (21), the head noun, *owiža* 'quilt,' is internal, inside the clause modifying it, the one with the verb *kaǧe* 'make.' It is also indefinite (= nonspecific), as indicated by the marker *wą*. This latter fact is crucially demonstrated by the unacceptability of the conversion of the head noun to definite (= specific) (Williamson 1987: 171):

22. ?? Mary owiža ki kaǧe ki he   ophewathų.
    Mary quilt Def make ki Dem I-buy
    ?? I bought the specific quilt that Mary made.
    Lit. I bought the-particular-Mary-made-quilt.

There is additional evidence for this specificity restriction: None of the standard singular terms may be the head of a relative cause. As Williamson explains (1987: 175): "Exactly these quantified expressions are excluded from the position of internal head: traditionally definite NPs . . . proper names and definite pronouns . . . , and various universal quantifiers."

It appears, then, that Lakhota translates the specific/nonspecific distinction into a *structural restriction on its relative clauses*. Williamson speculates that this may be a universal feature of languages with internally headed relatives, but this more general point remains to be seen.

Three factors other than definiteness, then, correlate with the specific/nonspecific distinction: factivity, negation, and restrictive modification. The first two reflect the difference between actual and nonactual mood; the third reflects uniqueness of reference. Their connection to specificity follows from the referential determinateness of specific entities and their association with verifiable information.

3.214.   Summary

In this section, we have seen the semantic and morphosyntactic characteristics of specificity. Specificity refers to the uniqueness, individuation, or referential accessibility of an entity in a mentally projected world. Both philosophical and linguistic accounts agree that specificity is an independent property, if not always inherent in an entity (as in a proper name) but inducible from the linguistic and pragmatic context (e.g., by mood and tense). Specificity often correlates with definiteness, and we have examined Givón's proposal that specificity and definiteness form an encoding scale. Specificity also surfaces in conjunction with factivity, negation, and restrictive modification. The overriding principles of actuality/nonactuality and the inherent delimitation of conceptual domains condition specificity in these contexts.

3.22. Boundedness

If entities are relatively atemporal regions in conceptual space, we can ask about whether or not the region has a *determinable limit*. This is the problem of *boundedness*. Some entities are inherently demarcated and come with their limits already specified. Such entities are said to be semantically *bounded*. On the other hand, some entities are inherently open and denote uncircumscribed regions in conceptual space. These entities are said to be semantically *unbounded*.

We can see the difference clearly in (23):

23. The gas escaped.

In the bounded interpretation, (23) means 'a kind or quantity of gas escaped,' and has a paraphrase in terms of units: *a gas escaped*. In the unbounded interpretation, however, (23) means something like 'an indeterminate extent of gas escaped,' and has a quite different paraphrase: *(some) gas escaped*. The noun *gas* thus has two readings, one denoting an inherently delimited entity and another an open entity.

3.221. Seven Features of Boundedness

The distinction between bounded and unbounded entities has been thoroughly discussed by Langacker (1987a, 1987b), and we consider his views in what follows. Langacker has noticed that the bounding of entities has a number of distinct ramifications. We first look at four characteristics of the bound itself; thereafter, we consider three more general features of the internal structure of bounded or unbounded entities.

3.2211. Four Features of the Bound

First, bounded entities are delimited only within their normal construal. Langacker argues that bounding must be in effect only in the *primary domain,* or the universe of discourse that is neutral at the time of speech. For example, the entity represented by the noun *a sound* is bounded in ordinary discourse: *a sound, two sounds, the sounds,* and so on. But in technical discourse, say in acoustics, the entity may be actually unbounded—*some sound*—because sound is a *continuous flow* of energy. This contrast does not vitiate boundedness per se, but relegates delimitation to the universe of discourse in effect at the time of speech.

Second, in addition to being restricted to a primary domain, boundedness may be *virtual* as well as *real*. Consider the entity denoted by *idea*. Although this entity has no material existence, it is still a bounded entity: *the idea, the ideas, two ideas, some ideas. Idea* is pluralizable, countable, and unitized, but its bound is *virtual*, unlike the *real* bound of the denotation of *table*, for example. Bounding may be virtual, so any kind of abstract delimitation counts as a bound, and abstract containment, like class membership or typing, is sufficient to induce bounding. Consequently, *gasoline* represents an unbounded entity, but when it is understood as a type or abstract class, it is bounded:

24. Most gasolines are lead free (i.e., Texaco, Mobil, Shell, etc.).

Third, boundedness is an inherent property of entities, not derived solely from the linguistic context, and so is part of the content of the semantic representation of entities. Langacker points out (1987a: 59): "The bounding . . . cannot be merely the default-case limitation resulting from a restricted scope of predication," by which he means that boundedness is not inherited by an entity from the events it undergoes. The process denoted by the verb *notice*, for instance, is of inherently limited duration, punctual, and temporally bounded: ?? *I noticed the bird all afternoon.* In spite of the inherent boundedness of the process, the verb may take *either* a bounded or unbounded entity as its object:

25a. I noticed the container of gas.
  b. I noticed gas.

If boundedness were inherited from the events in which entities participate, then (25b) should be unacceptable. *Notice,* however, represents a discrete process irrespective of the discreteness of the entity undergoing the noticing, and so boundedness is a property of the semantic representation of entities, not of the linguistic context.

Finally, boundedness is fuzzy. To quote Langacker (1987a: 60) again: "Bounding . . . need not be precise or sharply defined." Consider the difference in bounding between the entity denoted by *county* and by *region*. The former has a sharply demarcated bound, defined geopolitically; the latter has no clear phenomenological bound, even though it is a bounded entity: *the region, four regions, a region,* and so forth. Bounding is fuzzy, and thus it is possible to override it (like all fuzzy categories). Under ordinary circumstances, the entity denoted by *wall* is bounded. But imagine that we are tearing down a house; the walls are in pieces and their delimitation has become indeterminate. In this situation, it is possible to say things like the following:

26a. There's still some wall left over there.
  b. There's wall all over the place.
  c. There's not much more wall here.

These four characteristics define the bound itself. We now look at some characteristics of the internal structure of bounded and unbounded entities.

3.2212. Three Features of Internal Structure

Bounded or unbounded regions of conceptual space have three distinct internal properties. Langacker notes that bounded and unbounded entities diverge on their *internal homogeneity,* their *expansibility,* and their *replicability.*

Bounded entities tend to have internal organization. They can be viewed as composed of parts and are thus *conceptually heterogeneous.* In contrast, unbounded entities are viewed as *homogeneous,* with no, or little, internal structure; they are relatively uniform, or internally undifferentiated.

Consider in this respect the difference between the bounded and unbounded senses of *chocolate.* In the unbounded sense, as a substance, the entity has no parts and is not composed of "chocolate constituents." This is decidedly different from the bounded sense of *chocolate,* for example, *a chocolate,* as a piece of candy, where the entity does have pieces: A chocolate (candy) is composed of an outer layer, a filling, and so on. These parts heterogeneously compose the entity in its bounded state.

The two other characteristics, *expansibility* and *replicability,* follow from this difference in homogeneity between bounded and unbounded entities. Bounded entities, because they have internal structure, cannot be conceptually expanded or contracted without losing their status. Again consider the noun *a chocolate.* If the pieces of its referent are removed—if the covering is eliminated or the filling is subtracted—it is no longer a chocolate: Any scaling of the parts affects the discreteness of the entity as a whole. Furthermore, when the pieces of a bounded entity are extracted and examined, the pieces themselves do not retain identity with the entity they compose. The filling of a chocolate or the covering of a chocolate cannot stand for the totality of the entity.

But this is unlike unbounded entities. Consider *chocolate* as 'a mass of chocolate.' If a piece of this entity is subtracted, or more added for that matter, the entity remains intact. There can be more or less of an unbounded entity because it is continuous, noncomposite, and thus scalable. Moreover, if a piece of an unbounded entity is extracted, that piece retains the properties of the whole.

A piece of a mass of chocolate is still chocolate in spite of its extraction from the mass as a whole.

The question of expansibility brings up *replicability*. Bounded entities can be repeated; unbounded entities cannot be repeated. Langacker calls this result *incrementation*, noting that bounded entities can be incremented in discrete units because the bounding serves to demarcate one unit from another. Unbounded entities, however, because they are inherently undemarcated, cannot be incremented or replicated. Repetition of an unbounded entity results only in *more of the same entity*, whereas repetition of a bounded entity produces *another instance of the same entity*. Compare the difference between *more chocolate* and *more chocolates*: The former is incremented continuously whereas the latter is repeated or iterated.

Homogeneity/heterogeneity, expansibility, and replicability work in conjunction with the features of the bound itself to produce the overall semantic effects of boundedness. When we look at the forms that the bounded/unbounded distinction takes, we see how these characteristics translate directly into grammatical structure.

3.222. Reflexes of Boundedness

The bounded/unbounded distinction motivates the *count/mass* distinction, which itself is closely tied to *grammatical number*. However, these connections are not direct, reductive, or isomorphic. Nonetheless, we begin with this connection.

3.2221. Countability in English and Indonesian

Bounded entities are generally *countable* because they have a delimitation and are thereby replicable. Therefore, bounded entities tend to receive the morphological trappings of number, in whatever manner a language construes this formal device. In English, countability is associated with the indefinite article, numerals, the distributive quantifiers *each* and *every,* and pluralization. Our familiar example *chocolate,* which can have either a count or mass reading, bears out these encoding possibilities in its count interpretation: *a chocolate* ('a unit of candy': indefinite article), *one chocolate* ('a single candy': numeral), *every/each chocolate* ('enumerated set of candies': distributive quantifier), *chocolates* ('more than one unit of candy': pluralization).

Unbounded entities, on the other hand, tend to be *uncountable,* or better, nonenumerable, because of their continuousness and expansibility. After all, how can nondelimited entities be enumerated when enumeration presupposes differentiation of the entities to be enumerated? Unbounded entities therefore overwhelmingly tend to be marked differently in the number systems of languages. In English, mass nouns tend *not* to take the indefinite article, numerals, and pluralization; if these devices occur on mass nouns, the entities they encode come to be viewed as bounded and hence counted. Mass nouns tend to occur either with no marker or with nondistributive quantifiers, like *some, much,* and *little*: *chocolate* ('unspecified extent of chocolate': no marker), *much chocolate* ('large extent of chocolate': nondistributive quantifier).

We can see the universality of these reflexes by looking at Indonesian, where the bounded/unbounded distinction surfaces fairly directly as the count/mass distinction and is sharply made in the coding system (examples from MacDonald 1976). Only bounded entities take numerals:

26a. dua anak.
     two child
     two children.
  b. ?? dua air.
      two water
      ?? two waters.

An enumerated unbounded entity must take a mensural or a sortal:

27. dua liter air.
    two liter water
    two liters of water.

The mensurals and sortals *unitize,* or semantically *type,* the unbounded entity, allowing its countability.

In Indonesian, as in English, morphological pluralization is also symptomatic of the bounded/unbounded distinction. Bare plurals are typically formed by reduplication (i.e., repetition of a form, a common process across the world's languages for pluralization), and incrementation of bounded entities can be brought about this way, though it is generally unacceptable for unbounded entities:

28a. orang- orang.
      person person
      persons.
  b. ?? air-air.
      water water
      ?? waters.

If reduplicated unbounded entities have an interpretation, it is in terms of *virtual bounding* by class membership or type:

29. minyak-minyak.
    oil   oil
    different kinds of oil.

And so reduplication forces a bounded reading.[6]

We may summarize the results as to the coding of the bounded/unbounded distinction as follows. Bounded entities tend to be countable, and are then realized as plurals; pluralization is a function of the counting of the bounds on the entities because counting relies on the differentiation of entities to be counted. Unbounded entities tend to be uncountable, or masses, and are then realized as singulars, or nonplurals. If the entire matter were this straightforward, we could stop here, but there are a number of other troubling examples that suggest that such a simple mapping from the semantics of boundedness onto the syntax and morphology is not as easy as it appears.

3.2222. Oats, Wheat, and Countability

It has often been noted that mass and singularity, and count and plurality, do not necessarily coincide (Allan 1980 presents a nice catalogue of divergences). First, it is possible to have *mass plurals, oats,* and *coffee grounds,* for example. These occur *only* in the plural, ?? *an oat,* and are peculiar plurals at that because they cannot be further enumerated even though they are otherwise plural: ?? *seven coffee grounds,* ?? *six oats.*

Second, there are *mass nouns that occur only in the singular,* like the canonical examples given earlier (*butter,* e.g.), but that nonetheless do not seem to have the same properties as the standard singular uncountables. Compare *meat,* which is a singular uncountable, with *furniture. Meat* may be a mass here because, as an unbounded substance, it is internally homogeneous, but *furniture* represents a *heterogeneously composed mass* and yet is encoded only in the singular. By all semantic measures, *furniture ought* to be pluralizable.

Third, there are *count nouns that occur only in the plural*: *scissors, pants,* and *woods,* for example. If countability allows productive number marking because countables may be encoded either as a single bounded entity or more than one

---

[6]Interestingly enough, when bounded entities in Indonesian are reduplicated, they may also take on the sense of virtual bounding:

i. buku-buku
   book book
   different kinds of books

Pluralization of a *real bound* may thus induce a *virtual bound*. Again, compare English, where the bare plural *books* implies not only an incrementation of bounded entities—*books are on the table* ('more than one unit of book')—but also an abstract type:

ii. Tom likes a good detective story, but I hate such books.

Here, the meaning of *books* is as a kind: 'I hate such kind of book.'

such entity, then why are ?? *a scissor* and ?? *one pant* disallowed? These ought to have singular forms to complement the enumerable plural forms: *seven scissors, twenty pants.*

Finally, there are *countables with no plural.* Again, if boundedness motivates countability, and countability motivates plurality, why are there nouns like *hair? A hair* is possible, but ?? *the hairs* is markedly odd.

In response to examples like these, Wierzbicka (1985) proposes a general solution that reinvigorates the argument that there is a close connection between semantics and surface form. She shows (though not in these specific terms) that once the locale of incrementation is understood as the controlling property of singularity and plurality, not internal homogeneity per se or continuousness, then the aforementioned irregularities disappear.

Why are there mass plurals (problem 1)? Wierzbicka says that all entities coded as mass plurals have individual constituents, but these constituents are just not relevant to their perception. Coffee grounds have pieces, but the pieces are *not worth counting.* Plurality follows from their *countability-in-principle,* because of the unitization of their constituents, but mass follows from the basic irrelevance of actually counting the pieces. Mass plurals are therefore fuzzy: unbounded, but with countable constituents.

A similar solution holds for singular masses (problem 2), though with a slight twist. Why should *furniture* be a singular mass term like the canonical *butter,* when furniture is radically different from butter in its internal structure? Furniture, unlike butter, *is* internally differentiated, but the entities that compose the class called *furniture* are *markedly different from each other,* a point brought home by the observation that a set of the same kind of furniture, say chairs, is not referred to as *furniture: Furniture* must refer to a set composed of *different* elements, say chairs *and* tables. Due to the internal heterogeneity of its referent, *furniture* ought *not* to be a singular mass because the singularity reputedly follows from the lack of internal differentiation (as for *butter*).

Wierzbicka points out, however, that if counting is derived from the enumeration of internal constituents, these constituents must be of the same kind. Hence, *oats* is a mass plural because its referent has pieces that are not only differentiated, but are also the *same kind* of entity. *Furniture* fails to meet this characterization because furniture must be composed of different entities. The same holds for such words as *cutlery* and *crockery,* whose denotations must have different internal parts, no matter how discrete. They should be singular masses, as indeed they are, ?? *crockeries,* ?? *cutleries,* but it is impossible to enumerate them, ?? *one crockery* and ?? *one cutlery.*

What about countables with only plural forms, like *scissors* (problem 3)? Again the answer lies in how boundedness bears on the entity. The entity represented by *scissors* has clearly differentiated constituents, and, moreover, constituents of the same kind: two blades joined at the center. The same goes for *pants,* which encodes an entity that consists of two discrete identical pieces. Likewise, *woods* encodes an entity consisting of discrete parts that are all the same: trees. Countability, obligatory plurality in this case, follows from the internal semantic structure of the entities coded. They are coded as plural *because they are inherently plural.*

We can explain countables with no plural (problem 4) by means of the same principle. If plurality is a reflection of bounded entities to be counted, whether internal to the entity or as a function of the counting of the entity as a totality itself, then there may be entities that are bounded as a whole, but whose constituents or aggregations are either not bounded or are irrelevant to bounding. Such an explanation accounts for the lack of pluralization with *hair.* Hair is bounded as a totality, but the constituents of hair are simply irrelevant to our concern. Hence the referent for *hair* is countable, but it is functionally and conceptually singular: a countable with no plural.

From these considerations, Wierzbicka proposes a fairly radical view of the connection between meaning and form: There is more iconicity between semantic structure and grammatical coding than might be expected. How else can the irregularities already discussed come out as regular as they do? Although the full thrust of iconicity is still a matter of theoretical debate, we can appreciate a more general point. Wierzbicka shows that the crucial semantic ramification of boundedness is what Langacker calls *incrementation.* Surface coding is related to the incrementability of the entity, which may be derived either from the *internal incrementation* of bounded constituents, as in the case of *oats,* or from the *external incrementation* of the entity as a totality, as in the (negative) case of *hair.* (Mufwene 1980 presents a related view on the basis of what he calls the *individuated/nonindividuated distinction*: see especially 1980: 1024.) Number signals the *extent of the relevance of boundedness.* Even irregularities in number coding systems can be understood from this more general principle. Of course, this understanding rests on allowing semantics and surface expression to be connected rather than modularized. But without this motivation of surface form by semantics, it is difficult to see that the apparent exceptions to the syntactic form of the traditional count/mass distinction are actually quite regular.

3.223.   Summary

This section has discussed the semantic factors associated with the inherent delimitation of entities. We have looked at a number of characteristics of the bounded/unbounded distinction: for example, virtual bounding, fuzziness, expansibility, and so on. We have also considered the count/mass opposition and its encoding as the singular/plural distinction. Finally, we have looked at the divergence of boundedness and expected surface forms, like mass plurals, and proposed a more general account of the exceptions in terms of internal or external incrementation.

3.23. Animacy

Having considered how entities may have a unique denotation and may be inherently delimited, we now turn our attention to *animacy*. This property has received considerable attention in the literature no doubt because it often interacts pervasively with the morphology and syntax of languages, and thus its effects are clearly observable (see Comrie 1981 for a good short introduction to the problem). We try to define the property and its subclasses and then describe several attempts, via hierarchies, to systematize the relation between animacy and morphosyntactic coding.

3.231. Linguistic and Biological Animacy

Linguistic animacy only imperfectly matches up with what counts for animacy in natural science. From a biological standpoint, animacy has two principal criteria, life and locomotion, and the former has priority because all things that have locomotion are generally alive, but not vice versa. Under this view, humans, fish, and paramecia are animate because they have both life and locomotion. Plants are also animate, though they have no locomotion, because metabolism is sufficient to support the classification. Pineapples and rocks are not animate because they have neither life nor attendant locomotion.

Things are not so nicely segmented in the linguistic world. Sometimes both biological criteria are applied: In most languages, humans are encoded as animate. But sometimes *neither* criterion is applied even though by strict scientific method, each can and should be: In Kirwina, female humans may be encoded like inanimate objects (the legacy of the demeaning effects of patriarchy). And sometimes *totally different* criteria seem to be applied: In Yagua, rocks and pineapples are animate!

The essential criterion for the assignment of linguistic animacy appears to be the *influence* that the entity has over the *execution* or *instantiation* of an event. If an entity is more potent and more influential, it is more likely to be coded as animate. (In Yagua, rocks and pineapples are influential: see next section.) Thus, the biological criteria of life and locomotion may be relevant, but they are only two among many other properties that go to determine linguistic animacy. Topicality, potency, cultural importance, and discourse salience also determine the relative animacy of an entity. But these all follow the overriding criterion of *influence*.

3.232. Animates Versus Inanimates

All languages apparently distinguish between animate and inanimate entities at a gross level (see Allan 1977: 299), making the animate/inanimate division not only universal but also primary (Adams 1986: 248). Languages that encode the distinction rather sharply are Bantu languages (e.g., Swahili), some Athapaskan (e.g., Navajo), Algonquian (e.g., Ojibwa), and Wakashan languages (e.g., Nootkan) (Allan 1977: 299).

Yagua, our odd case in point, does likewise, marking the following with animate noun classifiers: persons, spirits, animals, stars, the moon, months, mirrors, pictures, rocks, pineapples, brooms, and fans. The semantic motivation to this list is fairly transparent. Humans, animals, and their manifestations are animate: hence mirrors and pictures are animate. Culturally influential items are animate: Yaguas are lunar worshippers, and the moon, months, and stars are animate, whereas the sun is inanimate. Rocks are influential and valuable, for crushing food; pineapples are historically animate in related cultures; brooms and fans have motion like animates (D. Payne 1986).

Singular animates take the classifier *nu* (D. Payne 1986: 122):

> 30. junúuy-nu   jiy- nu   quiivą.
>   live   Animate/Sing this Animate/Sing fish
>   This fish is a live one.
>   More exactly: This animate fish is a live animate thing.

Inanimates are usually marked by the inanimate classifier, *rà* (D. Payne 1986: 120):

> 31. tá- rà-   quïï   cucháára.
>   one Inanimate Singular spoon
>   one spoon.
>   More exactly: one single inanimate thing: spoon.

Though (30) and (31) present the animate/inanimate distinction as rather neat, in Yagua, as in many other languages, the coding of animates and inanimates does not often surface so purely demarcated. Frequently, those entities classed as animates also encode properties like humanness; inanimates also encode features like shape and physical constitution. Yagua has several dozen inanimate classifiers that are more specific about the physical features of the inanimate entity expressed (D. Payne 1986: 126):

> 32. Celina- jựy suuta- jááy-   rà   sújay mḯï- jày.
>   Celina dual wash Near Past Inanimate cloth dirty Inan/2D
>   Celina washed the dirty cloth yesterday.

A number of interesting other problems are raised by (32), including the fact that married women who have produced children are marked with the dual in Yagua and that time is marked by remoteness (see chap. 8). But note that the noun for 'cloth,' *sújay,* takes a classifier that not only expresses inanimacy, but also dimensionality, and the verb is marked for agreement with the inanimate, by *rà*. Thus, (32) is quite complex and more literally means 'Celina, who is a mother, washed in the near past an inanimate entity, namely a two-dimensional thing: a cloth.'

3.233. Humans Versus Nonhumans

Much more common than the distinction between animates and inanimates is one between humans and nonhumans. The pervasiveness of this contrast prompts Comrie (1981) to use it as the basis of a universal scale of the encoding of animacy: *human > animal > inanimate* (encoding preference from left to right). A language may mark the distinctions more broadly, just animate versus inanimate, and if so, the first two categories on the scale are grouped together. To some extent Comrie's scale is a truer picture of the facts, as long as it is understood that it is technically a subscale of a more general distinction between animate and inanimate.

A sharp demarcation between humans and nonhumans is found in many languages. The Finnish pronoun system reflects this division in the third person: *han* ('he, she': human), *se* ('it': nonhuman), *he* ('they': human), *ne* ('they': nonhuman) (Comrie 1981). Khasi has two numeral classifiers, one for humans and one for nonhumans (Adams 1986: 248). Tzeltal and Yurok have noun classifiers to differentiate humans from nonhumans (Allan 1977: 299). Nung distinguishes, by classifiers, animates from inanimates in general, and specifically encodes *just the class of humans* (Saul 1980: 27).

Indonesian, however, is in some ways a perfect manifestation of Comrie's claim that the major distinctions in animacy are those encompassed by the tripartite scale of human > animal > inanimate. Though Indonesian has, in principle, a number of noun classifiers to differentiate kinds of entities, especially with regard to their shape and arrangement, in actual practice, only *three* classifiers are used: one for humans, one for animals, and one for all other inanimates. These are respectively illustrated here (MacDonald 1976: 82–3, 87):

33a. se- orang   mahasiswa.
     one Human student
     one student.

  b. se- ekor   kuda.
     one Animal horse
     one horse.

  c. se- buah   buku.
     one Inanimate book
     one book.

The Indonesian examples bring to light two interesting semantic universals.

Ekor, in (32b), literally means 'tail of an animal.' Adams (1986) observes that universally a word for a body part—and frequently the word for 'tail'—is used to encode the whole class of animates. *Buah,* which stands for basically round objects, has come to signal any object that is neither human nor animal. As we will see later, roundness has a universal role in the denotation of objects by shape and dimension (pp. 122–24).

Although these examples suggest that the human/nonhuman distinction can be tracked rather neatly, in fact this is not the normal case. Very frequently, subclasses of human entities are differentiated by sex, age, social status, and kin relation, not just with regard to their humanness. In such cases, the human/nonhuman distinction is blurred or is, at least, part of a more particular classification.

Jacaltec illustrates this composite encoding of humanness. The language has numeral classifiers for humans (*wan*), animals (*on*), and inanimates (*b*) (Craig 1977: 265), but differentiates the human class for sex, age, degree of respect, and nearness of kinship relation (Craig 1977: 264):

34. xul   naj   Pel   b'oj   ya?   Malin.
    came Adult/Male/Non-kin Peter with Respect/Human Mary
    Peter came with Mary.
    More exactly: An unrelated adult male, Peter, came with a respected
    human, Mary.

In (34), the noun for 'Peter' is coded for age, kinship, and sex, and the noun for 'Mary' is marked for its social status.

If the human class is unevenly realized semantically, so too are its surface manifestations. Comrie (1981) notes that in different languages, the human/ nonhuman distinction is not always relevant to the same extent. In Arabana, human entities have a separate form only in the accusative; in Chuckchee, only certain subclasses of human entities trigger a singular/plural distinction. Regularities in these coding schemes are more fully discussed later, under the Animacy Hierarchy, but here we should caution that the human/nonhuman distinction, although productive and influential, cannot be assumed to apply in simple form across the board.

3.234. Animals

If we look at the category of animals more closely, we find results analogous to those for humans and animates in general. Often languages distinguish *kinds of animals,* not just animals as a separate category. Denny and Creider (1986: 236– 7), for instance, in their reconstruction of Proto-Bantu, claim that the language has 17 distinctions for animals, with classifiers for ticks, grey parrots, snails, bees, crabs, elephants, monkeys, and antelopes. Regularities within the animal category are very hard to come by. Comrie (1981: 190) notes that some form for 'dog' frequently appears in the world's languages, but this seems to be the extent of the generalizations available. Terms for flora are quite typical, and some form for 'tree' is often found (see Adams 1986: 246–7; Allan 1977: 300; Berlin, Breedlove, and Raven 1974), but it is most likely associated with inanimates. No distinction between mammals and nonmammals is consistently observed, though if linguistic animacy does not match up neatly with biological animacy, then why should more specific biological taxa also match up?

3.235. The Animacy Hierarchy and Reflexes of Animacy

In denoting the animacy of entities, languages differentiate generally between animates and inanimates, and more specifically among humans, animals, and inanimate objects. When we look across the world's languages, we find remarkable regularities in the morphosyntactic reflexes of animacy. Here we survey the results on how animacy bears on grammar in general.

3.2351. Silverstein's Animacy Hierarchy

In pioneering work on the Australian languages. Silverstein (1976) has proposed a relationship between a universal scale of animacy and the prediction of *ergative* morphology. To understand Silverstein's work, we must first look briefly at ergativity proper (a fuller discussion may be found in chap. 5, under *agent*). A language is said to be *ergative* if it marks the subjects of transitive verbs alike in contrast to both the objects of transitive verbs and the subjects of intransitive verbs—these latter two are treated the same in marking (e.g., in Nepali and Samoan). Ergativity contrasts with what is called a *nominative/accusative* system, like that of English, where all subjects are marked alike, in opposition to all objects, regardless of the transitivity of the verb. Of those languages that are technically ergative, most are not strictly ergative, but *split ergative*: They mark some subjects as if the language had an ergative system and some subjects as if it had a nominative/accusative system. What accounts for this split?

Silverstein observes that the choice between ergative and nominative/accusative in split ergative languages is controlled by the *degree of animacy of the subject* (see also Comrie 1978 and Dixon 1979). He proposes that a hierarchy of the animacy of the entities expressed as subject—actually a hierarchy of natural agency of the subject—underlies morphological marking in split ergative languages. Silverstein's *Animacy Hierarchy* is as follows, with animacy decreasing from left to right:

1/2 Pronoun > 3 Pronoun > Human Proper Noun > Human Common Noun >
Animate Noun > Inanimate Noun

FIG. 3.3. Silverstein's animacy hierarchy.

The marking of ergativity is split ergative languages is *inversely proportional to the degree of animacy of the subject.* In such languages, there is a clear tendency for subjects higher on the animacy scale (to the left) *not* to be marked as ergative (but as nominative); there is also a clear tendency for subjects lower on the animacy scale (to the right) *to receive* ergative marking. Silverstein argues that ergative marking is more likely if the subject possesses semantic properties that are less conducive to the entity functioning independently as the influential potent doer (i.e., less animate). To put it another way: the more inherently animate, the more likely a potent doer, and the *less* likely to be marked for such status by ergative morphology—whence the inverse relation between marking and animacy. By this reasoning, the split in split ergative systems ought to occur *right in the middle* of the Animacy Hierarchy—as it in fact often does—because that is the fuzzy area for potency and influence.

3.2352. A Revised Animacy Hierarchy and Degrees of Animacy

Over the years, a number of problems with Silverstein's proposal have been identified. For one thing, it does not exactly account for all cases of split ergativity, and often pragmatic factors, like discourse topicality and direction of information flow, determine the split (see DeLancey 1981; see also chap. 5). For another thing, the hierarchy itself is inconsistent. A semantic difference characterizes the lower end of the scale (animate vs. inanimate), but a formal difference characterizes the higher end (pronoun vs. noun, and proper noun vs. common noun). Silverstein acknowledges, however, that the Animacy Hierarchy is not the whole picture and notes that his proposal is part of a more general program to account for a variety of agreement inconsistencies.

Nonetheless the Animacy Hierarchy has persisted because of its general empirical applicability. It bears on a number of phenomena other than split ergativity—subject–verb agreement, number, case assignment, and voice (see Comrie 1981)—and a wide variety of unrelated languages (e.g., Cree, Dyirbal, and Chuckchee) appear to be grammatically sensitive to the categories in their relative order. The general applicability of the Animacy Hierarchy makes it more of a statement about the regularities that a noun may have with regard to its *control over other forms in an expression* as a function of the relative animacy of the entity encoded by the noun itself.

The scale shown in Fig. 3.4 is an attempt to pull together the variety of recent claims about relative animacy and its effect on grammar. The scale is derived principally from accounts given by Comrie (1981) and Foley and Van Valin (1985), who acknowledge other research in their renderings. In languages sensitive to the Animacy Hierarchy, the primary speech act participants, first- and second-person pronouns, have priority in controlling morphological marking.

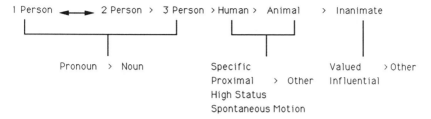

FIG. 3.4. Revised comprehensive animacy hierarchy.[7]

These are followed in priority by third-person pronouns and then by all other third persons (or entities "spoken about").[8]

Let us look more closely at the categories in their order of relative animacy and their morphosyntactic reflexes. Moving from left to right, we see that in some languages, the speaker has priority over the hearer (1 Per > 2 Per); in others, the reverse is true (2 Per > 1 Per). This is why the first category on the scale is notated as a *reciprocal relationship* (1 Per <———> 2 Per). In Mixe the speaker ranks above the hearer (and all other entities, as a matter of course) and thereby controls a number of morphosyntacic phenomena. The opposite facts hold for Plains Cree, where, as in most Algonquian languages, the *hearer* has grammatical priority over the speaker.

In Cree, subject and object are encoded by verbal agreement, but the order and interpretation of the subject and object morphemes are determined by the Animacy Hierarchy. In a sentence expressing a proposition with two entities, one of which is a speaker or hearer and one of which is lower than those on the hierarchy, the morpheme for the speaker/hearer *always precedes* that for the other entity (Foley and Van Valin 1985: 298):

35. Ni-tasam-ā- w   atim.
    I   feed Dir 3Per dog
    I feed the dog.

Here, the morpheme *ni* denotes the speaker and it precedes the verbal agreement

---

[7]Not all of these distinctions are realized in every language. In some, no distinction is drawn between third-person pronouns and nouns; in others, a very broad distinction is drawn just between humans and nonhumans. The revised hierarchy is meant to be summarial only.

[8]In some languages nonsemantic features, like "pronoun," often override the semantic ones. Comrie (1981) remarks that in both Chuckchee and Russian, third-person pronouns take morphology otherwise restricted to animate entities regardless of the animacy of the referent of the pronoun. The extent to which the Animacy Hierarchy is thus a purely formal scale is uncertain (see Comrie 1981: 188).

marker for the object, *w*, because the entity that the object denotes, 'dog,' is lower on the Animacy Hierarchy than the speaker.

What happens when *both* a speaker and hearer are expressed? No matter what the interpretation—whether the speaker is the subject or the object—the agreement morpheme for the hearer *precedes* the morpheme for the speaker (Foley and Van Valin 1985: 297):

> 36a. Ki- tasam-i- n.
>   You feed Dir I
>   You feed me.
>
>   b. Ki- tasam-iti- n.
>   You feed   Inv I
>   I feed you.

The different grammatical relations in (36) are signalled by an additional marker. If the verb is marked with the morpheme *i*, as in (36a), the order of morphemes *directly reflects* the Animacy Hierarchy [a variant of this morpheme, *ā*, signals this directness in (35)]; if the verb is marked with *iti*, the order of morphemes is the *inverse of the expected order* in relation to the Animacy Hierarchy. The presence of the Direct morpheme in (36a) shows that the hearer has priority over the speaker: That is, that the order of verbal agreement markers mirrors the Animacy Hierarchy as construed by Cree. This point is proven by its violation. When the speaker has priority, the verb takes the Inverse morpheme for inversion of expectations, as in (36b).

What factors determine the difference between a language with speaker over hearer, like Mixe, and one with hearer over speaker, like Cree? What are the typological characteristics of the languages that instantiate each kind of system? Very little is known in answer to these questions, though pragmatic and cultural factors may ultimately be responsible for these differences. Does this suggest that there are two types of cultures, one speaker-oriented and one other-oriented? We clearly need a systematic cross-linguistic study of the matter.

The second and third categories on the revised Animacy Hierarchy are humans and animals coded as nouns. We have already seen how humans and animals are formally differentiated in several languages, so there is no need to repeat the exercise here. Rather, we look at what might be called *degrees of humanness* and *degrees of animalness* to see how languages more finely differentiate humans and animals with regard to animacy.

In many languages, certain humans and animals are much more likely to be treated morphologically as animate than other humans. This differential treatment is frequently a function of additional semantic properties (though pragmatic factors, like topical salience, may also intervene). Those humans or animals with higher animacy are usually *specific* (proper nouns and names of humans and animals), *proximal* (spatially close humans or animals, near kin for humans, domestic or familially near animals), or of *high social status* (old, respected, or—patronizingly—male). Humans and animals without these properties are often treated as less animate.

A good example of this differential treatment is again found in Cree, where no distinction in verbal agreement is made between third-person *pronouns* and third-person *nouns*. Instead, third persons who are *proximal*, near to the speaker, are higher in animacy than those who are *distal* (or *obviative*, to use the Algonquianists' terminology), or far from the speaker. This means that in Cree, the Animacy Hierarchy is more exactly *Hearer > Speaker > Spoken About Proximal > Spoken About Distal* (Foley and Van Valin 1985; Wolfart 1973).

Interesting differential treatments come to light when two third-person nouns surface in the same expression. Recall that in Cree, if the order of morphemes follows the Animacy Hierarchy, then the Direct morpheme is used; if there is a mismatch, the Inverse morpheme is used. So, in an expression with two third persons, if the proximal precedes the distal, the morpheme indicating a direct relation between the Animacy Hierarchy and order of morphemes appears on the verb because proximals have higher animacy than distals:

37. Asam-ē- w   napew-Ø   atim- wa.
    feed Dir 3Per man   Prox dog Obv
    The man feeds the dog.
    More exactly: The near man feeds, as expected, the far off dog.

Here, the Direct morpheme *ē* appears [just a different surface form, or *allomorph*, of those in (35) and (36); proximal is indicated by zero-marking]. On the other hand, if the proximal and distal reverse position, the Inverse morpheme appears on the verb:

38. Asam-ekw-w   napew-wa atim-Ø.
    feed Inv 3Per man   Obv dog Prox
    The man feeds the dog.
    More exactly: The far off man feeds, contrary to expectations, the
       near dog.

(38) has the same verbal meaning as (37), so the Inverse morpheme cannot be a marker of passive voice, e.g. [note that (38) does not have a passive gloss]. Reversal of the expectations of the Animacy Hierarchy, with distal over proximal, triggers the Inverse.

Now we turn to the final category of the revised Animacy Hierarchy: inanimates. As with humans and animals, we have already seen how inanimates are grossly distinguished from other categories in several languages, so there is no need to repeat the examples. Instead, we look at *degrees of inanimacy*. Certain inanimate entities may be morphologically marked like animates in languages that make a fine enough distinction for degree of inanimacy to matter. Those inanimates that have higher animacy frequently are valued or influential objects in the cultures that speak the languages (as in Yagua, where rocks and pineapples are animate). Such entities may also have spontaneous motion, potency, or otherwise exhibit behavior reminiscent of animate entities. Thus, natural forces typically have higher status on the Animacy Hierarchy than inanimate objects.

A good example of finer differentiation of inanimates by degree of inanimacy can be seen in Navajo. In Navajo, an active verb is prefixed with *yi*, which also indicates that the subject is higher in animacy than the object; a passive verb is prefixed with *bi*, which also signals that the subject (actually *the logical object*) is higher than the object on the Animacy Hierarchy. In other words, Navajo has a general condition on its subjects, as do many languages (see Givón 1984), requiring them to outrank objects on the Animacy Hierarchy. The prefixes signal not only voice, but also the higher status of the subject in active (normal) and passive (inverted) word order (see Hale 1973; Witherspoon 1980).

Consider the following Navajo sentences (Witherspoon 1980: 10–1):

39a. tó   tsin a-   yi-   iłéél.
     water stick away Active/S > O float
     The water carried away the stick.
  b. ?? tsin tó   a-   bi-   iłéél
     stick water away Passive/S > O float.
     ?? The stick was carried away by the water.

The active form (39a) is acceptable, but the passive form (39b) is not acceptable. This must mean that the entities, water and stick, are unequal inanimates. If they were equal, then both the *yi* and *bi* forms should be allowed because animacy would make no difference. Only the *yi* form is acceptable, and so in Navajo, water must outrank sticks, even though both are technically inanimate.

Witherspoon explains that inanimates are divided into two categories in Navajo: *corporeal* (or having material existence) and *incorporeal* (or abstract), with corporeals outranking incorporeals. So, in Navajo, it is impossible to say *in the active form* something like *love killed him* because this requires S > O, but love, the S, is incorporeal and ranks the lowest among the inanimates. The corporeals are divided into two further groups: *activated* and *stationary*, with the former outranking the latter in animacy, obviously because activation entails motion and semipotency and stationariness entails the opposite. Here is where water and sticks part ways in Navajo. Water is an *activated corporeal;* a stick is a *stationary corporeal.* Hence water outranks sticks, and this difference has a formal reflex in the sensitivity of the nouns to the inversion rules in Navajo and the attendant verbal prefixation.

3.236.   Summary

In this section, we have seen the semantic factors associated with animacy and the regularities in encoding that animacy takes. We have noted the divergence of linguistic and biological animacy and we have seen the kinds of factors that underlie the distinction between animates and inanimates, humans and non-humans, and varieties of animals. We have also examined the Animacy Hierarchy, in original and revised versions, to see that certain predictions can be made about the surface form of animacy distinctions, including such things as the effect of animacy on split ergativity, the priority of speakers over hearers (or vice versa) in controlling agreement, and degrees of animacy among humans and inanimates in controlling syntactic constructions. These results point to a general semantic condition on animacy that returns us to our original definition of the property. Animacy is a measure of the relative influence and potency of an entity in the event expressed. In Plains Cree, hearers are more influential than speakers, and proximals more influential than distals; in Navajo, activated corporeal inanimates outrank stationary corporeals. More generally, languages are sensitive to the control properties of entities, and this translates into a correlation with a variety of structural phenomena.

3.24.   Sex and Gender

We have thus far surveyed the semantic and structural factors associated with specificity, boundedness, and animacy. In the present and following two sections, we turn to properties that are usually associated just with animate entities (and subsequently look at a range of properties typically associated with inanimate entities). Here we consider sex and gender. As with linguistic and biological animacy, we find that linguistic and biological gender match up irregularly, but again, just as with animacy, we find some general criterion—categorial differentiation—under which to unify the divergences.

3.241.   Sex Versus Gender

Animate entities are characterized by *biological sex,* or what Mathiot (1979: 1) calls *intrinsic gender.* Sex is to be differentiated, right from the start, from *grammatical gender,* which is a morphosyntactic category that some languages have for keeping track of nouns. *Sex* is a semantic property; *gender* is a formal or coding property. This is not to deny that sometimes sex and gender do match up. In many languages nouns for biological females are coded in one way, and those for biological males in another. But the direct manifestation of sex totally and only as a gender system is the rare case, for three reasons.

First, from the semantic side, the property of sex is associated with animacy and humanness, and so sex is not always coded directly into gender. A look at the English third-person, singular pronouns supports this point. *He* and *she* obviously distinguish male from female, as opposed to *it,* which codes neither, but *he* and *she* are normally understood to refer to humans. Nonhumans must be intimately known by the speaker before they can be referred to by the sex-sensitive pronouns (see Dixon 1982: 165; Mathiot 1979; McConnell-Ginet 1979).

Second, from the formal side, gender is purely a structural device with its own peculiar rules of operation, and just like syntax, it cannot be read simply or directly off semantic distinctions, even though there may be high correlations between biological sex and gender marking in some languages. In the Indo-European languages, grammatical gender historically derives from an earlier distinction in the animacy of nouns (Dixon 1982: 171), and this marking system has evolved into a general device for signalling formal subclasses of nouns. As a formal device, gender often interacts with other purely formal features, and it is not unusual to find gender connected with agreement and anaphora (what Foley and Van Valin, 1984, have called *reference tracking;* see also Greenberg 1978a), or even with phonological features: that is, properties even more remotely connected to meaning. In Yimas, gender is triggered by the phonological form of the noun ending (Foley and Van Valin 1984: 325–6); in Spanish, the *-ema* nouns, which end in *a* like most other feminine nouns, are nonetheless masculine: *el tema* versus *la mesa.*

Third, to put the semantic and formal sides together, even if biological sex is relevant to a language, there is no reason why sex has to surface as gender, or some such marking system. In English, for example, there are a number of verbs that accept only biologically male or female subjects:

40a. The man ejaculated.
  b. The woman gave birth.
  c. ?? The woman ejaculated.
  d. ?? The man gave birth.

But English verbs otherwise have no connection with grammatical gender. The lesson here is that sex and grammatical gender diverge. Not only is gender a formal device, but sex may be coded with other semantic properties and also have a morphosyntactic reflex other than what is traditionally understood as gender.

3.242. Male, Female, and Neuter

From the standpoint of cross-linguistic generalization as motivated by morpho-syntactic reflex, there are only three sex distinctions made in language: *male, female,* and *neuter.* The last, neuter, is associated not so much with sexlessness as it is with *underdevelopment* or *relative lack of salience of sex* (see Zubin and Köpcke 1986: 144–5). Clearly, there are other phenomenological possibilities, but these choices, though sometimes lexically manifested, do not have productive enough morphosyntactic ramification to merit a distinction. For example, many languages lexically differentiate castrated males, *steer* and *eunuch,* or entities with properties of both sexes, *hermaphrodite* and *androgyne*. But in these cases, the *lexical* differentiation is not productive morphosyntactically. There are no verbs that take only castrated males as their subjects, for example, and so this is not something adhering to the Grammatical Constraint.

When we look at how the three sex distinctions are realized in the world's languages, we see that *no language* has a tripartite coding system to reflect the division directly. That is, there is no language with one marking system for biologically male entities (all humans and nonhumans), another for all female entities (human and nonhuman), and a third for all sexless entities. Only one language, Lak, comes close to this picture. Dixon (1982: 174, citing Khaidakov) claims that older forms of Lak have a fourfold division in noun classes along the following lines: human males, human females, animals, inanimates. But this is fairly rare, and even in the case of Lak, such systematic cutting of nature at its joints no longer persists.

Sex is usually associated with other semantic properties, so sex distinctions are typically found within other kinds of entities, thus blurring the straightforward encoding of sex. A simple tripartite coding system based on sex requires that other significant distinctions be overridden, forcing humans and animals to be grouped together, for example. What is the distribution of the three sexes in terms of the other categories?

3.2421. Sex and Humanness

Many languages severely restrict the male/female distinction to the category of humans, leaving nonhumans undifferentiated. The Oceanic and Australian languages are characteristic in this regard. Dyirbal, a language with a productive noun classifier system, has four noun classes. The first includes a variety of animals (kangaroos and bats), culturally valued objects (boomerangs and moons), and all human males; the second includes water, fire, fighting implements, and certain other animals, plus all human females; the third class includes all nonflesh food; the fourth-class takes in all else (see Dixon 1982: 178).

More broadly borne out across languages with regard to the interaction of sex and other properties is the fact that females, unlike males, are often categorized among the less culturally significant entities. In some languages, females are classed with nonhuman animals. As if this were not degrading enough, in still other languages, females are marked for their marriageability, suggesting that their dependent reproductive function is all that is at stake. In Yagua, as we have seen (p. 90), the singular animate classifier, when associated with a noun for a female animate entity, signals that the female has no children; when the dual animate classifier is used, it signals that the female is a mother. None of this holds for males (see D. Payne 1986: 115–6).

To return to the question of sex and humanness proper, we can see the relevant differences for male/female among humans in the following Dyirbal examples (from Dixon 1982: 166):

41a. bayi nyalŋga.
    Cl1   child
    boy.

b. balan nyalŋga.
   Cl2   child
   girl.

In (41a) and (41b), the noun classifiers (*bayi* 'male human,' Class 1; *balan* 'female human,' Class 2) differentiate the head noun *nyalŋga* 'child,' which is vague for sex: The meaning 'boy' is produced *compositionally,* from 'male child'; 'girl' is constructed likewise.

When the neuter interacts with the class of human entities, more often than not, it singles out children, adolescents, or individuals for whom sex is otherwise irrelevant or nonsalient. That is to say, when a language can encode sex and does not do so completely across the class of human entities, the usual exclusions are those individuals for whom sex is less relevant. German is a good example of this principle. Adult males and females are differentiated formally for sex, with the article carrying the noun class:

42a. der   Mann.
    the/Masc man
    the man.

b. die   Frau.
   the/Fem woman
   the woman.

But the differentiation is not carried through for all humans:

43a. das   Kind.
    the/Neut child
    the child.

b. das   Mädchen.
   the/Neut maiden
   the girl.

Both children and maidens (unmarried girls) are not formally differentiated for sex (finer sex differentiation is also lacking for animals in general in German: see the discussion on p. 104). This is not to say that they are viewed as sexless in Germanic culture; rather, it points up the fact that humans for whom sex is less salient are often coded differently for this property from humans for whom sex is viable. In fact, in some languages, children as a whole group are categorized completely separately from other entities. This is apparently true in Vietnamese (Allan 1977; Thompson 1965: 198) and Nung (Saul 1980: 26).

3.2422. Sex and Animals

When we look at how sex is differentiated among nonhuman animals, we find, to a certain extent, results similar to those for humans. Many languages extend the male/female coding differentiation to nonhumans, but as expected, this typically obtains where the sex of the entity is relevant. Dyirbal and German again provide clear examples.

Whereas the male/female restriction is pretty watertight in Dyirbal, following the segmentation illustrated in (41), the male classifier, *bayi* (Class 1) can be used for nonhuman, animate entities normally assigned to other classes. Dixon (1982: 182) observes that the noun for 'kangaroo,' *yuri,* is usually assigned to Class 1, and hence put with the males, but when the issue of the sex of the kangaroo *is relevant,* the noun classifier may change to reflect finer differentiation:

44. balan yuri.
    Cl2   kangaroo
    female kangaroo.

The reverse may also happen. The noun for 'dog' is typically classified with female humans, so the normal form for 'dog' is *balan guda,* which may mean either 'dog' or 'bitch.' But when the male sex of the dog *is relevant,* the classifier may change:

45. bayi guda.
    Cl1   dog
    male dog ('stud').

In German, the differentiation of biological gender also extends to the nonhuman animals: *der Puter* 'the male turkey' and *die Pute* 'the female turkey.' But when the sex of the animal is not relevant, there is an expression formally in the neuter. Offspring of animals are coded in the neuter, just like the offspring of humans (Zubin and Köpcke 1986: 154–5):

46. das   Küken.
    the/Neut chick
    the chick (turkey or chicken).

In German, then, the principle of sex-irrelevance via the neuter extends into the
nonhuman animates.

3.243.   Gender and Categorization

The formal coding—the gender system—that differentiates biological males and
females also applies to nonhuman animals and inanimates as a group. This
extension of the gender system happens out of necessity because the encoding
that is motivated by intrinsic gender for some entities is also part of the general
formal marking system of nouns. This broad application of gender usually means
that its semantic basis is unfounded, that there is no semantic motivation to the
extension of the formal gender system to entities outside of those either with
inherent sex, but not differentiated for such, or totally without biological sex. But
recent work on gender systems suggests that there may be a pattern to it all,
though one that ultimately has nothing to do with sex per se.

Zubin and Köpcke (1986) observe that formal gender is bound up with conceptual categorization in general. From a detailed analysis of the German gender
system, they argue that for inanimates, neuter gender tends to be associated with
entities that represent *superordinates of categories*: that is, terms for a class of
entities as a whole. In contrast, masculine or feminine gender tends to be associated with *subordinates of categories,* or entities that are more specific members
of categories. Consider, for example, the terms in German for 'currency.' The
superordinate noun, the one for 'money in general,' is *das Geld* (neuter), but the
terms for subordinates, more specific members of the class of currency, are all
differentiated by gender: *der Frank* ('frank,' Masculine), *der Schilling* ('schilling,' Masculine), *die Lira* ('lira,' Feminine), *die Drachme* ('drachma,' Feminine). The same apparently holds for numerous other categories in German.

From this observation, Zubin and Köpcke argue that neuter gender is basically
associated with *nondifferentiation,* which is why neuter tends to code not only
superordinates, but also those entities whose biological sex is otherwise not
required to be differentiated. Neuter more broadly codes *conceptual* or *categorial
neutrality.* Masculine and feminine, on the other hand, are basically associated
with *differentiation*: finer conceptual distinctions are signalled by finer coding,
whether masculine or feminine. For biological sex, this finer differentiation
translates into males and females; for entities for whom biological sex is inapplicable or not immediately relevant, more general principles of conceptual
categorization take over, and subordinate terms—those that are more *finely
differentiated within a conceptual class*—are coded by the markers that otherwise code finer biological distinctions.

Zubin and Köpcke are quick to point out that this regularity does not support the simpleminded view that masculinely marked inanimates, for instance, are somehow masculine or, worse, somehow male. Quite the opposite: Males and inanimate masculines are alike only because of finer conceptual differentiation. At this level, it might be argued that males are not masculine either: only finely differentiated.

Whether or not Zubin and Köpcke's thesis is fully borne out across the world's languages remains to be seen. Nonetheless, it does provide a more general account of how gender and sex ultimately mesh, with the former as a morphological reflex of the latter. It also goes some distance toward supporting the position that semantic factors motivate structural factors. In this case, gender, originally motivated by biological sex, extends to categorial differentiation. Distinctions *within* categories of the mentally projected world are supported by male/female marking whereas distinctions *across* categories are supported by the neuter or undifferentiated form. In each case, we see the broader use of the formal noun-tracking system that languages have.

3.244. Summary

In this section, we have observed the basic distinctions in sex that language encodes—male, female, and neuter—and the correlation of these distinctions with humans, animals, and inanimates. Though we have distinguished sex and gender to begin with, we have also seen that a more general semantic principle may motivate their connection: namely that neuter gender encodes lack of differentiation and male/female supports differentiation, accounting for the correlation between neuter gender and superordinate terms and male/female and subordinate terms.

3.25. Kinship

The second semantic property normally associated with animates is *kinship*, the familial relations among humans. Kinship has a long tradition of study in semantics often with partisanship for a particular theory (see Greenberg 1987; Read 1984; Scheffler 1987). We rely heavily on the findings of the *componential approach*, which seeks to reduce kinship to a finite set of abstract concepts from which all kinship terms are combinatorially derived (Goodenough 1956; Greenberg 1980; Hirschfeld 1986; Lounsbury 1956).

All theories agree on two things. First, kinship is a *relational system* par excellence. No familial concept can be understood outside of its association with at least one other concept. For example, the term *child* is meaningful only as *child of a parent*. Therefore, whenever we analyze kinship, we must be aware of the focal point we have chosen from which to view the rest of the system, traditionally the *ego*. The point against which the ego is judged is typically called the *alter*: In *child of a parent, parent* is the alter and *child* is the ego because the view is from the child to the parent; *parent of a child* reverses the relation.

Second, because familial relations are intrinsic to humans, additional semantic properties often come into play in the definition of kin. Indispensable in this regard are biological gender and age, though gender appears to be more universal (see Greenberg 1966: 86–7). We simply assume the applicability of intrinsic gender and age and apply the appropriate distinctions wherever needed and without justification.

3.251. Consanguinity, Lineality, and Generation

The majority of all kinship relations can be understood in terms of three semantic properties: *consanguinity, lineality,* and *generation*. First, there is consanguinity, whether the family members are related biologically, by blood, or socially, usually by marriage, though close living and other nonmarriage familial relations may count here. If the relation is by blood, it is called *consanguineal*; if it is social, it is *affinal*. These two relations determine the way that the kinship hierarchy is formed: by *direct descendance* or by *socially approved association*.

We can see the distinction between consanguineal and affinal relation in the kinship system of English. *Mother, father,* and *daughter* all principally denote a biological relation between the ego and the alter: for example, a mother is usually biologically related to a daughter (the exception is adoption, in which the legal relation supersedes the biological relation). In contrast, there are terms that are purely affinal, *husband, wife, sister-in-law,* and *stepmother,* which are meaningful only through a nonblood relation between ego and alter: a husband comes about as a consequence of a social relation between the husband as ego and the wife as alter (and vice versa, of course).

The second property is *lineality,* or the nature of the relation between ego and alter. If the relation is *vertical,* with the ego and alter sharing a descendency relation, then the connection is *lineal*. Hence, the terms *father, child, daughter, mother,* and *grandchild* are all lineal: For example, a father is such by a direct relation to a child. If, however, the relation is *horizontal,* with the ego and alter sharing a nondirect, or lateral relation, the connection is *collateral*. The terms *brother, sibling, uncle,* and *niece* are all collaterally related: For example, a brother is such by virtue of a nonlineal connection to another sibling.

The third property is *generation,* or the parentage group to which the ego or alter belongs. Generation involves two more specific features. The first is the *direction of the generation*. If the ego generationally precedes the alter, then there is an *up-to-down* or *descendancy* relation: as in 'father of a child,' where the father descends into the child. If the ego generationally follows the alter, then there is a *down-to-up* or *ascendancy* relation: as in 'child of a father,' where the

TABLE 3.1
Synopsis of Properties Underlying Kinship Systems

Property	Criterion
1. Consanguinity (source of relation)	
a. consanguineal	blood
b. affinal	nonblood (social)
2. Lineality (nature of relation)	
a. lineal	vertical relation
b. collateral	horizontal relation
3. Generation (parentage group)	
a. direction	
i. descendancy	up-to-down
ii. ascendancy	down-to-up
iii. equals	neither
b. removal	
i. zero	same generation
ii. one	one generation difference
iii. . . . etc.	

child ascends to a father. If there is no directional relation between ego and alter, then they are *equals*.[9]

The second feature of generation is *removal*, or distance between generations. We can judge not only the direction of a generation, but also the *immediacy of the generation* or the *degree of removal from the ego or alter*. The generational difference between *parent* and *child* is zero; that between *grandparent* and *grandchild* is one; that between *great uncle* and *grand nephew* is one; and so on. Many languages have subtle ways of counting the degree of removal, not the least among which is English, with such terms as *first cousin* and *second cousin twice removed*, which encode variations on how removal is counted (see pp. 108–109).

These three properties, their subcategories, and their criteria are summarized in Table 3.1.

3.252. English, Seneca, and Mari'ngar

Consanguinity, lineality, and generation can be seen in operation by looking at how they underlie some kinship terms in radically different languages. Here, we consider kinship in English, Seneca, and Mari'ngar.

---

[9]Sometimes further distinctions are made, for example between equals within a consanguineal generation: *co-lineals*, like siblings; or equals in a consanguineal but collateral relation: *ablineal*, like cousins. See Miller and Johnson-Laird (1976: 360–73) for good discussion.

3.2521. English

The three properties, in combination with sex, define a wide range of English familial relations. The combination of Female, Affinal, and Collateral underlies the denotation of *wife, mother-in-law*, and *daughter-in-law*, which can be further differentiated by directionality of generation. Taking the speaker as ego (*my wife,* e.g.), *wife* is then Female, Affinal, Collateral, and Equal; *mother-in-law* is Female, Affinal, Collateral, and Ascendant; *daughter-in-law* is Female, Affinal, Collateral, and Descendant.

Similar regularities can be found among the terms defined by Male and Consanguineal. Both properties underlie *brother, nephew, uncle,* and *great grandfather,* which can be further individuated (with the speaker as ego) as follows: *brother* is Equal (more specifically, Co-lineal: see n. 9, p. 107); *nephew* is Collateral and Descendant; *uncle* is Collateral and Ascendant; *great grandfather* is Lineal and Removal of Two.

Two general problems surface when we look in detail at these partial semantic representations for English kinship, however:

1. we often need more specific semantic properties to do justice to the subtlety of the range of familial relations;
2. not all possible kinship relations are actually instantiated.

As to the first general problem—the need for more specific properties—we should note that English has a way of differentiating consanguineal collaterals in terms of the *minimum number of generations required before the ego and alter share a common ascendant.* This more specific property appears as the ordinal modification of collaterals, such as *first cousin* and *second cousin.* If the ego shares a cousin relation with an alter (i.e., a consanguineal collateral relation via a sibling of some parent of the ego), and the minimum number of generations to be traversed in the hierarchy to find the *common ancestor* of the ego and the alter (i.e., the parent of the ego's parent and sibling) is two, then the alter is the ego's *second cousin,* with the ordinal reflecting the number of generations counted to find a common ancestor. This procedure, for *second cousin,* is illustrated in Fig. 3.5. The ordinals increase with the number of generations required. So, a person's fourth cousin requires four generations beyond the immediate to find a common ancestor.

English may be even more specific with regard to removal by generation. Suppose that your second cousin has a child. The relation between you and that child is still as a second cousin because the minimum number of generations required to be traversed to find a common ancestor is still two (from you as ego). But there is a decided conceptual difference between you and your second cousin's child. For this relation, English has the term *removed,* which differentiates

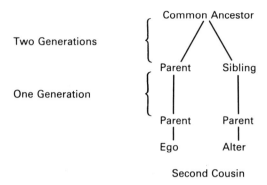

FIG. 3.5.   Hierarchy for *second cousin.*

relations otherwise undifferentiated by a common ancestor. A second cousin's child is a *second cousin once removed;* that child's child is a *second cousin twice removed,* and so on.

In actual practice, English speakers do not effectively use these distinctions, but they show that English has a number of other familial relations that are, in principle, given overt expression. This ultimately requires that our array of properties for the analysis be a bit more specific and include such things as *extent of removal within a common ancestor.*

In addition to needing more specifics to capture subtle kinship relations, we also need to concern ourselves with the second general problem listed on p. 108: Not all possible kinship relations are given overt expression in all languages. Kinship is more fully differentiated with subtle contrasts in some languages, and glossed over and undifferentiated in others. As to the lack of differentiation, note that English has no productive way of representing 'spouse of a cousin,' nothing like *spousin*. Nor is there any way of encoding 'uncle of a spouse,' no term *uncle-in-law,* for example. Unlike many other languages, English draws no morphological distinction between kinship on the mother's side (matrilineal and matrilateral) and that on the father's side (patrilineal and patrilateral) and so is technically known as a *bilateral* or *cognatic* system (see Keesing 1975). Thus, there is no encoding distinction between an uncle who is a sibling of a mother and an uncle who is a sibling of a father. We can identify the two if we choose— *uncle on the father's side* or *paternal uncle,* for example—but patrilineality is encoded separately. Maternal and paternal uncles are called just *uncle,* and perhaps more importantly, both have equal cultural significance. This is in stark contrast to many other languages, which formally differentiate matrilineality from patrilineality.

If other languages do give expression to relations not represented in English, this is because the universal kinship space may be gerrymandered as a specific language and culture wills (though there are limitations: see the discussion on universals later; see also Greenberg 1980). We can in fact see all these principles and problems of kinship clearly by examining languages with quite different kinship structures from English. The literature is full of dozens of representative studies, so we cast our net narrowly here.

3.2522. Seneca

One of the most widely discussed systems is that of Seneca, which has come to the fore because it has been the basis of Lounsbury's (1964) early studies (see also Kay 1975; Woolford 1984). In Seneca, there is *one term* to cover *all* relations defined by Paternal, Male, Consanguineal, and One (generation above the ego): *ha?nih* denotes 'father,' 'uncle on the father's side,' and even, to make the possibilities even more bizarre but in line with the principle, 'ego's great grandfather's brother's son's son' (I leave it to the reader to see that this is a patrilateral male, one generation above the ego). There is another single term for all relations defined by Maternal, Female, Consanguineal, and One (generation above the ego). *No?yēh* denotes 'mother,' 'aunt on the mother's side,' and even 'daughter of the brother of the mother's mother' (that is, 'mother's female cousin'). When the sex of the source of the genealogy shifts, so do the terms. If the relation is Maternal, Male, Consanguineal, and One (generation above the ego), one term, *hakhno?sēh*, denotes both 'uncle on the mother's side' and 'mother's male cousin.' When the relation is Paternal, Female, Consanguineal, and One (generation above the ego), another single term, *ake:hak* denotes both 'aunt on the father's side' and 'father's female cousin.'

Clearly, Seneca divides up the kinship space in a manner quite different from English, not differentiating certain areas in comparison. Sex and degree of removal by generation control the denotations. More detailed examination of the language shows that age also enters the picture, but we do not pursue it here (see Lounsbury's work).

3.2523. Mari'ngar

In his comprehensive study of Australian kinship systems, Scheffler (1978) notes that Mari'ngar has 18 basic kin terms:

1. *tyan'angga* father's father/mother's mother
2. *tamie* mother's father/father's mother
3. *it:a* father
4. *it:a ili:ingeri* wife's mother's brother (maternal "uncle-in-law")
5. *ngaia* father's sister (paternal aunt)
6. *ngaia ili:ingeri* wife's mother (man's mother-in-law)
7. *kela* mother

8. *kaka* mother's brother (maternal uncle)
9. *kaka boi* wife's father (man's father-in-law)
10. *ngauwe* brother
11. *ngaka* sister
12. *manggen* female cousin
13. *do'goli* male cousin
14. *bange boi* wife's brother (brother-in-law)
15. *nea* man's child
16. *mulugu* woman's daughter
17. *magu* woman's son
18. *wam:a* any third generation relative, up or down

One of the most striking consistencies in Mari'ngar kinship is the predominance of biological sex as a controlling variable. There are two terms for grandparents, but they depend on the parallelism of sex. Whatever the lineal relation, parallel sex, male or female, is expressed by *tyan'angga*; mixed sex is expressed by *tamie*. If English were organized similarly, we might use the term *grandfather* for our father's father, but not for our mother's father: the latter we might call *grandmother*.

The influence of sex in Mari'ngar kinship also extends to the immediate ascendants of the ego. There are specific terms for a *man's* affinal relations, and collateral consanguineal relations are also differentiated by sex: maternal "uncle-in-law" is encoded, for example. At the level of equals, sex again controls the relations, with no differentiation by age of siblings or cousins, as is otherwise found in many languages.

Analogous facts hold in descendents. Mari'ngar has no generic term for offspring. Rather, sex of offspring and sex of progenitor combine to produce distinct forms: 'mother's daughter' is differentiated from 'mother's son,' for example. Interestingly, and in accord with the universal principles to be discussed later (pp. 112–113), when relations further than the immediate generation of the ego plus one are to be encoded, *all distinctions*—even sex—*are neutralized*. A generic term, *wam:a,* is used, functioning much like the generic term *ancestor* in English.

3.253.   Universals of Kinship Semantics

In looking at how the basic properties of consanguinity, lineality, and generation—and their subtypes—are variably deployed in different languages, we might naturally ask if there are any overall consistencies in kinship apart from the presence of these properties. Heated debate over this problem has raged in the anthropological literature; a few of the basic findings are mentioned here.

Greenberg's (1966) influential study (replicated by Nerlove and Romney 1967 and clarified by Kronenfeld 1974) reveals that of 15 possible systems of terms for grandparents, only three are commonly found (1966: 85):

1. *a single term* for all grandparents, regardless of sex or lineage;
2. *two terms,* one each for the paternal and maternal grandparent, regardless of sex;
3. *four terms,* one each for paternal male, paternal female, maternal male, and maternal female.

Murdock's (1970) study of 566 languages has similar results, but indicates that the single-term system is much less common than those differentiating by sex (1970: 167).[10]

These typological consistencies have given rise to the more general claims that there are four principal kinship patterns: the *Crow/Omaha-type,* the *Iroquois-type,* the *Dravidian-type,* and the *Eskimo-type* (see Lounsbury 1956, 1964; Woolford 1984). The four are determined by their underlying structural equivalences and semantic neutralizations. Crow-type systems, for example, have a structural equivalence between a woman's brother and her son, called a *Crow-skewing rule:* Unrelated languages that follow this pattern are Baniata and Akan. In Iroquoian-type systems, distinctions for paternal uncle and maternal aunt are respectively called by the terms for father and mother, and thus neutralized, with their offspring simply designated by the undifferentiated *child*: A number of Australian languages work this way (Scheffler 1978).

Beyond typological patterns, Greenberg (1966, 1980) proposes a number of more abstract regularities based on principles of *markedness*: that is, universal expectations derived from *frequency of occurrence, logical dependence,* or *overt morphological marking* (Greenberg 1987; Scheffler 1987).[11] In terms of markedness, the following kinship regularities hold:

1. Lineal terms are less marked than collateral ones.
2. Consanguineal terms are less marked than affinal ones.
3. Generations closer to the ego are less marked than those further away.
4. Ascending generations are less marked than corresponding descending ones.

---

[10]Murdock's (1970) further studies of other terms reveal clear distributions for collateral, consanguineal relations. For uncles, the most common patterns are either a single term for maternal uncle with paternal uncle encoded the same as for father, or two terms—one for paternal uncle and one for maternal uncle.

[11]An *unmarked* form, thought to be more universal, is more frequent, logically independent, or not signalled formally (zero morphology) (or some combination of these). A *marked* form has the opposite characteristics.

The first two regularities mean that a language will tend to have semantic differentiation for lineal and consanguineal relations; alternatively, collateral and affinal relations will neutralize distinctions. Note how English follows these two principles. *Uncle* and *aunt,* two collateral terms, are undifferentiated for connecting kin (paternal and maternal); affinal relations are similarly restricted in the extent of the connection encoded, with no term *aunt-in-law.* The second two regularities mean that a language will have more semantic differentiation for the generations nearer the ego and ascendants. Again, English follows suit: All differences are neutralized by the generic term *ancestor,* which specifies general removal from the ego.

The four universals conspire to produce a rather simple result in the long run. The unmarked system encodes near, direct, blood ascendants, or in less technical terms, "immediate true family."

3.254.   *Kinship and Culture*

We have seen that kinship systems can be generated from three basic properties, with the addition of more specific features as a language warrants. We have also noted a number of regularities in all kinship systems, such as the unmarked status of lineal and consanguineal terms. In all these observations, we should remember that kinship is closely tied to social and cultural organization. Familial relations often serve as a method of arbitration in legal contexts because degree of relatedness can be traced thereby. This fact is often raised in considerations of non-Western cultures, but kinship has the exact function in cases of child custody and inheritance in the West, where nearness of kin determines the legal responsibilities and consequences. In some cultures, in fact, elaborate kinship systems function as surrogate number systems, so that counting is carried out by kin terms (see chap. 10).

Despite the clear connection of kinship semantics to culture, the semantic structure of kinship is not reducible to its cultural function. Otherwise, we would not be able to come to the consistencies we have or even begin to generate systems from a relatively small set of concepts. As Scheffler, elsewhere an ardent cultural reductionist, says (1984: 791): "Whatever the merits or demerits of these presumptions and procedures [of seeing kinship in a socially reductionist way], they have tended to deflect attention from the possibility that in some instances terminological structure may be a fully or semi-autonomous form of social culture." The universal semantic structure of kinship is evidence that linguistic semantics turns out to be, at base, independent of culture.

3.255.   *Summary*

In looking at the semantic structure of kinship, we have seen that all kinship terms are relational, requiring an ego and alter for definition. Three basic semantic properties underlie kinship: consanguinity, lineality, and generation. These determine blood line, hierarchy, and nearness of relation. We have seen how these properties work by looking at three widely different systems, English, Seneca, and Mari'ngar. Two general problems condition such comparative analysis: Some languages require additional, quite specific semantic properties and not all possible kinship distinctions are instantiated. Finally, we have seen a number of universals of kinship: The most unmarked system is that which reflects immediate, true family. Such universals argue for the claim that kinship semantics, though obviously connected to culture, is at base independent of culture.

3.26. Social Status

Recall that we are currently analyzing three semantic properties associated with animacy. We have just seen how language encodes familial relations. Here we turn to a related property, *social status,* the encoding of the nonfamilial, *social relations* of entities.

In all languages, there are ways of signalling relative social rank. Interestingly enough, social rank is not restricted to humans, but can apply equally well to animals, inanimate objects, and even to situations and bystanders. The encoding of social status takes a variety of forms because status itself is tied to a number of other social processes, each of them potentially deserving separate encoding. A representative list of these other social processes includes *politeness, social distance, formality, sympathy, face-saving, deference,* and *impersonalization* (Brown and Gilman 1960 is the classic study). We concentrate on the encoding of social status in a separate morphosyntactically productive form, however: the *honorific.* We do so because honorifics adhere to the Grammatical Constraint. As Brown and Levinson (1987: 179) remark, honorifics are "direct grammatical encodings of relative social status."

3.261. Four Aspects of Social Status

Before we look at honorific systems directly, we make four general observations about the semantics and formal features of social status: It is stable, narrowly structured, gradient, and encoded in a variety of forms.

3.2611. Social Status as a Contextually Stable Relation

Social status is technically a *relation between two entities,* not just a static property of entities. More specifically, it is a relation between the *speaker* of the sentence and (1) a *hearer* (a *Speaker/Hearer System*), (2) an *entity spoken about* (a *Speaker/Referent System*), (3) a *situation* (a *Speaker/Situation System*), or (4) a *bystander* (a *Speaker/Bystander System*) (Brown and Levinson 1987: 180–1; Comrie 1976a).

Social status always involves the speaker, so it is often argued that it is best understood as a problem of *social deixis* (Fillmore 1975b; see chap. 6), or the contextual anchoring of speech participants relative to each other. Sometimes social status is given a purely pragmatic definition; Brown and Levinson (1987) argue that honorifics are frozen conventional implicatures (1987: 33; see chap. 2 for definition of *conventional implicature*). Nonetheless, if social status is a purely pragmatic and contextualized notion, it is difficult to see why it takes the forms it does.

For one thing, social status markers are invariably triggered by other *semantic* properties, like age, sex, and nearness of kin. In Japanese, for example, a noun denoting a human of advanced age relative to the speaker *always* triggers an honorific, no matter what the actual social relation is, and so social status has a *semantic correlation,* not just a pragmatic function. For another thing, the encoding of social status is *relatively stable,* and thus carries *decontextualized meaning.* It is not a function of the intentions or judgments of the speaker. Honorifics, for example, *entail,* not implicate, social status (see chap. 2).

The contextual stability of social status lets Brown and Levinson (1987) argue that honorifics are derived from *frozen conventional implicatures* (cf. the Scale of Background Information, p. 43) or inferences triggered about context by inherent properties of forms. But social status cannot but be conveyed by the form chosen, and so honorifics are perhaps best understood as *contextualized entailments* rather than as frozen implicatures.

3.2612.   The Narrow Structure of Social Status

Now that we have seen that social status is a stable *semantic relation,* we can turn to our second general observation. How is this semantic relation structurally carried out? Markers of social status encode the social rank *difference* between the speaker (S) and another entity (X, whether hearer, referent, situation, or bystander). In principle, there are four possible ways to express this rank differential:

1. S is marked higher than X.
2. S is marked lower than X.
3. X is marked higher than S.
4. X is marked lower than S.

Although each method brings about the differential, only (2) and (3) are normally found in any language. Types (1) and (4) are rarely encountered, no doubt because they effectively require egotism and condescension on the part of the speaker: type (1) signals speaker superiority and type (4) signals X's inferiority. This does not mean that it is impossible to elevate the status of the speaker or lower that of the nonspeaker. On the contrary, languages do have ameliorative (elevating) and pejorative (derogating) markers. But the more common tack is to bring about rank differential by *showing deference on the part of the speaker* (2) and *respectability on the part of X* (3). Brown and Levinson (1987) observe that· these narrower possibilities are in line with a more general pragmatic principle of not overburdening the nonspeaker: Both (1) and (4) require that X be put in a compromising position, whereas (2) and (3) do not. Conversational organization appears to favor the hearer, and the rules of exchange (e.g., Grice's Maxims: see chap. 2) arguably function to prevent overburdening of the nonspeaker. As a consequence of this more general principle, only deference and respect are semantically encoded, with speaker superiority and nonspeaker inferiority pragmatically implicated, not explicitly signalled. Relative to its full possibilities, social status has a rather narrow structure.

3.2613. Social Status as a Gradient

Social status is also a *gradient*. Usually languages have ways of marking rank differential as a matter of degree, most commonly with the difference coded only by the marker of the higher status of X. That is, the gradience lies in the nonspeaker.

Ladakhi provides a clear example. The language has a variety of honorifics for nouns, pronouns, verbs, and even some adjectives and postpositions (Koshal 1987). Although the usual semantic opposition is between the normal and the honorific form, a number of entities can take an *extra-honorific marker,* or *highest grade social status* (Koshal 1987: 155, 158): *khar-ji* 'normal food,' *don-tang* 'great food,' and *sol-tshig* 'honored food' (extra-honorific). Ladakhi also has some forms that express degree of derogation, but, in line with our general observation that degree of status favors the ameliorative, the pejorative forms are decidedly restricted (see Koshal 1987: 155).

Many other languages have graded honorific systems. However, it is important to remember that in all cases, social status is a scalar notion.

3.2614. Variety of Surface Forms

Finally, encoding itself may take a variety of forms. The most obvious forms are pronouns because they represent speaker and addressee, but rank can also be signalled more generally on nouns, verbs, and modifiers. Japanese, for instance, productively marks verbs for the social status of the subject, direct object, and indirect object (Harada 1976; Kuno 1987a). Status is associated with entities and entities tend to surface as nouns; thus it is also quite common to find status signalled by syntactic processes that involve nouns. Passivization, for example, deemphasizes the agent of the action and is frequently correlated with honorific marking (Shibatani 1985: 829).

The most well-documented formal correlate of social status, however, is a *shift in number and/or person*. Elevated status of an entity almost universally triggers pluralization or a shift to a third person, both of which functionally induce distance. The former conveys lack of discrete individuation and the latter marks a nondirectly involved participant in the exchange. Anyone who has studied the Western European languages has observed this correlation. *Vous* in French signals higher status of the addressee in the singular and is also the generic *plural* addressee pronoun. The same holds for Spanish *Usted* and German *Sie*.

A particularly nice example of social status motivating pluralization process can be seen in Nepali, where the status difference between *tā* ('you' familiar) and *timī* ('you' middle grade) has a correlate in verb agreement. *Timī* takes the plural, whereas *tā* takes the singular (after Clark 1977: 71–81):

47a. tā   kahā̃ cha?
     you/Fam   where be/Sing
     Where are you?
     More exactly: Where is you (familiar)?
  b. timī   kahā̃ chəw?
     you/Middle Gr where be-Pl
     Where are you?

The difference in rank has a formal correlate, with higher status realized in the plural.

3.262. Honorifics

Now that we have a good sense of the general semantic and formal features of social status, let us look at them in a unified way in actual practice. We concentrate, as promised, on honorifics, specific markers of the social status of an entity. To simplify matters, we follow Comrie's (1976a) typology and look at examples of each of the four types of honorific system: Speaker/Hearer (S/H), Speaker/Referent (S/R), Speaker/Bystander (S/B), and Speaker/Situation (S/S).

3.2621. The S/H System

In the S/H system, the status differential is restricted to markers of direct address ('I' and 'you'). Languages infrequently have the S/H system as the only marking of social status; more often, addressee honorifics are bound up with an S/R (see sec. 3.2622) system because it is difficult to encode the Speaker/Hearer relationship independently of the referential context of utterance (see Brown and Levinson 1987: 276–7 for nice discussion here). For this reason, in fact, Comrie argues that the social status distinctions among pronouns in Western European languages are not connected with direct address, *contrary to all pedagogical grammars*, but are really S/R systems, because the forms that encode the status differential are not restricted to the vocative (direct address), but can refer to any participant.

Nonetheless, there are languages where the S/H system functions independently of reference. Japanese is a standard example here, with six levels of formality for the pronoun 'I' and five for the pronoun 'you.' Remarkably, neither the speaker nor the hearer has to be explicitly encoded for the rank differential to be triggered (Kuno 1987a: 99):

> 48. Ame ga   huri-masi-   ta.
>   rain Subj fall Hearer Status fall
>   It rained.
>   More exactly: Speaking from me to you, and you have higher
>   status, it rained.

In (48), there is no explicit form for speaker or hearer, but the verb nonetheless carries a marker of status difference, *masi*. What matters for honorific choice in this example is that the hearer be *the acknowledged object of speech,* not that the hearer be explicitly expressed.

Other languages that productively encode the S/H relation directly are Javanese, Madurese, Korean, and a number of Southeast Asian languages. Baek (1985) gives a clear description of Korean.

3.2622. The S/R System

The S/R system, where the participants *spoken about* are encoded for status, is by far the most common, for the reason just given, that it is difficult to separate the hearer or any other nonspeaker from the referential context of utterance. Thus, Japanese not only has the S/H markers described earlier, but also a number of other markers to denote the status of an entity referred to or spoken about. In Japanese culture, teachers are accorded high social status, and a noun denoting 'teacher' automatically triggers honorific agreement (Kuno 1987a: 99):

> 49. Yamada-sensei ga   tegami o   o-   aki- ni   nar- u.
>   Yamada teacher Subj letter   Obj Hon write Subj High Pres
>   Teacher Yamada writes letters.
>   More exactly: Respected teacher Yamada writes letters.

In (49), we see how honorifics follow the Grammatical Constraint. *Ni nar* indicates that the *grammatical subject* is high in social status. The language has other forms for other grammatical roles.

3.2623. The S/B System

The third kind of system is S/B, or one that encodes the status relation between the speaker and the bystanders, participants who are neither speakers nor hearers, nor spoken about. They are *overhearers.* This type of system has come to light from work on Australian languages (Dixon 1982), and although it is productive in those languages, it has apparently not been found anywhere else.

In Dyirbal, there are two speech styles. One, *Guwal,* is used in everyday contexts; another, *Jalɲuy,* is used only in the presence of taboo relatives: that is, only in the presence of a certain kind of bystander (Dixon 1982: 68). Given the conditions on association and communication imposed by the social system of the Dyirbal, a speaker must use Jalɲuy in the company of a parent-in-law, child-in-law of the opposite sex, or a cross-cousin of the opposite sex.

Many Dyirbal verbs have two forms, one for normal use, Guwal, and one for the S/B restricted, Jalɲuy use. A speaker may thus draw an explicit distinction between two kinds of bystanders overhearing the proposition 'the dog goes uphill.' In the everyday context of a normal relation between speaker and non-speaker, the Guwal form for the verb is used:

50. balan guda waynyjin.
     Class dog go uphill
     The dog goes uphill.

But in the company of taboo bystanders, there is a change in verb form:

51. balan guda dayubin.
     Class dog go uphill
     The dog goes uphill.

Dixon (1982) and Brown and Levinson (1987) both note the rarity of S/B systems. Certainly, S/B styles can be invented on the spot by speakers who wish to include or exclude overhearers, as in deliberate *code-switching*—the change from one language to another in midsentence to exclude overhearers. But productive S/B systems are found only in the Australian languages: Yidiny and Guugu Yimidhirr also have avoidance styles analogous to Dyirbal's (see Dixon 1982: 65, fn. 2).

3.2624. The S/S System

Finally, let us consider the S/S system, one that marks the relation between the speaker and the status of the *circumstances,* irrespective of the nature of the participants in the situation. Though S/S systems may seem the most general because they are connected to the situation as a whole, and therefore ought to be the most productive, it is necessary to keep in mind the independence of the system itself and the semantic properties of the participants: S/S must be *purely a function of the circumstances* and moreover must have peculiar morphology and syntax that directly signal the S/S relation.

Brown and Levinson (1987) argue that *diglossia* is a classic example of an S/S system. In diglossia, to put the matter simply, there are two varieties of the 'same' language. One variety is the *high form* and is used in situations that demand elevated talk, whatever the participants; the other variety is the *low form* and is used in circumstances of ordinary talk. Well-known examples of diglossia are the differences between Classical (Koranic) Arabic and vernacular Arabic, Classical and Demotic Greek, Standard and Swiss German in Switzerland, and French and French Creole in Haiti (Britto 1986; Ferguson 1964).

We can see the S/S system at work in Arabic. The following sentences have the same propositional content, but the overt form varies depending on the S/S relation. Example (52a) is from Classical Arabic and reflects the high variety; example (52b) is from Cairene (Egyptian) Arabic and reflects the colloquial style (from Kaye 1972: 41):

52a. ra?aytu l- walad-a   dhaahiban.
      I saw the boy   Obj going
      I saw the boy going.
  b. šuft   il- walad raayiħ.
      I saw the boy   going
      I saw the boy going.

Not only are there lexical differences between the Classical and Cairene (cf. the verb roots for 'see' and 'go'), but also morphological and syntactic ones: In (52a), the Classical form, inflectional morphology signals the accusative case, but this is absent in the vernacular (52b). Crucial to the point at hand, the Classical version is chosen when the circumstance itself is elevated: formal speeches, high ritual, literary and learned discourse, and so forth.

3.263. Summary

We have considered how social status, with particular focus on honorifics, is a relation between a speaker and a nonspeaker (hearer, entity spoken about, bystander, or circumstance). We have seen how social status is a *semantic* property, in spite of its obvious connection to context, because its forms entail contextually stable meaning. Social status is, moreover, narrowly structured, with normal encoding only of speaker deference or nonspeaker elevation; status is also a gradient and can assume a variety of syntactic forms, frequently a shift in person or number. Honorifics come in four kinds of systems: Speaker/Hearer, Speaker/Reference, Speaker/Bystander, Speaker/Situation. S/R is the most common, no doubt because it is associated with the broader context of reference. S/B is least common, found only in the Australian languages. S/H and S/S are in between, the latter known more commonly as diglossia.

3.27. Physical Properties

The previous three sections have addressed semantic properties restricted to animate entities; the present section focuses on properties of inanimate entities. The *physical properties* of entities—their characteristics as spatial objects— have received considerable attention in the literature over the past 2 decades, and we try to present a unified, if somewhat simplified, picture of their nature and behavior. Our investigation relies particularly on the typologies proposed by Denny (1976, 1979, 1986) and Allan (1977), though the latter's work is a bit loose in places (and even wrong, according to Dixon 1982: 226, fn. 13). Fortunately, Denny appears to pick up where Allan falls down, so a judicious combination of the two works out nicely.

We consider four general physical properties of entities: *extendedness, interioricity, size,* and *consistency.* These four subsume a number of other properties—extendedness covers *shape,* for example—all of which appear to be universally distributed. Several other properties are given minor attention— *arrangement, quanta,* and *material,* for example. We do not consider one category at all, *location,* even though it is often studied along with the other physical properties presented here. Location is reserved for the more general discussion of the semantics of space (chap. 6).

3.271. Extendedness

The first property is *extendedness,* or whether or not some entity occupies a physical position or is determinately extended in space. Traditional treatments of physical properties address extendedness only indirectly, focusing instead on what turn out to be subclasses—shape and dimensionality (see, e.g., Friedrich 1970; Allan 1977 also follows this line of thought). But Denny (1979) makes a convincing case for the priority of extendedness when shape and dimensions are otherwise identified.

There are two reasons for taking extendedness as fundamental. First, logically, shape and dimensionality express *a way in which space is occupied,* whereas extendedness expresses the more basic fact *that space is occupied.* Second, from an empirical view, many languages draw an overt distinction between extendedness and nonextendedness, with shape dependent on the priority of extendedness. Thus, extendedness has both logical and distributional priority.

Denny (1979) notes that Tarascan, Eskimo, Toba, Ojibway, and Western Apache mark nonextended entities in one way and extended entities in another.

In Toba, entities that are in the visual field but do not distinctively occupy space, for example, by protrusion, are marked by the noun classifier *ñi,* signaling *nonextendedness.* But those entities in the visual field that have distinctive spatial position, and hence are extended, are coded otherwise, by *ra* (from Klein 1979: 89; see also Denny 1986: 304):

> 53a. ?ongay ha- ñi-   hala.
>   good   Pref Non Ext fruit
>   The fruit is good.
>   b. ?ongay ha- ra- hala.
>   good   Pref Ext fruit
>   The fruit is good.

Examples (53a) and (53b) differ crucially in meaning, with the difference riding on extendedness. Example (53a) more exactly means 'the fruit sitting somewhere is good,' with nonextendedness correlating with *static spatial position.* On the other hand, (53b) means something like 'the fruit hanging on the tree is good,' whence the extendedness classifier *ra* (which also conveys direction: see p. 124) correlates with *dynamic spatial position.*

Extendedness has two subcategories: *dimensionality/shape* and *direction.*

3.2711. Dimensionality/Shape

There are obviously only three possible values for dimensionality: *one-dimensional, two-dimensional,* and *three-dimensional.* In traditional accounts, these values are often labelled *long, flat,* and *round,* respectively, to capture their association with the *shape* of the entity (though technically there is a difference between dimensionality and shape).

The literature is full of examples of languages where dimensionality is directly encoded. We look at only one language because there is an embarrassment of riches here. Japanese has numeral classifiers for each dimension, though the marker itself conveys physical information besides dimensionality. The classifier *hon* signals extension in one dimension (and thinness); the classifier *mai* encodes two-dimensionality (and thinness as well); the classifier *ko* marks three-dimensionality (and smallness). These three are illustrated here (after Downing 1984, 1986):

> 54a. banana ni- hon.
>   banana two one dimension
>   two bananas.
>   More exactly: two long thin things: banana.
>   b. syatu ni- mai.
>   shirt two two dimensions

two shirts.
More exactly: two flat thin things: shirt.
c. ringo ni- ko.
    apple two three dimensions
    two apples.
More exactly: two small round things: apple.

Dimensionality has been studied in detail, so we know some of the regularities of its distribution. Denny (1979) argues that languages encode one and two dimensions more often than three dimensions: $1/2 > 3$. Japanese bears out the generalization as the three-dimensional classifier *ko* occurs with considerably less frequency than do the one- and two-dimensional classifiers (Downing 1984, 1986). These facts suggest a cognitive or perceptual priority of one and two dimensions that is reflected in the linguistic distribution. In the received theories of vision, three-dimensional visual perception is *derived* from perceptual mechanisms that first deliver one- and two-dimensional representations (see Marr 1982 and the discussion on p. 134); in some languages, three-dimensionals overlap with nonextendeds, suggesting a neutralization of dimensionality beyond two dimensions (see Denny 1979: 99). The regularity that if a language encodes three dimensions, it encodes the other two, but not necessarily vice versa, appears to be grounded in the kinds of physical representations that the visual system computes.

Dimensionality is closely connected to shape. In the usual case, dimensionality and shape overlap so that extended one-dimensional entities are also long, extended two-dimensional entities are flat, and extended three-dimensional entities are round or curved. But shape and dimensionality are not necessarily related. Denny points out that in many analyses of classifier systems, the results are vague as to just how shape is connected with dimensionality: Salience in one dimension, for example, does not have to imply a long shape.

Are there languages where dimensionality and shape diverge? We can illustrate the difference in English, where it is possible to encode dimensionality *and* shape: *a curved row of corn, a long round pane of glass, a square block of ice*. In the Algonquian languages, dimensionality and shape are clearly separate. Denny (1979) argues that in Cree and Ojibway, length and unidimensionality can be independently predicated. The following example is from Cree (Denny 1979: 99):

55. kinw-ēk-   an.
     long two dimensions it is
     It is long (i.e., like a piece of cloth).[12]

---

[12]Shape, though, obviously has *some* connection with dimensionality, if not one of logical dependence. In some languages, dimensionality neutralizes shape: In Bantu languages, flatness is

The divergence of shape and dimensionality accounts for the fact that many languages have a variety of *nondimensional shape* markers: that is, shapes that are not measurable or determinable in the standard geometric sense—nonangular and irregularly angled. Compare the following from English:

56a. a wad of gum.
   b. a shard of glass.

Wad encodes nonangular shape: ?? *square wad of gum*; *shard* encodes an irregularly angled shape: ?? *symmetrical shard.*

By far the most commonly occurring nondimensional shape in language is *curvature*, especially *curvature of the exterior*. Allan (1977) points out the range of such expressions in English: *heap of clothes, lump of coal, mound of dirt.* D. Payne's (1986: 117–8) study of Yagua supports the cross-language productivity of curvature and shows that curvature cuts across all geometric dimensions in the Yagua classifier system. One-dimensional entities may be cylindrical; two-dimensional objects may be disclike; three-dimensional entities may be hollow. Thus, the separation of shape from dimensionality is important because curvature may be independently predicated and interact with dimensionality to produce a variety of more specific denotations.

3.2712. Direction

The second subcategory of extendedness is *direction*. A number of languages make a distinction between entities that are *vertically extended* and those that are *horizontally extended*. These basic axes of space determine the particular orientation an entity has in its spatial extension.

In Toba, vertically extended entities are marked by *ra;* horizontally extended ones take *ǰi.* Two different perspectives on the same event can thus be conveyed by the choice of noun classifier. If a liquid is spilled downward, for example, it is marked for verticality because of the trajectory (after Klein 1979):

57. nkotragañi ra-   wakalče.
    he spills   Vert Ext milk
    He is spilling milk (downward) (i.e., he is spilling the milk down).

---

derived from length extended in two dimensions (Adams and Conklin 1973, cited in Denny 1979: 100). And no language explicitly contrasts round entities with polygonal or polyhedral ones; the preferred strategy is to neutralize the distinction by putting both in the class of three-dimensional objects, which is why square houses are often classified with round objects in many languages (Allan 1977: 300). Once again, the third dimension neutralizes the distinctions that are relevant elsewhere, which suggests that three dimensionality is less specific semantically.

But if the liquid spreads out horizontally, the noun is marked for lateral extended-ness (after Klein 1979):

58. nkotragañi ǰi-   wakalče.
    he spills   Horiz Ext milk
    He is spilling milk (across) (i.e., he is spilling the milk out).

Another language that explicitly differentiates the directional orientation of an entity is American Sign Language. By hand position, the vertical or horizontal orientation of an entity is iconically represented (Suppalla 1986: 192–3).

3.272. Interioricity

The second major physical property is *interioricity* (the terminology is from Denny 1979: 108). This feature represents the *containedness* of an entity or the way that an entity *differentiates its inside from its outside.* Denny claims that there are two subcategories of interioricity: *solids* and *outlines.* The subclasses exhaustively define interiors.

Solid entities differentiate interiors from exteriors by the *substantiality of the interior.* Focus is on these entities as bodies, with their individuation from outward projection. Another way to think about this is that solids do not come with lines around them: Their edges are not explicitly demarcated because their interior density is sufficient to differentiate them from the surrounding environment. Consider the phrase *body of water.* Here, *water* is differentiated from its environment by means of its internal coherence, not by a conceptual line that separates a body of water from all other entities.

In contrast, there are *outlined entities,* whose differentiation from the surrounding environment is a function of explicit *delimitation from without.* In simple terms, outlined entities come with edges, unlike solid entities. Whereas *body of water* projects differentiation from the density of the interior (solid), *cup of water* relies on the explicit demarcation of an edge (outline). Similarly, *hunk of chocolate* differs from *box of chocolate* in that the former is differentiated by the solidity of the hunk whereas the latter is individuated from the imposition of a boundary.

Denny argues that there are two subtypes of outlined entities: *ring* and *holes.* Although his point is accurate, his explanation misses a more general point: Rings and holes are really exemplars of more *abstract types of outlined figures.* The former focus on the outline proper; the latter focus on the interior that is outlined. That is, a ring and a hole are different because *a ring is the outline of an interior* whereas *a hole is the interior of an outline.*

Many of these distinctions are morphosyntactically productive in Bella Coola, Trukese, Tzeltal, and Burmese. In Burmese, solid entities are coextensive with extended and nonextended entities; only two dimensions are explicitly marked, the third dimension neutralized with roundness. The numeral classifier *hca* marks extended two-dimensional solid entities (Cornyn and Roop 1968: 317):

59. pagan-bya: hna- hca.
     plate Plural two 2 Dim/Ext (= solid)
     two plates.
     More exactly: two two-dimensional solid extended things: plates.

There are separate classifiers for the two types of outlines, rings *kwin*, and holes, *pau?*. The often cited poetic form illustrates the former (Pe 1965: 174):

60. man   na- kwin.
     insolence five Curved Outline.
     five rings of insolence (i.e., five enwrappings of insolence).

The kinds of entities associated with the classifier for holes are windows, doorways, entrances, and holes in general (Cornyn and Roop 1968: 318):

61. daga: hna-pau.
     door two Hole
     two doorways (i.e., two door holes).

Note the logic behind associating doorways with outlined interiors where the outline itself is defocalized (vs. a ring): A doorway is an outlined hole in a wall, but the outline (the door jamb) matters less than the opening itself. Hence a doorway is more a hole than a ring.

3.273. Size

The third major physical property is *size*. This property is relatively easy to discuss and analyze because there are only two values: *large* and *small*. Languages apparently do not encode a middle value of medium, at least not in the grammar. The marking of large size is traditionally called the *augmentative,* that for small size the *diminutive*. Both values are pervasive and easily identifiable in the semantic systems of the world's languages.

More often than not the property of size is encoded along with other properties. The Japanese classifier *ko,* we might recall, marks not only round objects, but small round objects. Ekari has a numeral classifier for small *pieces* of entities, *tinee* (Doble 1987: 74–5):

62. mege tinee   wii.
     shell Small/Piece four
     four small pieces of shell.

Nonetheless, size is independently encoded in the classifier systems of certain African languages (Allan 1977), as Diola Fogny exemplifies. Among the noun classifier prefixes for mass nouns in this language, there is one for *small masses, ji,* and one for *large masses, jə* (Sapir 1965: 64):

   63a. ji-   rus.
         Small wind
         a breeze.

     b. jə- rus.
         Big wind
         gust.

3.274. Consistency

The last major physical property we look at is *consistency*. This refers to the *tractability of an entity* or its *plasticity under manipulation.* There appear to be two major values that languages use in encoding the consistency of an entity: *flexible* or *rigid.*

Many languages sharply draw the distinction between flexible and rigid consistency. In Tzeltal, for example, there are three numeral classifiers for rigid objects: one for one-dimensional entities and two for two-dimensional entities (with one each for thick and thin objects). A thick, rigid, two-dimensional entity is signalled by the classifier *pehč* (Berlin 1968: 99):

   64. h- pehč   latre.
      one rigid/2D/thick brick
      a brick.
      More exactly: one rigid thick flat thing: brick.

But when the entity is flexible, the classifier changes. *T'im* denotes thin, flexible, one-dimensional entities stretched between two points but not taut (Berlin 1968: 109):

   65. h- t'im   laso.
      one flex/1D/stretched rope
      a stretched rope (e.g., a lax clothesline)
      More exactly: one flexible, long, lax, stretched thing: a rope.

Allan (1977) notes that it is normal to find consistency lexicalized with other properties. Rarely do languages have a 'rigid classifier' alone, for example, though he says that the language of the Louisiade Archipelago does have a separate classifier for flexible objects (1977: 302).

Before we leave the subject of the tractability of entities, we should note that in addition to the major subtypes of flexible and rigid, there is a third less prevalent subcategory. Allan (1977) calls this *nondiscreteness,* by which he apparently means the *viscosity of entities.* In a number of languages, the surface tackiness of an entity is encoded, and mushy, sticky, and muddy substances are often formally differentiated. Navajo and Yucatec have separate noun classifiers for tacky substances. In Atsugewi, there is a special verbal root for the *motion of tacky substances, staq* (Talmy 1985: 74 ff.):

66. w-   uh-   staq-   ik-   a.
     3 Subj. from gravity tacky material on the ground 3Per
     Guts are lying on the ground.
     More exactly: Tacky material is located on the ground by its own
     weight.

3.275. *Additional Physical Properties*

Extendedness, interioricity, size, and consistency—and their subtypes, like dimensionality/shape, direction, and so on—cover a wide range of physical characteristics, but by no means do they exhaust the possibilities. In the interests of space, we merely note some frequent occurrences.

Many languages have ways of encoding what Allan (1977) has called *arrangement,* some noninherent or resulting configuration. English *coil of rope* is a good example, encoding not only a resulting arrangement but also curvature. Burmese has a special classifier for *pleats* and one for *folds*; Japanese and Tzeltal have unique classifiers for *objects that are strung together,* like beads and necklaces. Ekari has a special numeral classifier just for *tied bundles.* Yagua has classifiers for *netlike* and *featherlike arrangements.*

Languages also have markers for what Allan (1977) calls *quanta,* or aggregates of entities. A simple run through English shows the variety of quanta that are possible: *bunch, set, flock, group, mass, throng, cluster,* and so forth. In Ekari, there is a numeral classier just for *clusters of bananas and palm nuts.* The full range of possibilities is too unwieldy to enumerate here, but it is clear that quanta, like arrangements, tend to interact with other semantic properties and surface in association with properties like shape. *Cluster,* for example, encodes not only a quantum, but one irregularly shaped and relatively dense.

Depending on the preferences of the culture speaking a language, more particular physical properties may be encoded. Many languages have classifiers for different *natural forces* and detailed varieties of *flora.* The *material* out of which an entity is constructed is also overtly encoded in a number of languages. In Vietnamese, Japanese, and Chinese, books receive a special classifier for *readable volumes. Time, units of value* (money, e.g.), and *spatial measurement* are sometimes marked as distinct entities in languages. And depending on what is highly valued in a culture or found very frequently in the environment, a language may have a specific marker just for a particular object. So, to show the extreme limiting case, in Ekari, whose speakers value sweet potato gardens, there are separate numeral classifiers for both gardens and sweet potatoes (Doble 1987):

67a. tai   poga benumi.
     garden Class six
     six gardens (i.e., six garden objects).
  b. nota   mani benumi.
     sweet potato Class six
     six sweet potatoes (i.e., six sweet potato objects).

3.276. Summary

Under the category of physical properties, we have considered how languages encode extendedness (how entities occupy space), interioricity (how insides are differentiated from outsides), size, and consistency (tractability of entities). All these properties have subtypes: respectively, dimensionality/shape and direction; solids and outlines, rings and holes; large and small; flexible, rigid, and tacky. We have also seen that other physical properties occur to a lesser degree: arrangement, quanta, material, and even some language-specific categories, like tied bundles. In spite of the apparent variety, there are some regularities, most notably that one and two dimensions are more common than three dimensions, that dimensionality is separable from shape, and that in nondimensional shape, curvature is the most frequently expressed.

3.28. Function

The final property of entities to be considered is *function*. Many languages have ways of singling out specific *uses that entities have* or the kinds of *actions that are performed on them*. A close look at functional properties, however, gives rather foreboding results. The range of functions that any language encodes is extremely wide, and the regularities are few and far between. Adams and Conklin (1973: 7) remark: "Many of the function-based classes are language-specific and reflect cultural orientations of the speakers." Denny (1976: 128) notes that "no specialized studies of functional classifiers has been undertaken," and so results in this area must remain a bit rough.

In spite of the disclaimers and doom, there are a few consistencies in functional properties. Many languages have markers that encode the *edibility* of entities. Berlin (1968: 169–70) lists some 25 such classifiers for Tzeltal, differentiating edibles by consistency, size, sweetness, and kind of mastication required for ingestion. Dyirbal, which has only four noun classes to begin with, has an entirely separate class for edibles. According to Dixon (1982: 178–9), the noun class marker *balam* (see p. 101) in Dyirbal signals all nonflesh food: vegetables, fruits, and the plants that bear them. Dixon (1982: 185–205) also notes that the related language Yidiny draws an overt distinction between two kinds of edibles: flesh food marked by one classifier and nonflesh food marked by another.

Another common functional property for entities is *cutting/piercing* and *instruments for these acts*. Berlin's (1968) description of Tzeltal lists some 20 different classifiers for acts of cutting and piercing. Burmese (Denny 1976) has a special classifier just for cutting tools; so do Nung and Dimasa Kachari (Adams and Conklin 1973). Yagua has separate classifiers for cutting instruments (*ray*) and piercing instruments (*roo*) (D. Payne 1986: 119). And Ekari makes a distinction between uncut items, marked by the numeral classifier *tegee,* and cut items, marked by *ma* (Doble 1987: 75).

Other commonly found functional properties are *vehicular transport, housing,* and *speaking*. Denny (1976) notes that Gilbertese has a separate classifier for transport, *wa;* Japanese has a number of numeral classifiers for vehicles, differentiating airplanes (*ki*), large boats (*seki*), small boats (*soo*), and train cars (*ryoo*) (Downing 1984: 52–4). Yagua (D. Payne 1986: 119) has a special classifier for shelters and huts, *tgy;* Japanese (Downing 1984) differentiates buildings (*ken*) from schools (*koo*) and houses (*ko*). Vietnamese (Thompson 1965: 199) has five classifiers for linguistic units; Japanese has a separate classifier for written documents (*tuu*) and even literary forms, with poems (*syu*) different from narrative scenes (*koma*) (Downing 1984).

Narrowing the focus to particular languages increases the idiosyncracy of functional properties. Tzeltal provides a limiting case. The language has numeral classifiers for all the following functions: planning, igniting combustible materials, jumping, mixing, cleansing interiors, squatting, grinding, pulling, rubbing, pressing, peeling, raising, grabbing, harvesting, and even producing onomatopoeic sounds (see Berlin 1968).

Just what the core semantic properties are that underlie varieties such as those found in Tzeltal remain to be discovered. Until that time, functional properties remain something of a grab bag category, if not the most interesting because of it.

3.29. Summary of Properties

We have covered a lot of ground in our inventory of the properties of entities, so let us briefly review the findings. Traditionally, the study of these properties is done under the rubric of noun classifiers, and we have gotten a good idea of the range and form of classifiers and their grammatical relevance. We have looked at the following broad classes of properties, their significant subclasses, and their important semantic and morphosyntactic characteristics: specificity, boundedness, animacy, sex/gender, kinship, social status, physical properties, and function. Along the way, we have remarked on notable regularities of these properties, paying particular attention to specificity and mood, boundedness and countability, the Animacy Hierarchy, gender and categorization, universals of kinship, social status and honorific systems, and the logic of physical structure. These properties give a thorough characterization of the semantics of entities as temporally stable phenomena.

3.3.   UNIFYING THE SEMANTIC PROPERTIES OF ENTITIES

This has been a complicated chapter thus far, and perhaps we can get a firmer hold on the descriptive facts by looking at some overarching theoretical matters. To facilitate our approach to theory, we look at *one general* theoretical issue and examine attempts to *unify the properties of entities*.

In section 3.2 we sometimes remarked on how the properties were conceptually integrated, for example, in the connection between boundedness and countability. Are there any overarching principles that we can use to get a more unified picture of the semantic properties of entities? To answer this question, we divide the problem in two: connections *internal* to the properties of entities (i.e., how the properties are unified *in relation to each other*), and connections *external* to the properties (i.e., how the properties are generalizable to or derivable from the semantic properties of *other linguistic phenomena and mental structure in general*).

3.31.   Internal Unities

We have already noted a number of hierarchical and implicational connections across the properties, for instance how the Animacy Hierarchy predicts the morphosyntactic reflexes of ergativity. Are there any more general hierarchies that cast a larger unifying net on the properties as a whole?

3.311.   *Two Typologies of Noun Classifiers*

Denny (1976) and Allan (1977) offer broad accounts of the internal unities of the properties underlying noun classifiers. Allan puts them into seven types (some of which we have borrowed earlier): *material, shape, consistency, size, arrangement, location,* and *quanta.* Animacy, sex, and social status are presumably material properties; extendedness is part of location; dimensionality falls under shape. Denny's (1976) view is a bit neater. He argues that the semantic properties coded in classifiers reflect the three ways humans *interact with their environ-*

ment: physically, socially, and functionally. *Physical interaction* includes all of Allan's categories (hence all of our physical properties) plus, presumably, boundedness, specificity, sex, and animacy. *Social interaction* subsumes kinship and status. *Functional interaction* is the same as our functional properties.

But these two typologies often fall short of explanation. Allan's typology, for example, is irregular and inconsistent: Arrangement is almost always associated with shape, but does not this defeat the assignment of a property to one or the other category? Denny's proposal predicts little about which properties are more likely to appear where and when. Are social properties more likely than physical properties? In fairness to Allan and Denny, neither really ever makes any pretenses to proposing ultimate explanations, though Denny (1979) notes the connection between extendedness and interioricity, as we have already stated (p. 125). At the highest level of generalization, it is safest to claim that all languages have animacy distinctions (Adams 1986). DeLancey's (1986) historical study of classifiers in Tai languages shows that the current languages can be reconstructed from two basic properties: animacy and shape. And Adams and Conklin (1973) observe that sometimes animacy distinctions are associated with shape distinctions. Does this mean that shape is as fundamental as animacy? Clearly, more work needs to be done on the overall connections across the most general categories of these properties as well as on a more detailed level of implications across subtypes. Does the presence of quanta imply the presence of arrangement? Do material properties precede shape properties? We attempt some answers by looking at cases of semantic neutralization and the historical development of properties.

3.312. Neutralization and Historical Derivation

At a finer level of analysis, there are a number of interesting connections that provide some unity. No distribution of linguistic phenomena is uniform, and according to markedness theory (see p. 112), some phenomena are primary; others are productively differentiated in one part of a system and neutralized in another.

If we look at the semantic properties of entities in this way, we can observe that extendedness has more differentiation than nonextendedness: Nonextendedness appears to *neutralize other semantic distinctions,* particularly roundness and three-dimensionality. In none of the languages that Denny (1979) lists, Bella Coola, Trukese, Proto Bantu, Tzeltal, Burmese, Western Apache, and Ojibway, are there any further distinctions among nonextended entities for such properties as consistency and size.

In contrast, extended entities have a number of further semantic distinctions, with direction, dimensionality, and consistency repeatedly distinguished. For example, Tzeltal has numeral classifiers for extended, one-dimensional rigid entities, extended two-dimensional rigid thick entities, extended two-dimensional rigid thin entities, and extended flexible entities. But there is only *one classi-*

fier for all nonextended entities. Similarly, Bella Coola differentiates one-dimensional and two-dimensional extended entities, but all nonextendeds have *no further differentiation.* These facts suggest the following implicational relation for semantic differentiation: *Extended > Nonextended.* That is, extended entities will have finer semantic differentiation.

Neutralization also carries over into dimensionality. We already know that languages tend to differentiate one and two dimensions before three dimensions: $1/2 > 3$. Internal to dimensionality, there are more semantic distinctions among one and two dimensions than among three. Burmese and Tzeltal differentiate consistency only in two dimensions (Denny 1979). Yagua differentiates both consistency and size for one- and two-dimensional entities, but consistency is neutralized for three-dimensional entities (D. Payne 1986: 116–9).

If such neutralization among three-dimensional entities is a general principle, then it makes sense in relation to neutralization in nonextendedness. Three-dimensionality tends to derive historically from nonextendedness, and so if nonextendeds are neutralized, three-dimensional entities are likewise. What is not known, however, is *which properties tend to be neutralized.* In Yagua, consistency is neutralized but size is retained in three dimensions; in Bella Coola, the opposite happens. Is there some more specific rule here? Does the status of three-dimensionality as a perceptual derivative entail loss of semantic distinctions? Do languages lack further differentiation among three-dimensional entities because these entities are separately lexicalized, whereas one-dimensional and two-dimensional entities are classed as kinds? (See Denny 1979 for some observations on this matter.)

In addition to neutralization, *historical derivation* accounts for other internal unities among the properties. Denny (1979) observes historical connections between extendedness and interioricity. In the languages he has studied the marking for *outlined entities* derives from the marking for *nonextended entities.* In his account, the class of extended entities is virtually coextensive with solids (non-outlined entities), which suggests that *outlined entities derive from nonextended solids* (there may be some cognitive support for this connection: see sec. 3.32).

Denny (1979) also observes that among the two types of outlined entities, *rings historically precede holes.* That is, containers with a specific outline give rise to containers that are individuated from the interior out. There is some logic to this. As previously noted, outlined entities derive from nonextended solids, so interioricity is a function of the internal density of the entity. However, when outlining proper is further differentiated, it proceeds *from the outline in,* with rings giving rise to holes. So, the outline class itself derives from the interior out, but when the interior is established, the outline itself takes precedence over the interior. In the following paragraphs we note the perceptual justification for this relationship in terms of the priority of shading, but here it is worth remarking that there are historical accounts—plus neutralization—that offer hope for internally unifying the properties.

3.32. External Unities

Many of the internal unities find a coherent explanation in *external,* or nonsemantic, unities of the semantic properties. For instance, a number of the physical properties have a clear anchor in the mentally projected world, and one cannot deny the overlap between Locke's proposed primary qualities of bodies—for example, solidity, figure, number and extension—and those properties already discussed—for example, consistency, shape, size, quanta (see Allan 1977). In this case, language maps neatly from ontology. But more specific connections, such as between extendedness and interioricity, also have a neat perceptual and cognitive underlayment. The current received theory of vision—Marr's *three-dimensional sketch* (Marr 1982)—provides a direct explanation of the aforementioned association in terms of how the mentally projected visual world construes entities in physical space.

3.321. Vision as an Explanation

According to Marr (1982, see also Baron 1987; Jackendoff 1983), low-level visual identification of objects proceeds through four stages. First, the peripheral visual mechanisms (receptor cells) differentiate light intensities; the calculation of peaks and valleys of light intensity results in the detection of *edges*: Where intensity falls off, there is an edge. From this information, or *edge detection,* the visual mechanisms construct a *one-dimensional sketch.* Second, one-dimensional information is then converted into a *two-dimensional sketch.* Though exactly how this is done remains unclear, it appears that surface differences in intensity are neutralized and angles, corners, and rudimentary blobs are detected. The visual mechanisms thereby determine fundamental surfaces, or two-dimensional objects. Third, this information on two-dimensionality is converted to what Marr has called the *two and one-half–dimensional sketch.* Put simply, surfaces are converted to round, curved, cylinderlike entities. In the perception of a human figure, for example, a flat figure is converted to cones. Fourth, the two and one-half–dimensional sketch is converted to a *three-dimensional sketch* with depth and recognition assigned from central mental processing.

The details of this process are less important to our purposes than the results. Visual identification of entities has the following sequence of perceptual/cognitive computations:

1 Dimension (edges from intensity) $>$ 2 Dimensions (surfaces) $>$ 2½ Dimensions (curved surfaces) $>$ 3 Dimensions (normal objects).

A number of explanations come to the fore in the connection between visual computation and the physical properties of entities that have semantic import. In both semantic and visual perception, *three-dimensionally is derived*; one-dimensionality and two-dimensionality have to be computed first. It is no surprise then that three-dimensionality is sometimes neutralized semantically because it is not a prime in the mentally projected world of visual experience. Likewise, it is not surprising that more semantic distinctions should occur among one and two dimensions because these are the primary building blocks of visual experience.

It is also interesting to note the role that curvature plays in visual computation. In the determination of three-dimensionality, the system constructs an intermediate two and one-half-dimensional sketch, which is basically a visual projection of curved or rounded surfaces. We also know of the pervasive role that curvature plays in the semantics of entities, particularly in relation to three-dimensionality. As we have seen, curvature and three-dimensionality are sometimes conflated in nonextendedness. Is this because curvature is connected to three-dimensionality itself in the construction of the two and one-half-dimensional sketch?

Semantically, outlined entities derive from solid, nonextended entities: Outlines come from the density of interiors. This is again in line with visual perception. Visually perceived objects are individuated from the interiors outward because variations in shading and light intensity *internal to the object* produce edges. Objects are not primarily perceived as if they came to the visual field with outlines and edges: because, in fact, objects do not come with edges! Outlines and edges are *projected outward from the interior* of an entity by calculating differences in the relative solidity of the entity via light intensity. We might thus say that a solid, a homogeneous area of light intensity, derives the outline, or the edge. Once outlined objects are established, then the outline takes priority. Hence, rings precede holes. Here the basic connection between the mechanisms of visual perception and the regularities of semantic properties of entities is undeniable.

3.322. *General Cognitive Processes as an Explanation*

A great deal is gained by seeing the ultimate anchoring of semantic properties in the mentally projected world because the properties thereby take on a unified character. But as part of *general cognitive mechanisms,* some properties of entities ought to apply to other linguistic phenomena. If so, then the number of different properties is severely reduced because the mechanisms are *reusable.* Boundedness is a case in point.

Langacker (1987a, 1987b) observes that boundedness is not properly restricted to entities, even though it is most clearly applicable to them, but affects a variety of linguistic forms and categories. When the bounded/unbounded distinction is applied to *events* (normally coded as verbs), the fundamental aspectual distinction between *perfective* events (complete) and *imperfective* events (incomplete) results (see Bach 1986; chap. 7). Consider the difference between the following:

68a. Tom spat on the ground.
  b. Tom resembles his uncle.

The action expressed by *spat* is perfective, a bounded process completable within a well determinable limit. On the other hand, the event expressed by *resembles* is not so determinable. *When* does Tom begin to resemble his uncle? *When* does he stop? *Resemble* is therefore an imperfective process, or unbounded.

A number of syntactic facts correlate with this distinction between bounded and unbounded processes. Boundedness entails completeness, so bounded events are more likely to occur in time intervals that are theoretically boundable: the past and future. The present, however, is ephemeral and cannot be bounded and viewed as an interval: Perfective events are odd in the present: ?? *Tom spits on the ground* (which is understandable only in a habitual or time transcendent reading). Conversely, imperfective or unbounded events are more likely to occur in the (unbounded) present, as per (68b), and are odd in other (bounded) tenses: ?? *Tom will resemble his uncle.*

Bounded entities are replicable whereas unbounded entities are continuous. These features also have ramifications for bounded and unbounded events. Note that *spit,* which is bounded, can be incremented: *Tom was spitting on the ground.* But unbounded events are generally immune to iteration: ?? *Tom is resembling his uncle.* The progressive (*be* + *-ing*) expresses inherently continuous action and thus is redundant in relation to unbounded events like *resemble.* If progressivized *resemble* is understandable at all, then it must be given a bounded interpretation: 'Tom is behaving such that his actions make him resemble his uncle.'

The bounded/unbounded distinction also applies to *spatial relations.* Consider the difference between the following in terms of the *trajectory* of the spatial relation:

69a. Tom ran across the street.
  b. Tom ran through the street

Example (69a) expresses an event in which the trajectory of Tom's running is necessarily bounded: *across* means 'from one point to another.' Example (69b), in contrast, expresses an event where the trajectory is unbounded: *through* means 'in the medium of,' and has nothing to do with the bounding of the trajectory. Hence English lexicalizes the bounded/unbounded distinction in its spatial prepositions as well as in its verbs.[13]

Langacker (1987a, 1987b) argues that the wide applicability of the bounded/

---

[13]Another area where the bounded/unbounded distinction has proven fruitful is in work on *generic expressions:* habitual, universal kind readings associated with *mass terms* (*fudge is sweet*), *bare plurals* (*professors are useless*), *definite singulars* (*the dog barks* 'the dog as a kind'), and *indefinite singulars* (*a dog barks*). Expressions such as these have received extensive treatment in the philosophical literature (Bunt 1985; Pelletier 1979) and in the linguistics literature (Carlson 1977, 1979; DeClerck 1986, 1988; Farkas and Sugioka 1983; McCawley 1981: 442–7; Schubert and Pelletier 1986). Generic interpretations differ from nongeneric ones in that the former have a kind- or type-reading whereas the latter have an instance-reading. This difference is basically between an

unbounded distinction to the denotations of nouns, verbs, and prepositions is the result of the *general cognitive mechanisms* that humans use to individuate objects and construct the mentally projected world. That is, semantic properties are a derivative of the larger organization of mental models. (Similar arguments are given by Jackendoff 1983 for the construction of #entities#: see chap. 2.) If this is the case, then more precise connections between boundedness and such things as specificity, extendedness, and interioricity seem to be worthwhile pursuits because all three bear on the relative discreteness of entities. But the larger lesson is that we can make discernible progress toward unifying the semantic properties of entities by couching them in terms of both perceptual and general cognitive processes. This goes a long way toward justifying the mentally projected world as the domain of reference.

3.33. Summary

We have considered the theoretical problem of the unity of the semantic properties of entities. We have focused on internal explanation (e.g., neutralization and historical derivation) and external explanation (e.g., the relevance of vision and general cognitive mechanisms). We have seen how the wide applicability of certain semantic properties suggests that they derive from the mechanisms that humans use to construct mental models.

SUMMARY OF CHAPTER

In this chapter, we considered the semantic properties associated with entities. We presented a revised notional definition of *noun* based on three accounts of

---

unbounded sense—generic or continuously extended—and a bounded one—individuated and discrete. Carlson's influential formal solution to generics follows the spirit, if not the letter, of the bounded/unbounded dichotomy.

Carlson proceeds deductively, first postulating an ontology and then deriving the phenomenological facts therefrom. Carlson argues that denotations must make reference to three kinds of formal entities: objects (individuals, like *chair*), kinds (classes, like *chairs*), and stages (temporal instantiations of individuals and kinds, like *the chair broke* or *chairs break*). Now, which of these formal entities are subject to generic readings? Carlson argues that generics—specifically bare plurals—involve reference to kinds. To capture this kind/nonkind difference, Carlson proposed that there is a *generic nonquantificational operator, G,* that operates on stages to produce kinds and therefore produces generic readings. In contrast, there is also another *nonquantificational operator R,* which is the simple instantiation of a stage in an individual that produces the *instance-reading* (nongeneric). The difference between generic and nongeneric readings is accounted for in terms of how *kinds can be produced and represented.*

The larger point is that the instance-readings are bounded; the kind-readings are unbounded. And so Carlson's account follows the more general proposal that broad cognitive processes are at work in the semantics of entities, even if it does not explicitly propose such a tack.

categories and their typical denotations. Nouns tend to denote *entities*, relatively atemporal individuals in discourse, ontology, and conceptual structure.

We then described eight classes of semantic properties:

1. Specificity: the accessibility of an entity in a mentally projected world. Here we surveyed the philosophical and linguistic accounts of singular reference and the connection of specificity to definiteness, factivity, negation, and restrictive modification.

2. Boundedness: the inherent delimitation of entities. We looked at virtual bounding, fuzziness, expansibility, incrementation, and the like; the count/mass opposition and its encoding in number; the divergence of boundedness and expected surface forms.

3. Animacy: the relative influence and potency of an entity in the event expressed. We noted the divergence of linguistic and biological animacy and the factors bearing on the distinction between animates and inanimates, humans and nonhumans, and varieties of animals. We also examined the Animacy Hierarchy and its predictions for split ergativity and agreement.

4. Sex and Gender: male, female, and neuter. We observed the correlation of these distinctions with humans, animals, and inanimates and saw the relation between gender and superordinate and subordinate terms.

5. Kinship: familial relations. We noted three basic semantic properties, consanguinity, lineality, and generation, and saw them at work in English, Seneca, and Mari'ngar. We also noted that the most unmarked kinship system reflects immediate, true family.

6. Social Status: social rank and honorifics. We claimed that social status is a *semantic* property, normally encodes only speaker deference or nonspeaker elevation, is a gradient, and has a variety of syntactic forms. We discussed four kinds of systems: Speaker/Hearer, Speaker/Reference, Speaker/Bystander, Speaker/Situation, with S/R the most common and S/B the least.

7. Physical Properties: the physical structure of entities. We considered extendedness, interioricity, size, and consistency as well as their subtypes: dimensionality/shape and direction; solids and outlines, rings and holes; large and small; flexible, rigid, and tacky. We have also saw other physical properties to a lesser degree: arrangement, quanta, material.

8. Function: the uses to which an object is put. We discussed how this property is quite diffuse, with edibility and cutting/piercing two of the major subtypes.

We closed the chapter with a discussion of one theoretical issue: unifying the properties. Here we examined internal and external unities, focusing on semantic neutralization and cognitive and perceptual correlates.

QUESTIONS FOR DISCUSSION

1. Consider the following two sentences from Chipewyan (Carter 1976: 29):

   i. tu   θe- ʔą.
     water sits Inanimate Solid, Uncontained
     there sits some uncontained water (e.g., a lake).

  ii. tu   θe- łtą.
     water sits Contained
     there sits some contained water (e.g., a bottle of water).

Discuss these examples in relation to what you know about the physical properties of entities. What are better glosses of 'contained' and 'uncontained'?

2. Given what you know about Lakhota (p. 80), why is the following anomalous?

   i. ?? Edwin kuže ki   he   lel   thi.
       Edwin sick Def Dem here live
    ?? Edwin who is sick lives here.

(Hint: What would Russell, Donnellan, or Kripke say about *Edwin?*)

3. Brown and Levinson (1987) claim that in Japanese, the honorific marker *masi,* on p. 118, which is part of a Speaker/Hearer system, is currently changing denotation and becoming part of a Speaker/Situation system. That is, the honorific is beginning to encode just an elevated speech situation, not a respected hearer. Is this shift from S/H to S/S understandable? What pragmatic and semantic factors might contribute to this change? In your answer, consider the relationship of the hearer to the speech situation. Can the Arabic data on p. 120 be viewed in this way, too?

4 Events

4.1. INTRODUCTION

In Chapter 3, we looked at entities and their typical encoding as nouns. In this chapter, we consider the basic counterpart of entities, events, along with their typical encoding as verbs. We proceed in a manner analogous to Chapter 3, first discussing the semantic motivation of verbs as events, and then surveying three proposals for verbal categoriality: a discourse approach and two conceptual approaches. Thereafter, we take inventory of the kinds of events available to language, limiting our discussion to four principal classes: acts, states, causes, and motion. We describe such things as the nature of states, the logic of causation, and the connection of motion to sources, goals, and trajectories; we also look at the ways different languages translate these notions into grammatical form, and, more generally, how we can use the results of this analysis on other event classes, like transfer and possession. To close the chapter, we consider various attempts to unify classes of events through typologies based on their meanings and their distribution over a time interval. We see how the treatment of events as temporally sensitive phenomena meshes nicely with their typing by interval and produces an explanation of events and their associated structural reflexes.

4.11. Verbs and Events:
The Notional Definition of *Verb*

A verb is traditionally defined as the grammatical category that represents the action in a sentence, a definition that raises the same problems as the notional definition of *noun* in the previous chapter. There are many verbs that do not
140

represent actions, at least not in an intuitive sense of action as *some kind of process carried out relatively deliberately,* but are still verbs:

1. Donna is sad.

It is difficult to see the *action* in (1) because, in the situation described, Donna is not really doing anything.

As with *noun, verb* may be defined irrespective of the notions it encodes *as a form class,* with syntactic criteria for identification. Under this view, a verb is something that takes a subject or object. We know that *has* is a verb in (1) because its form is a function of the singularity of the subject. If the number of the subject changes, the verb form changes in response: *Donna and Bob* **are sad.**

Purely formal definitions of *verb* work because at some level, verbs are entirely structural phenomena. But if the traditional definition of *verb* is reversed, as is possible for that of *noun,* then the notional definition of *verb* goes through. Not all verbs are actions, but when actions are expressed, they overwhelmingly tend to surface as verbs.

The success of notional definitions of *noun* suggests that we follow suit for *verb.* Nouns represent *entities,* a cover term for all relatively atemporal regions or individuals, including persons, places, and things. Verbs encode *events:* a cover term for states or conditions of existence (e.g., *be sad*), processes or unfoldings (e.g., *get sad*), and actions or executed processes (e.g., *sadden*).

The definition of verbs as events has a near perfect illustration in Kalam. According to Pawley (1987), Kalam has a very small number of verbs, only 90, but these 90 verbs combine to compositionally produce all the event notions required for adequate expression in Kalam. Even more remarkably, only about one-third of the 90 are *commonly used,* so in practical fact, Kalam has about 30 verbs.

Pawley (1987: 336--7) notes that these 30 verbs "are sharply distinguished from all other parts of speech by numerous morphological and syntactic criteria," and so Kalam verbs meet the formal criteria for identification, such as subject agreement. More to our purposes, Kalam verbs denote *only states, processes, or actions.* For example, the verb *nŋ* refers to *all internal states.* If the concepts of seeing, hearing, feeling, thinking, smelling, and so on are to be expressed, an additional form appears to derive the more specific denotation from the generic internal state:

2. wdn nŋ.
   eye Internal State.
   see.

Kalam simply divides the event space more generally than does English. In Kalam, there is one verb for all resulting events, *d,* denoting such things as holding, having, and ending; one verb for all actions, *g,* denoting acting, doing, making, causing, and so on. Thus, Kalam is the limiting case of the claim that verbs are semantically motivated by events: A small number of verbs directly encodes only states, processes, and actions.

One way to think about the semantic motivation of grammatical categories is to say that there is something about the essence of their denotations that forces some things in the mentally projected world to be coded one way and other things to be coded in another. Nouns select relatively static particulars that persist in unchanged form. What is the essence of verbs as events? Or, as Davidson (1980) puts it: How can we *reliably re-identify* events? According to Davidson, entities, what he calls *substances and objects,* are individuated by their *sameness in spatial coordinates.* Events, on the other hand, are *essentially tied to change,* either changing themselves (as in the case of their own derivation by cause and effect) or bringing about a change in the entities associated with them.

Davidson's view that change is the essential criterion of events, and hence of the prototypical form that events take—verbs—recalls our discussion in Chapter 3 about the basic semantic difference between nouns and verbs: respectively, temporality versus atemporality. If Davidson is right, then change is associated with temporality, and temporality and change therefore motivate the categoriality of verbs, just as atemporality and persistence motivate the categoriality of nouns. So, with this reinvigorated notional definition of *verb,* we return to categoriality itself and the three accounts we reviewed in Chapter 3—Hopper and Thompson's, Givón's, and Langacker's—to see what they observe about events and their usual encoding.

4.12.   Three Accounts of Verbal Categoriality

Events, via change, motivate the categoriality verbs. How does this mesh with larger considerations of categoriality itself? As with nouns and entities, verbal categoriality is a function of the degree of change, the relative temporality, or the degree of "eventhood" of the action, process, or state motivating the verb.

4.121.   Events in Discourse

Hopper and Thompson (1984, 1985) argue that the informational requirements of discourse motivate the categoriality of nouns and verbs, with overt form reflecting the relative individuation of the information encoded by the form. Overt verbal categoriality then reflects the degree to which the event reported is individuated in discourse.

Supporting evidence is fairly easy to marshall. The overt markings associated with verbs as a grammatical category are often reduced when the events that these verbs report are informationally less significant to the ongoing discourse, just like incorporation for nouns (see p. 64). Many languages have a syntactic construction in which verbs are strung together in listlike fashion, one after the other, but constitute a *single grammatical unit*. Such constructions are called *serial verbs* (Foley and Olson 1985). Often the informational status of the constituents of the serial construction is reduced, and the separate verbs do not denote individuated events. Furthermore, the members of the serial-verb construction are usually not marked with normal verbal morphology, thus following Hopper and Thompson's informational principle and indicating that only the event *as a whole* has full informational status. In serial-verb constructions, the time of the events *in sequence* is frequently reduced, with time attributed *only to the entire construction:* that is, to the event that has *full informational status.*

Yoruba serial verbs bear out this point. Tense, the verbal encoding of time, is restricted to the first member of the serial-verb construction (Hopper and Thompson 1984: 735):

3a. Mo Ḿ- mú ìwé bọ̀
    I   Prog take book come
    I am bringing the book.
    More exactly: I am take-coming the book.
  b. ?? Mo Ḿ- mú ìwé wá.
      I   Prog take book came
    ?? I am take-caming the book.

Example (3b) is unacceptable because the second verb, *wá*, carries tense [cf. (3a) with tenseless *bọ̀*). Assigning time to a *constituent* of a serial verb-construction (*bọ̀* → *wá*) violates the logic of serial verbs, where the verbs are sequenced *in order to express one event*, hence reducing the individuation of the contributing events. (The same facts hold in other languages, for example, Yimas and Akan: see Foley and Olson 1985: 23).

The Yoruba data implies that the assignment of time, via tense, *increases* the informational status of the event encoded by the verb, or its "eventhood." Thus, time is a crucial signal of the status of an event as such, so much so that its encoding alone can serve to individuate events. Davidson's (1980) insights thus return: Prototypical events are associated with change, and change is measured *over time;* less prototypical events have a decrease in time and change less. For Hopper and Thompson's account, this *degree of eventhood* is reflected in the *degree to which the forms in discourse surface as verbs.*

4.122. *Temporal Stability and Conceptual Relations*

Hopper and Thompson's *functional* picture of the relative categoriality of verbs falls short of giving a full referential account of verbs as events. If a verb reports an event in discourse, what are the criteria that determine the event to begin with? We return to Givón and Langacker, whom we treat together because both offer the same criterion for verbal categoriality—the temporality of events—though each arrives at this result in a slightly different way.

For Givón (1979, 1984), grammatical categories are motivated by the perceived temporal stability of their typical referents (see the Scale of Temporal Stability, Fig. 3.1., chap. 3). In contrast to nouns as entities, there are "experiential clusters denoting rapid changes. . . . These are prototypically events or actions, and languages tend to lexicalize them as verbs" (1984: 52). Givón's position, like Davidson's, assigns priority to stability or change, though for Givón, the essential criterion for eventhood is *change over time*.

Langacker (1987a, 1987b) takes a related stand. On his view, two basic objects—*things* and *relations*—constitute the mentally projected domain of reference. The former correspond to what we have called *entities* and are encoded as nouns. Relations are either *temporal* or *atemporal*, with the latter underlying prepositions, adverbs, and adjectives, and the former corresponding to verbs. Langacker says: "A verb is a symbolic expression whose semantic pole designates a process" (1987b: 244).

Givón privileges change and Langacker privileges process, but each presupposes the essentiality of time. Givón's measure of stability is stability *within time*. Langacker's position relies on the priority of time by defining a process as something with a *temporal characteristic:* "A processual predication has a positive temporal profile" (1987b: 244). Thus both the ontological (Givón) and conceptual (Langacker) underpinnings of verbs support their denotation of events.

4.123. What Verbs Denote

We can put Davidson's, Hopper and Thompson's, Givón's, and Langacker's accounts together into a unified definition of *event* and *verb*. An *event* is a *relatively temporal relation in conceptual space*.

The priority of time in defining events, and hence accounting for the semantic motivation of verbs, can be brought home by demonstrating that time is independent of both process and change. A *process* is a series of states that in sequential or successive grouping constitute a phenomenon as a whole. Time is not relevant to this construal, only to its realization as an event and hence as a verb. We can see this by comparing nominal and verbal encodings of the same process. Consider the verb *arrive* and its nominalization *arrival*. Each denotes constituent states progressing toward a resulting state (the endpoint of the arrival), but only the verb highlights (or *profiles,* to use Langacker's term) the constituent states in their interrelations; the noun profiles the states as a totality. To put it another way, both forms highlight the result, but only the verb retains access to the states leading to the result, whereas the noun presents the states as one unified episode (see Langacker 1987b: 244–74).

In like manner, time and change are independent, as evidenced by the fact that there are events that are static, no change, but still involve time. Consider the verb *persist*, which encodes an event that by definition requires no change over time. Nonetheless, this lack of change is measured *only with reference to time* because *persist* means something like 'have the same properties at *two different times*.'[1]

Change and *process* refer only to the *relational aspects* of an event. A process involves the dependency and connection of component states, and change, insofar as it is a type of process (see fn. 1), involves the dependency of component states in differential connection. Thus, when Davidson (1980) claims that change is essential to identifying events, he is really saying just that events are relational.

Time is required for events, so it is possible to convert an atemporal relation into an event *by adding time*. Compare the preposition *toward* with the verb *approach*. Both have the same relational content: If X is toward or approaches Y, X bears an approximative spatial relation to Y. *Toward* and *approach* differ, however, in that *approach* construes the relation as *unfolding through time*. Hence relations must be given time to become events.

4.13. Summary

In this introduction we have looked at the traditional notional definition of *verb*, trying to use the lessons gained from earlier discussion (chap. 3) of the notional definition of *noun*. We have seen that events—actions, processes, and states— overwhelmingly tend to surface as verbs, thus corroborating the reversal of the traditional definition of *verb*. In further examining the criteria for identifying events as such, we have looked at Davidson's proposal—that change is essential to eventhood—in light of three linguistic accounts of verbs and events: (a) Hopper and Thompson's discourse view of verbal categoriality as a function of the informational requirement of reporting events; (b) Givón's ontological view of verbs as encoding less temporally stable phenomena; (c) Langacker's cognitive view of verbs as processes. We have settled on a unified account in terms of events as relatively temporal relations in conceptual space.

4.2. FOUR KINDS OF EVENTS: ACTS, STATES, CAUSES, AND MOTION

With a revised notional definition of *verbs* under our belts, we now examine the types of events that languages encode typically as verbs. We look at four kinds of events—*acts, states, causes,* and *motion*—to define the range of semantic phenomena associated with events and the variety of surface expressions that events

---

[1]We might also argue that process and change are *types of events*, not criterial to eventhood itself. A *process* is an event whose constituent states are related by time; a *change* is an event whose

assume. In this project, we should keep in mind that the list of events that follows is *representative*, not exhaustive. Acts, states, causes, and motion are major classes of events that languages encode, but by no means are they the only ones. As we examine a particular language in finer detail, we discover finer classes of events. English, for instance, has a large set of verbs expressing 'destruction'— *ruin, raze, eradicate, dismantle,* and so forth—but this seems to be a narrow fact about English, or at least of the culture that speaks English. The level of analysis of events is quite abstract, with the goal of identifying the more general events underlying verbal encoding.

4.21.   Acts and States

The first two kinds of event that we examine derive from a fundamental distinction between *acts* and *states*. Consider these sentences:

4a. Harry stole $10.
  b. The book cost $10.

In (4a), *stole* expresses an event that is *controlled, executed,* or *carried out,* with a distinct effect on the participants. But similar things cannot be said for (4b), where the event encoded by the verb *cost* is more a *condition of existence* or an *attribute* than it is a procedure that is enacted or controlled.

Examples (4a) and (4b) respectively illustrate *active* and *stative* events. We owe this distinction to early work by Lakoff (1965), who called them *nonstative* and *stative,* which is perhaps more appropriate because stativity is the issue here (see also Ross 1972). But we use *active* and *stative* (and synonymously, *acts* and *states*) in our subsequent work to define the types more precisely.

4.211.   Internal Structure, Scope, and Time

There are a number of conceptual differences between acts and states (Langacker 1987a; Smith 1983). Stative events are internally uniform, in marked contrast to actives, which appear to be heterogeneous and internally structured. Compare the verbs from (4) on this matter. *Cost* does not imply a series of internal states that lead ultimately to the attribution of price; on the contrary, to assert that the book cost $10 is to indicate that the book *already has a price,* not that it has come to be that way through a sequence of events (cf. *Harry priced the book at $10*).

---

constituent states are different at two different times (vs. a *state,* where there is no difference at different times). We might even argue that changes are types of processes: Events with constituent states that are related by time such that one constituent state occurs at one time and then a different constituent state at another (see p. 183, on inchoatives, acts, and states; see also Langacker's discussion of perfective and imperfective processes, 1987b, 254–67).

However, *stole $10* implies the execution of a series of different subprocesses resulting in the stealing of the money. Thus, the active event is built up out of constituents, and any uniformity is a consequence of the upshot of the subprocesses, not the event as a whole.

This difference in uniformity between actives and statives is a difference in *scope*. For statives, the scope of the event is the event as a totality; for actives, the scope of the event is its components. We may observe this scope difference by converting a stative to an active:

    5a. Fred likes rutabagas.
      b. Fred is liking rutabagas (more and more).

In (5a), the verb *like* expresses a mental state, 'a continuing mental condition of Fred is such that he likes rutabagas,' where the entire event is denoted as an undifferentiated phenomenon. But in (5b), an active interpretation is forced by the progressive (*be* + *-ing*). If (5b) is understandable at all, it is so only in the sense that there is a series of substates that now contribute to a final result: that is, something like 'Fred is trying, exerting some effort, or executing some actions so as to ultimately like rutabagas.' Hence (5b) is more acceptable with the adverbial *more and more,* which explicitly marks the series of substates in the scope of the event.

The scope difference between actives and stative contributes to the sense that actives are more associated with temporal change and dynamism of their substates. In contrast, statives typically do not unfold over time, have no internal dynamics, and are thus more stable in time than actives. We should immediately note how these observations fit with our initial characterization of events as relatively temporal relations. There ought to be some events that are more temporally sensitive than others because a gradience of temporality underlies events themselves.

Actives and statives differ in degree of temporal sensitivity. Consequently certain features of tense—the grammatical encoding of time—are associated with each type. Normally, actives are found in the nonpresent tenses (assuming that the language has ways of marking such things: see chap. 8). In the present tense, actives tend to receive a habitual or play-by-play interpretation, as a comparison of the nonpresent and present tense versions of (4a) show:

    6a. Harry stole $10. [= (4a) Past: Nonpresent]
      b. Harry will steal $10. (Future: Nonpresent)
      c. ?? Harry steals $10. (Present)

In the past and future (6a) and (6b), the active event has perfectly acceptable interpretations. But in the present (6c), *steals* must be given either a habitual reading ('Harry habitually steals $10') or a play-by-play reading (right at this very moment, the commentator is now saying about Harry's immediate actions: 'now Harry steals $10': cf. *Now the Yankees take the lead . . .)*. If actives are relatively more temporal, then it stands to reason that they usually appear only in nonpresent tenses. The present is ephemeral. Only the nonpresent is cognitively graspable, or unitized, so events that are temporally sensitive should therefore be restricted to appear in only the logically realizable tenses.

The opposite facts hold for statives. They are relatively less temporal than actives, so they should have fewer restrictions on what times they may encode. Note that the original example of a stative (4b) may occur in all tenses:

7a. The book cost $10. [= (4b) Past: Nonpresent]
 b. The book will cost $10. (Future: Nonpresent)
 c. The book costs $10. (Present)

Significantly, when the stative *cost* appears in the present tense, it does not receive any special interpretation, as is necessary for the active. It is possible to express statives at any time interval, because they are inherently less sensitive to temporal distinctions: They are characterized by continuous or homogeneous distribution of time over *all parts* of the interval in which they occur (see Dowty 1979; Mourelatos 1981: 192; Vlach 1981: 273; and sec. 4.42).[2]

A variety of semantic facts come together in the examination of the structure of actives and statives: internal structure, homogeneity, continuousness, the relevance of subprocesses and substates, distribution over a time interval, extension,

---

[2]The careful reader should have noticed by now that the active/stative distinction is reminiscent of the bounded/unbounded distinction treated at length in Chapter 3. Actives work very much like bounded entities, and hence like count nouns. Statives, on the other hand, function like unbounded entities and thus like mass nouns. Actives, like bounded entities and count nouns, are characterized by internal heterogeneity (the relevance of subprocesses) and unitization or *boundedness in time*. Statives, however, are characterized by internal homogeneity and continuousness; they are *unbounded in time*, just as mass nouns are unbounded in space.

Langacker (1987a) notes that these convergences account for several other properties of actives and statives. Statives, like masses and unbounded entities generally, have extensibility, and it is therefore possible to encode this continuation directly:

i. The book cost $10, and still does.

But such continuation is disallowed for actives because, like bounded entities and count nouns, they are not extensible:

ii. ?? Harry stole $10, and still does.

Moreover, actives, like bounded entities and count nouns, may be incremented, or repeated as discrete units:

iii. Harry repeatedly stole $10.

The adverb *repeatedly* signals the replicability of the event, but it is disallowed for statives:

iv. ?? The book repeatedly cost $10.

Example (iv) is sensible only under an interpretation where the cost as a total event is repeated: that is, where it is forced into a bounded meaning.

and incrementation. Given these characteristics as the basis of a preference rule for identifying actives and statives in any context, we now turn to a consideration of the surface forms associated with these two kinds of events.

4.212. Diagnostics and the Encoding of Acts and States

The surface forms of actives and statives have been widely discussed in the literature (Dowty 1979: 52–60, 163–89; Gruber 1976; Lakoff 1965; Miller and Johnson-Laird 1976: 472–9). There are a number of fairly consistent diagnostic tests in English of the difference between actives and statives. Five are considered here. For our larger purposes, these diagnostic tests may be seen as structural reflexes of the semantic distinction between acts and states. Alternatively, we can say that these structures are motivated by the semantic facts already presented, and where possible, we clarify the semantic motivation.

4.2121. Progressive

The first test is the *progressive,* which is a verbal structure composed of some form of the verb *to be* plus a present participle ($V + -ing$). Actives generally allow the progressive and statives disallow it. So verbs like *run, attack,* and *drive* represent active events:

  8a. Harry is running home.
   b. The dog is attacking the mailman.
   c. Fred was driving to the store when the rain started.

But verbs such as *know, weigh,* and *have* are stative because they disallow the progressive:

  9a. ?? Bill is knowing French. (cf. Bill knows French.)
   b. ?? My car is weighing a ton. (cf. My car weighs a ton.)
   c. ?? We are having a new house. (cf. We have a new house.)

The sensitivity of actives and statives to the progressive is understandable from their semantic structure. The progressive marks *extension in time,* and so a progressivized verb can represent a very large time interval into which smaller time intervals can be inserted—*I was running when it started raining,* where the progressive stretches the time interval of running and permits another event to occur simultaneously (see chap. 7 for more on this property of the progressive). But statives are *already extended and continuous* by definition. The use of the progressive with statives is superfluous because states are inherently extended, but acts are heterogeneously composed and are therefore amenable to extension.

4.2122. Pseudo-cleft

The second consistent diagnostic test for actives and statives is the *pseudo-cleft* construction: a sentence in the form *What X do be Y*. Actives tend to allow the pseudo-cleft, unlike statives:

   10a. What Harry did was steal $10.
      b. ?? What we did was have a new house.

As with progressivization, there appears to be a neat semantic fact that motivates the pseudo-cleft for actives and disallows it for statives. The pseudo-cleft brings into focus the action itself, *what X did was . . . ,* and *unitizes the event*. As we already know, only actives are unitizable because of their sensitivity to the time interval, and so the pseudo-cleft is disallowed for statives because statives are not unitizable.

The utility of the pseudo-cleft comes through nicely in a comparison of the active and stative versions of the same situation. The pairs *look/see* and *listen to/hear* illustrate the distinction. *Look* and *listen to* are active and allow the pseudo-cleft, whereas *see* and *hear* are stative and disallow the construction (see Gruber 1967):

   11a. What I did was look at the picture.
      b. ?? What I did was see the picture.
      c. What I did was listen to the music.
      d. ?? What I did was hear the music.

4.2123 What Happened?

The third structural reflex of the active/stative distinction is their sensitivity to the question *What happened?*. Only actives, for the most part, are expressed in answers to this question:

   A: What happened?
   B: Harry stole $10.
      ?? The book cost $10.

A question like *What happened?* asks about the unitized act, and thus statives, which are not unitized, are ruled out.

The *What happened?* diagnostic shows that English has many stative verbs that are not obviously stative at first glance. The following examples fail the *What happened?* test, though they seem to be acts:

A: What happened?
B: ?? Bill received a letter.
    ?? Bill believed his brother.

Receive and *believe* are semantically states, though conceptually they require some action to be carried out. Here again we see the divergence of semantic and conceptual structure.

4.2124. Imperative

The fourth test is sensitivity to the *imperative*. Actives allow the imperative; statives normally do not. Consider the difference between the following:

12a. Steal $10!
   b. ?? Cost $10!

Certainly, it seems odd to ask something to have a price because the very fact of having a price is out of the control of the thing priced. This is not true for an event like stealing, which can be controlled and thus requested to be performed. Actives are executed and have doers. But statives are not executed; rather, they are *embodied:* whence their similarity to attributes (see Dowty 1979).

Significantly, the same verbs that fail the *What happened?* test also fail the imperative test:

13a. ?? Receive a letter!
   b. ?? Believe your brother!

Believe represents a stative event, though, phenomenologically, belief appears to require effort to come into being. To believe something, you must think about it and exert some mental effort to come to the result of belief. But only the contributing event of 'thinking about' is active:

14. Think about your brother!

So extended action lies in one of the phenomenological constituents of belief—thinking about. Belief itself may require effort and action, but semantically, it is not an act at all, at least in English.[3]

---

[3]Related to the imperative test is that actives can appear as object complements (clausal objects) of the verbs *force* and *persuade* while statives cannot:

i. Bill forced Harry to steal $10.

ii. ?? Bill forced the book to cost $10.

Force and *persuade* represent events that *necessarily result in the execution of a subsequent*

4.2125. Carefully and Deliberately

The fifth and final diagnostic is the sensitivity of the active/stative distinction to the adverbs *carefully* and *deliberately*. Active events may be encoded in verbs that take these two adverbs, but stative events may not:

15a. Harry carefully/deliberately stole $10.
  b. ?? The book deliberately/carefully cost $10.

It might be thought here that the acceptability of *deliberately* or *carefully* is a function of the *animacy* of the subject of (15a) because deliberateness and care are normally associated with animates, humans moreover. This would make the acceptability of (15a) over (15b) unrelated to the active or stative nature of the event encoded. But if *deliberately* and *carefully* are dependent on the humanness of the entity represented by the subject, then why are the following disallowed?

16a. ?? Karen carefully received a letter.
  b. ?? Bob deliberately believed his brother.
  c. ?? Donna carefully inherited $1 million.

The sensitivity of actives to these two adverbs is the result of the fact that actives are executed. *Deliberately* and *carefully* have within their scope the level of intensity or control that a doer has in carrying out an action proper. This is not necessarily a function of the animacy of the doer because a nonhuman doer may still execute an act with care or deliberateness, *as long as the act is executed: The paper shredder carefully destroyed the incriminating evidence.* Statives, on the other hand, because they are not executed, cannot take a form that has scope over their execution.

We have seen five consistent diagnostics of the active/stative distinction: progressive, pseudo cleft, What happened?, imperative, and *carefully/deliberately*. The success of these tests is related to the semantic structure of the events in question: Acts have internal structure and may be executed; states are continuous and attributed rather than executed.

4.213. Exceptions and Degrees of Acts and States

From these five tests, we can divide all events as they are encoded in English into the two broad categories of acts and states. A sample list is given here:

Acts: lose, fly, run, eat, attack, annoy, drive, sneeze, look at, listen to, destroy, change, buy, prepare, bury, sweeten, paint, etc.

---

event. Seen this way, it is understandable that their complements require verbs that encode active events.

States: have, be, exist, know, understand, receive, seem, weigh, cost, like, inherit, belong, believe, etc.

A natural thing to do with these lists is to run them through the five tests like a diagnostic machine and see what happens. In the best of all possible worlds, *all the acts* meet *all the active tests* and *all the states* meet *all the stative tests.* Unfortunately, things do not turn out so well. (See Mufwene 1984 for excellent comparative data on this point: Some verbs/events are consistently active or stative across languages, but other, borderline cases are quite mystifying and vary from language to language.)

Drive meets all the tests for an active event, and *know* meets all the stative tests (as the reader may verify), but many verbs satisfy only some of the diagnostics. For example, *relax* meets some of the stative tests:

17a. ?? What happened? I relaxed.
  b. ?? I carefully relaxed.

But some active constructions allow *relax:*

18a. Relax!
  b. I am relaxing.

The same can be said for *sit,* in the locative sense, which allows the progressive even though it otherwise is a stative: *The box is sitting in the corner,* but ?? *What the box did was sit in the corner.* How do we deal with these exceptions, especially when not all of them center on the same diagnostic test?

4.2131. Statives in the Progressive: Logical Form and Derived States

One way to deal with the exceptions is to regularize them by identifying other semantic properties that underlie the events. This is Dowty's (1979) tack in his study of *stative verbs that allow the progressive.*

Dowty (1979) notes that verbs like *lie, sit, stand,* and *rest,* which otherwise look very much like stative events, permit the progressive, although they fail to meet other tests for active events, like the pseudo-cleft:

19a. The book is lying on the table.
  b. ?? What the book did was lie on the table.
  c. The vase is sitting on the mantle.
  d. ?? What the vase did was sit on the mantle.

His solution to this problem is complicated, but we can summarize it without too much harm to his main point. Verbs that are exceptions to the progressive restriction on statives attribute a relatively temporary positional state to an entity. If (19a), for example, is put in the nonprogressive, a habitual (or nontemporary) interpretation results: *The book lies on the table.* Moreover, entities that are normally thought to occupy positions for extended periods of time do not trigger the exceptional progressive: ?? *Philadelphia is lying on the Delaware River* (cf. *Philadelphia lies on the Delaware River*).

Dowty explains these facts through Carlson's (1977) logic of generic expressions (see also fn. 13, chap. 3). Carlson's formal semantic theory has a tripartite ontology: objects (individuals), kinds (classes, types, and attributes), and stages (the temporal instantiations of objects). Dowty says that progressivizable statives are logically stages: That is, they range over temporal instantiations of objects, like actives normally do, which is why they have a temporary interpretation. In contrast, nonprogressivizable—that is, typical—statives do not range over stages, but objects, and thus have *no temporal instantiation at all:* whence their stative (temporally continuous) nature. So the verb *know,* for instance, disallows the progressive because *know* does not express a stage, a temporal instantiation of an object, but simply an attribute of an object: *Know* ranges over an entity.

Dowty proposes two kinds of statives (actually three: see 1979: 177–86): those that range over objects and entities, like *know,* and disallow the progressive; those that range over stages, like *lie,* and allow the progressive. The latter are derived by the conversion of a stage into a kind, or a generic expression, via an abstract logical operator. The insight here is the logical relation between statives and generic entities: Both are relatively timeless attributions, just that the former apply to events. Dowty notes that the stage *is lying* has a logical relation to the kind *lies.* The kind entails the stage: If Philadelphia lies on the Delaware then it is lying on the Delaware, but not vice versa. Hence the stage version, *is lying,* is more elemental, in the same way that all basic semantic properties are entailed. So Dowty proposes that the kind be semantically derived.

The exceptions are thus explained away in the formal account. An abstract generic operator derives the kind (stative) from the stage (progressive). Problems with the active/stative diagnostic tests are regularized by an appeal to other semantic properties, like the ontology in Carlson's theory.

4.2132. Degrees of Acts and States

The logical approach solves the problems by postulating additional discrete properties that interact with the extant properties to produce gradient results. Another way to approach these exceptions is to focus less on additional discrete properties that override the active/stative distinction, but instead allow for *degrees of active/stative events.* In this case, the exceptions are regularized because *some events are more active or stative than others.*

The five diagnostic tests actually define three basic characteristics. The progressive encodes *extension;* the pseudo-cleft and the What happened? test encode *unitization* of an act; the imperative, and the adverbs *deliberately* and *carefully* all single out the *execution* of the act. Seen this way, acts allow extension, unitization, and execution; states disallow these. But not all three characteristics have to be present or absent to define an active or a stative because the events are defined *preferentially,* not categorically.

There may be statives that are not unitizable and not executable, but are nonetheless extendible. These are encoded in the verbs that Dowty accounts for by logical means. As noted, *lie* allows the progressive and is extendible, but disallows the pseudo-cleft. The event encoded by *lie,* therefore, might be more properly called a *semistative.*

Likewise there are some actives that disallow the progressive (extension), although they take the tests for execution and unitization. *Remain* is such a verb:

20a. ?? I am remaining in the house.
  b. What I did was remain in the house.
  c. Remain in the house!
  d. I deliberately remained in the house.

The event expressed by *remain* might be best understood as a *semiactive:* It is unitizable and executable (much like *stay*), but it is not extendible, probably because it is inherently extended like canonical statives and thus precludes extension.

A solution such as this, in terms of a *gradience,* raises a number of other problems. One is the relative ranking of extension, execution, and unitization. Are semistatives more likely to be generated by the presence of extension (and progressive) with simultaneous absence of execution and unitization? Does the opposite hold for semiactives? Is there a scale of activity: extension > unitization/execution?

In addition, even *within these three characteristics,* some verbs allow some tests but not others. For example the semiactive *remain* allows the pseudo-cleft, but not What happened?:

A: What happened?
B:?? I remained in the house.

Does this mean that there are subtle degrees of unitization (and thus of extension and execution)?

Whatever the status of degrees of active/stative events, we should observe that such a solution returns us to one of the larger points of this book: Meaning is gradient. Extension, unitization, and execution define the active/stative distinction via a *preference rule*—a probabilistic statement about the selection of a referent in any context—that determines a scale of activity on which events may fall. The presence of semiactives and semistatives does not mean that we have abandoned absolute predictability. If we allow a number of properties in conjunction to determine successful reference, this gives us more leeway to investigate how a speaker may structure a mentally projected world to meet his communicative needs. Not all events are categorically either actions or states, just as not all events are categorically events per se because a scale of temporality underlies events proper (cf. sec. 4.1). We thus get a scale (active/stative) within a scale (eventhood via temporality).

4.214. Active Languages and the Medio-Passive:
Chickasaw and Spanish

Now that we have seen the basic semantic structure of acts and states, their surface encoding, and exceptions thereto, we briefly look at some data from languages other than English to underscore the universality of the properties. We have come to two general conclusions: Acts can be differentiated from states; the active/stative distinction is a gradient. Here we observe an example of each: the sharp distinction between acts and states in Chickasaw and degrees of activity via the Spanish medio-passive.

4.2141. Active Languages

The active/stative dichotomy is found in all the world's languages, though how it surfaces depends on the structure of the particular language in question. The straightforward encoding of active versus stative is relatively rare. The usual place to look for a clear and relatively pure encoding of active versus stative is in so-called *active languages* (see also chap. 5, under *agency*), those that morphologically differentiate acts from states by marking either the predicates or the subjects (or both) for the status of the event. A number of Amerindian and Caucasian languages distinguish active from stative in this manner.

Chickasaw has a set of subject affixes that to a large extent correlate with the active/stative semantic structure of the event expressed by the predicate. In the first-person singular, a distinction is made between the subject of an active verb (marked by the suffix *-li*) and that of a stative verb (marked by the prefix *sa-*). Although the full range of facts is much more complicated than this account suggests, with the syntax not directly mapped from the semantic distinctions (see Munro and Gordon 1982), in a number of cases, the affixes are sufficient to distinguish active and stative construals of the same conceptual content. For example, the meaning 'good' is encoded as *chokma* in Chickasaw, but a semantic difference between active or stative 'goodness' can be signalled by differentiating the affix (Munro and Gordon 1982: 84):

21a. chokma-li.
      good   Active-I
      I act good.

b. sa-   chokma.
Stative-I good
I am good.

Abstractly, each event predicates goodness of the speaker, but in (21a), the event is executed by a controlling subject: 'I behave in a good manner.' In (21b), the event is not executed by, but *attributed to,* the speaker, making a more exact gloss something like 'I have goodness.'

4.2142. Medio-passive

Whereas Chickasaw rigidly differentiates active from stative, in some languages it is possible to encode something like *a decrease in the degree of activity of an event.* In Spanish and many other languages (Italian, Russian, and Chichewa), there is a way to take a transitive verb, detransitivize it, and thereby make it semiactive. This is done in Spanish via the *medio-passive* construction, formed with the reflexive pronoun *se.* Compare the following:

22a. Juan abr- e   la   puerta.
John open 3Per/Pres the door
John opens the door.

b. Se   abr- e   la   puerta.
Refl open 3Per/Pres the door
The door is open.

Example (22a) has the full active interpretation, with the event executed by the subject. Example (22b), however, attenuates the activity of the event: 'The door has come to be in a state of openness,' where the predicate has both active and stative characteristics. Moreover, the reflexive construction in (22b) is not really a passive in the usual sense. Its voice, the syntactic relation of subject to object via the verb, is still active and can in fact be converted to a more typical passive:

23. La   puerta fué abierta por Juan.
The door   was opened by John
The door was opened by John.

The event in (23) is still semantically active, just in a syntactic passive construction. This is unlike (22b), where the reflexive produces a *semantic passive* by reducing the activity level of the event, which nonetheless has an active syntactic form.

These examples from Chickasaw and Spanish provide two lessons. First, it is possible to encode the distinction between active and stative directly, as in Chickasaw. Second, it is possible to encode degrees of activity, as in the Spanish medio-passive. Both results are in accord with our more general findings. Active languages polarize the semantic gradience into acts and states, but this does not rule out the possibility of encoding values between the poles.

4.215. Summary

This section has looked at the distinction between actives and statives, focusing on the relative temporality and internal differentiation of acts and stats. We have also observed five structural tests for actives versus statives—progressive, pseudo-cleft, What happened?, imperative, and *deliberately/carefully*—and we have remarked on the semantic motivation of these structural reflexes. The five tests do not apply uniformly to all actives and statives, forcing us to consider exceptions in two ways—as overlooked regularities (Dowty's logical solution to statives in the progressive) and as degrees of acts and states (semiactives and semistatives). Finally, we have considered some data from other languages to see differences in the surface encoding of states and acts and found that active languages sharply differentiate acts from states and that the medio-passive decreases the activity level of an event: a semantic passive.

4.22. Causes

We have discussed the semantic and structural factors associated with acts and states. Here we examine a subclass of acts: *causes,* or in their verbal form, *causatives.* Events that are causative express some *relation of determination* between two events, with a prior event resulting in or giving rise to a subsequent event. Causality is a *relation,* and thus some linguists have argued that it is not a discrete event at all (see Dowty 1979; Talmy 1985). But the relational status of an event does not thereby reduce its eventhood. Motion, for example, is also a relation between a mover and the act of moving, and it is clearly an event.

All languages encode the causative relation, and usually do so verbally. But because a causative event is a *relation between two events,* the semantic systems of languages may construe this relation more or less directly, and, given the differential encoding possibilities of languages, the causative itself may assume an independent surface form to a varying degree.

We keep these two characteristics in mind as we examine the formal structure of causatives (antecedent and consequent), the nonformal structure (figure, ground, and semantic unity), the expression of the degree of involvement of the participants in a causative event, and the directness of the cause itself.

4.221. Logical and Linguistic Accounts of Causatives

The study of causation has a long history in philosophical and logical work, and we can by no means do justice to that tradition. Instead we raise some general points about causatives distilled from the logical, philosophical, and linguistic work, always with an eye toward the specific linguistic instantiation of causation. We first look at several logical accounts, for example, Lewis's (1973) and Dowty's (1979), and then one comprehensive linguistic account, Talmy's (1976, 1985).

4.2211. The Logical Structure of Causatives

If a causative event is a relation between a precipitating event and a result, then we can analyze it by the logic of antecedence and consequence: *logical implication* (also called *material implication*). Under this view, a causative event is abstractly an *if/then relation:* underlying the causative expression *Mary forced Bill to get a job* is the logical form $X \rightarrow Y$: 'If Mary forced Bill, then Bill got a job.'

This is an appealing solution because it captures the implicational dependency that characterizes causative relations, but, unfortunately, that is about all. Consider the expression *Smoking causes cancer.* Phenomenologically, there is a dependency between smoking and cancer, but the translation of that dependency into logical form, 'if smoking, then cancer,' misses a great deal. For one thing, smoking does *not necessarily result* in cancer, so the implication simply does not hold. If we can somehow restrict the semantic space between X and Y and thus force the precipitating and resulting events to be more related, we can perhaps salvage the implicational account of causatives.

Such a restriction is essentially what Lewis (1973) and Stalnaker (1968) propose. In these accounts, causative events are implicational, but *negative*—to rule out intervening factors—and conceived of in the *closest possible world* to limit the domain further: more formally, $-X \rightarrow -Y$, in the closest possible world.[4] Consider, for example, the events represented by *Rain increases water reserves.* Simple material implication fails to capture the causal dependency involved because 'if rain then increase in water reserves,' is not always true. If the ground is hard and the water runs off after the rain, we have rain and no increase in water reserves. But if we view the events negatively, we get a better result. If there is no rain, then there is no increase in water reserves: $-X \rightarrow -Y$. (Alternatively, it is impossible to have both no rain and an increase in water reserves *and* rain and no increase in water reserves: see fn. 4.)

But note that 'if no rain then no increase in water reserves' ($-X \rightarrow -Y$) still does not get all the facts straight. There may still be an increase in water reserves without any rain: That is, 'if no rain, then no increase in water reserves' might be false if, for instance, there is an unpredicted rise in the water table. To eliminate

---

[4]The rationale here is that causative events are relations of *necessity* and *sufficiency* within some well-defined universe of discourse that limits the range of necessity and sufficiency. To say that a precipitating event is both necessary and sufficient for a resulting event is to say that it is impossible to have both *no precipitating event* and *the resulting event* and a *precipitating event* and *no resulting event:* more formally, Impossible (not-e & e) & (e & not-e) (see Miller and Johnson-Laird 1976: 498).

such possibilities, we make the following stipulation: *in the closest possible world.* That is, in the closest possible world of rain impinging on the water reserves, without rain, there is no increase in the water reserves.

Once more, a little thought shows some problems with this formal account. For one thing, a great deal hangs on what is meant by *closest possible world.* If we have to specify the nature of the causative relation to begin with (e.g., in the connection between rain and water reserves), doesn't this beg the question? In any case, there are still examples that fall outside of this formal account, even accepting its restrictions. Reconsider *Smoking causes cancer,* now rendered 'if no smoking then no cancer in the closest possible world between smoking and cancer.' This does not rule out the possibility of developing cancer in spite of not smoking, even by restricting the facts to the closest possible world, say to *lung cancer:* 'If no smoking, then no *lung* cancer.' Again, this is not true. Asbestos may cause lung cancer in people who have never smoked. We might respond to this counter by limiting the closest possible world even further, to those worlds where smoking and lung cancer both occur in relation to each other. But then we really beg the question, because *the causative issue is the very relation between smoking and lung cancer to begin with!* Restricting the possible world in this way just pushes the solution back, and does so in a harmful way, because it produces a tautology—smoking that causes lung cancer results in lung cancer!

In response to objections like these, Dowty (1979; see also McCawley 1976 and 1981: 316) proposes that causal relations be viewed as *reversed negative implications in the closest possible world.* The problem with negative implication is its heavy reliance on the precipitating event *at the expense of the resulting event.* The crux of causatives, however, lies in the *results* they produce, not the causes. Arguably, it is impossible even to identify a causative event unless there is a result, regardless of the cause.

The logical structure of causatives is thus: $-Y \rightarrow -X$, in the closest possible world. *Rain increases water reserves* is derived from 'if no increase in water reserves, then no rain, in the closest possible world of rain and water reserves.' This seems to work quite well because it allows the result to be differentially caused, depending on how the closest possible world is determined. The same holds for the causal relation between smoking and cancer: In the closest possible world that you don't develop cancer, you don't smoke.

In reversing the implication and focusing on the results, Dowty's proposal loosens the logical criteria and allows for *possibility rather than strict dependence.* That is, it makes the connection a preferential relation between cause and effect and sidesteps the inflexibility of logical accounts of causality.

We want more flexibility because *semantic causes* may not exactly match up with either logical causes or physical causes. *Smoking causes cancer* can be semantically expressed, but only problematically put into logical form because the logical accounts ultimately try to tie causality to necessity and sufficiency. A proposal like Dowty's thus goes some way toward meshing logical and non-logical accounts of causatives because we want to be able to say that causation is not a categorical dependency, but a *preferential result.*

It is a tack such as this that motivates a purely linguistic account of causatives. When we look at Talmy's (1976, 1985) work, we see that it accommodates both the logical and the "looser" empirical facts.

4.2212. The Linguistic Structure of Causatives

In two studies of causation in language, Talmy (1976, 1985) proposes an account of the structure of prototypical causatives that is nonformal but still sensitive to the logical facts. In his theory, causation is not an abstract predicate (or an operator, as in Dowty's work), but a relationship. Specifically, causatives involve the relation of a *precipitating event* (Ep) and a *resulting event* (Er). Two basic issues surround this structure that determine the major semantic facts associated with causatives:

1. the nature of the shared information that constitutes the relationship of Ep and Er;
2. the way the entities that carry out the causative events are involved in Ep and Er.

The term *causative* thus does not refer to a discrete event or even to an abstract logical structure; rather, it is a cover term for a particular arrangement of information shared by two events and the orientation of participants to those events.

4.22121. *Shared Information of Ep and Er*

In all causatives, Ep and Er must have things in common. First of all, in canonical causatives, there must be *unity of cause and effect,* and Ep must be *semantically near* enough to Er in order for successful causation to occur. So (24a) expresses a more prototypical causative than (24b):

24a. The bike fell from the ball hitting it.
  b. ?? The bike fell from the ball hitting the car.

The oddity of (24b) lies in the fact that the connection between Ep ('the ball hitting the car') and Er ('the bike falling') is tenuous in normal circumstances. Of course, because we are not making categorical claims, (24b) is by no means absolutely ruled out, but, crucially, in order for it to be sensible as a causative, Ep ('the ball hitting the car') *must be construed* as *not remote from* Er ('the bike falling').

Along the same lines, there is typically *unity of circumstance* (time and space) and *participants* (doers and receivers). Note the anomaly of the following:

25. ?? The bike fell today from the ball hitting it yesterday.

The unity of temporal circumstance for Ep and Er is disturbed from the assignment of different times to Ep and Er (*today* and *yesterday*, respectively). Example (24b) can be made acceptable if the participants are united:

26. The bike fell from the ball hitting the car and glancing off onto it (the bike).

These points about unity are analogous to the logical escape clause of "the closest possible world." Talmy is just more specific about what *closeness* means: *unity of event-structure*. So, the expression *Smoking causes cancer* may represent a causative event if the Ep ('smoking') is not remote from the Er ('cancer') in terms of cause and effect, circumstance, or participant. This is equivalent to, and more explicit than, logical attempts to restrict the semantic domain.

4.22122. *Involvement of Entities in Ep and Er*

The second structural feature of causatives is the *orientation of participants to the events* via their *Figure/Ground relationships*. Every event can be thought of as an abstract scene in which the entities that participate in the event can either *emerge as salient*—Figure—or *recede* and form part of the background—Ground. Compare the following:

27a. The car is near the tree.
  b. The tree is near the car.

In the events of (27), the car and tree have equal logical status: If the car is near the tree, then the tree is near the car, and vice versa. But the car and tree are *oriented differently* with respect to each other and the event expressed: In (27a), the car (Figure) conceptually stands out in relation to the tree (Ground); in (27b) the Figure/Ground relationships are reversed (see chap. 5).

In canonical causatives, *the Ground of the Ep becomes the Figure of the Er*, or the entity that is part of the background of the precipitating event itself becomes the salient or emergent participant in the resulting event. This is why causes seem to have effects: Something that is acted on (Ground) then emerges (Figure) as a consequence of being acted on. Consider (28):

28. Tom shot the arrow.

Example (28) may be glossed 'Tom acted on the arrow, by shooting it, such that the arrow flew through the air.' The Figure of the Ep is Tom, and the Ground is the arrow: that is, 'Tom acted on the arrow, by shooting it.' But in the Er, the arrow is the Figure, 'the arrow flew through the air.' The crux of the causative event thus appears to lie in *the conversion of an entity acted on into an entity that acts*. Hence *Tom shot the arrow*, like all causative expressions, is abstractly: Ground$_{ep}$ → Figure $_{er}$.

This requirement of a Figure/Ground shift is a nonformal way of describing the formal observations of Dowty, Lewis, and others. The most adequate formal account of causatives focuses on the resulting event, and Talmy's theory fits nicely with this finding because the Figure/Ground shift likewise centers on the resulting event. The Ep's Ground must *execute the resulting event*, Er, for causation to occur. So both the formal and nonformal accounts are compatible on this point, though the nonformal account provides more specifics about how the resulting event is affected by the causation.

Talmy (1976, 1985) and others note how this basic causative structure can interact with other semantic properties of the events and participants to produce a variety of causative types. For example, if the Er is a motion event whose Figure moves as the result of a sudden impulse, the causative is known as a *ballistic causative*, such as *launch, shoot, fire, blast off*, and *throw*. If the Figure and Ground of the Ep and the Figure of the Er are *all the same*, then there is the *self-agentive causative*, as in *I walked home*, 'I performed an act on myself such that I walked home': cf. *walk, run, swim*, and so on (see Shibatani 1976; Talmy 1976, 1985).

Although the interaction of causative structure with other semantic properties produces a variety of semantic causative types, we are primarily interested in *causative structure per se*. We have seen how this structure can be described in terms of its logical form: logical implication, negation, reversed negation, and the closest possible world. We have also seen how a nonformal account provides additional details of causative structure while still accommodating the logical facts: unity of Ep and Er and Figure/Ground reversal in the connection of Ep and Er. Let us now consider the structural reflexes of causation and how more subtle details of this semantic structure take surface form.

4.222. *The Encoding of Causatives*

The surface form of causatives has two basic characteristics:

1. encoding of the *directness of the relation* of Ep and Er;
2. encoding of the *degree of involvement* of the participants in Ep and Er.

These two features readily follow from Talmy's analysis of causative structure as a whole. The first characteristic is a restatement of his claim about the unity of Ep and Er: how directly the precipitating event impinges on the resulting event. The second characteristic is a broader phrasing of Talmy's claim that causatives are associated with Figure/Ground shifts, only now we understand it as a condition on the nature of the involvement of *all* the participants in the events underlying causative expressions. More simply, we are concerned not only with the directness of the causation but also the directness of the *causer* and *causees*.

4.2221.   Directness of Ep and Er

Consider the difference between the following two sentences:

29a. Fred moved the vase.
  b. Fred made the vase move.

Both express the same causative event—'Fred did something to the vase (Ground) such that the vase (Figure) then moved'—but the directness of the Ep to the Er is not the same in each. In the situation expressed by (29a), Fred's actions cause the vase to move directly; in those of (29b), however, Fred's actions seem less imposing on the moving of the vase. Nonetheless in each there is distinct causation.

We find analogues to (29) in many other languages. Bemba has the following alternation (from Givón 1976: 332):

30a. Naa-ship- ishya Mwape.
  I   brave Cause Mwape
  I emboldened Mwape.
  Lit. I braved Mwape.
  b. Naa-leenga Mwape uku-shipa.
  I   made Mwape be   brave
  I made Mwape brave.

Example (30a) expresses a direct relation between the Ep and Er; in (30b), the precipitating event indirectly impinges on the result.

The distinction between direct and indirect causation has been the subject of a fair amount of work in linguistics (Comrie 1981; Shibatani 1976), where it is termed *manipulative causation* (direct) and *directive causation* (indirect). To avoid terminological difficulties, we use the terms *direct* and *indirect*. The difference between direct and indirect causation motivates a universal distinction in surface form. The degree of overtness of the expression of the causative event proper correlates with the directness of the relation between the Ep and Er. In other words, if the causative construction is *periphrastic* (many forms for the expression of a single meaning), or *polymorphemic* (surfacing in many forms), the Ep/Er relation overwhelmingly tends to be indirect; conversely, if the causative construction is *monomorphemic* and *lexical* (or *nonperiphrastic*), the Ep/Er relation tends to be direct. Examples (30a) and (30b) support this principle. In Bemba, the indirect causative, *naa-leenga* ('I made'), is periphrastic, with the causative event ('make') expressed as a separate form; the direct causative is not periphrastic: *naa-ship-ishya* (I-cause-brave) is one word.

Japanese is a frequently cited example of this correlation between surface form and directness of causation. Japanese has a lexical causative, where the causative event is fused into the verbal stem and, as expected, is a direct causative, and it has a periphrastic causative, where the causative event surfaces as a bound morpheme that expresses indirect causation (Shibatani 1976).

This difference in directness of causation, as signalled by relative overtness of surface encoding, has an additional effect on the grammar that recalls the discussion of animacy in Chapter 3. In periphrastic or indirect causatives, the *causee*, the entity carrying out the result (i.e., the entity that is the Ground in the Ep and the Figure in the Er), *must be animate* (see Shibatani 1976):

31. ?? Boku wa hon o   oti- sase- ta.
    I   Top book Obj drop make past
    ?? I made the book fall down (indirect cause).

Example (31) is unacceptable because of the inanimacy of *hon* ('book'). But if we make the causee animate or convert the periphrastic causative structure to a lexical or direct structure, the construction becomes acceptable:

32. Boku wa hon o   otosi-ta.
    I   Top book Obj drop past
    I dropped the book (direct cause).

The logic behind this grammatical effect is fairly straightforward. If the connection between the Ep and Er is direct (and hence lexically expressed), the status of the causee for animacy does not matter. Lexical causatives in Japanese take either animate or inanimate causees because the directness of the causation precludes any independent action by the causee: The causee has no choice but to carry out the consequences of the Ep. On the other hand, when there is an indirect connection between the Ep and Er, as in periphrastic causatives, the causee has some leeway to carry out the act precipitated by the causer because of the very indirectness. In this case, the animacy of the causee *should matter*. As we know, animate entities are more likely than inanimate entities to have influence and the potency to execute acts. Consequently in a situation where a choice can be made to execute the act, animate entities ought to be conditioned to appear as the causee. To put the matter in slightly different terms, if there is a choice to be made in executing an act, it stands to reason that an inanimate entity should be disallowed in the position to execute the choice. Japanese grammar follows suit here, with the grammatical facts closely aligned with the semantic characteristics.

Japanese is by no means alone in respecting a close connection between the semantics and syntax of causatives, and the animacy condition is not the only further structural ramification of the directness of the connection between Ep and Er. Periphrastic causatives frequently allow a loosening of the unity of time, place, and participants that characterizes causative events as a whole, as the following demonstrate:

33a. John, who was in the kitchen, made the vase, which was in the living room, move. (indirect cause, disunity of place)
  b. ?? John, who was in the kitchen, moved the vase, which was in the living room. (direct cause, disunity of place)

As in the case of the animacy condition on the causee in Japanese, the loosening of unity in indirect causatives has a pretty straightforward explanation. Indirect causatives express causation through more than one explicit event (e.g., *make* + *move*), and so the permitted disunity of place in (33) is a function of the presence of additional events that can have additional places and times within their scope. That is, because indirect causatives tend to be expressed with multiple surface forms, additional locations of events (and hence times and participants) can therefore associate with these additional events.

Thus, we see that a number of structural facts follow from the first semantic feature motivating encoding. Directness and indirectness of causation correlate with degree of overt form, and this affects such things as the nature of the participants in the causative event and the structural unity of the events that compose a causative event as a whole.

4.2222. Degree of Involvement of Participants in Ep and Er.

The second semantic characteristic that motivates the surface form of causatives is the degree of involvement of the participants in the events that compose the larger causative expression. *Degree of involvement* is illustrated by the following sentences:

34a. The nurse had the patient move.
  b. The nurse had the patient moved.

The expressions in (34) are indirect causatives, because they are periphrastic, but the degree to which the nurse and the patient are involved in the events varies. In the precipitating events of (34), the nurse does not act directly in the precipitating event. Both could be true, for example, if the nurse simply brought the patient's movement about by administrative order. Hence the causer in (34) is not directly involved in the precipitating event.

Similar results hold in a comparison of the resulting events in (34), where there is differential involvement of the patient (the causee) in the event of moving. In the events of (34a), the patient carries out some act as a consequence of the nurse's indirect cause. But in (34b), the patient seems to be even less involved in the events, and an appropriate gloss for (34b) is something to the effect of 'the nurse brought it about (e.g., by issuing a directive) that somebody else move the patient.' In Figure/Ground terms, we might say that the patient is, as required, the Figure of the Er in both (34a) and (34b), because the patient does the moving, but in (34a), the patient seems *more of a Figure* than in (34b). Example (34b) represents the causee as less involved in the Er, under less direct control of the causer.[5]

Many other languages explicitly encode these distinctions in involvement, most often by signalling reduced involvement of the causee by a change in grammatical case (see, e.g., Cole 1983). For example, in Hungarian, if the causee has little control over the resulting events, and hence is *more involved in and affected by* the Ep, the noun representing the causee is marked by the accusative (Hetzron 1976):

35. Lemondattam őt   az elnökségről.
    I-cause-resign him (Acc) the presidency
    I caused him to resign the presidency.

The situation of (35) is such that the causer directly affects the actions of the causee, for example, by deliberately forcing the resignation, and so the causee, őt ('him'), is marked in the accusative case, indicating less involvement in the resulting event of resigning (alternatively, more control by the causer over the causee in the precipitating event). However, if the situation is such that the causee retains some control over the resulting act (and hence is less involved in the Ep), the causee is encoded in the instrumental case:

36. Lemondattam vele   az elnökségről.
    I-cause-resign him (Instr) the presidency
    I had him resign the presidency.
    More exactly: I had something to do with him resigning the
       presidency.

---

[5]Note that degree of involvement is not the same as directness of causation:

i. The nurse moved the patient.

ii. The nurse made the patient move.

Moved expresses a direct causative in lexical form and *made move* expresses an indirect causative in periphrastic form. But although the strength of the causal relation expressed by each differs, the degree of involvement of the events' causer (the nurse) and causee (the patient) is constant. In both situations, the nurse directly enacts the causing even though the relation between that causing and the effect of moving may be indirect.

The *instrumental* here marks *less involvement of the causee in the Ep;* converse-ly, the *accusative* encodes *more involvement of the causee in the Ep* (see chap. 5 for more discussion of grammatical case and semantic involvement).

We can state fairly simply the full range of possibilities available for degree of involvement of causer and causee: high involvement of the causer or causee (what we might label *Causer+* and *Causee+*) or low involvement of the causer and causee (*Causer−* and *Causee−*). In principle, a language could encode all four of these options as independent structures, as listed here:[6]

1. Causer+ and Causee+ (high involvement of each)
2. Causer− and Causee− (low involvement of each)
3. Causer+ and Causee− (high Causer and low Causee)
4. Causer− and Causee+ (low Causer and high Causee)

In at least one language, Hindi, all four are encoded (Saksena 1982.) In Hindi, degree of involvement of the causer is signalled by a verbal marker of degree of causation. High involvement of the causer (Causer+) requires the Direct Causative *aa;* low involvement of the causer (Causer−) requires the Indirect Causative, *vaa.* Degree of involvement of the causee is encoded by grammatical case. High involvement (or affectedness) of the causee (Causee+) is encoded by either the accusative or dative case, *koo* or Ø; low involvement of the causee (Causee−) is signalled by the instrumental, *see.* This gives us four encoding possibilities:

1. Causer+ and Causee+: *aa/koo* or Ø
2. Causer+ and Causee−: *aa/see*
3. Causer− and Causee+: *vaa/koo* or Ø
4. Causer− and Causee−: *vaa/see*

The following examples from Hindi illustrate these choices (Hindi is SOV, so the causee precedes the causer):

37a. mãĩ-nee raam-koo   khaanaa khil-aa-   yaa.
     I   Agt Ram Causee+ food   eat Causer+ past
     I fed Ram dinner.

   b. mãã-nee naukar- see   kaam kar-aa-   yaa.
     I   Agt servant Causee- work do Causer+ Past
     I made it that the servant did the work.

---

[6]These possibilities refer to the structure of the Ep, the causation itself, and thereby affect the causative event as a whole. Generalizations about involvement of participants are restricted to the Ep for two reasons. First, the Ep is the only constituent event of the causative that shares participants:

c. māī-nee raam-koo   khaanaa khil-vaa-   yaa.
   I   Agt Ram Causee+ food   eat Causer- Past
   I had Ram eat dinner.

d. māī-nee naukar- see   kaam kar-vaa-   yaa
   I   Agt servant Causee- work do Causer- Past
   I had the servant get the work done.

The English glosses do not do justice to the semantic detail. In the situation of (37a), there is high involvement of each (the causer controls the causee), and so the interpretation is a prototypical causative: *fed* means 'caused to eat.' In the events of (37b), the involvement of the causee is attenuated, allowing the causee more control over the resulting event. English does not have an exact correlate of this, but the gloss captures the idea that the causer acts fully while the causee retains some independence from the Ep. In the events of (37c), the causer's involvement is attenuated, but the causee's involvement remains high. This is the Hindi analogue of the typical periphrastic English causative with deemphasis on the causer (*had X do Y,* e.g.). Finally, in the situation of (37d), both the causer and causee have their involvement attenuated, the effect of which is to suggest a semantically passivized causative: 'I brought it about such that the servant brought it about that the work got done.'

Saksena (1982) notes that there are further semantic and pragmatic restrictions on these constructions, such as the fact that Causer+ and Causee− encodings are conditioned by the nature and surface form of the Er. The verb for 'teach' in Hindi, for instance, cannot take Causer+ and Causee− because it is mono-morphemic (and hence direct causation) and logically requires immediate uptake by the causee. (There is apparently no such thing as 'made him be taught' in Hindi). Nonetheless, in spite of the restrictions, Hindi is a clear case of the full possibilities of the encoding of involvement.

These examples bring us full circle in our study of linguistic causation. Facts like these necessitate an account of the semantics of causation different from that available in formal terms because we have to be sensitive to the specific constituents, by degree, that make up causation as a semantic dependency between a precipitating and resulting event.

The causer is the Figure of the Ep and absent from the Er; the causee is the Ground of the Ep and the Figure of the Er. So, *only in the Ep are the participants relative to each other,* and thus only there can relative involvement in the event be judged. Second, there are certain redundancies of participants with regard to the Ep and Er. Causee+ in the Ep typically implies Causee− in the Er. That is, a directly involved causee, under the control of the causer in the precipitating event, in turn implies a causee with less control over the resulting event. It is this logic that underlies the Hungarian accusative, which signals less involvement of the causee in the Er (though more involvement in the Ep). Similarly, Causee− in the Ep suggests Causee+ in the Er. Such a relation underlies the instrumental case in Hungarian for the causee, where the causee is under less control of the causer and hence more involved in the Er.

4.223. Summary

We have examined the relational semantic structure of causatives, looking at both formal and linguistic accounts. The logical view of causation as an implication between two events in the closest possible world takes us some distance toward a thorough account of the semantic representation of causatives, but we have seen the value of Talmy's view of causatives as a relation between an Ep and Er with a Figure/Ground shift. Two properties of causatives—directness of causation and degree of involvement of participants—have a systematic effect on the way that causatives surface in language. Directness of causation (i.e., nearness of the Ep to the Er) correlates with monomorphemic or lexical causative form; periphrastic causatives correlate with indirect causation. Participant involvement also follows an encoding scale, with involvement of the causer and causee often marked by a shift in grammatical relation. Hindi provides the limiting case in this respect by encoding the full range of causer/causee involvement.

4.23. Motion

Now that we have examined actives, statives, and one subclass of actives—causatives—we describe an event type that cuts a bit more broadly across events as a whole, though in its usual form it is, like causatives, predominantly associated with actives rather than statives: *motion*. Obviously motion is bound up with space in general (see chap. 6); nonetheless, there are some distinct aspects of motion that require discussion in terms of events, like a time interval. So, the mere fact of space, which otherwise seems static, does not preclude event structure.

In what follows, we describe the difference between static and dynamic motion (position vs. movement) and the structure of motion as displacement of an entity. We briefly describe eight semantic factors bearing on displacement—theme, source, goal, path, site, cause, manner, and conveyance—and look at how these factors are differentially encoded, especially with regard to universal conditions on their fusion into the verb of motion.

4.231. Movement Versus Position

When we speak of *motion,* we normally mean 'movement,' but not all spatial events have to involve movement per se: *The boy sat against the wall.* This event is a semiactive, passing all the active tests except What happened? (?? *What happened? The boy sat against the wall:* cf. *The boy is sitting against the wall.*) But the expression still involves a spatial event and a time interval, though the movement is pretty much indiscernible. When spatial events make reference to statives and semiactives, the result is a *positional event* or a *location* (see Gruber

1976). This is why semanticists often claim that there are no motional statives. There simply cannot be motional statives because stativity is incompatible with *dynamic movement through space,* but not incompatible with *static position in space.*

Following tradition, we concern ourselves, for the most part, with movement. Fortunately, the majority of our observations also hold for nonmotional spatial events: both take direction, for example (*I flew back, I sat back*). We just have to be sensitive to the fact that when we talk about the structure of a motional event, we also include *dynamism* (to whatever degree), and this affects the other semantic components of the events.

4.232. The Structure of Motion: Displacement and its Attendant Properties

Motion entails the *displacement* of some entity, or *positional change,* by which we mean '*conceptually relevant* positional change.' Obviously, in terms of physics, every entity is in constant positional change, but this does not thereby prohibit nonmotional events in the ordinary semantic universe. Positional change is also relative to the grain of analysis in effect. If a person is sitting in a chair and twisting his torso continually, he is not thereby not sitting simply because of attendant positional change. Compare the event of walking, which requires positional change of the whole entity as an essential feature.

The elemental structure of a motion event is abstractly *Displace(x).* But expression of the bare motion event seems quite untypical:

38 a. The dog moved.
   b. My family traveled.
   c. Fred went.

Even in (38c), the minimal motion event of 'go' implies something about the *direction* of the motion. It is difficult, in fact, to use *Fred went* to mean motion toward the speaker in the here-and-now:

39 a. ?? Fred went here.
   b. ?? Fred went to me.
   c. ?? Fred went from over there toward me.

Motion events are invariably analyzed with regard to constituents of motion beyond the core notions of displacement of an entity because of such facts (Gruber 1976; Jackendoff 1983; Miller and Johnson-Laird 1976; Talmy 1975, 1985).

The full semantic structure of motion requires the specification of *eight semantic properties* in addition to displacement itself:

1. the thing displaced: theme or figure
2. the origin of the motion: source
3. the destination of the motion: goal
4. the trajectory of the motion: path, including direction
5. the location of the motion: site and medium
6. the means by which the motion is carried out: instrument or conveyance
7. the way the motion is carried out: manner
8. the cause of the motion: agent

In practice, languages allow their speakers to express some of these notions inherently in other forms, thus reducing the sheer quantity of expression of a full motion event. Nonetheless, it is possible to encode each separately.

Here we examine the gist of these eight features, their relative centrality to motion as a whole, and the universal conditions on their encoding. In doing so, we can kill two birds with one stone: We can see the more detailed semantic structure of motion and, at the same time, get a picture of the expected grammatical reflexes of this structure. Our description of the encoding facts is guided (though not uncritically) by Talmy's (1985) hierarchy of inherent coding in motion events.

4.2321. Theme or Figure

Every motion event involves a *displaced entity,* called the *theme* (roughly the *figure* in Talmy's work, or the conceptually salient entity: see p. 162). In English, as in the majority of the world's languages, it is normal to encode the theme *separately from the event,* as in *Tom threw the ball* or *The bird flew,* where the displaced entities, 'ball' and 'bird,' surface independently (Talmy 1985: 72–4). There are instances, however, of the theme fused into the verb, as in *It rained last night* ('rain was displaced last night'), where the theme, 'rain,' is inherent in the predicate. Compare *It rained onto the porch last night,* where the locative phrase *onto the porch* picks out the theme by assigning its movement a resulting site.

This fusion of the theme into the weather expression is a quirk of English. In Polish, the standard expression for the event of raining *must encode the theme separately:*

40. pada   deszcz.
    falls rain
    It's raining.
    More exactly: Rain falls.
    (cf. ? pada 'it falls,' with no weather implied)

Talmy (1985) argues that in Atsugewi and Navajo, it is quite common to fuse themes more generally into the motion event, a procedure, he says, that is not particularly productive for the Indo-European languages. This broader conclusion should perhaps be tempered with some concern for *relative rarity*. With a little thought, we can come up with a number of verbs in English that fuse the theme and the motion:

41a. Tom buttered the bread. ('displaced butter onto the bread')
  b. Fred painted the wall. ('displaced paint onto the wall')
  c. The workers paved the road. ('displaced tar onto the road')
  d. The farmer seeded his fields. ('displaced seed onto his fields')

Depending how motion itself is construed, the following arguably have fused themes:

42a. Bill lectured. ('displaced words')
  b. Ellen hinted. ('displaced a secret')

Nonetheless, if Talmy's generalization, properly constrained, is true, its logic is easy to trace. Displacement itself is embodied in the theme, so it stands to reason that the theme will be encoded separately. The motional event is constituted by two basic features of displacement and the entity displaced, and the separate encoding of each is the unmarked case.

4.2322. Source and Goal

In all languages it is possible to encode both the origin of the motion, the *source*, and the destination of the motion, the *goal*. The following expression makes this clear:

43. John ran from the back door to the front door.

Talmy (1985) groups source and goal into one category: *ground* (the entity that the figure moves with reference to: see p. 162). So, in (42), the source, 'back door,' and the goal 'front door,' are the entities in relation to which the figure, 'John,' moves.

From detailed cross-linguistic work, Talmy (1985) argues that in no language does the ground fuse with the verb to form part of the language's basic means to express motion. This is because the ground is the backdrop of the motion event, what Talmy calls the *unvarying component in a situation*, and its conceptual importance thus dictates an individuated form.

This restriction, like the previous one on fused themes, may be more a matter of *degree of the specificity of the ground* and the pragmatic circumstances of expression than the semantic structure of motion itself. We certainly can form English expressions where the ground is fused into the verb, as, from Talmy's paper, *The passengers deplaned* ['passengers (figure) displaced themselves with reference to a plane (ground)']. So the process seems much more productive than Talmy is ready to acknowledge. Sources and goals can easily fuse:

> 44a. Ellen boxed the books. ('displaced into a box')
>   b. We housed the product in Iowa. ('displaced into a storage area')
>   c. The police exhumed the body. ('displaced from the ground')

Spanish provides some clear comparative examples of these points. In many Spanish verbs, the ground can be expressed in a fused form, with the verb root signalling both the motion and the ground, and a prefix differentiating source from goal:

> 45a. La policia en-carcel-ó   a-   l   prisionero.
>   the police in jail   3Per/Past Animate the prisoner
>   The police jailed the prisoner (emprisoned).
>   b. La policia ex-   carcel-ó   a-   l   prisionero.
>   the police out of jail   3Per/Past Animate the prisoner
>   The police released the prisoner from jail.

The verb root *carcel* expresses both the ground, 'prison,' and the action; the prefix *en-* marks the goal and *ex-* the source. English has constructions analogous to (45a), *emprison, jail,* but there is no equivalent for (45b): ?? *dejail,* ?? *exjail,* ?? *deprison.*

4.2323. Location

Related to source and goal, insofar as these are spatial locales, is *location,* or the *fixed site* of a motion event. Under location we also include the *medium* in which a motion event takes place because the medium often expresses the general surroundings of an event, as in *We swam through the waves* and *My hat flew through the air.*

In English it is common to express location as a separate form, no doubt because location is less inherent to the motional event itself, unlike, say, a theme, source, or goal. But it is possible to think of verbs with fused locations if we limit the context so that the location is then pragmatically predictable. Take the verb *orbit,* whose normal location is celestial space. Example (46) is anomalous because the noncelestial location contrasts with the inherent location of the verb:

> 46. ?? The fly orbited my finger. (cf. The planets orbited the sun.)

In contrast, the medium appears to be more frequently fused into the verb probably because the medium is part of the expected general locale of a motional event. Arguably, *swim* and *fly* encode not only motion of a particular sort, but motion that takes place *in a specific medium: swim* normally evokes 'water' and *fly* evokes 'air.' But in Kobon, the expression for 'swim' *necessarily makes reference to the medium* (Davies 1981: 244):

47. ñig   pak.
    water strike
    swim.

In Kobon, the verb has compositional meaning, derived from forms that mean 'strike' and 'water.' Thus, in Kobon, 'swimming' is close to the denotation of English *splash*.

4.2324. Path

A frequently encoded feature of a motion event is *the trajectory of the theme*, technically known as the *path*. English encodes a variety of paths, with specific semantic features, as the following expressions indicate:

48a. I went along the river.
  b. I went by the river.
  c. I went across the river.

Along denotes parallelism of the trajectory of the motion and the ground; *by* denotes that the theme merely passes the ground; *across* denotes a bounded path 'from one side to the other.'
　　What are the possible paths of motion in any language? We can get an answer by looking at the relative contribution of three factors that compose all paths (see Talmy 1983):

1. the nature of the figure (the entity trajected along the path)
2. the nature of the ground (the reference object for the trajectory)
3. the nature of the trajectory itself[7]

4.23241. Figure

In all languages, the nature of the figure is the least important factor in the determination of paths. Many of the figure's semantic properties that otherwise are crucial to linguistic structure—for example, dimensionality, animacy, and

---

[7]A fourth factor may be the connection between the figure and ground via the trajectory (e.g., nearness, contact, and so on). We do not consider these factors here.

countability—often fail to contribute to the selection of the path. Thus, we can predicate *across* of a linear, nonlinear, animate, inanimate, countable, or noncountable figure:

49a. The golf ball went across the road. (nonlinear, inanimate, countable figure: golf ball)
b. The alligator went across the road. (linear, animate, countable figure: alligator)
c. Some gasoline went across the road. (as in an accident) (nonlinear, inanimate, noncountable figure: gasoline)

4.23242. Ground

Such unrestrictiveness is not the case, however, for the ground, whose internal semantic properties often control choice of path. English draws a distinction between liquid and solid entities as the ground in the selection of certain paths:

50a. The alligator went inside the box.
b. ?? The alligator went inside the water.

The only difference between (50a) and (50b) is the nature of the ground; apparently the path expression *inside,* 'a trajectory past the boundary and to the interior of the ground,' is restricted to nonliquids. The test case is an entity (as ground) with either a liquid or solid state. Only the solid-state interpretation is acceptable if *inside* is the path:

51a. The knife went inside the block of chocolate.
b. ?? The knife went inside the pool of chocolate.

This restriction on *inside* is a *semantic fact* about English and not a phenomenological derivative. There is nothing about liquids per se that makes them less reliable containers than solids. It is just that English *construes them this way.*

Countability of the ground also affects the choice of path in English, as *between* shows:

52a. The ant ran between the plates. (count)
b. ?? The ant ran between the hamburger. (mass)

It is understandable that the ground should matter more semantically than the figure in the long run. After all, it is the ground that provides the reference point for the movement of the figure: There can be a ground with no figure, but it is difficult to imagine a figure with no ground.

4.23243. *Trajectory*

In addition to features of the figure and ground, the nature of the trajectory itself matters to the selection of the expression of path. Curvature, boundedness, and interioricity all affect the nature of the path, as the following expressions respectively illustrate:

53a. Magellan circumnavigated the globe. (curvature)
  b. The dog ran across the street. (boundedness)
  c. Tom ran in the gym. (interioricity)

In the event of (53a), Magellan's motion traces out a curved path, as signalled by the prefix *circum*. In those of (53b), the dog's running has a path bounded by the lateral borders of the street: 'from one side to the other' (cf. *The dog ran over the street* and *The dog ran through the street*). In the events of (53c), Tom runs in the interior traced out by the gym.

4.23244. *Incorporation of Paths*

The nature of paths feeds back into their regularities in encoding. According to Talmy (1985), paths are the most likely component of a motion event to be incorporated into the event in overt expression. In fact, the degree to which a language incorporates its paths—however that is to be measured—is held by Talmy to be something of a yardstick by which to evaluate the structural differentiation of languages. He claims that the Germanic languages (English, German, Dutch, etc.) tend to incorporate path into motion much less than the Romance languages, and these in contrast to the Semitic, Polynesian, and Amerindian languages.

We can see Talmy's point with a short comparison of Spanish and English:

54a. Sub-   í   la   escalera.
    move up I/Past the stair
    I went up the stairs
  b. Baj-   é   la   escalera.
    move down I/Past the stair
    I went down the stairs.

The verb roots *sub-* and *baj-* in Spanish inherently encode the path, respectively upward and downward direction of the figure in relation to the ground. A number of other Spanish verbs do likewise: *entrar* 'move in,' *salir* 'move out,' *juntar* 'move together,' and *cruzar* 'move across.' In English, however, the normal means of phrasing these notions is in separate forms: *go up, go down, go out of, go into, go across,* and so on.

In spite of the immediate evidence, we should be careful about a generalization such as Talmy's. This difference in encoding between Spanish and English apparently holds only for colloquial speech. More formal English does have a number of verbs that inherently express the path, *ascend, descend, enter, join, cross,* though these are all borrowed from French, which is like Spanish. Furthermore, it is possible to express paths in a *nonincorporated form in Spanish:*

> 55. La gente se va.
>   the people Refl go
>   The people are going away.

The reflexive pronoun *se* in this case indicates motion away from the ground by the figure. So the incorporated form is not the only possible construction in Spanish. In other words, this difference between Spanish and English—and between Romance and Germanic languages more generally—is a matter of degree and depends on many factors, including the register of speech.

More importantly, Talmy points out that paths are universally allowed to appear in bound or inherent form in motion verbs. No doubt this is because the path seems to be an integral part of the motion event itself and thus can be recovered from the nature of the motion expressed. Such productivity in bound form of the path is a characteristic feature of the verbs in Slavic languages, which have large sets of verbal prefixes to encode finer path differentiation of the motion event expressed by the verb, as the following Polish verbs show: *dojexać* 'arrive,' lit. 'to + ride'; *objexać* 'ride around' or 'circumride,' lit. 'around + ride'; *przyjexać* 'come,' lit. 'near + ride.' The issue, however, is that paths, themselves determined by the nature of the figure, ground, and trajectory, are quite frequently incorporated into the expression of motion itself.

4.2325. Conveyance

Motion events can be structured not only by means of their figure, ground, location, and path—obvious spatial properties—but also by means of *how they are carried out,* or *conveyance.* Universally, the basic distinction in conveyance is between *vehicular* and *nonvehicular* transport. The distinction is clear in English, in *ride* 'go by vehicle' versus *walk* 'go by foot' (nonvehicle).

Conveyance distinctions are easy to locate in other languages. Polish, for example, has different verb roots for 'generic vehicular transport'—*jexać* (if the motion also has a determinate goal)—and 'generic nonvehicular transport'—*iść* (if the motion also has a determinate goal).

4.2326. Manner

Motional events are also constructed with reference to the *manner of the motion.* In many languages, there are distinct forms for motion as a function of such things as the speed and intensity of the motion independent of the other features, like conveyance or path.

English lexicalizes a number of separate motion events as a function of their manner of execution. For example, the difference between *Bill knocked on the door* and *Bill hammered on the door* is in the *intense manner* of the motion and contact. Many other verb pairs signal this difference in the motional intensity: *close, slam; wiggle, writhe; turn, wheel around.* Speed differences also motivate differential encoding of the motional event, as in *The truck went by the hitchhiker* versus *The truck blew by the hitchhiker.* Again, in English there are a number of such verb pairs that inherently encode difference in speed of execution of motion: *pick up, snap up; blow* (as wind), *whip; toss* (as 'throw'), *fire.*

In Talmy's (1985) view, manner is the second most frequent motion constituent that languages encode inherently in the verbal expression of the motion event (though among the Western European languages, the process is much less productive in the Romance languages than in others). We can see this incorporation in Margany (Breen 1981: 373), where the verb for 'walking,' *waba,* denotes 'generic, nonvehicular motion.' But when this motion changes in *manner* to 'slow' nonvehicular motion toward a goal'—'creeping'—there is an entirely different form: *ḏina binga* (though there is also a more transparent form: *gaṇḏiny waba*).

The tendency toward incorporation may be because manner is very much like a path in its own right. If motion is rapid, it is the traversal of the trajectory that is rapid. In like manner, if the motion is intense, the trajectory is attributed a density of execution. In fact, in some considerations of how manner relates to a predicate, manner is said to be the nonspatial path of the act (see Starosta 1988; chap. 5). So it may be that conceptually paths and manner converge, which would account for their similar behavior in motion events.

4.2327.   Cause

The final characteristic of motion events is their causation. It is quite common for motion to interact with causation because it can easily be the result of the application physical force.

In English, there are many verbs that are derived by means of inherent encoding of the causation of the displacement of the theme: *throw* ('cause to be displaced through the air'), *blow up* ('cause to be displaced into pieces), *roll* ('cause to be displaced in a circular motion along a surface'), and so on. Talmy (1985) notes that the incorporation of causation into the expression of motion events is common in the world's languages, especially if manner is also incorporated. This fact is understandable if we consider that causation itself is also an event, unlike, say, path and location. Thus, the conflation of two events— causation and motion—is likely as a result of their similar semantic nature.

However, there are languages where causation is much less likely than other semantic characteristics to be expressed as an inherent property of the motion event. Talmy (1985) claims that this is typical of the Romance languages, though we again run into the problems of usage and register that plague such a generalization for paths. If we want to see productive distinct encoding of causation and motion, we should turn to a language that tends more generally to separate causation from *all* other events, motion or not. Such is the case in Western Tarahumara, where the causative event, the motion performed by the causer, and the resulting event that the theme (the causee) carries out *all have separate surface forms* (Burgess 1984: 108):

> 56. né simí reká- ba   alué rió.
>   I   go   push Cause that man
>   I pushed that man.
>   More exactly: I made that man go by pushing on (him).

In Western Tarahumara, pushing motion—that is, the application of force and contact in motion—is lexicalized purely, in contrast to English, where some causation is implicated in the expression of the motion event. Compare the difference between *I pushed that man,* where a resulting effect is suggested (i.e., that the man moved) and *I pushed on that man,* where simple contact is encoded. The verb root *reká* in Western Tarahumara is thus more adequately translated as 'push on' because this expresses simple contact; causation is added to the motion independently in Western Tarahumara.

We have seen the details of the structure and encoding of motion events, by looking at eight additional semantic features associated with displacement: theme, source, goal, location, path, conveyance, manner, and cause. We have seen a number of regularities (and the semantic motivation thereto) in the incorporation of certain of these semantic factors into the motion expression. According to Talmy (1985), the most likely characteristic to be inherently coded in motion expressions is the path, followed by manner and cause. Then comes the figure and, thereafter, the least likely to be inherently coded, the ground. These tendencies translate into a hierarchy of inherent coding for motion: Path > Manner/Cause > Figure > Ground. Though this hierarchy has been something of a guiding principle in the discussion of the grammatical reflexes of motion, we have been careful to look critically at these generalizations. Often the hierarchy depends on a number of other conditions, like specificity of the property (ground = source and goal), level of speech, and the definition of the core means of expression of the language in question.

4.24. Summary

In our discussion of motion, we have considered the elemental semantic structure of motion—displace(x)—and the variety of other semantic properties that go hand in hand with displacement: theme, source, goal, path, location, cause, manner, and conveyance. For some of these properties, we have identified major subtypes, such as for paths, where we have observed how features of the figure and ground, for example, affect path choice. In all cases, we have noted encoding regularities for the constituents of motion events, for example, the fairly common incorporation of cause and manner. We have concluded by critically examining Talmy's hierarchy of inherent coding for motion events, arguing that many languages do not meet the hierarchy when they are examined in detail.

4.3. USING AND EXPANDING
THE SEMANTIC REPRESENTATION OF EVENTS:
TRANSFER AND POSSESSION

In this description of event types, we have spent considerable effort in looking at the details of acts, states, causes, and motion. For the sake of this detail, we have sacrificed range of coverage. This is not meant to imply that these four kinds of events exhaust the possibilities (though see the theoretical discussion on pp. 182–94, for what might be construed as attempts in the direction of radically paring down the types). On the contrary, as we examine any particular language more closely, many idiosyncratic features arise, not the least among which are more particular kinds of events.

If we use the tools and results thus far developed, we can go some distance toward a more comprehensive analysis of events. A case in point is the description of transfer and possession in motional terms. We have dealt with motion as *concrete displacement,* and our discussion of motion events has consequently examined physical movement. But if we loosen the reins a bit and allow displacement to be construed abstractly, beyond just physical movement, we broaden the range of events that fall under motion. From this more general position, all verbs of transfer and possession are motion events: *Give* denotes 'displacement of an entity into the possession of another'; *sell* is the *commercial analogue* of *give,* 'give via legal tender'; *teach* denotes 'displacement of information in a socially approved manner.'

By construing verbs of transfer and possession as abstract motion, we simplify the problems of semantic description and explanation. *Give, sell,* and *teach* all orient transfer and possession *from the source to the goal.* The same abstract motion, transfer, and possession can be oriented *from the goal,* as in *get, buy,* and *learn.* Such a regularity as between *give* and *get, sell* and *buy,* and *teach* and *learn* is known in semantics as a *converse relation.* A process or relation is said to be the converse of another if each has the same conceptual content, but the orientation of the entities to the events is reversed, as in *give* and *get. Give* may be characterized as: A, the source of the motion, is involved in the transfer of B, the theme, to C, the goal. *Get* is composed of the same process, only with a reversal of the source and goal: C, the goal, is involved in the transfer of B, the theme, from A, the source of the motion.

Seeing motion more abstractly allows a wide range of expressions to be captured in the same descriptive framework, thus giving a simpler overall account of events. Moreover, with respect to converses in particular, many languages *encode converse processes and relations exactly the same,* but just switch the encoding of the reversed participants. So the encoding facts parallel the semantic facts. Note that *rent* denotes a transaction from both the source's and goal's viewpoint, with no change in attendant form: *Tom rented the apartment to Bill* versus *Bill rented the apartment from Tom.* Polish works analogously, with no encoding difference in the verb roots for 'teach' and 'learn':

57a. ucz- ę   polski- ego.
      teach 1Per/Pres Polish Gen
      I teach Polish.

  b. ucz- ę   się polski- ego.
      teach 1Per/Pres Refl Polish Gen
      I learn Polish.

In each case, the verb root is *ucz,* meaning roughly 'transfer of information.' But crucially for our point at hand, the conversive events have the same conceptual content and are thus motivated to take the same surface encoding.

So we see that the semantic analysis of motion can be applied elsewhere in language with productive results. The elemental structure of motion underlies a variety of other events and its applicability demonstrates the usefulness of a clear analysis of the basics. Work remains to be done as to just how the semantic facts associated with acts, states, and causes can be likewise applied more broadly, though in the following discussion of even typologies, we see how these other event types can be both generalized and derived themselves from more general principles.

4.4. TYPOLOGIES OF EVENTS

In sections 4.1–4.3, we have focused only on a few basic event types, but have also noted that the events themselves may be multiplied indefinitely provided that we take the time to study individual languages. Theoretically, this tack is problematic because it sacrifices unity and exhaustiveness for length and representativeness. There is a payoff, however, because it gives us clear criteria by which to proceed to make theoretical claims to begin with.

Can we distinguish event types more concisely and narrowly? Is it possible to pare down the apparently open-ended list of events by observing unities in events and then noting how the long list is really a derivative of this (hopefully small) set of fundamental events? Positive answers to these questions have been the force behind a number of proposals in the philosophical and linguistics literature. Here we address more theoretical matters to provide a unified account of the phenomena we have thus far uncovered. Our goal is to establish a manageable *typology of events* based on: (a) internal event-structure; (b) time interval.

4.41.   Event Structure and Typology

The philosophical literature has a long history of attempts to simplify the kinds of events—more particularly verbs—in language by factoring out the constancies of their internal semantic structure (Aristotle, Kenney 1963; Ryle 1949; Vendler 1967). We ourselves have done this to some extent by drawing a distinction between actives and statives, for example, with most of the subsequent discussion focusing on types of actives: causatives and motion events.

Many linguists and philosophers have observed that whereas actives and statives characterize a broad and rather clear distinction between events, we must recognize two other fundamental events determinable by their internal structural features (in particular, their *aspectual properties:* see chap. 7 for more): *processes that develop through time* (where events become other events) and *processes that unfold and also come to a result* (see Dowty 1979 for clarifications; Bach 1989).

In addition to acts and states, with which we are already familiar, there are also pure processes in which entities change states, or enter into a new state from an old one—*inchoatives*—and processes that necessarily come to an end—*resultatives.* We know the first two types, so let us exemplify the latter two:

58a. My circumstances changed.
  b. My circumstances changed into a nightmare.

The events of (58a) are such that the circumstances proceed from one state into another, different state. The event expressed by *change* is said to be *inchoative,* a process of becoming, or a transition from the absence of state to the presence of a state (see also chap. 1, p. 12). Compare this with the events in (58b), where there is not only a change of state but also a *necessary resultant state,* with the nightmare as the obligatory result.

With the addition of inchoatives and resultatives to acts and states, we get a four-part typology of events (these categories are meant to be supplementary, not mutually exclusive; further analysis in section 4.42 shows overlaps):

1. States: static events (*statives*)
2. Acts: events that are executed (*actives*)
3. Inchoatives: events that unfold (roughly Vendler's *achievements* and Ryle's *achievements without an associated task*)

4. Resultatives: events that come to an end (roughly Vendler's *accomplishments*, Kenney's *performatives*, and Ryle's *achievements*).

This typology carves up the event space a bit more neatly than our earlier descriptions. Motion, for example, as displacement of an entity, however abstract that displacement is, may hold in any one of these four types. As *states*, motion events have a *positional interpretation: the lamp stood in the corner.* As *acts*, motional events have an *agentive reading: Tom threw the ball.* As *inchoatives*, motion events appear as *simple processes: the lizard moved* (i.e., 'went from one position to another'). As *resultatives*, motional events come to a *necessary conclusion: Bob arrived* (i.e., 'came to an arrival point'). With a typology like this, we can claim that there is a small set of fundamental events that underlie the apparent wide surface variety in language. This simplifies and streamlines the kinds of semantic representations we need to account for events as a whole.

4.411. Structural Correlates of the Typology

The literature on event typologies is full of additional discussion of the logical and syntactic facts that follow from the aforementioned four-part division. Indeed a number of additional structural tests productively differentiate the four (see Dowty 1979 for a full list and discussion). We already know the basic tests for distinguishing states from acts, so they are not repeated here. But there is another diagnostic for states and acts, as they are expressed in English, that bears on their relation to inchoatives and resultatives. States and acts may take the preposition *for* with a time frame to express the temporal duration of the state or act:

59a. I was happy for an hour.
  b. Tom threw the ball for an hour.

But states and acts may *not* take the preposition *in* with a similar time frame:

60a. ?? I was happy in an hour.
  b. ?? Tom threw the ball in an hour.

Hence it appears that acts and states are very much alike when it comes to their duration, at least insofar as these encoding restrictions indicate so, but differ radically with regard to their execution and extendibility: whence the fact that acts allow the progressive and pseudo-cleft, unlike states.

These characteristics of the semantic structure of acts and states take on significance in comparison with inchoatives and resultatives, which have quite different behavior with regard to expressions of temporal duration. Inchoatives pass the tests for actives (see Dowty's 1979 claim, p. 130, note 8, where he shows it is true that inchoatives take the progressive), but they do not take *for:*

61. ?? My circumstances changed for an hour.

However, inchoatives *do* allow temporal duration with *in:*

62. My circumstances changed in an hour.

In contrast, resultatives, which also pass the tests for acts, allow both *for* and *in:*

63a. My circumstances changed into a nightmare for an hour.
  b. My circumstances changed into nightmare in an hour.

Additionally, inchoatives and resultatives differ in their sensitivity to interruption. If inchoatives are interrupted, the event itself can still take place, but resultatives cannot be interrupted and successfully obtain. Consider the fact that if my circumstances are changing, and something happens in the middle of this changing, then it is still true that my circumstances have changed. However, if my circumstances are changing *into a nightmare,* and something interrupts this process, then it is *not true* that my circumstances have changed *into a nightmare:* The interruption precludes the result. Hence, resultatives, unlike inchoatives, cannot be successfully interrupted because the result is part of the event proper.

Furthermore, the two crucially differ with regard to how they interact with the adverb *almost.* Resultatives are ambiguous with *almost:*

64. We almost went to New York

Example (64) may represent at least two situations. In one, we proceed through the motions and never reach our destination: 'We went and almost reached New York.' In another, we never even leave, and the destination is irrelevant: 'We almost went, much less get to New York.' But when the result—*to New York*—is deleted and the verb is reduced to a simple motional process, there is no ambiguity:

65. We almost went.

Hence the resultative construction itself interacts with *almost* to induce ambiguity.

These structural ramifications of the four event types are summarized in Table 4.1.

TABLE 4.1.
Diagnostics for States, Acts, Inchoatives, and Resultatives

Event Type	Pass Active Tests	For	In	Interruptible	Almost Ambiguity
State	NO	YES	NO	N.A.	N.A.
Act	YES	YES	NO	N.A.	N.A.
Inchoative	YES	NO	YES	YES	NO
Resultative	YES	YES	YES	NO	YES

Note: Two clarifications of the table are in order. First, *N.A.* means 'does not apply.' The *almost test* is just odd for statives, for example: *I almost was ten years old.* If this expression is interpretable, however, there is no ambiguity: It simply refers to the state never obtaining. The same holds for actives, *I almost walked,* where, if this is interpretable, it is so in the sense that the action never began, not that it unfolded or unfolded but never reached an end. Thus, if we are to be thorough, we should list NO for states and acts. The matter of interruptibility works likewise. It is simply odd to say *Tom was happy, but he was interrupted.* If in the events expressed, Tom is interrupted, he is still happy. Similarly, if I am interrupted while walking, I have still walked. So here, the notation should be more properly YES, though again the test seems simply not to apply.

Second, the active tests are sometimes said to hold and sometimes not to hold for inchoatives. Dowty (1979: 130, fn. 8) notes that the progressive often sounds fine with inchoatives: *My father is dying.* So, too, the What happened? test works—*What happened? My father died*—as do the pseudo-cleft and imperative—*What the weather did was change* and *Die, scoundrel!*

4.412. *Regularizing the Regularities (and the Exceptions)*

What are we to make of these structural regularities? After all, they seem to be a bit of a mish mash, with differential behavior for prepositions lumped in with the ambiguous readings induced by a particular adverb. One answer is just to leave well enough alone and say that these are four different event types and these differences ought to be reflected in structural differences, no matter how disparate. This has the advantage of not forcing us into an infinite regress in a search for an explanation. On the other hand, it still leaves us with an odd grab bag of results. Are these different surface forms at all motivated by semantic factors? Or is this an instance of where form and content severely diverge? Another answer is to look further into the internal structure of the events for a more comprehensive explanation. Do internal characteristics motivate the surface forms?

The ambiguity of resultatives with *almost* follows from the fact that resultatives are complex events and logically contain inchoatives: A result requires *a process leading up to a result.* The ambiguity of *almost* with resultatives is a function of what *almost* modifies—more technically, *what the adverb has in its scope:* either the inchoative process itself or the endpoint. In turn, inchoatives are unambiguous with *almost* because processes have only *one constituent feature,* the process itself, and hence the adverb may have only the process within its scope and only one interpretation.

So much for the peculiar adverbial, but what about the anomaly of *in* with states and acts, and the acceptability of *in* with inchoatives—all this even though inchoatives also pass the tests for acts? We might say that states and acts have duration, which is why they allow *for* because that preposition appears to encode something of a generic interval of time. Then again, why is *in disallowed* for acts and states, because this preposition also appears to encode something about the duration of the event? Moreover, if duration is the key, why is one marker of duration (*in*) allowed for a process but another (*for*) disallowed?

If we seek an explanation for these facts in terms of the internal semantic structure of events thus far characterized, we ultimately run into circularity. Why do inchoatives take durative *in,* but not durative *for?* Because they are inchoatives, that's why! What is it about inchoatives that forces this distinction, but does not do so, say, for resultatives? Perhaps there is something about the kind of durations that *for* and *in* signal. And perhaps this is also applicable to states and acts. It is this way of thinking that has motivated another typology of events, one built on time intervals. The event typology goes only so far as an explanation. For a more comprehensive—and even simpler—theory, we need to return to the basic criterion of an event itself: *distribution in time.*

4.42. Typology of Events by Time Interval

In seeking a unified account of the structural facts that accompany event typologies, linguists like Dowty (1979) and Bach (1986) and philosophers like Taylor (1977) propose an event typology that relies on the way that the event is *distributed over a time interval.* Before we examine this claim, let us reconsider how this approach fits with the arguments of this chapter in general. In our introductory discussion, we observed that events, unlike entities, are relatively temporal relations in conceptual space. Another way to say this is to say that events are crucially defined by their association with a time interval. If we can determine a typology of events based on how events occur over an interval of time, then we are very much in line with our original claims and get down to the heart of the matter, both ontologically and conceptually.

To understand an event typology derived from a time interval, we must first examine the time interval itself. In accounts like Dowty's and Taylor's, time is viewed as a line composed of elementary points called *moments.* A group of moments along the time line defines a *subinterval,* and any grouping of subintervals results in an *interval.* Subintervals are optional, so an interval may be

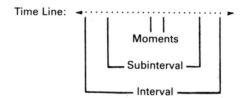

FIG. 4.1. Structure of the time line.

composed directly of moments, depending, of course, on the nature of the event distributed over the time line. These definitions are diagrammatically presented in Fig. 4.1. How are the four types of events discussed earlier distributed over the time line? Do they pick out different pieces of the time line and does this account for the structural reflexes in a more unified way? We return to the four events discussed in the previous section—acts, states, inchoatives, and resultatives—to see their interval structure. Throughout, we make reference to the findings summarized in Table 4.1 to anchor the discussion.

4.421. States, Acts, and the Time Interval

States *saturate*—that is, are in effect throughout—*the time interval* in which they occur *all the way down through the moments.* By this claim, we mean that if states are true at an interval, then they are also true at every moment comprising the interval. This feature contrasts sharply with the way that acts are distributed over the interval in which they occur. Acts *saturate the interval only down through the subinterval,* or more technically, if an act is true at some interval, it is also true at any interval larger than the moment.

We can see this difference between states and acts clearly in comparing a stative and active version of the same conceptual content:

66a. The door was open this morning. (State)
  b. The door opened this morning. (Act)

In the events of (66a), the state 'being open' takes place in the interval represented by *this morning,* and holds *at all relevant times during that interval:* If the door was open this morning, then it is true that it was open *throughout the relevant moments of this morning.* In contrast, in the situation of (66b), even though the event takes place in the same time interval, it is not distributed as fully throughout the constituent moments. Thus, if it is true that the door opened this morning, it is *not* also true that it opened throughout the morning. An act appears to hold only for the subinterval of the larger interval in which the act occurs, but a state saturates the interval *all the way down to the moments.*

Several other tests make this difference clearer. First, if we expressly indicate the saturation of the interval down to the relevant moments for the state, we get a redundancy: ?? *I knew French for every second of my childhood.* But if the expression of saturation is associated with an act, a specific interpretation results:

67. The door opened all throughout the morning.

Example (67) expresses a series of discrete events taking place at individuated subintervals of the larger interval.

A second test supports this restriction of acts to the subinterval. We can convert a state into an act in English by adding a participial ending to the adjective, and in doing so, change the way the event is distributed over the interval:

68. The door was opened all morning.

The events in (68) are distributed *only down to the subinterval* because according to the intended meaning there is a discrete series of individuated events, just as in the active version.

How do these characteristics bear on the structural reflexes of the act/state distinction discussed in section 4.21 and elsewhere? First, acts may be progressivized whereas states may not. What progressivization does is to extend an event throughout an interval. If a state already extends down to the elementary moments of an interval, then there is no need for the progressive. But because acts do not saturate time intervals down to the moments, they can be extended. Hence acts are logical candidates for the progressive because they normally extend only to the subinterval.

The two other structural reflexes of acts and states discussed earlier also fall out nicely from an examination of these events in terms of their distribution over an interval. Both acts and states allow durative *for,* but disallow durative *in.* The temporal expression with *for* encodes the *whole interval.* If I say *I ran for an hour,* I mean that the entire interval in which the running took place is an hour, and the temporal expression with *for* picks out the largest unit of time. However, *in* singles out *internal states of the interval,* or the moments and subintervals. If the expression *I ran in an hour* is at all understandable, it is so in terms of how the running is viewed as *contained within an interval,* not as simply having a generic interval. Thus, *in* encodes temporal distribution lower than the interval itself.

Both acts and states extend below the interval level, or inherently denote subinterval events. Therefore, their internal structure as determined by their distribution over the time interval is redundant in relation to overt specification of reference to the constituents of the interval itself. In plainer terms, acts and states do not select for *in* because they inherently select for pieces of the interval anyway.

Another way to say this is to observe that events select structural reflexes that are a function of the largest and smallest time units they allow. Acts and states denote both intervals and temporal units less than intervals, and thus they should permit temporal expression with *for*, because *for* denotes the generic interval, and disallow temporal expression with *in*, because *in* denotes units within larger intervals. An event that does not make essential reference to the generic interval itself ought to allow *in* and disallow *for*, as is true for inchoatives. Furthermore, events composed of other events ought to inherit the interval properties of their constituents: This is the case for resultatives, which are really complex events made up of acts and inchoatives.

We see how these predictions are borne out in the next two sections, but let us first note something about the place of states in the larger scheme of events. States are perhaps "the most basic" of the four basic events because they saturate the time line; they satisfy the full range of temporal distribution. In Dowty's (1979) theory, in fact, states are the elemental event from which all others are derived. For example, causatives are compositionally produced by an abstract CAUSE operator that acts on states to derive a causative event; inchoatives are derived from the output of the BECOME operator. We could also say that states, saturating down to the moment, are the most timeless of the temporally sensitive phenomena (events) by holding everywhere on the time line. More specific temporal phenomena, like causes, are then derived from them as a base. Although the idea is not pursued any further here, we do note that this unifies the event typologies even more by ranking the elemental events.

4.422. Inchoatives and the Time Interval

Inchoatives are defined by how they denote *an interval between two intervals*. Even though they occur within a time interval like all events, they saturate the space between the intervals required by other events. We can see this by considering that what makes an inchoative a process of becoming is *entry into a new state from an old state*, or the crossing of the boundary of one state into another. Hence if I say *The weather changed*, I mean that the situation is such that weather was in one state at one interval and then in another at a different interval. What is *not* at issue is the nature of the new state, only that a boundary has been passed. Chafe (1970: 122–5) makes this point nicely when he says that inchoatives involve *entry into a new condition*, though the character of the new condition itself is not significant. Similarly, Dowty (1979: 180–7) notes that inchoatives are change-of-state events, but they are simplex and indefinite, by which he means that they are homogeneous (like states) and the nature or direction of the change of state is irrelevant to the event itself, unlike resultatives, for example, where the endpoint does matter.

We can see that inchoatives are *non-subinterval events* (see Dowty 1979 for this terminology), or more precisely, *between interval events*, through a detailed example. Consider the following:

69. My circumstances changed this morning.

Though the expression represents the interval as 'this morning,' the precise time frame for the change of circumstances is not this morning proper, but *between two states within the interval* designated by the cover term *this morning.* Consequently, an adequate gloss of (69) is 'my circumstances went from one state to another at some time during this morning,' where the necessary reference to the intermediate interval is made explicit.

Moreover, the inchoative is not distributed lower than this interval, down to the moments. Explicit expression of this saturation gives an interpretation much like that for acts: *My circumstances changed all through this morning,* which implies that there is a discrete series of changes at subintervals, not that every moment of the morning is saturated with the change. Inchoatives thus are distributed *across the entry into a another interval,* the transition from one interval to another, or the crossing of the lower bound of the interval of the new state.

If the temporal domain for inchoatives is between intervals, several other structural facts beyond their sensitivity to contained intervals with *in* also fall out. For one thing, inchoatives should take the progressive. They do not extend fully down to moments. Consequently they should (like acts) allow the syntactic device that induces temporal extension, as, indeed, they do. For another thing, they are interruptible, which is compatible with their temporal structure because no endpoint is built into the inchoative. What matters for the inchoative is the transition of the lower bound of the subinterval of the new state, not reaching the end of the new state. Similarly, because only one bound—that traversed in the transition into a new state—is implicated in the interval structure of inchoatives, ambiguity with adverbs like *almost* is ruled out. For inchoatives, *almost* modifies only the transition point interval to the event, and thus no ambiguity is possible.

4.423. *Resultatives and the Time Interval*

Unified accounts of the structural factors associated with resultatives also follow from construing them in terms of time intervals. From a conceptual standpoint, resultatives are *complex events* (see Dowty 1979: 18–7), consisting of *both acts and changes of state.* Consider the following resultative:

70. Bill painted a picture.

We know that *paint a picture* is resultative because it is not interruptible: If Bill is painting a picture and is interrupted, then he cannot be said to have painted a picture. This is unlike the simpler expression *paint,* which can be interrupted. The mere expression of the goal, *the picture,* makes the event resultative.

Paint a picture involves both action and change of state. When we say (70), we express a state of affairs where Bill executes *an act* that goes through *a process* and reaches *an end.* Consequently, resultatives pass the active tests and the inchoative tests, allowing temporal expressions with *both for* and *in:*

71a. Bill painted a picture for an hour.
  b. Bill painted a picture in an hour.

These facts make sense because resultatives take on the interval properties of both acts and inchoatives.

Resultatives should *not saturate down to the moment* because they are composed of both acts and inchoatives. Indeed, they do not, as the following illustrates:

72. The soup cooled off this afternoon.

Example (72) means 'the soup came to an end in the cooling process in the interval of this afternoon.' It is not true, however, in the situation described, that if the soup cooled off this afternoon, it then also cooled off at every relevant moment during the afternoon. The resultative makes *cool off* is unlike the state *be cool,* which does saturate to the relevant moments, and the inchoative *cool,* which is confined to the space between intervals like all inchoatives:

73a. The soup was cool this afternoon. (state)
  b. The soup cooled this afternoon. (inchoative)

Example (73a) means 'the soup was in a cool state at all relevant moments of the afternoon.' (Even though the resultative—*cool off*—is semantically related to the state, the presence of the result prevents saturation down to the moment.) *Cool,* as an inchoative, also does not saturate down to the moment because if the soup cooled this afternoon, it is not thereby true that it cooled at all moments: The soup could have cooled sporadically.

Resultatives do not completely saturate the interval because their constituent acts and processes do not. But they extend up to the interval because their constituent acts do likewise. The boundary of the upper interval in which resultatives occur is itself the endpoint of the process encoded by the inchoative. If I say *Bill painted a picture for an hour,* I mean that he engaged in the process that came to an end when the interval expressed also came to an end. If I say *Bill painted a picture in an hour,* Bill may complete the act before the hour ends. In this way, resultatives are very much like inchoatives with an upper bound in the interval, adduced from the presence of their constituent acts. Hence because resultatives are both acts and processes, they should allow the tests for both, as indeed they do, because resultatives accept both *for* and *in.*

Why do resultatives disallow interruption and have ambiguity with *almost?* Essentially the same answer can be given for each problem. The lower bound of

TABLE 4.2.
Events and Their Intervals

Event	Largest Unit		Lowest Unit
State	Interval		Moment
Act	Interval		Subinterval
Inchoative	None		None
		(i.e., between intervals)	
Resultative	Interval		Interval
		(Act + Inchoative)	

the interval of the act containing an inchoative must be reached for the resultative to occur, and any interruption of this procedure prevents the bound from being reached. That is why an interrupted resultative still has an inchoative interpretation, because the change of state internal to the resultative is not affected by the interruption: *only the culmination is*. In the situation expressed by *The soup cooled off*, if the cooling off is interrupted, the soup then does not cool off, but it still may cool. Here, the inchoative that is a constituent of the resultative survives the interruption, as all inchoatives do, because the interruption is not sensitive to the internal bound of the interval, but the endpoint of the resultative event.

In like manner, the adverb *almost* is ambiguous with resultatives because it may have within its scope either the bound to be traversed in the inchoative or the limit of the interval specified by the act. *The soup almost cooled off* is ambiguous: Either the soup never got to cool or it did get to cool, but never reached a culmination. The complex event structure—and thus the complex time interval structure—of resultatives thus accounts for this structural peculiarity and unifies this event semantically and structurally.

4.424. A Schematic Interval Typology

We have seen that we can explain the four basic events of the event typology by an appeal to their patterning within an interval of time. Apparently disparate semantic and grammatical facts remarkably come together in this view. We can summarize the general approach rather succinctly. By talking about how these events are distributed over a time interval, we are defining them in terms of the *largest* and *smallest* time units they allow. The results of our discussion, in these terms, are in Table 4.2.

The value of a typology such as this lies not only in its unification of extant data, as we have shown, but also in its applicability to new data. Punctual events, like that expressed by *punch*, take *neither for* nor *in:*

74a. ?? I punched Tom for an hour.
   b. ?? I punched Tom in an hour.

Why is this? Punctual events are *confined to moments,* and because they do not take place in an interval, they do not allow *for;* because they are not between intervals, they do not allow *in.*

Moreover, we can create special interpretations of events otherwise criterially defined by shifting the interval specifications. Take the event expressed by the verb *own,* which in normal usage is a state:

75a. I owned the house for a day.
  b. ?? I owned the house in a day.

Owning saturates down to the moments of the interval, so it typically rules out the expression of contained time: *in.* But if we force this interpretation, we make it into an inchoative. If (75b) as interpretable, it must be understood as the transition from one state into another state by the traversing of the lower bound of the interval containing the new state: 'I passed from nonowning to owning during the day.'

So we see the ultimate advantage of unifying events in a manageable typology. We can accommodate new data and make predictions about new interpretations. In this way the interval typology becomes an explanation of events, not just another description.

4.43. Summary

In this section we have described several ways of unifying events by typing them according to semantic features. The typology of acts, states, inchoatives, and resultatives seeks unification by internal semantic structure; the typology by time interval unifies through distribution on the time line: States saturate to the moment, acts extend to the subinterval, inchoatives apply between intervals, and resultatives take on the interval properties of acts and states. These approaches allow us to reduce significantly the number of possible events that language encodes and "regularize the regularities" even further by providing an abstract and consistent underlying semantic structure for all events.

SUMMARY OF CHAPTER

This chapter concerned the semantic structure of events and their typical encoding as verbs. We revitalized the notional definition of *verb* by demonstrating the truth of its reversal: Not all verbs are actions but all actions are verbs. In the process, we considered several treatments of events and verbal categoriality: Davidson's view of events and change, Hopper and Thompson's view of verbs as forms that report events in discourse, Langacker's and Givón's views of events as time-bound phenomena.

Having settled on a definition of an event as a relatively temporal relation, we examined four principal classes of events: acts, states, causes, and motion. We discussed the semantic and logical content of each class and regularities in their encoding. We saw the relative temporality and internal differentiation of acts and states and how these relate to five structural tests (and the exceptions thereto) for actives versus statives—progressive, pseudo-cleft, What happened?, imperative, and *deliberately/carefully*.

We then looked at causatives, formally (as an implication between two events in the closest possible world) and linguistically (as a relation between an Ep and Er with a Figure/Ground shift). We considered directness of causation and degree of involvement of participants and their correlations with grammatical form.

Following this, we turned to motion, defined as displacement, in relation to its theme, source, goal, path, location, cause, manner, and conveyance. We observed how features of these constituents of motion events affect their incorporation into the expression of motion. We also looked at the application of the results of the analysis of motion to transfer and possession.

We closed the chapter with a description of several ways to unify events: a typology of acts, states, inchoatives, and resultatives and a typology of time interval. These approaches reduced significantly the number of possible events that language encodes.

QUESTIONS FOR DISCUSSION

1. Discuss the interpretations of the following sentence:

    i. The kitten ran under the table.

Is *under* ambiguous or vague? How do the different interpretations of (i) relate to our findings about paths and locations in the expression of motion? Is there a single form in English meaning 'under run'?

2. Consider the following sentence from Mojave (Schachter 1985: 19):

    i. ?i:pa-č   homi:-k.
       man Subj tall   Pres
       The man is tall.

The attribute 'tall' is inflected for tense, so (i) literally means 'the man talls.' What does this say about the way that Mojave treats attributes and adjectives? How does this relate to the definition of events as relatively temporal relations in conceptual space?

3. In many languages, there is an encoding relationship among statives,

causatives, and inchoatives. In some languages, statives and inchoatives are encoded alike, in contrast to causatives: that is, S + I versus C. In others, inchoatives and causatives are encoded alike, in contrast to statives: that is, I + C versus S. However, *in no language* are statives and causatives encoded alike, in contrast to inchoatives: * S + C versus I. What reasons can you give for these patterns? Note that inchoatives may be encoded like either statives or causatives. Are inchoatives semantically similar to these other two events? Are there any semantic reasons for the failure of statives to pattern like causatives? (Hint: see the discussion of sec. 4.4; see also Talmy 1985.)

5 Thematic Roles

5.1. INTRODUCTION

In Chapters 3 and 4, we looked at the semantic properties of entities and events. The former were viewed as relatively atemporal individuals in conceptual space, typically, but not necessarily, taking the form of nouns. We also observed that events, temporally sensitive relations in conceptual space, included states, processes, acts, and conditions of existence, again typically, but not necessarily, surfacing as verbs. In this chapter we ask the following questions: How do entities carry out events? What roles do entities play in events?

To answer these questions we turn to the study of *thematic roles* (also called *semantic cases* (Fillmore 1968, 1977), *semantic roles* (Dillon 1977), *thematic relations* (Gruber 1976; Jackendoff 1972), and, from a purely syntactic perspective, θ (*theta*) *roles* (Chomsky 1981; Marantz 1984). *Thematic roles* are semantic relations that connect entities to events (more particularly, arguments to predicates: see sec. 5.11)

In the discussion that follows, we present a broad sketch of the nature and function of 12 thematic roles, focusing first on predication as the basis of the relationship between entities and events and then on the difference between grammatical roles (like subject) and thematic roles (like agent). Following this introductory material, we consider the 12 thematic roles according to the two categories of participant and nonparticipant roles. We describe the semantic structure of such roles as agent, patient, instrument, benefactive, source, goal, and the like with illustrations from widely divergent languages to show the kinds of grammatical reflexes that thematic roles have. We complete the chapter with some discussion of theoretical attempts to unify thematic roles (through localism and macroroles) and systematize their connection to grammatical roles (through linking theory).

To understand the role of entities in events, we must first get a grasp of two more fundamental ideas. The first is *predication,* or the abstract way that individuals may be involved in events. Predication motivates thematic roles because it is the very possibility of a relation between entities and events. The second idea is the difference between *grammatical roles* (formal, syntactic relations of nouns and verbs) and *thematic roles* (semantic relations of entities and events). It is tempting to try to read thematic roles off grammatical roles, because they both are relational, but the value of keeping the two distinct should become evident.

5.11.   Predication and Thematic Roles

Predication is the way that individuals *instantiate*—embody, carry out, take on, or are linked to—properties, actions, attributes, and states. A simple way to understand predication is to go back to formal semantics (sec. 2.3) and ask the basic question of this approach to meaning: What kinds of things can linguistic expressions denote? We might answer that there are only *two kinds of things:* things that are independent and can stand alone, or individuals; things that are dependent and cannot stand alone, like qualities, relations, acts, properties, and states.

Consider the word *hat.* The referent for *hat* can be understood outside any circumstance, time, or person because 'hat' does not have to be attributed to anything or anyone: It is an individual. Now consider the words *red, on,* and *fell.* The denotations for these words cannot be grasped outside of their *association with an individual.* We attribute these denotations to things: *red hat, on the hat, the hat fell.* These denotations are intrinsically dependent: More technically, unlike individuals, they must be instantiated.

The inherently dependent phenomena are *predicates;* the independent individuals are *arguments.* The instantiation of a dependent phenomenon in an individual—the linking of a predicate to its argument(s)—is known as *predication.* In the simplest cases, events correspond to predicates and entities to arguments. For example, in the expression *The boy is eating the pizza,* the event 'eating' is the *predicate* because 'eating' must be done *by someone* and *of something.* Each entity, 'boy' and 'pizza,' is an *argument* of the predicate because they instantiate the 'eating.' Of course, these arguments instantiate the predicate in different ways. It is the purpose of the rest of this chapter to provide a typology of the different ways that arguments instantiate predicates, now that the mechanism of predication itself is clear.

Thematic roles are grammatically relevant relations of arguments to predicates, not simply the connection of entities to events. We need predicates and arguments because, on closer inspection, some things that we might classify as events by virtue of their overt form in sentences are really not predicates and therefore take no thematic roles. Likewise, some things that might appear to be entities are really not arguments at all and hence bear no thematic relation to the predicate.

What is the predicational structure of *The ball is red?* We might say that the predicate is represented by *is,* with *ball* and *red* standing for the arguments, as if the predication on the whole were something like 'being, by the ball, of red.' But how does 'red' instantiate 'being?' In point of fact, *the ball is red* is not about 'being,' but about 'color' (compare *the ball exists,* which is about 'being'). Predicationally, then, the expression is rather like 'redness, by the ball': The entity denoted by *the ball* thus has a thematic role in relation to the predicate expressed by *red,* itself not an event as such. The form *is* simply irrelevant here, and in many languages, *is* has no surface form in such expressions (cf. Russian *mjač krasny,* lit. 'ball red,' where there is no verb 'to be').

Just as not all events are predicates, so not all entities are arguments. What is the predicational structure of *It rains ice in Chicago?* We might say that there is one predicate, represented by *rains,* with three arguments, represented by *it, ice,* and *Chicago.* But whereas we can observe the individuals denoted by *ice* and *Chicago,* it is difficult to pick out that denoted by *it,* though we might guess 'weather,' 'clouds,' and so forth. But we are hard pressed to decide exactly how the referent of *it participates* in the situation: that is, how *it instantiates rain. It* does not represent *an argument* here because *it* does not participate at all semantically in the situation as expressed. Thus, we have an overt form that putatively denotes an entity, but is not an argument and cannot therefore have a thematic role. Dowty (1986) states the case nicely in saying that the features of arguments are very different from the features of the *referents* of arguments. The features in the world that *it* may pick out really have no bearing on whether *it* has a role in the predication. In contrast, *ice* and *Chicago* do stand for arguments of the predicate: 'raining, by ice, in Chicago.' Hence, these entities do have thematic roles in relation to the predicate.

If we now see the necessity to consider predicates and arguments in the analysis of thematic roles, how do we begin to describe these roles? Let us first take the cautionary route into grammatical roles to see that we have to develop an independent semantic vocabulary for thematic roles and not simply read predicate/argument relations directly off sentence form.

5.12. Grammatical Roles and Thematic Roles

If thematic roles are grammatically relevant relations between predicates (often events) and arguments (often entities), we might look for them in the typical *grammatical roles* like *subject, direct object,* and *indirect object.* After all, these are well-studied relations between things typically representing entities (nouns) and events (verbs). However, the domain of grammatical roles is *syntax;* they are features of *sentences,* not predications. *Subject,* for example, is a relation between a noun and verb such that the noun typically *governs,* or controls, the morphological form of the verb. In the sentence *It rains ice in Chicago, it* is the subject because it determines the singular form of the verb: ?? *It were raining ice in Chicago.* But we know that *it* does not represent an argument in this case and thus has no thematic role. Thematic roles require predicates and arguments, not necessarily nouns and verbs; we cannot take thematic roles directly from grammatical roles (Fillmore 1968; see sec. 5.33)

Just as thematic roles cannot be read off grammatical roles, so they cannot be derived from *morphological cases,* like *nominative, accusative, dative, genitive,* and so on, those forms that signal sentential relationships. Like grammatical roles, morphological cases do not map simply onto thematic roles. In the sentence *I have the book, I* and *the book* are in the nominative case (English has morphologically marked accusative case only for certain pronouns, *him, her*). But in Russian, where the semantically equivalent expression has the form *u menya kniga* (lit. 'at me book'), the word for 'I,' *menya,* is coded morphologically in the *dative case* and the word for 'book,' *kniga,* is coded in the *nominative.* In Polish, a language very closely related to Russian, the equivalent expression surfaces as *mam książkę* (lit. 'have-I book'), with 'I' marked by a verbal suffix, *m,* and 'book', *książkę,* coded in the accusative. In English, Russian, and Polish, the *same predication is expressed:* the predicate 'having' instantiated by the arguments 'I' and 'book,' and so the thematic roles are constant. But the morphological cases across the three languages are not comparable.

Thematic roles must be found elsewhere, outside the system of morphological cases, just as they have to be outside the system of grammatical relations. This conclusion is not meant to imply that morphological cases, grammatical relations, and thematic roles are completely unrelated. On the contrary, thematic roles follow the Grammatical Constraint and so are linked up with grammatical roles and morphological cases at some point. It just means that thematic roles cannot be simply read off surface form.

What we need, and what neither grammatical roles nor morphological cases provide, is a way to think about how the pieces of any situation go together in our mental models, beyond the variability in the machinery that languages have for putting forms together into *expressions about situations.* Thematic roles "configure" the projected world of reference, linking predicates to arguments in particular ways, much like an operating system formats a disk for a microcomputer, by setting allowable relationships, or like the lenses and settings of a camera affect perspective and organization in a photograph by modifying the relationships of the constituents of the picture, zooming in on some, defocalizing others (see Fillmore 1975a, 1977).

We want to find the content of the *constant semantic relationships of predicates and arguments,* those things that come built into the predication and hence are unaffected by contextual shifts, yet affect the grammar. This is not an easy task, if at least clarified. The conceptual content of thematic roles has been notoriously difficult to specify, causing some linguists to reject them out of hand for lack of precision (see Carlson 1984: 260; Fillmore 1977). We define thematic roles later just as we have defined all other semantic units: not with essential definitions but with preference rules (see chap. 2), or, as Dowty (1986) says, in terms of criterial properties extracted from instances.

Linguistic semantics considers meaning coded in grammar, and as the coding schemes of languages differ, so thematic roles surface in different ways in many languages: in word order, affixation, and particles. English relies on prepositions (particles) and word order for the most part; Polish relies on affixation. In spite of the variety of possible mechanisms for coding thematic roles, the variation is, in practice, quite limited. We examine typical grammatical manifestations of thematic roles and offer some reasons for why the roles surface as they do. So, although the comparative illustrations from different languages show a diversity of mechanisms, the best advice to the reader is: Don't get lost in the mechanisms; remember the principles and the content.

5.13. Summary

In this introductory material, we have defined thematic roles as grammatically relevant semantic relations between predicates and arguments. We have seen the need to look at predication to differentiate predicates from events and arguments from entities. We have also seen the divergence of thematic roles from both grammatical roles (like subject) and morphological cases (like nominative).

5.2. TWELVE THEMATIC ROLES

In this section, we discuss the semantic and grammatical characteristics of 12 thematic roles: agent, author, instrument, patient, benefactive, experiencer, theme, source, goal, locative, reason, and purpose. Though the literature on thematic roles lists anywhere from 18 to 25 roles, we limit our discussion to these 12, what I take to be the major thematic roles. Our analysis is guided by a distinction between two general categories of thematic roles: *participant* and *nonparticipant* roles. We briefly define these two categories before we proceed to the roles proper.

5.21. Participant and Nonparticipant Roles

There are two broad classes of thematic roles: *participant roles* and *nonpartici- pant* (or sometimes *circumstantial*) *roles*. The former are the roles of arguments necessitated by the predication itself, those that generally answer the question,

"Who did what to whom?" The latter are optional roles necessitated by the semantic context more than by the predication. They generally answer the question, "Why, where, when, and how?"

The distinction between participant and nonparticipant roles can be seen in the following sentence: *Tom hit the ball in the stadium.* The predicate, coded in *hit,* takes three arguments, represented by *Tom, ball,* and *stadium.* Which of these arguments are more central to the predication? Which of these are nondeletable or nuclear? My own intuition tells me that the logical doer and receiver, those entities represented by *Tom* and *ball,* are more germane to the predication than is the location signalled by *stadium.* A simple test confirms these intuitions. If the logical doer and receiver are eliminated, the predication fails, something not the result of eliminating the location. That is, 'hitting' cannot be successfully predicated without both a "hitter" and a "hittee"; the specific locale of the predication is optional and can be deleted without any real harm. Thus, the doer and receiver are in this case *participants* and have *participant roles;* the location of the predication has a *nonparticipant role* because it is selected by the semantic context, not the predication itself.

Standard treatments (e.g., Halliday 1970) view participant roles as obligatory and nonparticipant roles as optional. Though the terminology is a bit slippery, there is a more precise sense in which the obligatory/optional distinction can be understood. Some member of the class of participant roles must be expressed in every predication; the nonparticipant roles may be deleted or determined by context. This is because the participant roles stem from the compatibility of the properties of the argument with the properties of the predicate.

One consequence of this notional distinction between optionality and obligatoriness in the predication is their grammatical coding. Participant roles tend to be coded in the *direct grammatical relations* (subject, direct object, and indirect object) and all can surface as subjects. Nonparticipant roles, however, tend to be coded in the *oblique grammatical relations* (all others than the direct ones, e.g., object of preposition) and in grammatical adjuncts (e.g., subordinate clauses); it is unusual for nonparticipant roles to appear as subjects.

Perhaps Halliday's (1970: 149) own example summarily states the case:

1a. He was throwing stones at the bridge.
 b. He was throwing stones on the bridge.

In the events of (1a), the bridge is the goal of the action. Although the bridge is realized as an oblique grammatical relation as the object of the preposition *to,* it may surface as a subject:

2. The bridge is what he was throwing stones at.

This is unlike (1b), where the situation described has the bridge as the fixed locale of the act (a nonparticipant relation: *where,* or the locative). Consequently, there is no corresponding paraphrase with the bridge realized as a subject:

  3. ?? The bridge is what he was throwing stones on.

There is then a difference between goals and locations of predicates. The former are participants and can be subjects; the latter are nonparticipants and generally cannot be subjects.

What kinds of roles tend to be participant roles and are selected by the predicates themselves? What kinds of roles tend to be determined by the semantic context? How do languages code these arguments? We now turn to the 12 major thematic roles to see their semantic and grammatical structure.

5.22. Participant Roles

Here we examine nine major participant roles, grouped according to their function in the predication. Three concern the logical actor or doer of the predication; three concern the logical recipient or undergoer of the predication; three have properties of both and are best understood in spatial terms.

5.221. *Logical Actors*

5.2211. Agent

The *agent* is the deliberate, potent, active instigator of the predicate: the primary, involved doer. Normally, the agent is human, and agency is therefore often connected with volition, will, intentionality, and responsibility. Agents are also typically animate, though animacy has less crucial a place than does volition (DeLancey 1984). The prototypical agent is thus that argument that is the self-driving force for a predicate.

Agency may be seen in the following sentences:

  4a. Tommy drove the car.
  b. Our food was eaten by raccoons.

In (4a), *Tommy* stands for the agent because, in the situation expressed, Tommy carries out the act with deliberateness and primary involvement. Even in a situation where he is forced to drive the car illegally and involuntarily—*The terrorists held Tommy at gunpoint and forced him to drive the car, even though he was underage*—he still is the agent of driving because agency is concerned with the execution of the predicate, not with the circumstances that give rise to predicate or the argument. Similarly, in (4b), *raccoons* represents the agents, the active instigators of the eating, even though the form itself is not, as in (4a), the grammatical subject.

Where should we find good examples of agency? The direct mapping of the agent/nonagent distinction, pure agency, is relatively rare and found only among a handful of the world's languages, those known as *active languages* (e.g., Dakota, Wichita, Finnish, Batsbi, and Eastern Pomo, and Chickasaw (p. 156): Anderson 1971: 52–3; DeLancey 1981; Fillmore 1968; Trask 1979: 387). The following Dakota sentences are intransitive, so any marking differences are due not to syntax but to the semantics of agency (Foster 1979: 499–500):

5a. wa- ka-   hą.
    I Agt outer force sore
    I gave myself a sore by doing something.
    More accurately: I did the sore.

 b. ma- ka-   hą.
    to me outer force sore
    I got a sore unintentionally (from something or other).

In (5a), *wa* is an *agentive* pronoun; in (5b), when agency disappears, the pronoun changes to a nonagentive form, *ma*.

Another particularly clear example can be seen in Batsbi (DeLancey 1981: 629). When the execution of a predicate is not volitional or intentional, the argument is marked in the absolute, as in (6a). But the use of the ergative signals volition and intention on the part of the individual denoted by the argument— that is, pure agency—as in (6b):

6a. Ø- txo- naizdrax kxitra.
    Abs we   to ground fell
    We fell to the ground unintentionally.

 b. a- txo naizdrax kxitra.
    Erg we to ground fell
    We fell to the ground intentionally ('threw ourselves').

Given our discussion in Chapter 3 of the Animacy Hierarchy and how semantic influence and potency systematically relate to grammatical form, we might also look for distinct agency in *ergative/absolute languages*. These languages, as discussed in Chapter 3, mark the subjects of transitive verbs alike (in the *ergative* case) in opposition to both the objects of transitive verbs and the subjects of intransitive verbs, which are marked similarly (in the *absolute* case). In contrast to ergative/absolute languages, there are *nominative/accusative* languages, like English, which uniformly mark all subjects (nominative) as opposed to all objects (accusative).

Whereas ergative/absolute languages are widely distributed across the world—Basque, Eskimo, Nepali, and Samoan work similarly—by far the most common pattern is what is known as *split ergativity,* whereby a language encodes only certain arguments as ergative/absolute and others as nominative/accusative. As we know, the split in split ergativity follows the rule that ergative marking is inversely proportional to the degree of influence the entity in question has over the predication (see our discussion of the Animacy Hierarchy, p. 93; Dixon 1979; DeLancey 1981). Crucially for our discussion of agency, the mere agentive properties of the agent per se are not sufficient to trigger the split ergative encoding. Sometimes ergative marking is inversely correlated with the inherent agency of the argument: More typical agents (those that canonically embody agentive properties) are less frequently coded as agents than less typical agents, and so lack of overt coding is a consequence of the implicit presence of the properties of volition, potency, and so forth. But as DeLancey (1981) shows, ergativity is bound up with notions other than just the inherent properties of the arguments executing the predicate. Ergativity depends on other semantic properties, like aspect and directionality of the event, and pragmatic properties, like speaker's viewpoint, topic salience, and information flow (DuBois 1987). So, pure agency is not likely to be read directly off its ostensible coding. In the common case of split ergativity, a number of other factors complicate the singling out of pure agency.

What characterizes agency, like all thematic roles, is the manner in which the argument participates in the predication. A convenient way to summarize the constellation of properties constituting agency, based on Keenan's (1984) work on the semantics of absolutes, is to say that agents are semantically *independent.* Agents deliberately, intentionally, responsibly, and potently execute and control acts: They generate the effects themselves (DeLancey 1984: 193), making them relatively independent of those acts.

The independence of agents comes through clearly in purposive clauses. When there is an agent, the purpose for the event is associated with the agent because the agent has independent status as the source of the act. In *John floated down the river to get to the waterfall,* the purpose ('to get to the waterfall') is associated with the *agent's* motivations and goals. But when there is no agent, the purpose is associated globally, outside of the predication and as a part of the entire act, because there is no independent actor to accept the purpose. Consider ?? *The canoe floated down the river to get to the waterfall.* To make this meaningful, we associate the purpose with an unspecified agent external to the predication 'floating' (i.e., '*somebody* floated the canoe down the river to get *it* to the waterfall'), and in this sense, the inferred agent becomes the required independent instigator of the predication (Gruber 1976).

5.2212. Author

If the primary executor of an act has all the characteristics of an agent, but is not the direct cause of the act, the argument is the *author* (also called *effector:* Broadwell 1988: 116–7; Foley and Van Valin 1984: 51). This distinction between agent and author is made to accommodate differences in participation between those arguments that carry out acts for reasons internal to the arguments (agents) and those that carry out acts for noninternal reasons.

The author has a variety of properties, most of which are best understood in opposition to agency. The author is the sufficient, but not the necessary, cause of the predication; hence it is often understood as the *inactive cause*. Animacy, intentionality, and responsibility are not required of the author. Thus, whereas the agent is the direct doer, the author is simply the enabler, or the indirect cause, often differentiated from the agent by degree of involvement in the act (see DeLancey 1984 for comprehensive discussion).

These properties surface in the difference between the doers of the (otherwise similar) predicates in the following sentences:

7a. Bill floated down the river.
 b. The canoe floated down the river.

In the state of affairs of (7a), Bill directly effects the floating, as the paraphrase *Bill kept himself afloat down the river* brings out; if Bill does not volitionally carry out the act—if he is dead, for example—the nature of the agency changes, as does the nature of the relation between the arguments and the predicate. The paraphrase changes likewise: *Bill's body floated down the river*. In the situation represented by (7b), the canoe does not really carry out the act. So the paraphrase for (7a) that brings out the volition of the agent is unavailable for (7b): ?? *The canoe kept itself afloat down the river*. In their respective states of affairs, both Bill and the canoe carry out the event of floating, but only Bill is the agent: The canoe is the author.

Many languages syntactically distinguish authors from agents. In Russian, expressions with agents as subjects in the active voice may be passivized by inverting the subject and object and putting the agent in the instrumental case:

8a. Raboči   udivili   menya.
     workers surprised me
     The workers surprised me.
 b. Ja udivil-   sja   raboči- mi.
     I surprised Refl workers Instr
     I was surprised by the workers.

Raboči, the agent in (8a), is in the instrumental form, *rabočimi*, in (8b). But if the subject is an author, and passivization is necessitated, Russian uses the so-called "flip construction," a syntactic process analogous to the medio-passive in Spanish (see sec. 4.214). Compare the expressions in (9) (Schwartz 1988: 176):

9a. Strannyj eë kostjum udivil   menya.
    strange her outfit surprised me
    Her strange outfit surprised me.

  b. Ja udivil- sja   strann- omu eë kostjum-u.
    I surprise Refl strange Dat her outfit   Dat
    I was surprised at her strange outfit.
    More accurately: I got surprised from her strange outfit.

The dative marking of the author in (9b), *kostjumu,* contrasts with what otherwise happens if the active voice subject is an agent, as in (8b), where it takes the instrumental.

In Russian, then, as in English, the thematic role of author can be seen through its effect on the syntax of the language. Certain constructions are sensitive to the semantic properties that differentiate direct, volitional doers from indirect, nonvolitional ones.

The previous examples bring two other characteristics of authors to light. First, semantically, authors fall on a gradient between agents and *instruments* (the means of a predication: see sec. 5.2213). Agents are the direct instigators of the predicate. Instruments are the tools used by agents to carry out acts directly. Authors are somewhere between the two: Authors carry out acts relatively independently, but indirectly; however, their relation to the action is not so dependent as to deprive them of their effectuality. Thus agency may be best understood as a gradient of directness of execution of the predicate: agent > author > instrument.

This generalization is nicely illustrated by the language Hare (after DeLancey 1984). Agents take a transitive marker on the verb:

10. Joe lánj-h-   we.
    Joe die Trans 3Per
    She/he killed Joe.
    More acurately: she/he made Joe dead.

But authors are marked by a separate postposition:

11. kǫtúé' k'é   lánj-we.
    liquor Author die 3Per
    Liquor killed him/her.
    More accurately: she/he died from liquor.

Liquor is inherently potent enough to instigate the act of killing, but not high enough on the scale of agency to warrant agent coding. Conversely, arguments whose denotations are inherently volitional, and thus may directly execute an act because of their agentive properties, *cannot* take the author postposition:

12. ?? sa   k'é   lánj- we.
      bear Author die   3Per
    ?? He/she died from a bear.

Nor can arguments that are conceptually lower on the agency gradient, and are inherently instruments, take the author coding:

13. ?? gofį k'é   yejai tá'enįse.
      axe Author glass broke
    ?? The glass broke from the axe (i.e., 'someone used an axe to break the glass').

Semantically, an axe must be wielded *by an agent,* so it cannot enter a predication as an indirect cause, as an author, only as a secondary one, an instrument.[1]

5.2213. Instrument

If an argument is the means by which a predicate is carried out, it has the thematic role *instrument.* Instruments may look like agents and authors in that, as the method by which the action is executed, they are closely associated with both. But instruments, unlike agents and authors, must be *acted upon by something else* in order to participate in the situation; their energy source is external to them.

Instruments exert no action of their own, and consequently Fillmore (1968) originally defines them as inanimate forces or objects *causally involved,* not causing per se. The responsibility for the action is ultimately attributable to an agent (either elsewhere in the expression or recoverable from the context). Consider the following:

14a. Ellen cut the salami with the knife.
  b. Bob succeeded through his father's influence.

In the situation of (14a), although the knife directly performs the act of cutting, it does so only because of the action of Ellen, who exerts the necessary energy on the instrument. In the situation of (14b), although influence is the basis of the success, it has no role in the predication unless it is put into play by Bob's father: Again the action is wholly external to the instrument.

---

[1]This discussion of agency and causation is reminiscent of our analysis of causative events and directness of involvement of causers and causees (sec. 4.222). Indeed, another construction where authors tend to be found is the mediated or indirect causative. One way to analyze the difference, in Hindi, between direct causation (with *aa*) and indirect causation (with *vaa*) is that the former takes an agent whereas the latter takes an author as the causee, an individual whose directness has been usurped.

Niuean provides good comparative data on this matter. In this language, instruments are marked by a specific preposition, *aki* (after Seiter 1979: 28–38):

15. Ko e tohitohi a au aki e titipi.
    Pres Erg write Abs I Instr Abs knife
    I'm writing with a knife ('carving').

But when the participant in question does not depend on action executed by another—when its instrumentality is lost—the marking itself changes:

16. Kua mate a Sione he titipi.
    Prfct die Abs Sione Cause knife
    John died from a knife.

In (16), the more accurate reading is something like 'the knife killed Sione,' where the knife functions as an author.

Niuean morphology is thus sensitive to the difference between instrumental arguments and those that may exert a force of their own, in line with the agency scale already described (p. 207). In the events of (16), the knife is an author, and its weakly causal status is signalled (by *he*). This is unlike direct agency, which is marked by the ergative, as the subject of (15) demonstrates, and secondary agency, the instrumental, marked by *aki*.

Instrumentality is not a necessary consequence of any particular internal property of the denotation of the argument. Although some properties more than likely contribute to instrumentality, the absence of volition, for example, instruments may vary greatly in their internal characteristics, as (17) shows:

17. The administration dazzled us with improbable ideas.

What principally matters is *the role the argument plays in the predication* (though it must be stressed that some properties may contribute more significantly to this role). Consequently, instruments are no more likely, in principle, to occur with agents than with authors:

18a. The boy dried the clothes with the blow dryer. (agent)
  b. The truck ran over the rose bushes with its back tire. (author)

As long as one argument may be construed as exerting proper influence over the instrument, instrumentality is maintained.

It is crucial that there be, implicitly or explicitly, *another argument* to exert the proper influence, a condition that affects the overall grammatical coding of instruments. By far the most common pattern is to mark instruments obliquely, less commonly as objects, and even less commonly as subjects (see Givón 1984:

39). The logic to this pattern is clear. Clauses with obliques must have at least *one other grammatical role*—subject, if intransitive—to be well-formed, and the chances are high that the required external agent will be coded in that role. The same is true for instruments as objects. In the next example, a syntactic variation of (14a), the agent surfaces as the subject, with the instrument as *object:*

19. Ellen used a knife to cut the salami.

But *instrumental subjects* are rare because the coding tendencies of agents are the inverse of those for the instrumental. To put it simply, if the instrument appears as the subject, where is the required additional argument going to appear? Instrumental subjects are thus more likely in cases where the required additional argument—say, the agent—is pragmatically deducible, as in (20):

20. The rock broke the window.
     (i.e., 'somebody broke the window with the rock')

The predicate 'break' has a pragmatically inferrible agent, so the instrument can assume the subject position. The coding tendencies of instruments have discernible semantic correlates. The preference for oblique grammatical roles is related to the semantic requirement of an additional argument to denote the necessary external force for instrumentality.

5.222.   *Logical Recipients*

The three thematic roles of agent, author, and instrument are all associated with the *logical actor* of the event. We now proceed to three thematic roles associated with the *logical recipient* of the event: *patient, experiencer,* and *benefactive.* We begin with the canonical recipient, *patient.*

5.2221.   Patient

If an argument undergoes, is changed by, or is directly affected by a predicate, it is a *patient*. This choice of terminology reflects the fact that a patient *suffers* the situation, or comes out changed as a result of the action of the predicate. Just as the agent is the primary executor of the event, so the patient is the primary recipient.

The following are some examples from English that illustrate the patient:

21a. The man cleaned the car.
  b. The boy broke the glass.

In the situation represented by (21a), the car undergoes the cleaning and comes out changed by the act. Similarly, in the situation of (21b), the glass is directly affected by the actions of the predicate *break;* clearly, the glass comes out changed because of the action. In contrast, in the events of *I received the letter,* the letter does not undergo anything and is not changed by the act of receiving. Therefore, even though the letter is subject to some action, it is not a patient in this predication.

It is no coincidence that the patients in (21) are syntactically direct objects. A variety of pragmatic, semantic, and syntactic conditions conspire to have patients surface in that grammatical role. Givón (1984: 169–83) notes that patients as direct objects tend to be the secondary pragmatic focus of the sentence. Anderson (1984) defines direct objects dependently, as nonsubjects; Keenan (1984) argues that what semantically characterizes objects is their lack of autonomy in the predication. The generalization thus appears to be that pragmatic, syntactic, and semantic *dependency* converge on patients as direct objects, unlike agents, their logical counterpart, characterized by semantic autonomy.

The convergence of direct objects and patients is no doubt a consequence of the connection of patienthood to *transitivity,* syntactically, the presence of a direct object, and semantically, *the degree of effect an agent has on a patient via a predicate.* Hopper and Thompson (1980) argue that transitivity is derived from a constellation of factors, such as the degree of activity of the predicate, the potency and volitionality of the agent, and affectedness and individuation of the patient. Clauses high in transitivity have more canonical patients, so although these sentences are both transitive, (22a) conveys a more typical patient than does (22b):

22a. The Marines wiped out the small battalion.
  b. The Marines bought some flowers.

In (22a), the action is expressed by a verb of high activity, with a potent agent and a totally affected, individuated patient. Contrary facts hold for (22b), where the verb does not express potent action by a volitional doer and the patient is not individuated or totally affected. Consequently, the object in (22a) more typically evinces patienthood than does the object in (22b): Even though both clauses are transitive, the former is transitive *to a greater degree.*

These examples show not only that patienthood itself is scalar, but also that patients are conceptually tied to agents, though not vice versa. There can be agents without patients (e.g., *John ran*), but patients themselves are sensible only against a *transitive background,* one in which some potent agent or author is presumed to have acted.

Let us now turn to another language, Tagalog, for comparison and exemplification of the clear coding of *patient.* Tagalog is a *topic prominent* language, which means, in simplified terms, that the language signals sentence

topic as a separate grammatical relation—often in lieu of subjects—and topic
controls a variety of syntactic phenomena that, in subject-oriented languages like
English, are controlled by subject (e.g., deletions, agreement, coreference: see
Li and Thompson 1976; Schachter 1976). In Tagalog, all arguments are marked
by a preposition for thematic role. In addition, one argument in every predication
is marked as the topic, by the topic preposition, precluding its normal marking
for thematic role. The verb is then marked for the thematic role of the argument
that is also the topic. So, if an argument is a patient, it is marked as such, but if it
is also the topic under discussion, the argument is instead marked for topic, and
the predicate is then marked to show that its patient is the topic of discussion
(Foley and Van Valin 1984: 72; see also Gil 1984: 91, though Gil's explanation
conflicts with Foley and Valin's):

23. binsang-Ø   ng   lalake ang   baso.
    broke   Pat/Topic Actor   man   Topic   glass
    The man broke the glass.
    More accurately: The glass, it's what the man broke.

In (23), the verb takes a zero marking; this indicates that the patient is the topic.
So in Tagalog, the semantic content of the thematic role has a clear grammatical
reflex.

Given this discussion of patients and their canonical form, an additional
question arises. If canonical agents have a "weak form," authors, do canonical
patients have a similar "weak form"? The answer appears to be *maybe*. In the
recent theoretical literature, Wilkins (1987) and Lebeaux (1988) argue for a weak
version of patient called *affected*.[2] Although the validity of this role is still a
matter of debate—it has not been tested cross-linguistically and is not a received
term—there is some evidence that a distinction must be made between fully
affected (patients) and nonfully affected arguments (affected).

A patient is an argument that is acted on by an agent and changed by a
predicate. The affected argument is simply acted on, but not altered. Note how
the direct object in (24a) is a patient, but it is only affected in (24b):

24a. John burned the book.
  b. John picked up the book.

That is, in the state of affairs of (24a), the book undergoes the burning and is
changed by it, but in that of (24b), the book is simply affected by the action, not
changed. Wilkins (1987) observes that an *ergative paraphrase* (which means, in

---

[2]Specifically, Lebeaux argues for *affected* as a property of a thematic role, not as a special role
itself, while Wilkins appears to claim that it is a separate role.

means, in her terms, that an object of a transitive becomes the subject of an intransitive with full active reading) is possible for only (24a):

25a. The book burns (easily). [= ergative of (24a)]
  b. ?? The book picks up (easily). [= ergative of (24b)]

Example (24b) must have a *middle paraphrase* (where the transitive object becomes the intransitive subject with a passive reading). The distinct middle reading is clearer with *get* in English; note that (25a) does not have the middle reading:

26a. The book gets picked up (easily). [= middle of (24b)]
  b. ?? The book gets burned easily (easily). [= middle of (24a)]

Wilkins (1987) claims that middles take affected arguments whereas ergatives take patients. Whether this is true across the board remains to be seen; the facts do, however, seem to be related to, and perhaps derivable from, degree of transitivity: For example, *burn* is a more active predicate than *pick up*. But it is worth noting here that the affected, or weak patient, is distributed very much like the author, or weak agent. All patients are affected, but not vice versa; so all agents are authors, but not vice versa. If the patient/affected distinction turns out to have the pervasive grammatical consequences that the agent/author distinction does, then this new thematic role will be worth refining (see also chap. 1, p. 13, for additional discussion).

5.2222.   Experiencer

If a predicate affects the *internal state or constitution* of an argument, then the argument has the thematic role *experiencer*. Sentence (27) has either an experiencer or nonexperiencer reading:

27. Buddy smelled the flowers.

In one situation, Buddy goes out and sniffs the flowers; in that case, he is an agent because the event is attributable to Buddy as a volitional instigator. In another sense, the situation is such that the smell of flowers *comes over* Buddy and registers in his head; in this case, Buddy does nothing volitionally, but experiences the event. In the experiencer reading, Buddy's internal constitution is affected by the external event, and the event itself takes place only insofar as Buddy registers it internally.

Because internally affected entities have to have an internal state to register the effect, experiencers frequently turn out to be human, or at least animate (Fillmore 1968). But because what counts as an internal state is fuzzy and may be construed differently by a culture or domain of discourse, experiencers are not necessarily animate. It is necessary only that external experience be registered internally, or that experiencers *have a disposition.*

Nonetheless, experiencers are overwhelmingly found among human and animate arguments of predicates of internal effect, precisely because of a bias toward animate entities as possessors of complicated internal states. So Brekke (1988: 176, n. 2) argues that experiencers are specifically humans who can perceive and interpret external data (i.e., have a working disposition), take in the data uncontrollably (i.e., lack volition and do not instigate the event), and respond subjectively (i.e., have private worlds). Although it takes no imagination to see that these criteria also apply to machines, they do predict that experiencers will be associated with psychological or emotive predicates.

Brekke (1988) uses these criteria to argue that certain morphological facts about *ing-adjectives* are predictable from what he calls the *experiencer constraint:* Verbs have corresponding *ing-adjectives* only if they select for experiencers. Hence (28a) is allowed, but (28b) is not:

28a. a very arresting thought.
   b. ?? a very arresting policeman.

The former is acceptable because the underlying predicate, *arrest,* means 'cause a disturbing internal state *to someone'* and selects an experiencer. The latter is ruled out because the underlying predicate means 'cause the arrest of,' which has no experiencer. In Brekke's view the recognition of an action by an experiencer licenses the *ing-adjective.*

Experiencers are logical recipients of action—actions flow into them—so languages often mark them in oblique syntactic forms: that is, those grammatical relations and forms other than subject and direct object, like the dative. In Spanish for example, the proposition 'I like the cake,' which clearly requires an experiencer because liking involves the mental registration of pleasurable input, surfaces with the experiencer in an oblique case:

29. me   gusta el   pastel.
     to me please the cake
     I like the cake.
     More accurately: The cake is pleasing to me.

Similarly, in colloquial Polish, the proposition 'I am sad,' another internally registered state, surfaces with the experiencer also in the dative:

30. smutno mi
     sad   I/Dat
     I am sad.

A look at other languages shows a wide variety of experiencer constructions. In Kannada, a whole series of internal-state predicates take experiencers, not only the expected predicates of liking, but also those of possession and knowledge (Hermon 1984: 200–9):

> 31a. Sōma-nige tānu tumba ishṭa.
> Soma Dat self much liking
> Soma is very fond of himself.
>
> b. ava-ḷige āru makkaḷu iddāre.
> she Dat six children are
> She has six children.
>
> c. Asha-ḷige nāvu gottu- dīvi.
> Asha Dat we   know Past/3Pl
> Asha knew us.

Even predicates of "general occurrence" or happenstance, because they refer to registered internal states derived from external factors, take experiencers in Kannada:

> 32. ava-nige Koppa-kke varga   āyitu.
> he Dat Koppa-to   transfer happened
> He was transferred to Koppa.
> More accurately: He happened to be transferred to Koppa.

Data such as that from Kannada indicates that many more predicates in English than ordinarily thought take experiencers: *have, seem, think,* and so on. Genitive structures also, like *John's book,* are probably best analyzed as implicit experiencers because possession appears to be universally viewed as an internal state. The crucial fact, of course, is the construal of *internal.* Disposition to register external experience seems to be the key factor.

5.2223.   Benefactive

We have thus far considered two kinds of recipients: those that undergo acts (patients) and those that are affected internally (experiencers). There is a third kind: those that derive actions or entities from the actions of another. Such recipients are called *benefactives.*

This thematic role may be seen in the following sentence, which is ambiguous between a benefactive and nonbenefactive reading:

> 33. Dr. Frankenstein made his son a monster.

On one reading, the nonbenefactive one, Dr. Frankenstein's son is a patient: 'Dr.

Frankenstein converted his son into a monster.' On the other reading, the benefactive one, Dr. Frankenstein's son comes into the possession of something
because the actions of Dr. Frankenstein bring it about: 'Dr. Frankenstein made a
monster *for* his son.' In this latter reading, *his son* is an argument with a benefactive relation to the predicate.

Benefactives may be viewed, alternatively, as arguments inherently dependent
on surrogates. As Fillmore (1968) observes, benefactives typically require an
agent elsewhere in the predication. In the situation expressed by the benefactive
reading of (33), Dr. Frankenstein is a surrogate, or substitute performer, for his
son, carrying out the requisite actions so that subsequent states of affairs may
result. The surrogacy may even be so strong as to preempt or preclude action by
the benefactive, as in the following examples, where the benefactive indirect
objects are co-opted:

34a. Tom lost the game for his team.
   b. Mary bought lunch for Bob.

In (34a), the event is such that the losing affects all participants, but only one of
them, Tom, actually carries out the act expressed: The team derives the result
from the surrogate act of Tom. Similarly, in the event of (34b), only Mary
actually carries out the act. Bob is the benefactive: He derives a result from
Mary's actions and is, in fact, *prevented* from doing the act of paying because of
Mary's agency.

The examples in (34) raise two additional points. First, despite the nomenclature, benefactives do not necessarily *benefit* from the surrogate actions of
others, as (34) illustrates. Benefactives, more generally, relate to the "benefit"
of surrogate action, not to the goodness of the result. In this way, benefactives
look very much like instruments, only where instruments are secondary agents,
benefactives are secondary recipients.

Second, the co-optation illustrated in (34) is not a necessary feature of benefactives, just an example of extreme surrogacy. In the state of affairs expressed
by *Harry did Tom a favor,* Tom is a benefactive, though it is unlikely that Harry
has co-opted Tom's actions because Tom has done nothing, only benefitted. It is
fundamental to benefactives that the state of affairs be the result of another's acts
whether or not those acts go so far as to preempt or preclude the acts of the
benefactive.

These observations provide a key to the kind of predications that select for
benefactives. Benefactives co-occur with agents, and thus are likely to be found
in nonstative predicates, especially nonstative predicates of result. Consequently,
resultative, motional, and transactional predicates quite commonly select for the
benefactive, in contrast to simple states, as these examples illustrate:

35a. ?? I was tall for John. (state)
   b. I sang the song for Fred. (result)

c. I sent the letter for Bill. (motion)

d. I paid the bill for him. (transaction)

Benefactives overwhelmingly tend to be human, and so if they are secondary recipients, they are unlike their counterparts in agency, instruments, which tend to be inanimate. The logic to the animacy of benefactives is fairly straightforward. Benefactives have surrogates; were it not for the surrogates, the individuals having the benefactive role would have carried out the acts themselves, which requires potency, and hence animacy. This is in contrast to instruments, which cannot carry out acts independently. Example (36a) is therefore possible, but (36b) is not:

36a. I cut the salami for Bill. ('instead of Bill doing it')

b. ?? I cut the salami for the knife. (?? 'instead of the knife doing it')

Benefactives are relatively easy to find in the world's languages. They frequently occur with motional and transactional predicates, so they are often not formally distinguished from markers of 'motion toward' (see the discussion later on *goal*). In Niuean, however, benefactives have a distinct form, as the difference between (37a) and (37b) shows (Seiter 1979: 32 and 36):

37a. Gahua a   au ma e   tagata kō.
     work Abs I Ben Abs man that
     I work for that man.

b. Fia tutala a   au ki a   Sione.
   want talk   Abs I to Humn Sione
   I want to talk to John.

In (37a), the benefactive is marked with *ma,* but in (37b), the nonbenefactive spatial recipient of the motion is marked differently, with *ki* ('to'). Just as in English, Niuean sentences with benefactives convey the sense of surrogacy, further support for Fillmore's (1968) contention that benefactives often depend on the presence of agency elsewhere in the predication.

5.223.  Spatial Roles

Up to this point, we have examined samples of two general classes of thematic relations: those that are roughly associated with *actional doers* and those with *actional receivers.* There are three additional thematic roles that share many of the properties of those already described—indeed, are sometimes formally indistinguishable from those already mentioned—but are best understood in primarily spatial terms. These are the thematic roles *theme, source,* and *goal,* which we have already considered briefly in our discussion of motion (p. 170).

The overlap of these three roles with others, like agent and patient, is well-known, and the admission of such an overlap is not meant to diminish their importance or to call into question otherwise clearly differentiated roles. On the contrary, this overlap highlights the conceptual connections across all roles and suggests that an adequate theory of thematic roles must accommodate this overlap (more on this in sec. 5.3).

Even though theme, source, and goal are described in terms of their spatial structure (or the "where" of a predication), they are still participant roles because they are often associated with actors and recipients and frequently surface in the direct grammatical roles of subject and direct object. By these measures, then, they deserve attention under participant roles.

5.2231. Theme

We begin our discussion with *theme*. As we know, in the prototypical situation of motion, some entity is displaced as the result of an initiator's influence and moves from some resting point along a trajectory, often to another resting point. The displaced entity is the *theme* of the predication of displacement.

The following sentences illustrate themes:

38 a. Tom shot the arrow through the air.
   b. Bill rolled the ball across the floor.

In the event expressed by (38a), the arrow is the displaced entity and hence is the theme; the same holds for the ball in the situation of (38b).

These examples raise the question of how to differentiate theme from patient. After all, in the shooting of the arrow, the arrow not only moves, but is also affected by the act. The two are usually differentiated by explaining that the theme is much like the patient in that each undergoes an act, but the theme is *unchanged* (Fillmore 1977). Themes undergo acts because of the need for an external force for their displacement, but they are not modified by the displacement itself. This difference may be seen in the following:

39 a. Bob loaded the paper onto the cart.
   b. Bob ripped apart the paper.

In the situation represented by (39a), the paper is displaced from a starting point to a resting point as a result of the act of an agent, Bob; crucially, the paper is not changed by the act of loading. In contrast, in the situation of (39b), the paper comes out changed *because of the action:* not only displaced but also altered in its constituency. Strictly speaking, in (39b), the paper is a patient, not a theme.

If themes look like patients because of the presence of an external energy source operating on them to displace them, then they may also look like agents and authors if the energy source is self-contained, that is, if there is self-displacement (see Jackendoff 1972: 20–43 for good discussion):

40a. Fred rolled down the hill.
  b. Mr. O'Hara flew in from Ireland.

Example (40a) has either a volitional or nonvolitional reading. In one situation, Fred propels himself down the hill: the purely agentive reading. In the other situation, Fred is propelled down the hill by some external source. It is in this latter reading that the role of theme is assigned because Fred is an unchanged mover. In contrast, (40b) is basically unambiguous. In the event expressed, Mr. O'Hara moves unchanged in space from Ireland. Indeed, a rendering truer to the external facts is *Mr. O'Hara was flown in from Ireland*. In this sense, the argument in question clearly has the properties of theme: the unmodified, displaced entity.

The sensitivity of English syntax to the role of theme has been fairly well studied. English, like many languages, has a productive alternation of theme-as-patient and theme-as-instrument, respectively illustrated here:

41a. Bill wrapped the string around the package. (theme/patient)
  b. Bill wrapped the package with string. (theme/instrument)

The sentences are by no means absolute paraphrases; the theme in (41a) is more in focus. But in each case, the situation is such that the string is displaced unalterably.

The same kind of alternation is found in Bemba (Givón 1984: 116):

42a. a- à- cimine ifumo mu- ndofu.
    he Past thrust spear into elephant
    He thrust a spear into the elephant.
  b. a- à- cimine indofu ne- efumo.
    he Past thrust elephant Instr elephant
    He stabbed the elephant with a spear.

In each situation, the spear is the theme, the unaffected displaced object. In (42a), it surfaces like a patient; in (42b), more like an instrument.

A clear example of theme encoded directly can be seen in Choctaw, where the theme is productively marked in the verbal system. The auxiliary verb that indicates completed action has two forms, one for subjects that are nonthemes and one specifically for themes (Broadwell 1988: 124):

43a. habiinat tahli-   lih.
    receive complete/non-theme I
    I received them
  b. iyat ii- tahah.
    go we complete/theme
    We went

In (43a), the event is such that the subject does not perform the motion proper—is not a theme—and thus takes *tahli,* the auxiliary for nontheme subjects; in (43b), however, the picture changes: The subject is displaced, and the auxiliary is *tahah* to reflect the status of the subject as theme.

5.2232. Source

We have seen that a language may signal the object displaced in a predication. It is also common for a language to make reference to the point of origin of displacement. The argument with this thematic role is the *source.* In motion predicates, *source* is readily seen:

44a. The cat leaped from the bag.
  b. I received a letter from Mr. Smith.

In the event represented by (44a), the bag is the point of origin of the cat's leaping; in that of (44b), the transfer of the letter has its origin in Mr. Smith.

Sources, as the point of origin of a predication, are not restricted to purely spatial events and can be found in predicates that express any actional or stative source, whether or not motion is involved:

45a. Mr. O'Hara is from Ireland.
  b. The sun gives off heat.
  c. Wine can turn into vinegar.
  d. The publisher bought the rights from the author.

In the facts of (45a), Ireland is a source even though no spatial motion obtains (compare *Mr. O'Hara just came from Ireland,* where the event changes but the thematic roles are constant). In the situation of (45b), the sun is a source, though again the specific motion is indiscernible (hence the more motional paraphrase *Heat comes from the sun,* where the thematic roles are retained). In (45c), wine is a source, and there is no motion at all, just as in *Cheese comes from milk* and *Milk comes from cows* (these are often called *provenance relations:* see Evens et al. 1980). In (45d), the transaction is not spatial at all because what is expressed is abstract transfer; nonetheless, the transaction has an origin in the author.

Motion typically brings out sources, but the motion may be abstract, as in *His opinions run from liberal to Libertarian,* or not present at all, as in *My demons spur me into action.* Critical to the thematic role of source is a point of origin.

Similar semantic features characterize sources in other languages. In West Greenlandic Eskimo, motional and nonmotional points of origin are thematic sources and are marked alike (Fortescue 1984: 214):

46a. Fari- mit   allagar-si- vuq.
     Fari Source letter   get 3Per
     He got a letter from Fari (motional).
  b. tuttu-   mit   nassuk
     caribou Source horn.
     caribou horn ('horn from a caribou': nonmotional).

The situation of (46b) is very much like that of (45c): Caribou is the material origin of the horn, and this is sufficient to code it as a source in West Greenlandic Eskimo.

In many languages, the coding system for sources is also used to indicate whether the denotation of an argument is the topic of discourse—that is, source of information, or 'aboutness.' This use of source is often called a *reference-related* (or pragmatic) coding, as opposed to a *role-related* coding in the strict semantic sense (see Foley and Van Valin 1984; Schachter 1977). But the use is worth noting here because of its productivity. In English, the preposition *of* may mark semantic source, as in (47a), or discourse topic, as in (47b):

47a. The boat is made of wood. ('from wood')
  b. We talked of our pasts. ('about our pasts')

For comparison, consider Nguna, where the encoding of source expresses not only material and nonmaterial point of origin (semantic), as in (48a), but also discourse topic, as in (48b) (Schutz 1969: 39):

48a. au mari nakoau asa.
     we make pudding Source-it
     We make pudding from it.
  b. a noa ki sua   e   asa.
     I tell Obj Compl him Source-it
     I told him about it.

The thematic role of source appears to have a very general function, from the source of motion, to material and nonmaterial origin, to the topic of discourse. These results lend support to the overall model articulated in Chapter 2 of a continuum of pragmatic and semantic information. This thematic role is the convergence of discourse and propositional sources.

5.2233. Goal

If the origin of a predication can be marked as a distinct thematic role, so too can the destination. This is called the *goal*. The sentences in (49) all contain goals.

As with theme and source, the goal surfaces very clearly in predicates of concrete motion:

49a. My wife went to England last summer.
  b. Bob ran to the corner.

In their respective states of affairs, England and the corner are the goals of the predicates because they are the endpoints of the events.

Like sources, goals are not restricted to motion predicates. If the predication involves a destination, whether or not the means to that destination is spatial, then the argument denoting the destination has the role of goal. So, nonspatial conveyance also selects for goal:

50a. I told Ellen the story.
  b. Two new ideas came to me.
  c. The highway runs to the sea.

Sentence (50a) represents a case where Ellen is the goal of my words, though it is difficult to see how Ellen is the destination of any concrete motion; sentence (50b) expresses the fact that I am the goal of the ideas, and again, concrete motion is indiscernible. The absence of motion is especially clear in (50c), where the highway is said to merely reach the endpoint of the sea, not actually move toward it. What matters for goal, just as what matters for source, is lexicalization of a point, in this case an endpoint.

Given the nature of goals as endpoints, they are very likely to overlap with other thematic roles. Goals look very much like patients because both are "destinations" of actions; similarly, goals evoke the properties of benefactives because the latter, requiring surrogates, are logically the intermediate goal of an agent. These convergences underlie a well-known syntactic alternation, the *dative shift,* whereby obliquely coded indirect objects, as in (51a), have an alternate direct object form, as in (51b).

51a. Bob did the favor for Tom.
  b. Bob did Tom a favor.

When benefactives surface in this alternation, they look like patients, or direct recipients of the action. What stays constant, however, in this benefactive/patient alternation are the *goal properties* of the argument. So, in each situation of (51), Tom is the goal: The destination of the action is constant under the syntactic transformation.

A particularly interesting marker of goal occurs in Mandarin Chinese. Spatial expressions occur either preverbally or postverbally. With motion predicates, the preverbal form indicates static location—the fixed spatial position of the event;

in postverbal position, however, the phrase indicates the goal. This difference is illustrated here (Li and Thompson 1981: 399):

52a. tā   zài zhuōzi shang tiào.
     3Per at table   on   jump
     S/he is jumping (up and down) on the table. (preverbal; location of
       event)
  b. tā   tiào zài zhuōzi shang.
     3Per jump at table   on
     S/he is jumping onto the table. (postverbal; goal of event)

This positional constraint carries over into expressions of pure goal. *Dào* ('to') may occur pre- or postverbally because it inherently expresses the goal (and thus can never be given a static locational reading), but if it co-occurs with a verb that also inherently expresses destination, the goal argument *must* occur postverbally (Li and Thompson 1981: 410):

53. wǒmen fēi dào shànghǎi le.
    we   fly to Shanghai Completed
    We flew to Shanghai.

The relevant semantic generalization for Mandarin is that postverbal position is invariably associated with the results and destinations of predicates (see Li and Thompson 1981: 390–414). Insofar as goals are spatial results, they are constrained to occur in that position.

5.224. Summary

In this section, we have discussed nine major participant roles: three associated with the logical actor (agent, author, and instrument), three with the logical recipient (patient, experiencer, and benefactive), and three with characteristics of both and best understood in spatial terms (theme, source, and goal). We have tried to determine the criterial semantic properties for each role: volitional action for the agent, nonvolitional action for the author, external force for the instrument, change for the patient, internal disposition for the experiencer, surrogacy for the benefactive, displacement for the theme, point of origin for the source, and point of destination for the goal. Throughout, we have looked at the grammatical reflexes of these roles (e.g., dative alternation for the benefactive) and their illustration in languages other than English. More detailed theories of thematic roles often have additional participant roles beyond these nine—for example, *comitative, complement, counteragent,* and so on—though all can be understood in terms of our basic distinction between actors and recipients in participant roles.

5.23.   Nonparticipant Roles

We now consider nonparticipant, or circumstantial, roles, which derive from the semantic context of the predication rather than inherent selection by the predication. Informally, we have said the participant roles signal "who did what to whom." Nonparticipant roles signal "where, why, when, and how."

By imagining all the details of the semantic context of a predication, we can determine a wide range of nonparticipant roles: for example, different kinds of locations, reasons, and times. In the interest of representativeness rather than exhaustiveness, we restrict our discussion to three nonparticipant roles—*locative, reason,* and *purpose*—and even within those three, our analysis is rather more global than fine-grained. Other important nonparticipant roles, like *manner, path,* and *time,* are treated elsewhere. Manner and path are considered in Chapter 4 in the analysis of motion; time is discussed in Chapter 8, on tense.

5.231.   Locative

In our discussion of participant spatial roles (sec. 5.223), we considered the initial point, destination, and displaced object. Here we examine the fixed spatial organization of a situation. The argument that denotes the spatial position of the predicate is the *locative;* it is the *site* of the predication, or its static position. The following sentences illustrate the locative:

54a.   The cloud floated in the sky.
  b.   I sat behind Sally.
  c.   My brother works at the store.

In the situation of (54a), the sky is the site for the floating; in that of (54b), Sally is the locational reference point for the sitting; in that of (54c), the store is the site for the working.

When we think of the variety of spatial positions that an object or event can assume, we might immediately conclude that there is a virtually unlimited number of locative roles that an argument may encode. A simple run through the English prepositions shows the startling number of possibilities: *in, on, above, over,* and so forth. But we are interested only in the fact that the locative is a relation between a predicate and an argument. Types of location are spelled out fully in Chapter 6, under location and deixis.

Locative itself is a unitary relation. From the standpoint of thematic roles, there is no difference among *next to, beside, along side of, on the right of,* and *two feet directly to the left of.* All these denote the relative fixed (lateral) position of the participants. They do differ on such things as the distance between entities (*two feet*) and perspective of the speaker (*right of*), but these differences do not affect the relative fixed positions of the participants and are all *thematically locative.*

In languages other than English, the forms of the locative role are often very numerous, though the semantic principles remain the same. West Greenlandic Eskimo marks 19 locative relations thematically. All the relations discussed in Chapter 6 are found, plus some more specific relations formed by combining locational and nonlocational properties (Fortescue 1984: 232–3):

55a. qajaq ilulissa- p   nala- a- niip- puq.
     kayak iceberg Rel level its be at 3Per/Indic
     The kayak was level with the iceberg.

  b. qiqirtar-su- up assu-   a- ni.
     island   big Rel windward its Loc
     on the windward side of the big island.

Example (55a) shows the combination of lateral position with vertical measurement ('level with'); example (55b) illustrates the fusion of lateral position and culturally defined source ('windward'). But in spite of the variation of semantic content, in each case, West Greenlandic Eskimo encodes fixed spatial position of the predication.

5.232. Reason

All predications are motivated by other events and facts. The arguments that denote the prior conditions of a predication have the thematic role *reason*. Reasons are good examples of nonparticipants roles because they are clearly located on the contextual level, outside of strict participant involvement in the predication. This is because reasons are connected to the *intentions of the agent* and as such rely on prior events themselves for their existence. Reasons may thus be said to link other events to a predication by means of the motivation of an agent. In this way, reasons seem very much like instruments, only contextually located.

The following sentences all contain reasons:

56a. I ran from fear.
  b. Bob jogs because of his need to keep fit.
  c. The murderer acted out of passion.

In the events of (56a), fear precedes and motivates the running; in those of (56b), the need to keep fit motivates the jogging; in those of (56c), passion motivates the actions. In all three cases, the reasons derive from events external to the predication and motivate the predication through the intentions of the agent.

Reasons are *prior conditions,* and thus they are often coded like sources. English is a language that conflates source and reason marking. Sentence (57) is ambiguous between a source reading and a reason reading:

57. We ran from the horrible art.

In one sense, with source, the sentence means 'the point of origin of our physical displacement was the spatial position held by the horrible art'; in the other, with reason, it means 'we ran because of the motivating prior condition of horrible art (whatever its spatial position).' Each sense may be differentiated by supplying expressions to pick out the relevant semantic properties:

58a. We ran from the horrible art down to the awful coffee shop in the museum's basement. (source)
   b. We ran from the horrible art so as to save our sensibilities. (reason)

The connection between reasons and sources is understandable. Reasons, like sources, *precede* events, but do so at the level of contextually determined action. Unlike sources, reasons do not necessarily initiate or originate the events, though their motivational effects can be traced through the agent.

We have characterized reasons as prior conditions for the predication. But a number of counterexamples immediately surface. Consider (59):

59. Tom is wearing a tie because he has a job interview this afternoon.

In the situation of (59), the job interview motivates the tie wearing, but doesn't the interview *follow,* not precede, Tom's action? To answer this properly, we must keep in mind the distinction between *reasons as semantic phenomena* and the *actual events themselves.* In the facts described by (59), it is the *anticipation* of the job interview that motivates the wearing of the tie, not the actual job interview. So, the interview is a prior condition *as an expectation,* as part of the *agent's intentions.* As an actual event, a reason may follow what it motivates, but as part of the semantic representation based on a mentally projected world, reasons precede their predications.

This interaction of precedence and subsequence in the establishment of reasons is clearer if we see that reasons, as prior conditions, are judged only in their subsequent results. Priority is a dependent notion and cannot be evaluated outside of consequence. No doubt this logical connection underlies the fact that languages often encode reasons and results alike (i.e., purposes, see p. 227): There is a natural connection between the goals of actions and their anticipation.

Although the easy differentiation of reasons and results may be unexpected, fairly straightforward marking of reason as a thematic role may be found in Southwest Tanna. This language has a "reason preposition" (Lynch 1982: 41):

60. i- ak- a- mha tukw   kamaam.
    I Pres Prog sick Reason fish
    I am sick from the fish.

Here, *tukw* marks something like a nonspatial or contextual source. Significantly, the form is also glossed as 'cause' and 'future' (Lynch 1982: 58), indicating its semantic status in linking events: that is, reasons are potential causes for future events.

5.233. *Purpose*

If reasons may be viewed as the motivational sources of predications, what, then, are the motivational goals? A language may thematically code the result or consequence of a predicate. An argument with this role is the *purpose*.

Here are some sentences illustrating purpose arguments:

61a. I went to the doctor for a checkup.
  b. Tom has a silk shirt for impressing his friends.

In the events of (61a), the checkup is the goal of the action; in (61b) impressing his friends is the result of Tom's having the silk shirt.

Though purposes and reasons seem very much alike, we must be careful not to confuse the two, especially because languages often sharply differentiate them. Purposes focus on the *contextual endpoints of predications*. In fact, the purpose arguments in (61) may be converted to reasons quite simply by shifting the focus of the predicates to their prior conditions:

62a. I went to the doctor because of my checkup.
  b. Tom has a silk shirt from impressing his friends.

The meaning of (62a) is now something like 'I went to the doctor as a result of the anticipation of the checkup'; that of (62b) is something like 'Tom is now in the possession of a silk shirt *because of his prior actions* of impressing his friends.' In (62b), the possession *follows the reason,* as contrasted with (61b), where the possession *precedes the purpose*. Reasons are the motivational sources of predicates whereas purposes are their motivational goals.

These semantic distinctions are not meant to imply that purposes are always easily sorted out from reasons in the coding systems of the world's languages. Reasons may be differentiated from purposes by overt marking. But because of the inherent dependency of results (purposes) on prior conditions (reasons), it is quite common for languages to conflate reasons and purposes in overt form.

Nonetheless, there are good examples of strictly coded purpose. The connection of purpose to subsequent action can be seen in West Greenlandic Eskimo, where the marker for the thematic role of purpose typically co-occurs with the marker for futurity (Fortescue 1984: 218):

63. aalisar-nir- mut aturtu-   ssa- t.
    fish   Nom Purp equipment Fut Pl
    fishing equipment
    More accurately: equipment that will be used for fishing.

The only other temporal marker to co-occur with purpose arguments is habituality (Fortescue 1984: 218):

64. aalisar-nir- mut atur-tar-   para.
    fish   Nom Purp use Habit 1/3Per
    I (generally) use it for fishing.

Habituality is a logical counterpart of futurity because it indicates extended action and therefore retains the property of *subsequence* that is basic to purpose.

5.234.   Summary

In this section, we have looked at the structure and grammatical manifestation of three nonparticipant roles: locative, reason, and purpose. Locative is the fixed site of the predication; reason and purpose are, respectively, the prior conditions and the contextual goals of the predication. We have not looked at the roles of path, manner, and time, normally considered in discussions of nonparticipant roles, because they are treated in detail elsewhere (under motion and tense).

5.3.   UNIFIED TREATMENTS
OF THEMATIC ROLES: LOCALISM,
MACROROLES, AND LINKING THEORY

We have developed a basic picture of the major thematic roles available to any language. Throughout this discussion, we have implicitly addressed two theoretical concerns.

First, there is the question of conceptual connections across the roles. We have treated the 12 thematic roles separately, but we have often noted that some roles share criterial attributes with others. This unity is one of the motivations behind the distinction between participant and nonparticipant roles. But among the particular roles themselves, we have seen that certain properties recur. Agents and authors share all properties but volition. We have also seen that goals and purposes are very similar: the former a spatial destination and the latter a motivational one. Is there any way to unify the roles, in the way that we tried to unify entities and events? Can we provide an integrated semantic picture of them, and in doing so, reduce their number to more manageable size?

Second, we have often remarked on the tendencies for some roles to surface in particular grammatical forms, the convergence of agency and subject, for example. Can we be more precise about how semantic roles map onto grammatical roles? And how does such an inquiry fare in relation to a unified semantic account of the roles themselves?

In this section we turn our attention to three proposals concerning the conceptual unity and regularities of grammatical encoding of thematic roles. All three are attempts to provide unified treatments of thematic roles, very much along the lines of those we studied earlier for entities and events. So, we pick up this way of thinking and examine localism (and its offshoots), macroroles, and linking theory. The first two are theories that seek to pare down the number of thematic roles to a small set and derive the full range therefrom; the third is a cover term for theories that account for the regular grammatical reflexes of thematic roles: The name derives from the linking of semantic roles to grammatical roles.

5.31. Localism

5.311. *The Nature of Localism*

Localism is the belief that semantic and conceptual information is reducible to concrete spatial information (whence the name *localism*, or locale). Adherents of localism point to the ontological primacy of the physical world to argue for the spatial base of all reference and predication. Abstract transfer has its origin in physical exchange. Temporal sequencing derives from spatial contiguity. Cause and effect are regularized precedence and subsequence: Spatial priority comes to be systematized as actional cause, and *post hoc ergo propter hoc* ('after the fact, therefore because of it') is turned into an axiom. Thus, Lyons (1979: 139) remarks: "It seems natural to assume that the spatial locative expressions are psychologically basic and serve as the structural templates, as it were, for the more abstract expressions." And certainly the psychological evidence is there: Piaget's theory of cognitive development shows how abstract notions derive from concrete spatial relations. Anderson is a true localist in this matter. The last sentence of his book is a dismissal of causation as an unanalyzable notion: "The notion 'causative' is thus not semantically primitive" (1971: 219) because it can be derived from spatial parameters.

Although localism is often touted as the ultimate epistemology, it is actually a rather traditional and even commonsense view of meaning and conceptual categories. All of our knowledge, semantic and conceptual, has a concrete perceptual base in sense data, information registered from the physical, spatial world (Anderson 1971: 5–9).

The premise of localist theories of the unification of thematic roles follows the spirit, indeed the letter, of the localist law: "Not only are there common principles underlying spatial and non-spatial cases [thematic roles, WF], but . . . also . . . the spatial variant has ontological . . . priority" (Anderson 1971: 12–3). In other words, all thematic roles derive from a small number of universal spatial relations, and overt case markings are superficial variations on the common, abstract spatial organization of a predication.

5.312.   *The Spatial Grounding of Predication and Thematic Roles*

5.3121.   Predication and Localism

To understand localism, we have to reconsider predication itself, but this time in entirely spatial terms. Let us imagine that every predication drives from an underlying spatial scenario, or a journey. Actions, for example, are localistically derived from motion, direction, and transference. States are derived from abstract containment. Thus, an active predicate like *eat* is abstractly '*transferral* of food from *outside* to *inside*'; a stative predicate like *be sad* is abstractly 'be *in* the mental state of sadness.'

Seen this way, spatial structures for otherwise nonspatial predications are relatively easy to construct. Some examples follow:

65a. Tom spoke to Harry.
       Localistic Structure: 'Tom originated the *displacement* of information through a *medium* to the *destination* of Harry'
  b. I saw the balloon.
       Localistic Structure: 'the balloon was the *source* of sense data impingement *on* my eyes (= me)'
  c. I am happy.
       Localistic Structure: 'happiness is *in* me'

The existence of a localistic base to all predication is supported not only by the common spatial paraphrases of otherwise nonspatial expressions—*I have the book* (nonspatial) and *The book is in my possession* (spatial)—but also by the standard use of spatial expressions for nonspatial meanings in many other languages. Possession in Russian can be expressed *only* in a spatial way:

66. U menya kniga.
      at me   book
      I have the book. (lit., 'the book is at me')

So predication itself, the basis of thematic roles, can be construed localistically.

5.3122.   Thematic Roles and Localism

If predication and the structure of events are localistic, then so too must be the relations of the arguments to the predicates. What are the fundamental components of any spatial situation, apart from the event itself? The answer is: the *location* of the event, the *origin* of the event, the *destination* of the event, the *displaced* object, and the object's *trajectory*. In terms more familiar to us, these are (respectively): locative, source, goal, theme, and path.

Nonspatial thematic roles are readily converted to these spatial terms. The agent is the volitional source of the action. The author is the nonvolitional source. The instrument is either the theme or the path: In the former sense, the instrument is the object used, and hence displaced, by the agent; in the latter sense, it is the means by which the event takes place and is thus much like the route of the action, the way it is carried out. The experiencer is the mental goal of the action; the patient is the physical goal. The benefactive is the secondary physical goal. The reason is the contextual source; the purpose is the contextual goal.[3]

The localist view of thematic roles unifies and simplifies the roles considerably, leaving us with an inventory of thematic roles much like those shown in Table 5.1. Every proposition can then be reduced to its localistic base, not only in terms of the motional and directional origins of the predication itself, but also with regard to the participant structure. So a sentence such as (67) can be given an entirely localistic gloss and the arguments assigned spatial roles:

67. Tuesday, I happily bought the car for $100 from Bob.
    Localistic Structure: 'The car came, via attendant happiness, to me on Tuesday from Bob via $100.'
    Localistic Thematic Roles: Source: Bob; Goal: I; Theme: car; Path: happily, $100; Location: Tuesday.

The easy construction of examples like the previous ones indicates that the validity of localism, in some form, is undeniable. But it is difficult to see what localism provides beyond this (though see Anderson 1973 for an attempt to derive all surface case marking from a combination of locative properties and negation). But languages do encode *action in addition to space,* and action and space do not always match up nicely. In point of fact, whereas localistic theories are incontrovertible in their basic finding, they miss the interesting fact that languages systematically *vary* their role assignment and that some languages have productive ways of *marking the difference* between localistic and nonlocalistic roles.

---

[3]Other thematic roles not discussed can also be given a localistic reduction. Manner is the path, in the sense that the manner of the action is the abstract trajectory of the act: how the act is carried out; time is locative: the temporal location of the event.

TABLE 5.1.
Localistic Reduction of Thematic Roles

Localistic Role	Nonlocalistic Role
Source	Agent, Author, Reason
Goal	Patient, Benefactive, Purpose, Experiencer
Locative	Time
Theme	Instrument
Path	Manner, Instrument

It is the difference between spatial and nonspatial roles that has given rise to a recent conception of thematic roles that, although localistic in its underpinnings, is designed to allow both spatial and nonspatial levels in a single model. This is what I call the *tier model* of case assignment. It is based on advances in modeling borrowed from autosegmental phonology, a theory of phonology in which phonological features are assigned in levels, rather than in the traditional linear segments (see Goldsmith 1976). The application of this hierarchical view of thematic roles has its most articulate rendering in Jackendoff's work (1985, 1987, 1990; see also Culicover and Wilkins 1986), to which we now turn.

5.313.   The Tier Model

5.3131.   The Theta Criterion and Multiple Roles

To understand the tier model, we must also understand something of current syntactic theory and its most influential form: Government and Binding Theory (GB). One of the fundamental principles of GB is the *Theta Criterion,* a simplicity condition on predication: *Every argument in a predication must be assigned one and only one thematic role.* The Theta Criterion is motivated by the general adherence to simplicity advocated by generative theorists—the fewest and most restrictive hypotheses the better—and so this one-to-one assignment of thematic roles is in principle the most appealing theoretical position (though it also appears to be a trumped-up rediscovery of an old principle in case grammar: Twenty years ago, Fillmore, 1968: 21, suggested the same thing).

Unfortunately for GB, it is fairly easy to come up with counterexamples to the Theta Criterion. Consider this sentence:

68. Bill bought the car.

In the events described by (68), is the car the patient or the theme? Is Bill the agent or the source? Or is Bill really the goal of the action, because buying involves transfer to the agent? How do we account for this, and the numerous other examples that we could contrive, in a theory that operates from a strict simplicity constraint like the Theta Criterion?

5.3132. Spatial and Actional Tiers

Jackendoff's (1985, 1987, 1990) answer to the questions at the end of section 5.3131 is to allow thematic roles to be assigned at different levels, in *tiers.* At one level, the *spatial tier,* there are spatial role assignments. This level then provides input into an *actional tier,* where nonspatial roles are assigned. (These tiers then provide input into other tiers, like morphological tiers for case marking, a procedure that does not concern us here.) Hence any predication has a dual thematic role structure: one spatial tier and one actional tier.

There are three descriptive payoffs of this loosening of the Theta Criterion. First, it allows for the common fact that two distinct roles may be assigned to the same argument, as illustrated in (68). Second, it allows for the inverse: The same role may be assigned to two different arguments. Consider the arguments of *symmetric predicates,* those in which the action is mutually distributed among the participants, like *kiss, marry, collide with,* and the like:

69. Bob debated Mary.

In the event of debating, Bob and Mary are separate arguments, but they both are really agents of the action. Even though Mary may be viewed as a patient in some sense, she still volitionally executes an act in response. Hence Mary is an agent by definition, as is Bob (for obvious reasons). How does a theory that requires one-to-one mapping of roles accommodate these facts?

Third, the tier model allows for the fact that grammatical coding is often sensitive to the *difference* between spatial and nonspatial roles. Consider the following sentence:

70. Bill heard the music.

In (70), from a spatial standpoint, Bill is the goal and music is the source. But unlike the previous examples, where arguments can be given both a spatial and actional role assignment, the arguments here cannot. Typical diagnostic questions for agent (*What did X do?*) and patient (*What happened to X?*) do not pick out any such argument in (70) (see Jackendoff 1987: 394–8):

Agent: What did Bill do?   ?? He heard the music.
Patient: What happened to the music?   ?? Bill heard it.
                                    ?? It was heard by Bill.

In (70) there is *no actional structure, only a spatial one.*

English is sensitive not only to the localistic nature of thematic roles, but also to the *difference between spatial and actional roles*. Some predicates map spatial roles totally onto actional roles, *throw*, for example:

71.		Bill threw the ball.
Spatial Tier:	Source	Theme
Actional Tier:	Agent	Patient

> Agent: What did Bill do? He threw the ball.
> Patient: What happened to the ball? Bill threw it.

Some map only partially from the spatial tier onto the actional tier, *enter*, for example:

72.		Bill entered the room.
Spatial Tier:	Theme	Goal
Actional Tier:	Agent	XXX

> Agent: What did Bill do? He entered the room
> Patient: What happened to the room? ?? Bill entered it

Some predicates do not map from the spatial tier onto the actional one at all, *receive*, for example:

73.		Bill received a letter.
Spatial Tier:	Goal	Theme
Actional Tier:	XXX	XXX

> Agent: What did Bill do? ?? He received a letter.
> Patient: What happened to the letter? ?? Bill received it

Observations such as these have led Jackendoff and others to propose that any theory of thematic roles must consist of at least two formal levels: a spatial tier, where motion and location are assigned, and an actional tier, where agency and patiency are assigned. Consequently an operating principle like the Theta Criterion must be abandoned to accommodate the descriptive facts. The Theta Criterion may be theoretically satisfactory, but it is not empirically adequate. Only a tier model, where localism is assumed and where spatial roles are systematically related to actional roles, accounts for both blatant counters to the one-to-one mapping of the Theta Criterion and the fact that the rest of the language (in this case, English) is sensitive to the difference between space and action.

5.314.   Summary

In this section, we have described localistic approaches to thematic roles. We have examined the basis of localism in its assumption of the spatial origin of knowledge and seen the application of this idea to predication and thematic roles. The ultimate benefit has been the reduction of thematic roles to a small set of spatial relations. We have also seen a version of localism, Jackendoff's tier model, which assigns thematic roles at two levels, a spatial tier and an actional tier. The tier model addresses the problems of the Theta Criterion and accommodates the ways that languages differentiate the spatial and actional sides of predication.

5.32. Macroroles

5.321. Actor and Undergoer

In contrast to localism and its derivatives, there is another influential proposal to unify thematic roles by looking at the convergences of their conceptual content. This is the theory of *macroroles* developed by Foley and Van Valin (1984).

The theory of macroroles is designed to present a unified picture of the relation between thematic and grammatical roles. Behind the theory of macroroles is the basic insight that all thematic roles fall into two broad categories, *actor* and *undergoer,* which conceptually parallel the grammatical notions involved in transitivity. The actor "expresses the participant which performs, effects, instigates, or controls the situation denoted by the predicate" (Foley and Van Valin 1984: 29); the undergoer is "the argument which expresses the participant which does not perform, initiate, or control any situation but rather is affected by it in some way" (Foley and Van Valin: 1984: 29). In this view, typical actors are agents and authors; typical undergoers are patients. As cover terms for this broad view of roles, *actor* and *undergoer* are thus *macroroles.*

5.322.   Semantic Content
and the Actor/Undergoer Hierarchy

Macroroles are *not* themselves thematic roles. Instead, they are prototypes or templates, with no semantic content, that subsume thematic roles, which do have semantic content. This means that macroroles per se are not selected by a predicate from compatibility of semantic content; rather the macroroles specify potential participants in a predication, potential thematic roles, and "their exact interpretation in any clause is a function of the nature of the predicate and, to a lesser extent, the inherent lexical content . . . of the NP argument serving as actor . . . [and] . . . undergoer" (Foley and Van Valin 1984: 32). These examples illustrate this point:

74a. Mary killed Tom.
   b. Leukemia killed Tom.
   c. The knife killed Tom.

    d. Having to go to work every day killed Tom.

    e. Monday killed Tom.

In each sentence, the subject codes the actor of the predication 'killing,' but clearly, not all the actors have the same degree of control in the situation. The specific instantiation of the actor—respectively as agent, author, instrument, goal, and location—depends on the inherent properties of the predication (e.g., whether 'killing' is seen as a more or less active predicate) and the semantic properties of the denotation of the argument (e.g., inherent potency).

    From this view, the macroroles form the poles of a continuum of properties instantiated by specific thematic roles. Both logical and typological work shows, for example, that actors are more likely to be interpreted by a language as agents than as patients; conversely, undergoers are more likely to be instantiated as patients than agents. In other words, the quintessential actor is the agent; the quintessential undergoer is the patient. Foley and Van Valin (1984: 59) argue that all the other roles form intermediate dependencies between agent and patient, resulting in an overall *Actor/Undergoer Hierarchy* (see Fig. 5.1).

    This hierarchy is to be read as follows: Likelihood of instantiation of the actor decreases from top to bottom; likelihood of instantiation of undergoer decreases from bottom to top. Canonical forms lie at each end. Less canonical, or fuzzy, forms are found in the middle: that is, some predicates ought to be variable as to whether sources or goals are actors or undergoers.

    The Actor/Undergoer Hierarchy has the benefit of not bifurcating thematic roles, but instead allowing for typicality effects and permitting the interpretation to vary according to the predication expressed. Similarly, the gradience of actor/undergoer allows languages to instantiate the roles differently according to their means. Thus, the hierarchy does not lock us into a categorical view of thematic roles and, indeed, accommodates localism and the tier model (sec. 5.313) because spatial and actional roles are both part of the probabilities of the hierarchy.

5.323. Involvement, Affectedness, and Syntactic Movement

Apart from the conceptual unity afforded by the Actor/Undergoer Hierarchy, the theory of macroroles captures a large range of syntactic and semantic facts. Semantically, the Actor/Undergoer Hierarchy provides a unified picture of the phenomenon of *semantic involvement,* or affectedness by the action, a long noted correlate of various syntactic movement rules. Hall (1965), Fraser (1971), Fillmore (1977), Salkoff (1983), and Jeffries and Willis (1984) all note that sentences like (75a) and (75b) are characterized by a difference in the strength of the involvement of the participants in the predication:

    75a. Tom sprayed the wall with paint.

      b. Tom sprayed paint on the wall.

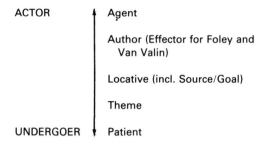

ACTOR ↕ Agent

Author (Effector for Foley and
Van Valin)

Locative (incl. Source/Goal)

Theme

UNDERGOER ↕ Patient

FIG. 5.1.   Actor/undergoer hierarchy.

Example (75a) implies that the wall is fully covered and totally affected. For (75b), the opposite interpretation appears: The paint seems to be totally affected, and the wall is less involved. In point of fact, an apt paraphrase for (75a) is something like *I covered the wall with paint,* but for (75b), there is no such total paraphrase because the wall may have unpainted areas. In contrast, an apt paraphrase for (75b) is something like *I totally sprayed the paint, on the wall.*

One account of these differences holds that the involvement effects are syntactic. In (75), the entity that is more affected is always the direct object: 'wall' in (75a) and 'paint' in (75b); the entity that is less affected is an oblique (object of preposition): 'paint' in (75a) and 'wall' in (75b). Many languages have this productive direct object/oblique alternation (Givón 1984), and one of the effects of this syntactic transformation is differential semantic involvement of the participants. This is because the traditional direct grammatical relations (subject, direct object, and indirect object) are often seen as more central to the predication than the oblique relations (object of preposition). Hence, Foley and Van Valin (1985) call the former *core* and the latter *peripheral;* Williams (1980) makes a similar distinction, calling the former *external* (outside of the verb) and *direct internal* (directly selected by the verb), and the latter *indirect internal* (optionally selected by the verb). To put the matter simply, if direct object is somehow more core or central, then it stands to reason that it ought to have more semantic involvement than an argument in an oblique or peripheral relation: The semantic results follow from the syntactic structures.

Unfortunately for the syntactic account, the involvement effects hold up under operations that *change* the grammatical relations. Passive and topicalization take direct objects and obliques and make them subjects:

76a. The wall was sprayed with paint by Tom. [passive of (75a)]
  b. The paint was sprayed on the wall by Tom. [passive of (75b)]
  c. The wall was what Tom sprayed with paint. [topicalization of (75a)]
  d. The paint was what Tom sprayed on the wall. [topicalization of (75b)]

In (76), the affected participants are subjects, but the involvement effects remain as in (75). So, the semantic facts cannot simply be read off the grammatical relations.

Here is where the Actor/Undergoer Hierarchy comes in. Some arguments are interpreted as more semantically involved in the predication—whatever their grammatical roles—because involvement reflects the macrorole of undergoer: "There is a clear correlation between the occurrence of an argument as an undergoer and a reading of total affectedness. . . . Affectedness is part of the . . . semantics of undergoer" (Foley and Van Valin 1984: 61). In (75) and (76), the arguments remain undergoers, and affected, in spite of the shift in grammatical role.

Semantic effects are derived from a shift on the Actor/Undergoer Hierarchy, not a shift in grammatical role. So, the following sentences all have manipulatable direct objects, but the entities represented are not uniformly involved in the predication. Involvement and affectedness *increase* as the examples proceed:

> 77a. I saw the ball. (Source)
>   b. I threw the ball. (Theme)
>   c. I tore the ball apart. (Patient)

Note that the examples also proceed down the Actor/Undergoer Hierarchy, from Source to Patient, and this gives the different effect for semantic involvement.

The Actor/Undergoer Hierarchy thus makes some nice predictions about semantic facts: Involvement is a function of "undergoerhood," not the result of purely syntactic transformation (though they are related because patients tend to be objects). Hence there are two interpretations of the following sentence, depending on the place of the subject on the Actor/Undergoer Hierarchy:

> 78. The box gives off heat.

On one interpretation, the box itself is not affected by the heat, but is, rather, a heat generator. On this reading, the box is toward the top of the hierarchy, as an author. But on another interpretation, the box itself is affected by the heat: that is, the box itself is also hot and is affected by the heat that it gives off—'this box is hot and the whole thing gives off heat.' On this interpretation, the box is a patient (or a source). But significantly, the increase in affectedness of the box in the predication is a function of the lower status of the box on the hierarchy, toward the undergoer end. On both readings, the syntax remains constant: *The box* is a subject.

5.324.   *Actor/Undergoer as a Typology: English Versus Tagalog*

We have seen how the Actor/Undergoer Hierarchy accounts for some semantic and syntactic facts quite nicely. Foley and Van Valin observed that the gradience of actor and undergoer has some interesting broader typological results. Consider the problem this way: If the Actor/Undergoer Hierarchy represents the gradient space in which languages instantiate thematic roles, do languages carve up the hierarchy in incommensurable ways, some having more formal distinctions on one end than another?

English, they argue, is a language where the morphological coding of actor is relatively underdifferentiated, in contrast to that for undergoer, which has a great deal of coding. This is different from Tagalog, which heavily codes the actor end and underdifferentiates the undergoer end. Note the variety of undergoers in English: *from Spain, to Spain, in Spain, across Spain, inside Spain,* and so forth. But agents are normally unmarked morphologically, and even when they are coded by a preposition, that preposition is semantically empty. An agentive passive may take *by* (*The book was read by John*), but the preposition has no content because it signals the thematic role of the original active form: cf. *The book was seen by Tom,* where *by* still codes the experiencer. So, the putative agentive form is transparent; coding is not differentiated on the actor end in English.

Tagalog, on the other hand, has an elaborate system of verbal prefixes to distinguish kinds of actors, volitional from nonvolitional ones, and the interaction of these properties with properties of the predicate: for example, permanent states, transitory states, perception and nonperception (see Foley and Van Valin 1984: 72). Foley and Van Valin argue, therefore, that Tagalog and English are opposite languages in a sense, as far as the explicit coding of the Actor/Undergoer Hierarchy goes. English prefers the undergoer end; Tagalog prefers the actor end.

The Actor/Undergoer Hierarchy thus leads to the general morphosyntactic prediction that there will be a range of languages typologically: those that prefer to code one or another end of the hierarchy more productively. In this way, the unified semantic view is integrated more into the theoretical claims about the form of any possible human language. The Actor/Undergoer Hierarchy is a general semantic constraint on syntactic and morphological expression of thematic roles.

5.325. Summary

In this section, we have discussed the theory of macroroles, a continuum of thematic roles from typical doer, actor, to typical receiver, undergoer. We have looked at the Actor/Undergoer Hierarchy, which ranks thematic roles between agent and patient, and we have seen how the hierarchy accounts for semantic involvement effects as a function of the change of position of an argument on the hierarchy irrespective of grammatical role. Finally, we have seen how the Actor/Undergoer Hierarchy provides a framework for typing languages according to their encoding preferences, with English highly differentiating the undergoer end and Tagalog the actor end.

5.33.   Linking Theory and Thematic Hierarchies

We have seen two ways to unify thematic roles conceptually: via localism and its offshoot, the tier model; via macroroles. The latter also make some predictions about the connection between thematic roles and their surface appearance. Here we pick up this last line of thought and address linking theory, a general account of the systematic links between thematic roles and grammatical roles.

The study of the translation of thematic roles into grammatical roles has induced a fair amount of theoretical controversy and extremism over the years. Rosen's (1984) position is typical in this regard. She argues: "Grammatical relations cannot be reconstructed by means of any possible algorithm that refers to meaning alone" (1984: 55). In support, she provides copious examples where thematic roles remain constant but grammatical roles change and says: "There is no universal alignment between semantic roles and initial GR's [grammatical roles]" (1984: 67).

Obviously, we cannot have a theory in which grammatical roles are read directly off thematic roles not only because it is unfeasible empirically, but also too binding theoretically. The real goal is not to demonstrate independence of thematic and grammatical roles, but to account for the numerous convergences between the two.

Linking theory is an attempt to provide a unified picture of how some thematic roles tend to surface *consistently* as certain grammatical roles. Linking Theory is designed to observe the correlations between thematic roles and grammatical roles, with the full understanding that this connection is a tendency.

A number of interesting proposals have been made over the years. All involve *thematic hierarchies:* natural dependencies across thematic roles that specify the likelihood that certain thematic roles will surface more often than others in a particular grammatical role. In this section, we look at three thematic hierarchies—Fillmore's Subject Hierarchy, Givón's Topic Accessibility Hierarchy, and Jackendoff's Thematic Hierarchy—and how they account for regularities in the linking of thematic and grammatical roles.

5.331.   Two Accounts of Subjects: Fillmore and Givón

Some 15 years apart, Fillmore and Givón gave similar accounts of how thematic roles surface in the grammatical role of subject. We look at their proposed hierarchies here.

5.3311.   Fillmore's Subject Hierarchy

One of the first thematic hierarchies is Fillmore's (1968) Subject Hierarchy: [Agent > Instrument > Patient] > Subject. The Subject Hierarchy is to be read as follows: Agents are more likely than instruments, which are themselves more likely than patients, to surface in the grammatical role of subject.

The Subject Hierarchy is best understood in relation to the *case frame* of each verb, the abstract specification of the thematic role possibilities for each predicate. For example, the predicate *open* optionally takes an agent and instrument, and obligatorily takes a patient, as the following sentences attest:

79a. He opened the door with a key. (agent, patient, instrument)
  b. The key opened the door. (instrument, patient, but no agent)
  c. The door opened. (patient, but no agent or instrument)

But *open* cannot appear with just an agent and instrument:

80a. ?? He opened with a key.
  b. ?? The key opened by him.

By these facts, the predicate *open* must have the following case frame: *Open* [Patient (Inst) (Agt)] (parentheses indicate optionality).

This case frame for *open,* if conditioned by the Subject Hierarchy, makes certain predictions about surface grammatical roles. If the agent is not selected, then the instrument will take subject position, a choice borne out by (79b). It also accounts for sentence (79c), where the patient surfaces as the grammatical subject, but only in the absence of both agent and instrument. So, by this example at least, the case frame and the Subject Hierarchy seem powerful tools for linking theory.

Unfortunately, it is easy to find counterexamples to the Subject Hierarchy. Consider this sentence:

81. The door opened with a key.

In this case, the patient surfaces as the subject in spite of the presence of the instrument, against the predictions of the Subject Hierarchy (see van Voorst 1988 for a catalogue of objections).

We might argue, however, that (81) does not disprove the Subject Hierarchy as much as require that it be fine tuned. Example (81) is allowed not because the patient surfaces as a subject in spite of the presence of an instrument, but because the argument in question is *an author,* a kind of agent. At the time that Fillmore wrote his original paper, the thematic role of author was yet to be discussed. So the Subject Hierarchy cannot be dismissed for not being sensitive to things then unknown.

If we modify the likelihood of subject assignment by introducing a new class of agents, namely authors, we can more carefully resolve issues of subject assignment. Updated, then, the Subject Hierarchy should more appropriately be: [Agent > Author > Instrument > Patient] > Subject.

The Subject Hierarchy obviously focuses on the tendency for thematic roles to surface as one grammatical role: subject. A more recent version of this hierarchy, with additional thematic roles, is given by Givón.

5.3312. Givón's Topic Accessibility Hierarchy

Givón (1984: 139) proposes that, for simple active clauses, there is a "ranking order of the various semantic case-roles according to the likelihood of their becoming the more continuous topic in discourse; more specifically, however, according to the likelihood of their occupying the pragmatic case-roles of subject or direct object." This ranking is the Topic Accession Hierarchy. Adjusted to be consistent with the terminology of this chapter, it is as follows: Agent > Benefactive (incl. Experiencer and animate Goal) > Patient > Locative (incl. Source and Goal) > Instrument > Manner. That is, if the simple active clause has an agent, it will tend to be the subject; if it has no agent, but has a benefactive, then the benefactive will be the subject; if the clause has no agent or benefactive, then the patient will be the subject; and so on.

For illustrative purposes, let us look at a few simple, active clauses, with two arguments, where the subject is higher than the other argument on the hierarchy (after Givón 1984: 141):

82a. Tom daydreamed in the backyard. (Benefactive > Locative)
  b. Tom daydreamed with gusto. (Benefactive > Manner)

The Topic Accessibility Hierarchy makes predictions about which thematic roles will be found as subjects, so paraphrases of (82) with arguments lower on the hierarchy and still in subject position ought to be disallowed:

83a. ?? The backyard was daydreamed in by Tom. (Locative > Benefactive)
  b. ?? Gusto was daydreamed with by Tom. (Manner > Benefactive)

This prohibition is a consequence of the fact that the hierarchy prevents the change of the grammatical roles of the arguments that the paraphrases require.

Like all hierarchies, the Topic Accessibility Hierarchy not only predicts dependencies internal to the thematic roles dependencies (e.g., agent over benefactive when the choice has to be made), but also more global typicality effects. The hierarchy embodies a general claim about the likelihood of subjects across the board, not just in relation to arguments competing for subject assignment within a predication. Subjecthood in general increases as the hierarchy moves to the left; alternatively, for all languages, subjecthood tends to be associated with arguments higher on the hierarchy.

Where, then, do languages tend to draw the line for subjects? Givón (1984: 139, fn. 7) says: "The dividing line as to access to subjecthood in active clauses

[is] either with patient or—much more rarely—locative case roles. To my knowledge, no clear cases exist of the instrumental or manner ever becoming subject." This is surely a bit overstated, given examples like *The key opened the door,* but where the instrument is a subject, the spirit of the observations seems to be correct. Locative, instrumental, and manner are decidedly in the minority when it comes to subjecthood (Fillmore observed long ago that English is unusual in allowing instrumental subjects). Locative and manner subjects are allowed in English, but the sentences are marked in focus:

84a. In the house is where he is.
  b. With gusto is how he did it.

Givón observes that similar restrictions apply to other languages. Bantu languages, for example, may have locative subjects only for stative verbs (1984: 142).

Given the Topic Accessibility Hierarchy, we can make predictable connections between thematic roles and grammatical roles. This is not a reductionist linking theory, but one sensitive to typicality.

5.332.   The Thematic Hierarchy Condition: Jackendoff

Although Givón's proposals are designed to account for typicality effects in the surface realization of semantic roles, Jackendoff's proposals are motivated by a desire to state global semantic conditions on syntactic operations: that is, to account for the interaction of syntax and semantics more generally. In his 1972 book, he describes a number of syntactic phenomena that require explanation with reference to semantic structure. Two that concern us here are passivization and reflexivization, because these two operations appear to be sensitive to hierarchies of thematic roles.

5.3321.   Passivization and the Thematic Hierarchy

Jackendoff observes that not all actives have passive counterparts, and the disparity is in large part accountable to the thematic roles of the arguments of the predicate to be passivized. Consider the following sentence:

85. Tom brushed the wall.

In this, the active version, the sentence is ambiguous. On one reading, the subject is an agent: 'Tom used a brush on the wall.' On the other reading, the subject is a theme: 'Tom's body inadvertently brushed against the wall.' Interestingly enough, only the first reading, with the subject as agent, is retained when the expression is put in the passive:

86. The wall was brushed by Tom.

Sentence (86) can mean only 'Tom used a brush on the wall.' Why is there this restriction on interpretation?

Jackendoff notes that in the allowable passive, (86), the argument of the *by-phrase* is an agent and the derived subject is a goal or patient. But if the nonagentive version of (85) were passivized, the argument of the *by-phrase* would be a theme and the derived subject a goal. This difference is schematized here:

87a. Agentive Reading (allowed):
     The wall was brushed by Tom.
     Goal   Agent
  b. Nonagentive Reading (not allowed)
     ?? The wall was brushed by Tom.
     Goal   Theme

Jackendoff suggests then that agents have priority over themes in passivization. An active sentence with the subject and object as agent and goal respectively may be passivized with the derived subject as goal and the *by-phrase* as agent: Schematically, $agent(S)$, $goal(O) \rightarrow goal\ (S)$, $agent(by\text{-}phrase)$. But when the active has the structure $theme(S)$, $goal(O)$, there is no passivization: $?? goal(S)$, $theme(by\text{-}phrase)$. This indicates that agents are more likely to be passivized than themes: agent $>$ theme.

Now consider another set of examples:

88a. John received the letter.
  b. The letter was received by John.

The active version, (88a), has the thematic structure $goal(S)$, $theme(O)$. This may be passivized, (88b), to $theme(S)$, $goal(by\text{-}phrase)$. Hence, a goal may become the argument of a *by-phrase*, and a theme may become the derived subject of a passive. But now consider the following examples:

89a. John reached the corner.
  b. ?? The corner was reached by John.

The active version, (89a), has the thematic structure $theme(S)$, $goal(O)$. But the passive, (89b), has the derived structure $goal(S)$, $theme(by\text{-}phrase)$, and this sentence is disallowed. It thus appears that themes are generally restricted from appearing as the argument of a *by-phrase* in a passive and have less priority than agents and goals in passivization: goal $>$ theme.

Jackendoff takes these observations, coupling them with other evidence for (1) the similarity of goals, sources, and locations, and (2) the priority of agents over these spatial roles, to state a thematic condition on the surface syntax of the English passive: Agent > Location, Source, Goal > Theme. This is the Thematic Hierarchy Condition, which restricts the argument of the passive *by-phrase* to a position higher than the derived subject on the Thematic Hierarchy. Note that all the acceptable examples given meet this condition; the disallowed passives violate it.

The Thematic Hierarchy Condition is valuable because it gives a more precise view of the passive. In traditional treatments, the English passive is viewed as a syntactic operation that derives a subject from an object and puts the original subject in an agentive *by-phrase*. But it is clear that the *by-phrase* is not agentive and has no semantic content at all. Fillmore (1977), Marantz (1984), and Dowty (1989) all observe that the argument of the *by-phrase* in English passives retains the thematic role of the active version and is therefore semantically transparent. Note that in *The book was read by Tom,* the argument of the *by-phrase* is an experiencer, as it would be in the active version. The *by-phrase* is a morphological correlate of passive, but thematic roles are assigned elsewhere. In this view, the syntactic and semantic domains of the passive are more clearly separate. The passive is a formal operation conditioned by a hierarchy of thematic roles, not an operation that induces thematic role change.

5.3322.   Reflexivization and the Thematic Hierarchy

Jackendoff is looking for consistent semantic conditions on syntactic structure as a whole. His emphasis on the syntactic impact of thematic roles can be further seen in the more widespread effect of the Thematic Hierarchy Condition. Jackendoff notes that reflexivization is also sensitive to the Thematic Hierarchy. Although it is clear that a great deal of reflexivization is accountable to syntactic structure (i.e., the domain of antecedent control for bound anaphors: see van Riemsdijk and Williams 1986), it is equally clear that the meaning of the predications in which reflexivization takes place also has an effect on the possibility of using a reflexive pronoun at all.

Consider the following sentences:

90a. I talked to John about himself.
  b. ?? I talked about John to himself.

Why can *John* be the antecedent for the reflexive pronoun in (90a) and not (90b)? There is apparently no syntactic explanation for this. Wilkins (1988: 208) observes, for example, that both arguments after the verb are assigned the same formal predicate relation (*predicate internal,* in Williams's 1980 terminology: see p. 237). By the syntactic facts, reflexivization ought to be allowed. This problem is further complicated by sentences like the following:

91a. I talked to myself about myself.
  b. I talked about myself to myself.

Why is the inversion of the two prepositional phrases allowed, with reflexivization maintained, when the semantic content of the arguments changes to 'speaker' (*myself*)?

The solution lies in the fact that certain thematic roles tend to control the
antecedents for reflexive pronouns. Example (90a) has the following thematic
role structure:

92. I talked to John about himself.
    Agent   Goal   Theme

Jackendoff argues that *himself* represents the theme here because the predicate
talk is abstract motion and thus selects for a source, goal and theme (see 1972:
152; see also Wilkins 1988: 208–9). In this predication, then, the antecedent,
John, is a goal and the reflexive pronoun, *himself,* is a theme. In (90b), however,
the sequence is reversed:

93. ?? I talked about John to himself.
       Agent   Theme Goal

The fact that the antecedent is the theme prevents reflexivization. Significantly,
the theme is lower than the goal on the Thematic Hierarchy we found necessary
for explaining the passive. It must be the case, then, that the antecedent of a
reflexive pronoun has to be higher on the Thematic Hierarchy than the pronoun
itself, just as passivization required a similar adherence to the hierarchy. Jackendoff (1972: 148) puts it specifically: "A reflexive may not be higher on the
Thematic Hierarchy than its antecedent."

This adherence to the Thematic Hierarchy is also what allows the sentences
with *myself,* in (91), in any permutation. Their thematic structures are shown
here:

94a. I talked to myself about myself.
     Agent   Goal   Theme
  b. I talked about myself to myself.
     Agent   Theme Goal

The prepositional phrase alternation with reflexives is allowed because the antecedent is the *agent, I,* not the theme or the goal. The agent is higher on the
Thematic Hierarchy than the other two arguments, theme and goal. Thus the
ranks of these other two are irrelevant to the choice of antecedent for the reflexive

pronoun. Hence, any structure with an agent as an antecedent should allow the alternation in (91):

95a. John talked to himself about himself.
  b. John talked about himself to himself.
  c. John talked for himself about himself to himself.

The Thematic Hierarchy also accounts for sentences where arguments positionally intervene between the antecedent and reflexive:

96. John talked to me about himself.
    Agent   Goal   Theme

Here, the *agent* controls the reflexive, not the nearest syntactic form (*me*), so that assignment of antecedents must, in at least some cases, be sensitive to the relative position of the arguments on the Thematic Hierarchy.

The exact details of the connection between thematic roles and reflexivization are more complicated than presented. Wilkins (1988), for example, notes that the Thematic Hierarchy must be augmented with the roles of patient and affected (see sec. 5.2221) in order to account for the full range of facts (see her revised hierarchy, 1988: 211). Kuno (1987b) argues that reflexivization must be sensitive to a hierarchy that includes additional undergoer categories, like experiencer and benefactive (see his hierarchy, 1987b: 176). But both of these revisions retain the spirit of the original proposal: The position of the thematic role of the antecedent on a universal hierarchy of thematic roles predicts the grammaticality of reflexivization itself.

5.333. Summary

We have now been through three versions of linking theory that rely on hierarchies of thematic roles: Fillmore's Subject Hierarchy, Givón's Topic Accessibility Hierarchy, and Jackendoff's Thematic Hierarchy Condition. The first two concentrate on those thematic roles that have a high tendency to surface as grammatical subject; the third focuses on how the relative ranking of thematic roles conditions the syntactic operations of the passive and reflexive. Hierarchies of thematic roles have very general effects on the predictability of overt form. They are crucial to linking theory itself because they specify the likelihood of the mapping from thematic roles to grammatical form. Whether or not linking theory itself can be united with the various proposals to simplify the thematic roles remains to be seen. But in all cases the goal is to account for the convergences of the roles that an argument may have in a predication and the surface forms that those roles take.

SUMMARY OF CHAPTER

In this chapter, we defined thematic roles as grammatically relevant semantic relations between predicates and arguments. We looked at predication itself and the differentiation of predicates from events and arguments from entities. We also saw the divergence of thematic roles from both grammatical roles and morphological cases.

We then surveyed nine major participant roles: three logical actors (agent, author, and instrument), three logical recipients (patient, experiencer, and benefactive), and three spatial roles (theme, source, and goal). We determined the criterial semantic properties, for example, volitional action for the agent, and noted the grammatical reflexes of these roles. Thereafter, we looked at three nonparticipant roles: locative, reason, and purpose.

We the turned to attempts to unify thematic roles, looking first at localism, or the theory of the spatial origin of knowledge and meaning. We noted the possibility of the reduction of thematic roles to a small set of spatial relations; we also described a version of localism, Jackendoff's tier model, which assigns thematic roles at two levels, a spatial tier and an actional tier, and addresses problems with the Theta Criterion.

Then we turned to the theory of macroroles, a continuum of thematic roles from typical actor to undergoer. We looked at the Actor/Undergoer Hierarchy, which ranks thematic roles and accounts for semantic involvement effects as a function of the change of position of an argument on the hierarchy irrespective of grammatical role.

To close the chapter, we considered three versions of linking theory that rely on hierarchies of thematic roles: Fillmore's Subject Hierarchy, Givón's Topic Accessibility Hierarchy, and Jackendoff's Thematic Hierarchy Condition. The first two concentrated on predicting surface grammatical subject; the third focused on how thematic roles condition passive and reflexive.

QUESTIONS FOR DISCUSSION

1. Identify the predicates, arguments, and all the thematic roles of the arguments for the following expressions:

i. The clothes dried from the sun.

ii. The seismograph sensed the earthquake.

iii. Tom loaded the truck with hay.

Do some arguments have both spatial and actional roles? Can you organize these roles in tiers? Now look at the following variations on these expressions. How do their thematic-role structures account for the acceptability and unacceptability of the expressions?

iv. ?? The clothes dried from the new dryer.

v. The clothes dry easily.

vi. The earthquake was sensed by the seismograph.

vii. Tom loaded hay onto the truck

(Hint: Remember semantic involvement, affectedness, and thematic hierarchies.)

2. The following data are from Georgian, a split ergative language (from DeLancey 1981: 648):

ia. kaceb-i   çeren çeril- s.
  men Nom write letter Dative
  The men are writing a letter.

ib. kaceb-ma daçer- es çeril- i.
  men Erg wrote 3Pl letter Nom
  The men wrote a letter.

Why do you think that the subject, *kaceb*, is marked by the nominative in (ia) and the ergative in (ib)? Is the meaning more agentive in (ib)? Does the difference between 'are writing' and 'wrote' affect your answer? Note that in (ia), the object, *çeril*, is marked by the dative, and so a more accurate gloss of (ia) is something like the archaic English 'the men are writing of a letter,' as if the letter is somehow less affected by the action. How do thematic roles and linking theory relate to this interpretation?

3. The following is a sentence from Emai with the literal meanings of the words supplied, but no full gloss (Schaefer 1986: 486):

i. oli omohe la shan vbi   ukpaode.
  the man   ran Path Contact road

Give an English translation for this expression. (Emai syntax is SVO, so *omohe* is the subject: 'the man ran . . .') Does English have a way to express path and contact? Give a number of ways to express these notions in English.

6 Space

6.1. INTRODUCTION

In this chapter, we are going to investigate how language encodes spatial concepts. We have already discussed space to a certain extent in our considerations of the spatial structure of entities (chap. 3), motion events (chap. 4) and spatial thematic roles (chap. 5). Here, we go into spatial notions in much more detail, focusing on location and deixis.

We begin by outlining two fundamental ideas about space and its representation in language: (a) that space is a *relational concept* and (b) and must be understood against the backdrop of a *canonical and naive conception of space and physics,* or the mentally projected world of space.

With an understanding of these essentials, we turn to the nature of location and deixis and their grammatical encoding. *Location* is the relative spatial fixedness of entities; we want to identify the universal places and positions that language allows its speakers to represent. We see that there are two types of locations: *topological* and *projective,* respectively, spatial positions independent of a viewer and those dependent on a viewer.

Deixis is the way that language allows its speakers to refer to the relation between an entity or event and properties of the context in which it is spoken: for example, the speaker and the hearer or the time and place of utterance. We consider *spatial, personal,* and *temporal deixis;* all require analysis in terms of a reference point, remoteness, and direction.

The spatial system of language "imposes a fixed form of structure on virtually every spatial scene" (Talmy 1983: 229), where "only certain notions and not

250

others are permitted representation" (Talmy 1983: 228). As with all semantic notions, the universal structure corresponds indirectly to the phenomenal world and privileges certain notions over others. Our goal is to tease out this structure and discuss the spatial notions that are allowed to be represented by language locationally and deictically.

6.11.   The Relational Character of Space

The semantic structure of spatial expression is a *dependency* between two or more entities or events, as can be seen in the following expression of location:

1. the cat on the sofa.

Sentence (1) denotes a situation where one entity, a cat, bears some spatial dependency ('on') to another entity, a sofa. Following Herskovits (1986), we refer to the first member in the relation as the *located object* [cat in (1)] and the second member as the *reference object* [sofa in (1)]. The location itself [on in (1)] is thus the relation between the located object and the reference object. Hence the notions of position and place, which intuitively appear to be stable points in our projected world, are in truth *dependencies between a located object and a reference object,* not static positions or places at all.

A similar account holds for deixis. Consider the following expression:

2. that cat.

In (2), the form *that* requires a relation between the located object (cat) and the reference object, here the speaker of the utterance. Example (2) more particularly means 'the cat removed from the speaker,' and so deixis, as well as place, is relational in character.

The constant relational nature of space can be expressed as an abstract formal relation between (at least) two participants: *X Spatially Relates To Y,* where *X* is the located object, and *Y* is the reference object. But we also want to ask about the *content* of the variables in the abstract spatial relation. What is the content of the abstract relation *Spatially Relates To?* Is there a finite, and small, set of recurrent spatial relations that all languages encode? Do the relations tend to be coded in specific ways? Do only certain semantic properties of the located and reference objects bear on the interpretation of spatial expressions? How does the content of the located object and the reference object interact with the content of the spatial relation? To answer these questions, we need to consider the mental framework of space itself.

6.12.   Canonical Conception of Space

We have made a case for the semantics of space as a fixed relational form and have indicated that the interpretation of spatial expressions depends on the content of the variables in the spatial expression. Where does this content come from? All spatial expressions in everyday language are understood with reference to a canonical conception of space. This view of space has two principal components: a *naive conception of geometry and physics* and a *projected ideal spatial world*. We look at how each component grounds the content of spatial relations and their participants (the discussion is based on Herskovits 1986, Miller and Johnson-Laird 1976, and Talmy 1983).

6.121.   Naive Geometry and Physics

Science teaches us that the physical world is organized quite differently from how we ordinarily perceive it. In school we learn that everything is in motion and the perceived stability of objects is an illusion because their constituent molecules are in constant movement. Space is not really empty and, even though solid objects appear to support other objects, this is a fortuitous result of their current material state: A solid can easily be a liquid, given enough heat. Objects do not really fall, but instead move toward the place of highest density. After all, if there is no ultimate ground, how can things fall?

Although such ideas are the mainstays of modern science and technology, they are not at all fundamental to the way ordinary language structures space. Quite the contrary, the content of our spatial expressions relies on a nontechnical, or naive, conception of geometry and physics, encompassing such principles as the following:

A. space is empty;
B. solids have no spaces in them;
C. the ground is stable and supports things;
D. Earth is immobile and is the bottom line.

Though these principles are false, they are absolutely essential to the interpretation of spatial expressions. Consider the following:

3. The nail was in the wall.

Two interpretations of (3) are 'the nail was embedded in the wall either fully or partially' and 'the nail was contained in the space between two surfaces of the wall (inside)'. One interpretation that does not come up is 'the nail's molecules were in an arrangement such that each matched a space between molecules in the wall: thus the nail was in the wall.' Science allows us to conceive of the location of the nail in this way because, technically, both the nail and the wall have internal spaces that may conceivably be lined up. But our naive model of geometry and physics simply rules this out: As per principle B, solids have no spaces (I let the reader imagine expressions that exemplify the other principles.)

Certainly our untutored conceptions of how the world works are not always useful and in fact may hinder our learning of more abstract notions (McCloskey 1983). Nonetheless, it is this naive model of geometry and physics that invests our spatial expressions with content, even though this model is probably false in all its aspects when the technical aspects of physics and space are brought to bear.

6.122. Projected Ideal World

Our canonical conception of space is not only naive, it is also ideal and conceptually projected. For all intents and purposes, Euclidean geometry is enough to anchor our spatial expressions. The world is three-dimensional. Lines are parallel. Geometric figures—lines, points, surfaces, cubes, and all variations thereon—come in their ideal forms, though because ideal forms are a projection of our conceptual apparatus, they have typical values that admit a tolerance in their applicability.

The relevance of the projected ideal world to the content of spatial expressions can be seen in (4):

4. The lamp is in the corner of the room.

How much in the corner must the lamp be for (4) to be appropriate? The normal interpretation of (4) involves the conception of a corner as the intersection of perpendicular lines, with a range of allowable spatial positions in an area projected outward from the vertex of the intersecting lines that make up the corner. Rooms do not come with this range inherently demarcated, but speakers are able to use the expression *in the corner* with absolute accuracy because *in* has an ideal denotation.

All the mathematical apparatus of real-time geometry (like Riemannian geometry without parallel lines) may truthfully tell us that ideal geometric figures are nonexistent and Euclidean principles do not hold. But this apparently does not matter to the geometry underlying our language about space. The values for variables in the abstract relations that constitute spatial expressions rely on an ideal, if naive, model of how the world's objects are put together and occupy space.

6.13. Summary

To recapitulate, we have considered two important preliminaries to any discussion of spatial concepts encoded in language. First, spatial concepts are relational; we are interested in the content that the relation may assume as well as the interaction of the content of the entities in the relation with the relation proper. Second, spatial expressions are grounded in a canonical picture of geometry and physics: a naive and idealized model of spatial relations. With these preliminaries in mind, we now turn to a description of location and deixis.

6.2. LOCATION

Here we look at the locations that language may encode. In this task, both the relational character of space and the ideal model of spatial content provide the necessary framework.

First recall that the abstract relation underlying spatial expressions is *X Spatially Relates To Y*. For location, this relation concerns all the relatively fixed places and positions of entities. If we take the Newtonian conception of space— that space is a continuous, stable three-dimensional container, that is, *a cube*— as the ideal backdrop to this relation, we can define eight locations for a geometric figure. These are schematically represented in Fig. 6.1. (In the figure, the spatial relation is labeled, and a sample preposition from English is given to illustrate the encoding of the relation.)

Three of these locations are *topological:* That is, they are constant under any change of the ideal cube—*coincidence, interiority,* and *exteriority.* The remaining five, *inferiority, superiority, anteriority, posteriority,* and *laterality,* are *projective:* That is, they require a viewpoint and thus are not constant under change. We follow this distinction between topological and projective locations as we discuss the semantic and grammatical facts associated with each of the eight possible spatial positions.

6.21. Topological Locations

Topology is the study of the geometric properties of objects that are invariant under change of the object. Imagine an ideal donut, whose cylindrical, curved shape is technically called a *torus.* If we stretch the torus, many things happen to the form—for example, the length and width change—but what does *not* change is the torus itself. Under stretching, the donut is still donutlike. Thus, the torus feature of the donut is a topological property because it remains invariant under transformation of the figure embodying it.

Three of the locations illustrated on the cube of Fig. 6.1, coincidence, exteriority, and interiority, are likewise topological, holding no matter how the spatial relation is viewed. Consider the expression *The ball is in the box,* which represents a spatial relation of interiority between a located object (ball) and a reference object (box). If, in the situation described, the box is turned on its side or twisted, the interiority of the ball with reference to the box is not thereby

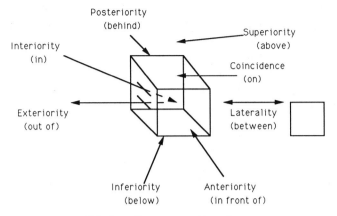

FIG. 6.1. Taxonomy of locations.

modified. Interiority is immune to transformations, so it is a topological location. (Similar comments may be made for coincidence and exteriority, and I leave the exercise to the reader.)

We now consider the topological locations. In the following discussion, we detail their ideal denotation and give some examples of how they are encoded.

6.211. Coincidence

The first topological location is *coincidence,* the near or total spatial overlap of the located object and the reference object. These expressions represent the relation of coincidence:

5a. The fly is on the wall.
 b. Harry is at the fence.

In (5a), the situation is such that the fly (the located object) has contact with the wall (the reference object); contact entails spatial overlap, so an expression of coincidence is allowed. In (5b), the located object (Harry) does not necessarily have direct contact with the reference object (fence): Harry may just be standing sufficiently near the reference object to evoke the true description and thus fall within the tolerance that the ideal denotation of coincidence allows. What counts for the coincidence is that the located object and the reference be *conceptually projected as sharing the same ideal space.*[1]

---

[1]Note that mere proximity does not suffice to guarantee coincidence, nor does remoteness rule coincidence out, as (i) shows:

 i. Voyager II is at Saturn.

Types of coincidence can be differentiated on the basis of the content of the located object and the reference object. English has two kinds of coincidence, *at* and *on*. *At* has a number of semantic conditions. First, the coincidence of the located and reference objects is the overlap of *points*. The punctual nature of *at* comes through clearly if we consider the interpretation of the following, where the located and reference objects are geometric figures with spatial extension and hence are not punctual:

6. The highway is at the corner.

The scene evoked by (6) is of some ideal *point of coincidence* of the two figures, in spite of their inherent extension. So (6) means 'the highway intersects at some point with the corner.'

At requires coincidence of points, so the objects involved must be *bounded* because punctual entities, by their nature, have inherent limits. Thus, the following are disallowed because of the unboundedness of the located object, in (7a), and reference object, in (7b):

7a. ?? Water is at the fence.
 b. ?? Harry is at water.

However, when the objects are denoted in bounded form, the expressions are then acceptable:

8a. The water is at the fence.
 b. Harry is at the water.

In (8a) and (8b), 'water' is given a bounded state: Respectively, 'some container or body of water is coincident with the fence' and 'Harry is at the body or container of water.'

Where punctuality and boundedness interact with coincidence to produce *at*, three different properties interact with coincidence and underlie *on*. First, *on* requires that there be some *contact*, either direct or derived, between the located object and reference object. Consider the possible interpretations of the following:

9. The apple is on the table.

For (9) to be true, the apple must be either directly on the table or on another

---

Example (i) may be true even though the actual distance between the located object (Voyager II) and the reference object (Saturn) is thousands of miles. This is because Voyager II and Saturn are in the same ideal space.

object that itself has contact with the table. (Of course, pragmatic features determine the allowable extent of indirect contact.)

The second property is *dimensionality of the reference object*. The located object must have contact with either a one-dimensional or two-dimensional (but not three-dimensional) reference object for *on* to be appropriate. Consider the following:

10a. The clothes are on the clothesline.
   b. The picture is on the wall.

In the situation of (10a), the clothes have contact with a *linear reference object*, the clothesline. In the events of (10b), the located object has contact with the *surface of the reference object*. The two-dimensionality of the reference object is crucial: If the reference object is expressly three-dimensional, *only its surface properties* are relevant to the expression:

11. The picture is on the cube.

Sentence (11) means 'the picture has contact with a surface of the cube.' The volumetric properties of the three-dimensional reference object are not relevant for *on*.

Finally, the located object must be typically *supported by the reference object*, as (12) indicates:

12. The gum is on the table.

Example (12) evokes a scene in which the gum has contact with the surface of the table and the table is somehow supporting the gum, or preventing it from falling. Note that if the gum is stuck to the underside of the table, and thus not supported in the usual sense, it is odd to say (12).

English, then, differentiates types of coincidence by relying on the semantic content of the located object and reference object. Dimensionality, support, and contact are all implied by *on* in addition to coincidence; punctuality and bound-edness bear on the appropriateness of *at*.

In languages other than English, the expression of coincidence often encodes simply the mere fact of coincidence and is vague for other properties; the prag-matic and semantic context then determine the spatial overlap more precisely. This lack of further distinctions in coincidence is frequently found in languages with an all-purpose location marker that can be more precisely differentiated wherever need arises.

In Indonesian, there are three basic space markers, one for motion away from the speaker, one for motion toward the speaker, and one for general location. This last form, *di*, may occur with other more specific markers of location, like those for 'inside' and 'outside.' But it may occur alone to mark simple, un-differentiated spatial coincidence, and the full interpretation is then a function of the semantic and pragmatic context (MacDonald 1976: 112–4):

13. di rumah.
    Loc house
    coincident with the house.

Example (13) may mean 'at the house,' 'in the house,' or 'on the house,' with more specific meanings signalled by additional forms, of which Indonesian has a variety:

14. di dalam rumah.
    Loc inside house
    in the house.
    Lit. coincident with the inside of the house.

But when the locative appears alone, as in (13), the default value for interpretation is undifferentiated coincidence.

This general locative function of coincidence in languages like Indonesian suggests that the relation is somehow basic or unmarked. It might be argued, in fact, that the eight relations diagrammed in Fig. 6.1 (p. 255) all involve coincidence to some extent. For example, *above* means '*coincident* to the domain extended over the reference object,' *beside* means '*coincident* to the domain lateral to the reference object,' and so on. If all spatial relations presuppose coincidence in their ideal denotations, then it is no surprise then that some languages do not distinguish coincidence more finely and, further, that finer differentiations often presume coincidence (see the theoretical discussion, pp. 283–91).

6.212. *Interiority*

The second topological location is *interiority,* which we may define as inclusion or containment of a located object in the reference object. In principle, interiority may: (a) be either partial or total, (b) range across objects of any dimension, or (c) either real or virtual.

We can see these three possibilities in the following examples, all of which use the standard English marker of interiority, *in:*

15a. The books are in the box.
  b. There's a crease in the paper.
  c. Delaware is in the Eastern United States.

Sentence (15a) has two interpretations: one is a situation where the located objects, books, are *totally* contained in the reference object, box; the other is where the books are *partially* contained in the box, but are nonetheless viewed as connected to the interior of the box. In each case, there is some degree of inclusion. In (15b), the one-dimensional located object, crease, is contained in a two-dimensional reference object, paper: 'There is a lengthwise fold included in the surface of the paper.' Importantly, the dimensional properties of the located and reference object do not preclude the expression of interiority. In (15c), the reference object is not precisely defined either geographically or politically, but it is still possible to locate an object in its interior because 'the East' is a container in a mental projection of the United States. So (15c) shows that interiority may be virtual as well as real.

Expressions of interiority normally imply that the located object is *smaller* than the reference object no doubt because total containment of the located object by the reference object is the expected value. Thus, the interpretation of (15a) as partial containment, with books protruding from the box, is more exactly rendered with a *hedge* (cf. chap. 2):

16. Technically, the books are in the box.

So although containment is the core of the denotation, it is also closely associated with a size differential.

Herskovits (1986) notes that interiority often interacts with other semantic properties to produce finer differentiations of inclusion. For instance, *in* cannot take a reference object that is a noninherent piece of a surface:

17. ?? The check mark is in the page.

Example (17) is prevented because the area of containment is some noninherent subdivision of the page proper. However, a reference object with a semantically inherent subdivision allows interiority:

18. The check mark is in the margin.

A margin is an inherent subdivision of a page, so the requirement of containment and inclusion is met thereby.

English also encodes *total* interiority. Compare (19) with (15a):

19. The books are inside the box.

Although (15) has two interpretations, total containment or partial containment, (19) has only one, 'the books are totally contained in the box.'[2]

---

[2]Other semantic factors interact with interiority, like the nonliquid state of the reference object for the use of *inside:* see chap. 4 (p. 176).

A look at other languages gives similar principles and results. An interesting example of interiority can be found in Manam. Spatial relations in Manam are marked by the general locative morpheme *o*, which, notably, is also the same as the marker for coincidence, making Manam very much like Indonesian, where general location and coincidence also converge. Finer spatial relations may be encoded in Manam·by expressions that denote more precise locations. Interiority is one of these, and is encoded by *iló*, 'space inside' (see Lichtenberk 1983: 587):

> 20. boi?ísi móne iló-   Ø   na-   lo.
>   box   money space inside 3/Inalienable Liaison Locative
>   the money in the box.
>   Lit. the money in the box's inside space.

Example (20) shows not only that interiority may be encoded purely and straightforwardly, but also that Manam associates interiority with *inalienable possession,* or semantic inseparability, because the spatial marker takes the additional marker of close possession, ø in this case.[3]

Apparently, in Manam, *all relationships of close proximity,* kinship, body parts, mental states, and the like, are marked with inalienable possession. Certain spatial relations are also signalled by inalienable possession: all topological locations and those projective relations that are nonvertical, for example, 'in front of,' but not 'above.' There thus appears to be a very general constraint in the semantics of Manam to mark as inalienable all very close relations, whether spatial or not, assuming here that the vertical relations are more alienable. This point is brought home by the fact that the relation 'near' is *not* marked for inalienable possession, but the relation 'very near' *is* marked for inalienability (see Lichtenberk 1983: 584–85). The association of interiority in Manam with inalienability thus has a certain logic. As a topological relation of containment, there is a necessary conceptual nearness between the located object and the reference object. It is arguably this spatial overlap that motives the marking of inalienability in this language.

6.213. *Exteriority*

The third and last topological location is *exteriority,* a spatial relation whereby the located object is external to the reference object. Though exteriority might

---

[3]Inalienable possession is a phenomenon whereby possessed items are marked for their inseparability from their possessors. In Spanish, the meaning 'my hand' is rendered as *la mano,* literally 'the hand': The explicit possessive marker is disallowed in such cases because hands, as body parts, are inalienably possessed; that is, they are inseparable from their possessors. In point of fact, the expression *mi mano,* literally 'my hand,' is ungrammatical in Spanish.

appear to be the simple negation of interiority, it is actually the *converse*. Recall from Chapter 4 that converseness is a logical relation in which the conceptual content of the relation remains constant while the relative positions of the participants switch. This definition holds for interiority and exteriority: If *X* is interior to *Y*, then *Y* is exterior to *X*, and vice versa (cf. *give* and *take;* Bennett 1975 remarks that exteriority requires more than converseness to be adequately described, but for most cases, the intuition of converseness holds).

The constancy underlying conversives gives us good reason to expect that exteriority will borrow all the properties that are true of its converse, interiority, just reversing the positions of the located and reference object. Consider the properties of totality or partiality, which are relevant to interiority:

21a. The ball is out of the box.
  b. Bill is outside the room.

Sentence (21a) may refer to a situation in which the located object is either totally or partially exterior to the reference object, and so *out of* is the converse of *in*, both vague for totality. In contrast, (21b) marks total exteriority—the located object must be completely uncontained in the reference object—making *outside* the converse of *inside*. (I leave it to the reader to verify the other properties of dimensionality and real/virtual exteriority: see p. 258.)[4]

If we turn to different languages for examples of exteriority, we see results analogous to our cross-language comparisons for interiority. In Chamorro (Topping 1973: 116–19), as in Indonesian and Manam, there is a general locational marker, *gi*, which can be amended with more specific indications of spatial relation, like exteriority:

22. Gaige gué gi   hiyong gumá.
    is   he   Loc outside house
    He is outside the house.
    More accurately: He is located outside the house.

The same phenomenon can be found in Indonesian, where, as we know (see p. 258), the general location marker, *di*, can be amended with more specific indications of space. In the case of expressions of exteriority, the standard marker *di* is replaced by *dari*, which means 'from' (MacDonald, 1976: 114):

---

[4]Another English form that looks very much like a marker of exteriority is *away*, as in the following:

   i. Maria is away from her desk.

But even though *away* implies that the located object is exterior to the reference object, *away* does not represent a converse of interiority. If *X* is away from *Y*, then it is not true that *Y* is in or inside *X*. *Away* appears to encode the *simple negation* of coincidence: If *X* is away from *Y*, then *X* is not at *Y*.

23. dari luar   rumah.
    from outside house
    outside the house.

This substitution of *dari* 'from' for *di* 'generic location' raises an interesting point. The spatial relation encoded by *from* is typically analyzed as inherently negative (see Gruber 1976), as something like 'not to.' If exteriority bears a converse (and hence negative) relation to interiority, then it stands to reason that a language might explicitly encode this negation. Notably, in Indonesian, the specific marker for interiority, *dalam*, does not take the general location marker *di* either. Instead, it requires *ke*, 'to,' the 'positive' version of 'from.'

Exteriority and interiority are semantically related by converseness, and the negation inherent in converseness is expressly encoded in the Indonesian locational markers that precede the specific manifestations of exteriority. In English, in contrast, this negation is fused into the expressions of the spatial relations proper.

6.214.   Summary

In this section we have discussed the nature of topological space and examined three topological locations: coincidence, interiority, and exteriority. We have seen further that these basic spatial concepts often interact with other semantic properties to produce finer spatial distinctions (e.g., 'punctual' + 'coincidence' = 'at'; 'totality' + 'containment' = 'inside') and all these distinctions bear on the encoding of the relation in surface form. We have also seen how two of the topological locations, exteriority and interiority, are related to converseness. Throughout, we have observed comparisons of English semantic structure and encoding with data from unrelated languages.

6.22.   Projective Locations

We now turn our attention to the nontopological, or *projective,* locations, those that vary in value and interpretation depending on how they are viewed. Topological locations are constant regardless of how they are seen by a viewer, but such constancy is not possible with other spatial relations, which rely on a framework *projected by the viewer.*

Think about the situation in Fig. 6.2. Given this state of affairs, is it acceptable to say *The circle is next to the square?* The truth of the expression depends on *how the circle and square are viewed.* If we are placed in the situation proper, not above it, at point 1, and view in the direction of the arrow, then the expression is true. But if we are at point 2, and view in the direction of the arrow, the expression is not true—in this case, it is more appropriate to say *The circle is*

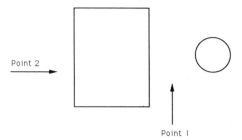

FIG. 6.2. Illustration of projective location.

behind the square. Therefore, the denotation of the spatial expression *next to* depends on a *projected viewpoint.*

Projective locations thus involve a *frame of reference,* or a vantage point against which to judge the relationship of the located object to the reference object. There are two frames of reference: that *inherent to the reference object* and that *inherent to the viewer* (see Fillmore 1975b; Herskovits 1986; Miller and Johnson-Laird 1976). Each frame of reference is a function of outward projection, from the "face," front, or central point of the viewer or the reference object (in whatever way *face* may be construed).

The difference between the two frames of reference can be seen in the interpretations of the following:

24. The ball is in front of the chair.

In one sense, (24) represents a situation where the viewer is facing the chair—that is, projecting outward from the viewer's face—and the located object is between the viewer and the reference object. For this interpretation, the frame of reference *inherent to the viewer* determines the meaning of *in front of:* 'in front of the viewer.' But (24) has another interpretation, one where the inherent frame of reference of the reference object overrides that of the viewer. Suppose that the situation is such that the ball is at the front part of the chair—that is, where the seat is. Whatever the frame of reference of the viewer, (24) is still appropriate, because the *inherent frame of reference* of the chair determines the spatial relation. In this case, *in front of* means 'in front of the reference object.'

Now that we understand the basic semantic facts involved in projective location, we can proceed to catalogue these types of spatial relations and to remark on their additional semantic and formal qualities. Just as with the topological locations, we give a core definition of each projective location in ideal space, note the interactions of this definition with semantic properties of the located object and reference object, and discuss how additional properties may produce finer projective locations.

6.221. *Inferiority*

A located object may have the relation of *inferiority* to the reference object if the located object occupies the space projected from the bottom of the reference object. Crucial to this definition is *bottom,* which we define as 'the lowest side of the reference object, either from a viewer or from the object itself.' If we project ideal space downward from this side, we get the area that the located object must occupy for inferiority to hold. Occupation of this space may be partial or total, although a language may encode precise distinctions along these lines.

The following expression encodes inferiority, so defined.

25. The cat is below the table.

In (25), the situation is such that the located object occupies the ideal space projected downward from the reference object, but because inferiority is a projective relation, we may change the frame of reference and bring about a slightly different interpretation. Consider (25) with a frame of reference projected from the viewer. In this case, the located object, cat, does not have to be directly in the ideal space projected downward from the reference object per se, only located in the area lower than both the table and the viewer. A more precise rendering of this situation is something like *The cat is below the table from where I'm standing.* Even in this case, the ideal meaning of 'occupation of downward projected space' still accommodates the denotation, just with the projection taken from the viewer.

Inferiority may interact with semantic properties of the reference object. In normal interpretations, the space that the located object occupies is a projection of the *lowest part* of the reference object, however *lowest part* is to be construed. A three-dimensional reference object projects the area of its lowest surface as the penumbra into which the located object may fall, as in (25). But consider (26):

26. The treasure is under the water.

Sentence (26) means either 'the treasure is located in the space projected downward from the *surface* of the water' or 'the treasure is located in the space projected downward from the *body* of water (e.g., 'buried under the lake'). The latter meaning makes reference to the lowest part of the reference object of the body of water and so meets the description given earlier. The former does also in that 'under the surface' makes reference to the *only projectible part* of water as a mass: The upper surface of the water becomes the lowest part by default.

In addition to making reference to surface properties of the reference object, inferiority may also interact with total or partial containment. Consider (27):

27. The cat is underneath the table.

Example (27) requires an interpretation in which the located object is entirely contained in the downwardly projected space, even in the situation where the frame of reference lies in the viewer. English thus encodes not only finer properties of the reference object, as per (26), but also more specific features of the spatial relation itself.

Similar facts about inferiority may be observed in West Greenlandic Eskimo. According to Fortescue (1984: 231–2), Eskimo has a basic marker for inferiority, *ata/ati,* which may denote downwardly projected space from either the reference object or viewer:

28. nirrivi-up   ata-   a-   ni.
    table   Rel Case below Poss Loc
    under the table.
    More exactly: below the table's location.

The more specific gloss of (28) singles out the role of the reference object in projecting the ideal space for the located object.

The surface properties of the reference object also have a bearing on the expression of inferiority in Eskimo. When the surface of the sea is the reference object, a special expression, *iki,* must be used to indicate reference to the space projected downward *from the sea's surface:*

29. imma-p   iki-   a-   ni.
    sea   Rel Case below Poss Loc
    under the sea.
    More exactly: under the sea's surface.

Iki denotes 'a layer between two other layers,' that is, a stratified view of an object, making (29) more precisely 'at the level beneath the layer of the sea.'

The Eskimo examples are worth noting for two reasons. First, they show that, as in English, the space projected from the lower part of a reference object and the surface properties thereof can determine the projective meaning. Second, they illustrate the obvious influence of culture. It takes little imagination to see how a fishing culture should develop ways to encode finer properties of the domain of its livelihood.

6.222. Superiority

Just as interiority and exteriority are in a converse relation, so superiority is the converse of inferiority. We can see this relationship by the simple reversal test: If *X* is inferior to *Y,* then *Y* is superior to *X* (and vice versa).

For superiority, the located object occupies the upwardly projected ideal space from the reference object. In that way, superiority involves the ideal space higher than the highest limiting point of the reference object, as (30) exemplifies:

30. The shelf is above the table.

Like its converse counterpart, superiority may interact with other semantic features and produce a finer projective relation. For example, coincidence may interact with superiority to denote contact of the located object and reference object in a vertical relation, as in (31):

31. The shelf is on top of the table.

In the situation of (31), not only is the located object in the upwardly projected space from the reference object, but there is also surface contact between the two. No doubt this is observable because of the morphological transparency of *on top of,* where contact and coincidence, *on top,* are overt.

We might make the stronger claim here that superiority and coincidence are intrinsically likely to interact. Note that there is no equivalent English expression for the interaction of coincidence and inferiority: ?? *the gum is underside the table.* In the naive model of physics that underlies superiority, a world where the ground is the ultimate bottom line, lower objects sustain and support higher objects, and so superiority of the located object to the reference object suggests contact between the two.

The extreme likelihood of contact and support in the superiority relation accounts for a number of other frequently observed meaning correlations with superiority. Sometimes, an expression for superiority implies 'covering' (Bennett 1975; Brugman 1981):

32. The newspapers are over the table.

One reading of (32) is 'the newspapers *cover* the surface of the table'; another is 'the newspapers are in the space above the table, with no contact.' The "covering reading" of (32) is *pragmatically* expected because superiority is associated with support via coincidence in the naive model of space.

Eskimo again provides good comparative data for illustrating the basic properties of superiority. Fortescue (1984: 231) notes that the language has a marker for simple superiority, with no contact:

33. qiqirta-p   qula-   a-   ni.
    island Rel Case superior Poss Loc
    above the island.
    More exactly: in the space located superior to the island.

The form in question, *qula,* is related to the Eskimo nominal for 'upwards,' so here we can see, as with English *above* and *over,* that superiority is associated with a space higher than the reference object.

Eskimo may also encode the interaction of superiority and contact. The form *qa* is used only where there is contact between the located object and the upper surface of the reference object:

34. illu- p   qa-   a- ni.
    house Rel Case super/contact Poss Loc
    on top of the house.
    More exactly: in contact with the upper surface of the house.

There is no contact counterpart of inferiority in Eskimo, as there is also none in English. This absence looks like a promising candidate for our theoretical discussion (sec. 6.4) because contact may be universally associated with certain spatial relations.

6.223. Anteriority

Anteriority obtains if a located object occupies the ideal space projected in front of the reference object. Crucial to this ideal meaning is the interpretation of *front.*

As we have seen in (24), with the discussion of frame of reference, the *front* is determinable either by intrinsic properties of the reference object or by the frame of reference of the viewer. So *Bob is in front of the museum* means either 'Bob is located in the space projecting outward from the entry of the museum,' the intrinsic front of the reference object (*at the museum's front*), or 'Bob is in front of the museum as you view it,' the intrinsic front via the frame of the viewer. In this latter meaning, Bob may even be at the *intrinsic back*—rear—of the museum, though he is still in front of the museum *by the viewer's standards.*

What makes something frontal, given that anteriority has to be a projection? In the case of the viewer's frame of reference, the preceptual apparatus, or "face," determines the front. In no language, for instance, does the term for 'back' refer to the human face. But for properties inherent to the reference object, the decision is not so clear cut. How is anteriority determined, especially when the object has no obvious front?

A number of solutions to this problem have been proposed (Bennett 1975; Herskovits 1986; Hill 1982; Miller and Johnson-Laird 1976). Basically all rely on the *asymmetry of* (or the attribution of asymmetry to) *the reference object.* In an object that is intrinsically asymmetrical, such as a truck, the part that lies in the direction of motion of the object (should it be put in motion) or otherwise is associated with salient or important features (such as visibility) is considered the front. Hence for a truck, the cab is the front because that is the spearhead of the motion—the point that arrives first—and the place where the control lies.

But for symmetrical objects, the situation is problematic. Where is the front of a ball? In such cases, cultural and pragmatic factors intervene and determine frontal properties, but they do so usually by attributing the characteristics of asymmetrical objects to the objects in question. So, at least in the case of English, the front of a ball is the place that is in the direction of its motion.

These points can be nicely seen in some comparative data. Hausa contrasts markedly with English on the attribution of anteriority (and other projective locations: see Hill 1974, 1982). In expressions of anteriority, where the frame of reference is inherent to the reference object, symmetric reference objects are assigned a front that projects *away from the viewer*. This contrasts with English, where the position nearer the viewer is usually the source of the projection of anteriority.

Consider a situation with a viewer, a spoon, and a pumpkin, as shown in Fig. 6.3:

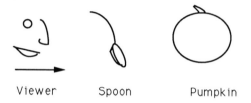

FIG. 6.3. Schematic of situation for 'front.'

How do we make reference to the position of the spoon in relation to the pumpkin, given that the objects do not intrinsically differentiate themselves on frontal properties? We can say two things:

35a. The spoon is in front of the pumpkin.
  b. The pumpkin is behind the spoon.

In each case, the reference object is viewed as facing the speaker. In (35a), the pumpkin faces the viewer, and the spoon is in front of the reference object. In (35b), we convert the spoon into the reference object but maintain the rule for the determination of anteriority. Here the front of the spoon is the part facing the viewer, and thus the pumpkin is behind the spoon. Note that we do not say *The pumpkin is in front of the spoon* for this state of affairs.

The *reverse facts* hold for Hausa, where frontal properties are projected from a position *away from the speaker*. So the Hausa equivalents of (35a) and (35b) are (Hill 1982: 21):

36a. Ga cokali can baya da k'warya.
    look spoon there back with pumpkin
    There's the spoon behind the pumpkin.
    More accurately for English: The spoon is in front of the pumpkin.
  b. Ga k'warya can gaba da cokali.
    look pumpkin there front with spoon

There's the pumpkin in front of the spoon.
More accurately for English: The pumpkin is behind the spoon.

Although Hill (1982) gives a more elaborate, and clearly more adequate, account of the Hausa facts in terms of the projected visual field, the contrasts nonetheless remain. Anteriority is a projected location, and the projection is a function of the choice of frame of reference. Thus different languages may privilege different versions of the projection. In this way, Hausa is the reversal of English, and, of course, vice versa.

6.224. Posteriority

The converse of anteriority is *posteriority:* If X is in front of Y, then Y is behind X. Posteriority may then be defined in a manner analogous to that for anteriority: The located object occupies the ideal space projected from the rear of the reference object.

We should expect the same semantic effects to hold because posteriority can be viewed on analogy with anteriority. First, there is a clear effect for projection, depending on where the frame of reference is located. Consider the following:

37. Bob is behind the house.

Sentence (37) has either a viewer-centered or reference-object-centered interpretation. On the former, the situation may be such that Bob is anywhere in relation to the house, just as long as he is not visible to the viewer. With the frame of reference thus projected from the viewer, posteriority is associated with lack of visibility of the located object. On the latter interpretation, the situation is such that Bob is located with relation to the intrinsic rear of the house as the reference object, or more explicitly: *Bob is at the back of the house.*

We have already inquired into what makes a front a front. Two characteristics make a back a back. First, there is lack of visibility. Posteriority is overwhelmingly associated with hiddenness. Second, backs are frequently the point of an object that is located away from the focus or the direction of motion. This feature corresponds to the converse of the frontal characteristic of headedness.

We can see these characteristics in an examination of Hausa. The same reversal (in comparison to English) of frame of reference for anteriority holds for posteriority, as can be seen in (36) (p. 268). But also in Hausa, the lack of visibility of the located object may induce posteriority *irrespective of the reference object.* Consider the following example:

38. Go   kwallo can   baya da   itace.
    look ball   there back with tree
    There's the ball behind the tree.

Example (38) represents the situation shown in Fig. 6.4.

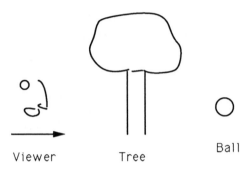

Viewer   Tree   Ball

FIG. 6.4. Schematic of situation for 'back.'

By our previous discussion of anteriority in Hausa, we should expect this state of affairs to be encoded by *Go kwallo can gaba da itace* 'the ball is in front of the tree': A ball behind a tree to speakers of English is in front of a tree to speakers of Hausa. But only (38) is appropriate because the located object, the ball, is hidden from view by the reference object, the tree. Lack of visibility overrides the frame of reference and forces an interpretation in terms of posteriority (see Hill 1982).

6.225.   Laterality

The final projective location to be examined is *laterality,* and one of its subtypes, *mediality.* If laterality obtains, the located object occupies a position in the ideal space projected horizontally outward from a side of the reference object. This ideal meaning underlies (39):

39. Donna is beside the car.

Example (39) represents what might be called *generic laterality.* There is no obvious further restriction on usage, apart from relative closeness in ideal space. After all, in a certain sense, San Francisco is beside New York City.

As with all projectives, the frame of reference can be brought to bear explicitly. Consider the following.

40. Donna is to the right of the car.

Sentence (40) has two interpretations, depending on where the frame of reference for the projection is located. Is Donna to the right of the reference object from the viewpoint of the speaker or the reference object? Either state of affairs is compatible with (40), though English can explicitly differentiate the frame of reference:

41a. Donna is to the right of the car from where I'm standing.
  b. Donna is to the car's right.

Sentence (41a) encodes the viewer-centered projection, (41b) the reference-object-centered projection.
Laterality may also interact with other locational properties, like coincidence:

42. The picture is against the table.

Example (42) holds only where the located object has lateral *contact* with the reference object and may never be used to represent a situation in which the located object is on the table top, and thus in nonlateral coincidence.

Many of these characteristics can be observed clearly in Manam, which, as Lichtenberk (1983) notes, has three expressions of laterality. One, *zagé,* marks generic laterality and, like all locations in Manam on the horizontal axis (see p. 260), appear in constructions of inalienable possession (Lichtenberk 1983: 588):

43. zagé-   gu-   o   go-   túi.
    space beside 1Sing Loc 2Sing stand
    Stand beside me.
    Literally: Stand in my lateral space.

Manam also has expressions for 'left' and 'right,' likewise obligatorily in the inalienable construction because they are on the horizontal plane. Unlike English, however, 'left' and 'right' are viewed *only from the standpoint of the reference object* (Lichtenberk 1983: 590):

44. ?áti péra ŋasí-   Ø   n-   o   i-   éno.
    canoe house space to the left 3Sing liaison Loc 3Sing be
    The canoe is to the left of the house.
    Literally: The canoe is in the house's left lateral space.

The restriction of frame of reference to the reference object does not thereby make the Manam laterals nonprojective. Significantly, if the reference object is shifted on its axis, laterality does not remain with the side shifted, as it would if it were a topological relation. For example, a house on its side now has laterality projected from the upturned base, not from the overturned side. In Manam, the projection is *always made from the reference object outward.*

As we have already noted, in Manam, topological and horizontal projective relations are marked by inalienable possession; vertical projectives are marked as alienable. This encoding fact may help us to draw a further distinction in Manam between two types of expressions of nearness, one of which denotes 'lateral nearness.' The form *saringa,* 'near,' does not occur in the inalienable. Therefore, *saringa* must encode either vertical nearness or a nonprojective location. In contrast, *sa?é,* 'very near/next,' *must* occur in the inalienable. Inalienables can never be associated with vertical projectives, so *sa?é* must be a horizontal projective (it is certainly not topological, because it depends on a frame of reference). Consider the following:

45. ?áti   péra   sa?é-   Ø-   n-   o   i-   éno.
    canoe   house   space very near   Sing liaison Loc Sing be located
    The canoe is right next to the house.

Example (45) may have either a lateral ('right beside') or anterior/posterior ('right in front of/right behind') interpretation. But in each case, the meaning makes reference to the horizontal axis, so (45) may never mean 'right on top' or 'right under.' In this way, Manam is very much like English, where *right next to* and even *next to* have a horizontal interpretation only: either 'beside' or 'in front/behind.' We also see here the value of tying meaning to form. The formal correlates allow us to observe a denotation that we might otherwise overlook: namely, the association of 'nextness' with the horizontal axis because of the requirement of the marking of inalienable possession for horizontal locations in Manam.

To close the discussion of laterality, let us briefly look at one subtype: *mediality,* which is the ideal overlapping space projected laterally from two or more reference objects and occupied by a located object. The following expressions encode mediality in English:

46a. The cat is between the couch and the table.
  b. The flower is among the weeds.

The situation of (46a) is such that the located object, cat, occupies the intersection of the ideal space projected laterally from both the couch and the table. The expression *between* also requires that the number of reference objects be precisely two. A similar account holds for (46b), where the located object, flower, occupies the laterally projected space of the weeds. *Among* carries a different restriction from *between:* The reference objects must be more than two.

Occupation and intersection play such a fundamental role that expressions of mediality often imply containment. More specific, if pleonastic (linguistically redundant), renderings of (46a) and (46b) are *The cat is in between the couch and the table,* and *The flower is in among the weeds.* Simple containment and mediality are different because in the latter, the space for containment must be a lateral projection.

The ideal denotation of mediality holds for other languages. Spanish is a good example, although unlike English, it does not have a number restriction on the reference objects in expressions of mediality. There is one form in Spanish, *entre:*

47. El gato está entre   los pajaros.
    the cat is   Medial the birds
    The cat is between/among the birds.

Entre denotes only occupation in the intersecting, laterally projected space of the reference objects. Pragmatic factors sort out the specific number.

The same phenomenon is found in many other unrelated languages. Greenland-ic Eskimo has one form for mediality, *akunniq,* 'the space between' (Fortescue 1984: 234). Manam has a single form, *mara,* 'space between or among' (Lichten-berk 1983: 589), and, like all horizontals, it must occur in the inalienable construc-tion. Mam has one form, *t-xool,* 'between,' which, interestingly, is related to the noun root for 'interval' (or a unit between two other units), *xool-b'aj* (England 1983: 71). Yapese (Jensen 1977: 242) has a single form for mediality, *fidik',* glossed as 'midst.' It thus appears that English is unusual among the world's languages in its number restriction on reference objects of expressions of mediality.

6.226. Summary

In this section, we have considered the nature of projective space and its associa-tion with a frame of reference either centered in the viewer or inherent to the reference object. Using this information, we have discussed five projective loca-tions: inferiority, superiority, anteriority, posteriority, and laterality (plus its sub-class, mediality). We have observed the converse relation between four of these and noted their interaction with other semantic properties, like coincidence and number. The projectives are dependent on a frame of reference and we have seen how different languages select different options in viewpoint: for example, the Hausa "reversal" of English viewpoint for 'front' and 'back.'

6.23. Summary of Location

Our study of location has focused on the fixed site of an object. We have seen the need for a basic formal structure involving a located object, one or more refer-ence objects, and the projected, ideal space in a naive model of the geometric and physical world. We have looked at two kinds of locations: topological and projective. The former are invariant spatial relations and the latter are dependent on a viewpoint, or frame of reference. These two categories subsume eight locations: coincidence, interiority, exteriority, inferiority, superiority, anteriority, posteriority, and laterality. For each location we have given an ideal denotation in terms of the located object and the reference object(s), and we have observed how this denotation interacts with other semantic properties, such as number and punctuality. Examples from a variety of languages (Hausa, Indonesian, Eskimo, and Manam) illustrate the range of encoding possibilities available to languages as well as the subtle differences in frame of reference that must be invoked to differentiate languages in the semantics of location.

6.3. DEIXIS

Having seen how language denotes and encodes the spatial position of an object, we turn our attention to *deixis,* the way an expression is anchored to some essential point *in context.* We consider deixis here under our larger discussion of language and space because this contextual anchoring can be entirely spatial, with a located point and reference point.

The possible kinds of deixis are a function of the possible contextual properties that serve as anchors. Typically, there are three such properties: *who* is speaking or hearing the expression—*personal deixis; when* it is being said— *temporal deixis;* and *where* it is being said—*spatial deixis.*[5] Inasmuch as we are concerned in the present discussion with how language encodes space, most of our effort is put on spatial deixis, but even in so limiting our focus, we learn a great deal about the other two because the same (or closely related) semantic principles characterize all deictic expressions (see Anderson and Keenan 1985; Fillmore 1975b; Klein 1980; Levinson 1983; Weissenborn and Klein 1982).

In the discussion that follows, we outline the necessary preliminaries for the study of deixis: the here-and-now and relation thereto. We then consider spatial deixis in detail, focusing on its universal components: reference points, remoteness, and direction. We see from comparative illustrations that languages vary within these deictic parameters, though often they have quite detailed and idiosyncratic denotations for deictic terms. We close with a short discussion of how personal and temporal deixis follow the spatial parameters.

6.31.   Semantics, Pragmatics, and the Universal Requirements of Deixis

To get a preliminary sense of deixis, consider the difference between *Be here at 9:00* and *Be there at 9:00.* The former denotes a position *toward the speaker,* and the latter a position *away from the speaker. Here* and *there* thus make essential reference to the spatial context of the speech event. Deictics do not intrinsically denote a static location, but some *relationship* whose precise position is to be determined relative to the participants and locations in the situation represented.

Our goal in this section is to examine the principal features of these contextual relationships. Before we proceed, however, we should clarify two things: the

---

[5]Sometimes a fourth property appears: *what* is being said, or the topic of discourse, giving rise to *textual deixis:* see Weissenborn and Klein (1982).

connection between deixis and the semantics/pragmatics dichotomy; the universal core of all deictic expressions.

First, deixis lies on the semantics/pragmatics border. Even though deixis concerns properties of the context, and may thus appear external to semantics, the forms that encode deixis do so *intrinsically: here,* for example, makes *essential reference* to context. Thus, in spite of having pragmatic force and a contextual denotation, deixis also has a traditional semantic structure in that it brings its effects with it into any context.

Second, all deictic expressions have a common core: the *reference point,* sometimes called the *origo* (Klein 1980), from which the speech event and its relation to context are judged. The reference point is the deictic analogue of the reference object for location and the contextual anchor for the located object. For spatial deixis, the reference point is a *contextual location* from which to judge the speech event and the situation expressed. In the expression *Be here at 9:00,* the issue is how to judge the denotation of *here* relative to a particular locale: one coterminous with the speaker? with the hearer? with neither?

We need a catalogue of reference points, at first glance a limitless project. But in actual practice, the canonical deictic anchor is very narrowly defined as *the speaker in the here-and-now.* Deixis overwhelmingly takes as its base the face-to-face encounter of speaker to hearer/other and projects outward from the speaker as the origin of the speech event in the present time at the present locale. So, *Be here at 9:00* has a preferred interpretation where *here* denotes 'the place of the speaker.'

Given this basic structure, we now turn to the specifics of spatial deixis, and, with much less emphasis, personal and temporal deixis. In all cases, the core denotation of 'the speaker in the here-and-now' interacts with a variety of other semantic features, all of which go differentiate more precisely the anchoring of an expression to points in context.

6.32. Spatial Deixis

The basic semantic structure of spatial deixis can be understood in terms of three concepts: the reference point, remoteness, and direction. These three organize the following discussion.

6.321. Reference Point: Speaker and Hearer

All languages have ways of identifying contextual locations in a speech event by using the location of the *speaker* as the reference point. In fact, in a few languages, there is a single spatial deictic (so it is said of Czech), and this single term invariably takes the speaker as the frame of reference. The constant in spatial deixis is clearly *situatedness radiating outward from the speaker.*

Speaker-centeredness underlies the difference in English between *here* and *there*. As we observed with *Be here/there at 9:00, here* denotes that the position of the located object ('you') is *near the speaker; there* reverses this relationship, signalling a position *away from the speaker*. In both cases, however, the speaker is the reference point. Even in an interpretation of *Be there at 9:00* where the located object is viewed as near the hearer, as 'Be over there by you at 9:00' the essential reference point is the speaker: 'over there by you and hence away from me, the speaker.' The same holds for an interpretation in which the located object is close to a third party, as 'Be over there by Harry at 9:00.' The location is still judged with essential reference to the speaker: that is, 'over there by Harry and thus not near me, the speaker.' *There* is never interpreted as a location judged from the nonspeaker's position.

Though the speaker is the unmarked reference point for spatial deixis, it is not thereby true that the reference point must always be the speaker. In some languages, there are forms to encode the *hearer* as the reference point, though they are much less common, and even in such systems there is always speaker-centered judgment, too (Anderson and Keenan 1985). Certainly, there is a logical explanation for these facts. If the speaker is the canonical center, then the nonspeaker is deducible therefrom.

One language that explicitly encodes nonspeaker reference points is Chamorro. According to Topping (1973: 114–5), Chamorro has three deictic adverbs of nonmotional space: *guine* 'here' indicates speaker-centeredness; *guenao* 'there' indicates hearer-centeredness; *guihi* 'there' indicates a location other than speaker or hearer. Compare the following:

48a. Mata'chong yó guenao.
      sat down   I   there: hearer
      I sat down there by you.

   b. Mata'chong yó guihi.
      sat down   I   there: neither
      I sat down there away from us.

The English glosses do not exactly capture the Chamorro semantics. Examples (48a) and (48b) respectively encode contextual locations judged from the hearer and from a third party.

Specific reference to the location of the hearer is also found in Japanese, which has demonstratives (*this/that*) and locative adverbs (*here/there*) that take the speaker as the reference point and then a different set that take the hearer as the reference point: *kono* 'this, near speaker,' *sono* 'that, near hearer' (i.e., 'this by you'), *koko* 'here, near speaker,' *soko* 'there, near hearer.'

Although we can vary the value for the reference point for spatial deixis from the universal, speaker-centered value to others, like the hearer, the choice of a value for the reference point is not sufficient to account for all spatial deixis. Two other properties must be taken into consideration: *remoteness* and *direction,* respectively the degree and direction of removal in space from the reference point.

6.322. Remoteness and Direction

6.3221. Remoteness

How far from the reference point may the located object be positioned? The simplest solution to this problem is to have only two values: far or not far, more technically *distal* and *proximal.* This distinction underlies the English demonstratives, with *this* denoting proximal space in relation to the speaker and *that* denoting distal space.

But certainly we can imagine degrees of remoteness more subtle than this binary one. What about great removal from the reference point, something like *distal + +?* What about great nearness, something like *proximal + +?* If we think a bit more about English, we can see that many degrees of remoteness can be explicitly encoded, as the following illustrate:

49a. Tom is right here.
  b. Tom is way over there/yonder.

Sentence (49a) encodes a situation where the located object (Tom) is in close proximity to the speaker; in contrast, in (49b), the located object is extremely distal relative to the speaker. In each case the *relative remoteness* of the located object in the reference point motivates the form.

A rich system of remoteness distinctions may be found in Malagasy, which has seven different forms for varying degrees of distal and proximal relation to the reference point (Anderson and Keenan 1985: 292). There are three degrees of nearness to the speaker: *eo, eto,* and *ety,* respectively encode increasing nearness to the reference point:

50. Mipetraka eo/   eto/   ety   Rakoto.
   is sitting   here+/here++/here+++ Rakoto
   Rakoto is sitting here/right here/right next to me.

There are also four distinction of remoteness from the speaker, with increasing distal relation signalled by *etsy, eny, eroa, ery*:

51. Mipetraka etsy/   eny/   eroa/   ery   Rakoto.
   is sitting   there+/there++/there+++/there++++ Rakoto
   Rakoto is sitting there/over there/way over there/way way over there.

6.3222. Direction

In addition to remoteness, the direction of the orientation to the reference point is often encoded. For this property, there are just two possibilities: *toward the reference point* and *away from the reference point*. So taking the speaker as the canonical reference point, we can see how English encodes the two directions:

52a. Tom came.
  b. Tom went.

In the event of (52a), Tom moves in a direction toward the reference point, in this case the speaker, as the unexpressed and unmarked origin. We can see this by explicitly violating the directionality:

53. ?? Tom came from me.

Similar effects can be seen in (52b), where the orientation of the motion is necessarily away from the reference point, again in this case the unmarked speaker. The violation test proves the rule:

54. ?? Tom went to me.

Example (54) is odd because contradictory directions are encoded: *went* intrinsically signals motion away from the reference point, but *to me* signals direction toward the reference point.

Chamorro once again provides a good comparative example. In motional expressions, direction toward the speaker as reference point takes *magi* [vs. the form for static position in (48)]:

55. Matto gué magi.
    came he here: toward speaker
    He came here.
    More accurately: He came to me.

The reverse direction, away from the speaker as reference point, is signalled by a different form:

56. Humanao gué guatu.
    went   he there: away from speaker
    He went away.

We also know, from (48), that Chamorro can explicitly encode a shift in the canonical reference point to the hearer, so we ought to expect an additional form that indicates motion in the hearer's direction. Indeed, there is such a form:

57. Humanao gué guatu   ġuenao.
    went   he there: away from speaker there: hearer
    He went towards you.
    More accurately: He went away from me to your position.

6.323. Interaction of Deictic Components with Semantic Properties

The three combining factors of reference point, remoteness, and direction may interact with other semantic properties to produce finer and apparently more idiosyncratic systems of spatial deixis. Many languages have ways of differentiating contextual locations by how *visible they are to the reference point*, usually the speaker, though sometimes the hearer. Kikuyu, for example, makes such a distinction in speaker-centered distal deictics (Denny 1978: 73–4):

58a. handū haarĩa   he na nyeki.
     place visible/there is with grass
     that visible place with grass.

  b. handū harĩa   he na nyeki.
     place non-visible is with grass
     that out of sight place with grass.

The same distinction of locations by their visibility to the reference point is found in Kwakwalla and Bella Bella (Anderson and Keenan 1985: 290).

  In addition to visibility, vertical and horizontal positions are also frequently encoded in spatial deictics. A relatively generic system of this sort of interaction can be found in Eipo. According to Heeschen (1982: 84–5), Eipo has a strictly speaker-centered system of spatial deixis, with one form for proximity to the speaker, and three forms for space distal to the speaker. The three latter forms are further differentiated not by degree of remoteness, but by horizontal or vertical location, as illustrated here:

59a. ei-   binmal.
     up/distal from speaker he goes
     he is going way up there.

  b. u-   asik.
     down/distal from speaker village
     the village way down there.

  c. ortam   dit lebnanam.
     across/distal from speaker song we two will sing
     We two will sing a song from way across there.

Eipo thus applies three projective notions to the reference point and remoteness: superiority, by *ei;* inferiority, by *u;* and laterality, by *ortam.*

Similar interactions with horizontal and vertical space may be found in many other languages, often to an extreme effect. Daga has 14 demonstratives: 1 each for space proximal to the speaker and hearer and then 12 that differentiate by remoteness and horizontal/vertical level. There are 5 forms in Daga for degree of superiority to the reference point, and 3 of these are differentiated by degree of remoteness. The difference is paralleled in the forms for inferiority (see Anderson and Keenan 1985: 291).

The closer we examine particular languages, the more idiosyncratic the interactions turn out to be. In some languages, the boundedness of the locale interacts with spatial deixis to produce finer differentiations, as in Eskimo, where there is a formal difference between contained and noncontained space that is distal to the speaker (Denny 1978). In other languages, the basic components of spatial deixis interact with measures of distance. Dyirbal has a number of forms for degrees of remoteness downhill, downriver, uphill, and upriver (Anderson and Keenan 1985; Dixon 1972).

It is important to note that even these more specific systems can be accommodated by the machinery we have thus far proposed. All make essential use of a reference point, usually the speaker; degrees of removal from this reference point are also encoded, as are, frequently, orientations with regard to this reference point. Different cultures add to these basic properties, but these modifications assume the elemental structure of spatial deixis.

6.33.   Personal and Temporal Deixis

Now that we have seen the universal components of deixis and their manifestation in spatial deixis, we briefly consider personal and temporal deixis. Though these two do not raise necessary questions of the semantics of space, as deictic systems, they share the semantic properties of spatial deixis—in particular, the reference point and remoteness.

6.331.   Personal Deixis

All languages have ways of directly encoding the *participants in the speech act:* the speaker ('I,' first person), the hearer or addressee ('you,' second person), and the nonspeaker/hearer or the spoken about ('he/she/it,' third person) (see also the discussion of social status and rank in Chapter 3). These three persons comprise the set of contextual anchors for deictic reference to speech act participants, and all languages encode all three. For example, there is no language that encodes just speaker and hearer, and eliminates the third person, although in many languages, explicit encoding of the third person is by a zero-form.

Personal deixis is judged with the speaker as reference point. In all languages, person distinctions ultimately depend on the presence of the speaker of the utterance as the baseline of the context.

Remoteness also bears on the encoding of contextually referential persons. In some languages, there is a formal distinction between third persons who are near to the participants in the speech event and third person who are far away. These forms are often called the *proximative* and *obviative* (near and far, respectively) or *fourth persons*. The Algonquian and Athapaskan languages are typical in this regard, and we have seen illustrations of this phenomenon in our discussion of the Animacy Hierarchy (chap. 3, p. 93). Interestingly, degrees of remoteness in personal deixis appear to be restricted to the third person. No language has a form, as far as I know, to differentiate a near hearer from a far one; nor does any language have such forms for speakers.

Just as with spatial deixis, nondeictic properties interact with the deictic components to produce more finely differentiated personal deixis. Animacy, gender, number, inclusion, and social rank frequently are found in systems of personal deixis. Some languages distinguish not only singular and plural number in contextual participants, but also *dual* (exactly two) and *trial* (exactly three). Hopi has the dual; Fijian has the dual and trial. Notably if a language has a trial, it also has a dual, but not vice versa. In many languages, there is a formal distinction between first-person encoding that *includes the hearer* and first-person encoding that *excludes the hearer*.

There is no formal mechanism to differentiate the two in English, but in Malagasy, 'we will go,' can be explicitly encoded for its inclusion or exclusion of the hearer (Anderson and Keenan 1985: 264–5):

60a. H- andeha izahay.
    Fut go we(excl)
    We, but not you, will go.
  b. H- andeha isika.
    Fut go we(incl)
    We, plus you, will go.

Diyari (Austin 1982) works likewise, with separate forms not only for the meanings glossed in (60), but also for duals: 'we two excluding you' and 'we two including you.' Fijian, a language with a trial, extends this number differentiation to that for inclusion, and there are separate forms in Fijian for 'we three including you' and 'we three excluding you' (Anderson and Keenan 1985).

Though Fijian and Diyari seem a bit extreme in this respect, they bring us back to our original points about deixis. The core property of deixis is found in all deictic systems: the reference point. Remoteness from the reference point also functions in systems of personal deixis, as well as more specific semantic properties, like duality and the inclusion of the hearer in the denotation.

6.332. *Temporal Deixis*

The final kind of deixis is temporal deixis. The details of temporal structure are treated at greater length under tense and time (chap. 8). Nonetheless, it will do us some good to consider how temporal deixis appropriates the core notions of deixis and yet takes on its own idiosyncrasies.

The principal reference point for temporal deixis is the present, the contextual time at which the utterance occurs. Consider (61):

61a. John is here now.
   b. John was here then.
   c. John will be here then.

In (61a), the temporal deictic *now* indicates the coincidence of the time of the event ('is') and the contextual time of the uttering of the expression. Sentences (61b) and (61c) show that English does not make a formal deictic distinction between past and future, both signalled by *then*. In terms of temporal deixis, English may be said to have a form that encodes the convergence of event time and utterance time, *now,* and one that encodes the divergence of event time and utterance time, *then* (either forward or backward event time).

Temporal deixis may also be sensitive to degrees of remoteness, as in the following:

62a. John is here right now.
   b. John was/will be here right then.

Right now/then is a proximal temporal deictic. It has distal counterparts, but apparently only in the past:

63a. John was here way back then.
   b. ?? John will be here back then.
   c. ?? John will be here up then.

The structure of temporal deixis in a language is influenced not only by the invariant properties of any deictic system, but also by how the language construes time in general. We discuss time in more detail in Chapter 8, but it is worth pointing out here that there are two basic ways that time is chunked in any language: *vectorially* or *metrically.* In a vectorial system, as in English, time is a simple extension from a point of origin, for example, "backward" from the present point or "forward" into the future. In other languages, time is encoded as inherent units or measurements, as in Manam, which has markers for different measurements of *days* in the past and *days* in the future.

Note that English *then* does not denote a specific unit of time removed either to the past or future, only that time is *extended as a vector from the present.* This is unlike Manam, which has two temporal deictics for the present, both of which refer to the unit 'today': one for 'any time today' and one for 'time prior to the time of utterance but still today.' Temporal deictics in the past in Manam also denote metrically and, furthermore, interact with remoteness by degree. There are six past time deictics, two specifically metric ('yesterday' and 'day before yesterday') and four that encode degrees of remoteness relative to the day before yesterday: 'not long ago,' 'some time ago,' 'a long time ago,' and 'a very long time ago.' The future temporal deictics in Manam are not so diverse. There are three, but again they are metrically driven: one for 'tomorrow,' one for 'the day after tomorrow,' and one for 'any time after the day after tomorrow' (Lichtenberk 1983).

Temporal deixis thus follows the requirements of all deictic systems. The reference point and remoteness underlie the denotations and languages capitalize on these to provide more specific temporal deictics.

6.34. Summary

We have looked at the structure and encoding of deixis, the anchoring of an expression in contextual space, time, and participants. We have considered three universal components of deixis—the reference point, remoteness, and direction—and have discussed their operation principally in spatial deixis, though to a lesser extent in personal and temporal deixis. We have seen a number of cross-language regularities in spatial deixis—the prevalence of speaker-centeredness, for example—and we have noted the interaction of deictic components with other semantic properties, such as visibility, inclusion, and number.

6.4. UNIFYING THE SEMANTICS OF SPACE

We now have a good idea of the range of meanings available to any language for expressing spatial concepts as well as a sense of how these notions surface in coded form. Given this descriptive basis, we turn to more theoretical matters and concern ourselves with questions similar to those raised in the theoretical sections of other chapters. Is there any way to pare down these spatial notions into a smaller set? Are there hierarchies of relationships, dependencies that might lead to predictions about the semantics of space in any language? To answer these questions, we look at a handful of internal connections among the concepts that comprise locational systems and spatial deixis.

6.41. Conceptual Unities in Location

Here we four examine conceptual unities in the meanings that comprise the semantic systems of location:

1. the prominence of coincidence;

2. the relationship between surface features (two-dimensionality) and coincidence;
3. the relationship between contact and superiority;
4. the relative number of semantic distinctions made on the horizontal, vertical, and lateral axes of space.

We see that the explanations for these unities lie in the nature of the naive model of space that grounds spatial conceptualization.

6.411. The Prominence of Coincidence

Coincidence holds a primary place in the semantic system of any language. Significant support for this generalization comes from the fact that in many languages, the marker of coincidence does double duty, indicating not only coincidence itself but also *any general locative relation.*

This general function of coincidence is found in Chamorro, where the all-purpose locational marker *gi* also means 'on' (Topping 1973). The same is true of Manam (Lichtenberk 1983), where the morpheme *o* is not only the marker of coincidence, but also the marker of any locative relation; in Kobon (Davies 1981), both coincidence and general location receive a zero-form; in Vietnamese (Thompson 1965), the marker of coincidence, ỏ', also indicates generic location.

The conceptual primacy of coincidence is further demonstrated by the fact that coincidence may co-occur with the overt expression of *all other spatial relations.* We can see this in English, where all locative relations have a rendering in which coincidence may be expressed: for example, interiority: *at/on the inside;* exteriority: *at/on the outside;* superiority: *at/on (the) top;* and so on. In Chamorro, the marker of general location co-occurs with *all other spatial expressions:*

64. gi halom guma.́
    Loc inside house
    inside the house.
    More exactly: At the inside of the house.

Why is coincidence primary? Coincidence expresses the state of a located object *at rest.* In fact, in a number of languages, the marker of coincidence encodes *lack of motion* or the *canonical rest position* of the located object (in Eskimo and Vietnamese, for instance). Whereas the scientific model of space has all objects in motion, our naive model of space takes the rest position as the base form from which to judge motion and all other spatial positions. Furthermore, in the naive model, Earth is the ultimate immobile reference point. The conceptual reason for the primacy of coincidence and its association with generic location is that coincidence reflects the rest position of a located object, and this default option in our naive model of the spatial world translates into the default option in our semantic systems.

We might put the whole issue a bit more broadly by observing that the primacy of coincidence may reflect the primacy of topological over projective relations. Coincidence is not only the generic spatial relation, but also the generic topological relation, co-occurring even with other topological relations. Given that topological location is a spatial constant, it is the baseline against which to judge spatial change. Moreover, children appear to acquire the topological before projective relations. Under the assumption that conceptually simpler or more atomic notions are the first acquired, we can claim a conceptual explanation for our semantic facts. The rest position of objects is conceptually primary, so the encoding of locations at rest ought to have prominence in the semantic system of space.

6.412.   Surface Features and Coincidence

There is a consistent relationship in languages between coincidence and surface properties of the reference object. This suggests that coincidence itself may be more properly associated with two-dimensionality.

In some languages, the marker for coincidence is related to forms that express surface properties. In Mam, *t-witz* 'on' is formally related to the form for 'face': *witz-b'aj*. So here we see the direct derivation of coincidence from surface properties.

Furthermore, in many languages the marker of coincidence also implies contact between the located object and the surface of the reference object. In Manam, for example, *o* 'on' entails *only surface contact*. The same is true of Northern Paiute (Snapp and Anderson 1982: 49):

65.   usu samupi huciba'a punni sɨɨ bi-ma-ku.
      he   mostly bird   see   tree Abs on habitual
      He saw mostly birds in the tree, as a rule.

The English gloss misses much of the semantics of Northern Paiute. English construes the events represented *volumetrically,* and the located objects, birds, occupy a position *in* the ideal geometric space of the tree: 'birds *in* the tree.' But in Northern Paiute, *ma* entails simple coincidence with surface contact, and so (65) is more adequately glossed 'he saw mostly birds *on the surface* of the tree.'

We can explain the connection of coincidence and surface properties again by an appeal to the naive conception of space that serves as our mental model. In this view, two dimensions are the upper bound of contact, the maximum number of dimensions relevant to the expression of coincidence. If we want to express the coincidence of a located object with a *three-dimensional* reference object— *and make reference to the three-dimensionality of the reference object*—we then imply containment because three dimensions are also associated with volume and depth. Coincidence is lost when the reference object exceeds two dimensions. In no language that I know of is there a way to encode coincidence with reference to a three-dimensional object because the object itself is composed of surfaces.

Further support for two dimensions as the upper bound of contact may be found in the generality of its reference. In languages that make the distinction between surface and point contact, the form for surface contact may subsume the meaning for point contact, but not vice versa. Compare the following:

> 66a. The boat is on the river.
>   b. The boat is at the river.

Sentence (66a) may mean either that the boat has surface contact with the river ('floating on') or point contact with the edge of the river ('resting near the edge'). But (66b) entails only point contact. Hence surface contact subsumes point contact, but not vice versa.

Conceptually, the surface of an object corresponds to a crucial perceptual region. All objects have a well-defined surface that separates their insides from their outsides. The surface of an object is thus criterial to the individuation of the object itself, unlike volume and depth. The surface is therefore a *conceptual upper bound* of an object in general, and this conceptual generality translates into semantic primacy.

6.413. Contact and Superiority

In many languages, contact (particularly surface contact) and superiority are highly associated, as we can see in the possible interpretations of (67):

> 67. The book is on the table.

Example (67) represents a situation with surface contact between the located object, the book, and the reference object, the table, but also suggests that the reference object *supports* the located object: 'The book is *on top of* the table.'

The same phenomenon is found in a wide variety of unrelated languages. In Kobon, there is a special form for indicating surface contact in a relation of superiority. Eskimo differentiates between mere superiority (without contact) and superiority with surface contact:

> 68a. illu- p   qula- a-   ni.
>   house Rel Case above Poss Loc
>   above the house.
>   More exactly: superior to the house's location (no contact).

b. illu-   p   qa-   a-   ni.
house Rel Case above/contact Poss Loc
on top of the house.
More exactly: on the top surface of the house (contact).

Interestingly enough, the opposite phenomenon is not very widespread, and few languages associate inferiority and contact. Note that neither *The gum is under the table* nor *The gum is underneath the table* expresses necessary contact between the located object and the reference object. The same asymmetry is found in Eskimo, which lacks a form for inferiority parallel to (68b).[6]

These findings are again accountable to the naive model of space. In this view of the world, gravity and support pervade space, and these two notions are built around a *vertical construal of support* and the necessity of *contact to maintain support*. The naive model disallows free-floating objects. Even in these cases there must be a medium that has contact with both the located object and the reference object: planets float *through* space, which also *touches* us. The ultimate yardstick in this view of vertical support is Earth, which is the immobile backdrop that, crucially, lies *below* all supported objects. We are supported by the fact that we have a superior contact relation to Earth as the bottom line. The naive model of space naturally associates vertical positions and contact, and this underlies the convergence of contact and superiority.

6.414. Semantic Distinctions by Axis

Our final observation concerns the number of semantic distinctions made on the various axes of the ideal spatial projection. The cube in Fig. 6.1 (p. 255) has three basic axes: superiority/inferiority, or *vertical;* anteriority/posteriority, or *horizontal;* laterality/mediality, or *lateral.* A survey of the semantic distinctions made along these axes in unrelated languages suggests that the lateral and vertical axes are more differentiated than the horizontal.

Many, many languages make quite specific distinctions along the lateral axis, encoding such common notions as 'left/right,' lateral geographical orientations among laterals, and even fine distinctions in mediality, such as for number and animacy. Manam distinguishes four kinds of laterality and two kinds of mediality. Northern Paiute differentiates at least four kinds of laterality/mediality, perhaps five, depending on how things are counted. Eskimo and Kobon distinguish a number of specific positions on the lateral axis, including lateral contact.

---

[6]Curiously, Kobon encodes inferior contact, but the language has forms for *all kinds of contact:* lateral contact included. The association of contact and inferiority in Kobon appears to be the result of a more widespread process. The more likely result is the asymmetry of contact/superiority and simple inferiority.

Similar claims hold for the vertical axis. Mam encodes two kinds of superiority and two kinds òf inferiority. Kobon distinguishes this axis for contact, yielding two types of superiority and inferiority. Eskimo distinguishes three kinds of superiority and one kind of inferiority. Yapese differentiates two types of superiority and inferiority: one each for the standard relation and one each for 'uphill' and 'downhill.' Dyirbal (Dixon, quoted in Anderson and Keenan 1985: 292) apparently distinguishes five kinds of superiority and inferiority.

In marked contrast is the relative lack of differentiation on the horizontal axis. In Kobon, where there are four distinctions on the vertical and three on the lateral, there are only two on the horizontal: generic anterior and posterior. Eskimo, Yapese, Northern Paiute, and Chamorro all distinguish only two values on the horizontal axis: again, generic anterior and posterior.

Why should there be greater differentiation on some axes and less on others? From the standpoint of the canonical view, all areas on the vertical and lateral axes are within view and are open to differentiation. But this is not true for the anterior/posterior axis. Posteriority, as noted in section 6.224, is often bound up with visibility, and so the horizontal axis is more tied to projection from the viewer. We might then propose that there is more differentiation on the vertical and lateral axes because they cannot be projected otherwise. In contrast, projection from the canonical speaker can dominate the horizontal axis and preclude more differentiation. This leads to a tentative hierarchy of differentiation: Lateral/Vertical > Horizontal. This hierarchy and its predictions are tied into the projection of space outward from the viewer for the horizontal axis: After all, if posterior positions are not visible, why make further distinctions?

6.415. Summary

We have seen four ways to unify the notions underlying semantic systems of location: the primary role of coincidence, the connection between contact and two dimensionality, the relation of contact to superiority, and the greater semantic differentiation of the vertical and lateral axes (vs. the horizontal). All four are ultimately accountable to the naive model of space that underlies spatial expression: the primacy of coincidence, for example, relates to the "rest position" of an object as the default option in the naive view of space.

6.42. Conceptual Unities in Spatial Deixis

We have made some general claims about the conceptual unities of spatial position. Now, we turn to generalizations about spatial deixis. A number of linguists have made comprehensive proposals on spatial deixis. Anderson and Keenan (1985) observe that the maximum number of terms in a deictic system is five, and note the kinds of semantic notions that tend to be associated with a quantitatively defined system. Three-term systems, for example, invariably encode 'near the speaker,' 'far from the speaker/near the hearer,' and 'away from both.'

Denny (1978) attempts to unify systems of spatial deixis by four parameters (Denny's terminology is listed in parentheses):

1. Reference Point (speaker's field or hearer's field)
2. Visible/Invisible (in field or out of field)
3. Proximal/Distal (here or there)
4. Other semantic features (e.g., verticality, boundedness, etc.)

According to Denny (1978), these four categories, arranged hierarchically in the order listed, generate most systems of spatial deixis.

Although these descriptions are well and good, they fall a bit short of an explanation. Why are there only certain distinctions made? What semantic and cognitive explanations can we propose for facts about deixis? Here we examine two generalities about spatial deixis that in some sense precede the general characterizations just articulated: (a) universals in reference point; and (b) regularities in number of distinctions along the proximal/distal dimension.

6.421. *Universals in Reference Point*

All languages distinguish the speaker as a reference point in spatial deixis. Some languages, though far fewer, also distinguish the hearer. Some also distinguish a third position—'away from both speaker and hearer'—and often within this last distinction, they distinguish by remoteness: 'way away from neither.' This sequence leads to the following hierarchy for reference points in spatial deixis: Speaker > Hearer > Neither (near/far).

Some languages, like English, encode no lower on the hierarchy than the speaker: *There,* for example, refers to a position by the hearer as a consequence of being *removed from the speaker,* and so *there* is still speaker-centered. Languages with no explicit way to encode hearer-centeredness approximate this meaning by using remoteness and directionality in combination with speaker-centeredness to evoke the hearer. Hearer-centeredness in this way is weakly equivalent to 'speaker distal,' as in English. The entire semantic system comes to the rescue in this matter to produce, in a composite way, notions that other languages simply encode directly.

In languages that encode hearer-centeredness, that is, necessary reference to the position of the hearer as the reference point—it is customary to find additional semantic distinctions beyond simply speaker and hearer as reference points. More common is for hearer-centered distinctions to occur in three-term systems, with both speaker- and hearer-centered forms, plus others, like 'away from speaker,' or 'away from both (neither).'

The category 'neither' is even more restricted. No language has a single form for a position near a third party, as projected out from the third party itself. In all cases, 'neither' is a *negation* of the first two categories: *neither* speaker *nor* hearer. In languages where the hearer is not explicitly encoded, 'neither' is normally associated with extreme distance from the speaker; in languages with hearer-centeredness, 'neither' makes reference to both speaker and hearer, but only as a *derivative* from them, not as a reference point in its own right.

Thus, if we want to be more precise, there are really only two possible values for the reference point: Speaker > Hearer. The third possibility is their negation, not an independent notion (see Batori 1982).

The ultimate explanation for these regularities comes from pragmatics. The canonical speech encounter radiates outward from the speaker in face-to-face interaction. The universal distinctions in reference point follow that conversational dictum, with hearers defined in relation to speakers. If hearers and others have any status at all as a reference point, then the speaker must also be included. So the pragmatic facts of conversation parallel the hierarchy of reference points.

6.422. *Semantic Distinctions in Remoteness and Direction*

We have seen that some of the axes of location are more finely differentiated than others. Does a similar principle hold for deixis? Let us look at how remoteness and direction are further differentiated.

If we look at how the world's languages treat remoteness, we see that they make more distinctions in the distal than in the proximal. Malagasy (p. 277) is a case in point, with four distal distinctions compared to three proximal ones; moreover, one of the proximal distinctions appears to be leaving the language, so Malagasy really has a four/two opposition of distal and proximal. Northern Paiute has an analogous asymmetry, with one proximal and two distal demonstratives. Spanish has one proximal demonstrative and two distals. Diola Fogny (Sapir 1965: 58) has four distinctions in its distal adverbials: *u* ('there'), *a* ('right there'), *aɲa:* ('over there'), and *aɲa:mɔ* ('way over there'). But there is only one marker for proximal: *ɛ* ('here'). Clearly, languages differentiate distal more finely than proximal.

In contrast to this differential carving up of remoteness, languages appear to make only two distinctions in direction—toward the reference point and away from the reference point—and not differentiate orientation any further. Diyari is a nice case in point (Austin 1982). The language makes four distinctions in remoteness, but has only two for direction: *yarra* ('toward the speaker') and *yada* ('away from the speaker').[7]

---

[7]Some languages encode *parallel direction*, just as some also encode static level position. The extent of this distinction in the world's languages is not known, nor is its relation to directionality in general. See D. Wilkins (1988).

How can we account for these patterns? There may be more distal than proximal distinctions because objects removed in space may be more amenable to explicit demarcation. Nearness to the speaker may require less differentiation because the distinctions are visible and within access to the speech act participants.

The lack of differentiation in direction appears to have a simple, though not particularly logical, explanation. The two directions parallel the anterior/posterior distinction in location. 'Toward the speaker' is akin to anterior, or 'facing'; 'away from the speaker' is like posterior or 'away from.' For the same reason that the anterior/posterior distinction tends to have a binary value, so too does directionality in spatial deixis: It is a projection outward from the reference point.

In many cases, direction and remoteness overlap. If something is *far from* the reference point it is also likely to be seen as *away from* the reference point. Thus it might be that the relatively finer differentiation of the distal accounts for the lack of differentiation in movement away from the speaker: Conversely, the lack of differentiation in the proximal coincides with the general lack of differentiation in orientation toward the reference point.

At present these observations must remain speculative, but they fit well with a model of speech exchange driven by the canonical speaker-centered utterance in an ideal present context. These basic possibilities then give rise to the regularities in the systems that we do see and limit a priori the kinds of distinctions made and the places where finer differentiation might be even attempted by a particular language.

6.423. Summary

We have proposed two regularities in spatial deixis: the primacy of speaker-centeredness in selection of reference point and the relatively finer semantic differentiation of the distal in remoteness (vs. the lack thereof in the proximal and in direction). These patterns have an explanation in the speaker-centered pragmatic structure of exchange.

SUMMARY OF CHAPTER

In this chapter we have looked at how languages encode space. We first investigated two important preliminaries to any discussion of spatial concepts: (a) Spatial concepts are relational and (b) spatial expressions are grounded in a naive and idealized model of space.

We then discussed the nature of topological space and the three topological locations of coincidence, interiority, and exteriority. We saw the interaction of these topological meanings with other semantic properties (e.g., punctuality and totality) and that two of the topological locations, exteriority and interiority, are converses.

Following this, we considered projective space and its connection to a frame of reference in the viewer or in the reference object. We discussed five projective locations—inferiority, superiority, anteriority, posteriority, and laterality (plus its subclass, mediality)—and observed the converse relation between four of them.

From location, we turned to deixis, how an expression is anchored in context. We considered three universal components of deixis—the reference point, remoteness, and direction—and discussed their function in spatial deixis, and to a lesser extent in personal and temporal deixis. We saw a number of cross-language regularities in spatial deixis—the prevalence of speaker-centeredness, for example—and we noted the interaction of diectic components with other semantic properties, like visibility and inclusion.

To close the chapter, we discussed four ways to unify the notions underlying the semantics of location: the role of coincidence, the connection between contact and surfaces, the relation of contact to superiority, and the greater semantic differentiation of the vertical and lateral axes (vs. the horizontal). All four were accountable to the naive model of space.

We also proposed two regularities in spatial deixis: the speaker-centeredness in selection of reference point and the finer semantic differentiation of the distal (vs. the lack thereof in the proximal and in direction). These patterns were explained through the pragmatics of exchange.

QUESTIONS FOR DISCUSSION

1. Consider the following sentence from Ewondo (Redden 1980):

i. Móán atoá á   tébɔ́le.
   baby sit Loc table

Example (i) may mean either 'the baby is sitting at the table' or 'the baby is sitting on the table.' Discuss these meanings using what you know about the semantics of coincidence. The latter gloss is the preferred meaning. Why?

2. Discuss the semantic properties of *along* in the following sentence:

i. The picture is along the wall.

What kind of location does *along* denote? What other semantic properties of either the located or reference object does *along* require for interpretation? Is the following anomalous?

ii. The picture is along the rock.

If (ii) is meaningful, what states of affairs must be the case?

3. Consider the following Hopi demonstratives: *ima* 'near animate things': that is, 'these individuals here'; *puma* 'far animate things': that is, 'those individuals there'; *mima* 'very far animate things': that is, 'those individuals way over there.' How do these Hopi forms reflect the principles of spatial deixis we have discussed in this chapter?

7 Aspect

7.1. INTRODUCTION

The topic of this chapter is *aspect,* which is the nontemporal, internal contour of an event. The current literature contains number of excellent surveys of the subject (Chung and Timberlake 1985; Comrie 1976b; Dahl 1985; Talmy 1985), and we rely on these studies in our subsequent discussion of the issues and facts surrounding aspect.

We begin our discussion with a definition of aspect and some illustrations of its relation to other semantic phenomena. Thereafter, we develop an inventory of major aspectual types and their semantic and grammatical properties. We focus on six aspects: perfective/imperfective, telic/atelic, punctual/durative, iterative/semelfactive, progressive, and habitual, with short discussion of five minor types (intensive, incipient, terminative, prospective, and retrospective). We close the chapter with some theoretical discussion of typology and the conceptual underpinnings of aspect.

Aspect is closely associated with events, so we should begin by recalling our discussion of events to get the proper context. An event is a relation that makes essential reference to time. Aspect, however, is *the way that an event is distributed through the time frame* in which the event occurs (see Talmy 1985). We can get a better grasp of this picture of aspect by trying to imagine how we can modify an event without affecting its basic event structure. To phrase it more technically, what additional computations can we perform on an event to make it into a new event, without losing the character of the original event?[1]

---

[1]The literature on aspect frequently draws a distinction between two kinds of such computations on event structure: those that derive from modification of the event proper, called *Aktionsart* ('kind of

One thing we might do is to extend it, or "widen" it. Take a motion event in an *extended state,* as in the following expressions:

1a. John ran.
 b. John was running.

Both expressions represent the same active motion event, 'run,' in the past tense, but they differ in the way that event is put together *within the past time-frame.* Example (1a) simply expresses the motion event as a completed act. In (1b), however, the event is necessarily extended or stretched into a continuous event, even though it is still relegated to the past. Examples (1a) and (1b) differ not on their temporal framework (their event properties), but on their *patterns within their temporal frames* (their aspectual properties). Aspect thus *operates on* event structure like a mathematical procedure that adds properties to basic expressions to derive new ones. In a sense, *was running* is a semantic equation *run + extension.*

Aspect is conceptually distinct from tense, and thus it is generally understood as the *nondeictic structure of an event,* as compared to tense, which is an event's deictic structure.[2] Sentence (1a), for example, says nothing about the internal composition of the event, unlike (1b), which indicates how the event is put together whatever its deictic structure.

Our goal in this chapter is to enumerate the kinds of nondeictic internal contours that events may have. Languages deploy a relatively small set of distinctions to compute event contours and the major aspectual distinctions are related to other properties that we have already used to describe different semantic phenomena.

7.2. SIX MAJOR ASPECTS

In this section we look at six major types of aspect: *perfective/imperfective, telic/atelic, punctual/durative, iterative/semelfactive, progressive,* and *habitual.* These six do not exhaust the possibilities because many languages have more particular aspectual computations on event structure. We later consider five of

---

action') or *lexical aspect,* and those that are a function of a perspectival change on an event as induced by discourse structure and information flow. There is little agreement on the proper terminology here, though see Bybee (1985) and Brinton (1988), and it is not always clear that this distinction can be drawn consistently (Comrie 1976b). In what follows, we simply use the term *aspect* to refer to *all such modulations of the internal contour of an event,* whatever the proper locale, lexicon or discourse, of the computation.

[2]Tense is deictic because it concerns the relative ordering of events in time, and thus relies on the anchoring of an event in relation to a temporal reference point: see chaps. 6 and 8 for how such a definition accords with deixis.

these briefly (in sec. 7.3), but do so in aggregate, under the rubric of minor types. Throughout this discussion, we try to define the particular aspect criterially and then illustrate the grammatical constructions that are sensitive to the kind of meaning expressed by the aspect (the interested reader should see Dahl, 1985, and Talmy, 1985, for observations on the morphological regularities of aspectual meaning).

7.21.   Perfective/Imperfective

Perhaps the most widely discussed aspectual distinction is the *perfective/imperfective* dichotomy. Many unrelated languages (Russian, Arabic, Chinese, Hawaiian, Hungarian) draw productive and overt distinctions between perfective events, those viewed as *complete,* and imperfective events, those viewed as *incomplete.* English, unfortunately, does not make the distinction so straightforwardly and is therefore difficult to use to illustrate the phenomenon. But we can get a feel for the difference between perfective and imperfective aspect in (2):

> 2a. I have written the letter.
> b. I was writing the letter.

The event of (2a), 'write,' has a perfective interpretation: It is a *complete, viewable unit* (cf. ?? *I have written the letter, but it's not finished*). The complete event in (2a) contrasts markedly with the event of (2b), where the action is seen as *still in progress,* or at least *nonunitized* and *without bounds* (cf. *I was writing the letter, but it's not finished*). Example (2b) thus has an imperfective interpretation. The event is incomplete, nonunitized, and not viewable as a totality.

English does not have a productive morphological distinction between perfective and imperfective aspect and relies on other grammatical and semantic phenomena, like tense, to encode this aspectual opposition.[3] Other languages more directly encode the perfective/imperfective dichotomy. Perhaps the most widely discussed languages in this regard are those of the Slavic family.

In Russian, the perfective and imperfective versions of (2) are directly encoded:

> 3a. Ja napis   al   pismo.
>   I write/Perf Past letter
>   I have written the letter. (perfective)
> b. Ja pis-   al   pismo.
>   I write/Imperf Past letter
>   I was writing the letter. (imperfective)

---

[3]Example (2a) is in the *perfect tense,* which may have the interpretation of perfective aspect: see chap. 8.

Like the Slavic languages in general, Russian differentiates perfective from imperfective events by encoding the verb root for the former, often by prefixation, as in the case of *na-pisal,* or by internal root modification (see Timberlake 1982). In any case, the Russian data clearly indicate the direct encoding of complete and incomplete versions of the same event.

7.211. Complete Versus Completed

Before we proceed, we should clear up a problem that frequently arises in the study of perfective and imperfective aspect. The perfective/imperfective distinction is *independent* of the *termination* of an event. When we say that perfective events are complete and imperfective events are incomplete, we do *not* mean, respectively, *completed* and *not completed.* Perfective aspect is not the same thing as the cessation of an event (nor is imperfective aspect the lack of cessation). The idea is rather that perfective aspect construes an event as a complete unit, whether or not this event has itself come to an end, and imperfective aspect requires that an event be viewed as nonunitized, again whether or not the event is finished.

This difference between complete and completed (and incomplete and not completed) is readily seen again in the Slavic languages, where it is possible to represent the specific cessation of an event in *either perfective (complete) or imperfective (incomplete) aspect.* Compare the following examples from Polish, where, as in Russian, the perfective is often formed by prefixation:

4a. skonczy- łem   piwo.
    finish/Perf 1Per/Past beer
    I have finished the beer. (perfective)
  b. konczy-   łem   piwo.
    finish/Imperf Past/1Per beer
    I was finishing the beer.

The perfective, (4a), conveys that the act of terminating itself is complete whereas (4b) indicates that the termination is still in progress. Clearly, perfective aspect is different from the completion (and imperfective from the noncompletion) of an event proper because the aspects co-occur with the very at of completion itself.[4]

7.212. Perfective/Imperfective as Bounded/Unbounded

The character of perfective and imperfective aspect as complete and incomplete events brings us to a more detailed definition of these two aspects, one that recalls our earlier discussion of the nature and structure of entities (chap. 7.3). If

---

[4]A related confusion is the equation of the duration of an event and perfective/imperfective aspect. If perfective events are complete, then it seems logical that they be of short duration; if

an event is in the perfective aspect, it is *bounded;* if an event is in the imperfective aspect, it is *unbounded.* Perfective aspect, when computed over an event, makes the event a *single unanalyzed whole.* As such, a perfective event is understood from a conceptual distance, or, as Comrie (1976b) notes, from a position *outside the event proper.* Perfective aspect induces a view of an event as a totality, so the event's internal complexity—its beginning, middle, and end—is much less relevant to the interpretation than its unitization. In contrast, imperfective aspect induces the view of an event as internally complex. Imperfective events are viewed *from within,* or as *in progress,* and their *internal properties* are much more relevant to their expression than their unitization (cf. Langacker 1987b for more discussion of the connection between boundedness and aspect).

Many of these basic differences emerge nicely in a language that rigidly distinguishes the two aspects. In Kusaiean, bare verb roots typically express events in the imperfective aspect. Kusaiean, however, has a rich system of directional suffixes which, when added to the verb root, make the event perfective. Compare the following (Lee 1975: 285):

5a. Eltahl kang   ik ah.
     they   eat/Imper fish the
     They are eating the fish. (imperfective)
  b. Eltahl kang-lah   ik ah.
     they   eat up/Perf fish the
     They ate up the fish. (perfective)

In (5a) the bare verb encodes the event in the imperfective form and thus has the unbounded interpretation, an ongoing, presently unfolding, continuous activity. In (5b), however, the addition of the directional suffix *-lah* converts the event into a perfective, with the resultant interpretation of a bounded and unitized event, so (5b) is glossed as past and complete: Only its boundary conditions are relevant to its interpretation.

By using directional markers in this way, Kusaiean is very much like both English and the Slavic languages, where directional affixes also induce perfectivity. Consider the effect of the directional marker *up* on English verbs: *eat/eat up, fill/fill up, shut/shut up.* The latter form in each pair has a decidedly perfective meaning, in the sense of the event coming to a complete or totalized state. Likewise, Polish induces perfectivity by the attachment of directional prefixes to otherwise imperfective verb roots: *jexać* 'go' (imperfective) versus *przyjexać* lit. 'toward go,' 'come' (perfective). The logic of this phenomenon lies in the fact that the directional marker indicates a spatial goal, and with perfective aspect

---

imperfective events are incomplete, then they should also be long (or, at least, not short). However, complete events can have relatively long duration and incomplete ones relatively short duration: cf. Russian *Ja stojal tam minut* 'I was standing there for a minute' (imperfective).

bounding the event, the goal functions as the bound. Conversely, events with no direction are unbounded, and hence have imperfective interpretations.

A number of regular and understandable semantic effects follow from viewing perfective and imperfective aspect in terms of boundedness. Boundedness delimits events and forces unitization. Thus, perfective aspect is often connected to the beginning, end, results, goals, and even the specificity of the participants of events: in short, the event's *determinateness*.

In Kusaiean, the perfectivizing directional affix *-lah,* 'up,' when attached to a verb of making, regularly induces a resultative reading: that is, an interpretation in which some object comes into a determinate state as a consequence of the making. Compare the following:

6a. Eltahl oruh   lohm sac.
    they   build/Imp house the
    They are building the house. (imperfective)

 b. Eltahl orwac-lah   lohm sac.
    they   build up/Perf house the
    They build the house. (perfective)
    More accurately: They brought a house into existence by building.

The effect of the perfective aspect is not only to induce unitization of the event, but to focus on the determinate bound itself, in this case the resultant object of the event of making.

Opposite effects hold for imperfectives, which tend to be associated with continuous, habitual, and nonresultative actions: that is, an event's *indeterminateness*. Imperfectives regularly co-occur with nonspecific entities because they are indeterminate and thus functionally unbounded. Moreover, imperfectives are often compatible with adverbs of manner because such modifiers refer to the internal constituency of the event—how the event is carried out—and imperfective aspect requires an internally situated view of the event (unlike perfective aspect, which forces a view from without).

Both these latter two effects—nonspecifics and adverbs of manner—can be seen in Russian. Nondeterminate plurals, functionally unbounded entities, normally occur with imperfectives (Dahl 1985):

7a. On pis-   al   pism- a.
    he   write/Imper Past letter Plural
    He wrote letters. (imperfective)

 b. ?? On na- pis- al   pism- a.
       he   Perf write Past letter Plural
       He wrote letters. (perfective)

If (7b), the perfective, is to be interpreted at all, it must refer to a specific, delimited, and determinate set of letters: that is, 'he wrote *those* letters,' not 'he wrote some letters' (see Dahl 1985: 75).

Adverbs of manner, which pick out features internal to the event proper, are more compatible with imperfectives than perfectives:

8a. On pis-   al   pismo medlenno.
    he write/Imp Past letter slowly
    He wrote the letter slowly. (imperfective)

  b. ?? On na- pis- al   pismo medlenno.
    he Perf write Past letter slowly
    He wrote the letter slowly. (perfective)

Dahl (1985) observes that (8b) is unacceptable because the perfective aspect bounds the event and forces a distanced view of the act, whereas the manner adverbial requires focus on the inside of the event.

The connection of perfective aspect with determinateness, and imperfective aspect with indeterminateness, bears directly on the associated tenses and time reference of these two aspects. Perfective events, because they are inherently bounded, usually occur in either the past or the future. Rarely do they occur in the present, and when they do, it is usually in a stative event. As we know from Chapter 4, statives are very much like unbounded events anyway, so the stativity of the event apparently overrides the effects of the perfective aspect.

The general absence of perfectives in the present is accountable to the nature of the aspect. How can bounded events occur in the present tense, which itself is fleeting and ungraspable? But why should the future and past be the default choices? Obviously the past is bounded and viewed from without. In fact, the perfective is universally more likely to occur in the past, no doubt because the past is the prototypical removed or distant state of affairs. But the future is likewise bounded because the future is equally removed from the unbounded present.

In the Slavic languages, perfective verbs have productive past-tense and present-tense marking, but crucially, the present tense of perfective verbs signals *future time*, as in the following Polish example:

9. Ja prze-czyt- am   książkę.
   I Perf read Pres/1Per book
   I will read the book. (perfective)

Though *przeczytać*, 'to read,' is in the perfective aspect in the present tense, it can have only a future meaning. Similar effects may be observed in unrelated languages, such as Mandarin Chinese, where the perfective is also compatible with a future time interpretation (see Li, Thompson, and Thompson 1982: 23). So we again see how the logic of boundedness supports a variety of semantic phenomena. Events that are determinately distributed through time take determinate time reference.

7.213. *Perfective/Imperfective and Foreground/Background*

Before we leave perfective and imperfective aspect, we should note one final broader effect of the distinction. A number of linguists, most pointedly Hopper (1979, 1982), have observed that certain discourse structures correlate with each aspect. Events in the perfective are used to represent foregrounded or narrated information whereas events in the imperfective represent background or contextual information.

We can see this difference with an example from English, although we must recall that English does not have a productive perfective/imperfective dichotomy and instead uses other aspects and tenses:

10. While the telephone was ringing, John left the house.

In the situation of (10), the event in the subordinate clause (*while* . . .) is background information and encoded in the continuous form, the English version of the imperfective. The event in the main clause (*John* . . .) is foregrounded information, the event that constitutes the narrative episode, and is in the simple past, the English equivalent of the perfective. This correlation of background/imperfective and foreground/perfective is underscored by a reversal of the forms of (10):

11. ? While the telephone rang, John was leaving the house.

Example (11) is odd because the foregrounded event is in the continuous form and the background event is in the simple past.

In languages with productive perfective/imperfective aspect, the foreground/background correlation holds right down the line. Russian and Mandarin perfectives are overwhelmingly associated with foregrounded events; imperfectives are associated with background (see Hopper 1982).

Without taking sides on the argument over the primacy of pragmatics and semantics, we might observe that the use of perfective events as foregrounded information is compatible with the bounded and determinate nature of the perfective. Narrated events are sequenced and therefore required to be distinct from each other, so it stands to reason that foregrounded, sequenced events should be in bounded and delimited form. On the other hand, because background events establish a continuous backdrop for narrated events, it is logical that they be unbounded and associated with indeterminate events.

There is a larger lesson, however. We can provide a unified view of perfective and imperfective aspect if we see the distinction along the lines we have chosen for bounded and unbounded entities. One major pattern of distribution of events through time is their polarization into complete, determinate, bounded phenomena on the one hand, and incomplete, indeterminate, and unbounded phenomena on the other.

7.22. Telic/Atelic

Another major aspectual distinction is the contrast between *telic* and *atelic* events. We have already considered this distinction in Chapter 4 under resultatives and accomplishment verbs (Dowty 1979; Vendler 1967). We pick up the idea here and look at the telic/atelic distinction more as a feature of the internal contour of events.

Telic events are *resultative*, which means they have built in goals that they *must reach* in order be successfully asserted. (Naturally, atelic events have no such inherent consequence.) This property has given rise to a number of more precise definitions of telic aspect. Nedjalkov and Jaxontov (1988) observe that telic events denote states that also *necessarily imply previous events*. So, for example, in the expression *I baked a cake,* the state of the cake being baked is entirely dependent on the prior events of mixing ingredients, putting the cake in the oven, and so on. Accounts proposed by Comrie (1976b) and Dahl (1981, 1985) also exploit this dual structure of telic events: *the process* **and** *the requisite result*. According to their observations, telic events are characterized by *processes that exhaust themselves in their consequences*.

7.221. Structural Reflexes of Process and Result

The requirement of *both* the process and the result allows us to distinguish some rather tricky cases on the basis of three resultative tests: noninterruption, ambiguity with *almost,* and durative *in* (outlined in chap. 4, pp. 184–86). First, telics are generally not interruptible because they require consequences; if they are interrupted, the process that precedes their results holds, but the consequent is nullified. Compare (12a) and (12b):

12a. Bill reached New York.
  b. Bill drove to New York.

Both events appear to be telic because they are exhausted by their results: If Bill reaches or drives to New York, then there is no more action by Bill. But they differ crucially on the interruptibility of the process leading to that result. Sentence (12a) represents only the endpoint of the entire event, and so if Bill is interrupted in reaching New York, the entire event fails, making *reach* atelic. In contrast, (12b) denotes both the process and result, and so if Bill is interrupted in driving to New York, then the prior event of driving holds while the result of arriving in New York is nullified: *drive to* is therefore telic.

Second, resultatives are ambiguous with *almost* because the adverb can refer either to the result ('almost the result') or to the process ('almost the event leading up to the result'). Compare the following:

13a. Bill almost reached New York.
  b. Bill almost drove to New York.

Example (13a) is not ambiguous, meaning only 'Bill nearly achieved the result of getting to New York.' But (13b) is ambiguous, meaning either 'Bill nearly started the process of driving' or 'Bill nearly came to the result after doing the driving.' *Drive to* has the proper dual semantic structure, and so is predictably ambiguous with *almost*.

Third, telic events allow temporal expressions with *in* and marginally allow such expressions with *for*. Atelic events allow only such expressions with *in*. Consider (14):

14a. Bill reached New York in two hours.
  b. Bill drove to New York in two hours.

Both allow the durative time expressions with *in,* showing that each selects for a volume of time (see chap. 4), but they differ with durative *for:*

15a. ?? Bill reached New York for two hours.
  b. Bill drove to New York for two hours.

Only *drive to* permits durative *for* and is thus telic. We find such durative collocations because expressions with *in* require a bound to denote intervals of time. Both *reach* and *drive to* have results (bounds), so they both allow *in*. However, expressions with *for* focus on the duration itself. *Reach,* as pure result, has no such process and so cannot accommodate any durative expression that selects for the process. *Drive to* does have the requisite internal process, and allows durative *for*.

7.222. Two Structural Correlates of Telics: Perfect Tense and Passive Voice

Now that we have a sense of the meaning of telic aspect, let us consider two other factors that accompany and induce telic interpretations: perfect tense and passive voice.

7.2221. Telics and the Perfect Tense

The *perfect tense* (in English, *have* + past participle) induces telic meanings. Consider this expression:

16. Donna has driven.

Sentence (16) is "weakly resultative," as the success of the "*almost* diagnostic" shows. *Donna has almost driven* can mean either 'Donna has driven a little and not reached a completed state' or 'Donna never got to the process of driving at all.' But the test fails to induce ambiguity on the nonperfect form, *Donna almost drove,* so it must be that the mere introduction of the perfect tense generates telic meaning.

Many of the world's languages have a similar correlation between perfect and telic events. Analogous structures can be found in Evenki, Georgian, Tongan, German, Russian, and Lithuanian (see Nedjalkov and Jaxontov 1988). A particularly clear example of this perfect/telic convergence can be seen in Mongolian, where, as Dugarova and Jaxontova (1988: 218) note, the perfect tense is formed by adding a participial suffix to the verb and inserting a perfect auxiliary:

17. Gurvan cagt bi max- aa   čana-san   baj-san.
    three   by I meat Acc boil Prtcpl Aux Perf
    By three o'clock I had boiled the meat.

Example (17) can have a number of more specific interpretations—for example, 'I had *already* boiled the meat' or 'I had the meat boiled'—but in all cases, the meaning of the verb is telic: The necessary result of the process of boiling is that the meat is now in the state of being boiled. As in the English perfect of (16), the telic interpretation appears to be wholly a function of the perfect tense because in Mongolian, the verb root *cana* 'boil' is atelic by itself.

Why should the perfect induce telic aspect? The perfect tense, as discussed in Chapter 8, requires that the event in its scope be composite. The perfect relates two times, the present moment of speech and some other past or future time, as a more accurate gloss of (16) indicates: 'Donna's past driving is now relevant for assertion at the present moment.' In relating two times—and, by implication, two events—the perfect is functionally equivalent to the telic, which, as we know, requires a dual event structure. The ambiguity with *almost* in the perfect follows from the fact that the adverb has two times to choose from for its scope: for (16), 'Donna has almost driven as of now' or '. . . as of then.' The perfect induces telic aspect because of its dual temporal structure (see Maslov 1988 for similar observations).

7.2222. Telics and the Passive Voice

A second syntactic structure that may induce the telic is the passive, especially ergative or middle voice constructions (see chap. 5), those that look like intransitive passives:

   18. The door was closed.

Example (18) denotes a telic event because there is both the resultant state ('closed') and the process leading to that result ('came to be in a closed state'). It is also ambiguous with *almost*. *The door was almost closed* may mean either 'the door almost reached the resultant state of closure,' where the adverb has the result in its scope, or 'someone nearly began the closing the door,' where the process is in its scope. Hence passive forms convey telicity because of their intrinsic dual structure of both process and result.

In languages with the proper morphological means, the passive and telic are frequently associated directly (see Nedjalkov 1988 for ample evidence from the world's languages). Golovko (1988) observes that Aleut has three passive markers: two form nonresultative passives and the third is restricted solely to the telic:

   19a. umla-sxa- ku-   q.
        wake Pass Non-fut I
        I am being woken.
    b. su- ĝa-   ku-   q.
        hold Pass/Telic Non-fut I
        I am being held.

Example (19a), a passive formed by the atelic passive affix *sxa,* has no resultative meaning and is interpreted as 'I am in the process of being awakened, but no result reached.' In contrast (19b) is formed with the telic passive affix, *ĝa,* and is understood to denote not only the process leading to 'holding,' but also the resultant state 'being held.' Hence (19b) is more accurately 'I have come to be being held.' Aleut thus nicely exemplifies the connection of results and passives by differentiating telic from atelic passives.

The convergence of passive voice and telic aspect is fairly readily explained. The logic of the passive is to promote the recipient of the action to subject position. In doing so, the passive focuses on the result of the process encoded by the verb insofar as the recipient is the result of the action. After all, one simple way to evoke a telic reading is to add a recipient to an event, either actionally (bake *a cake*) or spatially (drive *to New York*). The presence of and focus on the recipient provided by the passive produce the telic interpretation.

7.223. *Resultative Markers*

We have seen a variety of ways that languages construct and encode the telic. Let us close with the most transparent. In many different languages (German, Armenian, Nivkh), there are simple and direct ways of converting an atelic event into a telic one by inserting a morpheme of result. Nivkh forms the telic by inserting a verbal infix to indicate that the event is interpreted resultatively. Compare the following (Nedjalkov and Otaina 1988: 140):

    20a. imŋ mud'.
         they die
         They are dying.
      b. imŋ mu- ʒ əta-d'.
         they die   Telic
         They are dead.

Example (20a) denotes the process of death, 'dying,' whereas (20b), encoded as it is with a telic marker, focuses on the resultant state of dying, 'dead.' So we see how a language can straightforwardly convert events with no inherent goals into events that must be exhausted in their consequences.

7.23 **Punctual/Durative**

We have thus far examined two kinds of internal contour of an event: boundedness or unitization (perfective/imperfective) and goal-directedness (telic/atelic). We now turn to the *extent* or "volume" of an event. If an event is momentary and has no temporal duration, it is *punctual;* if it is necessarily distributed over time, it is *durative*.

The punctual/durative distinction is very much the event-analogue of the *extendedness* of entities (chap. 3): whether they occupy a salient position in spatiotemporal coordinates (pp. 121–22). The same idea can be applied to events. Punctual events have no temporal extension; durative events do.

The punctual/durative distinction may be seen in the following expressions:

    21a. Lisa received the package.
      b. Lisa climbed the tree.

The event in (21a) is punctual because it denotes a momentaneous act. Note that it is odd to ask specifically about the length of time required for Lisa to receive the package—?? *How long did it take Lisa to receive the package?*—because *receive* denotes only the point of receipt. *Climb,* on the other hand, denotes a durative (or nonpunctual) event because climbing occupies time. It is reasonable to ask about the exact length of time required for this event to unfold: *How long did it take Lisa to climb the tree?*

7.231. Two Structural Reflexes:
Measure Phrases and Momentaneous Adverbials

These preliminary observations correlate well with two consistent diagnostic tests for the punctual/durative distinction: measure phrases and momentaneous adverbials (Brinton 1988; Carlson 1981; Comrie 1976b; Dowty 1979). First, because durative events are inherently extended, they should be compatible with phrases that measure temporal extension: phrases like *for an hour, all afternoon, for awhile,* and so on. However, punctual events, because they are momentary, should be incompatible with such phrases. These expectations are borne out:

22a. Lisa climbed the tree for a while.
  b. ?? Lisa received the package for a while.

Sentence (22a) allows the measure phrase *for a while,* but the punctual expression (22b) disallows it because the extension inherent in *for a while* is incompatible with the momentaneousness of the event of receiving.

Second, if duratives allow measure phrases because of their inherent extension (while punctuals disallow such phrases), then punctuals ought to permit phrases that encode momentaneousness. Expressions with punctual events take phrases that encode the specific point of time at which they occur, adverbial phrases such as *at once, at noon,* or *at that point:*

23. Lisa received the package at once/at noon/at that point.

Durative events are also compatible with such markers of punctuality, but with an interesting twist. Consider (24):

24. Lisa climbed the tree at once.

The phrase *at once* refers only to *part* of the entire durative event: specifically, to the *beginning point.* Thus (24) is aptly glossed 'Lisa immediately began the climbing of the tree,' where the initial *point* is in focus. Thus, even when a momentaneous adverbial phrase modifies a nonpunctual event, it selects a punctual feature of that event, in this case the moment of inception.

7.232.   Three Cautions
with the Punctual/Durative Distinction

These two structural correlates—measure phrases for duratives and momentaneous adverbials for punctuals—bring up three cautions. First, we should
be careful to remember that the punctual/durative distinction concerns only *the
fact of the extension of the event,* not any specific measurement of the event's
quantity or length. Very short events, no matter how short, are not thereby
punctual; nor are events that consist of a single undifferentiated act punctual
simply because they are unitary. Consider (25):

25a. The worm inched along.
  b. Fred sat.

The event in (25a) is of extremely short duration, but in spite of its conceptual
brevity, *inch along* is durative: *the worm inched along for a while.* So, too, the
event in (25b) is not punctual just because it is unitary. Sitting is a noncomposite
state, but despite its lack of internal structure, sitting is still extended and durative: *Fred sat all day long.*

Second, the punctual/durative distinction is independent not only of the specific magnitude of the event, but also of both boundedness and telicity. Though
punctual events are momentary and nonextended, they are not thereby perfective
or bounded. Similarly, durative events, though they are extended, are not thereby
imperfective or unbounded. Brinton (1988: 25) puts the issue nicely: "Punctuality and durativity are inherent features of the meanings of verbs or of situations signified by verbs; perfectivity and imperfectivity are means of viewing
situations (be they punctual or durative) as whole and complete or ongoing and
incomplete." In languages that draw a productive distinction between perfective
and imperfective aspect, we also find both perfective and imperfective punctuals.
In Polish, there are perfective and imperfective forms for the meaning 'to
knock,' though the meaning itself is punctual.

Furthermore, punctual events are not necessarily telic. Even though momentaneous events appear to be goal-directed (a goal is an end*point*), momentaneousness does not translate into telicity. The verb *reach* is, as we know,
atelic, but it is also punctual:

26a. We reached New York at once.
  b. ?? We reached New York for a while.

Third, though the punctual/durative distinction is at base independent of other
aspectual distinctions, because no language encodes all semantic distinctions
separately, in many cases, specific punctual/durative encoding is absent and
other aspectual and event properties cover these needs. In English, we can

convert punctuals into duratives by progressivization (see sec. 7.25): *Lisa was receiving packages all afternoon.* In languages where the perfective/ imperfective distinction is primary, durative events are compatible with imperfectives and punctuals with perfectives. This is apparently the case for certain verbs in Russian (see Comrie 1976b). Furthermore, stative events, because of their internal continuity, have a tendency to be durative, whereas actives may be either durative or punctual. In short, the punctual/dual distinction is in principle autonomous, but in practice it frequently is associated with events and aspects with similar semantic structure.

7.233. *Comparative Illustrations*

These facts about the punctual/durative distinction can be seen in comparative examples from languages other than English. Hungarian has a number of verbal suffixes that function to convert a nonpunctual event into a punctual one, typically by restricting a durative event to a single occurrence (a *semelfactive* event: see sec. 7.24). A similar nondurative marker is found in many of the Australian languages (Heath 1981). Douglas (1981: 234) notes that Watjarri has a kind of all-purpose punctual marker, *pa*, that can affix to any grammatical category to indicate a punctual interpretation of an event, entity, or proposition. Consider (27), where the punctual marker *pa* is attached to the subject, though the effect is to induce a punctual reading of the whole state of affairs:

27. njinta-pa   wangka.
    you Punc say
    You say it at once.

English lacks an appropriate lexical item for the meaning of 'punctual say,' though a close rendering may be something like *blurt:* ?? *He blurted it all afternoon/ He blurted it at once.*[5] Presumably without the punctual marker *pa*, (27) has a durative interpretation, something like 'you say it whenever you want,' where there is no restriction on the extension of the event of saying.

A crystal clear example of the punctual/durative opposition can be seen in Northern Paiute, where verb stems represent events with no aspects. By affixation and other modifications, the stems can be compositionally converted into aspectualized events. One way to signal durative aspect is to devoice the last consonant in the unaspectualized stem. The bare stem *yaga* 'cry' is made durative as shown here (Snapp and Anderson 1982):

---

[5]*Blurt* is not only punctual, but also intensive (see sec. 7.35)—'intense punctual saying'—and thus is still not an entirely appropriate equivalent.

28. usu yaka-   kwi.
    he cry/Dur Fut
    He will be crying.

The last consonant of the stem, *g,* is devoiced to *k: yaka* is the durative form of 'cry.' But when the punctual version of this event is to be encoded, a separate suffix is added to the neutral stem:

29. usu yaga-hu-   kwi.
    he cry Punct Fut
    He will cry at that point.

The Paiute data thus show that the punctual/durative distinction is an independent aspect. In this language at least, the opposition can surface in distinct forms to convert an event that is otherwise neutral for aspect into an aspectualized one.

7.24. Semelfactive/Iterative

We have just seen how events may be either temporally extended (durative) or nonextended (punctual). This distinction is at the level of the gross magnitude of the event, irrespective of the amount of extension that an event may have. Many languages make further aspectual distinctions with regard to the quantity of an event.

If the event consists of a single act, it is in the *semelfactive* aspect. If the event has multiple subevents, or is "plural," it is in the *iterative* (sometimes called *frequentive*) aspect (Brinton 1988; Chung and Timberlake 1985; Comrie 1976b; Talmy 1985). Quite commonly, languages encode multiple subevents as a regular collection, as events in a *phase* or *cycle.*

We can get a good idea of these features of iterativity by the following English examples:

30a. Bob shrugged.
  b. Bob wiggled.

Example (30a) expresses an event composed of a single subevent. *Shrug* denotes the single raising (with optional lowering) of the shoulders and so is technically a semelfactive: More than one unit of raising and lowering cannot be denoted by *shrug.* In (30b), the event denoted *must* occur more than once. *Wiggle* refers to multiple movements of the body. Note that *Bob wiggled once* is sensible only if *once* denotes a single unit of multiple movements. If Bob performs a single body movement, then *wiggle* is inapplicable (and something like *twitch* is appropriate). Hence *wiggle* is inherently iterative or frequentive.

7.241. Phases, Cycles, and Repetition

The multiplicity of the denotation of *wiggle* illustrates a larger point about the kinds of quantities that iterative and semelfactive aspect may encompass. Not only can language encode the simple cardinality of an event (its "singularity" or "plurality"), but also the cyclicity, or pattern of repetition through time. Consider verbs like *rebound, reverberate,* or *blink,* which represent events that must be conceptualized in a phase: complementary positions or states of affairs that constitute a single event, much like the phase or cycle of a sound that has both positive and negative amplitudes.

Sometimes languages encode exactly two subevents (just like the encoding of precisely two entities in the dual), as in *sway,* which denotes 'dual lateral motion'—back and forth. Significantly, it is rare for languages to encode more than two subevents, just as they infrequently encode trials for entities, and never do languages encode more than three subevents: that is, there is no verb *bisway* ('sway twice' = two cycles) or *triblink* ('blink three times' = three cycles).

Iterative aspect involves the repetition and extension of events, and so it is sometimes confused with other aspects, such as the durative, which, as we know, denotes extended events. But the iterative must be kept apart from these other aspects. Simple duration does not induce iteration—*sit* is durative, but not iterative—and iterative events can be simultaneously encoded as durative, as in *Bob was wiggling all afternoon.*

7.242. Comparative Illustrations

A look at other languages reveals a variety of iterative and semelfactive structures. Nahuatl (Sullivan 1988), like many languages, employs morphological reduplication to bring about iterativity. Example (31) encodes a simple non-enumerated durative event:

31. qi- tequi.
    it   they cut
    They cut it.

But when the situation requires that cutting be seen as iterated into a series of discrete subevents, the first syllable of the verb is reduplicated:

32. qui-tetequi.
    it   they cut/Iter
    They cut it up.

Example (32) is perhaps more accurately glossed 'they sliced it up'; *slice* may suggest the repetition of the simple durative event of cutting (cf. *slice into*, which is semelfactive).

Similar facts hold for Eskimo, which, as Fortescue (1984) notes, has a variety of iterative affixes: two to denote generic iteration and several others to signal particular kinds of spatial or temporal repetitions of an event. Eskimo can denote the *serial iteration* of a motion event:

33. nivinnga-jurar-   pai.
     hang   Iter/Serial 3Sing/3Pl/Indic
     He hung them up one after the other.

As usual, the English gloss does no justice to the Eskimo construction, which is perhaps more accurately rendered 'he hung one, and then another, and then another. . .' The affix *jurar* indicates that the action is to be seen as a series, and so we have a clear instance of how iteration can be compositionally and transparently derived.

7.25. Progressive

The fifth aspect we consider is the *progressive*. This aspect has been widely discussed in the semantics literature, and there are about as many proposals and terminological differences for the progressive as there are individuals who write on the subject (Bach 1986; Brinton 1988; Carlson 1981; Dowty 1979; Parsons 1989). We limit our discussion just to the essentials of the progressive, hopefully the concepts that all the writers basically agree on (see also chap. 4, verb typologies).

The traditional definition of the progressive is the aspect that encodes action *in progress, on-line,* or *ongoing*. This intuition is corroborated by an example from English, where the progressive surfaces, as in the vast majority of languages (Dahl 1985), as a separate, periphrastic form [the verb *to be* plus the present participle (*-ing*) of the main verb]:

35. Maria is watching a bird.

The event in (35) is understood to be on-line or in progress, whatever the exact time of the activity: cf. *Maria was watching a bird* and *Maria will be watching a bird*.

Insofar as the progressive encodes ongoing activity, it is frequently argued to be preferentially connected to dynamic events, themselves characterized by progress (Chung and Timberlake 1985; Vlach 1981). Indeed the appropriateness of the progressive in (35) seems motivated by the fact that 'watching' is a dynamic act, unfolding through time, requiring change and on-line presence (cf. the discussion of active events, pp. 146–58).

The connection of the progressive to the continuous unfolding of events has led to the received formal definition of the progressive aspect (Dowty 1979). An event is in the progressive aspect if the event itself is true at a point in time that is contained by a true nonprogressive version of the same event. More strictly, the point t of the progressive is true in the interval I of the concomitantly true nonprogressive: t $\supset$ I (Dowty 1979: chap. 3; Parsons 1989). The progressive thus logically requires that an event be in effect at some interval extending beyond the exact point at which the event is asserted to be on-going: that is, at some interval containing the point of the progressive. For example, if Maria was watching a bird (progressive at a point in the past), then it is also true that Maria watched a bird (nonprogressive) at some time either prior or subsequent to the point at which she was watching a bird (true at the nonprogressive interval containing the progressivized version.) This more formal definition captures the sense that the progressive event is *continuous* and *extended* (indeed, sometimes the progressive is referred to as the *continuous*) from a point into an interval larger than itself.

7.251. *Progressive and Extension from the Inside*

The formal definition of the progressive as truth at a larger interval containing the point of the event implies that the aspect temporally elongates the event, but from an *interior viewpoint,* given its containment in a larger interval. The progressive is an operation that *extends an event from the inside,* much like the blowing up of a balloon. This view of the progressive aspect as extension from the inside of an event accounts for a number of other well-known effects. We look at four: iterativity, simultaneity, stativization, and temporariness.

First, when the progressive is applied to a punctual event, an *iterative* interpretation results. Consider (36):

36. Maria was bumping her head.

Bump represents a punctual event—?? *Maria bumped her head for a while/At that point, Maria bumped her head*—but progressivized, as in (36), it takes on an iterative reading: 'Maria performed a series of discrete acts of bumping.' The iterative reading is a natural result of the progressive extending an event from the inside because punctual events *have no insides.* They are momentary and thus have no internal structure to be extended, so the only possible result of extending a punctual event is to repeat it in a series.

Second, the progressive allows for *simultaneity* because of its internal perspective (Langacker 1982). Consider a durative event in the progressive:

37. Tom was walking.

The event represented in (37) not only has duration, but also has extension within that duration. Sentence (37) suggests that the event is open to be simultaneous with another event: *Maria bumped her head while Tom was walking*. In extending the event from within, the progressive makes additional "event space" to accommodate another simultaneous event.

Third, because the progressive extends events from within, it is often interpreted as a *stativizing* operation on dynamic events (Langacker 1982). In many unrelated languages (e.g., Thai, Quechua, and Welsh), the progressive is formally similar to the marker of 'static position' (Traugott 1978). Even the present-day English progressive is historically related to forms like *is a-going* ('is in going') and *is a-doing* ('is in doing'), where the connection to static position is clear (much like the French progressive *en train de* 'in the process of'). This effect of stativization is related to the fact that the progressive is preferentially associated with the internal structure of an event. As we already know, statives are characterized by continuous internal structure, so it stands to reason that extension from within should produce stative effects.

The fourth and last effect of the progressive is its frequent association with temporary or contingent events. Compare the following:

38a. Fred lives in Texas.
  b. Fred is living in Texas.

Example (38a) denotes a relatively permanent state, and is in the nonprogressive. But the progressive version, (38b), represents a temporary state of affairs, suggesting that in the events represented, Fred's place of residence is contingent or nonpermanent: that is, 'Fred is living in Texas for the time being.' This effect follows from other facts about the semantics of the progressive. Brinton (1988: 9) notes: "A situation in progress is one which is *not* complete." Thus, even though the progressive gives any event duration—punctuals and duratives alike—the duration is limited because of the internal perspective and the on-line unfolding of the event. To put it simply, on-line events may be stretched out, but they do not last very long in that state (Mufwene 1984).

7.252. *The Progressive in Other Languages*

The progressive in English covers a wide range of internal contours of events that are frequently coded separately in other languages. In English, the progressive may have a durative, imperfective, and even a habitual meaning: For example, *Maria was buying a new coat every year* is roughly equivalent to the explicit English habitual, *Maria used to buy a new coat every year*. English otherwise has few productive signals of these additional aspectual distinctions, so the progressive does double and triple duty, as a sort of all-purpose "event extender." But the same generality does not hold in other languages, where the progressive often surfaces independently of these other aspects and where the semantic space as a whole is structured differently.

Verbs that are progressivizable in English are sometimes not progressivizable in other, related languages. Weather expressions in English and Spanish are standard in the progressive: *it is raining* and *está lluviendo*. But in Icelandic (related to both English and Spanish), the otherwise productive progressive is disallowed for weather verbs (Comrie 1976b: 35).

The opposite facts also hold: What cannot be progressivized in English can often be progressivized in other languages. So, English generally fails to progressivize verbs representing mental states, such as *see, know, believe,* and the like. However, such progressivized forms are allowed in Portuguese (Comrie 1976b); certain of these are likewise allowable in Sesotho. Machobane (1985: 62) observes that the progressive marker *se* in Sesotho may co-occur with the verb *tseba* 'know' in the present tense:

39. Teboho o-   se   tseba Sesotho.
    Teboho Subj Prog know Sesotho
    Teboho is knowing Sesotho. ('still knows')

The progressive form in (39) is acceptable under the interpretation that the 'knowing' had been suspended and then reinvoked, as in the case of Teboho leaving the country, coming back, and it then turning out that he still in fact knows Sesotho. In this way, the verb for 'know' is directly progressivizable because, interestingly, a contingency or transience has been introduced into the state of affairs to warrant the use of the on-line form.

Though we might argue that Sesotho and English differ on the degree to which they allow mental states to be viewed as on-line, this would miss the remarkable convergence between the two languages elsewhere with regard to the progressive. In Sesotho, this aspect serves the same wide range of semantic functions as in English: iterativity, repetition, and habituality. It even marks intentionality, as it also does in English: *If Fred comes tonight, then I'm leaving,* where the progressive signals the intentions of the speaker through the implication that the on-line activity will hold at a future state (see also Dowty 1979).

A look at other languages reveals clear and more widespread divergences from English in the treatment of the progressive, especially in relation to other aspects. Let us recall that Northern Paiute productively distinguishes the durative by a separate marker (see sec. 7.23). The progressive also has a distinct realization, as in the following example (Snapp and Anderson 1982: 75):

40. usu saa- wini- na   o   pɨ-pɨ'-a-mɨ tɨka.
    he cook Prog Simul his friends   eat
    He was cooking while his friends were eating.

Northern Paiute distinguishes continuous action by the marker *wini* (the durative has a different form). Moreover, the progressive here is compatible with the marker of simultaneity in Paiute, *na*. This is entirely in line with our previous observations that the extension of an event from within produces the event space that accommodates simultaneous action. In Paiute, simultaneity itself just re-ceives explicit encoding along with the progressive.

So here we see that Northern Paiute encodes the progressive aspect differently from other, conceptually related aspects. In Northern Paiute, incomplete and nonmomentary events are semantically and formally distinct from events that are extended from within.

7.26. Habitual

The last aspect to be discussed is the *habitual,* which, unlike the progressive, *extends an event from without.* Habitual aspect indicates the *persistence of an event irrespective of time,* unlike the progressive, which signals extended action *within* a temporal interval. This definition accords with the observations of other linguists on the semantic structure of the habitual. Comrie (1976b) notes that the habitual signals the *indefinite protraction* of an event. The habitual is not associ-ated with any specific moments, but with a whole period. Dahl (1985) notes that the habitual encodes the *quantification of a set of occasions,* and the event asserted in the habitual is understood to hold in the *majority of these occasions.* Again, this implies that the habitual is removed from, or exterior to, the time interval with which its asserted event is otherwise associated. Brinton (1988) observes that the fundamental characteristic of the habitual is that it expresses the *repetition of an event on different occasions,* or the event is *distributed over a number of times.*

The habitual removes an event from any specific reference to time, yet ex-tends the event nonetheless. Consider (41), with the English habitual marker, *used to:*

41. Maria used to buy a coat every winter.

Example (41) means something like 'Maria bought a new coat over numerous winters in the past,' where persistence over a time period is implied. The habitual appears to be removed from time, or exterior to the time interval over which it holds. Consequently, expressions in the habitual aspect are quite similar to gener-ic statements. So, the habitual in (41) may be interpreted very much like a generic aspect, some kind of the extension of an event into customary or usual practice, and removal from temporal contingency.[6]

---

[6]Although these examples show how the habitual may denote the generic status of an event, in some languages, though markedly few, there is a distinction between those events that are simply habitual and those that are generically habitual. Dahl (1985) claims that Wolof, Greenlandic Eskimo, Isekiri, and Maori differentiate generic from nongeneric habitual events. In the only example that I

7.261. *Habitual versus Progressive and Iterative*

Though the habitual extends events, much like the progressive and iterative, we must be careful to distinguish the habitual from these two aspects. The progressive extends action *within* a temporal interval. We can see the distinction between progressive and habitual precisely by examining an expression that encodes them both:

42. Maria used to be buying a new coat every winter.

The progressive, *be buying,* signals extension of the event inside an interval in the past. But this extension is different from what the habitual does in conveying that the event persists *over* the time period that contains the on-line progressivized action. So (42) may be more precisely glossed 'persistently over numerous winters in the past, Maria engaged in the on-going activity of buying a coat.'

The habitual is also distinct from iterative aspect. Habituality is not a function of the simple repetition of an event, no matter how frequent or whatever the rate of the iterative. Compare the following:

43a. Fred was bumping his head a thousand times.
 b. Fred used to bump his head.

Sentence (43a) progressivizes a punctual event and thereby makes it iterative. But in spite of the great magnitude of the repetition (*a thousand times*), the iterative still does not produce a habitual interpretation. This is because the iterative is the result of the progressive, which restricts the repeated event to *inside the frame of the interval.* Sentence (43b), however, does have the habitual interpretation, with no indication of the exact amount of iteration, because *used to* encodes the critical feature of extension *over* or *outside* the interval.

The progressive and the iterative are conceptually independent of the habitual. Though languages sometimes allow the iterative and progressive to convey habitual meanings—because meanings and structures often do double duty—the three aspects have quite different domains and operate differently on events.

7.262. *The Habitual in Zapotec and Northern Paiute*

Many languages have a specific form to signal the habitual aspect. Zapotec, for instance, draws a clear formal distinction between progressivized and habitual events (Bybee 1985: 142):

---

have been able to verify, Eskimo, Fortescue's (1984) grammar does not differentiate habitual from generic habitual, letting the marker that Dahl cites, *sar/tar* (phonetically related), stand for both kinds of habitual aspect. Nonetheless, it is worth noting that claims are made for some languages differentiating the two types of habitual aspect by productive surface form.

44a. ku- ka?a- beé.
    Prog write 3Sing/human
    He is writing.

  b. ru- ka?a- beé.
    Habit write 3Sing/Hum
    He usually writes.

Presumably (44a) locates the event in the on-going present and associates it with a particular moment. Example (44b), on the other hand, removes the event from any particular temporal moment and represents it as a generic, customary habit.

Northern Paiute has a similar structure. We already know that the language overtly differentiates the progressive from other aspects, but it also has separate forms for the habitual: one for perfective habitual events, *yai,* and one for imperfective habitual events, *yakwi.* Snapp and Anderson (1982: 75–6) cite examples of each:

45a. nɨ nano'ooɨ tɨnawakɨno ɨ   punni-yai-   dua.
    I every   Monday   you see   Hab/Perf Unrealized
    I will see you every Monday.

  b. sɨsɨmɨna   nɨ cikana   noho awamua tɨka-yakwi.
    sometimes I   chicken egg morning eat Hab/Imperf
    Sometimes I eat eggs in the morning.

Example (45a) encodes habitual bounded events, with futurity marked by a morpheme for 'unrealized action.' It is therefore more precisely 'I will have seen you every Monday,' where the perfectivity of the future event is clearer. Example (45b), however, takes a different habitual, one for imperfective events, so this extension must refer more to the internal properties of the event. Though it is hard to get a more precise gloss in English, perhaps something like 'sometimes I am eating eggs in the morning' is a bit closer.

7.263.   The Habitual, Other Aspects, Tense, and Modality

Throughout this chapter, we have observed that many aspects frequently overlap with each other and additional semantic categories, like tense/time. The same holds for habitual aspect. Quite often the meaning of habitual aspect is taken up by the imperfective. This happens in Spanish, as the possible interpretations of (46) show:

46. Jug- aba   al   béisbol.
    play 1Per/Imperf/Past to the baseball
    I played/was playing/used to play baseball.

The verb is marked in the past imperfective, *-aba* suffix, but this is compatible with a number of meanings: simple past durative ('I played'), past progressive ('I was playing'), and past habitual ('I used to play').

The convergence of the habitual and imperfective, as in Spanish, is possible because the imperfective signals incomplete action. Insofar as lack of completion conceptually correlates with extension of action, the habitual is a likely function to be taken up by the imperfect. Indeed, Bybee (1985) remarks that in languages that have both an imperfective and habitual, the habitual follows the imperfective historically, as a specific meaning that develops after the more general imperfective meaning.

Pawnee illustrates this historical connection. Here, the habitual is a subclass of the imperfective (Bybee 1985: 144, though Parks 1976: 201 slightly diverges from this generalization if the usitative is also counted as habitual): It must also be affixed to an imperfective, and must be ordered further away from the root than the imperfective (this latter fact is important to Bybee, who follows the iconist belief that forms nearer the root are historically earlier: see also Baker 1988). We can see how Pawnee works in the following (Parks 1976: 199):

47. herikspawaki- us-   u:ku.
    they say   Imperf Hab
    They used to say.

In (47), the imperfective affix, *us,* attaches to the verb root for 'say,' and the habitual marker, *u:ku,* follows the imperfect. Hence (47) is more properly glossed as 'they used to be saying.'

In some languages, tense and the habitual have certain close connections. By far the most common tense in which the habitual occurs is the past, and some languages, like English, overtly distinguish the habitual only in the past: ?? *He uses to go to the movies* and ?? *He will used to go to the movies.* This convergence of the habitual and the past is related to the fact that the habitual frequently conveys that action *no longer holds* (see Comrie 1976b). Not only does *Bob used to go to the movies* represent a state of affairs extended over a period of time, but it also implies that the action is no longer in effect: If he used to go, then it is also very likely that he does not go now. Though Comrie argues that the *lack of current effect* of events in the habitual is an implicature and not an entailment of the habitual, this meaning is compatible with the tendency for the habitual to occur in the past, where events, as removed and complete, also no longer hold.

In tenses other than the past, the habitual is often formally indiscernible. In the present, the habitual typically is signalled by the narrative present—*He goes to the movies.* Zapotec and Nahuatl, however, do distinguish the habitual formally in the present (Bybee 1985). In the future tense, matters are less clear, and Dahl (1985) notes only one language, Isekiri, that differentiates the future habitual (though this paucity may be the result of lack of a widespread sample rather than a semantic or conceptual motivation). In any case, the more prevalent tendency of the habitual to be formally differentiated in the past is worth noting, and may indeed be the result of the connection of the habitual with events that no longer hold, even though they are asserted to have persisted over a period of time.

Finally, the burden of expressing the habitual is sometimes taken up by modality, forms that mark a speaker's knowledge or belief: *would, can, must, should,* and so on (see chap. 9). According to Brinton (1988), in Old and Middle English, habitual aspect was regularly signalled by the modals *sceal* 'shall,' *sceolde* 'should,' and *wolde* 'would.' Over time this association diminished as the specific marking of habituality was taken over by the periphrastic forms *be accustomed/used to.* We can still see this connection of modality to habituality in some current expressions:

48. He would go to the movies.

Sentence (48) is technically in the *conditional,* as encoded by the modal *would,* related to the Middle English form *wolde,* already cited. But (48) has a decidedly habitual interpretation, which must be the result of the modal itself.

The convergence of modality and habituality is understandable. As Brinton (1988: 140–1) notes, habituality extends an event from without and distributes it over an entire time period. This carries the force of a *prediction:* for example, the extension of an event over the past into the present suggests that the event can be predicted at any time in the past. As such, habituality has the effect of a belief. If I say (48), the hearer can expect that the asserted actions would have occurred at some then-future times. The semantic function of belief and prediction is normally within the purview of modality, so it is no wonder that the modals should take up the slack of encoding habitual aspect: Their semantic functions overlap with those of the habitual.

7.27. Summary

We have looked at six major classes of aspect in some detail: perfective/imperfective, or the bounded/unbounded distinction applied to events; telic/atelic, or the goal-directedness of an event; punctual/durative, or the inherent extension of an event; iterative/semelfactive, or the singularity and plurality of an event; progressive, or the extension of an event from within; habitual, or the extension of an event from without. For each aspect, we have seen how the criterial definition interacts with grammar: for example, how perfective aspect correlates with certain tenses because of boundedness, how telic aspect relates to perfect tenses and passive voice because of their connection to endpoints and resolution, and how punctual aspect evokes momentaneous adverbials and durative evokes volumes of time. We have also seen how many languages press aspects into the service of related denotations: the progressive, the iterative, and the habitual converge in many languages because of the meaning of 'extension' necessary for all three.

7.3. FIVE MINOR ASPECTS

The six aspects we have thus far studied in no way exhaust the kinds of aspect found in the world's languages, though they do represent the principal distinctions that any student of semantics will find. To imagine other kinds of aspect, all we have to do is to pose our original definition of aspect in question form: in what ways (other than by bounding, extension, and so on) can the internal contour of an event be modified? We close this section with a brief consideration of five minor aspects: inceptive, terminative, prospective, retrospective, and intensive.

7.31. Inceptive

Many languages have ways of encoding just the initial point of an event, the point at which an event begins to obtain. This is *inceptive aspect,* also known as *incipient aspect,* or *ingressive aspect* (though the last term is frequently restricted to stative events, 'entry into a state'). Eskimo, for instance, has a verbal affix, *lir,* which denotes the initial point of an event (Fortescue 1984: 282):

49. uqaluqatigii- lir-   put.
    talk together Incip 3Pl/Indic
    They began to talk together.

7.32. Terminative

Just as the initial point of an event can be selected, so can the endpoint, or the point at which an event ceases to obtain. This is known as *terminative aspect* or, especially with regard to stative events, *egressive aspect.*

According to Fortescue (1984), Eskimo has two terminative aspects, one for a habitual event, *ssaar,* and one for a nonhabitual event, *junnaar.* The latter is illustrated here:

50. uqaluqatigii- junnaar-put.
    talk together Termin 3Pl/Indic
    They stopped talking to each other.

7.33.   Prospective

Languages encode not only the beginning and end of an event, but also a point *just prior to* the beginning of an event. This is known as *prospective aspect,* though it is sometimes called the *intentive* because it indicates that an event is expected. The prospective denotes that an event is about to take place or is on the verge of obtaining.

Nkore-Kiga has a bound form, *ka* (which Taylor 1985 calls the *impending aspect*), that signals the prospective status of events:

51. ti- ba- ka-   riire.
    Neg they Prosp eat/Perf
    They are about to eat.

Two additional facts underscore the prospective meaning of this form. First, *ka* requires that the verb be negative (*ti*), making another gloss of (51) 'they haven't eaten yet.' The function of the negative is to signal that the event itself is still prospective or has *not yet* come to pass. Second, the prospective aspect is associated with perfective events (*riire*), those *about to be bounded.* So the prospective signals that some "event bounding" is about to obtain, and a more precise gloss of (51) is probably something like 'they are about to have eaten.'

7.34.   Retrospective

Just as inceptive aspect has a complement in terminative aspect, so prospective aspect has its analogue in *retrospective aspect:* the encoding of a point *immediately subsequent to* the endpoint of an event.

Some languages have productive retrospective aspect, but, compared to the prospective, they are much more difficult to locate. England's (1983: 162) discussion of Mam indicates that the language has such a form, though it may be indistinguishable from a tense that expresses recent past:

52. ma   chin   jaw tz'aq- a.
    Retro 1Sing Dir slip   1Sing
    I slipped just now.

England claims that *ma* signals an aspect of recency or the immediate retrospective view of an event.

Perhaps the relative absence of the retrospective occurs because it can be accommodated by other notions more readily than its counterpart, the prospective. Viewing an event from the standpoint of its completion can perhaps be accommodated by the perfective and punctual aspects, as well as past tense. In any event, the asymmetry of the distribution of prospective and retrospective is conspicuous.

7.35. Intensive

The final aspectual category we consider is the *intensive,* which indicates that an event is magnified or performed with a degree of intensity or rate that is greater than normal.

Manam has one intensifier for nouns and one for verbs. The latter, *tina,* denotes an increase in the magnitude of the event (Lichtenberk 1983):

53. tamóata i-   panana-tína.
    man   3Sing run   Intense
    The man really ran. (= 'sprint')

Nahuatl, like many languages, employs reduplication to signal the intensive aspect. The verb root *toca* means 'follow,' but when its initial syllable is reduplicated, *totoca,* it means 'pursue,' understandably related to 'intense following.' Similarly the root *itta* means 'see,' but in reduplicated form, *iita,* it means 'stare,' as staring is equivalent to intense seeing.

7.36. Summary

We have briefly considered five minor aspects: inceptive (beginning point), terminative (endpoint), prospective (approaching the beginning point), retrospective (reviewing the endpoint), and intensive (magnification). These aspects spell out the full phase of an event: its beginning, growth, and end. Many languages encode these aspects rather specifically, by particular bound morphemes.

7.4. UNIFIED TREATMENTS OF ASPECT

In sections 7.2 and 7.3, we surveyed the principal aspects, their meanings, and some of the ways they are encoded in the world's languages. We now attend to theory. Our goal here is to unify the numerous generalizations made with regard to aspect and to put our descriptive material in a more streamlined framework, hopefully one that affords us a certain degree of predictability, as all explanations require.

We concentrate on two theoretical tacks. First we provide a manageable and workable typology for aspect based on semantic notions. Though we consider several kinds of typologies of aspect, particularly aspect hierarchies and matrices, we settle on a "looser model" that types aspects as open, closed, and phase, and orders more specific aspects hierarchically under these categories.

Second, we try to account for aspectual notions in terms of conceptual structure so that diverse semantic phenomena can be given a unified conceptual treatment. This goes some way toward justifying the claim that mental models ground semantic systems, or at least that our internal models of the world deliver the components that allow us to fix the referents for our expressions.

7.41. Typologies of Aspect

The literature is replete with studies proposing unified accounts of aspect and related notions. The work as a whole is so voluminous that it is impossible for anyone to summarize it thoroughly, much less assimilate it without duplicating others' already published efforts (though Brinton 1988 makes an admirable try). Frequently it appears that many linguists reinvent each other, sometimes consciously, and not very charitably at that.

In this section, we look at an aspect typology based on three categories: open aspects (unbounded), closed aspects (bounded), and phase aspects (internal structure). Within each of these categories, aspects are organized hierarchically to reflect logical and distributional dependencies.

7.411. Why No Aspect Typology Is Perfect

Before we begin, we must concede that no aspect typology is watertight. One reason for this is an undue emphasis on either binarism (on/off values of features) or strict hierarchical organization of abstract properties (i.e., attempts to pigeonhole aspects into discrete categories and dependencies) in accounting for aspectual distinctions (see Brinton 1988: 55). We ultimately settle on a mixture of characteristics of the hierarchy and matrix because this affords us coverage without sacrificing predictability.

In addition, aspects, although intimately associated with events and their attendant verbs, are not necessarily a singular function thereof (Brinton 1988; Verkuyl 1972, 1989). Quite often, an *entire expression* assumes an aspectual interpretation because of factors not inherent in the verb/event itself, as in the conversion of an atelic event into a telic one by the simple addition of an appropriate patient or goal: *Bob ran* (atelic) → *Bob ran to the store* (telic). Likewise, we can make a nonhabitual event into a habitual one by expressing the agent and patient in generic form and exploiting their compatibility with the habitual as a "generic aspect": *A squirrel hid a nut* (nonhabitual, nongeneric) → *The squirrel hides nuts* (habitual, generic). Observations like these motivate Verkuyl's (1972) view of aspect, what he calls the *compositional approach,* whereby aspectual interpretations for expressions are derived from a constellation of factors in an expression—not just the event properties—including semantic features of entities (nouns) and durative/nondurative modifiers (adverbs, e.g.) (see also Mourelatos 1981; Verkuyl 1989).

The compositional character of aspect, however, does not vitiate our basic approach to aspect as a property of events, even if it does clarify it. Even if the aspects are, in some cases, constructed from the compositional semantics of an entire expression, the definitions and diagnostics we have provided nonetheless hold. For example, even if telics can be constructed from the interaction of an event and its patient or goal, telic events are still uninterruptible. In any case, a compositional approach to aspect must still be reconciled with the fact that the aspects in sections 7.2 and 7.3 can be found simply as properties of events and events must in many cases be compatible with the elements forming the constructed meaning. An expression with a stative event cannot be assigned a durative interpretation—a compositional durative aspect—just because one of its components is durative: ?? *The book was expensive all afternoon.* So, *the properties of the event do matter,* even in cases where aspect is compositional.

With this caveat in mind, we now discuss several proposals to unify aspect: the hierarchy, the matrix, and ultimately some combination of the two.

7.412. The Logical and Distributional Facts: Hierarchies and Matrices

All accounts of aspect must explain two logical and empirical facts. First, the perfective/imperfective distinction is the principal aspectual opposition, both empirically and logically. It is the most widespread aspectual opposition in languages, as both Bybee (1985) and Dahl (1985) observe. Bybee (1985) further argues that of all aspects, the perfective/imperfective split is more central in terms of meaning-form correspondences because it is likely to surface in derivational changes of verbs and as modifications of the root and stem—that is, processes that make *new lexical items.* Thus, the perfective/imperfective split is arguably the most unmarked on both distributional and morphological grounds.

Moreover, the imperfective logically contains the habitual, durative, progressive and all aspects that *protract events.* As we have already noted (pp. 319), Bybee (1985) argues that the imperfective is historically earlier and more general semantically than the habitual and continuous. In some languages (like Nahuatl) habituals and duratives form a semantic and morphological subset of the imperfect. So there is a logical hierarchy of durative events.

Second, the other aspects have distributional regularities. The second most frequent opposition in language, after the perfective/imperfective, is one between habitual and continuous (Bybee 1985). Inceptive aspect is very frequently found in languages, by Bybee's (1985) account (if I understand it), the most frequent after the habitual/continuous split. Iterative aspect is farther down the list in distributional frequency. Thus, any unified model of aspect must accord with the distributional facts from the highest to lowest levels.

To account for these regularities, Comrie (1976b) proposes the following aspect hierarchy, founded on the perfective/imperfective opposition and branching into subclasses of the imperfective:

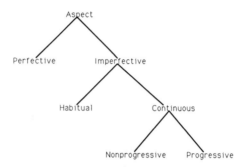

FIG. 7.1.   Comrie's aspect hierarchy.

Although the hierarchical model neatly sets out the categories, and accords with many of the basic typological and distributional predictions for aspect, the model creates a number of problems. Some aspects cannot be derived from the fundamental perfective/imperfective split, no matter how unmarked or logically central the distinction. On the contrary, some aspects, like the inceptive, telic, and progressive, must apply to *both* categories, which appears to call into question the original motivation for having a branching model. In Comrie's defense, we should note that the hierarchy can be read criterially rather than strictly, and it does accommodate the facts at a gross level. Perfective/imperfective is more frequent than habitual/continuous, which itself is more frequent than progressive, and so there is an implicational scale for aspectual distribution: Perfective/Imperfective > Habitual/Continuous > Progressive. Perhaps we should let these facts stand as they are without forcing dependencies in a hierarchy.

Another frequently proposed model of aspect is a matrix, a table of abstract semantic features with binary values that, in combination, generate all aspects. An adequate matrix model naturally hinges on the set of abstract semantic atoms from which the aspects themselves are constructed. For example, Friedrich (1974), in one of the first comprehensive studies of aspect, derives the major aspectual distinctions from a combination of three abstract features: *durative/nondurative, completive/noncompletive,* and *stative/nonstative.* His proposal is meant to capture the regularity that languages encode the opposition of *point versus extension, termination versus continuation,* and *act versus state.* A finite set of abstract components in combination can in principle generate all the aspectual distinctions required by languages.

Similar matrix models have been proposed to account for Vendler's typology.

Dowty (1979), for example, tries to reduce Vendler's categories to binary values for the abstract features [change], [definiteness], [momentariness], [agency], and [complexity] (see 1979: 184). Carlson (1981) likewise offers a matrix account of Vendler's typology, proposing to generate all event types from a combination of binary values for three features: [point], [extended], and [continuous].

Like hierarchies, matrices fail to meet the needs of an adequate aspect typology. The lure of binarism and efficient generation prevent matrices from accommodating the wide range of aspectual types that we actually find in languages, like intensive, telic, and iterative. Brinton (1988: 57) proposes that additional abstract features be added to matrices to generate more particular aspectual forms, for example [telic] for resultatives and [multiplicity] for iteratives and seriated events. But where do the features stop? If they are invented just to generate specific aspect types, why not leave the aspects as they are? Aren't we reinventing the wheel here?

Furthermore, a matrix cannot account for the fact that languages *prefer* the perfective/imperfective distinction, and thereafter the habitual/continuous. Thus, Brinton (1988) objects to matrices in principle because they fail to cover hierarchical relations *across the features that comprise the matrix.* (After all, this is what makes a matrix a matrix: an array, rather than a dependency.) The lack of hierarchical relation internal to the features of aspectual matrices means that observed overlaps and convergences of aspects cannot be generated, but must be stipulated.

Due to the need to accommodate the logical and distributional facts, and the inadequacy of both the hierarchy and matrix, we turn to a model that combines the favorable aspects of the matrix and hierarchy, while avoiding their pitfalls.

7.413.   *Open, Closed, and Phase*

The typology of aspect that we examine assigns all aspects to three major categories: *open, closed,* and *phase.* Within each of these, subcategories are ordered relative to each other, according to distributional criteria:

Open: A > B > C > . . .
Closed: A > B > C > . . .
Phase: A > B > C > . . .

FIG. 7.2.   Schematic of aspect typology.

Two notable examples of such a model are Brinton's (1988: 53) and Chung and Timberlake's (1985). Brinton (1988: 57) puts the matter concisely when she says that any model of aspect must be both compositional, in that it has to accommodate the generation of aspectual categories from abstract notional categories, like a matrix, but it also has to account for "secondary systems of aspectual marking" (p. 57), like a hierarchy.

This model is driven by the basic insight that there are three principal kinds of aspect: one that *opens* events, one that *closes* events, and one that refers to their internal structure, or *phase.*[7]

Open aspects are the *imperfective, durative, progressive, habitual,* and *iterative.* They all express the *extension of an event over a time frame.* Consider how the progressive functions to protract the event beyond the simple moment of its occurrence: The event in *I am spitting* is extended with regard to the present moment, even though *spit* denotes a punctual event. The progressive thus has an *open function.* (I leave the rest of the open aspects to the reader's imagination for testing.)

In contrast, *closed aspects* are the *perfective, punctual, telic,* and *semelfactive.* These all express the *restriction of an event to a time frame,* even down to a moment. For instance, the perfective forces us to view the event as contained and hence "from without," as we have noted, because the perfective completes and bounds the event. Its natural restriction to nonpresent times is thus a function of its requirement to be *framed by a time interval.* The fleeting present is open by definition, so an aspect with a closed function, like the perfective, is unlikely in the present tense. (Again, the reader can test the others for their closure properties.)

The *open* and *closed* aspects are complemented by *phase.* As Brinton (1988) and Talmy (1985) note, events may also be characterized in the distribution over time with regard to *how they change status inside or outside the time frame,* by their *beginnings, middles,* and *ends. Phase aspects* are the following: *inceptive, terminative, prospective, retrospective,* and *intensive.* For example, intensive aspect functions to modify the magnitude of the event, much like changes in amplitude affect the phase of a sound wave. Incipient aspect denotes the start of the phase, prospective denotes a point just prior to the start of the phase, and so on.

These three basic aspectual categories form the backbone of this combinational model. They are notional categories, as required by the matrix model. But given the distributional and logical facts, we can then order their subcategories by dependencies, introducing the benefits of the hierarchical model and meet the requirements of any aspect typology.

7.4131.   Hierarchies within Open, Closed, and Phase

If we look at the logical and distributional findings of Dahl (1985), Bybee (1985), and Comrie (1976b), we can order the subcategories of open, closed, and phase aspects as follows in the hierarchy/matrix model of aspects:

OPEN: imperfective $>$ durative/habitual $>$ progressive $>$ iterative

CLOSED: perfective $>$ punctual/telic $>$ semelfactive

PHASE: intensive/inceptive $>$ prospective $>$ terminative/retrospective

---

[7]Brinton (1988) uses the more traditional terminology by calling the first two possibilities *perfec-*

More detailed distributional studies will no doubt require modification of these dependencies, but let us take them as they stand and provide a short commentary.

The imperfective is the most widely found open aspect; it is also logically primary. As Bybee notes, the second most frequent distinction is that between habitual and durative, and hence they are assigned equal status on the implicational scale. These are followed by the progressive, which on both Bybee's and Comrie's accounts is less frequent. Finally, the iterative is assigned the last position by default.

For the closed aspects, the perfective is acknowledged as the most frequent, and the semelfactive the least, so these form the bounds of the scale. In between, we have put the punctual and telic because they are, by my intuition, more frequent than the semelfactive, but because there is no data to differentiate the two by frequency, they have equal position.

In phase aspects, we assign the incipient aspect first position because of Bybee's findings; the intensive has equal status on the scale from the intuition that many languages have such an aspect. Both the terminative and retrospective aspect are infrequently noted in distributional studies, unlike the prospective, which is occasionally identified. Thus, the prospective is ordered before the terminative and retrospective, which are listed together.

This account allows us to combine both the matrix and hierarchical models. We begin with the major notional categories, and then order the aspects relative to each other on the basis of distributional evidence. This lets us accommodate the basic distributional findings and predictions: for example, that languages prefer perfective/imperfective distinctions overall. It also allows us to apply aspects across categories: There is no reason why phase and open aspects should not interact, for example.

We can also account for aspectual convergences both conceptually and distributionally. In most languages, aspects do double duty, as for example, in Spanish, where imperfective forms cover all the open functions. In many languages, the intensive and the iterative overlap. Does this mean that there is a connection between the phase and the open function? We might in fact argue that phase aspects are really something like *semiopen* or *semiclosed* events, much like geometric rays, closed on one end and open on the other. If this is the case, the intensive may be a kind of swing category in a helical organization of aspect, between open and closed, much the way definiteness, specificity, and genericity are related for entities (see chap. 3). In short, a model in this form satisfies both the logical and distributional requirements for a typology of aspect.

---

tive and *imperfective,* respectively. Chung and Timberlake (1985) relate aspect more directly to its definition as the pattern of the distribution of an event with respect to time. They see open aspect as the event *contained within the time frame* of the interval of the event itself and closed aspect as *the time frame included* in the event.

7.4132. Open and Closed Languages

This model introduces a number of other predictions that may serve useful explanatory purposes. Chung and Timberlake (1985) observe that, given their simpler model of only a binary opposition between open- and closed-frame aspects, the distinction between inside the frame and outside the frame predicts that there are two kinds of languages with regard to the encoding of aspect. A language "will choose to define one of these possibilities in relatively narrow terms, in the sense that it will impose additional semantic restrictions; the opposite possibility will be defined in broad terms" (p. 239). That is, a given language will choose to differentiate, and thus more narrowly restrict semantically, one of the two basic classes. The other will be left more relatively unencumbered and have broader applicability.

Chung and Timberlake argue that Russian defines the perfective (closed) narrowly and the imperfective (open) broadly: The former has more tense restrictions and is usually telic; the latter, in contrast, may apply without restrictions on tense and other event types. Therefore, they say that Russian is a *closure language:* that is, it *narrows the closed aspect.*

English is the opposite. The productive open aspect in English, the progressive, has a number of restrictions, including requirements that the event be a process, that it be nonstative, and so on. In contrast, nonaspectualized forms have fewer semantic restrictions: They may be either telic or atelic, for example. With greater restrictions on the open aspect, English is, according to Chung and Timberlake's terminology, a *dynamic language,* or, in our terms, an *open language* because it *narrows the open aspect.*

How the rest of the world's languages fare on this choice of restricting aspect is unknown. But the principle leads to a number of important questions that deserve the attention of those working in semantic theory. Are there more open languages than closed languages? More specifically, are there universally more distinctions in closed aspects than open aspects? What are the other semantic characteristics of open or closed languages? Are there languages that have no phase categories? How do phase aspects interact with open and closed aspects? Can languages be typed according to the kinds of phasal distinctions they allow?

These are the sorts of questions that a semantic typology of aspect raises, provided that the proper framework is first established. In my view, the best such framework is one that has the advantage of both the matrix and hierarchy, makes new predictions, and raises new theoretical questions as well.

7.414. Summary

We have considered the logical and distributional requirements of any typology of aspect: the perfective/imperfective split is central and other aspects have logical and distributional regularities in relation thereto. We have looked at an aspect hierarchy and an aspect matrix, and their problems, most notably their inability to account for all the aspectual distinctions covered in sections 7.2 and 7.3. A typology that relies on the categories of open, closed, and phase subsumes more particular, hierarchically organized aspects, like perfective, progressive, and incipient. This typology that combines both hierarchy and matrix has the benefits of these two, avoids their pitfalls, and makes some interesting predictions with regard to the preference languages have for open or closed forms.

7.42. The Conceptual Structure of Aspect

We have just seen how purely semantic approaches to aspect result in fairly succinct and efficient typologies of languages by their aspectual properties. These accounts seek to couch aspectual systems in terms of basic *semantic* categories, like perfective and progressive, but we should recall one of the lessons of linguistic semantics: Semantic distinctions ultimately have their explanation in conceptual structure.

If we look closely, we see that many of the same notions that we have used elsewhere to carry out semantic description and explanation can be applied to the distinctions required for aspect. Importantly, these same notions have in most cases already been given conceptual and perceptual grounding. The upshot is that we can perform a sort of conceptual reduction of the semantic categories required for aspect, and this allows us to integrate aspectual system into our more general project of a semantics based on the mentally projected world of speakers.

7.421. Unitization

The prime aspectual distinction in language is between perfective and imperfective aspect, or generic closed and open events. As we have already noted (pp. 297–301), this distinction has a direct correlate in the bounded/unbounded distinction for entities. Seen this way, the major aspectual opposition in language is the same as the major distinction among entities: *unitized* versus *nonunitized* entities. Our perceptual and cognitive systems make a fundamental distinction between discrete and continuous phenomena, forcing events and entities to deploy the same mechanisms to carve up the world.

This convergence does not mean that semantic systems are the same things as conceptual systems. Certainly events in the perfective aspect are different from count nouns even though they each derive from the same perceptual process of unitizing phenomena. But all along we have maintained that the semantic system is a *function of the conceptual system,* and the mentally projected world uses the bounded/unbounded distinction broadly.

7.422. Extendedness

A similar account can be given for the punctual/durative distinction, which is obviously related to extendedness, the basic conceptual category for entities. Just as entities may or may not have extension in space (extended or nonextended), so may events have (or have not) temporal extension by virtue of the nature of their internal contour. Durative events are extended; punctual events are nonextended.

Both progressive and habitual aspect involve extendedness: The former extends from within the event, the latter from without. We can explain this difference in the location of extendedness by applying two other notions from spatial systems. Progressive aspect is a function of the combined operation of extendedness and *interioricity;* habitual aspect derives from extendedness and *exterioricity.*

The mentally projected world motivates the semantic system by providing a unitary process that differentially translates into the denotations of linguistic expressions. Conceptual structure categorizes phenomena by their capacity to occupy a position (extendedness); the mental world then further differentiates by interior and exterior. When these conceptual mechanisms are applied to spatially stable phenomena, entities, we get the distinction between salient and nonsalient objects with insides and outsides. When the same conceptual mechanisms apply to temporal phenomena, we get certain aspects. Punctual and durative categories emerge, and may do so with respect to the insides (progressive) and outsides (habitual) of events.

Again, this is not to say that semantic structures can be exhaustively read off conceptual structure. It takes some doing and a lot of extra information to derive progressive aspect from interior extension, much less determine the hows and whys of its overt form. But such an account is less the point than the observation that interior extension itself motivates the semantic structure of entities as well as of events. This connection allows us a unified picture of semantic structure as a function of the mechanisms that construct the projected world to which we apply our expressions.

7.423. Remoteness and Proximal Space

Unitization and extendedness capture a number of the major aspects discussed in section 7.2. Two of the minor aspects discussed in section 7.3 are accountable to remoteness and proximal space, considered in our discussion of deixis (chap. 6). Prospective aspect encodes a position just prior to the initial point of an event, the *proximal positive boundary condition* for an event (or more ordinarily, *near the beginning*). Retrospective aspect is the *proximal negative boundary condition* because it denotes a position just after the termination of an event (*near the end*).

We have already seen the utility of the category of proximal in a number of other areas, such as deixis. Its applicability here suggests that it is connected to a more general conceptual category. The mechanism that constructs our mental world of reference deploys proximality, and when this notion is joined with such things as starting points and endpoints and applied to events, we get prospective and retrospective aspect. This is not to say that the notions of proximal, beginning, and end thoroughly define these aspects. On the contrary, they are just a part, but a fundamental part, and one that surfaces elsewhere in the conceptual and semantic system.

7.424.   *Other Conceptual Unities and a Tabulation*

With a little thought, we can observe further conceptual reductions of the aspects. Intensive aspect may be a product of the same mechanisms that produce the semantic property of *size*. Iterative and semelfactive aspect are ways of *enumerating* events: just as entities can be assigned singularity or plurality, so too can events be qualified. Telics have inherent goals, and as we already know, goals are crucial to other parts of the semantic system, in thematic roles, for example. When applied to events, goals generate necessary outcomes or limits.

A useful way to summarize our observations on the conceptual structure of aspect is in tabular form. Table 7.1 lists the aspects and their putative conceptual categories:

TABLE 7.1
Summary of Conceptual Structure of Certain Aspects

Aspect	Conceptual Category
perfective/imperfective	unitization
punctual/durative	extendedness
progressive	extended + interior
habitual	extended + exterior
resultative	goal
iterative/semelfactive	quantity and number
intensive	size
prospective	proximal space and initial point
retrospective	proximal space and endpoint

An examination of Table 7.1 reveals the predominance of spatial notions motivating aspectual distinctions. We can appreciate the priority of space if we also understand that our mentally projected world of reference is initially constructed from the notions delivered by our perceptual mechanisms (see chap. 5, on localism; Miller and Johnson-Laird, 1976: chaps. 1–2). These mechanisms are more directly connected to the physical world, so there ought to be noticeable commonalities between the output they deliver and the properties of the objects they operate on. That is not to say that perception merely reads properties off the physical world in some sort of blind tabulation. Certainly, the perceptual mechanisms impose their internal structure on the objects that impinge on them. The world is as fine-tuned to the mechanisms of perception as the mechanisms of perception are fine-tuned to the world. However, it is interesting to note that the concepts that emerge from this accommodation can be found throughout the mental models that anchor our linguistic expressions.

7.425. Summary

We have discussed the conceptual unities of aspect, noting particularly how unitization, extendedness, remoteness/proximal space, size, goals, and quantity motivate certain aspects as well as entities and space in general. These convergences suggest that the perceptual and cognitive mechanisms that construct our mental models are also implicated in our semantic models.

SUMMARY OF CHAPTER

In this chapter, we defined aspect as the way an event is distributed over time. We looked at six major classes of aspect: perfective/imperfective, telic/atelic, punctual/durative, iterative/semelfactive, progressive, and habitual. We saw the structural correlates of each aspect and the way that some aspects cover related denotations, as in the convergence of the progressive, the iterative, and the habitual.

We then briefly considered five minor aspects: inceptive, terminative, prospective, retrospective, and intensive. These aspects cover the beginning, development, and end of an event.

Following this description of aspects, we looked at the requirements of all aspect typologies: the logical and distributional predominance of the perfective/imperfective opposition and the distributional regularities of other aspects. We considered the aspect hierarchy, matrix, and a combination of the two, the last built on the categories of open, closed, and phase, with hierarchies of aspects therein. This typology makes predictions with regard to open and closed languages.

We completed our theoretical discussion with the conceptual unities of aspect. Unitization, extendedness, remoteness/proximal space, size, goals, and quantity underlie certain aspects. These convergences suggested that our mental models are involved in our semantic systems.

QUESTIONS FOR DISCUSSION

1. In section 7.21, we saw how adverbs of manner in Russian are more compatible with imperfective events than perfective ones (see example (8)). This is due to the fact that adverbs of manner refer to the internal structure of an event

and imperfectives have internal focus by definition. Consider the following, however:

i. On na- pis- al   pismo bystro.
   he Perf write Past letter   quickly
   He wrote the letter quickly. (perfective)

Example (i) is acceptable in Russian, unlike its counterpart in (8b), which has an adverb of manner with the opposite meaning. Using what you know about perfective and imperfective aspect, explains this difference. Does 'quickly' refer less to the internal structure of the event than 'slowly' (thus letting the perfective appear here)? Example (i) may be more accurately glossed 'he wrote out the letter quickly.' How does this gloss affect your answer?

2. In section 7.223 (example (20)), we discussed how Nivkh encodes telic aspect directly with the verbal infix ɟəta. Consider the following Nivkh sentence:

i. k'e teqa- ɟəta-d'.
   net strong Telic
   The net remains strong.

Without the telic marker, ɟəta this expression means 'the net is strong.' Why does the telic marker induce the meaning of 'continuation' here? In your answer, consider the meaning of teqa 'strong.' Is this stative or active? Can 'strong' be seen as an "already attained state," and does this affect the telic interpretation of (i)?

3. Compare the imperfective and progressive versions of the same proposition in Godie (Marchese 1986):

i. ɔ 6lɨ   sʉkʌ́.
   she pound/Imperf rice
   She is pounding rice. (imperfective)
ii. ɔ kʊ   sʉkʌ́ 6lɨ   dʌ.
   she Progr rice   pound place
   She is pounding rice. (progressive)

What differences are there in Godie between the imperfective and progressive? What does the form dʌ 'place' in the progressive say about the relation between the progressive in Godie and the universal structure of this aspect (hint: consider English *is a-doing*)? Grammars of Godie note that kʊ is sometimes glossed 'be at.' How does this affect your answer? Give more accurate English glosses of (i) and (ii).

8 Tense and Time

8.1. INTRODUCTION

In this chapter, we inquire into how language structures and encodes time. The analysis of linguistic time has an involved history, with logical and structural/typological camps (Comrie 1985; Dahl 1985; Prior 1967; Reichenbach 1947; Rescher and Urquhart 1971). In our own foray into the matter, we try to extract the accepted findings from both practices in an attempt to present the necessary elements of any linguistic system of time.

We restrict our study of time to the mechanism that assigns time to events: *tense*. This focus on tense affords us a number of advantages. Most immediately, it allows us to contrast the internal temporal contour of events with their nontemporal internal contour, aspect, discussed at length in the previous chapter.

If aspect is the way that an event patterns within or over a time frame, tense is the way an event is *explicitly indexed for a time frame,* the grammatical and morphological means that a language uses to locate an event in time. Aspect encodes the nondeictic contour of events; tense signals the deictic contour insofar as such concepts as 'location in time' and 'relative order' are deictic because they require reference points for their determination. We thus get considerable use out of our previous discussion of deixis now that we are required to apply it to the structure of events and their temporal location.

Our investigation proceeds as follows. First, we spell out the basics of time and its encoding in any language. Here, we discuss the canonical model of time that underlies linguistic expressions and the elemental deictic requirements of any tense system. Thereafter, we see how the deictic structure of tense translates into linguistic form. The deictic reference point and located point relate to how languages assign absolute and relative values. Remoteness between the reference point and the located point determine the ways that languages choose to measure temporal distance, either through simple extension, as a vectorial system, or through intervals, as a metrical system.

Once we have an idea of the kinds of tense and time systems allowed by language, we turn to more theoretical matters for unified treatments of tense. We briefly discuss the conceptual structure of tense and its relation to space and aspect and look at the gist of the extensive work on tense logic to see how the formal study of tense and time accords with the basic descriptive and conceptual data. Tense as a scope-bearing item makes it amenable to treatment as an operator (like quantifiers) and the pronounlike features of tense give it a coherent explanation in terms of anaphora.

8.11. Naive Time

In our study of how language encodes space, we noted that spatial expressions are motivated by a mental model of space that diverges markedly from the school-based picture of the physical and geometric world. This naive, idealized model of space has a counterpart in a naive model of time for temporal expressions.

In school, we learn that time is relative and there is no simultaneity. The temporal overlap of any two phenomena is a convenient fiction because objects and events come with their own spatiotemporal coordinates. We also learn that time is flexible because, as physics teaches us, time is connected to space, motion, and the point from which time is measured. A body moving in a direction opposite to our stationary vantage point appears to slow down, relative to us as observers, because the space occupied by the body dilates from our position of measurement (see Salmon 1980). Constant time, part of our everyday life, is another a convenient fiction.

Speakers of ordinary language perform quite well without expert knowledge of time. Arguably, such knowledge gets in the way of our everyday talk. But if our everyday world is made up of convenient fictions about time, what do they look like and how do they work? Here we examine two principles of the mentally projected world of time that forms the backdrop for temporal expression: (a) time is a line; (b) linguistic time is not cultural time.

8.12. Time is a Line

The stereotypical, ideal time line is an entirely adequate model of linguistic time. Events in linguistic expressions are located on an unbounded, unidimensional extent that stretches outward from a central zero-point, the here-and-now (see Fig. 8.1). In the expert model of real time, there is no central zero-point because

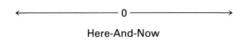

Here-And-Now

FIG. 8.1.   Basic time line.

all bodies are in motion. But we need a central zero-point, the temporal equivalent of the spatial baseline of Earth, when we say such simple things as *I wrote the letter*. The past tense, *wrote,* is understandable only as projection from the baseline of the present, 'write before the present,' just as *will write* means 'write after the present.' Ordinary speakers are unperplexed by the fact that the present zero-point itself is a moving target in real time.

Moreover, all languages appear to rely on the time line, in spite of the argument that some languages are tenseless and timeless or that the people who speak the languages have no conception of linear time. Some languages structure the time line differently, or assign different values to different parts of the line; some languages interpret the significance of the time line in a way that clashes dramatically with the way that we think that time fits into our lives. But not a single language dispenses with the line, because the naive model itself merely claims that *time is an ordered scale of precedence and subsequence relative to a baseline.* This minimal schematic is filled in differently in different systems, but the *structural system of tense* nonetheless obtains.

The grounding of the naive model of time in the abstract time line, and not real time, gives rise to two other expectations: linguistic time is constant and imprecise. First, the time line is inflexible and stable. Linguistic time is a *constant,* because the time line is an unwavering backdrop. Note, for example, that if we express an event in the past tense, as in *I wrote the letter,* we are not thereby allowed to choose a range of values for the past simply because we know that time is, in reality, flexible. A language hands down to its speakers certain temporal constants—what Comrie (1985) calls the *essential meanings* of tenses—and this is a reflection of the essential immobility of the time line.

Second, though linguistic time line is inflexible, it is also *imprecise.* The time line is underdifferentiated, and the kinds of times that constitute linguistic time are not very exact by expert standards. No language has a tense marker for 'nanoseconds,' much less one for 'hours.' Instead, the time line is a simple extent, and very gross units of time are sufficient to capture the temporal notions that speakers require. Note how *I wrote the letter* makes no reference to the exact moment of time in the past. Certainly, we can lexicalize exact moments—*I wrote the letter at 2:17*—but no language has a mechanism for grammatically encoding such a precise interval (and even languages that encode time in units, metrical systems, choose broad and fuzzy intervals for the denotations). The time line is thus a kind of midlevel, gross schematization of temporal extent, underdifferentiated and inflexible, but sufficient nonetheless.

8.13. Linguistic Time Is Not Cultural Time

According to the second principle of naive time, linguistic time is different from *beliefs about time* determined by culture or cosmology. Everyone has the same naive model of time, because linguistic time is a structural constant deriving from the computations and form of our mental models. Cultural or cosmological time, however, is a value imposed on our mental models by the contexts we grow up in.

As Comrie (1985) observes, there is a great difference between time as a linguistic construct and *progress,* a cultural construct derived from inherited beliefs. Many cultures have little or no idea of advance through time. Many cultures also have little sense of history as a series of events removed from the present, but this absence appears to be a function of the concurrent absence of schooling, literacy, and history as a written object, not at all related to the ways that the languages of the peoples in question structure event-time through tenses (see Frawley 1987).

In this debate over cultural and linguistic time, Hopi has now reached mythical proportions from the popularization of Whorf's relativity hypothesis, based on his claims about the connections between Hopi time, culture, language, and cosmology (see chap. 2). The nonscholarly view of Hopi holds that it is a tenseless and timeless language that forces on its speakers a cyclic view of the future and the past. Such claims about Hopi turn out to be correct for Hopi *cosmology,* but irrelevant to the *structural mechanisms that convey time* in the Hopi language. Malotki's (1983) detailed analysis of the Hopi tense system shows that, compared to the rest of the world's languages, Hopi has a pretty traditional tense structure, one based on a future/nonfuture distinction with a number of degrees of remoteness. Hopi, like all languages, distinguishes the temporal notions that its speakers *value* from the concepts of time that its speakers *must encode.* English cosmology can no more be read into (or off) English tense than Hopi tense can be read off (or into) Hopi world-view.

Language requires a naive, schematically structured linear extent, derived from the mechanisms that build our projected models of the world. Naive time is thus a form of ideal time because it is removed from real-time processing. The speaker of Hopi and English alike has the same problem: how to represent events in terms of precedence and subsequence on a scale with a zero-point, which is done whatever the cosmology.

8.14. Summary

In this preliminary discussion, we have defined tense as the grammatical means for locating events in time and seen how the naive ideal model of time underlies this definition. The time line is an adequate model of linguistic time, accounting for the stability and imprecision of tense denotations; linguistic time differs from cultural time in that the structural encoding of time is unaffected by the significance of time to the speakers of a language.

8.2. TENSE STRUCTURE AND TENSE SYSTEMS

Now that we have an idea of the conceptual structures that underlie the semantics of temporal expressions, we can turn to the mechanisms by which all tense systems operate and to an enumeration of the kinds of tense distinctions found in language. Our goal here is to specify the universal structure of tense, the semantic distinctions available to any language in constructing tense systems, and the range of possibilities actually chosen by languages when they encode the time of events. We first look at the deictic structure of time and then use this deictic structure to organize all subsequent discussion of tense systems. We see how choices made for reference and located points in the deictic structure, and the directional and remoteness relations between those points, determine all possible tense denotations: Absolute and relative tense derive from the choice of temporal reference point; perfect tenses denote two located points on the time line; metrical systems rely on measured temporal remoteness. In preparation, we review the basics of deixis and see how this translates into grammaticalized time.

8.21. The Deictic Structure of Tense:
Tense Locus, Event Frame, and their Relationship

Structurally, tense is rather simple and straightforward, borrowing its mechanisms directly from the concepts that organize space and deixis. Recall from Chapter 6 that deictic systems have two principal components:

1. deictic points: the contextually situated *reference point* and the *located point*;
2. the *direction* and *remoteness* of the relation between the reference point and the located point.

Tenses *locate* events in time with respect to a fixed *temporal reference point* and then specify the relation of the event to that temporal center by some *direction* and some *degree of remoteness*. A simple English example illustrates these ideas:

1. Bob bought the cake.

The event in (1) is *located* in the past, and hence is the temporal equivalent of the spatially located object. Following Chung and Timberlake (1985), we call this temporal position the *event frame*. But the past event frame of (1) must be judged relative to a reference point or temporal center—the moment of speech—which is the temporal equivalent of the spatial reference point (or origo) required for spatial deixis. We call this contextual, temporal reference point, again following Chung and Timberlake (1985), the *tense locus*. Using these ideas, we can say that the past tense signals that *the event frame precedes the tense locus*; in the present tense, however, *the tense locus coincides with the event frame*; in the future tense, *the event frame follows the tense locus*.

This elementary account of tense by their deictic points brings up direction and remoteness. The connection between the tense locus and the event frame is an *ordered relation*—past tense: event frame < tense locus; present tense: event frame = tense locus; future tense: event frame > tense locus. By this ordering, direction is built into the very relation of deictic points. Direction may be augmented by the degree of remoteness of the relation. We can get a feel for the applicability of remoteness by the following:

2a. My father would get up at 5:00 A.M.
 b. My father just got up.

Examples (2a) and (2b) assert that the event frame precedes the tense locus, but in (2a), this relation is *distal* ('some time ago') and (2b) it is *proximal* ('just'). Tense appropriates entirely the basic structure of deixis, as summarized here:

Reference Point: Tense Locus
Located Point: Event Frame
Direction: Precedes, Coincides, Follows
Remoteness: Distal and Proximal

We want to know how languages exploit these possibilities of the deictic structure of tense. The obvious choices fall out: Languages vary as to how they assign tense locus, event frame, directionality, and degree of remoteness. We address these choices in that order.

8.22. Deictic Points: Tense Locus and Event Frame

8.221. Choice of Tense Locus:
Absolute Versus Relative Tense

There are just two possibilities for the tense locus. If the present moment of speech is the tense locus, this is *absolute tense*. If some other event or some moment not the present moment of speech is the tense locus, this is *relative tense.* This terminology, though standard, may be a bit confusing because it suggests that absolute tense is somehow independent when such a possibility is decidedly contrary to deixis, whose components *depend* on a reference point. All tenses are relative in that they all depend on a temporal reference point for judgment of the event frame on the time line, but for absolute tense, the tense locus is a *constant* and hence is absolute through this single default choice. On the other hand, the tense locus for relative tense is a *true variable* in that its value is a function of any event, the present moment or not, as the language or situation dictates. We explore the details of each of these in the next section, but here it is important to note that we have not compromised the deictic structure of tense by calling one *absolute* and the other *relative.*

8.2211.   Absolute Tense

Absolute tense relies on the here-and-now to determine the tense locus. We might also say that absolute tense reaches directly into the speech event by determining the event frame, direction, and remoteness on the basis of the time of the encoding of the expression containing the event. *John ran home* and *John will run home* denote that the event of running is in the past or future *relative to the present position of the speaker in encoding this event,* regardless of the time of the event frame. In this way, absolute tense, like spatial deixis, assigns temporal distance *outward from the speaker* as the deictic center.

Absolute tense is the principal means by which any language assigns time to events, and so we can cast our example net anywhere to find a comparative illustration. Consider the following from Yapese (Jensen 1977):

3. Gu waen nga Donuch.
   I   go   to   Donuch
   I go/went to Donuch.

Like a number of languages, Yapese bifurcates the time line into future and nonfuture. The bare verb in (3) is compatible with either a present or past reading, as the gloss indicates, but the main lesson is that absolute tense holds sway. The tense locus for the event frame, regardless of its position on the time line, is the present moment.

8.2212.   Relative Tense

Consider (4):

4. The man sitting in the chair was rich.

Sentence (4) encodes two events, 'being rich' and 'sitting.' The former event has absolute tense; *was* indicates that 'being rich' is unalterably prior to the moment of speaking. But what about 'sitting'? By its overt form, a participle or nonfinite verbal form, it is has no inherent temporal reference. Sentence (4) may be glossed 'the man who *was* sitting in the chair was rich,' where the event in question is assigned a position prior to the moment of speaking, just as 'being rich.' But crucially, *sitting* does not come with an obligatorily past time interpretation, as *was rich* does. So (4) is just as likely to be glossed 'the man who *is sitting now* in the chair was rich,' where 'sitting' and 'being rich' are asserted to hold at different times (cf. also *The man sitting in the chair tomorrow will be rich,* where the event may even have a future reading). In other words, the present moment of speech, which is essential to the absolute tense of *was rich,* does not apply by default to *sitting,* and so the form has relative tense. *Sitting inherits its tense locus* from some other event or some other specified time (though, of course, we may assign it the present moment of speech if we choose).

Relative tense may select the tense locus from other than the here-and-now, so it is sensitive to constructions that shift deictic reference points as a rule. Expressions of *reported speech,* or *indirect discourse,* where the original speech of a situation is incorporated into the language of the describer of that situation, often rely on deictic shift. Imagine a situation where you report having asked another person why his hands are shaking and both events—the asking and the shaking of the hands—are prior to the present moment of speech. In using indirect discourse to report this event, you might say the following, where the second verb is incorporated into your report of the actual question:

5. I asked him why his hands were shaking (cf. I asked him: "Why are your hands shaking," which has direct discourse).

Both events are in the absolute past tense because their tense locus is a function of the here-and-now (i.e., both the asking and the shaking prior to the moment of speech). Now suppose that the asking is in the future and the shaking of the hands is in the present. To report this scenario, we say:

6. I'll ask him why his hands are shaking.

Here again the events are assigned absolute tense—future and present, respectively—because they take the moment of speech as the tense locus and come with inherent tense assigned.

In Russian, however, the situation is very different. The event in reported speech does not have absolute tense. On the contrary, the event in the reported or indirect discourse *must occur in the present tense* and inherit its temporal interpretation from another event, even though denotationally that other event may actually precede the moment of speech and thus logically require past tense. So (5) in Russian is as shown here (Chung and Timberlake 1985: 211):

7. Ja spros-il   počemu u nego trjasutsja   ruki.
   I ask   Past why   to him tremble/Pres hands
   I asked him why his hands were shaking.

Assignment of past tense here to *trjasutsja* 'tremble' is ungrammatical in Russian. Instead, the verb takes its tense from the first verb.

This use of relative tense in reported or secondary events is in fact quite a widespread phenomenon. But it underscores the main characteristic of relative tense. The tense locus is inherited from a point other than the moment of speech.

8.2213.   The Choice of Relative Versus Absolute

Having seen the basic mechanisms of absolute and relative tense, we might inquire as to where they occur and when languages that have the option choose one over the other. According to the surveys made by Comrie (1985) and Chung and Timberlake (1985), the general rule seems to be that absolute tense is associated with *syntactically and semantically autonomous events*. Consequently, absolute tense is overwhelmingly found in main clauses (Comrie, 1985, notes only one language, Classical Arabic, where relative tense surfaces in the main clause). It appears, then, that the "absoluteness" of absolute tense is connected to the "semantic absoluteness" or independence of the constructions in which it appears.

Relative tense, in contrast, is usually found with events *dependent in both meaning and form* on other events and structures [cf. (7), where the reported speech is in a subordinate clause]. An excellent example of the association of relative tense and dependency can be seen in verb serialization (typically found in West African, Oceanic, and Papuan languages). Let us recall from Chapter 4 that verb serialization is a syntactic device by which several verbs are strung together in sequence but act as a single verbal unit. Evidence for their unified structure lies in the fact that in spite of their multiple constituency, serial verbs frequently have a single tense, even though there are several event candidates in the construction to assign tenses. Consider the following expression from Yimas (after Foley and Olson (985: 31):

8. na-   bu-   wul- cay- pra- kiak.
   Obj/3Sing Subj/3Pl afraid try   come Past
   They tried to make him afraid as he came.

Example (8) is a single sentence with a complex verbal unit functioning as a single verb. In effect, the event in (8) in 'try-be afraid-come,' and though there is obviously no appropriate English gloss, we can render it approximately with the subordinate structures indicated. Importantly, the Yimas expression has a *single tense,* past, which percolates across the entire verbal construction, assigning past time reference to *all the events encoded.* One event in (8) takes absolute tense, probably the last, *pra* 'come,' because Yimas is a verb-final language, and this tense is then inherited by all the other verbs, just as verbs in reported speech in Russian inherit their temporal assignment from the verb of the main clause.

Though there is a correlation of absolute tense with autonomous events and relative tense with subordinate ones, we must be careful to paint this picture with a broad rather than narrow brush. To a certain extent, this difference between autonomy and subordination depends on how a language construes these notions. For example, in Quechua (according to Comrie 1985, who cites Cole 1982), main clauses take absolute tense and subordinate clauses relative tense, except for relative clauses, which, though syntactically dependent, take absolute tense. Similar facts hold for Russian, though, like Quechua, it also requires absolute tense in relative clauses (Chung and Timberlake 1985).

There is a conceptual correlation to the absolute/relative tense opposition. If the event assigned tense is conceptually autonomous, then it is more likely to take its tense locus as a function of the moment of speech. Conversely, if the event is conceptually dependent, it is more likely to inherit its tense locus from some other event or time.

8.2214. Summary

We have seen how languages assign values to the deictic temporal reference point, or tense locus. Absolute tense relies on the moment of speech for tense locus; relative tense selects the moment of speech or another event as tense locus. Absolute tense is the principal means by which languages assign tense, and it tends to be found in main clauses. Relative tense is a secondary means of assigning tense, and is usually found in subordinate clauses. One way to think about this choice in tense locus is to say that absolute tense correlates with autonomous meanings and structures and relative tense with dependent ones.

8.222. *Choice of Event Frame:*
Simple Tenses and Perfects

We have seen the options available to languages in their assignment of tense locus. Now, we turn to the possible event frames, or temporally located points. Before we do so, we should note that we are still concerned only with the universal *structure* of tense as a deictic system, and thus we are simply inquiring into the number of formally defined temporal positions that any language has in structuring time. As we proceed, we describe the actual temporal values that languages select along the time line, but we need to explore the abstract structures first.

There are only two options with regard to event frames: Languages may choose a *single point* or *two points* on the time line to bear a relation to the tense locus. The first option has no received nomenclature, so I call it *simple tense*; the second is known as *perfect tense*. We discuss both of these in the next section, spending much of our time on the perfect because its dual event frame produces a number of interesting semantic effects.

8.2221.   Simple Tenses

In simple tenses, the event frame consists of a single position on the time line in relation to the tense locus. The tenses in the following expressions show how the event frame can be simple:

9a. Andy jumped.
 b. Andy is jumping.
 c. Andy will jump.

Sentences (9a–c) differ markedly in what values they assign to the event frame on the time line and in the direction of the relation between the tense locus and the event frame. But they are exactly alike on one count: Their tense locus in the present moment of speech bears a relation to a *single position* on the time line.

Other languages assign different values to the simple event frame. English selects any position on the time line with the proper direction in relation to the tense locus. Yoruba assigns the event frame a specific interval—for example, 'yesterday,' 'tomorrow,' etc. (see sec. 8.232). But in each case, the structure of the event frame is simple, and such simple tenses are the basis of any tense system.

8.2222.   Perfect Tenses

Although simple tenses are fundamental, they are not the only possibility. In many languages, the event frame may consist of *two located positions on the time line*. Consider (10):

10. Tom had seen the movie.

Sentence (10) locates the event frame, 'see,' not only in the past relative to the moment of speech but also relative to *another past event*. We use Reichenbach's (1947) terminology and call this third event the *reference time*.[1] Sentence (10)

---

[1]Reichenbach (1947) proposed that all tenses have a reference time. Simple tenses, like those illustratred in (9a–c), simply collapse the event time and the reference time, or fail to differentiate the two. My claims are mute on this possibility, and I simply want to introduce a second event frame to account for the structure of the perfects. See section 8.3, where Reichenbach's model is discussed more fully.

thus means something like 'Tom saw the movie [event frame] and this event occurred *before* some other unspecified event in the past [reference time],' where the tense locus bears a relation to two points on the time line. Such a tense is called a *perfect*.[2]

8.22221.   *The Dual Structure of the Perfect*

Perfects require a complex event frame, which in all cases and in all languages conveys that the event frame is to be judged as *prior to,* or *temporally up to,* a projected reference point. This *dual structure* of the event frame is one reason why certain adverbial constructions are preferentially compatible with the perfect, as in (11):

11. Tom had already seen the movie.

The adverb *already* in (11) suggests there is an interval of time in the past, defined by the space between the event frame, 'see,' and the requisite reference time. Indeed, *already* means something like 'up to a point' or 'from a prior position to a later position.'

The compatibility of adverbs like *already* with the perfect is underscored by the fact that in many languages, the perfect is formed *solely by means of this adverb* (or its equivalent). Dahl (1985) observes that Yoruba and Karaboro work this way. Ewondo does likewise (Redden 1980: 91):

12. medí-   ya   zoag.
ate/1Per already elephant
I have eaten elephant.

In (12), the verb is suffixed with the form for 'already,' producing the perfect. Significantly, (12) without the suffix for 'already' denotes the simple past 'I ate elephant.' Hence the perfect marker specifically introduces the reference time needed to derive the perfect from the simple tense.

The dual structure of the perfect is further highlighted by the fact that certain constructions select *only parts* of the complex event frame. For instance, we can encode the reference time itself:

13. Tom had seen the movie by ten o'clock/before he arrived/etc.

---

[2]The perfect is also called the *anterior* (Bybee 1985; Reichenbach 1947) because of the requirement of the later reference time, and *absolute-relative tense* (Comrie 1985). This latter term is understandable given that perfects assign tense on the basis of a tense locus in the moment of speech—absolute—but also require a second tense locus in the reference time for the event frame—hence relative by definition.

Some punctual adverbs of time are ambiguous with perfects precisely because the perfect denotes a dual event frame (after Comrie 1985):

14. Tom had seen the movie at ten o'clock.

Example (14) has two interpretations, depending on whether the punctual temporal phrase *at ten o'clock* associates with the point of the event frame or the point of the reference time. On one interpretation, (14) means 'Tom saw the movie at ten o'clock and this was prior to another unspecified event,' where the event frame takes the temporal phrase. It may also mean 'Tom saw the movie and this was prior to ten o'clock,' where the temporal phrase selects the reference time: That is, *Tom had already seen the movie by ten o'clock.* The ambiguity of (14) provides further support for the dual event frame of the perfect.

8.22222.   *The Perfect and its Temporal Associations*

We have viewed the perfect thus far as an arrangement of points in temporal deixis, whatever the exact values for these points. This formal definition of the perfect lets it equally structure any part of the time line, past, present, or future. The event frame must only be formally complex and "proceed" from one point up to another. English, in fact, has four different perfects, whose interpretations depend solely on where the dual structure of the event frame falls on the time line: That is, position is the only variable. *Past perfect,* or the *pluperfect,* situates both the event frame and the reference time prior to the tense locus. *Present perfect* shifts the dual structure toward the tense locus, situating the event frame prior to the tense locus and the reference time coincident with the present: whence the intuition that an expression like *Fred has seen the movie* conveys 'present relevance.' *Future perfect* tense shifts the complex event frame to a position subsequent to the tense locus, and the *conditional perfect* (*would have X-ed*), shifts the structure event farther away from the tense locus.

The formal structure of the perfect makes it independent of more specific temporal associations that might arise from an examination of the time line itself. For example, we might think that the past perfect, because it appears to be so removed from the tense locus and pushed into the past, is equivalent to a very remote past. But no matter how remote we make a simple past, we do not thereby create a perfect:

15. Tom saw the movie 10 years ago.

The event in (15) is very remote from the tense locus, but it lacks the proper structure of the time line for a perfect and so cannot convey a perfect meaning.

This is not to say that all temporal associations are compatible with perfect tenses. Indeed, there are a number of well-known effects in English in this regard. The English present perfect disallows adverbs of specific past time:

16. ?? Tom has seen the movie yesterday/last week.

We might argue that such past time adverbs are ruled out because in the English present perfect, the reference time coincides with the present, so if any temporal adverb is acceptable with the present perfect, it is one for present time: *Tom has seen the movie today.*

However, other languages freely allow past time adverbs with present perfects (Dahl 1985: 137):

17a. Bulgarian: Pratkata e pristignala predi tri   dena.
delivery is arrived   before three days
The delivery has arrived 3 days ago.
   b. Swedish: Jag har   mött din   bror   igår.
I   have met your brother yesterday
I have met your brother yesterday.

Moreover, such restrictions do not apply to all the perfects in English, only to the present:

18a. I had seen your brother yesterday/today (when you called).
   b. I will have seen your brother today/tomorrow.
   c. I would have seen your brother next week/today/yesterday (had he been here).

The adverbial restriction on the present perfect in English may be the result of things other than the structure of the perfect itself, perhaps the close pragmatic association of the perfect and present relevance. In any case, this adverbial restriction is not universal, and not even widespread in the rest of the English perfect tense system.

8.22223. *The Perfect and its Implicatures*

Now that we understand the formal structure of the perfect, let us turn to a few of its frequently discussed interpretations. We see that the formal structure of the perfect as a complex event frame is consistent with these interpretations as implicatures. Semantically, the perfect denotes only that *two event frames are evoked in relation to a tense locus.*

The semantics literature is full of claims that the perfect tense, especially the present perfect, has uses such as the following (Comrie 1985; Dahl 1985; McCawley 1971, 1981):

1. to express results: *Donna has come to a decision.* (cf. sec. 7.22, on telics)
2. to express present relevance: *Einstein has taught at Princeton* (even though he's now dead).

3. to express an experiential state: *I've met your brother before.*

4. to express persistent action: *Donna has jogged for years.*

Although there have been many perceptive analyses of these uses, we side with Comrie (1985) on the matter and claim that these interpretations are pragmatic, and not the result of any inherent semantic meaning of the forms, though motivated by the semantic structure of the perfect.

Comrie (1985) observes that many of the uses of the perfect are implicatures, not entailments (see chap. 2), and as such can be cancelled, given the appropriate discourse context. For example, it is entirely possible to negate the uses in (2) and (4) and nonetheless retain the perfect:

19a. Einstein has taught at Princeton, but who cares about that now?!

b. Donna has jogged, but only for a minute or two.

These are interpretations *consistent with the perfect,* but *not required* by it. As implicatures, they are determined by the context of use, and are not inherent to the forms.

A second argument against these effects as necessary semantic features of the perfect comes from the fact that in some languages, interpretations like (1–4) are not signalled by the perfect at all. In Indonesian there is one verbal construction to encode the perfect tense, the auxiliary *sudah* plus the verb, and another to encode experiential states, the auxiliary *pernah* plus the verb. Thus, Indonesian unlike English, draws a formal distinction between a straightforward perfect interpretation of a sentence like *I've met your brother* and an experiential one ('I've had the experience of meeting your brother'). Moreover, even in languages like English where the perfect carries these additional interpretations, it is possible to evoke the meanings without the perfect: *Well, Einstein DID teach at Princeton, for your information.* We might then argue that the additional interpretations of the perfect can be dispensed with, because they are not built into the tense proper.

These pragmatic interpretations correlate with some structural facts of the perfect. The dual event frame of the perfect has the functional consequence of inducing a time interval or some temporal extension on the time line. We have already noted how this characteristic of the perfect accommodates and even engenders a resultative reading by mimicking the process/result structure of the telic (sec. 7.22). So, it is understandable that there is a perfect of result, as per (1) (p. 349). The dual structure of the perfect accommodates the perfect of present relevance, (2) (p. 349), because the reference time of the present perfect is coincident with the present tense locus: Present relevance falls out of the way the perfect structures the time line. Similar arguments from the form of the perfect account for both the experiential perfect and the perfect of persistent action, which require that an event be extended through time. As we know, two ways to extend events are via the progressive and habitual aspects. The perfect functionally imitates these two aspects by extending the event frame into an interval.

The perfect, through its dual event frame, functionally reproduces the structural requirements of the extension of events. Thus it is no surprise that perfect tenses should be compatible with interpretations that necessitate temporal extension. The structure of the tense parallels the functional requirements of discourse and allows a number of possible interpretations based on implicature.

8.223. Summary

We have discussed the nature and function of simple and complex tense. The simple tenses have a single point on the time line for the event frame and complex tenses, perfects, have a dual event frame. We have put most of our attention on perfects, noting their association with the meaning 'already' or 'up to'; the complex event frame accommodates expressions that select only parts of the frame, like punctual temporal phrases. The formal structure of the perfect makes it compatible with any time reference, and this structure underlies the standard implicatures of the present perfect—for example, result, present relevance, experiential state, and persistent action—because the complex event frame mimics temporal extension.

8.23. Direction and Remoteness:
Vectorial and Metrical Tense

We have seen how one half of deixis—the deictic points—is appropriated by tense and translated into a temporal system. Languages select a tense locus, equivalent to the deictic reference point, and an event frame, the temporal analogue of the located point. We now turn to the other half of deixis: the relationship of deictic points via *direction* and *remoteness*. Here we consider how languages assign values to points on the conceptual time line within the basic formal structure of tense.

There are many imaginable ways that a language may denote and encode the time line—in days, months, seconds, and so forth. Of all the choices, languages select just two as part of their grammatical systems: (a) undifferentiated extension from a zero-point, a *vectorial system;* and (b) definite intervals, a *metrical system*. Both kinds of system operate within the general constraint of direction because all require that the time line be conceptualized as an ordered relation with respect to the tense locus: prior to, coincident with, and subsequent to. So, when we consider values on the time line, we are speaking of two different measures of remoteness within a constant framework of tripartite direction: unmeasured (vectorial) and measured (metrical) remoteness.

Traditional studies of tense usually restrict considerations of remoteness to metrical systems, though this seems to be because degrees of temporal distance are more often found in this kind of system, for the obvious reason that metrical systems measure time to begin with, and thus are likely to encode fine differentiations. In the discussion that follows, however, we assume that remoteness (or temporal distance) applies equally to both kinds of systems because of their deictic structure, but they assign temporal distance different values on the time line.

8.231. Vectorial Tense

Most of the world's languages do not radically differentiate the time line, but simply extend it in each direction away from the present moment, giving tripartite directionality: before, during, and after the tense locus. This term—*vectorial*—which invokes physics and geometry, is transparent and useful. A vector is technically defined as anything with direction and velocity, and this is exactly how a vectorial tense system construes time. The present is the point of origin for two rays, the past and the future, both of which extend in undifferentiated remoteness away from the present with equal "temporal velocity," and neither of which is bounded.

Vectorial tense is scalar and gradient; the categories of past, present, and future are determined relative to each other and located on the time line statically as a matter of convenience only. Within each of these scalar categories, we can discern a number of consistencies, some more obvious than others. Here we discuss the criterial definition of past, present, and future, their typical encoding, and their larger semantic effects.

8.2311. Past Tense

The past tense in a vectorial system is an undifferentiated temporal extent moving away from the present moment into the already known or completed, and, with enough temporal removal, into the unknown and hypothetical. Consequently, the past tense is regularly associated with bounded events, no doubt because the tense locus is the present moment, and so the past offers a view of events as a totality. Other properties associated with the past tense are temporal removal, nonactuality, hypotheticality, dissociation from the present, counterfactuality, improbability, and even desire, insofar as desire can be seen as a dissociation from the present, or as-yet-unrealized action. James (1982) and Fleischman (1989) survey these uses of the past tense and provide an overall characterization: The past tense is generally consistent with *distal events,* in whatever way that a language or culture may construe or require temporal removal.

Some illustrations from vectorial tense systems point up these basic properties of the past tense. In Spanish, the preterit, the past tense connected with completed and past events, denotes incontestable temporal distance. Consider this example:

20. La Grecia produj- o   grandes filósofos.
    the Greece produce Past/3Per great   philosophers
    Greece produced great philosophers.

The event in (20) is encoded in the preterit, by the suffix -o. As a consequence, this expression may refer *only to Ancient Greece,* that is, an entity that itself is completed and removed from the present. If (20) is to refer to present-day Greece, then the interpretation requires us to fill in some deleted contextual parameters, such as a specification of an interval during which the event was true. Thus, if we use the preterit in an expression that otherwise refers to an existing entity, we invoke a special interpretation:

21. ?? Los Estados Unidos produj- eron   grandes autores.
    the states   united produce Past/3Pl great   authors
    The United States produced great authors.

Example (21) implies either that the United States no longer exists or that it does not produce any more great authors (after the endpoint of some contextually given interval). But in each interpretation, the sense of removal, completion, and distance is conveyed (thanks to J. P. Lantolf for this discussion).

In many languages, the past tense assumes a variety of functions that are consistent with its basic meaning as 'distal time.' The past tense is commonly associated with certain aspects, like the perfective, and certain moods, grammatical indications of truth value or a speaker's orientation toward the denotation of an expression. James (1982) observes that the past frequently indicates hypotheticality, a speaker's lack of expectation about an event, or, in general, nonactuality or the improbability of an event. Consider (22) (after James 1982: 383):

22. I wish I owned a car.

The event in the subordinate clause, 'own,' has in absolute terms a future meaning: That is, the speaker does not presently own a car and projects the desire into the future. But it is encoded in the past, and cannot in fact be put in any other tense:

23. ?? I wish I own/will own a car.

Similar facts hold for Cree (James 1982: 384):

24. nipakose:lihte:n ki:takošinokopa:ne:.
    I wish   past/he/come/past
    I wish he had come.

Though (24) is translated in the more standard English form with the pluperfect (so called *sequence of tenses*), it more accurately means 'I wish he came.' Importantly, the true time reference for 'come' is the future with reference to the first event of wishing. Nonetheless, because of its hypothetical and unrealized nature, it is encoded in the past.

The dissociative function of the past tense can be clearly seen in its connection to politeness and social distance. Fleischman (1989) observes the respectful and attenuative effect in French of a request encoded in the past tense (here in the imperfect aspect also):

> 25. Je voul- ais   parler avec vous.
>   I   want Imper/1Per speak with you
>   I want to speak with you
>   More accurately: I was wanting to speak with you.

But such a request in the present tense is blatantly peremptory and imposing:

> 26. Je veu- x   parler avec vous.
>   I   want Pres/1Per   speak with you
>   I want to speak with you.
>   More accurately: I wanna speak with you!!

The generalized distal function of the past tense comes through in all languages in a variety of ways, in this case extended to an indicator of social distance. Overall, however, past tense is associated with distal time, and this temporal removal is compatible with a number of other semantic effects.

8.2312.   Present Tense

The present tense is an area of the time line simultaneous with the moment of speech. The present is neither a specific point nor a vector itself, but an ideal temporal segment that fixes the reference of the vectors of past and future. Bull (1969) argues that the present is an abstract unit with inferred limits. Comrie (1985) likewise observes that the present tense only inexactly encodes the present moment of speech and really is *larger than the present time*; it *includes* the present moment of speech and thus extends slightly into the past vector and slightly into the future vector, outward in both directions from the canonical present moment of speech.

The present is idealized, and thus constructions that specifically mark the true simultaneity of the moment of speech and the event frame are fairly unusual and restricted in use. One such is the performative, the speech act (see chap. 2) that indicates simultaneous encoding and execution of an event: *I hereby pronounce you husband and wife.* Another such construction is the in situ narrative: *Now he steps up to the plate, and the pitcher releases the pitch.* . . More common is for the present tense to have an inexact correspondence between the moment of speech and the time of the event encoded in the present.

The nature of the present on the vectorial line gives rise to a number of associations. The present is frequently connected to on-line activity, actual events, and likelihood of occurrence. To a certain extent, the present is also associated with incomplete events and those with some degree of inherent extension, like states. For this reason, the present tense frequently expresses generic and timeless events as well as habituality. The aspectual and modal properties of the present therefore contrast markedly with those of the past. The past implies removal; the present implies effectuality and persistence.

Many of these properties can be seen in Nahuatl, which, as Sullivan (1988) indicates, marks the present tense by the absence of any form other than the verb stem (this is quite common for present tense as a rule: see Bybee 1985), though number is explicitly marked in the plural. Present tense in Nahuatl may signal that the moment of speech exactly coincides with the event represented, much like the performatives or in situ narrative:

27. izcatqui nican ompehua- Ø   in cronica   mexicayotl.
    behold here begin/Pres 3Per the chronicle mexican
    Behold, here begins the Chronicle of the Mexicans.

Example (27) is uttered at the beginning of the legendary narrative of the Nahuatl people and so corresponds exactly to the moment of the event expressed. The present tense may also encode the more standard inclusion of the event frame in the present moment:

28. ye qulz-
    now leave/Pres Plural
    Now they are leaving.

It may have a habitual or generic use:

29. icuac ocelotl quitta- Ø   anqui, amo cholog- Ø.
    when jaguar see/Pres 3Per hunter Neg flee/Pres 3Per
    When the jaguar sees the hunter, he does not flee.

Example (29) has the interpretation of a timeless state of affairs, where the tense locus always coincides with the event frame, and hence is in the present by definition. Thus, Nahuatl functions very much like English in this respect, where the vectorial present has a variety of interpretations compatible with its location as an area on the time line that includes the present moment of speech.

8.2313. Future Tense

The future tense is a vector stretching outward from the present moment in an undifferentiated extent into the unknown or unrealized. The future thus typically "looks ahead" in time from the stable present moment. This characterization suggests that the future is the symmetric counterpart of the past, and indeed, the future conveys many of the same semantic notions as the past. For example, future tenses are customarily associated with hypotheticality, nonactuality, and even politeness.[3] The future is remarkably like the past in that both convey distal notions, and the expected implications of temporal distance follow therefrom for each.

However, the symmetry of the past and the future stops with their convergence in temporal distance. Fleischman (1982, 1989), Ultan (1978a), and others note that future tenses often convey meanings of inception, prediction, intention, imminence, potential, volition, and supposition, concepts not usually connected to events removed to a point in time prior to the tense locus. As a corollary, future tense systems tend to be marked and unstable historically, unlike the past. Furthermore, languages tend to make finer semantic distinctions in the past more so than in the future, which they frequently leave undifferentiated.

All the evidence points to a conceptual *asymmetry* between past and future because the future tense is much more connected to the unknown. As a consequence, the future more often than not fails to express pure futurity and is instead bound up with modality and the expression of belief and possibility. The general historical development of future tenses bears this out, wherein futures tend to derive from markers of desire, inception, change, and even goal-directedness. Indeed, this latter fact has a clear parallel in the frequent use of the verb *to go* in many languages to indicate futurity—*I am going to leave,* where the goal-directedness of the motion is the indicator of futurity (see Fleischman 1982; Ultan 1978a; sec. 8.31).

Any number of examples from English support this characterization of the future tense. Consider the possible interpretations of (30):

30. Alan will buy the car.

---

[3]As to the last, consider the following from French (Fleischman 1989: 19):

i. Vous ser- ez   bien gentil de fermer   la   porte.
    you   be   Fut/3Per   well kind   of to close the   door
    Would you be so kind as to close the door?

Though the gloss of (i) indicates the relevant English translation, it literally means 'you will kindly close the door,' not exactly the form of a polite request in English, though in French, the future tense is sufficient to signal politeness by temporal removal from the present.

Sentence (30) might have a simple future time gloss, 'Alan's buying of the car is to occur at a point in time after the present moment,' a prediction, 'if he has enough money, (my guess is that) Alan will buy the car,' or an obligation, 'Alan *will* buy the car (I guarantee).' The very form *will* derives from the Proto-Germanic marker of volition, 'want,' and so it is pretty clear that the future in English also conveys desire (cf. Modern German *Ich will* 'I want').

The same facts can be found in other languages quite readily. Again let us look to Nahuatl for a comparative illustration. Verbs in the future tense in Nahuatl are marked by the suffix -*z,* and the future tense can have the interpretation of simple future time:

31. ni- cochi- z.
    I   sleep Fut/Sing
    I will sleep.

It can also denote any of the other attendant properties of the future, such as obligation (32a) or uncertain action, especially in regard to volition (32b):

32a. inic ti- nemi-   z.
     thus you go around Fut/Sing
     You have to go around like that.
     More accurately: You are obliged to go around thusly.

  b. monequi amo quitta- z   in   tlein tecualani.
     desirable Neg see Fut/Sing this what annoys
     It is not desirable that she see what annoys people.

More accurately, and in terms of the future orientation, (32b) means something like 'it is desirable that she will not see what annoys people,' where the future requirement of the volitional state comes through.

Expressions of purpose or events with an actional goal also require the future in Nahuatl:

33. tic- cahua telpochti-   z.
    we   leave be a young man Fut/Sing
    We are leaving him to become a young man.

Example (33) is interesting on two counts. First, it shows how a more precise future gloss is required to do justice to the obligatory future tense in Nahuatl: 'we leave him now so that he will become a young man.' Second, it shows that the future tense itself, because of its connection to potential events and probability, is sufficient to convey the purposive sense of this expression. Sullivan (1988: 58–9) points out that (33) dispenses with the explicit marker of purpose, *inic* 'so that,' because the future tense alone signals the expectation and goal-directedness otherwise required by the purposive marker.

So here we see how the future tense is generally compatible with a number of futurelike meanings: volition, purpose, obligation, and uncertainty. Though formally the opposite of the past tense, and compatible with distal time, the future is actually quite distinct from the past denotationally.[4]

8.2314. Encoding Vectorial Systems

In the previous sections, we have covered the kinds of distinctions that vectorial tense systems make on the time line and certain additional semantic implications of these distinctions. Now we turn to a brief discussion of the structural regularities of vectorial systems.

There are six logical possibilities of encoding:

1. A Three-term System: past, present, and future all encoded differently.
2. A Two-term System:
   a. past and present encoded alike vs. future.
   b. present and future encoded alike vs. past.
   c. past and future encoded alike vs. present.
3. A One-term System: past, present, and future all encoded alike.
4. A Zero-term System: past, present, and future not encoded at all.

In practice, we find only four of these possibilities, and of those four, only two have any regularity. One-term systems and two-term systems with a present versus past/future opposition simply never appear, for reasons that have to do with the conceptualization underlying tense and the time line (see sec. 8.23144). Of the four remaining possibilities, the zero-term system appears, but rarely. Such a language is *tenseless,* and pidgins and certain creoles are claimed to be so (Bickerton 1981); Comrie (1985) argues that Burmese and Dyirbal are likewise tenseless. In these infrequent systems, the semantic requirements of tense are taken up by other structures. In pidgins, aspect supersedes the tense distinctions, and in Burmese and Dyirbal, the modal system of realis/irrealis oppositions substitutes for tense (see chap. 9 for more on these ideas). Thus, even in the case of tenseless languages, functionally equivalent two-term systems take over. The remaining options are the three-term system and two two-year systems.

---

[4]At this point, we should call attention to another construction that is often considered in discussions of tense: the *conditional,* formed in English by *would,* as in *Bill would eat all day.* From a grammatical standpoint, the conditional is the past tense of the future *will,* and thus arguably encodes remote futurity. But the conditional may also encode the remote past—*When my father was alive he would watch the Giants*—and so is not properly restricted to a particular time, as with other tenses. Moreover, the conditional normally occurs in conjunction with hypotheticals, which have no time: *If you were rich, you would be Donald Trump.* For these reasons, we do not treat the conditional as a tense, but as a *mood,* as a marker of *irrealis,* and consider it in Chapter 9.

8.23141.   Three-term Systems

Three-term systems have separate encodings for each of the three relations
between the tense locus and the event frame and so allow no overlap of time
reference along the vectorial scale. This kind of mechanism seems the simplest
and most efficient possibility, but it is rather infrequently documented in surveys
of the world's tense systems (Chung and Timberlake 1985: 205).

The relative rarity of the three-term system may, however, be a quirk of the
counting procedure. Two-term systems are usually derived from three-term systems with a zero-marked present that associates either with the past (as in 2a) or
the future (as in 2b). But zero-marking may itself be a distinct operation and so
the function of zero-marking needs clarification (see Ultan 1978a). Furthermore,
it is often difficult to discern whether the tenses themselves actually overlap
denotationally, given the shallow level of analysis that sometimes characterizes
grammatical description. Nonetheless, what epitomizes a three-term system is
three denotations with *three* surface forms. Ultan (1978a) lists a number of
candidates: Lithuanian, Hausa, Bassa, Berber, Coos, Cuna, Eskimo, Haida,
Hupa, and Tlingit (see also Bybee's 1985: 158 survey, though it focuses on
surface form only).[5]

The standard example of a three-term system is Lithuanian. Note the surface
forms of the following examples (Dambriunas, Klimas, and Schmalstieg 1966:
26, 67, 76):

34a. jìs skaĩt-o.
      he read Pres/3Per
      He reads.

   b. jìs skaĩt-ė.
      he read Past/3Per
      He read.

   c. jìs skait-ỹs.
      he read Fut/3Per
      He will read.

Each tense has a distinct suffix. Moreover, each expression has a distinct absolute time reference: Example. (34a) denotes only the event frame prior to the
moment of speech, example (34b) the event frame included in the moment of
speech, and (34c) the event frame following the moment of speech. Thus,
Lithuanian meets the definition of a three-term system by having no overlap of
denotation for three separate surface forms.

---

[5]One of Bybee's candidates is Nahuatl, which is not a three-term system by definition. Though
the present is unmarked in this language and thus formally distinguishable from all other tenses, the
present in Nahuatl may be used for past time reference (Sullivan 1988). However, this overlap may be
restricted to relative tense.

8.23142.   Past/Nonpast

Much more frequent than three-term systems are binary tense systems, defined by how the present tense patterns with time reference in addition to the here-and-now. One such pattern is to associate the present tense with future time, thus resulting in the opposition of past versus present/future. Such a pattern is known as a *past/nonpast system,* for the obvious reason that the past tense stands out in distinct opposition to the future/present as a complex unit. (Ultan, 1978a, calls these systems *prospective* because the collapsing of distinction occurs in the future.)

Past/nonpast systems are characteristic of the Indo-European languages, and English is therefore as good an example as any of this kind of pattern. Consider the fact that the future tense, *will,* is unmarked morphologically—*I will, you will, he will,* and so forth—and so is very much like the present tense, which is also morphologically reduced. This formal manifestation contrasts with the past tense in English, which receives morphological marking across the board: *I walk-ed, you walk-ed, he walk-ed,* and so forth. Moreover, the present tense is compatible with future meaning, *I go tomorrow,* but never past, *?? I go yesterday.* All signs therefore point to English as a system that associates, both formally and referentially, the present with the future, in contradistinction to the past.

Many other languages have past/nonpast tense: for example, Yidin, Finnish, Hungarian, Korean, Tongan, Mandaic, and Miwok (Chung and Timberlake 1985; Ultan 1978a). The following Finnish examples clearly exemplify the system:

35a. me laula-mme.
       I   sing Non-Past/1Per/Pl
       We sing/are singing/will sing.
   b. me laula-imme.
       we sing Past/1Per/Pl
       We were singing.

Example (35a) may refer to an event frame either coterminous or subsequent to the tense locus. Example (35b), on the other hand, is restricted entirely to the past.

8.23143.   Future/Nonfuture

Just as languages may collapse the present and the future in opposition to the past, so they may align the present with the past in contrast to the future. This results in the *future/nonfuture system* (which Ultan 1978a refers to as *retrospective* because the neutralization occurs in the past). Future/nonfuture systems are widely found, particularly among the Amerindian and Oceanic languages: Takelma, Dakota, Guaraní, Hopi, Onondaga, and Rotuman have future/nonfuture systems (Chung and Timberlake 1985; Ultan 1978a).

We can see this kind of patterning clearly in Kusaiean. Lee (1975) notes that the unmarked forms of verbs have either a past or present interpretation, as indicated by their compatibility with a specific adverb of either past or present time:

36. Sepe el   mas ekweyah/ingena.
    Sepe Subj sick yesterday/now
    Sepe was/is sick yesterday/now.

In marked contrast, however, the language has a variety of explicit surface forms for future time reference, differentiating degrees of certainty of future action. Compare the following:

37a. Sepe el   ac   misac.
     Sepe Subj Fut/Certain die
     Sepe will surely die.
  b. Sepe el   fah   misac.
     Sepe Subj Fut/Probable die
     Sepe will probably die.

The Kusaiean examples are noteworthy on a number of counts. First, they show that the language clearly differentiates future from nonfuture because the present and the past are collapsed into a single form, in contrast to the variety of different surface forms for specific future meanings. Second, they show that the language follows the general meanings of the future sketched in section 8.2313. Kusaiean not only differentiates the future uniquely, but also has finer distinctions within the tense as a function of the level of probability of the event frame asserted to hold subsequent to the tense locus.

8.23144. Why These Patterns?

Before we leave this discussion of vectorial tense, let us briefly remark on the logic of three-term and two-term systems and what this might say about semantic structure in general. By far the most frequent tense systems are the binary systems. Typological studies such as Ultan's (1978a) in fact do not show a preference for one type over the other, with past/nonpast as well represented as future/nonfuture. But the fact that binary systems tend to be restricted to these specific choices underscores an interesting fact about the semantics of time and its grammaticalization as tense.

There are no discontinuous systems. No language chooses encoding option 2c on p. 358, wherein the present stands in structural opposition to the future/past: There is no present/nonpresent tense system. Surprisingly, there is no a priori reason to rule such a system out. After all, the present is conceptually distinct from the past and future; moreover, the past and future do share a number of semantic associations in that both are consistent with distal time, and both are used to signal politeness and hypotheticality. Why not then have a system that unifies the past and future in contrast to the present, which generally does not have these additional semantic associations?

We might propose a strictly formal solution here by noting that of all the tenses, the present is universally the most likely to surface in zero-form. Coming as it does, unspecified, the present understandably converges with other tenses because it is not encoded for inherent temporal reference. Although this is appealing from a formal standpoint, such an answer treats the symptoms more than the disease. Why do these things happen at all?

A more conceptual account relies on the naive model of time, where the present *always intervenes between the past and future,* and in the tense systems that do surface to grammaticalize this conceptual structure, the present retains this position and is never singled out on the scale. This result follows, more generally, from cognitive studies of scalar phenomena of which the time line is representative. In his analysis of the acquisition of scaled nominal properties, Keil (1979) proposes that conceptual scales follow what he calls the *M-Constraint,* a principle whereby any scale maintains the continuity of its constituents, and any grouping thereon proceeds locally, without redirecting the inherent order of the scale. With respect to the time line, the present is conceptually real and cannot be bypassed, no matter how phenomenologically transient. If any grouping or reordering of the time line is to take place, it must be done *as a function of the present.* Given the M-Constraint, the only possible binary systems are those that we actually find because past/nonpast and future/nonfuture do not disturb the continuity of the scale.

For similar reasons, we fail to get option 3, whereby all tenses are marked the same. This possibility is functionally equivalent to the zero-term system because, if all times are encoded similarly, then there is no differentiation. The time line is a scale comprised of constituents *in opposition,* and thus time is defined *in relative terms,* and without at least two units, there can be no determination of the relativity. Hence it is understandable that tense should surface in multiples because this is consistent with the relativity of temporal determination itself.

These options show that in encoding time, languages follow the general conceptual constraints that operate on all cognitive scales. This is why when time surfaces, it overwhelmingly does so in coherent multiples.

8.2315. Summary

We have discussed the definition and grammatical ramifications of vectorial tense, which is the way language structures the time line as an undifferentiated extent outward from the present moment. The past is associated with distal time and removal, or a general dissociation of the event from the tense locus. The present is an area of the time line that includes the present moment; it is associated with effectuality, persistence, and extension. The future denotes unknown or unrealized subsequent time and though it is intuitively like the past tense in terms of distal time, the future is connected to volition, prediction, and intention.

In addition to the criterial definition of the three tenses, we have also examined their encoding regularities. Four of the six possible encoding systems are actually found in language, and only three of these with any frequency: three-term systems (one form for each denotation) and two two-term systems (past/nonpast and future/nonfuture). In the latter, the present is associated in both form and denotation with either the past or future. We have also seen some logical and conceptual reasons for these patterns, most notably that the two- and three-term systems do not interrupt the continuity of the time line.

8.232. *Metrical Tense*

In the previous section, we examined how languages construe the time line as an undifferentiated extent, marking only past, present, and future. Here we look at how some languages take the basic time line and measure it in intervals. Tense that operates in this manner is known as *metrical tense* (Chung and Timberlake 1985), though it is also frequently discussed under the rubric of *remoteness systems* (Dahl 1985) or *degrees of remoteness* (Comrie 1985). Compared to the number of languages that use vectorial tense, metrical tense is much less widespread, though frequently found in the Bantu, Amerindian, Oceanic, Aleut, and Caucasian families.

In metrical tense, the time line is segmented into intervals with varying degrees of specificity. One way to think about metrical tense is to say that all tense systems are vectorial in that they presuppose the time line and extents thereon, but some languages compute fixed lengths on these vectors and then grammaticalize these measurements in the verbal system. Alternatively, we might say that metrical systems *measure the relation* between the tense locus and event frame, rather than simply locate the event frame as a point.

Even though metrical tense measures the time line, it is still a system of temporal deixis and brings with it the same semantic and formal associations as a vectorial system (no doubt, also, because a metrical system can be seen as an interval overlay on a vectorial system). In metrical systems, intervals in the past have the typical associations with completeness, removal, hypotheticality, and, in general, distal time. Likewise, the measures of the future imply potentiality, nonactuality, and the like.

Moreover, the regularities of encoding that we have observed for vectorial systems also apply generally to metrical systems. There are many examples of binary metrical systems. Luvale, for example, appears to be basically a future/nonfuture system, even though it is metrical. Horton (1949) observed that the meanings of the present have been appropriated by the past and the past and the present pattern together, in contrast to the future: a classic future/nonfuture system. Hua and Guaraní, two metrical systems, are also future/nonfuture (Comrie 1985; Ultan 1978a).

With the fundamentals of metrical tense established, we can turn to an enumeration of the kinds of intervals denoted in metrical systems. Our goal here is to examine the temporal values that are consistently grammaticalized and the nature of the cut off points on the time line that determine the intervals.

We look at three broad classes of metrical division: hodiernal tense, or today/not today; hesternal tense, or yesterday/not yesterday (and its complement, tomorrow/not tomorrow); multiple divisions beyond these (four or more intervals).

8.2321. Hodiernal Tense: Today/Not Today

The basic distinction made in metrical tense systems is between today and not today, and so the time line is initially carved up from the center outward, as we might expect to be the case in any deictic system, where the reference point is the here-and-now. Systems that make the distinction between today and not today are generally known as *hodiernal systems* (from the Latin *hodie*, 'day').

The crux of a hodiernal system is the criterion for deciding what 'today' covers. The determination often has cultural restrictions, but even there it is a function of how the naive model of time construes the boundaries of the interval of today. In most cases, however, the boundary between today and not today is determined by the solar day.

In Nkore Kiga, there is a tense distinction between earlier today and yesterday; the latter is defined, according to Taylor (1985: 152), as "anything occurring prior to the speaker's awakening from the previous night's rest." Thus, in Nkore-Kiga, the today/not today boundary is a function of the experience and consciousness of daylight. In Ewondo (Redden 1980), the distinction between today and not today is drawn on the basis of the previous sunset: the new day, today, begins with the setting of the sun of the previous day. Nkore Kiga and Ewondo thus choose opposite sides of the same boundary to define the today/not today distinction: in Nkore Kiga, the presence of new daylight forms the denotation; in Ewondo, the expiration of old daylight has the same effect.[6]

The hodiernal system can apply equally to the past or the future. That is, the interval of not today can be projected equally backward (yesterday) or forward (tomorrow) from the interval of today. Though the general principle in all studies

---

[6]Interestingly enough, it appears that the intrusion of Western culture and temporal measurement on Ewondo has begun to affect the tense system. Redden (1980: 84) remarks that only older Ewondo draw the today/not today boundary with the previous sunset; younger speakers now tend to measure the time line by the Western clock and draw the line for the today/not today interval at midnight. This semantic variation thus has a neat parallel in stratified usage.

of tense and time is that more distinctions tend to occur in the past than in the futurᵒ, thus suggesting that the today/not today distinction ought to arise most frequently in the past, as today/yesterday, it is very easy to find numerous examples of today/tomorrow encodings.

Grebo illustrates the symmetry of the today/not today opposition applied to both the past and future. An event in the present is encoded in the today tense (all examples from Innes 1966: 55; tones not indicated):

38. ne du-   e   bla.
    I   pound Today rice
    I pound rice today.

Example (38) is compatible with any subinterval of today, earlier or later, and so (38) may also mean 'I pounded rice, but still today,' or 'I will pound rice, but still today.' When the event frame precedes today, the event is encoded in the yesterday tense:

39. ne du-   dǝ   bla.
    I   pound Yesterday rice
    I pounded rice yesterday.

When the event frame follows today, the event is marked in the tomorrow tense:

40. ne du-   a   bla.
    I   pound Tomorrow rice
    I will pound rice tomorrow.

Grebo nicely illustrates the application of the hodiernal interval to all parts of the time vector, but we should note here that in making a split between today and not today, languages often encode past and future subintervals in the interval for today, and this narrower division can take the place of a specific and well-defined measurement of today. We have seen this with the Grebo data (38), where the interval for today can take a future or past reading, provided that this subinterval is contained in the interval of today. To put this another way, often the today/not today split is captured by splitting 'today' itself, and then letting the subintervals contrast with 'yesterday' and 'tomorrow.'

A language that follows this option is Aghem. Hyman (1979: 86–93) notes that the language is metrical, but has no basic today interval. Coincidence with the tense locus is handled either by aspect or by one of two subintervals of today. There is the recent past, 'past on today,' signalled by *mɔ̀*:

41. ò   mɔ̀   bò fíghâm.
    he Past/Today hit mat
    He hit the mat earlier today.

And there is the recent future, 'future on today,' signalled by sì:

42. ò sì   bòó fìghàm.
     he Fut/Today hit   mat
     He will hit the mat later today.

These subintervals contrast on the time vector with a well-defined interval for not today, both in the past and future. So an event frame located before today—and thus before the subinterval 'past on today'—takes *mɔ*, but with a different tone:

43. ò mɔ́   bò fíghâm.
     he Past/Today hit mat
     He hit the mat before today.

The same result is found in the future, though there is a separate form, not a tone change, and this signals that the event frame is situated in an interval that begins some time after the end of the subinterval 'future on today':

44. ò lɔ́   bóo fìghàm.
     he Fut/Today hit   mat
     He hit the mat after today.

This interpretation of the today/not today split (more exactly, the today/after today and before today split) points up a larger issue in considerations of metrical tense. What we are really talking about here is a remoteness system that functionally assigns values to sections of a scale. As long as the proper intervals are structurally present—*as long as a boundary is drawn*—the system meets the definition of a today/not today distinction. That is, subintervals of today are sufficient to capture the today interval.

8.2322. Three Intervals: Hesternal and After Tomorrow

The simplest metrical cut of the time line is into a hodiernal interval. But most languages do not stop there and customarily encode some temporal area more removed from the not today interval into the past, the future, or both, yielding three-interval systems: 'today' plus two before or after. However, because of the general prevalence of past time over future distinctions, the most widely found system is a three-term metrical past: today, not today (=yesterday), and before yesterday; the rarer three-term future is today, not today (=tomorrow), and after tomorrow (Comrie 1985).

When the language has a yesterday/before yesterday distinction, it is said to have *hesternal tense* (from the Latin *hesternus*, 'yesterday'). No received terminology exists for a tomorrow/after tomorrow boundary. Typically, the area of the time line beyond the not today interval (yesterday or tomorrow) is also aligned with some sense of general remoteness.

The time line is a scale, and so the interval of not today in the past is only roughly equal to yesterday and is thus more like a near past. Some languages may choose to denote this interval by assigning a more particular value, as 'yesterday,' but if the denotation is a bit vague or the boundary more fluid than that, no harm is done to the metrical nature of the system. The same observations hold for not today in the future, and for the intervals beyond those. A three-term system in effect sets up a structure that sequences time periods by culturally defined boundaries on the vector. Actual practice sometimes allows these units to correspond with traditional solar units, but there is no reason to require this correspondence, because intervals by degrees of remoteness work just as well on the scale *as a scale*.

Grebo, which we used to illustrate the hodiernal interval and its oppositions, nicely exemplifies the tendency toward a three-way opposition. We already know that Grebo encodes both kinds of not today, specifically yesterday and tomorrow, as per (39) and (40). But it can also encode an interval extending beyond each, following the unbounded vector into the past and future (examples from Innes 1966: 55; tones deleted in (45a), but tense marker in (45b) has tone to differentiate from (39)):

45a. ne du-   da   bla.
     I   pound Before Yesterday rice
     I pounded rice before yesterday. (i.e., some time in the
        nonimmediate past)
  b. ne du- $də_2$ bla.
     I   pound After Tomorrow rice
     I will pound rice after tomorrow.

A similar pattern can be seen in Luganda. Ashton, Ndawula, and Tucker (1954: 122–24) observed that the language encodes two degrees in the past, a not today interval whose boundary is defined by roughly the past 12 hours before the moment of speech, and a more general past tense that extends beyond this 12-hour past. The two take the same infix, -*a*-, but differ on the form of the stem, with the simple form associated with the more remote past:

46a. w- a-   labye ki.
     you Near Past see   what
     What did you see (in the past 12 hours)?
  b. w- a-   laba ki.
     you Far Past see   what
     What did you see (some time ago)?

The same oppositions hold in the future, where it is possible to encode an event as situated in the interval of tomorrow, by the infix -naa-, or in some interval after tomorrow, by the infix -li- [the verb stem in (47) changes to *raba* because of phonetic reasons]:

47a. a- naa-   laba ki.
     he Near Fut see   what
     What will he see (tomorrow)?

   b. a- li-   raba ki.
     he Far Future see   what
     What will he see (at some time in the future)?

By these examples we can clearly see how language treats the time line metrically beyond the today/not today split. 'Before yesterday' and 'after tomorrow' are associated with general remoteness, though more languages distinguish yesterday/before yesterday, or have a hodiernal system.

8.2323. Four or More Intervals

Some languages, though comparatively few, divide the time line into four or more intervals on each side of the present. Regularities in these tenses are fairly hard to come by, a problem complicated by the paucity of representative systems. According to Comrie (1985), Mabuiag has a four-term past and Bamileke-Ngyeboon has a four-term future; Yagua has a five-term past; Kiksht, depending how it is evaluated, has a six- or seven-term past tense. Apparently, no language has more than six or seven distinctions, so there is at least one regularity: Metrical systems prefer a smaller number of intervals over a larger number.

For the purpose of illustration, let us just consider the tense markings for the past in Yagua (Comrie 1985: 99):

48a. jásiy past on today
   b. jáy   yesterday
   c. siy   within a few weeks
   d. tíy   within a few months
   e. jadá   distant past

Even with the multiple past tense, Yagua still follows the basic rule of a today/not today distinction, notably executed through a subinterval for today. The Yagua tense system then encodes time before yesterday, as expected.

Though the data on systems with four or more intervals seems a bit unwieldy, we can nevertheless attempt a few generalizations to close this discussion. First, metrical tense systems do not use equal interval scales. Unlike the scale on a ruler, for example, where the distance between each kind of subdivision is the same for any instance of the subdivision (i.e., the distance between inch one and inch two is the same as between inch four and inch five), metrical tense does not subdivide the time line into equal segments. The absence of equal intervals is heightened by multiple-term systems, where it appears that the size of the interval *increases* as the degree of removal from the tense locus increases. Intervals at the very remote ends of the time line are quite unspecific and cover rather wide ranges of time, from weeks to months, to generic distant past. We might then characterize multiple interval systems as having a *positive correlation between degree of removal from the tense locus and size of the interval encoded.*

Moreover, the increase of terms in multiple interval systems does not seem to be restricted to any particular position on the time line. Comrie (1985) observes that in three-term systems, the tendency is for additional subdivisions to be located in the interval of not today: That is, the interval of today is not usually subdivided to increase the number of terms. This suggests that proliferation of terms in metrical systems is to be found at intervals removed from the present (=today). But such a generalization does not hold very well for systems with four or more intervals. Some have more distinctions closer to today, and increase the metrical units by finely dividing the vector close to the center. Others, however, divide the scale further out. In Comrie's data, Yandruwandha has a five-term system in the past, but three are close to the today interval. On the other hand, Araona also has a five-term system, but three appear to be more skewed toward the remote end of the past. Work clearly needs to be done here to see where multiple-term systems and metrical tense in general tend to have finer differentiation.

Finally, some languages choose rather idiosyncratic intervals as they increase the units. Mabuiag has a special tense for 'last night'; Kiksht has one for 'last week.' The most remote past tense in Yagua evidently also denotes 'legendary time.' Whether or not there are implicit limits on such choice of intervals remains to be seen, though clearly in many cases the answer may lie in how the cosmology of the culture speaking the language necessitates finer and more peculiar intervals.

8.2324. Summary

This section has discussed metrical tense, or the measuring of the time line by intervals. We have seen that metrical tense presupposes the basic extension of the time line characteristic of vectorial tense and indeed appropriates the semantic associations of those tenses (e.g., past time and removal) as well as the encoding regularities (e.g., binary tense). We have also seen the kinds of distinctions that characterize metrical tense: today/not today, or hodiernal, is the basic metrical opposition, and frequently languages further divide the interval for today; three-term systems with today versus yesterday/before yesterday (hesternal) and tomorrow/after tomorrow are also found, though the former type is more common. Multiple interval systems are the least frequent, though they are regular in that the size of the interval denoted increases with its removal from the present.

8.3.   UNIFIED TREATMENTS OF TENSE

We have surveyed the nature and distribution of tense, observing how any tense system must be organized and how different languages make use of these fundamental requirements. In doing so, we have emphasized the deictic organization of tense in its superimposition on the naive mental model of time that a speaker brings to the task of expression. We have seen how the basic elements of deixis translate into temporal organization in terms of tense locus, event frame, directionality and remoteness of tense, absoluteness or relativity of the temporal reference, and so on. We have also seen how languages may construe the time line as either an undifferentiated or unitized extent. All along we have tried to point out how these semantic notions tend to be encoded by looking at the surface regularities of tense.

Given this descriptive work, we now turn our attention to theoretical issues in the study of tense systems. We concentrate on the kinds of unities derived from tense logic and formal accounts of the temporal anchoring of events. In particular, we look at how tense can be accounted for by the mechanisms of logical operators and anaphora. The reduction of tense to these two severely limits the descriptive and theoretical issues surrounding tense. However, before we look to the logical work, we should remark that the applicability to tense and time of notions used in the analysis of space and aspect is quite striking and cannot be sheer coincidence. Space, time, and aspect appear to rely on a single conceptual substrate.

8.31.   Conceptual Treatment of Tense

8.311.   The Unity of Space, Time, and Aspect

The semantic, philosophical, and psychological literature is full of testimonies to the remarkable conceptual unit of space, time, and aspect, as well as to the empirical priority of spatial notions with regard to tense and time. We ourselves have tried to give aspect an entirely spatial explanation (chap. 7). Piaget (1970) observed that children's temporal notions derive from the cognitive extension of identical spatial concepts; Clark (1973) argues the Piagetian doctrine more closely with respect to semantic development. Bennett (1975) devotes an entire book to the unmistakable convergence of spatial and temporal prepositions; Traugott (1978) argues for the historical priority of spatial meanings in the emergence of temporal meanings. Perhaps most pointedly, a localist theory of language takes space as axiomatic and seeks to derive the major linguistic categories therefrom (Anderson 1973; chap. 5 on localism).

Certainly, the deictic structure of tense itself underscores this connection. Traugott (1978) notes that past tense is generally understood to be the temporal *source,* and the future the temporal *goal,* in relation to the present as tense locus: "one comes from the past [to the present] . . . ; one goes toward the future" (Traugott 1978: 376). Some languages use this directionality as the principal means to determine tense. In Basque, Scottish, Gaelic, and Tibetan, for example, source relations express the past tense; in Egyptian, Irish, Hebrew, and Arabic, goal relations express the future.

Perhaps the strongest evidence for this directional component to tense lies in the fact that many languages have a periphrastic future expressed by *go,* so called *go-futures,* where the *goal orientation* of future time is unmistakable. Languages also have *come-futures,* though less common, but note how this possibility underscores the relevance of directionality to tense. In *come-futures,* the directionality of time shifts its deictic center. It is significant, however, that this is a relatively infrequent choice, suggesting that futurity and movement away from the deictic center, the present, is the dominant cognitive structure for the future (Fleischman 1982).

8.312.   The Emergence of Time

What do such convergences of space, time, and aspect get us beyond the mere suggestion of a unified mental model? These unities accord with a number of accepted facts about the structure and development of tense systems. In emergent linguistic systems, aspectual distinctions tend to precede and ground tense distinctions: implicationally, aspect > tense. The literature on children's acquisition of tense and aspect has long supported this connection (see Aksu-Koç 1988 for a recent review) as does work on the evolution of creoles from pidgins (Bickerton 1981).

We know from the developmental data that aspect is encoded before tense because aspect is more closely allied with *the event as a whole* (its internal contour) whereas tense appears to be an operator secondarily assigned to an event. Nevertheless, aspect and tense are conceptually related because aspect is the pattern of an event *through time* whereas tense is the grammaticalization *of time.* Rephrasing the implicational hierarchy of aspect and tense, we might then ask how nondeictic time (aspect) gives rise to deictic time (tense). Creole languages provide a basic answer to this question. In the development of creoles from pidgins, closed and open aspects (what Bickerton calls *punctual* and *nonpunctual*) engender tense distinctions, with the past tense, for example, emerging out of closed aspects.

The same pattern is found in the developmental data, though more of the specifics are known. Children's tense systems begin with a lack of differentiation between tense locus and event frame. Events are first distinguished *only with relation to each other,* by their internal properties or aspect. Temporal ordering then proceeds gradually *outward from the tense locus,* first of all into the past, where perfectives and telics (as in creoles) derive past tenses. For children, past time is a simple extension into remoteness with immediate pasts preceding remote pasts. The encoding of this elementary temporal ordering is first carried out by deictic adverbs of proximal and distal time. As the deictic structure of time comes under control—no doubt also as the result of cognitive developmental factors as outlined by Piaget—more complex tenses emerge: whence the fact that perfects overwhelmingly follow simple tenses in the developmental sequence.

We can summarize the development of tense from aspect by saying that remoteness and temporal extension give rise to simple temporal ordering, which then gives rise to complex differentiation. In other words, the time line is first established as an extent into remoteness, then differentiated by simple ordering carried out by proximal/distal markers, followed by complex ordering and deictic time. The simplest way to explain this pattern is by appeal to an underlying conceptual unity in space, time, and aspect. If a single *spatial* mental model underlies aspect and tense, then the differentiation of aspect from tense ought to proceed as it does, on spatial grounds.

8.32.   Formal Approaches to Tense

In section 8.31, we looked at a unified treatment of tense in terms of a single mental substrate. Here we look at another kind of unification of tense notions—that done through logical analysis. Formal approaches to tense seek to reduce the surface variety of tenses in language to a small set of formal objects and operations.

In what follows, we examine a few of the basic findings of tense logic to see how the formal analysis of tense may shed light on linguistic time. In doing so, we take up two principal concerns: the relation of tense to quantification, and therefore to scope; the connection of tense and anaphora and the role of reference time in tense systems. Before we go to this work, we look at Reichenbach's (1947) seminal study of tense logic for a statement of the basic formal issues.

8.321. Reichenbach's Formal Representation of Tense

In one of the seminal works on the formal representation of tense, Reichenbach (1947) proposed the basic logical machinery needed to analyze tense systems. All tenses are generated from the grouping and relative ordering of three positions on the ideal time line: the *point of speech, S* (our tense locus), *the point of event, E* (our event frame), and *the point of reference, R* (our reference time).

With a series of simple formulas built from this notation, he represented all tense relations in a simple and unified manner.

The simple tenses require that the reference time associate with the other two points on the ideal time line. The simple past is fundamentally R,E → S (this notation differs slightly from Reichenbach's but captures the ideas). The reference and event time are indistinct because the simple past requires only that the event be seen as removed from the point of speech. The simple present coalesces all temporal positions, requiring no differentiation of event, moment of speech, and reference time: $\overrightarrow{\text{S,R,E}}$. The simple future tense uses the reverse of the mechanisms for the past tense, splitting the point of event from the point of speech and reference time and forcing the moment of speech and reference point to coincide: S,R → E.

The perfect tenses are defined by the relative position of the reference time. The pluperfect requires both that the point of speech look back on the point of event and the point of reference, and that the event precede the reference: E → R → S. This representation contrasts with that for the present perfect, which in implying some relevance of a past event on the present, bring the reference time of the past event into the point of speech: E → S,R. Future perfects are like pluperfects, with the ordering of temporal positions reversed: S → E → R.

The benefits of such a formal account should not be underestimated. Reichenbach's representations capture the basic issue of tense—the relative ordering of temporal positions on a time line—and do so in an efficient manner through the regular application of a rule of ordering with symmetric results. This picture of tense is appealing from its logical simplicity. However, whereas Reichenbach's formal account of tense often lacks specifics and overlooks subtleties of meaning that come part and parcel of the tenses it proposes to represent, his basic insights still underlie much of the current work on formal (and even non-formal) accounts of tense. To get the proper coverage, we are forced to bring in additional logical apparatus. Recent approaches to tense build on Reichenbach's work and improve our view of the formal structure of tense. We consider two more specific advances: tense as a logical operator and the relation of tense to anaphora.

8.322. *Tense and Scope*

8.3221. Tense as an Operator

In the current formal literature, tense is a *logical operator* whose domain is the sentence (though see Bach 1980). For our purposes, this means that tense can be extracted from an expression and occur as a higher-level function that has scope over the other elements of the expression, much like negation, quantification, or conjunction. We may analyze a quantified expression by extracting the quantifiers as operators with scope over the individuals and events and order them relative to each other to produce different interpretations (*Every boy saw a girl*: Every, A (. . .) vs. A, Every (. . .), see chap. 2). Tense is also an operator, so we can analyze it with the same mechanisms, extracting the tense from the expression and letting everything following it fall within its scope. Hence, formally, *John ran* is Past (run (John)).

Now consider (49) (after Enç 1986):

49. Every prom queen knew Tom.

Sentence (49) is ambiguous, depending on when the prom queens are prom queens. On one reading, (49) means 'all prom queens knew Tom in the past,' and is paraphrased by something like *Every then-prom-queen knew Tom then*. But (49) may also mean 'every prom queen who is such now knew Tom then,' where there is a split between the time of knowing and the time of the status of the prom queens. In this case, (49) has a paraphrase in *Every current prom queen knew Tom in the past*.

Formally, the ambiguity of (49) is just like the ambiguity of *every boy saw a girl* and has the identical solution. The two interpretations of (49) are a function of the interaction of the tense and quantifier as operators. On the first reading, the tense has scope over all the elements in the expression: Past (know (Tom (Every (prom queen))). That is, all information—knowing, prom queens, and Tom—is in the past: whence the proper paraphrase. On the second reading, the relative scope of the past and quantifier shift: Every (prom queen (Past (know (Tom)))). In this case, not every prom queen is in the past, precisely because the quantifier is outside the scope of the tense as an operator. As with different relative scope of quantifiers, the contrasting interpretations of the effect of tense on the elements in the expression can be captured by a scope difference (see McCawley 1981: 357 for additional discussion).[7]

One great theoretical benefit of this account is its provision for a unified logical treatment of tense in terms of all operators. The same mechanisms that produce interpretations for quantifiers and negation, for example, can be reused for tense, and their interactions can be predicted. In this way, proposals for the logical semantics of natural languages are severely reduced because the mechanisms can be generalized across different areas of the semantic system.

8.3222. Tense and Semantic Content

If tense can be treated like quantification, and thus like any other operator, then we ought to expect the same semantic effects that apply to the logic of quantification to apply to the logic of tense. Recall that the semantic content of both the

---

[7]The fully correct analysis for the second interpretation is different in many details from what I have given here. The main point of differential scope of operators remains, however. See Enç (1986).

quantifier and the entity quantified affect the interpretation of quantification as a whole (see chap. 2). Does the same phenomenon hold for tense as an operator? Enç (1986) spends considerable effort pointing out that it does, though not exactly in these terms. Not all expressions allow the scope shift identified in (49). Consider (50) (after Enç 1986):

50. Every fugitive is in jail.

Sentence (50) must have an interpretation in which the quantifier is outside the scope of the present tense because (50) can mean only 'every past fugitive is now in jail': Every, Present (. . .). In point of fact, with the scope shift—Present, Every (. . .)—the expression is a contradiction: ?? *All current fugitives are in jail.* How can a fugitive be in jail, if part of the meaning of fugitive is 'someone who is not in jail'?

This problem is known as *the missing tense operator* because there appears to be a phantom past tense lurking somewhere to provide the proper temporal domain for *fugitive*. The solution is to assign the missing temporal meaning to the entity itself, as Enç (1986) argues. Interestingly enough, when we use an expression for an entity with no such inherent temporal property, we do not get the scope restriction:

51. Every boy is in jail.

Example (51), though false, may have an interpretation where the present tense has scope over the quantifier. In making the temporal restriction part of the entity, we produce a solution that is analogous to that proposed for variable scope of quantifiers: We allow the semantic content of the element within the scope of the operators to affect the interpretation. This is exactly what we need to account for quantification, and thus the generalizability of the operator solution to tense is further supported (see Enç 1986 for much more on this).

This approach to tense as an operator raises a number of interesting theoretical questions that remain to be answered. What kinds of entities tend to fall outside the scope of tense? (In Enç's terms, what are the indexical properties of entities that preclude a scope solution?) Moreover, do languages mark these scope relations at all? Some languages, like Turkish, apparently signal the domain of scope for certain operators, like those for focus. Does such a device overtly differentiate these scope variations associated with tense? And what about languages that are said to be tenseless? Do they lack such scope variations? Does aspect produce similar results? (If not, then aspect may not be an operator: that is, may be a different logical object from tense.) Are scope variations with tense more likely to occur with certain tenses over others? How does scope interaction relate to vectorial and metrical tense? Does the specificity of the interval in metrical tense preclude or engender scope interactions?

The answers to such questions remain to be seen. But it is eminently clear that the questions would never have been asked had tense not been analyzed in logical terms. So, the very possibility of tense as an operator and the logical and empirical questions that follow therefrom owe their existence to formal theories like Reichenbach's and those of recent tense logic, which seek a unified account of tense as a formal object.

8.323.   Tense and Anaphora

8.3231.   Time and Coindexing

The scope of operators is one logical phenomenon whose function has shed light on a unified formal account of tense; another is *anaphora,* or the means by which language keeps track of the identity of individuals in expressions. A classic example of anaphora is pronominalization, which is the referential dependency between a full expression for the entity, an *antecedent,* and a reduced form, or *pro-form,* that refers to the same entity, as illustrated in the following example:

52. $Mary_1$ hates $Fred_2$ and he_2 hates her_1.

In (52), *Mary* and *Fred,* in the first clause, are the antecedents of the anaphoric, referentially dependent forms, the pronouns *he* and *her,* in the second clause (the subscripts indicate co-reference).

Such coindexing, or sharing of identities, is not restricted to nominal anaphora. Even the most cursory observation indicates that temporal phenomena can also be involved in the same anaphoric dependencies as entities:

53. $Fred_1$ saw $Mary_2$ yesterday$_3$ and he_1 spoke to her_2 then$_3$.

In (53), not only is the identity of entities tracked through pronouns but the time of the first sentence is also reinvoked, and done by means of a referentially dependent pro-form, *then.*[8]

The anaphoric possibilities of time make it a prime candidate for logical analysis because truth via correct reference is at the heart of formal accounts of meaning to begin with (see chap. 2). The tracking of identities through coindexing must therefore be part and parcel of logical semantics because the truth value of an expression like (53) depends on the recovery of the identities of individuals.

The connection between tense and anaphora has long been observed, and there have been a number of proposals to treat temporal anaphora along the same

---

[8]Space can also be involved in antecedent/pro-form dependencies:

i. $Fred_1$ saw $Mary_2$ at the store$_3$. He_1 said hello to her_2 there$_3$.

lines as nominal anaphora (Partee 1973). According to the basic argument, tense itself is anaphoric, or, as Partee (1984) says, tense is like a pronoun that refers to some temporal antecedent, and subsequent temporal anaphors, like *then,* reinvoke this temporal antecedent.

One advantage of this kind of analysis is the fact that it provides a unified treatment of all anaphoric devices. The formal mechanisms for indexing the identities of all elements in an expression are the same at base, but just apply to different domains. As in the general analysis of logical operators, the similar treatment of temporal and nominal anaphora provides a simplified analysis and reduces both the descriptive and explanatory task considerably. As Partee (1984) remarks, the unification of apparently disparate phenomena, like temporal and nominal anaphora, is a major advance in itself.

8.3232. Indefinite Antecedents and the Role of Reference Time.

The lesson of formal studies of anaphora for tense in general might stop with the important claim to a unified analysis if there were not some additional critical problems with the formal study of nominal anaphora that spill over into tense. Partee (1984) surveys a number of issues in nominal anaphora; one critical issue is the fact that coindexing of entities may occur *even when the antecedent entity is indefinite.* This may be seen in the famous "donkey sentences" (Geach 1962):

54. Every farmer who owns a donkey$_1$, beats it$_1$.

There are a number of problems with the logical form of (54) that make a straightforward coindexing of entities difficult. For example, the indefinite article in *a donkey* ought to be logically represented as $\exists$, but the interpretation is more like $\forall$—that is, there is a specific donkey for every farmer. More to our purposes, note that the antecedent for the pronoun is not really referential (in formal analysis, it is *existentially quantified*). In simple terms we may ask: What does *it* refer to? In the events of (54), there is in fact *no specific donkey* to serve as the antecedent of the pronoun, so how can identities be tracked by anaphora if there is no particular individual to anchor the indexation?

To complicate matters, the same phenomenon is found in temporal anaphora. Consider the following:

55. Allan drank during his sophomore year$_1$ and had a good time then$_1$.

The temporal anaphor *then* is referentially dependent on the temporal phrase in the first clause, *during his sophomore year,* but we may legitimately ask: When is the time specified by *during his sophomore year?* This interval is just as indefinite as the entity serving as the antecedent in (54). How can there possibly be successful tracking of temporal identity when the antecedent has no identity?

This problem, and others like it, has been given a unified solution in formal semantics, and the analysis raises some interesting issues for tense as a whole. The gist of the solution is to change the nature of the antecedent in such expressions so as to maintain anaphora to specific individuals and thereby eliminate the problem (see Heim 1982; Kamp 1981; Partee 1984).

The details of the solution are complex and a full explanation will take us far afield. Nonetheless we can get a feel for the proposal. Kamp argues that the domain of antecedent/proform dependencies for nominal anaphora is *discourse, not logical form* (i.e., not truth conditions or formal interpretation, not semantics, as such). In this view, discourse sets up a running file of entities spoken about, all of which are specific, no matter how indefinite they appear in logical form. These *discourse entities* serve as antecedents for anaphora (see also Givón 1984; Seuren 1985; chap. 3). So, an expression like (54) introduces two discourse entities, 'farmer' and 'donkey,' and the pronoun takes the latter as its antecedent, regardless of the logical and semantic properties of the entity that *donkey* represents. From the standpoint of its logical form in discourse, *a donkey* in an expression like (54) may serve as the antecedent to a pronoun not because of its logical specificity but because it has an *address in the ongoing discourse.* Only when *a donkey* is interpreted logically does it become indefinite (or existentially quantified). So, Kamp's solution to "donkey sentences" and related phenomena is to delete the indefiniteness of the antecedent by drawing a distinction between its *logical representation,* where is *is* indefinite, and its *discourse representation,* where it is specific and individuated. Hence, nominal anaphora is carried out at the level of coindexing of addresses in discourse. Nominal anaphora is possible because the nature of the antecedent has been changed.

For temporal anaphora, Partee (1984) proposes that we adopt a solution similar to Kamp's but just apply it to time. She argues that we still treat nominal and temporal anaphora in a unified manner, but, as in the case of nominal anaphora with indefinite antecedents, we again change the nature of the antecedent. Following Reichenbach's model, she argues that all tenses have not only an event frame but also a reference time (see sec. 8.321), and *the reference time is the antecedent for temporal anaphora* (not, as might be expected, the event frame). Consider (55) again. Why is the temporal anaphor *then* acceptable? *Then* refers not to the event frame of drinking, but to the overtly specified reference time, *during his sophomore year.* In (55), the event frame is expressed by *drank,* and its reference time in the past is the interval indicated by the adverbial phrase. Note that if we delete the adverbial phrase, temporal anaphora is questionable:

56. ? Allan drank$_1$ and he had a good time then$_1$.

If (56) is to be understood at all, it must be interpreted with reference to a specific, though *unstated,* time in the past. In such a case, *then* means 'the time when Allan drank,' which is, of course, the implicit reference time for the event frame. Note further that the more usual explicit indication of the reference time uncontroversially allows the temporal anaphor:

57. Allan drank yesterday$_1$, and he had a good time then$_1$.

Partee thus points out that it is wrong to claim that temporal anaphora can take an indefinite antecedent, which complicates matters in the same way that "donkey sentences" complicate nominal anaphora. Rather, *the antecedent for all temporal anaphora is the reference time of the event frame.* Furthermore, drawing on the mechanisms that Kamp proposes for nominal anaphora, she argues that every instance of an event in discourse brings its own reference time. Hence, just as discourse entities are freely introduced and may serve as individuated antecedents for nominal anaphora, so every event introduces its own reference time, which likewise serves as the antecedent for all temporal anaphora. In this way, nominal and temporal anaphora are *re-unified,* though with a bit of a twist in logical machinery (the antecedents are now discourse entities vs. reference time), and this allows a more comprehensive solution to all anaphora, while avoiding the problem of indefinite antecedents.

8.3233.   The Lessons of Tense and Anaphora

What do these results do for our larger considerations of tense? Most pointedly, they suggest that we ought to pay more attention to how the reference time works in relation to tense because the reference time is the temporal equivalent of the unquantified discourse address for nominal anaphora. Focus on the reference time allows us to explain the fact that in many languages, narrative discourse requires that the time of an event in the narrative be explicit only when there is a change of time. Quite often in languages, the first event in the narrative is encoded for time, and the time of this event percolates to all subsequent events—themselves unspecified for tense/time—until there is an explicit change. If there is a tense change, the newly introduced time then serves as the temporal anchor for the subsequent events.

Such a process happens in Sùpyíré. According to Carlson (1987), Sùpyíré narratives mark the time of the first event in the narrative through tense on the verb, and subsequent events, encoded as verbs, inherit that time reference even though their overt forms lack any tense marking. This short narrative illustrates the process:

58. ceè- ŋi wà u mà?a pyà si
    woman Def Indic Pro Past child give birth to
    kà u ú fáá̗.
    and she Seq paralyzed
    A certain woman gave birth to a child and then she became paralyzed.

Though the details of Sùpyíré narrative are much more complicated than this, especially because the language has markers of event sequencing and thematic continuity, the basic principle of temporal antecedence is clear. Only the first verb is assigned tense, the past in this case. The verb in the second sentence is unmarked, but it nonetheless inherits its time from the first verb.[9]

We can explain this temporal dependency in Sùpyíré through the formal mechanism we have already outlined. The first event in (58) introduces an event frame, *si* 'give birth to,' *and* a reference time, abstractly R_1. A subsequent narrated event has its respective event frame—unspecified for time, like *fáá* 'paralyzed'—and its own reference time, R_2. The second event has a past time interpretation because the reference time for all these events is the value for R_1, the past, whatever the encoding of the events for event frame. What anchors Sùpyíré discourse is *coherence of past reference time*. In this way the reference time serves as a general temporal antecedent for all the events, which refer back to this original reference time for their temporal value.

Two lessons surface here. First, tense is anaphoric, and its antecedent is the reference time. We would not have known this had not the formal analysis of tense as anaphora been modified in the ways that Partee has done, relying on the unified approach to all anaphora derived from Kamp's work on anaphora and discourse representation.

Second, we now have to reexamine the place of definiteness in anaphora as a whole. The solution to "donkey sentences" and indefinite temporal antecedents has been to make definiteness and indefiniteness secondary to the whole matter to begin with. This suggests that we might want to analyze languages across the board for how they treat definiteness and indefiniteness in relation to their nominal and temporal antecedents. Many languages, as is well known, do not mark nominals for definiteness or indefiniteness. Given that the solution to English antecedents requires that English be analyzed exactly like such languages on an abstract level, we might want to pursue the structural consequences of the difference. As Partee (1984: 266) notes: "Our temporal system is . . . more like the nominal system of languages that lack the definite and indefinite article." What other languages are like English in this regard? What are the properties of languages like English, where explicit definiteness or indefiniteness matters to the nominal system, but appears not to have any grammatical ramification in the temporal system? Are there languages where definiteness and time interact in the

---

[9]This sequence is very much like the English colloquial narrative voice:

i . . You know what happened to me yesterday? This guy comes up to me and says . . .

In (i), the explicit time of the events is introduced in the past, but all subsequent events are in the narrative present. However, they are interpreted as in the past and hence inherit their temporal reference in the same way that events in Sùpyíré do (I am indebted to Eggers, 1989, for this observation).

grammatical system? Are there some languages where reference time has a more explicit role? How can this be charted, and what predictions fall out?

Again, we do not have the answers to these questions, but they are interesting problems for future analysis. The linguistic study of time thus owes a great debt to tense logic and its current extensions. Without this work, the precise relationships of definiteness, reference time, temporal antecedence, and tense would have never come to light.

8.33. Summary

In the formal study of tense, we have outlined Reichenbach's proposal for the basics of any logical analysis of tense, the grouping and relative ordering of the point of speech, point of the event, and the reference time, and we have defined simple and perfect tenses in these terms. With these elements of the formal analysis of tense in hand, we have considered two problems in tense logic— tense as an operator and tense as anaphora—which result in a unified formal treatment of tense. As a logical operator, tense interacts with other scope-bearing items and is accountable to the general effects of quantification: relative order of operators and the content of quantified entities. As anaphora, tense functions like a pronoun, taking values from a temporal antecedent. The problem of non-specific antecedents in nominal anaphora ("donkey sentences") spills over into tense as anaphora and solutions similar to Kamp's discourse representation for anaphora apply to nonspecific temporal antecedents. This answer relies heavily on the role of the reference time in discourse to anchor tense. In both cases— tense as operator and as anaphora—we have seen how tense can be given a unified treatment as a formal object.

SUMMARY OF CHAPTER

We began this chapter by defining tense as the grammatical means for locating events in time. We saw how the naive model of time, which accepts the time line and differentiates linguistic time from cultural time, motivated temporal expression. We then studied tense as a deictic system, noting how the choice of the temporal reference point (deictic center), tense locus, determines absolute versus relative tense and how the choice of the temporally located point, event frame, determines simple tenses and perfects. We showed how these deictic points are complemented by direction (past, present, and future) and remoteness (distal and proximal).

For vectorial tense, language construes the relationship of tense locus and event frame as an undifferentiated extent, the most common tense system. Past, present, and future had a number of typical semantic associations, such as removal for the past and intentionality for the future, as well as regular patterns of encoding, with three-term systems, past/nonpast, and future/nonfuture the most common. Metrical tense structures the time line by intervals, usually in terms of today/not today, yesterday/not yesterday, and tomorrow/after tomorrow. Multiple interval systems—those beyond three terms—turned out to be fairly rare.

We saw how aspect precedes tense in emergent linguistic systems and this relation suggest a unified conceptual substrate for space, time, and aspect. We then considered formal approaches to tense: Reichenbach's formal representation of tense and improvements thereon. We spent some time examining the relationship between tense and logical operators and tense and anaphora. As to the former, we saw how tense behaves like other scope-bearing phenomena and adheres to the general effects of the relative order of operators and the content of entities under its scope. As to the latter, we saw how tense takes values from a temporal antecedent and how the problem of nonspecific antecedents in nominal anaphora (donkey sentences), and solutions thereto via Kamp's discourse representation, apply to temporal antecedents. The role of the reference time in discourse turned out to be crucial to the logical treatment of tense.

QUESTIONS FOR DISCUSSION

1. Consider the following sentence from Japanese (Soga 1983: 51):

i. samaku na-   ru   to   yuki ga   hut- ta.
    cold   become Pres when snow Subj fall Past
    When it became cold, it snowed.

(i) refers to a state of affairs where both events, 'become cold' (*samaku na-ru*) and 'snow' (*yuki ga hut-ta* lit. 'snow fell'), are prior to the moment of speech. Why is *na* 'become' in the present tense? Does it help to know that because Japanese is (SOV), *na* is in a subordinate clause? Discuss this example in relation to what you know about absolute and relative tense; compare it to the data from Russian in sec. 8.2212.

2. Consider the following:

i. Fred will have bought a new car tomorrow.

Does *tomorrow* refer to the event frame, the reference time, or both? Note that for (i) to be true, Fred does not actually have to buy the car tomorrow. When does Fred's buying of the car have to occur for (i) to be true? If Fred bought the car before the moment of speech (i.e., in the past), is (i) still appropriate? Once you have answered these questions, consider the relation between the tense in (i), which is the future perfect, and future time. Does (i) *entail* future time: that is, must the event be in the future? Does (i) *implicate* future time: that is, is it highly likely, though not required, for the event to be in the future? (See Comrie, 1985, for more on this.)

3. A cursory survey of metrical and vectorial tense systems suggests that perfect tenses are generally not found in metrical systems. Why should metrical systems not have perfect tenses? Is there any conceptual connection between the structure of perfect tenses and the structure of metrical tenses? Are perfects at all like intervals? Perfects and metrical tenses tend to appear in periphrastic forms, unlike the simple vectorial tenses. Does this encoding pattern affect your answer? If metrical tenses systems do not have perfects, then how do you think these systems express the usual semantic and pragmatic associations of the perfect?

9

Modality and Negation

9.1. INTRODUCTION

Up to this point, we have looked almost exclusively at the semantic structures found in straightforward, positive assertions of fact. But such statements are only a small portion of the entire picture of linguistic expression. Speakers often qualify their statements with respect to believability, reliability, and general compatibility with accepted fact. The area of semantics that concerns the factual status of statements is *modality*. The goal of this chapter is to survey the meanings associated with modality and the resources that languages have to express modal information.

To make this project manageable, we restrict our inquiry almost entirely to *negation, possibility,* and *obligation.* We begin with a short introduction to modality and modal notions, where we describe the variety of concepts subsumed by modality and differentiate modality from mood. Thereafter, we examine the basic parameter of modality, realis/irrealis, and discuss its interaction with other semantic phenomena, such as tense and specificity. With this preliminary information in hand, we proceed to a description of negation, epistemic modality (possibility) and deontic modality (obligation).

Negation is directly connected to factuality through falsity and denial, and so it naturally falls under the rubric of modality. We focus on logical denial and consider some of the well-known issues in negation, like the syntactic diagnostics of negation, variability in negative scope, and negative polarity items. We then discuss epistemic modality, or possibility and degrees of certainty, and deontic modality, or necessity and obligation. Under the former, we survey the kinds of judgments of fact and the evidence for such judgments that languages allow their speakers to express; under the latter, we consider the varieties and degrees of obligation that speakers may encode. Throughout, we try to enumerate the regularities in encoding patterns of these notions.

Once we have an idea of the possible modal notions that languages encode, we turn to theories of the development of modality. We look at the role of pragmatics and conversational implicature in the emergence of epistemic modality from deontic modality. We then use these accounts to propose solutions to the development of negative types, given that negation itself is a modality and therefore subject to the same conditions on development as epistemic and deontic modality.

9.11. Defining Modality

9.111. Modality and the Factuality of Statements

Palmer (1986) defines *modality* as *semantic information associated with the speaker's attitude or opinion about what is said.* Bybee (1985) gives a broader definition: *what the speaker is doing with the whole proposition.* Though these definitions diverge on the particulars, they agree that modality concerns *entire statements,* not just events or entities, and its domain is *the whole expression at a truth-functional level.* Grammatically speaking, modality is associated with the sentence more than its constituents, unlike aspect, for example, which is predictably found with verbs as events.

The notional content of modality highlights its association with entire statements. Modality concerns the *factual status* of information; it signals the relative *actuality, validity,* or *believability* of the content of an expression. Modality affects the overall *assertability* of an expression and thus takes the entire proposition within its scope. As such, modality evokes not only objective measures of factual status, but also subjective attitudes and orientations toward the content of an expression by its utterer.

We can see all these qualities in the following example, which is a fairly untraditional, yet clear, illustration of modality:

1. Apparently, Maria bought another cat.

Sentence (1) does not straightforwardly assert a positive fact. Though (1) is admittedly not negative or counterfactual, it is nonetheless *contingent* or, at least, *attenuated* in its assertability: 'I tentatively assert that Maria bought another cat.' This restriction on its factual status is entirely a function of the sentence adverb *apparently* because without this adverb, the expression is quite determinate: *Maria bought another cat.*

The sentence adverb *apparently* signals the *epistemic stance,* or state of knowledge, of the speaker (Biber and Finegan 1988). In McCawley's (1978) and Fauconnier's (1985) terms, the adverb is *world-creating:* That is, it sets up a *belief context,* or a *possible world,* against which the content of the proposition has to be judged. In more classical philosophical terms, the adverb conveys a *propositional attitude,* an indication of the orientation or commitment of speakers toward the content of their statement.

Natural language counts a wide variety of notions as modal. In one way or another, all the following have been proposed as part of modality (after Palmer 1986): hypotheticality, doubt, supposition, ability, conditionality, potential, counterfactuality, quotation, actuality, realizability, interrogation, negation, possibility, obligation, judgment, and necessity. To these we might add the long list of epistemic stances encoded by sentence adverbs (Biber and Finegan 1988; Koktova 1986): style (e.g., *honestly*), factive attitudinal (e.g., *actually*), nonfactive attitudinal (e.g., *allegedly*), domain (e.g., *biologically speaking*), and so on. Modality is so broad that we need a vocabulary to accommodate a range of criterial attributes like attitudes, worlds, evaluation, and factual status. As we proceed, we try to narrow this vocabulary to a more manageable and hence more useful size. But for now, we should be aware that a full account of modality requires sensitivity to the broad factuality of a statement.

9.112.   Mood and Modality

Frequently in the literature on modality, there is confusion between modality and *mood.* Now that we have a sense of basic content of modality, let us clear up this potential problem right away.

Modality is a semantic phenomenon: It is the content of an expression that reflects the speaker's attitude or state of knowledge about a proposition. *Mood is a grammatical phenomenon,* usually the inflectional expression of a subset of modal denotations (Palmer 1986). However, traditional accounts of mood equate it with modality: For example, subjunctive mood, a grammatical device, is often defined as the way a language *expresses* hypotheticality or uncertainty. But whereas there may be close connections between grammatical forms and semantic content in this regard, mood is a structural property of verbs in certain kinds of clauses.

Some languages have many moods, sets of inflections for verbs to mark the dependency relations between clauses. Bybee (1985: 187) notes that Yupik has moods for consequence, 'when,' condition, 'if,' concession, 'although,' and precession, 'before.' West Greenlandic Eskimo has an inflection, *kuni,* to signal the conditional dependency between two clauses (Fortescue 1984: 56):

2. apuuk- kuni   niri-uma- ssa- aq.
    arrive Cond eat want Fut 3S/Indic
    When he arrives, he will want to eat.

Insofar as mood is determined by *the nature of the overt form,* Eskimo has a conditional mood not because of the notions that the mood denotes, but because the conditional dependency between two clauses surfaces as an inflection on the verb. Mood is a morphosyntactic device that may overlap with or denote modality, but nonetheless is distinct from modality.

9.12. Realis/Irrealis:
The Basic Parameters of Modality

We have surveyed the range of notions that modality covers and examined the distinction between modality and mood. All the while we have been careful to maintain that modality has distinct semantic content. The basic denotation of modality is the opposition of actual and nonactual worlds, or more technically, *realis/irrealis.* The notions underlying deixis provide an explanatory framework for the realis/irrealis opposition.

9.121. Modality as Epistemic Deixis

The assertability of a proposition requires a judgment of relative factuality by the speaker, and this in turn necessitates a reference point against which to make the judgment. Modality thus exhibits all the classic symptoms of deixis. Indeed, Chung and Timberlake (1985) suggest as much; we will say that modality is a kind of *epistemic* (or knowledge-based) *deixis,* and this structure sets the basic conceptual parameters for all modal systems.

In Chung and Timberlake's (1985) view, modality is the way a language encodes the *comparison of an expressed world with a reference world.* If I say *John may go,* I am more particularly asserting: 'with *reference to* the present state of actualized events, I *express* the possibility of a nonactualized state of affairs, namely John going.' The *expressed world,* the state of affairs in the asserted proposition, is the modal equivalent of the deictic located point. The *reference world,* normally the actual world of speech, is the modal counterpart of the spatial and temporal reference point, the here-and-now.

Remoteness and direction likewise enter the picture, but with epistemic value. In saying *John may go,* a speaker indicates there is *distance* between the actual world (the present) and the nonactual world (going) and this nonactual world is *away from* the actual. Compare this account with that needed for *John might go,* which encodes the same epistemic points, but differs on the degree of removal between the actual and nonactual world. Although *may* indicates that the nonactual state of affairs is reasonably likely to happen, or that the speaker is reasonably confident of its realization and is committed to the truth of the assertion, *might* signals that the nonactual state of affairs is more epistemically removed from the present state of affairs, and this has the effect of attenuating the speaker's commitment to the proposition itself.

Modality is an epistemic version of deixis, with the values for the deictic points rewritten in terms of the speaker's state of belief and the relation between those points interpreted as degrees of commitment and likelihood of the actualization of a state of affairs. When the reference world coincides with the expressed world, we get actual modality, or *realis*. When the reference world does not coincide with the reference world, we get nonactual modality, or *irrealis*. This basic dichotomy is a scale, and thus the factual status of a proposition depends on the *extent to which* the two epistemic deictic points diverge; this divergence is translated into possibility, evidence, obligation, commitment, and so on.

Given the variety of structural possibilities that are imaginable from modality as a deictic system, we might expect that languages should differ markedly on what they take to be realis, irrealis, and epistemic distance. But there are many cross-language regularities in this regard. Languages make finer semantic distinctions in the irrealis than in the realis, for the logical reason that there are more ways that states of affairs "can be less than completely actual" (Chung and Timberlake (1985: 241) than actual.[1] In all cases, however, the basic parametric opposition remains: realis, or actual worlds, versus irrealis, or nonactual worlds.

In some languages, this elemental opposition surfaces directly, as in the Austronesian (Chamorro: Chung and Timberlake 1985; Bikol: Givón 1984) and certain Amerindian languages (Takelma: Chung and Timberlake 1985; Jacaltec: Palmer 1986, Craig 1977). We can see this basic distinction clearly in an Oceanic language, Manam. Lichtenberk (1983: 183–93) observes that the language marks the realis/irrealis distinction through subject agreement prefixes on the verb, as illustrated here:

3a. ?u-   púra.
    2S/Real come
    You came.

  b. go-   púra.
    2S/Irr come
    You will come.

The glosses in (3) are only approximate because English carries some of the weight of modality by its tense system. The realis modality is associated with facts, either in the present or past, so (3a) is compatible with any number of glosses—'you came,' 'you are coming'—just as long as the states of affairs have factual status. The irrealis modality, in contrast, is associated with imagined, future, contrary, or imposed events, so (3b) has a range of nonactual interpreta-

---

[1]Compare this with the greater number of distinctions in the past tense, away from today, and in distant space, away from the deictic center. Epistemic deixis follows suit with more distinctions in the irrealis.

tions—'you should come,' 'you ought to come'—again just as long as the factual status of the proposition is attenuated.

Interestingly enough, Manam has a number of further types of irrealis modality: definite, indefinite, and prospective. So Manam accords with Chung and Timberlake's (1985) general observation that finer semantic distinctions appear in the irrealis as opposed to the realis. There are no definite or indefinite realis counterparts in Manam.

9.122. Modality, Tense, and Specificity

Whereas the realis/irrealis poles are encoded directly in some languages, in others these denotations are taken up by different semantic phenomena. The view of modality as epistemic deixis has considerable value here because the other semantic phenomena that support modality are often those that have an obvious deictic structure. Tense, for example, sometimes carries the burden of epistemic stance, with the immediate past associated with removed (and thus realized) states of affairs, the remote past associated with remotely likely events, and future connected to the unachieved and the possible (see Palmer 1986; Vet 1983; Zalta 1987).

Deixis itself often interacts with modality, as can be seen in how personal deictics are restricted to particular epistemic stances. Consider *I may go,* which cannot denote 'permission.' Clearly this restriction results from the pragmatic structure of this kind of utterance, where the directive disallows the deictic center of speech (I, the speaker) to coincide with the deictic epistemic center (I, the speaker). In principle, we should be able to give ourselves permission, but the deictic clash evidently prevents this.

Modality also converges with semantic phenomena that do not have an obvious deictic structure. Frequently, definiteness and specificity interact with modality because definiteness is associated with referentiality and indefiniteness with nonreferentiality. Realis modality is compatible with referentiality insofar as factual states of affairs are more likely to evoke determinate entities. In some languages, nonspecific entities are more likely associated with irrealis modalities, as in Jacaltec, where the irrealis marker may attach to the indefinite article to indicate the nonreferential status of the entity in question (Palmer 1986: 45):

4. x'- 'oc heb ix   say-   a' hun-uj   munlabal.
   Asp start Plur woman look for Fut a   Irreal pot
   The woman started looking for a pot.

With the irrealis marker *uj* suffixed to the indefinite article *hun,* (4) can have only a nonreferential interpretation: 'any old pot.' So in Jacaltec, definiteness and modality converge with the irrealis supporting indeterminate reference.

As we proceed, we see more convergences of modality and other semantic phenomena. For now, it is enough to be prepared for such overlaps, aware as we also are of how modality as epistemic deixis motivates certain convergences to begin with.

We now consider three types of modality, their semantic associations, and their structural patterns. We restrict our inquiry to *negation,* or *contrary to fact information*; *epistemic modality,* or *possibly factual information*; *deontic modality,* or *necessarily factual information.* In terms of epistemic deixis, *negative modality* is constituted by a *divergence between the expressed world and the reference world. Epistemic modality* involves the *potential convergence between the expressed world and the reference world*—states of affairs that *may be actualized*—and issues of *evidence* and criteria for judging an actualized world. *Deontic modality,* or, to use the terminology of Chung and Timberlake (1985), how an event may be imposed on a speaker or addressee, concerns the *obligatory convergence of the expressed world and the reference world.* These three types in no way exhaust modality. They are, however, the traditionally discussed categories and are found in all languages.

9.13. Summary

In this introduction to modality, we have defined modality as the factual status of a statement. As such, modality subsumes a wide range of notions, including possibility, obligation, negation, hypotheticality, doubt, attitude, and the like. We have differentiated modality from mood, the latter a grammatical device for marking clausal relationships whose denotations sometimes reflect modal notions. Finally, we have considered modality in terms of the two parameters of realis and irrealis, which in turn are subsumed by the larger framework of modality as epistemic deixis. Modality requires a reference world, an expressed world, and remoteness and direction between the two. In many languages, this deictic structure surfaces purely in the realis/irrealis distinction; in others, these parameters overlap with tense, person, and specificity.

9.2. NEGATION

9.21. Logical Denial and Propositional Negation

The kind of negation that is usually studied under semantic considerations is *propositional negation* (sometimes called *sentential negation*: see Payne 1985; the basic terminology is from Klima 1964). This is the linguistic counterpart of *logical denial,* determined by the *law of double negation*: two logical denials produce a positive.

We can see the presence of logical denial in the following examples:

5a. The dog did not eat.
 b. The dog never ate.

Examples (5a) and (5b) both mean 'it is false that the dog ate.' Despite the different means for effecting propositional negation, *not* versus *never,* both expressions follow the test for logical denial because the negation of each results in a positive proposition:

6 a. The dog did not not eat. (= the dog ate)
 b. The dog did not never eat. (= the dog ate)

The effects of double denial make propositional negation stand out against other kinds of negatives, like *affixal negation,* the attachment of a bound negative marker to a lexical item. Consider (7), with affixal negation on the adjective:

7. Bob is unhappy.

Let us deny (7) to see if the proper positive effect falls out:

8. Bob is not unhappy.

Not unhappy is not equivalent to *happy* because a not unhappy person is not thereby happy, but could be simply in a normal mind set (see Langendoen and Bever 1973 for the classic study; Horn 1989: 273–308). Thus nonpropositional negation, as in (7), does not involve logical denial because the effect of double negation does not produce a positive result (see also the discussion of scope, sec. 9.22).

9.211. The Informational Structure
of Propositional Negation

These facts about propositional negation and logical denial bring to light a more general consideration of the meaning of propositional negation and our larger project of negation as a modality: the relation of propositional negation to the assertability of information in general. The basic informational structure of propositional negation supports its characterization as a modality. Even though logical denial operates on the entire proposition, it preferentially affects *only that part of the proposition whose factual status, assertability, and commitment could be in doubt,* or only that part of a proposition whose realis mode might be made irrealis.

From a discourse standpoint, all propositions have two informational constituents: the *given,* or background information, and the *new* or asserted information. In Payne's (1985) terminology, these are, respectively, the *contextually bound* and *contextually free* aspects of a proposition. Propositions assert contextually free information against the backdrop of contextually bound information, with *negation preferentially affecting the contextually free portion of a proposition* (see also Givón 1984).

The association of denial with contextually free information is the exact result needed for the view of propositional negation as a modality. Contextually bound information is the anchor for assertions and so is not the kind of information whose factual status can be reduced. It is just unusual for assertions to be built on denials. For these reasons, contextually bound items—for example, presuppositions and definite subjects—are, as a rule, immune to logical denial. Consider (9):

9. Bill did not see the man who came yesterday.

What is denied in (9) is the contextually free event, 'seeing,' not the information in the relative clause, 'who came yesterday.' Significantly, the information in the relative clause is contextually bound as a restrictive clause modifying a definite noun. Example (9) is thus most appropriately glossed 'I say of Bill and the man who came yesterday that it is false that Bill saw him,' where the contextually bound information ('Bill' and 'the man who came yesterday') is outside the scope of propositional negation (see Givón 1984; Payne 1985).

In short, the informational structure of propositional negation accords with its function and status as a modality. Negation affects only that information that could be affected—positive assertions—because, in terms of informational structure, logical denial binds the contextually given to the contextually free and takes only the latter within its scope.

9.212.   *Diagnostics for Propositional Negation*

We have just seen some of the basic semantic facts about propositional negation. The literature provides us with a number of fairly reliable structural tests for logical denial. Here we review these tests and point up how they suggest that we may need a scalar concept of propositional negation.

The basic tests for propositional negation are found in Klima's (1964) seminal study. Additional discussion is provided by Payne (1985) and McCawley (1988). Though these tests have been developed with English in mind, similar results have been found in their use on other languages (see Payne 1985: 198). We look at three of the syntactic diagnostics, all of which rely on how an expression with propositional negation may take a contrastive or noncontrastive continuation: by *too/either*, by *tag questions*, and by *not even*.[2]

---

[2]There is some debate in the syntactic literature over the precise structural domain of these tests—whether, for instance, the tag question indicates that propositional negation attaches to the verb or the

9.2121. Too/Either, Tag Questions, and Not Even

Expressions with propositional negation may generally be continued by *either* and some expression of contrast; they generally disallow continuation with *too* because that implies noncontrastive continuation of a state of affairs. Conversely, sentences without propositional negation take *too*, but not *either*. Compare the following:

10a. Maria did not get a new kitten, and I didn't either/ ??too.
  b. Maria got a new kitten, and I did too/ ??either.

Example (10a), in the negative, accepts *either* and disallows *too*; example (10b), in the positive, accepts *too* and disallows *either*.

Propositional negation is compatible with *positive tag questions*, whereas positive assertions allow *negative tags*. The converses of these diagnostics also hold:

11a. Maria did not get a new kitten, did she/ ?? didn't she?
  b. Maria got a new kitten, didn't she/ ?? did she?

This diagnostic may, of course, be violated for the sake of implicature or pragmatic effect: *So you're an ordinary businessman, Mr. James Bond, are you*? But obviously this is different from the semantic requirements, which force a positive tag for denial and a negative one for affirmation.

An expression with logical denial may be continued with *not even* for contrastive effect; *not even* narrows the domain of reference expressed by the propositionally negated expression (*even*) while maintaining logical polarity (*not*). The opposite effects hold for positive assertions:

12a. Maria did not get a new kitten, not even a cheap one.
  b. ?? Maria got a new kitten, not even a cheap one.
  (cf. Maria got a new kitten, even a cheap one)

These three diagnostics show that a variety of forms trigger propositional negation. Obviously the standard English verbal negator *not* allows the diagnostics, but a number of other forms do likewise. Certain *negative adverbs*, like *never*, have the proper results:

13a. Anna never wet the bed, and she never cried, either/ ?? too.
  b. Anna never wet the bed, did she/ ?? didn't she?
  c. Anna never wet the bed, not even when we expected her to.

---

entire sentence. We do not take up this debate, only because it is more syntactic than semantic. The facts about meaning stay roughly the same regardless of the exact structural effects (see McCawley 1988).

Negated quantifiers trigger the diagnostics:

14a. Not many babies were crying, and not many wet the bed, either/ ?? too.
  b. Not many babies wet the bed, did they/ ?? didn't they?
  c. Not many babies wet the bed, not even those we expected to.

Negative indefinites also are compatible with these structures:

15a. Nobody cried, and nobody wet the bed, either/ ?? too.
  b. Nobody wet the bed, did they/ ?? didn't they?
  c. Nobody wet the bed, not even those we expected to.

Given this variety, we might ask: What are the semantic or conceptual boundary conditions on the triggers of propositional negation? The answer to this question is complicated by the fact that not all negative forms actually trigger propositional negation, or do so to the same extent. Consider *deny,* which arguably means 'assert that something is *not* true.' In spite of its inherent negation, *deny* does not trigger propositional negation:

16a. Bob denied all guilt, and Harry denied it, too/ ?? either.
  b. Bob denied all guilt, didn't he/ ?? did he?
  c. ?? Bob denied all guilt, not even a little bit.
    (cf. Bob denied all guilt, even a little bit)

Nor do items with more overt, affixal negation produce the diagnostics. Consider *dislike:*

17a. Bob dislikes Harry, and Fred dislikes Harry, too/ ?? either.
  b. Bob dislikes Harry, doesn't he/ ?? does he?
  c. ?? Bob dislikes Harry, not even in a good mood.
    (cf. Bob dislikes Harry, even in a good mood)

On the other hand, *seldom,* an inherently negative adverb, triggers *some* of the diagnostics:

18a. Bob seldom went home, and Mary seldom went, either/too.
  b. Bob seldom went home, did he/ didn't he?
  c. Bob seldom went home, not even in the summer.

Seldom, 'not often,' allows both *either* and *too,* and both tags, unlike the usual case of propositional negation, but curiously the adverb allows *not even,* just as ordinary propositional negation should. Compare the behavior of *seldom* with that of *few,* a quantifier with an inherently negative meaning, 'not many':

19a. Few boys came, and few had a good time, either/too.
   b. Few boys came, did they/ didn't they?
   c. ?? Few boys came, not even at midnight.

By (19a), *few* is a propositional negative, allowing *either*, but it also allows *too*. According to (19b), *few* is indeterminate because it allows *both* kinds of tag. By (19c), *few* is not a propositional negator at all, because it disallows *not even*.

Assuming that the diagnostics are reliable, we are forced to say that not all potential propositional negators carry out denial to the same extent. Some are constant, like *not,* but others negate by degree. As McCawley (1988: 588) says, "The differences in their degree of unacceptability probably point to differences in their status as negative," and this comes through in their varied sensitivity to the three diagnostics for propositional negation.

9.2122. Two Factors Motivating Scalar Propositional Negation

It has long been known that a variety of factors affect the status of negation, though all these point to logical denial as a scalar value, with standard verbal negation as the place where all the factors converge. Scalar propositional negation has two principal sources: (a) degree of overtness of the negative; and (b) degree of irrealis modality.[3]

We can see the effect of the first factor, overtness of the negative, by comparing *few* with its more overt negative counterpart *not many. Few* behaves in a scalar fashion, as per (19), where it meets only some of the diagnostics. However, *not many,* as seen in (14), behaves like a standard negative quantifier and meets all the tests of propositional negation. The real meaning difference between *few* and *not many* lies in the overtness of the negative, so overtness itself must affect the strength of denial (note also that serial position is held constant in [14] and [19]).

If degree of overtness of negation contributes to the fuzziness of propositional negation itself, then we should expect languages to diverge markedly on this factor because, after all, degree of overtness is basically a *morphological question,* and obviously languages have different morphological resources. Indeed, Payne (1985) points out that Persian and a number of other languages do not have mechanisms for producing overtly negated quantifiers like *not many* and *not all.* In Persian, there is a form for 'many,' *besyar,* but this cannot take overt negation: ?? *ne-besyar.* Instead, there is a form for 'few,' *kam,* but this has no overt negation (just like its English counterpart) and thus is unlikely to induce full

---

[3]A third source, left-to-right ordering and scope, also affects the tests, but this is such an important issue that it is discussed separately, in section 9.22: see examples (13)–(15) for examples of the left-to-right effect of negatives.

propositional negation. To negate *besyar*, Persian must move it into the scope of verbal negation to functionally reproduce a form like *not many* by syntactic means. Insofar as degree of overtness of the negation of a quantifier correlates with degree of propositional negation, Persian and English markedly diverge in the way they carve up the space of negation, with English having fewer restrictions, in this case, on encoding canonical propositional negation.

Second, the degree of propositional negation is a function of the degree to which the form in question encodes irrealis modality. From the standpoint of modality as epistemic deixis, negation is the mismatch of the expressed world and the reference world, so the strongest propositional negation should be induced by forms that encode the total mismatch. Conversely, those forms that encode less mismatch between the reference world and the expressed world should display fuzzy behavior for propositional negation.

Consider the forms that encode total divergence of the reference and expressed world: *not, never, nobody, no one, none,* and so on. These forms also trigger the diagnostic tests for propositional negation. Now consider the forms that do not meet all the diagnostics: *seldom, hardly, few,* and so on. One thing that characterizes the denotations of these forms is the *partial mismatch* of the reference world and the expressed world. If I say *Bob seldom went home,* for example, I mean that there were times that Bob did not go home and there were times that he did. *Seldom* only partially induces irrealis modality: That is, it is semantically less irreal than the denotation of a form like *never.* Similar claims might be made for the other forms that do not meet all the diagnostics, like *scarcely* and *barely.* To put this in simple terms: The greater the extent to which irrealis modality is induced, the greater the likelihood of full propositional negation.[4]

It seems safe to say that no one knows which of these two factors is more critical for propositional negation. We might surmise, however, that the presence of both factors should induce the strongest propositional negation and the absence of both, or their reduction, should lessen the strength of negation as a whole. The broad scale in between these two poles will be sorted as the resources of the language in question demand, given what the language takes to be overt negation and even irrealis mode.

9.213.   Cross-language Regularities in Surface Form: Verbal Negation

With a sense of the basic semantic and structural facts of propositional negation, we look here at some cross-language patterns in surface expression. We draw on two major studies of surface patterns, Payne (1985) and Dahl (1979), and restrict our attention to negation that surfaces in association with the verb.

---

[4]Note that this difference between full and partial negation parallels the difference between strong and weak determiners: that is, operators that map totally or partially from set to set (see Bach 1989:

Verbal negation, sometimes called *standard negation,* takes a variety of forms, from a fully separate surface form to a bound morpheme. At the extreme, we find that some languages carry out propositional negation through *negative verbs*: that is, forms that encode only denial, but which pattern exactly like verbs. Negative verbs come in two basic forms: (a) a full, or *higher,* verb or (b) a reduced, or *auxiliary,* verb.

The Polynesian and certain Amerindian languages characteristically have higher negative verbs. In these languages, the negative verb functions much like any other verb that takes a sentential complement, like English *believe that, know that,* and so on, which have a clause boundary between the verb and object. For higher negative verbs, there is an identifiable clause boundary between the negative and the rest of the expression. Tongan and Fijian are the usual examples in this regard. Consider the following expression from Tongan (Payne 1985: 208):

20. Na'e 'ikai ke   'alu 'a   Siale.
    Asp Neg Asp go   Abs Charlie
    Charlie didn't go.

In (20), *'ikai* is a full verb because the second aspectual marker, *ke,* occurs only in subordinate clauses in Tongan. There is no other verb in (20), except for *'alu* 'go,' which is the verb of the subordinate clause proper, and so the negative must be functioning as a full verb itself: A subordinate clause has to be subordinate to another verb, and so the only candidate is the negative. Hence, the Tongan expression (20) is structurally [$_s$ [$_s$ na'e 'ikai] [$_s$ ke 'alu 'a Siale]], with the proper clausal bracketing as a result of the verbal status of the negative.

In far more languages, we find negation surfacing as an auxiliary verb. By this, we mean that the negative marker has some of the usual properties of a verb, such as agreement and tense, but it does not structurally select for a clause boundary, like the Tongan higher verb. A number of the Uralic languages work this way, though we can see the auxiliary negative clearly in Yapese (Oceanic) which, as Jensen (1977) notes, has a different negative marker depending on the tense of the main verb. In positive expressions, the future tense is signalled by *raa,* the future marker. But in a negative future expression, *raa* is replaced by a negator suffixed with *-b* to indicate the tense. Compare the following:

21a. ga   raa yaen.
     you Fut go
     You will go.

56–62). Perhaps there is a generalized function in language that maps from one world onto another in total or partial terms.

b. daa- b   ga yaen.
   Neg Fut you go
   You won't go.

In (21b), futurity is encoded by a bound morpheme on the negative marker. This suggests that the negative has verbal properties because it can carry tense, as any normal verb might. However, nowhere in Yapese is there any indication of a clause boundary between the negator and the rest of the expression. Hence, the negator is verblike, but not a full verb.

Much more common than negative verbs is negation either by a simple free form or by bound inflection on the verb. By Dahl's (1979) count, neither is significantly more frequent than the other. Verbal negation by a simple free form is traditionally known as a *negative particle*. English, of course, uses this mechanism, though it may be found in many other unrelated languages. The uninflected negative, *tago,* in Manam is a clear example (Lichtenberk 1983: 385):

22. tamóata tágo ŋá-   te- a.
    man   Neg 3S/Irreal see 1S/Obj
    The man will not see me.

In languages with more synthetic morphology, verbal negation surfaces as a bound verbal form. Bybee (1985: 176) cites Maasai, where the negator is prefixed to the verbal complex. The same phenomenon happens in Nkore-Kiga (Taylor 1985: 59):

23. t- a- ra-   nyweire.
    Neg he Remote Past drink
    He didn't drink a while ago.

These examples of particle and bound negation illustrate a more general distributional fact about the form of propositional negation. The negative generally tends to *precede the verb*. As Bybee (1985: 178) says: "Negation is a category where position with regard to other categories tends to be determined . . . in an absolute left-to-right fashion." We can understand this preference if we consider the scope properties of denial as a propositional operator. The widest scope is usually assigned to the earliest operator, and because the domain of denial is the entire proposition, as it is for any modality, we should find negators just where Dahl (1979) indicates: as early in the expression as possible (see sec. 9.22).

Verbal negation takes forms other than those just listed, but they are relatively rare. Some languages have double particles, like French *ne + Verb + pas.* Dahl (1979) observes that the double construction is also found in Celtic and some Mayan languages. But on the whole, this pattern is relatively infrequent; indeed, French appears to be losing the double particle in favor of simple *pas* (curiously, the retained form is not preverbal, so there may be other changes going on in the language accompanying the negative restructuring though, see Horn 1989).

Within languages, there may even be variations in form depending on the nature and function of the negation itself. Some languages have different negative markers for main clauses versus subordinate clauses. Other have variant forms for negative imperatives and negative existential statements. These facts support the view that the negative is sensitive to the proposition as a whole: Some languages choose to vary the nature of the negative form as a function of the nature of the propositional content.

9.214. Summary

Thus far, we have considered the nature and structure of propositional negation, or the linguistic counterpart of logical denial. We have seen how propositional negation accords with the informational structure of discourse by associating with the contextually free part of a proposition. We have gone through three diagnostics for propositional negation, *too/either*, tag questions, and *not even*, and we have discussed the range of forms that trigger these tests. Significantly, some forms give only partial results, and these facts, coupled with the degree of overtness of the negative and the degree of irrealis modality, suggest that propositional negation is scalar. Finally, we have considered some cross-language regularities in the form of verbal negation, higher negative verbs, negative auxiliary verbs, particles, and bound negators.

9.22. Scope

Having been through the basics of the meaning and form of expression of propositional negation, we now focus on a more particular and frequently debated issue in the study of negation: *scope*. Discussions of the scope of negatives have a long and detailed history (see Horn 1989 for a good survey). Here we simply try to outline the basic considerations and suggest what they mean for the analysis of negation as a modality. The issues in the scope of negation revolve around two principal factors: (a) the range of scope; and (b) the interaction of negative scope with other scope-bearing items.

By range of scope, we mean that a negative may apply to all or part of the meaning of an expression and thereby have variable scope. By interaction, we mean that insofar as negation has scope, it necessarily comes into contact with other scope-bearing items and thus has to compete for effect.

9.221. Range of Negative Scope

Why should the scope of negation have a range at all? Speakers need to assign irrealis mode to different things, and the reduction of the factual status of an entire statement is often not sufficient for the reduction of the factuality of a piece of that statement (nor vice versa).

The range of negative scope can be understood as a scale of values between the parameters of wide and narrow. Two general principles of the scope of negatives control interpretation of wide and narrow scope (Givón 1984; Horn 1989: 316): (a) the wider the scope of the negative, the more elements likely to be affected; (b) the closer the negative is to an element, the more likely the element is to be directly negated. This means that wide scope affects more but the degree of effect is proportional to the distance between the negative and the element negated. *Distance* can have either a structural or serial definition. Structurally defined, scope is a function of the attachment of the negative to a constituent that subsumes other constituents; the negative thereby affects everything dependent on the constituent immediately affected by the negative. Serially defined, scope is a function of left-to-right ordering: The first scope-bearing element has the widest scope.

We can see these principles and effects in the difference between propositional negation and affixal negation, as in (24):

24a. I don't run frequently.
   b. I run infrequently.

The propositional negative has wider scope in (24a) and ranges over more parts of the expression: the verb and its adverb. In contrast, the scope of the affixal negative in (24b) is narrow and affects only the adverb. These scope differences give the proper interpretive results. Example (24a) asserts a completely negative fact, or a denial: 'It is not true that I run frequently,' derived from the closeness of the negative to the event through structural and serial position. Example (24b) asserts an essentially positive fact with an inherently negative form: 'I assert that my running is not frequent,' where *in* precedes and negates only the adverb.

These basic parameters of wide and narrow scope have surfaced in a number of guises in the literature, and it is often difficult to keep them straight. In the philosophical work on reference and presupposition, for example, *wide* and *narrow* have rough equivalents in, respectively, *external* and *internal scope*. Let us recall from Chapter 2 that an expression like *The king of France is not bald* is given two accounts. From Russell's standpoint, the expression is false because there is no king of France, and hence the negative has scope over the whole proposition: Not[the king of France is bald]. This is *external scope* because the negative is external to the propositional constituents. But from Strawson's standpoint, the expression presupposes that there is a king of France and asserts only that he is not bald. Therefore, the negative is associated only with the portion of the expression regarding baldness: [the king of France is [Not bald]]. This is *internal scope* because the negative is internal to the proposition.

In the syntactic literature, wide and narrow scope have structural counterparts. *Sentential negation* is often understood to have *wide scope* for the obvious reason that it affects the sentence as a whole, as the structural diagnostics indicate. In contrast to this, there is *constituent negation* (or *term negation*), with *narrow scope*, whereby a negative marker attaches to and negates some structural member of a sentence smaller than the verb, as in *I saw lots of squirrels and no birds.*

In this proliferation of look alike terms for wide and narrow scope, we should be careful not to assume mutual substitution. The domains for these concepts differ in actual practice. *Wide* and *narrow* refer simply to the *range of effect*; *external* and *internal* refer to the *position of the negative in logical form*. *Sentential* and *constituent* refer to *syntactic structure*.

9.222. *Narrowing Negative Scope*

All languages have ways of narrowing the scope of negation by bringing a constituent into focus in a negative construction. Typically languages use one of two ways to effect narrowing: (a) a separate form with narrow negative scope; and (b) movement to bring the item within the scope of the negative.

English is a good example of the first way. The forms *not* and *no* can be associated with a particular constituent to indicate narrowed negative scope for the items that they precede: *I saw no birds* and *I want not many*. The same process happens in Eskimo, where it is possible to infix negatives in adverbs to induce narrowed scope (Fortescue 1984: 138):

25. akuliki- nngit-sumik tikit- ta-   aq.
    often   Neg often   come Habit 3S/Indic
    He came not often. (= seldom)

Normally, verbal negation in Eskimo would appear between *ta* and *aq*, but in (25), the negative is infixed in the adverb and thus the scope of the negative is narrowed to the adverb.

In contrast to this process, other languages narrow scope by moving the element to be narrowed *toward the negative* (see Davison 1978 on Hindi and other languages). We can see this mechanism clearly in Kusaiean, where both the negative and the element in its scope can move. According to Lee (1975: 315–6), explicit scope narrowing in Kusaiean requires that *the negative and the item* in the narrowed scope *move* to sentence initial position as in (26):

26. tiyac ma sac   eltahl molelah ekweyah.
    Neg   the thing they buy   yesterday
    It is not THE THING that they bought yesterday.

All other elements can be similarly moved to a position after the initial negative for narrowed scope. Note how this mechanism in Kusaiean underscores the basic principles of negative scope that we previously outlined. Narrowed scope relies on both a structural and serial definition of distance in Kusaiean. The element subject to the scope of the negative is put in construction with the negative and hence the negative is nearer to this item. Moreover, the negative is moved to sentence initial position and so the left-to-right principle manifests itself.

9.223. Interaction of Negative Scope and Other Operators

We have just seen the factors that contribute to the variable range of negative scope. Now we briefly consider how the scope of negation can interact with other scope-bearing elements. As we already know, the presence of more than one operator in an expression creates problems of interpretation because of the strength of their respective scopes. Similar facts arise in the case of negatives.

One of the customary examples given in this regard is the apparent *some/any* correspondence in English, derived from an examination of the paraphrase relationship between examples like the following:

27a. John has some money.
  b. John doesn't have any money.

Arguably, the presence of the negative in (27b) triggers a rule that converts the indefinite quantifier *some* to *any*. The negative of (27b) precedes and structurally dominates the quantifier *some,* and so the higher scope of the negative forces the surface change in the quantifier.

This account of the interaction of negatives and quantifiers would be all well and good if there were not a number of obvious counterexamples (Lakoff 1970). Most patently, it is not always true that quantifiers like *some* under the scope of negation are converted to a different surface form. Compare the following:

28a. John didn't like any of your comments.
  b. John didn't like some of your comments.

Why is (28b) immune to the *some/any* rule? Though the discussion of this finding is complex and often tedious (see McCawley 1988), we can observe that (28a) and (28b) differ with respect to the specificity of the quantifier. Sentence (28a) means 'John liked none of your comments,' where the quantifier is non-specific: Any comment will do for being disliked. This intuition is captured by the negative having wide scope over the quantifier: Not (some(comment)), 'there is not some (= no) comment that John likes.' Sentence (28b), on the other hand, means 'John liked some of your comments and disliked others,' where specific comments count for being included in the liking or disliking. Here, the quantifier has wide scope over the negative, allowing some of the comments to be nonnegated: some (comment(Not(. . .), 'there is some comment that John doesn't like (and some that he does).'

The lesson here is one that we have seen before. The *semantic content* of operators and items within their scope affects the scope relations. In this case, the content of the quantifier, as specific or nonspecific, affects its interaction with the negative. Scope thus cannot be applied in a mechanistic fashion, but must take into account the nature of the operators whose scopes are in competition, just as tense and quantifiers must.

The need to examine the content of operators comes through in cases of the wide scope of propositional negation in apparent violation of both the structural and serial definitions of scope. In many cases, a verbal negative can have scope over a quantified subject, even though the subject serially precedes the negative and is not structurally dependent on it:

29. Everybody isn't cheating.

Sentence (29) has two interpretations. One is where the quantified item has scope over the negative: everybody(Not(cheat . . .) 'all the people are not cheating.' But by my intuition, the preferred interpretation of (29) is one where the negative has scope over the quantified item: Not(everybody(cheat . . .) 'not everyone is cheating'—i.e., 'some people are and some aren't.'

Arguments over this phenomenon continue to occupy linguists (Horn 1989; Jackendoff 1971; Lasnik 1975). My goal is not to articulate the proposed solutions, most of which show that a semantic analysis is sufficient here (e.g., Hand 1985). Rather, I want to point out that it is the *content of the negative as an operator* that overrides the structural and serial conditions and induces wide scope.

Not all negatives with the effect of denial can have wide scope:

30. Everyone hardly ate.

Example (30) may mean only 'all people hardly ate,' everyone(hardly(. . .)), not 'hardly everyone ate' (= few people ate), where the scope of the negation is wider than the quantified item. Even though *hardly* has the effect of propositional negation (consider the diagnostics from sec. 9.2121) it does not have the wide scope possibilities of the verbal negator.

We might argue that the difference between (29) and (30) is a function of the content of the negator. *Not,* as a full denial, has more possibilities of wider scope and can override the structural and serial conditions on scope. However, when its epistemic force is reduced, as to *hardly* for example, a negative of lesser degree, the wide scope possibilities are lost. In this way, just as the scope interactions of the negative and quantifier *some* can be affected by specificity, so can the relative negative content of propositional negation affect scope interactions. For these reasons, we must concern ourselves not only with the formal apparatus that defines operators, but also with their semantic content.

9.224. Negative Content, Inherent Polarity, and the Variety of Negative Polarity Items

This discussion of the effect of semantic content on scope interaction brings up a related issue with which we conclude our treatment of negation. Many forms have *inherent polarity*; they obligatorily induce a negative reading and attendant scope phenomena because of their intrinsic negative properties. We examine such forms here to see what makes them inherently polar because this may shed light on what constitutes negation to begin with.

Many linguists have noted that some expressions are acceptable only in the negative form. They are known as *negative polarity items* (Horn 1989; Ladusaw 1979; Linebarger 1981; McCawley 1988):

31a. He didn't work a lick/?? he worked a lick.
  b. She didn't lift a finger/?? she lifted a finger.
  c. I couldn't eat a bite/?? I could eat a bite.
  d. The dog wouldn't budge/?? the dog would budge.

Many other expressions have a similar restriction: *can't ever, haven't yet, not so much as, isn't half bad,* and so on.[5]

What makes these items intrinsically polar? A simple answer is to say that the negative polarity items contain an implicit negative (whereas positive polarity items have an implicit positive). *Not lift a finger,* for example, really means something like 'fail to help,' where the negation is clearly in effect. *Budge* is used only in the negative because it refers to minimized and ultimately failed movement.

If these items are inherently negative, then we have a straightforward account of why negative polarity items trigger the diagnostics of propositional negation: for example, *She didn't lift a finger, and Bob didn't lift a finger, either/?? too.* But what are we to make of the fact that they are compatible with contexts other than those that are explicitly negative? Consider the following (after Linebarger 1981):

---

[5]There are also forms that occur only in the positive, *positive polarity items:*

  i a. The soup is pretty good/?? the soup isn't pretty good.
    b. The prime rib is delicious/?? the prime rib isn't delicious.
    c. I'd rather be in Florida/?? I wouldn't rather be in Florida.

There are many other such items: *be superb,* is *already,* and *had better,* for example.

32a. Did she lift a finger to help?
 b. He would leave rather than lift a finger to help.
 c. I'd drop dead if she lifted a finger to help.

Why is the negative polarity item *lift a finger* acceptable in a positive question (32a), positive replacive clause (32b), and positive conditional (32c)?

Before we answer this question, let us consider some further data. In section 9.223, we observed that when *some* has nonspecific indefinite reference under the scope of negation, it changes to *any* (specific indefinite remains *some*). Note that the same contexts as in (32a–c) also trigger *any*-conversion:

33a. Did she have any friends?
 b. He would leave rather than have any friends.
 c. I'd drop dead if she had any friends.

We might propose that questions, replacive clauses, and conditionals allow negative polarity items and trigger *any*-conversion because such contexts are themselves negative. That is, they provide the requisite propositional negation to trigger the appropriate effects. How so?

Questions like (33a), information questions, presume a negative state of affairs: the question is asked because the speaker *lacks* information. Replacive clauses, with *rather*, indicate the explicit *absence* of something: X rather than Y, which is absent. Conditionals, at least in the case of (33c), indicate an *unrealized* state of affairs, and thus signal another kind of absence. In short, all three constructions are *negative to some degree*.

If this analysis is correct, then we can make sense of the fact that a wide variety of phenomena trigger *any*-conversion and negative polarity items whereas closely related constructions do not. *Before*-clauses allow these structures, but clauses with *after, when,* and *while* do not:

34a. I knew Tom before he had any money/lifted a finger to help.
 b. ?? I knew Tom after/when/while he had any money/lifted a finger to help.

Before-clauses express an unrealized state of affairs and so allow *any; after, when,* and *while* presume that the state of affairs has either been completed or is in progress, in all cases realized.

Hypotheticals and generics allow *any* and negative polarity items, but concessives and purposives do not:

35a. Should he have any time, he will lift a finger to help.
 b. Whoever has any time lifts a finger to help.
 c. ?? Although he has any time, he lifts a finger to help.
 d. ?? He works hard so as to have any time to lift a finger to help.

The same explanation holds here as for the previous examples. Hypotheticals and generics express states of affairs whose factual status has been attenuated or is to some extent minimized. But concessives and purposives suggest no reduction of the factual status of the propositions they encode, and they thus are incapable of triggering *any*-conversion.

The overall explanation for these facts brings us back to the original argument of this entire section. Negation is a modality. In particular, it expresses the divergence between a reference world and an expressed world. The reduction of factual status that negation entails—whatever the form or degree of this reduction—triggers negative polarity items and related phenomena, like *some/any* conversion. Thus, we can understand why in some languages, question markers and negatives have the same form: Latin, Turkish, and Quechua, for example (Lehmann 1974: 153). Negation is a discrete modal category and anything that can count for the attenuation of the factual status of the content of a proposition may be analogously encoded. English, Quechua, and Turkish are no different: all treat negative irrealis—contrary to fact—as a unified semantic category.

9.225. Summary

We have surveyed the issues surrounding negative scope. We have seen that scope can vary from wide to narrow and the distance between the negative and the item affected determines the likelihood of effect; distance can have either a structural or serial definition. Languages have two principal means of narrowing scope: a separate form or movement of an item into the scope of the negative. Like all operators, negation interacts with other scope-bearing items (e.g., quantifiers) and, as expected, the semantic content of the items involved affects the interpretation of scope. So, negation can trigger *some/any* conversion depending on the specificity of the quantified entity; verbal negatives can have wide scope over quantified subjects (violating the structural and serial conditions) provided that the negative denotes full propositional denial. The role of negative content underscores the behavior of negative polarity items, forms with inherent negative meaning. These expressions not only trigger *some/any* conversion, but also occur in positive constructions whose semantic content has reduced factual status: questions, conditionals, hypotheticals, and the like. These results show that negation is a modality because the divergence of the reference and expressed world to any degree can trigger negative effects.

9.3. EPISTEMIC MODALITY

We have spent considerable effort exploring how language minimizes the factual status of statements through the divergence of the reference world and the expressed world. We now turn our attention to the *convergence of the two,* particularly to the *likelihood* of that convergence and the *evidence* that a speaker marshals to assert this convergence. This is *epistemic modality*: the structural and semantic resources available to a speaker to express judgment of the factual status and likelihood of a state of affairs.

We examine epistemic modality in the following way. First, we present an overview of epistemic notions, and some examples, to get a feel for the phenomenon. Thereafter, we look at the basic distinctions in epistemic modality—for example, possibility, necessity, and evidentiality—through a summary of Palmer's (1986) and Givón's (1982) typologies. Then we propose a new typology of epistemic modality, derived from its deictic structure, and built on the two parameters of source of knowledge and strength of commitment. We illustrate this typology with examples from a variety of languages and attempt to articulate some of the regularities in encoding associated with epistemic modality and evidentiality. Finally, we consider a few additional grammatical ramifications of epistemic modality: for example, the interaction of epistemic modality with tense and person.

9.31. A Survey of Epistemic Notions

The literature on modality has a number of admirably clear surveys of the basic distinctions in epistemic judgment that languages allow their speakers to express (e.g., Chafe and Nichols 1986; Chung and Timberlake 1985; Coates 1983; Givón 1982; Kiefer 1987; Palmer 1986). *Epistemic modality* is a handy cover term for the way that language denotes and encodes the following concepts, among others: possibility, necessity, inference, belief, report, hearsay, conclusion, deduction, opinion, commitment, speculation, quotation, doubt, evidence, and certainty.

Epistemic modality obviously concerns the expression of truth, but *truth relativized to a speaker*. Categorical truth—what we might customarily and naively assume to be the standard of certainty—is only one of many possible stances that a speaker may take toward the content of a proposition. As Palmer (1987) argues (after Givón 1982), linguistic truth is but a narrow segment of the larger scale of all potentially valid information (though see Frajzyngier 1985 and 1987 for a contrasting position). We are concerned with the *range of truthlike notions* through which language permits its users to speak.

We can begin to get a handle on this diversity by looking at the following examples:

36a. Bob must be home.
  b. Bob might be home.

Both expressions have roughly the same semantic content, namely 'possibly, Bob is at home,' but they diverge with respect to the speaker's confidence in the validity of the information. Sentence (36a) indicates that the speaker has come to some *strong* conclusion about the factual status of the proposition, or, in deictic terms, that the convergence of the reference world ('the speaker's here-and-now') and the expressed world ('Bob is at home') is fairly likely (and if the convergence does not turn out, then the speaker should be surprised or held accountable for the error). Sentence (36b), on the other hand, indicates that the speaker is less committed to the facts working out as expressed, or that the convergence of the reference and expressed world is less likely. These examples illustrate that epistemic modality *connects the speaker to the proposition* (unlike negation, for example, which *connects the given to the new*). Epistemic modality relativizes truth to speakers by relating their current state of knowledge or belief to the content of their expressions.

Our goal in this section is to analyze and enumerate the range of epistemic notions available to any speaker through language, aware as we are that epistemic modality is a relation between a speaker and a proposition. We see this structure again and again, most immediately in the distinctions that comprise two influential typologies of epistemic modality.

9.32.   Two Accounts of Linguistic Truth

Linguists agree that epistemic modality concerns possibility and necessity broadly construed, but modulated for commitment and evidence. These ideas underlie two influential accounts of epistemic modality, Palmer's theory of epistemic categories and Givón's theory of epistemic scales. We examine these in schematic form so as to provide the groundwork for a more comprehensive account. What we are attempting to do here is to outline the universals in the way that language treats possibility and truth as a conceptual/semantic system: not as a system that relates language to the world, but as one that connects language to its users.

9.321.   Judgments and Evidentials:
Palmer's Account of Epistemic Categories

Palmer (1986) claims that epistemic modality divides into two basic categories: *judgments* and *evidentials.* In *judgments,* Palmer includes all epistemic notions that involve possibility and necessity, particularly with regard to speculation and deduction on the part of the speaker as subject or perceiver of the information. Judgments assert the possibility of the truth of a proposition without any overt indication of the grounds for that assertion. Palmer further categorizes judgments by the degree of confidence that the speaker has in the assertion. This produces two subcategories: *necessary judgments* and *possible judgments,* respectively based on *inference* and *confidence, deduction* and *speculation,* or *strong* and *weak judgment.*

We can observe judgments in West Greenlandic Eskimo, which has a variety of verbal affixes to indicate the speaker's assessment of the content of the proposition. Compare the following (after Fortescue 1984: 294):

37a. qama-   junnarsi- vuq.
   seal-hunting probably 3S/Indic
   He's probably seal-hunting.

   b. tamma- quuqa-   at.
   get lost undoubtedly 3Pl/Indic
   They undoubtedly have gotten lost.

Though the two forms *junnarsi* and *quuqa* are glossed as if they are adverbs, in fact they are simply verbal affixes in Eskimo and are perhaps better translated as modal auxiliaries. *Junnarsi* is thus more accurately something like 'should,' as in *he should be seal hunting,* and *quuqa* is something like 'must,' *they must have gotten lost.* In any event, the two forms encode the *same degree of epistemic judgment* that the English modals *should* and *must* do: *junnarse* signals a less confident judgment than *quuqa.*

In contrast to judgments are *evidentials,* which encode the *grounds* on which a speaker makes an overtly qualified assertion. Unlike judgments, evidentials explicitly signal the collateral that a speaker takes as substantiating an assertion. Palmer divided evidentials into two subcategories: *direct* and *indirect.* In the former are all markers of a speaker's firsthand evidence, with sensory evidence carrying the main weight; indirect evidence encompasses all forms of secondhand fact. Many languages distinguish these two kinds of evidence by differentiating an auditory or reportive evidential (direct) from a quotative or hearsay one (indirect). Makah works in this fashion, as the following illustrate (Jacobsen 1986: 13–16):

38a. babaɫdi-'   xqad?i.
   be a white man Auditory
   He sounds like a white man.

   b. x̣ubiẗadibit-   wad.
   he was snoring Quotative
   I am told he was snoring.

In (38a), the suffix *xqad?i* signals that the grounds for the assertion 'he is a white man' lie in the speaker's direct auditory encounter with the event. In (38b), the truth of the event of snoring is asserted on the basis of hearsay, or what others have said or indirectly reported to the speaker.

Direct evidence typically subsumes visual, auditory, and other sensory modalities, with visual evidence by far the most prevalently encoded, attesting to the priority of visual perception as the arbiter of epistemic judgment (this is not universal, however: see Palmer 1986: 68 on Ngiyaamba). In fact, in some languages, all semantic distinctions in sensory evidence are neutralized after visual evidence: Makah works this way, with the marker of auditory evidence compatible with all nonvisual sensory information (Jacobsen 1986: 14). *Indirect evidence* encompasses report, quotation, hearsay, assumption, appearance, and all other types of supportive, auxiliary information. By far the most common are quotative and hearsay.

Palmer argues that the two basic categories of judgments and evidentials translate into a tripartite typology of epistemic modality. Languages may be *rather purely judgmental, rather purely evidential,* or *mixed* (both). English, he says, is basically a judgment language insofar as there are relatively few distinct evidential markers as compared to, say, Makah. Tuyuca (Palmer 1986) is a relatively pure evidential language because expressions in this language *must be marked* for their evidential status. Most other languages are mixed. Of course, a critical issue surfaces here: How are we to draw the lines across judgmental, evidential, and mixed? English does have a number of judgmental forms (*might, must*), but certainly evidentiality can surface in a number of overt ways: *I hear that Andy's in jail.* Similarly, languages on the evidential side of the contrast frequently have judgmental forms. Palmer (1986; 69–70) notes these convergences and in the end acknowledges that most systems are mixed. But this certainly does not vitiate the two basic categories, judgments and evidentials, as poles of the scale.

9.322. Degrees of Certainty: Givón's Theory of Epistemic Scales

Palmer gives the *categorial structure* of epistemic modality. Givón (1982) discusses its *scalar properties*. For Givón, epistemic modality is the way a language expresses the relative validity of propositions, and this depends in turn on how the language and the culture that the language is embedded in interpret a universal scale of epistemic choice.

Givón argues that there are three kinds of propositions, typed by their inherent certainty and need for substantiation:

1. those with *lowest certainty*: These are doubtful hypotheses and are *beneath challenge* and substantiation;
2. those with *medium certainty*: These are *open to challenge* and thus require supporting evidence and collateral;
3. those with *high certainty*: These are taken for granted, presupposed, and are *above challenge*.

These propositional types constitute an epistemic gradient that a language and culture can interpret as it chooses. For example, in some languages, given the contingencies of the culture, mystical or revealed knowledge is above challenge, as in traditional societies; in others, such as those dominated by empirical science, mystical knowledge is beneath challenge or unworthy of evidence. In both cases, the choices follow the invariant structure of the epistemic scale.

Epistemic modality maps onto this scale by tracking and encoding epistemic choice and justification. Givón (1982) argues, with copious evidence from unrelated languages, that evidential requirements are found *only in the middle range of the scale*. Languages marshal and encode evidence *only where they have to*: only where the propositions are open to challenge. The universal epistemic gradient clusters its evidential requirements shown in Fig. 9.1:

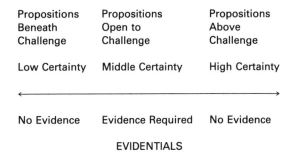

FIG. 9.1.   Adaptation of Givón's (1982) scale of epistemic space.

As a result of this construal, the distinction between judgments and evidentials is eliminated. Though Palmer (1986: 53) tries to appropriate Givón's model to his own uses, by equating judgments with low certainty propositions and evidentials with medium certainty propositions, the analogy just does not go through. There is no conceptual difference between judgments and evidentials *because all epistemically qualified assertions are evidential to some degree*. The real issue is: What is the evidence allowed and how is it chosen?

Givón's answer is: through another set of scales. He argues (1982: 43–4) that languages quantify evidence along four gradients:

1. Person: Speaker > Hearer > Third Person
2. Sense: Vision > Hearing > Other Senses > Feeling
3. Directness: Senses > Inference
4. Proximity: Near > Far

When languages have to make the grounds of their assertions explicit, as they must in propositions of midrange certainty, they force their speakers to choose evidence according to the aforementioned four scales and according to the internal order of the gradients: for example, vision over hearing. These scales are obviously an analytical rendering of Palmer's more general point that evidence is either direct or indirect: Indeed Givón's sensory scale (scale 2) corresponds exactly to our finding that vision supersedes all other categories in sensory evidence.

We do not exemplify Givón's claims per se; the interested reader is referred to his (1982) paper. Instead, we point up the broader lesson of his account. Whereas Palmer uncovers a set of universal *kinds* of epistemic modality, Givón elucidates their *extent*. A thorough account of epistemic modality can do without the judgment/evidential distinction—because judgment is only one kind of evidential—but it cannot do without *both categories and scales*. The natural logic of possibility requires a scale of justifications on a continuum of justifiable information. It is to this fuller picture that we now turn.

9.33.   A Deictic Account of Epistemic Modality

If we understand the requirements of epistemic modality by the *categories of source/direction of knowledge* and the *scale of strength of knowledge,* we can simplify and unify accounts of epistemic modality. To do so, we must first reexamine the basic deictic structure of modality, via deixis itself, which, as we know, has three components: deictic points, direction, and remoteness.

9.331.   Source, Direction, and Remoteness
of Knowledge

The convergence of the expressed world and the reference world is assessed and substantiated from the viewpoint of the *epistemic center,* the source of knowledge or the principal deictic point. Sometimes the *self* is the center of the epistemic stance (as in judgments) and sometimes the *other* (nonself) (as in hearsay). Hence the values that a language chooses to assign to the epistemic center dictate epistemic stance by providing the grounds for the source of the modality itself. From the standpoint of deictic points, there are two options for source of knowledge: self and other (= nonself).[6]

Languages have subtler ways of dividing up the source of knowledge than simply self and other. These additional categories can be accommodated if we apply directionality to the source of knowledge: *from the self, to the self, from the other, to the other.* Some epistemic judgments are made *wholly from within the self* (judgments: inference and confidence). These have no marking of data-source other than the self and knowledge appears sui generic. But other epistemic stances are a function of the evidence received *by the senses of the self* (i.e., to the self: direct evidence or sensory evidentials). In a third category is knowledge

---

[6]Languages may vary on the preferred deictic center, though the customary value is the self as speaker, as for all deictic systems. Schlichter (1986) argues, however, that Wintu privileges the other as the epistemic deictic center. It would be interesting to see if languages like Cree, which reverse the animacy hierarchy in a similar way, also privilege the other in epistemic modality.

that *proceeds from others* (indirect evidence: reports, hearsay, quotation, and so on). A final category is that which *proceeds to others*. Though this is infrequently attested, Palmer (1986: 76–7) does note that some languages force their speakers to modulate their assertions by the speaker *projecting to the hearer* (see the example from Kogi, p. 415).

The two parameters of deictic points and directionality describe all the epistemic *categories*. Now let us turn to the *scales*. Palmer distinguishes between direct and indirect evidence, and Givón scales evidence from the canonical source outward. We can incorporate these observations in a deictic account by enlisting the third component of deixis: remoteness. When we say that a speaker is *less committed* to a proposition, the evidence is *less strong or direct,* or the speaker is *less confident,* we mean that, just as in any deictic system, *the distance between the reference point and located point is relatively large.* Confidence, commitment, strength, and so on are ways of talking about the relative distance between the source of knowledge (the reference world) and the object of knowledge (the converging expressed world).

We can now scale every category of source/direction of knowledge by remoteness, from direct to indirect. Such scaling gives the proper results for an overall typology of epistemic modality, summarized in Table 9.1.

9.332. Two Illustrations: Tuyuca and Kogi Evidential Systems

The deictic account in Table 9.1 considerably streamlines typologies of epistemic modality. The benefits come through clearly if we recast some well-known systems in terms of these deictic categories and scales. One frequently discussed language is Tuyuca, which Barnes (1984), Palmer (1986: 67), and Malone (1988)

TABLE 9.1
Deictic Categorization and Scaling of Epistemic Modality

Source of Knowledge		*Strength of Knowledge*
Self		
	From	Scaled Categories of Inference necessary > possible
	To	Scaled Categories of Sensation visual > auditory > other senses > feel
Other		
	From	Scaled Categories of External Info. quote > report > hearsay > other
	To	Scaled Categories of Participants other > all else

argue has a basic five-term evidential system. According to Malone's recent reappraisal, the Tuyuca terms and their denotations are shown here:

wi-   firsthand visual knowledge
ti-   firsthand nonvisual knowledge
yi-   nonfirsthand direct knowledge
yigɨ-   nonfirsthand indirect reported knowledge
hīyi-   nonfirsthand indirect reported knowledge

We can readily translate these meanings into those of Table 9.1. First of all, Malone indicates that the distinction between firsthand and nonfirsthand knowledge, basic to the Tuyuca system, divides knowledge by source. By Malone's (1988: 124) definitions, firsthand knowledge *originates in the speaker* and thus is equivalent to the category Self; nonfirsthand knowledge *originates outside the speaker* and hence covers the category Other. By this distinction, *wi* and *ti* belong to Self, but because they further differentiate by sensory data, they belong under To Self, and are scaled therein. *Yi, yigɨ* and *hīyi* fall under the category Other and are scaled by directness. *Yi,* according to Malone (1988), encodes information from a direct external source, what Palmer and Barnes indicate as something like circumstantial evidence. *Yigɨ* and *hīyi* encode not only information from a source external to the self, but mediated by reportage and hence less direct than circumstantial evidence.

Given this construal, we can sketch the Tuyuca epistemic system in Fig. 9.2. This deictic hierarchy shows that the epistemic structure of Tuyuca is unified, not simply listlike, as descriptive accounts suggest. In fact, Malone's (1988) revision accords remarkably well with our more general observation that the basic categorial distinction in epistemic modality is the source of knowledge. He argues that the distinction between firsthand and nonfirsthand knowledge (Self vs. Other) motivates the entire epistemic system in Tuyuca and related languages.

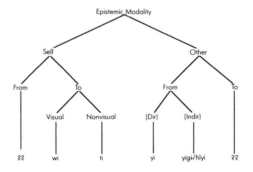

FIG. 9.2. Deictic structure of Tuyuca evidentials.

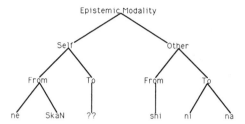

FIG. 9.3. Deictic structure of Kogi evidentials.

Similar unification can be found in languages that specifically encode properties of the addressee in their evidential systems. One such language is Kogi, which, according to Palmer (1986: 76), has a five-term system. The verbal affixes *ne* and *skaN* both indicate that the speaker is uncertain of the propositional content, and, with this restriction to the speaker, fall under From Self. They may be further differentiated for strength, with *skaN* 'doubt' (complete lack of knowledge) weaker than *ne* 'speculate.' (We need further work to establish this with certainty.) The three other forms, *ni, na,* and *shi,* explicitly make reference to the addressee. *Shi* 'ask' elicits information directly from another, and hence is under the From Other category. *Ni* 'remind' and *na* 'inform' take the other as the goal of knowledge and thus fall under To Other. Given this account, we can schematize the Kogi evidential system (see Figure 9.3).

These examples highlight a more general point about epistemic systems. Languages carve up the ideal, deictic epistemic space differently and use different structural resources to carry out their epistemic requirements.

9.34. Differential Structuring and Encoding of Epistemic Space

The examples of Kogi and Tuyuca show that not all deictic epistemic categories are instantiated in any language. Though we should be prepared for this result because we know that certain epistemic categories, like visual information, tend to have more frequent distribution, we should also describe the more common patterns of overlap we see in the world's languages.

Tuyuca differentiates relatively moreso the "middle" of the deictic hierarchy whereas Kogi differentiates "the ends." English, with its predominance of judgments, as per Palmer (1986), is skewed toward the "Self end" (*must, have to, may, might,* and so on), though there are clearly cases of encoding in the "middle": sensory markers (*see, hear*) and markers of external source (*hear that*). Hill Patwin, unrelated to English, looks a bit like English in that there are a number of evidential degrees in the From Self category: *m?a* ('must'), *mther* ('might'), *mte* ('less might'). The language also encodes degrees of indirect evidence, differentiating the From Other category: *boti* ('direct nonsensory evidence') and *mon?a* ('inference via appearance') (see Whistler 1986: 69).

All languages apparently distinguish Self from Other in some fashion. Indeed, in some languages this basic opposition is the only differentiation of epistemic space. Nichols (1986) observes that Chinese/Russian pidgin differentiates only direct from indirect evidence; Turkish (Aksu-Koç and Slobin 1986) apparently works likewise, with a basic distinction between inference (Self) and hearsay (Other). Further regularities are hard to come by, however. If the subcategories of Self and Other form a scale, then we ought to expect differentiation as follows: $Self_f > Self_t$, $Other_f > Other_t$. That is, languages ought to have more inference than sensory categories and more hearsay and reportive categories than other-directed categories. But his is a logical claim that awaits empirical test.

If not all languages carve up epistemic space equivalently, then it is also true that not all languages use the same structural means to carry out epistemic encoding. In the Tuyuca and Kogi examples, the epistemic categories and scales are all encoded by separate particles, but this is by no means the only, or even typical, case. Frequently, languages use *tense* to differentiate epistemic stance. In English, the strength of a speaker's inference can be attenuated by changing the tense from present to past: *may* versus *might, shall* versus *should,* and *will* versus *would,* where the second member encodes a reduction in strength. According to Woodbury (1986), a similar phenomenon is found in Sherpa, where the evidential *nok,* 'immediate evidence,' has its immediacy attenuated when it occurs on verbs in the past tense. In the present, *nok* signals experiential (direct) knowledge; in the past, it signals inferential (indirect) knowledge. In German, according to Palmer (1986: 63), the present tense of *mogen* 'may' signals weak epistemic judgment, whereas the past tense of the same form reduces the commitment:

39a. Er mag   gehen.
     he may/Pres to go
     He may go.
  b. Er möchte   gehen.
     he may/Past to go
     He might go.

This modal function of tense change is in fact quite a widespread phenomenon. Nichols (1986), for example, notes the overall correlation of evidentials of immediacy and imperfective aspect and evidentials of nonimmediate knowledge and perfective aspect: As we know, the perfective is likely to occur in the past tense. The connection of tense to modality is actually quite understandable. Tense is deictic, so temporal distance can substitute for modal distance. The present tense is likely to be associated with immediate evidence for the obvious reason that the present encodes the lack of temporal distance between the reference time and the located time. We know that the past tense is generally associated with removal and distancing, and so the use of past tense to attenuate the strength of evidence via removal is not surprising.[7]

What we do not know, however, is exactly how different tense systems interact with modality. Are metrical tense systems more or less likely to be used for modal purposes? Which past tenses tend to be associated with modal distance? Woodbury (1986: 195) puts the question of tense/modality interaction quite generally when he says that any difference between the time reference of an evidential category and tense will result in the assignment of a nonexperiential value to the evidential: That is, all mismatches of tense and modality attenuate the directness of the evidence. Even if this is true, we still need to determine if different tense structures induce different effects (see Carey 1989 for interesting discussion here).

Tense is not the only structural device that languages use to signal epistemic modality. Person (another deictic category), voice, emphatic markers, and definiteness are also frequently associated with epistemic modality. We look at the use of person as an example. Frajzyngier (1985) observes that Czech and Polish have *dubitative particles* to indicate the reduced factual status of a proposition that is *spoken by someone other than the speaker*. Compare the following Polish expressions containing the dubitative particle *niby* (Frajzyngier 1985: 245):

40a. Powiedział że   niby jest chory.
  he said   that Dub is   sick
  He said that he was sick, but that may not be true.

  b. ? Powiedziałem że   niby jestem chory.
   I said   that Dub I am   sick
   ? I said that I was sick, but I lied.

In (40a), the content of the proposition is attributed to a person other than the

---

[7]Obviously, similar claims may be made for the future tense, which indicates potential and unrealized events, and hence irrealis. In Spanish, the future tense inflection has taken on an entirely epistemic meaning:

i. hablar- é.
   speak   1Per/Fut
   I intend to speak.
   Lit. I will/shall speak.

Simple future time is signalled by *ir* 'to go' plus the infinitive:

ii. voy a hablar.
    I go to speak
    I am going to speak/I will speak.

See also Dowty (1979).

speaker, and here *niby* can attenuate validity. In (40b), however, the content of the proposition is asserted *by the speaker,* and the presence of the dubitative particle makes the expression a bit odd. The problem is: How can you put into doubt (by *niby*) what you assert about yourself? If (40b) is to be made sense of, it cannot have an interpretation where the factual status of the statement is simply reduced, but *controverted.* Hence, (40b) can mean only that the speaker has lied, not asserted a weak truth.

This person restriction in Polish and others like it in many other languages underscore the essentially deictic nature of epistemic modality, built as it is on the *situatedness of validity.* If truth is a function of its attribution to speakers and hearers—that is, the source of knowledge in a self or other—then it is understandable that parameters for the contextual participants themselves should interact with the assertability of the proposition.

These examples of additional structural mechanisms that induce modality point up an interesting summarial fact about the encoding of epistemic modality. The reason for the rather fluid nature of encoding may be that from an abstract position, modality itself is fluid. According to Givón (1982), epistemic modality is scalar at base, deriving as it does from a continuum of directness. The most direct and reliable knowledge is that found near the deictic center, From/To Self, or firsthand information; less direct, less reliable knowledge is found away from the center, From/To Other, nonfirsthand information. Given the scalar foundation of the basic epistemic categories of source/direction of knowledge, the two basic categories of Self and Other emerge as *points of stability,* criterially defined, and not discrete categories. If this picture is correct, then we can understand why mechanisms that simply induce distance, whether temporal, personal, or conceptual, have the effect not only of scaling down the assertion, but also changing the epistemic categories. Anything that can induce distance should potentially have a modal effect.

In providing a broad view of epistemic modality as a deictic system, we have curiously come across an overlap of formal and typological approaches to meaning. Both kinds of account of modality agree on one thing: "The truth of a statement does not depend [entirely, WF] on its meaning, but on the time and place at which the event it describes is supposed to happen" (Schlichter 1986: 57–8). Epistemic modality, as linguistic truth relativized to a speaker, thus buys into the situatedness of knowledge and relies on grammatical mechanisms and denotations that are likewise associated with speaker-based information.

9.35. Summary

This section has discussed epistemic modality, the likelihood of the convergence of the reference world and expressed world, and the evidence a speaker uses to ground the assertion of their convergence. We have examined the variety of epistemic notions—possibility, inference, hearsay, report, and so forth—and considered two typologies of epistemic modality: Palmer's theory of categories and Givón's theory of scales. We bring these two accounts together in a deictic account of epistemic modality built on the notions of source, direction, and remoteness of knowledge. We have seen how the deictic typology gives a unified account of different evidential systems and forms the basis of a broad view of the differential structuring of epistemic space. In closing, we have noted how other parts of the semantic system often take up the burden of epistemic modality: Tense and person, with their inherent connection to deixis, are frequent choices in this respect.

9.4. DEONTIC MODALITY

We have considered how language denotes and encodes negation and possibility; here we examine *obligation* and *permission,* otherwise known as *deontic modality.* We begin with a definition of deontic modality to circumscribe its conceptual domain, stressing the relation of descriptive/linguistic facts to formal deontic logic, and, ultimately, to deictic structure. Thereafter we examine three semantic characteristics of deontic modality: the categories of obligation and permission, futurity, and other-orientation. Finally, we close with some discussion of the forms of deontic modality, with particular focus on the convergence of epistemic and deontic modality in surface manifestation.

9.41. Defining Deontic Modality

9.411. Deontic Notions

Deontic modality covers a variety of notions that share the features of obligation and permission. Deontics themselves have long been the object of inquiry for logicians, and the major initial advances in the semantics of obligation come from the early work on formal deontic logic (the seminal paper is von Wright 1951; see also Follesdal and Hilpinen 1971; Hilpinen 1981; von Wright 1981). In one form or another, deontic modality is related to all the following: orders, rights, willing, duty, exhortation, permission, requirements, and even ability (see Chung and Timberlake 1985 for a list of representative notions). These concepts are appropriately labeled *deontic* because the term itself refers to obligation, duty, or *normative action* (see Follesdal and Hilpinen 1971).

We can get a good idea of deontic modality from the following example:

41. Ron must be an accountant.

Sentence (41) has two interpretations, depending on the modality assigned to the auxiliary *must*. In one sense, (41) means 'by my reasoning and judgment, Ron is an accountant,' where the auxiliary has an epistemic meaning because it denotes the mental state of the speaker with regard to the content of the proposition. But in another sense, (41) has the interpretation of described duty: 'Ron has no choice but to be an accountant (for whatever reason, say that his family is full of accountants).' On this reading, the modal auxiliary is deontic, expressing the obligatory state of affairs that the participant in the proposition must come to. In the deontic interpretation, the content of the proposition is a requirement to be satisfied, not, as in epistemic modality, a judgment to be validated.

Deontic modality expresses the *imposition of a state of affairs on individuals,* or, with the modality as deixis, the *imposition of an expressed world on a reference world.* To use Chung and Timberlake's (1985) account, deontic modality is the way that languages express the *restriction of possible future states of affairs to a single choice*: that is, the forced convergence of the expressed world and the reference world. This characterization is easy to see with regard to the deontic sense of (41). If Ron is obliged to be an accountant, then we are saying that, from the vantage point of the present state of affairs, there is only one possible future state of affairs: namely, that Ron is to be an accountant.

9.412. Semantics, Pragmatics, and the Deictic Structure of Deontic Modality

Insofar as deontic modality can be viewed as the *imposition* of an expressed world on a reference world, a number of scholars have suggested that deontic modality is more a pragmatic than semantic phenomenon: That is, imposition and obligation align deontics less with truth than with action. A full interpretation of (41), for example, requires us to delineate the normative conditions under which the statement is successful or under which the imposition of the expressed world comes about. This in turn demands that we examine the *outcomes and uptakes* of the participants and evaluate the statement as *a performance,* not as a representation of a state of affairs (for this reason von Wright argued that deontic logic concerns acts, not propositions; Forrester 1989 provides an account of deontics in terms of Gricelike maxims of dutiful speech). Palmer (1986) makes similar claims by saying that deontic modality is concerned with language as action, much like speech acts themselves, whereas epistemic modality concerns language as information.

Even though deontics have obvious pragmatic force, their informational (and hence semantic) side cannot be eliminated. Deontic modality expresses normative action and duty as a *function of the attitudinal state and judgments of the speaker.* Example (41), for example, indicates that the speaker has somehow judged and is committed to the convergence of the expressed world and the reference world, and so there is still a relation between the speaker and the content of the proposition. For this reason, deontics still have an arguable truth value. Note that (41) may be judged for its truth as a described obligation. Indeed, it is possible to *deny* (41) (unlike a purely pragmatic form, like a command, which has no truth value):

A: Ron must be an accountant!
B: Not true (he can be whatever he wants).
(cf. Be an accountant! ?? Not true.)

Though deontics appear to require determination through their conditions of satisfaction more than their conditions of validation, their validity as a function of their judgmental character still holds.

Truth conditionally is not precluded for deontic modality just because it has a preferential interpretation in terms of its pragmatic force. Indeed, from a deictic standpoint, deontic modality looks very much like (truth functional) epistemic modality, though with a modification or two. Epistemic modality encodes the relation between the speaker in a reference world and a proposition in an expressed world. As we have seen, languages make use of the basic deictic components to assign epistemic values to this structure. Deontic modality encodes the relation between a speaker in a reference world and two connected expressed worlds by expressing the *speaker's judgment of the emergence of an expressed world from the reference world*. The same deictic components in epistemic modality are required here, though distributed differently. There are *deictic points*: the reference world as center and the expressed world as located point. There is *direction*: The flow of the emergence of the expressed world is always away from the reference world, into any future, away from the speaker, toward the other. There is *remoteness*: The likelihood of the emergence of the expressed world is a function of the connection of the reference world and the expressed world and the speaker's judgment thereof.

Now that we have an idea of how deontic modality shares deictic structure with epistemic modality, we turn to the basic semantic characteristics of deontics. There are three features that deserve our attention: categories of deontic modality and their degrees, futurity, and other-orientation.

9.42.   Three Semantic Features of Deontic Modality

9.421.   *Deontic Categories: Obligation and Permission*

Deontic modality comes in two basic categories: *obligation* and *permission*. We can see these illustrated by a comparison of the following:

42a. Anna has to go home now.
  b. Anna may go home now.

Example (42a) encodes the obligatory emergence of the expressed world ('going home') from the reference world ('now'); example (42b) encodes the allowed emergence of the expressed world from the reference world.

Obligation and permission are separate semantic categories, so they normally surface in separate forms, as in the difference in English between *has to* and *may*. The same phenomenon is found in Albanian, where obligation may be expressed by the modal verb *do* 'want' (Newmark, Hubbard, and Prifti 1982: 102):

43. kjo këmishë do   larë.
    this shirt   want wash
    This shirt should be washed.
    More accurately: This shirt wants washing. (note the parallel between
        Albanian and dialectal English here)

Permission, however, is signalled by a different form, *mund* (Newmark et al. 1982: 106):

44. Ja   mund ta mbaroni.
    you may   it finish
    You may finish it.
    More accurately: You can (are allowed to) finish it.[8]

The significance of the divergent surface forms of this categorial difference between obligation and permission should not be overlooked. Intuitively, permission seems to be a weak version of obligation, and not a separate semantic category at all, something like 'obligation with options open to the hearer.' But the difference between obligation and permission is not a gradient. They are *categorially separate*, shown by the impossibility of grading permission into obligation and vice versa. A scale of obligation expresses deontic distance between the reference world and the expressed world in terms of duty; and a scale of permission expresses deontic distance between the reference and expressed world in terms of allowance. Crucially, the scales do not overlap: Weak obligation does not equal strong permission, for example.

Consider English in the respect. Obligation in decreasing measure may be seen in the following expressions:

45a. You must go home.
  b. You should go home.
  c. You might go home.

---

[8]Interestingly enough, just as in English, where the form *may* expresses either epistemic or deontic modality, so does *mund* in Albanian. Example (44) may also mean something like 'you will probably finish it,' where the epistemic judgment of the speaker is implied (see sec. 9.5).

Example (45a) has the highest strength, or the least deontic distance between the reference world and the expressed world; example (45c) has the least strength, accounting for its pragmatic force as a suggestion rather than an order (as when a teacher politely suggests an assignment for Monday's class: *you might want to read the chapter by then*). Example (45b) falls in between. Permission likewise has scalar values:

46a. You may go now.
  b. You can go now.
  c. You could go now.

We get the same decreasing measure of deontic distance as in example (45), though this time for permission. Example (46a) is the strongest permission, in that *may* signals that the permission is directly given, or that the distance between the reference world and the expressed world is small. Example (46b) is less strong in the respect, and (46c) is the least.[9]

Significantly, *may* and *might,* which have scalar epistemic value, are not related on the deontic scales. *Might* denotes 'weak' obligation'; *may* denotes 'strong permission.' They belong to *separate categories. May* can never have an obligational sense: *You may go now* does not mean 'you are obliged to go now'; *might* can never have a permissive sense: *You might go now* does not mean 'you are allowed to go now.' So, the weakest marker of obligation, *might,* cannot denote permission; the strongest marker of permission, *may,* cannot denote obligation. Deontic modality thus has two distinct categories, each composed of scales.

Analogous facts hold for other languages. We can illustrate this with another look at Albanian, restricting ourselves to the scale of obligation in the language. By Newmark et al.'s (1982) grammar, Albanian has two degrees of obligation:

47a. kjo këmishë duhet larë.
    this shirt   must wash
    This shirt must be washed.
  b. kjo këmishë do   larë.
    this shirt   want wash
    This shirt should be washed.

Newmark et al. (1982: 103) observe that *do* is milder in obligation than *duhet.*

---

[9]Note that, as with epistemic modality, tense functions to induce distance and lessen the degree of the category. In the permission sequence, the present tense form *can* has a greater degree of permissibility than its past tense, *could.* Similarly, we might argue that under obligation, the past tense form *should* has a higher degree of obligation when converted to its present tense counterpart, *shall.* By my intuition at least, *you shall go home* conveys more obligation than *you should go home.*

Hence, in Albanian, there is a scale of compulsoriness: *duhet* > *do*. But again scalar relations do not induce categorial difference: *do,* the weaker member of the scale of obligation, cannot denote 'permission.' For that, Albanian has the separate form *mund.*

9.422. Futurity

The second principal characteristic of deontic modality is futurity, or the *directionality of the events.* By this we mean that deontics always point to some upcoming state of affairs from the reference world: away from the deictic center and into some subsequent expressed world. This characteristic of deontics is a natural result of deontic meaning: the (future) imposition of a situation, the (future) convergence of two worlds, or the (future) emergence of one world out of another.

The inherent "forward" directionality of deontics is connected to the failure of deontics to accommodate past tenses. Palmer (1986: 100) notes that: "there are no past tense forms for the deontic modals, for obviously one cannot give permission or lay obligation in the past (as opposed to reporting that one did.)" Though Palmer is essentially correct, we should perhaps be a bit careful about the expansiveness of such prohibitions. In Spanish, it is entirely possible to encode obligation in the past:

48. deb- ías   ir.
    ought Imperf/2Per to go
    You were obliged to go.

Example (48) is perhaps most accurately rendered *You oughted to go,* to reflect the fact that the deontic modal in Spanish is inflected for past tense. Similarly in English, it is possible to encode deontics in the past: *You had to go yesterday.* The correct observation, however, is that *the direction of obligation itself cannot extend into the past.* The *description of the obligation,* like any other description, can of course be encoded in the past.

When we speak of the futurity of deontics, we really are indicating something of the characteristic deictic structure of this modality. *Futurity is one version of the forward directionality of events,* but certainly not the only one. It is entirely possible to locate deontics in the past as long as the forward direction of the modality is met.

We can see this independence of directionality and time in an examination of deontics in Aghem. According to Hyman (1979: 111), obligation is encoded in Aghem by the market *kí* 'have.' As we already know from Chapter 8, Aghem has metrical tense, and so the event under obligation is encoded for the *interval* in which it will occur. It is entirely possible to locate the deontic in the 'before today' interval:

49. ò mɔ̀   kí   álésù fíghâm.
    he before today have wash   mat
    He had to wash the mat, before today.

A more precise gloss of (49) is 'in the interval before today, he, at one point, was obliged to wash the mat at a later point from the obligation.' Crucially, the forward directionality of the deontic is maintained in spite the temporal interval, and the requirement of futurity is thereby met.

9.423. Other-Orientation

We have seen the two basic categories of deontic modality, their scalar composition as a function of deontic distance, and their futurity or forward directionality. Now let us look at the third principal feature: *other-orientation*. Epistemic modality is deictically defined by the source of the knowledge. The role of the self in epistemics makes them out to be subjective, encoding the mental states of speakers. Deontics, on the other hand, convey more a sense of objectivity than do epistemics. Consider the expression *Tom must go,* where the speaker appears to be *merely reporting this obligation.*

Whereas epistemic modality is basically speaker-situated and source-oriented, deontic modality is other-situated, and goal-oriented. Obligations and permissions denote the involvement of the speaker *in the other,* whereas epistemic modality crucially restricts the involvement to the speaker *in relation to the other.* In deictic terms, the difference between epistemic and deontic modality hinges on the directional connection of the deictic points. Epistemic modality selects sources and hence involves the commitment of the self. Even in cases where the source of knowledge flows from others, as in evidentials of direct report, the knowledge is registered in, and arbitrated by, the self. Deontic modality, however, is defined by goals, and it crucially involves the commitment of others, though, as a modality, this judgment may be modulated by the speaker's view of the facts: whence the strength of obligation and permission.

To put this all another way, we might say that both epistemic and deontic modality may be defined by sources and goals as deictic points, but, by their structure, they privilege these points differently. Epistemics privilege the source over the goal; deontics the goal over the source.

9.43. Forms of Deontic Modality

We have seen the basic semantic facts of deontic modality, and now we turn to its encoding patterns. There are two main findings in this regard, and both suggest something about the conceptual structure of deontic modality. First, deontics rarely appear as inflections; second, deontic and epistemic modality frequently overlap in surface form.

9.431. Deontic Modality and Inflection

According to Bybee (1985), deontic modality is infrequently realized as an inflection. To understand this claim, we must also understand Bybee's view of inflection. For her, an inflection is an obligatory grammatical marking on a verb whose semantic content directly affects the semantic content of the verb: that is, its status as an event (1985: 11). By this definition, aspect is an inflection because it is obligatory and its meaning affects the nature of the event encoded by the verb.

Given this definition, deontic modality generally does not appear as an inflection because its semantic content does not affect the status of the event *as an event*. To use Bybee's (1985) terminology, deontic modality is *agent-oriented*; it bears on how an event is to be *carried out by an agent,* not on the event proper. Deontic modality thus more particularly expresses a relation between the speaker and the agent of the proposition expressed. In this way, deontic modality is very much like so-called *dynamic modality,* or ability, like English *can* ('be able to') (see Palmer 1986: 102), which indicates a condition *on the agent of the event,* not a condition on the event expressed. Curiously, dynamic modality does not frequently appear as an inflection, either.

In contrast, epistemic modality often does surface as an inflection. Though some reasons for this are mentioned later (sec. 9.5), we should remark here that this difference in inflectional coding for epistemics is understandable from the nature of this kind of modality. Epistemic modality encodes the speaker's judgment of the factual status of an event, not the judgment of its execution. Therefore, epistemic modality is more strictly *event-oriented,* or, as Bybee (1985) calls it, *speaker-oriented.* It is not surprising then that epistemic modality should surface as an inflection because its semantic content is more compatible with the semantic content of inflection as a whole.

9.432. The Surface Convergence of Deontic and Epistemic Modality

Deontics and epistemics are very often encoded *in the same form*; alternatively, a marker of modality frequently has both a deontic and epistemic reading. We have seen this convergence repeatedly in our previous examples, where the English form *may* has either a deontic or epistemic reading and Albanian *mund* means either 'permission' or 'possibility.' The same overlap is found in Eskimo, for example (Fortescue 1984: 292–3). Why should there be such a convergence?

As Palmer (1986: 124) points out, a number of people have offered the same explanation, though Sweetser's (1982) is perhaps the most detailed and straightforward: deontic and epistemic converge in surface form because they derive from the same conceptual content. Her account relies first on a distinction between epistemic modality (identical to our notion) and *root modality* (which includes both deontics and dynamics: obligation, permission, and ability). She claims that both epistemic and root modality denote '*the overcoming of a potential or actual barrier by the exertion of force.*' When the barrier and force are in the sociophysical world, we get root modality, with notions of obligatory and permitted *action* and *ability to execute events*. But when the barrier and force are in the notional or informational world, we get epistemic modality, as in the case of strong epistemic judgment, for example, which expresses an inference about the likelihood that an event will "move" across the barrier of unrealization into realization: that is, achieve abstract factual status. Here we get cognitive force and dynamics. Consequently, deontic and epistemic modality converge in surface form because they have the same semantic content, but apply to different domains: epistemics to knowledge and roots to action.

One advantage of this account is its breadth. If there is a basic unity to deontic and epistemic modality, which then applies to different domains, we might then expect this difference and convergence to surface in other places, wherever there might be some need for the expression of modality or of a speaker's relation to a proposition or event. Indeed, Sweetser (1982) observes that the root/epistemic contrast applies quite generally in English. Many verbs not usually associated with modal readings do in fact have both root and epistemic senses. Consider the following expressions:

50a. The policeman indicated that we sped up.
  b. The policeman indicated that we speed up.

Examples (50a) and (50b) are very nearly alike on the surface, but they have quite different contents. Example (50a) describes a completed state of affairs presented with factual status. However, example (50b) describes an order: 'the policeman made an indication that he/she was obliging us to speed up.' *Indicate* thus is compatible with two senses, one that is associated with actualization, and hence is epistemiclike, and one that is aligned with obligation, and is deontic. This difference comes through in the grammatical structure of the complements. The epistemic reading takes the indicative mood in the complement, *that we sped up,* and the deontic takes the subjunctive, *that we speed up.* Indeed, there are many such verbs (and adverbs) in English that follow this pattern: *suggest, insist, expect,* and so on (see Sweetser 1982). Similar facts hold for other languages: for example, compare Spanish *insistir,* which has the same double sense.

This observation about the broad applicability of the deontic/epistemic contrast returns us to a basic point made in this section. Language has both an informational (epistemic) and actional (deontic/root) domain. We have just seen, further, that both are compatible with the more elemental modal concepts of realizability, actualization, or realis/irrealis. A simple and efficient encoding mechanism for language to exploit in this case is to encode simply the degree of actualization and let each domain sort out the interpretations. Under this view, the intensional—that is, world creating or belief-context inducing—properties of any expression should be compatible with these two readings.

9.44. Summary

We have defined deontic modality as the imposition of an expressed world on a reference world and seen how in spite of the clear pragmatic force of this definition, deontic modality nonetheless retains a semantic structure. Three semantic factors characterize deontic modality: obligation/permission, futurity, and other-orientation. We have also described the encoding regularities of this modality: the failure of deontics to appear as inflections and the frequent convergence of epistemic and deontic modality in surface form. The latter is accountable to the underlying conceptual unity of deontics and epistemics in the overcoming of an actual or potential barrier.

9.5. THE DEVELOPMENT OF MODALITY

Now that we have a fairly good command of the descriptive facts surrounding modality, we can try to put these ideas into a broader theoretical context. We conclude by examining one idea that has been something of the backbone of our exposition: Modality has an underlying conceptual unity and this in turn motivates its surface forms.

This basic point leads to an interesting area of theoretical inquiry. Given the conceptual unity of modality, we can make claims about the historical and logical emergence of some forms of modality out of others because they all derive from a common base. We focus on how deontic modality gives rise to epistemic modality on the basis of pragmatic strengthening and the subjectivization of meaning. We then take these results as grounds for speculation on the development of negative types and propose a solution to the problem of the historical and conceptual relationship between descriptive and metalinguistic negation.

9.51. From Deontic to Epistemic

The literature on semantic change indicates that epistemic modality *follows* deontic modality historically. We already know that deontic and epistemic modality are conceptually related by virtue of sharing the meaning 'overcoming a barrier,' as per Sweetser's (1982) argument, and this motivates their surface convergence to begin with (sec. 9.432). But why should the deontic meaning be *primary*? Is this relation between deontic and epistemic modality representative of a more general pattern of the emergence and differentiation of modality? (If so, is negation likewise subject to similar conditions of development?) A number of scholars—most notably Bybee (1985; Bybee and Pagliuca 1985) and Traugott (1989)—have proposed interesting answers to the puzzle of the developmental relation between deontic and epistemic modality. Their theories also provide some grounds for speculation about negation.

9.511. The Subjectivization of Meaning

Traugott (1989) argues that the course of the development of grammatical meaning—of which the deontic-to-epistemic shift is an example—involves the gradual *subjectivization of meaning*. This condition subsumes three tendencies (Traugott's view is slightly different here; I put the three together for expositional purposes: see Traugott 1982, 1989):

1. Meanings in the *external* (sociophysical) world give rise to meanings in the *internal* (e.g., mental) world;
2. Meanings in the *external/internal* world give rise to meanings in the *textual* or *metalinguistic* world;
3. Meanings in the *textual* world give rise to meanings in the *expressive* or *subjective* world.

In short, the course of grammatical meaning is subject to the following hierarchy: External > Internal > Textual/Metalinguistic > Expressive.

Traugott gives impressive evidence in support of this scale. For example, the English conjunction *while* originally meant 'at the time that' and thus was a wholly propositional, temporal marker (external/internal); it then came to mean to 'during,' and also took on a conjunctive function in texts (textual); subsequently, *while* developed a concessive meaning 'although,' and came to express speaker's attitude (expressive). So the historical course of the denotation of *while* follows the hierarchy of subjectivized meaning.

Traugott's theory offers a number of advantages. For one thing, it subsumes other competing accounts. Bybee and colleagues argue that the development of epistemics from deontics is part of the larger historical emergence of *speaker-oriented* modalities (such as epistemics, *where semantically general information is associated with the utterer of the proposition*) from *agent-oriented* ones (such as deontics, *where semantically specific information is associated with the executor of the proposition uttered by the speaker*). The generalization of meaning that characterizes Bybee's theory accords with gradual subjectivization: The relocation of agent modalities to speaker modalities is subjectivization par excellence.

For another thing, Traugott's account broadly cuts across language and unites a number of phenomena. Not only does the emergence of epistemics from deontics fit the pattern of subjectivization, but so also do other trends in the development of modal notions, such as the emergence of evidentials, epistemic adverbs, and speech act verbs (see Traugott 1989). For example, verbs that allow both assertive and directive meanings, like *insist* ('assert with force' vs. 'command'), typically derive the assertive meaning from the directive one (Sweetser 1982; sec. 9.432). Hence, Traugott (1989: 45) argues, the speaker's "belief attitude is later than the directive," or the deontic precedes the epistemic.

9.512. Pragmatic Strengthening and the Deontic/Epistemic Split

Traugott's proposal is motivated by the observation that in many cases, semantic change is the result of *communicative requirements*. The emergence of epistemics from deontics is the result of the gradual stabilization, or strengthening, of a *conversational implicature* (or a highly expected and codified pragmatic inference triggered by a form: see chap. 2). The epistemic sense is pragmatically implicated by the deontic, and this implicature comes to be conventionalized, or semanticized through time.

Consider the logical relation between deontic *may*, 'permission,' and epistemic *may*, 'possibility.' Permission does not entail possibility, as an examination of the inferential relations across the following shows: *John may ('permission') go $\nrightarrow$ John may ('possibility') go.* If John is allowed to go then it is *not* thereby true that it is possible for him to go: He may have permission but his going may be prevented. Thus, the development of the epistemic sense from the deontic cannot be semantically or truth-functionally driven because *may* as permission does not entail *may* as possibility. The pragmatic facts suggest otherwise, however. If John has permission to go, then it is pretty reasonable to expect that it is also possible for him to go. After all, why should someone give permission for something that is impossible to carry out? The inference from permission to possibility is thus not an entailment, but an implicature.

Traugott argues that implicatures of this sort become conventionalized into the semantic representation and split the deontic sense from the epistemic. By her account, semantic development is driven by the rules of conversation with meaning becoming more and more situated in the "speaker's attempt to regulate communication with others" (1989: 51): that is, in the conventionalization of subjectivized meaning, or what she calls *pragmatic strengthening*.

9.52. Pragmatic Strengthening and the Explanation of Negative Types

In Traugott's theory, pragmatic strengthening forms a general condition on the emergence of modality in subjectivized forms. Can we use this to explain the emergence of other modal phenomena? If so, then the unified view of the development of modality takes on additional force.

9.521. *Descriptive and Metalinguistic Negation*

It has often been noted that negation comes in two forms: *descriptive negation,* which *denies the truth* of propositional content (equivalent to propositional negation); *metalinguistic negation,* which *rejects aspects of context* and is thereby not truth-conditional (see Horn 1989). We can see these two types of negation in the following:

51a. Bill didn't paint the house.
  b. Bill didn't *paint* the house, he slapped it all over with cheap whitewash.

Sentence (51a) illustrates descriptive negation in expressing the falsity of a state of affairs: 'It is false that Bill painted the house.' Sentence (51b), in contrast, does not express a falsity, but a pragmatic contrast: The verb *paint* is rejected in favor of a different *form* of expression, *slap it all over.* . . The negation in (51b) signals that the *assertability* of the verb *paint* is to be *rejected,* and so here, the negation is metalinguistic, not truth-conditional.

These two kinds of negation have different properties. Descriptive negation, for example, triggers the *some/any* rule whereas pragmatic negation does not:

52a. Bill didn't say anything.
  b. Bill didn't *buy* something, he *procured* it.

But the two also have a great deal in common. Horn (1989), for instance, argues that the two have exactly the same meaning, 'negation,' but applied to different domains, with descriptive negation found in the propositional domain and pragmatic negation found in the contextual domain. Moreover, languages tend to give the two negation types the *same surface form,* letting the context sort out the specifics of interpretation, as in English, where both negatives surface as *not.*

These similarities in the two types of negation should immediately bring to mind the claims made previously about deontics and epistemics, which also have the same meaning, just applied to different domains, and tend to surface in the same form. Are descriptive and pragmatic negation thus related, just as epistemic and deontic modality? Is there the possibility of a unified treatment of negation types on the analogy of a unified treatment of epistemic and deontic modality? As Horn (1989: 443) says:

> One issue which remains is the directionality of the relationship between descriptive and metalinguistic negation: which use is primary and which is derivative? Or do both uses branch off from some more basic, undifferentiated notion? I have little to contribute to this etiology, given that the connection is explicable in either direction and that a full answer would appear to be buried in the realms of speculation.

9.522. Metalinguistic Negation
and Pragmatic Strengthening

Traugott's account of the development of epistemics out of deontics, and of semantic change in general, provides an interesting solution to this puzzle with negatives. First, we should note that just as with deontics and epistemics, there is no entailment relation between the two negatives: *Bill didn't paint the house* (denial) does not entail *Bill didn't **paint** the house, he slapped it all over with whitewash* (rejection). That is, the falsity of the state of affairs does not logically imply a rejection of the form of the expression. Nor does rejection imply denial: *Bill didn't **paint** the house, he slapped it all over with whitewash* (rejection) does not entail *Bill didn't pain the house* (denial). On the contrary, if, in the situation described, Bill slapped the house all over with whitewash, then he *did* in fact paint the house!

However, also following the pattern of deontics and epistemics, there is an implicature between the two kinds of negation. If it is false that Bill painted the house, then it is extremely likely that one will reject the usage of the expression *paint* to describe the situation. Denial thus implicates rejection, or, as Horn (1989) also calls it, lack of assertability. In point of fact, why assert things that are false? This restriction can be understood as a function of Grice's rules of rational discourse (see chap. 2).

The implicature does not work the other way around, moreover: rejection does not implicate denial. Quite the opposite, rejection implicates the affirmation. The rejection of the expression *paint* is grounded by the fact that the denial itself is false: *Paint* is rejected because the proposition is *true*, but improperly characterized or encoded. Denial thus implicates rejection. On analogy, then, with deontics and epistemics, descriptive negation is prior to metalinguistic negation, and the metalinguistic sense is the conventionalization, or strengthening, of a conversational implicature from denial.

A number of other facts further support this line of reasoning. Traugott (1989) observes that semantic change is conditioned by subjectivization, with metalinguistic senses following propositional ones (recall her scale; sec. 9.511). Under this view, metalinguistic negation ought to naturally follow descriptive negation because the latter is propositional by definition. Note also that metalinguistic negation adheres to the same conditions as other forms that emerge out of propositional domains. Metalinguistic negation is more subjective than descriptive (or propositional) negation because rejection lies in the speaker's judgment of what is assertable, not in truth value. Furthermore, metalinguistic negation can have a textual function and expressive function, as per Traugott's claims. The rejection of a form of expression by metalinguistic negation focuses on the text as a mode of expression: The contrast in (52) is designed to call attention to the text itself (cf. Traugott's discussion of *while* here). Moreover, metalinguistic negation can be used to express purely attitudinal meaning, as Horn (1989) points out when he observes that the negative can reject not only forms of expression but any feature of context, even surrounding nonlinguistic information.

The empirical and ontogenetic facts also match up with these predictions, though at first glance, it might not appear that way. Many acquisition specialists have shown that negation in child language begins in the pragmatic and contextual domain—as the negation of existence (*no toy!*) or refusal (*no more!*)—and then evolves into standard propositional denial (Bloom 1970; Horn 1989: chap. 3; Pea 1980). From this well-attested sequence, we ought to conclude that pragmatic negation precedes descriptive negation. But we should be careful to recall an even broader principle of semantic change. Many semantic categories begin as pragmatic ones, which means that, as Traugott (1989) argues, external (sociophysical) precedes internal (semantic) information. So to say that refusal precedes denial is only to say that child language accords with the general development of propositional information per se, from external to internal. In his synopsis of Pea's work, Horn (1989: 167) echoes this observation: "External prohibition then develops into internal (self-) prohibition."

There are *two types of pragmatic negation,* one the pragmatic external basis of denial and the other textual. As Horn notes (1989: 429); "not all uses of metalinguistic negation can be analyzed as semantic external," that is, as pragmatic in the first sense. It is the latter—that which negates the form of expressions or indicates attitude—with which we are concerned.

I am aware of no study on this matter, but my intuition tells me that such negation is ontogenetically quite late. Textual negation requires metalinguistic awareness, and this is generally a late cognitive operation because it also requires cognitive control and hypothetical thinking. As a result, metalinguistic negation should follow the development of denial (itself evolving from external factors) (thanks to Roberta Golinkoff for advice on this point).

Additional supporting data for the claim that metalinguistic negation of the sort we have identified is comparatively late should come from historical change, where if the predictions are correct, descriptive negation should precede metalinguistic negation. There is again little information available on the subject, no doubt because an adequate solution also requires a historical pragmatic grammar of a language, no mean feat in itself. But perhaps we can speculate on the basis of the information in historical dictionaries.

For *not,* the *Oxford English Dictionary* (OED) lists descriptive negation as the historically earliest form in English, with the first citations around 1340. Uses of *not* in a pragmatic/contrastive sense, of the sort that textual negation exemplifies, occur some time later. Assuming that the use of negation as contrast with a following *but* is indicative of this function—*it's not this, but that*—we see that such senses are first attested in 1579, some 200 years after the descriptive sense. Indeed, the OED documentation of the usage by J. Hayward comes pretty close to the sense we want: "Discovering that is not hid but vailed," where there is an explicit contrast of *form.* Hayward's citation is from 1635. Moreover, the first attestation of the use of *not* in a reflexive metalinguistic sense—the first citation of *not* as a form (e.g., "a *not*")—occurs in 1601 in Shakespeare. Thus, *not*'s own metalinguistic properties are not found until some 300 years after its descriptive sense is attested.

All these factors point to what we have predicted: the metalinguistic sense of negation, as a textual expressive marker, follows the descriptive sense. In this way, the types of negation closely parallel the types of modality. Indeed, Horn (1989: 443–4) argues as much: "There is a procedural sense in which the descriptive use of negation is primary; the non-logical metalinguistic understanding is typically available only on a 'second pass,'" by which he means that psychologically, the preferential reading is the descriptive. He also points out that the emergence of negation looks curiously like the emergence of epistemic modality from deontic (1989: 539, fn. 7). Horn's intuitions are borne out by the data. Indeed, they are predicted by Traugott's theory of the subjectivization of meaning and the role of pragmatic strengthening in the emergence of modality and other semantic categories.

9.53. Summary

We have discussed the historical development of epistemic modality from deontic modality and considered Traugott's theory of semantic change as a comprehensive framework. Traugott argues that the emergence of epistemics out of deontics is the result of the strengthening and subjectivization of the implicature between the two: Obligation implicates probability. We have applied this account to the relation between descriptive and metalinguistic negation, showing that the former likewise implicates the latter. Traugott's theory of subjectivization, as well as the historical and ontogenetic data, accords with this result. A unified theory of modality works side by side with a coherent theory of the development of modality under pragmatic conditions.

SUMMARY OF CHAPTER

This chapter has defined modality and discussed the range of notions it covers, such things as possibility, obligation, negation, hypotheticality, doubt, supposition, and inference. We distinguished modality from mood, a grammatical device for marking relationships across clauses, and defined modality more precisely through the realis/irrealis opposition. We then cast the whole issue in terms of deixis: a reference world, an expressed (or located) world, and remoteness and direction between the two.

We then turned to three kinds of modality: negation, epistemic modality, and deontic modality. First, we focused on propositional negation, logical denial, and saw how the informational structure of discourse associates negation with the contextually free part of a proposition. We noted three structural diagnostics, *too*/*either*, tag questions, and *not even*, and the range of forms that trigger these tests. We considered some regularities in the form of verbal negation, higher negative verbs, negative auxiliary verbs, particles, and bound negators, and the issues involved in negative scope (especially variations in wide and narrow scope and the role of semantic content) and negative polarity items and the variety of negative inducing forms.

Second, we discussed epistemic modality, the likelihood of the convergence of the reference world and expressed world and the evidence for such. We considered two theories of epistemic modality, Palmer's on categories and Givón's on scales, ultimately combining them into a larger deictic view of epistemic modality. Source, direction, and remoteness of knowledge form the basis for a broad view of the differential structuring of epistemic space. We also noted how tense and person, themselves deictic notions, often take up the burden of epistemic modality.

Third, we defined deontic modality as the imposition of an expressed world on a reference world and examined three basic semantic factors: obligation/permission, futurity, and other-orientation. We described the failure of deontics to appear as inflections and the frequent convergence of epistemic and deontic modality in surface form, explaining the latter via the underlying conceptual unity of deontics and epistemics in the overcoming of an actual or potential barrier.

In closing, we discussed the historical development of epistemic modality from deontic modality and Traugott's theory of semantic change through pragmatic strengthening and the subjectivization of implicatures. We applied this account to the relation between descriptive and metalinguistic negation and brought in historical and ontogenetic data for further support.

QUESTIONS FOR DISCUSSION

1. Discuss the following expressions in terms of what you know about modality:

   ia. When Dave was alive, he would go to the circus.
   b. If Dave were here, he would go to the circus.
   c. The King of France is un-bald.
   d. I hear that Bob is coming.

What is the denotation of *would* in (ia) and (ib)? How does *would* relate to the realis/irrealis distinction? What times is *would* compatible with? What does a deictic account of modality reveal about the meaning of *would*? For (ic), discuss the meaning and scope of the negative prefix *un*. Can (ic) ever mean 'there is no

King of France'? For (id), consider the kind of epistemic modality denoted by *hear*. How does this expression fit in with the theories of evidentials we have discussed? Compare (id) to *I hear Bob coming*. What does this expression mean? What does it indicate about evidentiality in English and its structural reflexes?

2. Consider the following expression from Manam (Lichtenberk 1983: 418):

i. ŋa-   múle- re.
   3Sing/Def/Irreal return Assertion
   He must come back!

Example (i) has a deontic meaning: 'he is obliged to come back.' Why does the verb, *múle,* take a marker of irrealis? Moreover, why does the verb also take a marker of assertion? One definition of an assertion is 'a statement that can be true or false.' How does this affect your answer? What does this say about the status of deontic modality as a semantic phenomenon?

3. Some verbs in English allow paraphrases between their own negation and the negation of their complements: so-called *negative transport*. *Believe* is one such verb; note the paraphrase relationship between the following:

ia. I do not believe he is here.
 b. I believe he is not here.

Say, however, does not allow this relationship, and the following are not paraphrases:

iia. I did not say he was here.
  b. I said he was not here.

Can you think of other verbs that allow negative transport and some that do not? What semantic characteristics do these verbs have (i.e., how is *say* different from *believe*)? With this information in mind, consider the following negated expressions:

iiia. It is not certain that he will go.
   b. It is not likely that he will go.
   c. It is not possible that he will go.

Which of these allow the negative to be transported into the complement (*that he will go*) and yet are paraphrases of the originals? Which do not allow the transport of the negative? Now, note that *certain, likely,* and *possible* form a scale of epistemic modality, from strongest likelihood to weakest: *certain* > *likely* > *possible*. How could such a scale affect negative transport? In your answer, consider also the following modal forms scaled from strong to weak: *must* > *supposed to* > *might* and *sure of* > *expect* > *hope*. Which allow negative transport and which do not? Can you formulate a general semantic rule for this phenomenon? (See Horn 1989 and Givón 1984 for help.)

10 Modification

10.1. INTRODUCTION

In this chapter, we turn to the final topic of our analysis of linguistic meaning: modification. The kinds of properties ascribed to entities and the ways that such ascription is carried out in language are perhaps the most unresearched areas in all of linguistics. We focus primarily on what we might call *property concepts* or *adjectival concepts*: those qualities that surface as adjectives or modifierlike forms.

By way of introduction, we examine the structure of modification and three definitions of property concepts and adjectives: Givón's theory of temporal stability, Thompson's discourse view, and Wierzbicka's semantic/conceptual account converge in terms of the noncriterial and unidimensional nature of property concepts. We complete the introduction by examining the relative and absolute structure of property denotation and the categorematic or syncategorematic relation of a property to the domain modified.

Following this introductory material, we provide an inventory of property concepts, based on Dixon's (1982) study of adjectival modification and corrections and improvements thereon (e.g., by Schaefer 1989; Wierzbicka 1986). Here we survey six broad categories of property concepts—value, human propensity, physical property, color, age, and quantity—as well as their regular subcategories (e.g., universals of color terminology). We spend considerable time on the last category, quantity, because theories of quantification have been influential in the development of semantic analysis itself.[1]

---

[1]There are several conspicuous absences in the discussion of property concepts: possession, adverbial modification, and morphological regularities. Their absence is not an indication of their

We close the chapter with an examination of the semantic basis of the order of modifiers in an expression. We look at several typological accounts of modifier order and explanations thereof based on subjectivity and scope. We then consider some of the formal claims about modification, with a focus on modifiers as logical functions. We look at how the logic of modification, by extension or intension, unifies the formal and typological claims about modifier order.

10.11. Modification: Domains, Properties, and Delimitation

What do we mean when we say that something *modifies* something else? We can provide some answers by looking at an instance of modification:

1. five red balls.

The expression in (1) encodes a *domain,* the item that is modified (*balls*), which is *delimited* by two *properties*: *numerical quantification* (*five*) and *color* (*red*). This illustration underscores two basic questions that drive our subsequent inquiry into modification:

1. What kinds of property concepts universally delimit domains in language?
2. How do property concepts delimit domains?

The goal of this chapter is to provide an inventory of properties and functions at the service of the grammars of all languages. These ideas, fundamental as they are, presuppose an even more basic inquiry. *What are property concepts to begin with*? Three influential answers to this question have appeared in the literature.

10.12.   Three Accounts of Property Concepts

What concepts underlie modification? The literature contains three principal answers: two in terms of semantic/conceptual structure and one in terms of discourse/information flow.

---

insignificance, only a symptom of the limits of space. The interested reader may consult Ultan (1978b) and Nichols (1988) for a thorough study of possession and McConnell-Ginet (1982) and Ernst (1984) for a survey of adverbial properties and structures. Dixon (1982), Schaefer (1989), and Lindsey and Scancarelli (1985) discuss the surface forms of modifiers.

10.121. *Modifiers and Temporal Stability*

Givón's (1970, 1984) solution to the nature of property concepts is in the spirit of his account of all grammatical forms. As we already know (chaps. 3 and 4), Givón views grammatical categories as motivated by their typical denotations, and these, in turn, are a function of the relative temporal stability of perceptual phenomena. Nouns encode temporally stable entities; verbs encode temporally unstable events. Between these two are adjectives, encoding qualities, phenomena that are *both temporally stable and unstable.* Adjectives and their attendant properties are cognitively, phenomenologically, and categorially *a mixture of nouns and verbs.*

A number of convincing illustrations support the gist of Givón's characterization. The adjectives *noisy* and *long* are both technically states, but the former is compatible with active expressions, and the latter takes statives (after Givón 1970; see also Dowty 1979, chap. 2):

2a. The children are being noisy.
 b. ?? The board is being long.

Givón accounts for this difference by arguing that "adjectives are not semantic primitives, while nouns and verbs are" (1970: 835). *Noisy* is more verbal because it is a property that is temporally sensitive and potentially under control of a doer: *Noisy* derives from *make noise. Long,* on the other hand, is a nominal derivative because it is a state of existence, is temporally stable, and cannot be executed or carried out: *Long* derives from *length,* not from *make long.* So, the difference between active adjectives like *noisy* and stative adjectives like *long* comes down to the essence of property concepts themselves. The intermediate position of adjectives and their associated property concepts on the continuum of time stability gives rise to a duality in English modifying expressions via the temporal characteristics of the property concepts that the expressions denote.

The intermediate position of property concepts, their expression as adjectives, and their general temporal heterogeneity are more clearly underscored in languages that do not have a productive class of adjectives, but instead encode property concepts as either nouns or verbs. In Chinese, adjectives function very much like verbs. Latin, which has a productive class of adjectives, nonetheless allows some adjectives to function like verbs if the situation requires explicit attention to the temporal instability of the property concept expressed (after Wierzbicka 1986: 376):

3a. rosa rubr- a   est.
 rose red   Fem is
 The rose is red. (Adjective)

b. rosa rub- et.
   rose red   3per/Pres
   The rose is red. (Verb)

In (3a), the property concept of color is encoded as an adjective, as indicated by
the agreement of the root *rubr* with the feminine noun *rosa*. Here the property is
temporally stable, making a more appropriate gloss of (3a) 'the rose is perma-
nently red.' But in (3b), the property concept is encoded as a verb, as signalled
by tense and person on the root *rub,* and the form comes with all the usual
semantic associations of temporal sensitivity that verbal notions entail. A more
exact gloss for (3b) is probably 'the rose reds': the redness of the rose is "a
momentary feature of the scenery" (Wierzbicka 1986: 376).

Latin exemplifies how the verbal encoding of the property concept is compatible with the temporal stability of the denotation itself. These choices are possible
because property concepts are denotationally heterogeneous to begin with. What,
then, are property concepts? Givón's answer is: temporally heterogeneous phenomena that are intermediate on the scale of time stability. This denotational
structure motivates their overt forms.

10.122. Modifiers and Discourse Structure

Thompson (1988) provides an alternative view of the nature of property concepts. The canonical denotations of grammatical categories are properly understood in terms of the information flow of discourse. Nouns encode discourse
participants and typically denote individuals; verbs encode narrated events and
denote actions. From an information-flow view of categories and denotations,
adjectives and property concepts modify individuals in order to anchor them in
discourse.

Thompson (1988) argues that the two basic adjectival forms—*predicative,*
following a copula (as in *The book is red*), and *attributive,* directly modifying a
noun (as in *the red book*)—are determined by discourse pressures. The most
frequent adjectival expression of property concepts is the predicative form, determined by the discourse function of predicative modification, which is to assign
properties to *established discourse participants.* An expression like *The book is
red* is overwhelmingly associated with the delimitation of a domain that is old
information. The second most frequent form is the attributive adjective, which is
used predominantly to assign property concepts to *new* (though not brand new)
discourse participants. Hence, an expression like *the red book* delimits a domain
that represents new information in the discourse.

What are property concepts? Thompson's (1988) answer is: attributes of participants subject to the informational requirements of discourse. Informationally,
there are two basic kinds of individuals in discourse: old and new. Likewise,

there are two kinds of property concepts: predicative, for old participants; attributive, for new participants.[2]

10.123. Modifiers as Single Properties (vs. Kinds)

A third account of property concepts is given by Wierzbicka (1986), who observes that traditionally, nouns denote substances and adjectives denote qualities. She argues, however, that this construal misses a critical point. Nouns and adjectives *both* denote properties. In fact, modern logic teaches us that nouns are predications as much as adjectives and verbs: To say that something is a bird is to say that it has the qualities of birdness or the set of "bird properties" (see sec. 10.3 for more on this point). But nouns and adjectives diverge in the means and purpose of the denotation of properties. Nouns refer to *kinds* by denoting a *complex of properties*. Adjectives denote *single properties* and thus *fail to refer to kinds*.

We can see this denotational difference in (4), which contrasts a nominal and adjectival expression of roughly the same conceptual content:

4a. Bill is an Irishman.
 b. Bill is Irish.

---

[2]Bolinger (1967) proposes a semantic solution to the distinction between predicative and attributive modifiers that is reminiscent of our original semantic considerations of property concepts and is also compatible with Thompson's discourse-oriented view. Modifiers whose denotations have temporal restrictions, or are occasioned, very likely occur in predicative position. On the other hand, modifiers expressing property concepts that are atemporal, customary, or, in general, less occasioned, are very likely to be found in attributive positions. Compare the following in this respect:

 i. This whiskey is straight.
 ii. This is straight whiskey.

Example (i), where the property concept is expressed in predicative form, conveys a temporary circumstance and is likely to be found as a description of a drink "readied for the occasion" (Bolinger 1967: 4). Example (ii), on the other hand, expresses the property concept in an attributive form and denotes a product, or a temporally stable phenomenon. This account returns us to Givón's view of property concepts and modifiers as occupying an intermediate position on the continuum of temporal stability: Predicative modifiers are verblike and temporally sensitive; attributive modifiers are nounlike, atemporal, and stative.

With a little imagination, we can make Thompson's (1988) discourse theory follow suit. Temporary properties (predicatives) are ascribed to established participants, and nontemporary properties (attributives) are ascribed to new participants. The logic of this correlation follows Grice's maxim of quantity: be as informative as possible, but not too informative. Temporary information, changeable and thus more inherently uncertain, is ascribed to established or known discourse participants; more permanent information, established and thus more inherently certain, is ascribed to unknown and unestablished discourse participants. Predication and attribution are inversely related to the informativeness and newness of the domains they modify. In this way, discourse structure is compatible with, and does not determine, semantic structure. Predication and attribution enter into discourse with inherent semantic content, and the information structure of discourse accommodates this by requiring informationally balanced domains for the modifiers.

In (4a), *Irishman* denotes a complex of properties that define membership in a class: for example, 'having Irish heritage,' 'having a certain appearance,' 'behaving in a certain manner,' and so forth.[3] In (4b), the adjective *Irish* denotes a single property, 'ethnicity,' and the modification functions to apply this single property to the individual denoted by *Bill*. As Wierzbicka (1986: 378): "The adjective specifies one feature. . . . The noun categorizes the person." More generally (1986: 366), "An adjective may restrict the domain to which the intended referent belongs, and to help identify this referent within that domain, but it can't replace that initial placement within an imaginable domain (i.e., a KIND)."

What is a property concept? According to Wierzbicka it is a single noncategorizing property that applies to a kind (versus a complex of categorizing properties, which is what a noun denotes).

10.124.   A Unified Account of Property Concepts

We can bring together these three accounts into a unified picture of property concepts. The denotations of modifiers are *singular, noncriterial, nonprimitive* qualities.

By *singular,* we mean that property concepts are unidimensional and apply to referents in a piecemeal fashion. Property concepts denote *only one thing at a time* and that denotation is always part of a larger denotation. For this reason, certain property concepts, like color, are more typically adjectival than others, like shape. Wierzbicka (1986) notes that shape may surface as an adjective, a singular property, but it is also frequently encoded as a noun classifier, a kind property, because shape can delimit an entire entity and thus may functionally induce a kind. Color, on the other hand, never denotes an entity as a totality and never delimits individual. As a consequence, color is rarely found as a noun classifier in languages, because color is more singular and less kindlike.

By *noncriterial,* we mean that property concepts do not substitute for domains or delimit them uniquely; rather, they *apply to* domains. Thompson's (1988) observations on the discourse function of adjectives fall in line here: Adjectival modification ascribes a single property to a non-information-bearing individual (either old or new, but not brand new) in discourse. Insofar as property concepts are noncriterial attributes, they cannot categorize and thus cannot, by themselves, distinguish new referents in discourse.

By *nonprimitive,* we mean that property concepts are functions, or are derived. Givón argues explicitly that they are heterogeneous and derivative; Thompson argues a similar position in seeing modifiers as a function of their

---

[3] A noun thus denotes what lexicographers call a *lemmatization,* or the union of relevant properties under a category label.

informational status; Wierzbicka concurs, claiming that property concepts apply to, but do not categorize, individuals. The literature on formal approaches to modification puts the same point more precisely. Parsons (1980) argues that modifiers are logical functions: specifically, ways of *connecting properties to sets of properties*. When we say *red shirt*, we are in fact saying that the form *red* stands for a function that maps the property of color onto the property of being a shirt (nouns themselves denote properties). Though we make more of the logical view of modification when we consider theoretical matters (sec. 10.33), we simply note here that all accounts converge on a single point: Property concepts *build complex denotations* more than they denote independently.

We now have a reasonably good idea of the nature of the denotation of modifiers: singular, noncriterial, nonprimitive properties with identifiable temporal, discursive, and conceptual characteristics. Before we proceed to an inventory of these property concepts, we should bear in mind two factors that traditionally drive the analysis of modification: the relative or absolute structure of the denotation of the modifier and the dependent or independent relation of the modifier to the domain.

10.13. Relative Versus Absolute Properties

Two kinds of property denotations are usually identified in the literature on modification: *relative properties,* those that can be scaled and hence are also called *scalar* or *gradable*; *absolute properties,* those that cannot be scaled and hence are also called *categorical* or *ungradable* (Sapir 1944 is the classic study).

Two tests fairly reliably differentiate relative from absolute properties. The first is the comparative construction. If a property is relative, it can be explicitly increased or decreased by comparative forms. An absolute property, however, is not amenable to comparison. Consider the following:

5a. Anna is Polish.
 b. Anna is happy.

The property of being Polish is absolute, as the anomaly of a comparative form indicates: ?? *Anna is more Polish than Mark.* Example (5b) expresses the property of happiness, which is clearly relative, as the acceptable comparative form attests: *Anna is happier than Mark.*

When we use the comparative test to differentiate relative from absolute properties, we must be careful not to be fooled by forms that look like they can be compared. We might argue that *Anna is more Polish than Mark* is acceptable, just like *This car is bluer than that one,* suggesting that color is also scalar. But we must pay attention to exactly what is being scaled by the comparative. *More*

Polish is acceptable as an indication of either 'scaled ethnicity' (in which case it *is* a relative property, but *forced to be so* outside of its normal interpretation) or 'incremented ethnicity' (as 'one quarter Polish,' in which case the property is not scaled but simply augmented in discrete units). *Bluer* is acceptable as a comparative of the *trueness of the color,* which is relative, not of the chromatic value of the color: A bluer car is closer to the truest blue, not more blue. For these reasons, we can put the comparative test in a more explicitly scalar context with an inchoative verb like *become,* which straightforwardly denotes a scale through growth. In this case, both *Polish* and *blue* fail the test, and so are absolute: ?? *Anna is becoming more Polish than Mark* and ?? *This car is becoming bluer than that one.*

The second test is negative implication, which works only if the form in question has an antonym and is tested against it. Absolute terms with opposites contrast with each other in a mutually exclusive fashion; technically, they are *ungradable antonyms,* or *complementaries.* In such pairs, the positive of one item implies the negative of the other, and vice versa, as for *dead* and *alive:*

6a. If someone is alive (Pos), he is not dead (Neg).
 b. If someone is dead (Pos), he is not alive (Neg).
 c. If someone is not alive (Neg), he is dead (Pos).
 d. If someone is not dead (Neg), he is alive (Pos).

This negation test yields a number of ungradables—*married/single, true/false,* and so on.

Relative properties are nonmutually exclusive opposites, or *contraries.* They are identified by half the negation test for ungradables, whereby the positive of one implies the negative of the other, but *not* vice versa. *Hot* and *cold* denote relative properties:

7a. If the soup is hot (Pos), it is not cold (Neg).
 b. If the soup is cold (Pos), it is not hot (Neg).
 c. ?? If the soup is not hot (Neg), it is cold (Pos) (tepid).
 d. ?? If the soup is not cold (Neg), it is hot (Pos) (tepid).

Gradable antonyms have middle terms between the two poles: *hot/tepid/cold, good/mediocre/bad,* and so on. For relative items, the negation test cannot split the scale as it does for absolutes, where there is no middle term, and hence mutual exclusion.

The dichotomy between absolute and relative properties has spurred much work to determine the *kinds of scalar denotations* present in languages (Cruse 1986; Rusiecki 1985). Cruse (1986: 204–20) nicely articulates the basics of these results. He points out that there are three kinds of gradients on which all scaled properties can fall: *polar, equipollent,* and *overlapping.* Polar gradients scale properties on a single, continuous dimension; equipollent gradients scale properties on a single dimension with a central gap; overlapping gradients scale properties on two scales, both gradients themselves, but only one of which grades into the other. There is a simple test for these types, one that operates by forcing the compatibility of direct expressions of gradience.

Polar gradients allow the contrastive expression of *both* the positive and comparative forms of each property, as shown in the next example:

8a. The box is heavy, but lighter than yesterday.
 b. The box is light, but heavier than yesterday.

Light and *heavy* must encode a single dimension, something like 'weight,' because they are compatible in comparison with each other. *Equipollent gradients,* however, *disallow both* kinds of expression, as *hot* and *cold* illustrate:

9a. ?? It is hot, but colder than yesterday.
 b. ?? It is cold, but hotter than yesterday.

These expressions are anomalous because the property that *hot* and *cold* expresses, for example, 'temperature,' has a cut off point in the center. *Semantically* (not conceptually), less heat does not produce coldness, nor does less coldness produce heat, and so the scalar property expressed by the terms must really consist of two subscales, one for *hot* and one for *cold,* with no intersecting middle ground (other examples from English that fit this test are *happy/sad* and *sweet/sour*). *Overlapping gradients allow one* of the expressions and *disallow the other.* Typical in this regard are English expressions of value:

10a. Bob is bad, but better than yesterday.
  b. ?? Bob is good, but worse than yesterday.

Good and *bad* have some scalar interaction, because they are compatible in comparison, but not a total connection. *Bad* can scale into *good,* as per (10a), where *bad* is compatible with *better.* But *good* cannot scale into *bad,* as per (10b), where *good* is incompatible with *worse.* (Note that if [10b] is to be made acceptable, then *good* must be scaled *explicitly with itself, not good: Bob is good, but not better than yesterday.*)

We do not pursue this work in any more detail, but merely note that the structure of the denotation of modifying expressions must be taken into account in any larger study of modification. It is important to know the kinds of property concepts that tend to be scaled or absolute, and how they are scaled, because not all languages treat the same properties in the same way.

10.14.   Categorematic
Versus Syncategorematic Modification

The second factor usually considered in studies of modification is the way the modifier applies to the modified domain. There are two such relations: *categorematic,* denotations *independent* of the domain modified; *syncategorematic,* denotations *dependent* on the domain modified (see Bloemen 1983; Martin 1986; Siegel 1980).

We can see the difference in the ambiguity of (11):

11. the wonderful singer.

Example (11) has two interpretations, depending on how the denotation of *wonderful* relates to the denotation of the domain, *singer.* In one sense, (11) means 'the singer who is wonderful irrespective of singing abilities': The modifier has a denotation independent of the domain and is thus categorematic. In another sense, however, (11) means 'the singer who is wonderful *as a* singer, or who sings wonderfully,' where the denotation of the modifier makes crucial reference to the denotation of the domain. In this interpretation, the modifier is syncategorematic because it essentially depends on the domain for its applicability.

A reliable test for the categorematic/syncategorematic distinction is the persistence of the modifier in set membership. A categorematic modifier is true of the set to which the domain belongs (the superset); a syncategorematic modifier is not. Consider (11) again. A singer is a member of the set of persons, but is a wonderful singer also a wonderful person? The persistence of the modifier *wonderful* to the superset of persons is true only in the categorematic reading of *wonderful.* But in the syncategorematic sense, *wonderful* is not true of its superset: A wonderful singer—one who sings wonderfully—is not necessarily a wonderful person.

We now have a good sense of the nature, structure, and function of modification and property concepts. Given these necessary preliminaries, we turn to an examination of the kinds of property concepts that languages encode.

10.15.   Summary

In this introduction, we have defined modification as the encoding of property concepts. We have looked at the structure of modification—domain, property, and delimitation—and considered three views of property concepts: Givón's theory of temporal stability, Thompson's view of modifiers as anchors for old and new information in discourse, and Wierzbicka's theory of modifiers as single properties. These three come together in the view that modification is the means by which a language restricts or delimits a domain by encoding singular, noncriterial, nonprimitive qualities. We have closed our discussion by looking at scalar versus absolute properties and categorematic versus syncategorematic modification.

10.2. SIX CLASSES OF PROPERTY CONCEPTS

This section describes six classes of property concepts that languages encode, usually as adjectives, though this depends on whether the language has a productive adjective class (Dixon 1982; Lindsey and Scancarelli 1985; Schachter 1985; Schaefer 1989). We hope ultimately to answer the two essential questions (sec. 10.11) of the kinds of property concepts that language have and the ways that property concepts delimit their domains. Along the way we bear in mind, and sometimes explicitly invoke, the relative or absolute nature of the property concepts and the categorematic or syncategorematic interpretation of the modifiers within the category.

Our inventory of property concepts is based on Dixon's (1982) extensive cross-language study of adjectives, though we emend his findings where necessary. We look at the following six categories of property concepts: color, value, age, human propensity, physical properties, and quantity. The first five of these categories are self-explanatory and are, moreover, five of the seven universal categories of adjectival concepts that Dixon finds in his cross-language work. (The other two are dimension—for example, size—and speed, which we do not consider here for reasons of space.) The first three of these categories, furthermore, are the "most universal," the property concepts that all languages tend to encode as independent modifiers (see Wierzbicka 1986).

The last category, quantity, deserves some explanation. Quantity includes determiners (the, that, etc.), nonnumerical quantifiers (all, most, etc.), and numerical quantifiers (one, two, first, etc.). Dixon puts these in a single category, "logical modifiers," and I follow him not only for consistency, but also because determiners and quantifiers have unified treatments in the literature in general. The category is divided into nonnumerical quantifiers, forms like much and many, and numerical ones, what we ordinarily understand to be numerals. In the discussion that follows, we spend about half the time on the first five categories and half on quantity terms; we devote such effort to quantity because of its influential position in semantic theory and analysis.

10.21. Color

Color vocabulary has been one of the most well-researched areas of the lexicon. Thanks to Berlin and Kay's (1969) seminal study, and improvements thereon by Kay and McDaniel (1978), we now know that all languages have a set of basic color terms chosen from a universal hierarchy of color denotations.

10.211.   Basic Color Terms
and the Universal Hierarchy of Color Denotations

A *basic color term* is a monolexemic (one morpheme) form that occurs in the idiolects of all speakers, is psychologically salient for them, refers to a wide class of objects, and has a meaning that is not included in the meaning of any other color term. Although these criteria have been the subject of some debate (see Crawford 1982), even in revision, the essential insights remain: A basic color term is typically a single, productive form used by all speakers, with stable and generalized color meaning and independent denotation. By these criteria, the color term *red* in English is basic, while the terms *slate blue, charcoal grey,* and *light green* are not basic.

The *universal hierarchy of color denotations* specifies a fixed order of basic color terms. From a survey of 98 languages, Berlin and Kay find that languages choose from a set of 11 denotations and these denotations follow the order in Fig. 10.1. This hierarchy is to be read as all other hierarchies we have studied in this book: Items to the right presuppose items to the left, but not vice versa. Alternatives in braces are mutually exclusive choices, where the one not chosen first becomes the next choice by default; alternatives in bars are selected in conjunction.

All languages distinguish *black* and *white,* though in many languages this amounts to a distinction between *dark* and *light.* Some languages have only these two terms and thus bifurcate the color space. If a language has three terms, it will have *black, white,* and *red.* A fourth term must be either *green* or *yellow,* and the fifth is the option not chosen from this set. Six-term color systems invariably have *blue,* and seven-term systems have *brown.* Systems with more than seven terms select denotations from the last set of four, meaning that languages with more than seven terms usually have no fewer than eleven.

Berlin and Kay (1969) argue that the hierarchy predicts that languages will choose one of seven possible color systems, which they call *stages* (the terminology reflects their interest in the evolutionary development of color vocabulary). The stages and examples of languages at each stage are given in Fig. 10.2. These stages bring to light a number of implications and interesting corollaries. We consider three.

10.212.   Three Features of Color Terms

10.2121.   Hue

The denotations of color terms are determined primarily by hue. Though other facts bear on the specific choice of color terms, such as brightness and saturation (purity) of the color, the essential reference of color terms is chromatic. The only

White		Green				Purple
	> Red > {		} >	Blue >	Brown >	Pink
Black		Yellow				Orange
						Grey

FIG. 10.1. Berlin and Kay's hierarchy of basic color terms.

real counter to this is at Stage I, where the two terms, *black* and *white,* accommodate 'light' and 'dark' generally. Kay and McDaniel (1978), in their revision of the Berlin and Kay hierarchy, note that this heterogeneity of denotation for Stage I terms, as opposed to the chromatic homogeneity of later stages, implies that the hierarchy itself is not a successive ordering: that is, three-term systems do not properly include two-term systems because the former denote only hue, whereas the latter may denote brightness. But this observation does not eliminate the hierarchy so much as fine-tune it. As Kay and McDaniel (1978: 617) note, if there is this lack of homogeneity from Stage I to successive stages, then the hierarchy has to be understood as the progressive differentiation of a continuum of color rather than the successive denotation of discrete categories. Color denotation must be fuzzy rather than deterministic.

10.2122. Variation and Universality

The denotations of the basic color terms admit both variation and universality. Speakers allow the denotations for color terms to fall within a range of values, but they all agree that (a) there is a *central value* as a focal color for each category and (b) the *boundaries between categories are clear* and determinable despite the variety of values internal to the color category.

Consider the English basic term *blue,* which accommodates a range of hues that are all "acceptably blue." *Blue* denotes a *color space,* or a conceptual region of color, whose boundaries are no doubt influenced by how the culture itself structures color. In contrast, the range of denotations for *azul* 'blue' in Mexican Spanish differs from those for English in that the Spanish term includes more of the space that English speakers encode by *purple* (see Berlin and Kay's comparative tables, 1969: Appendix I). But in both cases, the denotations for *blue/azul* have a typical and best value within that color region—each language has a true *blue/azul*—and the boundary between 'blue' and 'not blue'—wherever and however that is understood—is unequivocal for speakers of both English and Mexican Spanish.

The internal structure of color denotation is therefore scalar, like all prototypes, but the denotation of color terms themselves is absolute. Languages vary within a universal prototype structure for color. Culture and context may influence this variation, but perceptual and cognitive constancies determine the invar-

Stage I: black and white
              Dani: modla ('white'), mili ('black')

Stage II: black, white, red
              Bulu: fum ('white'), vin ('black'), re ('red')

Stage III: black, white, red, green OR yellow
              Mende: kole ('white'), teli ('black'), kpou ('red'), pune ('green')

Stage IV: black, white, red, green AND yellow
              Eskimo: gakurktak ('white'), girmitak ('black'), anpaluktak ('red'),
              tungajuktak ('green'), guksutak ('yellow')

Stage V: black, white, red, green, yellow, blue
              Hausa: fări ('white'), băķi ('black'), ja ('red'), algashi ('green'), nawaya
              ('yellow'), shuḍi ('blue')

Stage VI: black, white, red, green, yellow, blue, brown
              Malayalam: vellá ('white'), kaḍupə ('black'), čuwə́ppə ('red'), paččá
              ('green'), maṇṇá ('yellow'), niḷá ('blue'), tavíta ('brown')

Stage VII: all eleven basic colors
              English: black, white, red, etc.

FIG. 10.2.   Seven stages of color term systems.

iant structure of the color space in terms of typical values, focal points, and category boundaries (see Kay and McDaniel 1978).[4]

10.2123.   Uneven Distribution of Stages

Although all languages belong to one of the seven stages, not all stages are distributed evenly across the world. According to Berlin and Kay's tabulation (1969: 21), most languages are Stage II (three terms), Stage III (four terms, with *yellow* OR *green* as the fourth), Stage IV (five terms), or Stage VII (eleven

---

[4]As an aside, we should observe how the variant, but universal, structure of color denotations sheds light on a basic problem of semantics that we have discussed at length in earlier chapters, namely the relation between semantic information and conceptual structure. If color terminology is representative of the issue, then semantic structure and conceptual structure clearly diverge. Semantically, color terms are absolute in denotation, but cognitively and perceptually, they are relative: 'Green' fades into 'blue' perceptually, but not so denotationally.

The essential independence of semantics and cognition underscores a point made by both Dowty (1979) and Putnam (cited in Dowty 1979): *Intensions are not the same as concepts* (see also chap. 2). Intensions may be underdetermined with respect to concepts, as the case of color properties bears out. Color concepts are clearly wider than color intensions because the former admit a broad range of perceptual values that nonetheless have a single intensional property.

terms). Moreover, there appears to be a geometric increase in color terms after seven, with no language exhibiting eight, nine, or ten terms. What accounts for these somewhat odd distributional facts?

Stage I systems, with two terms, work from the basic logic of opposition, with two terms encoding the parameters of the generic color space. But why is there *red* after this, why the subsequent choices, and why the increase to eleven? Kay and McDaniel's (1978) revision of the color hierarchy provides an interesting solution. They argue that the neurophysiology of color perception makes four colors neurologically primary, or retinally underived: red, yellow, blue, and green. These they call *primary terms* (black and white are also, in a sense, primary because they are underived, but they rely on brightness, not chromatic values). The intersection of these primary colors gives what they call *derived colors* (e.g., brown, purple, and so on). The union of the primary colors gives what they call *composite colors,* those determined only by brightness. This means that the color hierarchy is based on three more elemental categories: *primary, composite,* and *derived.*

If we recast the stages in Berlin and Kay's theory accordingly, it turns out that the differentiation appears to be *away from* simple primary term systems and *toward* complex systems. This means that the hierarchy of color terms is best understood not from progressive numerical addition, but differentiation away from the primary terms by logical operations of union and intersection. If we add a third logical operation, as Kay and McDaniel (1978) do, identity, to account for the underived individuation of the primaries and black and white, these three logical operations—identity, union, and intersection—exhaustively characterize color vocabulary. We now have a more ordered picture of the sequencing and internal logic of color denotations and their apparently uneven distribution.[5]

10.213. *Categorematic Relation to the Domain*

Color terms appear to be principally categorematic in their interpretation. Consider the expression *blue shirt. Blue* ascribes color to the domain independently of any particular property of the domain: That is, a blue shirt is blue irrespective of the nature of the shirt as an entity. Of course, we might press the syncategorematic status of the color term and construe *blue shirt* as 'blue as a shirt,' but this requires special circumstances.

In some languages, the categorematic/syncategorematic distinction for color is rigorously enforced. Siegel (1980) notes that in Ngamambo, color terms have either an attributive form, which encodes the syncategorematic reading, or a

---

[5]Berlin and Kay (1969) discuss another regularity that may be more overarching. Languages with more terms have more technology, so the increase in color terms could be a requirement of increased colors in the environment to denote.

predicative form, which encodes the categorematic reading. Consider the following (Siegel 1980: 166):

> 12. iywid we nɔ wɛ baŋə ne.
>   fire   the that it   be red Rel
>   the fire that is red.

In (12), the color term *baŋə* is a verb, and the meaning is categorematic. The interpretation of (12) is something like 'the fire got red,' or 'came to have the entire property of redness.' Notably, the attributive form of 'red' is anomalous here:

> 13. ?? iywid bagə we.
>   fire   red   the
>   ?? the red fire.

Siegel (1980) explains that the attributive form with syncategorematic meaning is ruled out because, in the culture in question, fires have no inherent color. With no property internal to the domain for the color term to select, the only possible relation between 'red' and its domain 'fire' in Ngamambo is categorematic.

These observations lead Siegel (1980) to propose a general relation between the categorematic/ syncategorematic distinction and encoding. In languages like English, which as a rule do not formally differentiate the attributive and predicative forms, and have a unified adjectival category, the categorematic/syncategorematic distinction may also fail to be fully differentiated. In contrast, languages like Ngamambo, which radically differentiate attributive from predicative, the categorematic/syncategorematic opposition may also have a parallel differentiation. Although the full thrust of Siegel's proposal remains to be worked out, it does suggest that there may be a general form/meaning correspondence for modifiers, here borne out in the structure and encoding of color properties.

10.22. Value

We have just seen how languages denote color properties. Fortunately, the literature on color terms is considerable, and so we have been able to make some detailed claims about this property concept. The same benefit does not hold for the category of value (nor for the majority of the rest). So we have to make due with what is available and with what we can surmise.

Dixon (1982) observes that value properties encompass all meanings of evaluation or merit, to whatever degree. In this category are the expected generic meanings 'good' and 'bad' along with a number of other related concepts.

Though neither he, nor anyone else for that matter, has provided an exhaustive list of these further notions, the samples that Dixon does give indicate that the additions are all magnifications or extensions of the basic evaluative difference between 'good' and 'bad.' Hence, languages often encode degrees of goodness—*excellent, wonderful, fine,* and so on—as well as degrees of badness—*awful, horrible, atrocious,* and the like. Within the category, languages often encode more particular types of meritorious qualities, like 'purity' (*true* and *pure*) and 'propriety' (*proper, real*) (note how both notions may be neutralized by *good* in English: *a good blue* 'pure/true blue' and *good behavior* 'proper behavior').

Value properties exhibit two consistent features. One concerns the structure of their denotation and the other concerns the relation between value and the domain modified.

10.221. The Scalar Structure of Value

Value properties are scalar, as can be seen by subjecting the generic adjectival pair, *good* and *bad,* to the negation test for gradability. If something is good, it is not bad; if something is bad, it is not good. However, if something is not good, it is not necessarily bad; if something is not bad, it is not necessarily good. Value, unlike color for example, is a semantic gradient (through both may be conceptual gradients).

Much effort has been spent on identifying the precise kind of gradient that value embodies. Value properties turn out to be *overlapping* (as we saw in sec. 10.13): *Fred is bad, but better than Sam,* but ?? *Fred is good, but worse than Sam.* Cruse (1986) argues that the proper view of value denotations is one in which badness grades into goodness, but then goodness "takes off" on its own into a new scale that overlaps with, but is ultimately independent of, badness. He calls this second scale *merit,* giving the generic value terms in English an overlapping structure (see Fig. 10.3).

bad   good

FIG. 10.3. Overlapping scale for value terms.

Cruse (1986: 208) goes so far as to suggest that overlapping properties are coextensive with value terms in English: "Overlapping . . . antonyms have an evaluative polarity as part of their meaning: one term is commendatory . . . and the other is deprecatory."

Cruse's work on these scales shows that different languages structure the denotations of their value ascriptions differently. In English, Egyptian Arabic (Cruse 1986: 219), and Tamil (personal data), value concepts are overlapping.

But in German, value properties fall on a polar gradient; it is possible to assert the following with no anomaly (see Cruse 1986: 219):

14a. Peter is gut,   aber schlichter als   Johann.
     Peter is good but   worse   than John
     Peter is good, but worse than John.
  b. Peter is schlicht, aber besser als   Johann.
     Peter is bad   but better than John
     Peter is bad, but better than John.

This means that one major semantic difference between English, Tamil, and Egyptian Arabic on the one hand, and German on the other, is not the scalar denotations of value terms per se, but the *structure of the denotations of value terms*. In German and semantically alike languages, value properties are a true scale; in English and similar languages, the scale is overlapping.

10.222. *Syncategorematic Relation to the Domain*

The first main feature of value properties is the nature of the scale of the denotation and its use in comparison of semantic structure of languages. The second principal characteristic is the relation of value properties to their domains. Value concepts are universally syncategorematic.

The dependence of value concepts on the denotations of their domains has long been known, as even a cursory look at the philosophical and linguistics literature shows (Chafe 1970: 194; Ziff 1960: chap. 6). We can see the syncategorematic nature of value properties with a simple example:

15. atrocious writer.

In (15), the deprecatory evaluation is relative to the nature of the writer as a writer, whatever aspects of a writer that can be atrocious, not the writer as a whole.

If we press the issue further, we might ask: What properties of modified domains tend to be within the scope of value properties? Can the basis of the evaluation by syncategorematic modification be predicted? Dillon (1977, relying on Jerrold Katz's work) suggests that functional and instrumental aspects of the domain are typically used as the basis of the evaluation. In his view, the expressions *good father, good hammer,* and *good car* are syncategorematically identical in that they all rely on some norm of functional propriety as the basis of the evaluation: 'good, as fathers, hammers, and cars are judged for such.' Although this is appealing, it really offers little more than what Ziff (1960) came up with 30 years ago: *What is good is what answers certain interests.* So, whatever aspect of the domain may answer to certain interests—that is, be construed as valuable—can be the basis of the syncategorematic modification by value properties.

If Ziff was correct, then we might argue more generally that evaluative terms are simply *vague* as to the norm of evaluation, and the pragmatics of the situation sorts out the precise nature of the value. In this way, an expression like *good car* may have any number of interpretations within the semantic confines of a property "raised to certain interests." A good car may be good because it is cheap, solidly built, reliable, fast, red, blue, or whatever. Each of these intensional aspects of the meaning of *car* fits the criterion of meeting certain interests, though the precise interest is left to the speaker.

We certainly need a thorough assessment of the norms for value modification across languages. It may well turn out that some intensional properties of domains are *never* the basis for modification, and others typically recur. At present, we can only point to this gross distinction and note that value denotations are overwhelmingly syncategorematic in the way they apply to domains.

10.23.   Age

The third class of property concept typically found in languages is what Dixon (1982) refers to as *age,* which subsumes three basic meanings: 'old,' 'young,' and 'new.' His discussion suggests that the category is based on *chronological age,* but careful work by Wierzbicka (1986: 368–70) indicates that the category is organized by *newness* or *recency.* She gives two reasons for this view.

10.231.   Newness, Recency, and Chronological Age

Wierzbicka notes that in many languages, chronological age is frequently not encoded as a quality per se, but as a kind, making chronological age more compatible with the conceptual structure of nouns than that of modifiers (recall the discussion of her general theory; sec. 10.123). Many, many languages have words for 'old person' or 'young person' that are not transparently related to the form for modification by a property concept for chronological age. Consider the terms from Wargamay (Dixon 1981): *Bulbu* ('old person') and *gilan* ('old man') are both nouns, but *ganbaymu* ('old') is an adjective unrelated in form to these two nouns. This suggests that chronological age is more criterial and classificatory, allowing it to surface as a nominal. But as we know, property concepts as a rule are nonclassificatory, and so chronological age is an unlikely candidate for the dimension underlying the category of age.

Chronological age itself does not account for the broad range of meanings that are compatible with modification by age. Consider the possible interpretations of the expression *old teacher:* 'aged teacher,' 'experienced/established teacher,' 'former teacher,' or 'previous teacher.' Though *old* may denote a variety of agelike properties, only one is unequivocally associated with chronological age. In point of fact, with the meaning 'previous,' *old* may co-occur with *young: Our old teacher was young* ('our previous teacher was youthful').

In the Romance languages, the more specific denotations of age properties have surface correlates in differential placement and form. In Spanish, for example, *nuevo* ('new') and *viejo* ('old') may precede or follow the nouns to be modified, but their placement depends on the nature of the denotation of the modifier. Postnominally, *viejo* denotes 'chronological age,' but prenominally it denotes 'extent' or 'experience.' *Nuevo* 'new,' postnominally, denotes 'unused or unconsumed state'; prenominally, however, the form denotes 'recency' or 'sequential newness' (see, e.g., Klein-Andreu 1983 and the discussion in sec. 10.3).

Given facts such as these, Wierzbicka (1986) suggests that *one* dimension, *newness* or *recency,* underlies the category of age. All the meanings of *old* cited previously are compatible with something like 'non-newness': An aged teacher is non-new chronologically; an experienced teacher is non-new professionally; a former teacher is non-new occupationally; a previous teacher is non-new in terms of a sequence of teachers (i.e., before the present teacher).

This broader view of the semantic dimension underlying age allows us to account more perspicuously for variation in the world's languages in age modifiers. Northern Paiute (Snapp and Anderson 1982: 52–3) differentiates the chronological interpretation of newness in a formal way. When *pɨdɨ* 'new' specifically means 'young' (chronological newness), it may appear only in attributive position:

16. umɨ   pɨdɨ duaki.
    those new child
    those young children.

The predicative form, where the adjective takes a verbal marker, is unacceptable:

17. ?? umɨ   duaki pɨdɨ-tɨpɨ.
    those child   new be
    ?? Those children are young.

Otherwise in Northern Paiute, adjectives may appear in *either* attributive or predicative position. In fact, when *pɨdɨ* 'new' means simply 'new' or 'recent'— that is, when it has no association with chronological age and *encodes the generic underlying dimension*—it may appear in *either* predicative or attributive position:

18a. usu nagwi pɨdɨ- tɨpɨ.
     the dress new be
     The dress is new. (predicative)

b. usu pɨdɨ nagwi.
the new dress
the new dress. (attributive)

In both examples, the meaning of *pɨdɨ* is more appropriately 'recent' or 'just acquired,' not 'unaged.'

10.232. Scalar and Categorematic Age

Now that we have settled the nature of the denotation for this category, let us examine briefly the structure of the denotation and the relation of age properties to modified domains. Newness is a scalar property, and in English at least, the denotation appears to be a polar gradient:

19a. This book is old, but it's newer than that one.
 b. This book is new, but it's older than that one.

The opposites *old* and *new* are compatible with each other's comparative form, so they must fall on a single scale. This is not to say that more specific denotations of this scale are necessarily polar. It may well be that as chronological age or experience, newness has a different structure, though chronological newness also appears to be polar:

20a. This man is old, but he's younger than that one.
 b. This man is young, but he's older than that one.

Much work remains to be done on the details of the more particular denotations of expressions of newness as well as on descriptions of how different languages converge and diverge with respect to the structure of this semantic dimension.

Though the denotation of age as newness may be scalar, it is preferentially categorematic in the way it modifies a domain. Consider the phrase *new gun,* in the sense of 'brand new.' The ascription of newness depends on no intrinsic properties of the gun. The categorematic interpretation also appears to hold for chronological age: *old woman* and *young woman* both have categorematic meanings. But there is a sense of *old*/*new* that is syncategorematic, as the phrase *new teacher* illustrates. In the experiential sense, *old* and *new* are syncategorematic because a new (inexperienced) teacher is such by virtue of the nature of the denotation of teacher. A new teacher is new *as a teacher,* and hence this sense of *new* relies on some inherent attribute of the domain for proper modification.

Though we do know that some more particular denotations of age properties are categorematic and some are syncategorematic, we do *not* know which fall in each characterization. Again, more work remains to be done on this count, aware as we are that age, as newness, can be ascribed both dependently and independently to a domain.

10.24. Human Propensity

The fourth category of property concept is human propensity. This class covers a rather heterogenous collection of notions associated with human mental state and human behavioral characteristics. Dixon (1982) remarks on the wide internal variation of the category in observing that human propensity shows more variation from language to language than any other semantic type. There is, however, a general "region of semantic space" that the human propensity items in individual languages all refer to, and it is this that enables us to recognize a universal semantic type (Dixon 1982: 61)

The kinds of denotations that comprise the human propensity class have such a broad range that languages frequently have dozens, if not hundreds, of modifiers for human propensity concepts (see Dixon 1982: 46). This denotational heterogeneity is compounded by the variety in the structure of the denotations. In English, for example, some human propensity concepts are in polar opposition, some are equipollent, and some not in opposition at all.

As this class of terms is rather loose and uncertain in its membership, we begin with an attempt at subcategorizing the items that typically fall into this class. I am aware of no other such streamlining of this class of property concepts, so we are breaking new ground here, if only out of obvious need.

10.241. Three Types of Human Propensity:
Mental State, Physical State, and Behavior

Human propensity terms fall into three general subclasses: mental state, physical state, and behavior. These classes distinguish property concepts on the basis of their location and function with respect to the human to which they are ascribed. Mental state terms are cognitive, perceptual, and emotive; they are internal to the human, and reflect experiential states. Physical state terms are the internal, nonmental attributes of the human; they are corporeal qualities and not to be confused with physical properties, which are nonhuman attributes (see sec. 10.25). Behavioral terms are those properties that have overt consequences in human action. These three subcategories can be parameterized by orientation to the human body. Some properties are entirely internal (mental state); some are entirely external (behavioral); some are between internal and external (i.e., they have overt and covert effects: physical state).

We can see the utility of these subclasses by how they organize terms in English:

English Human Propensity Terms

> Mental State: jealous, happy, elated, downcast, ashamed, confident, loyal, drunk, kind, generous, clever

> Physical State: weak, strong, robust, itchy, sore, thirsty, hungry

> Behavior: wild, drunken, interruptive, disorderly, argumentative, funny

The subcategories are also applicable to languages other than English. Schaefer's

(1989) description of Emai human propensity terms also fits these subclasses, as the following sample indicates:

Emai Human Propensity Terms

Mental State: fun (kind), khoo (wicked), ghonghon (happy), ruru (stupid), hio (proud), ékéin (close minded) . . .

Physical State: étin (strong), i étin (weak) . . .

Behavior: ise (indulgent), toto (effective), eo (fierce), udu (bold) . . .

These subcategories are meant to be descriptive rather than explanatory. They sort the data more neatly than before, but they do not make any obvious predictions. For example, we do not know if languages have more mental state terms than physical state terms. Nor do we know if these subcategories make any predictions with respect to encoding or semantic structure (i.e., are behavioral properties structured or encoded one way, while physical ones another?). Thus, they have the status of operational definitions.

10.242. The Structure and Function of Human Propensity Terms

One certainty with regard to human propensity terms is the unusual structure of their denotations. Dixon (1982) notes that, unlike the other classes of property concepts, human propensity terms often have no lexicalized opposites. As he says (1982: 20), "Each HUMAN PROPENSITY adjective is best considered as a singleton, individually specifying an antonym-like parameter." The lack of antonymy can be seen in the English terms *jealous, lonely,* and *observant,* which arguably have no opposite. A similar fact can be seen in Emai, where, according to Schaefer's (1989) list at least, the terms *hure* 'pompous,' *ise* 'indulgent,' and *re* 'observant' have no opposite.

Despite the absence of opposites for some terms, human propensity items are scalar (Rusiecki 1985: 9, calls these single scales *unary scales*). Such terms as *kind, clever,* and *generous* have gradable denotations:

21a. Larry is kinder than Sam.
 b. Fred is less generous than his brother.

But so do terms without clear opposites:

22a. Bob is more jealous than I thought.
 b. Lori is less observant than Martha.

Though it is fairly easy to see the scalar structure of human propensity concepts, it is more difficult to assign them to a kind of scale. Most of the human propensity items in English are not polar gradients, and so their denotations exceed a single continuous dimension. Most terms are either overlapping or equipollent. *Polite* and *rude,* for example, are overlapping:

23a. Bill is rude, but he's politer than Sam.
   b. ?? Bill is polite, but he's ruder than Sam.

Proud and *ashamed,* however, are equipollent:

24a. ?? Bill is proud, but he's more ashamed than Tom.
   b. ?? Bill is ashamed, but he's prouder than Tom.

Cruse (1986) notes two interesting facts in this respect that may help us to regularize the findings on human propensity terms. First, he observes that equipollent antonyms "refer distinctly to subjective sensations or emotions . . . , or evaluations based on subjective reactions, rather than on 'objective' standards" (1986: 208). If Cruse is correct, then human propensity terms cluster on the equipollent scale because they denote subjective reaction and sensation par excellence. What we do not know, however, and what is arguably more important, is *which comes first*: the scale or the denotations? Do human propensity terms lend themselves to equipollent grading by their nature, or do equipollent scales more easily accommodate these denotations and thus "seek out" such concepts?

Second, in a potential answer to the questions we have just posed, Cruse (1986: 219) remarks that the three basic gradients themselves form a metascale of objectivity. Polar gradients encode the most objective denotations (like 'physical length'), equipollent gradients encode the most subjective denotations (like 'mental state'), and overlapping gradients encode an intermediate stage, objective/subjective denotations (like 'value'), giving the following objective-to-subjective ranking: Polar > Overlapping > Equipollent. Cruse argues that polar gradients are more conceptualized and removed from subjective facts; the opposite holds for equipollent gradients, which tend to encode, as he says (p. 219), "the raw psycho-physical facts." If Cruse's intuitions are correct, then it is the relative objectivity of the denotations that determine their denotational structure. For this reason, despite the heterogeneity of denotation for human propensity terms, they tend not to be polar, because they also tend not to be objective.

Finally, let us remark on the relation of human propensity modifiers to their domains. Human propensity terms can have either categorematic or syncategorematic interpretations. Consider the phrase *cruel person,* where the meaning seems to be categorematic, because a cruel person can be denoted as such irrespective of the properties of being a person. However, if we change the domain slightly, and make it more specific, we force a syncategorematic interpretation. Consider *cruel boss,* where the meaning of the phrase relies on the nature of the domain because not all cruel bosses are cruel people:

25. He was a cruel boss, but a kind person (i.e., 'he was cruel as a boss').

The possibility of either categorematic or syncategorematic readings for human propensity terms underscores a more general, metatheoretical point about the relation of modifiers to their domains. Syncategorematicity itself may be scalar. Siegel (1980) notes the variety of single-form modifiers that have both readings. Miller and Johnson-Laird (1976: 356) point out: "to classify all adjectives as either absolute (categorematic, WF) or relative (syncategorematic, WF), however, dichotomizes what is essentially a continuum. Color and shape adjectives are near one end, evaluative adjectives are near the other end, and the majority of predicate adjectives are somewhere in between."

Color ascription is prototypically categorematic; value ascription is prototypically syncategorematic. Human propensity ascription is intermediate. These three choices translate into three basic conceptual procedures. To find the denotation of a categorematically modified expression, it is possible to compute the denotation of either the modifier or the domain exclusively because both contribute independently to the denotation of the expression as a whole. To compute the denotation of a syncategorematically modified expression, it is necessary to compute the denotation of the domain first because the ascription depends crucially on the semantic characteristics of the domain. To compute the meaning of a modification that can have either interpretation, it is possible to compute the modifier and domain either separately or together: Hence the last subsumes both the first two options. Here we have a cognitive procedural complement to the semantic relations between modifier and domain.

10.25. Physical Properties

The fifth category is physical properties, which subsume all types of nonhuman physical attributes. This category is as heterogenous in constitution as the class of human propensity items. Indeed, Dixon (1982: 46) notes that physical property terms typically number "at least several score." So we are faced again with the problems we addressed in section 10.24. Is there some internal structure to this category? Can we assign useful and meaningful subcategories?

We have already considered physical properties to some extent in our examination of noun classifiers, so we should reuse those insights. Here we return to and adopt some of Allan's (1977) observations about physical properties surfacing as noun classifiers (see chap. 3); we add to these categories as we see fit, given the kinds of physical properties that tend to appear in modifying constructions in languages.

10.251. Seven Types of Physical Properties

Seven subcategories of physical properties tend to recur across the world's languages: sense, consistency, texture, temperature, edibility, substantiality, and configuration. Let us briefly look at the composition of each.

Under the subcategory of *sense* are all notions that concern properties determined by sense data. Particularly common here are ascriptions of taste and smell, although languages often have terms for properties from the other senses as well (e.g., visibility and audibility, as we saw with evidentials, chap. 9).

In *consistency*, we find terms for the physical manipulability of objects. Common terms here are those that refer to hardness, softness, flexibility, and degrees thereof.

Under *texture*, we find expressions for the surface properties of objects: roughness, scaliness, smoothness, and bumpiness. It might be argued here that this category ought to be included under *sense* because texture is determined by tactility. But so many languages seem to have specific terms for kinds of texture that it merits an independent subcategory. Moreover, texture can be determined not only by touch, but also by vision, so the denotation does not seem to be confined to one sensorial category.

For *temperature*, languages tend to encode the basic scale of heat, though there are usually many variations thereon. Numerous languages differentiate degrees of heat and kinds of heat as a function of heat source.

Under *edibility*, various qualities ascribable to food are found, like ripeness, rawness, and preparedness of food. Dixon (1982: 46) remarks, in fact, that one of the most recurrent properties in his entire inquiry is 'raw,' no doubt because this represents the basic physical state of edible items.

The subcategory of *substantiality* includes all terms that refer to the internal constituency, or relative solidity, of an entity. Here we find such notions as weight, thickness, hollowness, and fullness.

Finally, in the subcategory of *configuration*, there are terms to denote the physical utility of an object. Hence this subcategory denotes more particularly 'configuration for use,' or 'set up,' much like the configuration of a computer. Under this category, we typically find languages encoding sharpness (for knives and tools) and brokenness or wholeness to signal something of the overall configuration of an object.

We must keep two caveats in mind with this classification scheme. First, these seven subcategories are not exhaustive. Many languages have terms for 'wet,' 'dry,' 'clean,' 'healthy,' and 'position,' and it is unclear where such notions belong, if not in separate categories. No doubt a fuller analysis of physical property concepts will reveal further categories. Second, these seven subcategories are established primarily for heuristic purposes, to organize the data. They may have ultimate theoretical appeal, but at present they have only operational use. We do not know if languages encode these subcategories as such or differentiate them structurally; we also do not know if their denotations sufficiently vary to warrant discrete categorization. We *do know*, however, that these subcategories capture succinctly a large array of terms, and for that descriptive goal alone we use them here.

If we apply these seven subcategories to the physical properties encoded by English, we get results along the lines of the following:

English Physical Property Terms

    Sense: loud, soft, quiet, noisy, smelly, savory, salty, sweet, sour . . .

    Consistency: hard, soft, rubbery, .rigid . . .

    Texture: rough, smooth, tacky, bumpy, pitted, crusty . . .

    Temperature: hot, cold, cool, tepid, warm, lukewarm, icy . . .

    Edibility: raw, cooked, ripe, burnt, roasted, baked . . .

    Substantiality: heavy, light, fat, thick, thin, full, empty, runny . . .

    Configuration: sharp, dull, blunt, broken, whole, arable, primed . . .

Emai, completely unrelated to English, lends itself neatly to these subcategories (from Schaefer 1989):

Emai Physical Property Terms

    Sense: toto (loud), haa (quiet), nene (sweet), khenkhen (sour), laa (bitter)

    Consistency: ka (hard), huo (soft),

    Texture: mioghonmíóghón (smooth), sháshághá (rough/dry/scaly) fúyé (fine in texture)

    Temperature: tohia (hot), fo (cool)

    Edibility: nye (cooked), ogbon (raw), nwe (ripe), oban (unripe)

    Substantiality: khua (heavy), húsé (light, of animates), héghé (light, of inanimates), féféghé (very light, of inanimates), zeze (thick/solid), hóghó (hollow), von (full)

    Configuration: rie (sharp), gbe (blunt), gha (complete), kennokénnó (in bits)

10.252. The Structure and Function of Physical Property Terms

In structure, the denotations of many of these subcategories are scalar. Temperature, for example, is undoubtedly a gradient in all languages, as is weight and certain kinds of texture. But some other denotations are clearly absolute, 'broken' versus 'whole,' for example. Notable here is the universal denotation 'raw,' which in English is not a scalar concept—objects are either raw or not raw; this characteristic most likely holds for other languages as well. Some languages have more particular denotations that are undoubtedly nonscalar. My guess is that *kennokénnó* 'in bits' in Emai is absolute. Much comparative work remains to be done in this regard to determine what kinds of property concepts are or are not scalar.

Work also needs to be done on the kinds of scales that gradient physical property terms denote. Temperature, for instance, is a classic equipollent scale, and 'weight,' one kind of substantiality, is clearly polar (see the examples in sec. 10.13). Some forms of texture are polar:

26a. This board is rough, but smoother than that one.
  b. This board is smooth, but rougher than that one.

Some sense denotations are equipollent:

27a. ?? This sauce is sweet, but it's more sour than that one.
  b. ?? This sauce is sour, but it's sweeter than that one.

This variability is testimony to the fact that regular correlations between physical properties and scale types remain to be worked out.

Furthermore, some physical properties are preferentially categorematic (*full, empty, solid*), and some are preferentially syncategorematic (*light, hot, fat, thick*). Again, we do not know at present whether the kinds of gradients that structure these denotations have any other semantic motivation; nor do we know if the categorematic/syncategorematic distinction for physical properties follows the boundaries of other categories or subcategories. These unanswered questions make further semantic spadework exciting and essential.

10.26.   Summary of Properties Thus Far

In sections 10.21–10.25, we have looked at five kinds of property concepts. Under color, we have seen basic color terms, Berlin and Kay's hierarchy of color denotations (and its modification in terms of primary, composite, and derived colors); we have also seen the variation in color term systems and distribution as well as the association of color with chromatic denotation. Following this, we have studied value terms, noting their overlapping gradients and tendency toward syncategorematic modification. We then considered age, defined in terms of newness and recency rather than chronological age; we have seen the scalar and categorematic features of this property concept. The fourth category is human propensity, which we have divided into terms for mental state, physical state, and behavior. Human propensity terms tend to be relative and equipollent. The fifth category is physical properties, which we have further divided into seven types: sense, consistency, texture, temperature, edibility, substantiality, and configuration. Many, but not all, of these denotations are scalar, and the full range of gradients is attested.

10.27.   Quantity

The sixth and final category is modification by quantity. In this class, we include all kinds of denotations of amount, whether or not explicitly numerical. We are interested in the kinds of properties that are encoded in consideration of the questions "How many?" or "How much?" The study of quantifying terms has an influential history in semantics, especially in formal and model-theoretic treatments. This work has been so influential in fact that we cannot hope to present the results in anything like a synopsis. Instead, we simply examine the basics and suggest where these elementary ideas lead both descriptively and theoretically.

In this discussion, we divide quantity property concepts into two types: *nonnumerical* and *numerical* properties. The former subcategory is equivalent to what is usually known as *logical quantifiers*; the latter includes all *cardinal* and *ordinal* quantity modifiers. The distinction here is thus between those amounts that have a specific, determinate, and exact numerical value as their denotation (numerical quantities, like *three*) and those that do not (like *some*). This is not to say that nonnumerical quantities *cannot* have numerical values *in* their denotations, only that they cannot have numerical values *as* their denotations. The nonnumerical term *several* is a case in point. Its denotation has some relation to the numerical value 'three,' but whereas the numerical quantity *three* is exactly and only 'three' (i.e., has a cardinal value) *several* means something like 'at least three.' Hence *several* has a numerical quantity *in* its denotation, and thus is not essentially numerical; this is unlike *three,* which has an exact quantity *as* its denotation and is essentially numerical.

10.271. Nonnumerical Quantities

In this section, we consider the basic semantic facts of determiners (demonstratives, like *that,* and articles, like *the* and *a*) and logical quantifiers (*every, all, some,* and so on). For convenience, and following the usage in the literature, we refer to both determiners and logical quantifiers as simply *quantifiers.* Our inquiry is informed by two questions:

1. What are the denotations of quantifiers? That is, what kinds of nonnumerical quantities do quantifying terms denote?
2. What is the scope of quantifiers? That is, because quantifiers are scope-bearing elements (they have a range of effect, just like logical operators), what are the regularities of this effect and what factors contribute to scope?

We try to show that the answer to question 1 provides a partial answer to question 2. Our discussion relies heavily on Ioup's (1975) claims that many of the scope properties of quantifiers follow not from structural facts—not from the syntax— but from how the denotations of the quantifiers contribute to the inherent scope of a quantifier. We use Ioup's insights to answer question 2, but this of course first requires that we answer question 1. So now we examine the kinds of denotations that quantifiers may have.[6]

---

[6]The view that the denotations of quantifiers affects their scope is not universally accepted in linguistics. Hornstein (1984), for example, argues that there are only three types of quantified expressions, and these three types and their scope properties can be determined irrespective of their denotations. He notes that the three types of quantifiers parallel the three types of anaphoric expressions that syntax allows:

10.2711. The Denotations of Quantifiers.

10.27111. *Existential and Universal Quantification*

To get a sense of the kinds of denotations that quantifiers may have, we can turn to predicate logic, where there are two kinds of quantifiers, differing in how they refer to sets of entities: the existential quantifier ∃ and the universal quantifier ∀. Existential quantification characterizes forms that denote amounts of 'at least one,' like *some, a,* and *any*. Note that the expression *A man played golf* means 'there was at least one man who played golf.' Universal quantification, in contrast, characterizes forms that denote 'totality': for example, *all, every, each*. Note how the expression *All the men played golf* has a totalized interpretation: 'for every man, that man played golf.'

The properties and effects of existential and universal quantification are well known, as any logic book reveals (Allwood et al. 1977). It is also well known that these two logical quantifiers are insufficient to capture all the necessary nonnumerical denotations that exist in natural languages. How are the English quantifiers *many, most, a few, several, much,* and *a lot of* to be treated in terms of logical quantification? None of them is entirely consistent with either universal or existential quantification. Consider (28):

28. Many chickens died.

Certainly, the meaning of (28) fits somewhat with the existential interpretation: 'There is at least one chicken that died.' According to my intuition at least, the issue in (28) is not that at least one died, but that *more than one* died. The focus of *many* is on some quantity *beyond* existential quantification. Likewise, the meaning of (28) is somewhat compatible with universal quantification, but the totalizing aspect of 'for every' must be scaled down.

For *many,* existential quantification falls short of the necessary quantity whereas universal quantification exceeds it. This failure is related to the way that

---

A. expressions that are *namelike* and thus have denotations in any construction (i.e., they are syntactically free; Hornstein's example is *any*);

B. expressions that are *anaphorlike* (or like reflexive pronouns) and thus have denotations that depend entirely on the clause in which they occur (i.e., they are syntactically bound; Hornstein's example is *a*);

C. expressions that may have either (i.e., they are like pronouns in syntax; Hornstein's example is French *personne*).

We do not pursue Hornstein's argument here (see Aoun and Hornstein 1985; Hintikka 1986 is a reply; McCawley 1988: 618–28 is a clear synopsis of the basic issues). We do point out, however, that Hornstein's syntactic reductionism overlooks Ioup's (1975) remarkably similar solution proposed 10 years before but *in semantic terms,* relying crucially on the *denotations* of the quantifiers.

logical quantifiers denote. Existential and universal quantification denote by their truth conditionality in referring to sets. The former is true when it denotes at least a single member of a set, the latter when it denotes all the members of a set. Unfortunately for set theory and logical quantification, a large number of natural language quantifiers are denotationally *between* the two kinds of logical quantities. How many is *a few*? How many is *several*? (See McCawley 1977; see also Keenan and Stavi 1986 for a long list of related and derived quantities.)

10.27112. Total and Partial Quantities

If we examine the English quantifiers more closely, it becomes clear that we can describe them, first of all, by how they denote either *total* or *partial* quantities of a collection of individuals. Some quantifiers denote by means of no reference to other members of the collection. These are *total*. Others denote by essential reference to some other members of the collection. These are *partial*.[7]

Let us go through an example for clarification. To understand the meaning of *many birds*, we must know not only the amount of the collection of birds that *many* denotes, but also the remainder that makes up the rest of the collection of birds against which *many birds* is judged. In set theoretic terms, we would say that *many* evokes its *complement*, which is everything in a set other than what is explicitly represented (e.g., the complement of the set of positive integers is all the nonpositive integers). Another way of saying this is to note that an expression like *many* must be understood with reference to the amount that is outside the denotation proper, or, to follow Keenan and Stavi (1986), that *many* denotes an *implicit comparison*. For this reason, many denotes a partial quantity.

On the other hand, the meaning of *every bird* is determinable without reference to any remainder. *Every bird* is simply 'every bird,' with no implication of any additional members of the collection of birds. *Every* thus denotes an amount without reference to any other amount, or without an implicit comparison. For this reason, *every* denotes a total quantity.

If we apply this basic denotational distinction to the quantifiers already discussed, we get the categorization shown in Table 10.1.

---

[7]The astute reader will recognize that this distinction between partial and total quantities is, in spirit, the same made by Barwise and Cooper (1981) with regard to strong and weak determiners. Total quantities have an analogue in strong determiners—those that do not require reference to a world for denotation—and partial quantities in weak determiners—those that require a world for denotation. However, the analogy is not exact for a number of reasons. First, strong and weak determiners are derived from the logical analysis of determiners as functions, which is not at issue here; also, many more quantity terms than just those I have mentioned fall under the rubric of strong and weak determiners (e.g., *the* is a strong determiner, but it is unclear if it is a total quantity—though probably so). In any case, both approaches share the insight that the denotations of quantifiers are of two kinds.

TABLE 10.1
English Quantifiers as Total and
Partial Quantities

Total Quantities	Partial Quantities
All	Some
Every	A few
Each	Most
	Many
	A
	A lot
	Several

Only one term in Table 10.1, *a,* needs justification. Why does *a* denote a partial quantity, especially when it appears to single out only an individual, no quantity relative to the rest of a collection? The logical definition of *a* is 'at least one,' and so *a* does not denote a single entity, but 'one or more.' In this way, it makes essential reference to the remainder of a collection.

With this broad denotational opposition between total and partial quantities, we can more finely divide the denotations within the classes by asking *how* the individual terms denote total or partial quantities. For total quantities, the distinction depends on how a totality can be construed; for partial quantities the terms depend on how the denotation and remainder are judged.

10.27113.   Kinds of Total and Partial Quantities: Distributive, Collective, Maximum, and Minimum

How can a total collection be denoted? There seem to be only two ways: (a) by the collection in its *entirety* or (b) by *enumeration of all the individuals* that comprise the collection. Quantifiers that refer to collections as a whole are called *collective quantifiers*; those that refer to the elements of a total quantity are called *distributive quantifiers.* This distinction is clearly seen in the difference between *all* on the one hand and *each* and *every* on the other. *All birds* denotes a collection of birds by reference to the undifferentiated totality. *Each/every bird* also denotes an entire collection, but by reference to the individuals that comprise it; for this reason, *each/every bird* requires a singular verb: *each/every bird is here* refers to the entire collection by its singular elements. *Each* and *every* are distributive; *all* is collective.

How can a partial collection be denoted? The answer seems to be: in whatever way the cut off can be made between the denotation of the quantifier proper and the remainder of the collection. This is done in terms of the *maximum* and *minimum* values that satisfy the denotations of partial quantities. These values are not always tied to specific quantities, and they are best understood as kind of a blank check that the context of use fills in.

Consider the partial quantity *many*. How many is *many*? The usual guess is something like 'more than 50%,' where the minimum is assigned an exact proportion. But how much more than 50%? Is 51% *many*? Is 57%? And what about the upper bound? If a term denotes 82%, is that no longer *many*?

A variety of solutions to this problem have been proposed (cf. Barwise and Cooper 1981; Lappin 1988). The gist of the solution is that *many* denotes a range of values whose *minimum exceeds the expected norm for the situation* represented by the expression in which it occurs. This makes the whole interpretation of *many* asymmetric because there is a conceptual imbalance between the quantity that exceeds the norm and the remainder. Keenan and Stavi (1986: 258) make a similar claim when they observe that *many* involves a value judgment on the part of the speaker. The use of *many* indicates that the speaker considers the quantity *significant,* whatever the reason for the speaker's view, and whatever the exact amount. Significance is a function of the exceeding of an expected norm.

Many birds therefore denotes some range of unspecified values that exceeds the expected norm for whatever context in which the expression appears. In a birdless country, the appearance of two birds would surely evoke, correctly, *many birds,* precisely because the expected norm has been exceeded and there is a significant proportional asymmetry, the specifics of which are filled in by the context in which the expression appears.

Similar descriptions of the denotations of the other partial quantities are possible. *Some,* like *many,* denotes a range of values based on a minimum. For *some* to be successfully asserted, the quantity, at minimum, must be equal to or greater than 'one.' *Most,* in contrast, denotes by reference to a maximum. For *most* to be truthfully asserted, the quantity must asymptotically approach the totality of the collection. *Most* denotes a quantity whose maximum is judged as a shortfall of the total collection, again given the context of use. Once more in a birdless country, one thieving bird is surely sufficient to motivate *Most birds are thieves.*

These examples not only illustrate the basic sense of partial quantifiers, but they also point up the critical role that pragmatics has in their ultimate interpretation. As Keenan and Stavi (1986) note, partial quantities are essentially vague on many counts. Consider *many,* which is compatible with any situation that construes a collection in terms of a norm, whatever the cardinal value for the norm.

The role of context in these quantities is underscored by how pragmatics picks up where semantics falls off. *Most* denotes via a maximum—a quantity asymptotically approaching the totality of a collection—but we do not have to specify a minimum for *most* because the interaction of entailment and implicature takes up the burden here. *Most entails lesser values,* so if it is true that most birds are on the lawn, then it is also true that some bird is on the lawn.

However, the assertion of a lesser value *implicates the negative of a larger value* 'not most' (see Horn 1989 on scales of implicature): If it is true that some birds are on the lawn, then my having asserted the lesser value, *some,* implicates that I do not know the larger one, *most.*

Analogous arguments surface in the relationship of *most* and *many.* In spite of the fact that *most* refers to a maximum, and thus an apparently large quantity, and *many* to a minimum, and thus something included in a large quantity, *most* does not entail *many. Most birds are on the lawn* does not entail *many birds are on the lawn* because the near totality of the denotation of *most* does not have to make any essential reference to the exceeding of some norm, as *many* requires. Indeed, if *many* actually denoted something like 'more than half,' then there would be an entailment relation between *most* and *many.* But *many* makes no essential reference to midpoints or central values and hence cannot be included in the meaning of *most.*

However, *most implicates many*: If most birds are on the lawn, then it is quite likely that many birds are on the lawn. In this way, again via the rules of pragmatics, it is possible for terms that denote maxima, like *most,* to access or evoke terms that denote minima, without the semantic system having to build both maxima and minima into the denotations. This is a classic example of the interdependence of semantics and pragmatics: The denotations of some terms both require and implicate the denotations of others.

10.27114. Comparative Examples: Nkore Kiga and Yoruba

To summarize thus far, we have seen that quantifiers can be described by two parameters:

1. the total or partial denotation of a collection;
2. the nature of the total or partial denotation: total quantities can be either collective or distributive; partial quantities can be determined by minima or maxima.

The utility of these parameters can be observed in how they describe quantifiers in languages other than English.

Nkore Kiga (Taylor 1985) has three terms for total quantities. The bound form *-Vna,* often prefixed with a noun class marker, indicates collective totality; two other free forms, *buri* and *ibara,* denote distributive totalities. These are illustrated here:

29a. bo-ona.
      they all
      all of them.

   b. buri kwezi.
      each month
      each/every month.

   c. ibara kasheeshe.
      each morning
      each/every morning.

In Nkore-Kiga, the difference between distributive and collective totalities has a syntactic reflex. The collective term *-Vna* follows and agrees with the noun class of the form it modifies whereas the distributive terms precede their head and take canonical form.

Yoruba has three forms for the meaning 'many,' *ọ̀pọ̀, púpọ̀,* and *ọ̀pọ̀lọpọ̀,* which are differentiated by how they denote size and other features of the collection. Lawal (1986) observes that *púpọ̀* denotes an undifferentiated partial quantity that exceeds some expected norm, and thus is equivalent to generic 'many':

  30. èniyàn púpọ̀.
      people many
      many people.

Ọ̀pọ̀, in contrast, denotes a partial quantity larger than that denoted by *púpọ̀:*

  31. ọ̀pọ̀   èniyàn.
      many+ people
      a great many people.

This semantic difference between *ọ̀pọ̀* and *púpọ̀* has a formal ramification in the positional shift of the former. Finally, *ọ̀pọ̀lọpọ̀* denotes a quantity even larger than that denoted by *ọ̀pọ̀,* and this quantity is also internally variegated and animate:

  32. ọ̀pọ̀lọpọ̀   èniyàn.
      many++ people
      a very great many individual people.

We can see these restrictions on *ọ̀pọ̀lọpọ̀* by their violation:

  33a. ?? ọ̀pọ̀lọpọ̀ iyanrìn.
          many++ sands
          ?? many sands.

    b. ?? ọ̀pọ̀lọpọ̀ èfọ̀n.
          many++ mosquitos
          ?? many mosquitos.

Example (33a) is unacceptable because the domain, *iyanrìn* 'sands,' denotes an inanimate individual; example (33b) is unacceptable because, according to Lawal (1986), mosquitos are undifferentiated in Yoruba culture, and thus even though they are technically animate, their lack of individuation prevents them from quantification by *ọ̀pọ̀lọpọ̀*.

The Yoruba and Nkore Kiga data underscore the utility of partial and total quantities and their subclasses. Languages completely unrelated to English have grammatical reflexes of these semantic conditions.

10.2712. Scope of Quantifiers.

We have now provided the elements of an answer to question 1 (p. 465) regarding the basic denotations of quantifiers. Let us turn to question 2: What are the scope properties of quantifiers? We know that quantifiers are scope-bearing items, as we have seen in the scope interactions of expressions with more than one quantifying term. Before we proceed, let us restate the basic facts.

Consider the following:

34a. Many children saw a bird.
  b. A bird was seen by many children.

Sentence (34a) has two interpretations, depending on which quantifier is given widest scope. On one reading, there are as many birds as there are children, 'many children saw a bird each,' in which the quantifier *many* has scope over the quantifier *a,* and the wider scope of *many* produces a plural denotation for the domain modified by *a*. On the other reading, there is a single bird seen by a number of children: 'many children saw one bird.' Here, the quantifier *a* has scope over *many,* and the wider scope of *a* results in a singular meaning for the domain modified by *a*. For most speakers, this latter interpretation of (34a) is not the preferred; the former meaning, where *many* has scope over *a,* is the most readily available. However, when we look at (34b), we find that the same interpretations as for (34a) are available, but in *reverse order of preference*. The usual first reading of (34b) is the singular denotation, but with a little thought, the multiple meaning can be gotten, provided that *many* is seen as having scope over *a*.

What causes these differences? Though the literature is full of ingenious and detailed proposals, ranging from purely syntactic to pragmatic explanations, it appears that the best account is one that takes into consideration a number of factors at once.

10.27121. Two Factors Determining Quantifier Scope

Ioup (1975), Jackendoff (1983), and McCawley (1988), among others, have spelled out the factors affecting quantifier scope in the most succinct terms. We follow their proposals here, noting that quantifier scope is a function of at least two things: (a) the denotation of the quantifier; and (b) the denotation of the domain modified.[8]

10.271211.   Inherent Scope and Denotation.   Ioup (1975) observes that quantifiers can be scaled on the basis of their *inherent tendency to have wide scope*. Some quantifiers, just about wherever they occur and whatever they modify, tend to dominate scope assignment whereas others, again just about wherever they occur, tend not to. Ioup (1975) provides the following hierarchy of quantifiers, scaled on their inherent scope properties. Quantifiers on the left carry inherently wide scope, whereas those on the right carry inherently narrow scope (see Fig. 10.4).

each > every > all > most > many > several > some > a few

wide scope   ⟵⟶   narrow scope

FIG. 10.4.   Ioup's hierarchy of quantifiers by inherent scope.

We can see how the hierarchy in Fig. 10.4 captures the facts by simply changing the quantifier *many* in (34b) to one that has higher inherent scope:

35.   A bird was seen by each child.

In the original expression, the preferred reading is one where *a* has scope over the second quantifier, thus inducing a singular meaning. But note that with the change of *many* to *each,* we no longer have the wide scope of *a* as the first reading. Sentence (35) has a preferred interpretation in terms of the distributive quantifier, 'a respective bird was seen by each child,' with *each* wider than *a*. The only possible explanation for this shift is the change in quantifier, so it must be the case that some quantifiers can have wide scope whatever their context (see Ioup 1975 for further discussion and examples from languages other than English).

Ioup's hierarchy of quantifiers by inherent scope is actually related to the denotations of the quantifiers. Those with inherently wide scope denote total

---

[8]A third factor bearing on quantifier scope is the grammatical role of the quantified expression. Ioup (1975) observes that inherent scope increases as the quantified expression functions as a grammatical subject or topic and decreases as the expression functions as an object. She provides another hierarchy (modified for convenience) of scope by grammatical role, as follows:

Topic > Subject > Indirect Obj > Obj of Preposition > Direct Obj

Wide scope   ⟵⟶   Narrow Scope

Compare the preferred interpretations of (34) with this hierarchy.

quantities: *each, every,* and *all.* Those with inherently narrow scope denote partial quantities: *several, some, a few.* The more particular distribution of the terms along the hierarchy seems to be a function of how the terms denote *within these two basic categories.* For the inherently wide scope terms, distributive quantifiers have wider scope than collective quantifiers; in the narrow scope terms, those that denote via minima have less inherent scope than those that denote via maxima.

From these observations, we can recast Ioup's hierarchy of quantifiers by inherent scope in terms of their denotations (see Fig. 10.5).

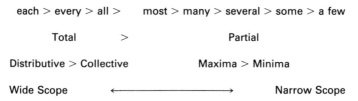

FIG. 10.5.   Ioup's hierarchy of quantifiers revised.

Inherent scope thus appears to be a function of totality and distributivity. Within partial quantities, wider scope depends on the *tendency toward totality,* which is why partials defined by maxima have priority over partials defined by minima. More broadly, it appears that *relative size* and *individuation* motivate the inherent scope of quantifiers.

10.271212.   Denotation of Domains.   If the denotations of quantifiers affect their scope possibilities, then so do the denotations of the domains they modify. Let us reconsider (34a), where *many* has scope over *a.* Suppose we change the domain such that the entity modified by *a* lends itself differently to the content of the prediction. Compare the following, where (36a) = (34a):

36a. Many children saw a bird.
  b. Many children saw a galaxy.

The preferred reading for (36a) is, as we know, one where *many* has scope over *a* (multiple birds). But this is not the case for (36b), where the preferred reading indicates that there is one galaxy: That is, *a* has scope over *many.* Even if we choose a quantifier of the highest inherent scope to modify *children,* we do not get a distributive reading:

37. Each child saw a galaxy.

Example (37) preferentially means: 'each child saw a single (= the same) galaxy.'

The reason for this result is fairly straightforward, and it brings home a basic point of this book regarding semantic content and logical form. Galaxies, unlike birds, are not things that are seen in multiples. Thus, the denotation of the modified domain can override even the inherently wide scope of the quantifier *each*. Consequently, we must admit that a second semantic factor bears on the scope of quantifiers: the denotation of the modified domain.

Whereas we do know that the denotation of the quantifier and the domain contribute to the interpretation of quantifier scope, we do *not* know the relative strengths of these factors. Does the inherent scope of the quantifier contribute more to scope than the denotation of the modified domain? Much work remains to be done here, but at least the proper questions are now before us.

10.2713. Summary.

This section has considered nonnumerical quantities. We have looked at how universal and existential quantification miss a large number of natural language quantities; we have analyzed quantifiers in terms of total quantities (distributive and collective) and partial quantities (maximum and minimum). Pragmatics plays a major role in filling in the basic semantic structure of quantifiers. Two semantic factors affect scope: the denotation of the quantifier (Ioup's hierarchy of inherent scope) and the denotation of the domain quantified.

10.272. *Numerical Quantities*

Here we turn our attention to numeral systems and the semantics of counting. We concentrate on the denotations of cardinal numerals, those quantities with a determinate numerical value for counting. We do not treat ordinal numerals— those with a numerical value for a succession of quantities—because ordinal numerals are invariably derived from cardinals. After all cardinal numerals have an inherent order in so far as they are related to the integers, where $1 < 2 < 3 < 4 \ldots$, and so the cardinal numerals are naturally prior to the ordinals.

There has been considerable interest in numerical quantification and numeral systems, no doubt because different languages count in quite different ways. Nonetheless, the extensive work on numeral systems in the linguistic and anthropological literature has revealed many regularities in the semantics and morpho-syntax of numerals. We explore some of these consistencies in the following pages, relying especially on the work of Stampe (1976), Greenberg (1978b), and Hurford (1975, 1987).

10.2721. Numbers, Numerals, and Counting.

We must first be aware that in the semantics of numerical quantification, numbers are not the same things as numerals. *Numbers* are *concepts,* all the theoretically conceivable numerical quantities. *Numerals,* on the other hand, are the basic *elements of the semantic and syntactic system of counting* in the language as a whole.

To see the difference between numerals and numbers, consider the expressions *nine* and *the square root of eighty-one.* The denotations of both are the same, 'nine,' but the former is a numeral and the latter is a number. *Nine* is a term in the numeral system of English because it is used as part of the ordinary counting system and is productively related to the rest of the system, as can be seen in the forms *ninety seven, nineteen,* and so on. But *the square root of eighty-one* has no such productivity. If someone asks you how many innings there are in a baseball game, you do not say: "The square root of eighty-one." Numbers are conceptual; numerals are semantic (see Greenberg 1978b for good discussion of this point).

Numerical quantification is a way of giving semantic shape and overt form to number concepts and the requirements of counting: that is, the assignment of determinate values, the ordering and sequencing of such values, the judgment of relative magnitude, and so on. In some languages, these necessities are carried out in very practical ways. Oksapmin, like many languages, uses body parts as the basis of numerical quantification, with 27 basic numerals corresponding to 27 cardinal points on the human body (see Hurford 1987: 78–81). In Mullukmulluk (Greenberg 1978b: 257), the term for 'twenty' means literally 'hand one, one, foot, foot,' transparently related to all the digits: $5 + 5 + 5 + 5$. In Western Tarahumara (Burgess 1984), the words for 'five,' *marígi,* and 'ten,' *makoé,* derive from a Proto-form *ma* meaning 'hand.' So counting here originates with the digits as external aids. Interestingly, in Aghem (Hyman 1979), the word for 'twenty,' *wó'ó,* also means whole body: that is, all possible digits, fingers and toes.

The few languages that are said to lack elaborate numerical quantification (certain Australian languages: Dixon 1980: 107–8, Hurford 1987: 68) have other ways of assigning cardinal values, through their complex kinship systems, for example, and this has the same functional result of assigning magnitude and sequence (see Dixon 1980: 108, quoting Hale). In any case, speakers of Australian languages who do learn other numeral systems in fact learn them quite well, easily, and regularly (see Dixon 1980: 108; Hurford 1987: 68–85). The insignificance of the relative absence of numerical quantification in the Australian languages is brought home by the excessiveness and equal idiosyncracy of certain Polynesian languages: Hawaiian and Tongan have numerical terms for the value 'one hundred thousand,' though it is doubtful that the speakers of these languages have any practical use for such a quantity (see Hurford 1987: 74).

Just as interesting as these exceptions, if more so, are the immense regularities that constrain the pairing of number concepts with numerical terms: that is, the construction of a denotation system for mathematical ideas. When we look at systems of numerical quantification across the world's languages, we find that numeral systems can be fairly well described in terms of their *numerical bases* and *atoms* and the *principles used to construct complex numerals* from these elementary units (see Greenberg 1978b and Stampe 1976).

10.2722.   Atoms and Bases

Greenberg (1978b) notes that all systems of numerical quantification are finite. This may seem surprising at first because some languages, like English, appear to allow for infinite counting. But Greenberg (1978b: 253) observes that every numeral system has a highest number, the *limit number,* to use Greenberg's phraseology, for which a numeral can be generated. In American English, it is *decillion* (= 10^{36}); in Northern Paiute, it is 'ten': *simi manoi*; in Watjarri (Douglas 1981: 267), it is 'three': *marnkurr*. The fact that languages have a limit number does not mean that higher numbers are inconceivable or inexpressible. In Watjarri, as in many other languages with small numeral systems, plurality takes over, and beyond 'three,' numerical quantities are simply 'many,' *yaljpa*.

The finitude of numeral systems is related to the fairly regular restrictions on the formation of numerical quantities across languages. All systems have what Greenberg (1978b) refers to as *atoms,* the simplest lexicalizations of number in a language, and those from which more complex numerals are constructed. In English, the atoms are the forms *one* through *ten*; all the other forms in the language can generally be derived therefrom: Compare *sixteen* (*six* + *ten*). Aghem (Hyman 1979: 34–5) works similarly, with atoms for the numbers from 'one' through 'ten,' and numerals for numbers thereafter productively derived from the atoms. For example, in Aghem, the form for 'ten' is *ghím* and 'three' is *tíghá:* 'thirty' is *n-ghím n-tíghá*.[9]

In some languages the entire numeral system is restricted to the atoms. Greenberg (1978b) observes that the universal range for systems of this sort is between 'five' and 'two.' Wargamay (Dixon 1981) is a good example, with three numerals—*yuŋgul* 'one,' *yaga* 'two,' and *gaṛbu* 'three'—and quantities beyond 'three' encoded by *guymaṛbari* 'many.' In Margany (Breen 1981), there are apparently only two numerals: *wakanyu* 'one' and *ura* 'two,' with the general quantifier for 'many,' *ḍiwala*, taking up the counting function thereafter.

In the vast majority of languages, however, the atoms can be used combinatorically to form complex numerals. In such languages, there are *bases,* which Stampe (1976: 600) describes quite nicely:

> Somewhere between 2 (the minimal plural) and 20 (the sum of the fingers and toes), and usually at 10, every language runs out of simple numbers [atoms, WF] expressing consecutive integers (units). To count higher it is necessary to start over

---

[9]English forms like *twenty,* which look like counters, actually support the rule. *Twenty* is morphologically related to *two* and counting in the twenties, as in all the decades, requires use of the atoms.

again at 1, somehow marking the units of the second cycle to distinguish them from the first. The usual way to do this is by combining the highest unit counted on the first cycle with the successive units of the second.

The *base* of the system is "that number from which counting starts over" (Stampe 1976: 601). This does not mean, however, that beyond the base, there are no new numerals; on the contrary, it is quite common for languages to have new terms beyond the base. Crucially, at a certain numeral, the previous numerals, the atoms, *begin to be reused*. This point of recycling is the base.

The most common base is 'ten,' or *decimal,* meaning that after the numeral for 'ten,' the atoms of the system recycle to produce complex numerals. English and Aghem are base ten. So are Mam (England 1983: 84), *kyajlaaj* 'fourteen' (lit. 'four-ten'), and Kusaiean (Lee 1975), *singuhul ahng* 'fourteen' ('ten' + 'four'). Base-ten systems predominate because this is the number of fingers (Stampe 1976).

Nondecimal systems are fairly easy to find, given enough searching. They typically come in one of three kinds: base four (*quaternary*), base twelve (*duodecimal*), or base twenty (*vigesimal*), though there are some variations on these types. Greenberg (1978b: 257) notes that the language of Dagur and Vatai, in New Guinea, begins to recycle its numerals most productively after the term for 'four,' making it technically a quaternary system. Sora is a duodecimal: simple numbers reach to *miggel* 'twelve' and thereafter complex numbers emerge from the simpler ones: 'fourteen' is *miggel-bagu* 'twelve-two' (Stampe 1976: 601). Ainu, the ancient language of the Japanese islands, is vigesimal, with complex numerals formed by subtraction downward from 'twenty': 'Fifty' is *wambi i-richoz,* literally 'ten from three twenties,' or 'sixty minus ten' (Hurford 1975: 240).

Other base systems are possible, through not all that widespread, and often derived from a combination of bases. Kobon (Davies 1981: 207) has a rather strange system, something like a double base-twelve system. The numerals are atoms up to *mögan* 'twelve.' At 'thirteen,' the numerals from to 'twelve' are used in reverse order, preceded by a constant form *böŋ,* to form the numerals up to 'twenty four.' At 'twenty four,' another constant form is introduced and precedes the numerals from 'one' to 'twenty three,' thus forming the next sequence of 24 numbers. This procedure goes on with different prefixes as the system increases. The phrase 'thirty-eight shells' is given here as an illustration (Davies 1981: 208):

38. köbap ñin ju-öl adog da ajɨp böŋ.
    shell   twenty-three   fifteen
    thirty-eight shells.
    More accurately: twenty-three-fifteen shells.

Closer to home, French combines both decimal and vigesimal systems in its expression for 'ninety': *quatre-vignt-dix,* literally 'four twenty ten.' Hurford (1975) argues that this kind of structure in French is the result of the historical interaction of the Romance decimal systems and the Celtic vigesimal one, producing a hybrid in the modern language.

10.2723.   Complex Numerals and Arithmetical Operations

The atoms and bases combine to produce complex numeral systems. Remarkably, languages follow the basic arithmetical operations in this regard, using addition, subtraction, multiplication, and division to combine atoms with bases to form complex expressions.

Greenberg (1978b) remarks that the most common arithmetical operation for forming complex numerals is addition: that is, the numeral is *added to the base;* this is followed in frequency by multiplication. The inverses of these two operations, subtraction and division, are then the next most frequent. This gives a hierarchy of operations in the construction of complex numerical expressions: addition > multiplication > subtraction/division.

Examples of addition are readily found. In Margi (Hoffman 1963: 106–8), a decimal system, numerals are explicitly added to the base ten by the meaning 'and put in':

39. kúm gà   pwá   fóɗʉ́
    ten and put in four
    fourteen.

Multiplication can be found in the Indoeuropean languages, where in French, 'eighty' is formed multiplicatively: *quatre vigant* (4×20).

The inverse operations are more difficult to locate, but are not rare. We have seen subtraction in the Ainu vigesimal system; Greenberg (1978b: 260) notes that subtraction occurs in Latin: *duodeviginti,* 'eighteen,' literally 'two from twenty.' Division is the least likely operation used for forming complex numerals and most often used in the formation of 'fifty,' as 'one-half of a hundred.' Oriya, however, uses division in the form for 'two hundred seventy five,' *pau ne tini šata,* literally 'quarter from three hundred,' where 'quarter' is understood to be 'one-fourth of a hundred' (Greenberg 1978b: 261).

The rationale behind the hierarchy of operations is understandable. Addition is the arithmetically simplest; multiplication is a derivative of addition. Both inverse operations are decidedly less frequent, no doubt because of their marked status arithmetically and because, as Stampe (1976) notes, they force the counting to go backward while counting itself goes forward. Hence, the operations that construct complex numerals out of atoms and bases follow the natural cognitive increase in magnitude at the base of cardinal numerals. Operations that go against this expectation are distributionally less frequent.

10.2724. Summary

In this section, we have looked at the semantics of numeral systems. We have differentiated numbers (concepts) from numerals (semantic and syntactic systems) and looked at how atoms, bases, and arithmetical operations produce systems of simple and complex numerals. Most languages have a base—the numeral at which the atoms begin to be reused—typically 'ten,' but also frequently 'twelve,' 'twenty,' and 'four.' Complex numerals derive from the addition, multiplication, subtraction, and division of the atom and base: the first two are the most common choices and also the simplest mathematically.

10.3. MODIFIER ORDER

Up to this point, we have discussed the major property concepts and denotations that underlie modifying expressions in language. Here we consider a broad theoretical issue bearing on these descriptive facts. Why do modifying expressions occur in certain orders? Why *big red car,* but not ?? *red big car?* Is there an answer to this problem in terms of the denotations of modifying expressions and the relative ordering of property concepts themselves?

We consider answers to these questions from both the typological and formal camps. We look at Dixon's attempt to describe the regularities in the order of adjectives, and Seiler's and Hetzron's more abstract explanations for these consistencies. All rely on some inherent conceptual dependency across property concepts: There is a "natural order" to modifiers.

With these proposals in hand, we turn to formal matters and ask the basic question of the logic of modification, indeed of the formal account of language in general: What kind of a formal object is a modifier? The solution we take up holds that modifiers are logical *functions* that map from domain to domain; they are not really properties at all. Modifiers have only a small number of formal functions. Some modifiers map extensionally, onto entire domains, and some map intensionally, onto parts of domains. We consider what this functional account of modification has to say about the typological facts of modifier order, and, in the end, we try to bring together the typological and formal results to make some suggestions about how each can help to solve the other's problems.

10.31. The Problem and Some Pitfalls

A look at the way languages string together modifiers reveals two basic problems. First, *within languages,* there are rather fixed orders of modifiers in modifying expressions. English is typical in this respect. We can certainly say (40a), but (40b) is anomalous because the order of modifiers is scrambled:

40a. those many little sick children.
 b. ?? many little those sick children.

The same general restriction holds in the completely unrelated language Watjarri (Douglas 1981: 241), where (41a) follows the preferred order of modifiers, and (41b) is anomalous because of scrambling:

41a. yaljpa mayu tjintjamarta pika pala.
 many child small   sick that (mid-distance)
 those many little sick children.
 b. ?? yaljpa mayu pika pala tjintjamarta.

Importantly, (40b) and (41b) are unacceptable from the ordering of modifiers, not for other structural reasons, because in each case we have kept the head of the modified expression—the noun denoting the domain—in the correct position for that language.

Second, even though the order of modifiers is fairly rigid within many languages, *across languages* there are somewhat different orders of modifiers (apart from those determined by the head/complement parameter of the language, which is entirely syntactic). Again, compare English and Watjarri. In English, as (40a) reveals, quantity expressions precede those for size, which in turn precede those for physical state: *many little sick*. But in Watjarri, where modifiers follow their heads as a rule, quantity precedes the head and, working from the outside in, physical state precedes size.

Our goal here is to see if there are any regularities underlying variations like these. We are motivated to search for consistency, in spite of the divergence in the simple comparison of English and Watjarri, because languages themselves tend to be so regular internally. However, before we go into that work to see how it bears on our general descriptive findings, we should be aware of a few pitfalls.

Morphology, syntax, pragmatics, and scope may all constrain the order of elements in a modified expression, irrespective of semantic conditions. In Telugu, modifiers carrying overt morphological derivation must precede nonderived forms, whatever the denotations of the modifiers (Dixon 1982: 26, fn. 27). Configurational languages (those with syntactic subject/object asymmetries as a consequence of having a VP in their syntax) are more prone to restrictions on the order of modifiers than nonconfigurational languages (those without a VP). Consequently, English has modifier order because it is configurational, but Hebrew, which is relatively nonconfigurational, has fewer such conditions (Gil 1983). Pragmatic factors, like focus and topicalization, may also intervene to determine modifier order: *It was an OLD big car, not a NEW one!* (cf. ?? *old big car:* see also Ney 1983 and Sichelschmidt 1986). Finally, modifier order may be affected by the internal scope of the modifiers themselves; *good sharp knife* has the order it does because *sharp* is within the scope of *good*: that is, 'the knife's sharpness is good,' structurally, [[good sharp] knife].

Without demeaning or dismissing these factors, we want to look at what semantic correlates there are, if any, to modifier order. Our goal is to see if the denotations of modifiers themselves have a bearing on how modifiers are strung together in languages that have restrictions on their modifier orders. Hence our larger project is not reductivist: That is, we are not trying to reduce modifier order to meaning; we want simply to see how semantics and structure work in tandem on this point.

10.32. The Order of Modifiers in English
(and Other Languages)

A number of studies have been done principally on the order of English modifiers according to their denotations (Bache 1978; Dixon 1982; Quirk and Greenbaum 1973). Though not all these studies agree on the details, and certainly they diverge as to their claims to universality, their generalizations are remarkably similar at a gross level.

Dixon (1982) offers the following characterization of English modifier order based on his eight classes of property concepts (we have discussed five of these: see sec. 10.2):

Logic > Value > Dimension > Physical Property > Speed > Human Propensity > Age > Color

FIG. 10.6.   Dixon's account of modifier order in English.

This scheme accounts for expressions like the next example:

42a. five good long smooth old brown tables.
  b. one small quick leap.
  c. many miserably clever green snakes.

Dixon (1982: 24–5) points out that although speakers show a general agreement on ordering across property concept type, they exhibit inconsistent intuitions within type. So dimensional properties generally precede physical ones— *long smooth table* versus ?? *smooth long table*—but within dimensionality, width, for example, is not more likely to precede height, or vice versa—*tall wide bridge* versus *wide tall bridge*. Dixon's account of modifier order thus places the organizing principle at the highest semantic category to which the denotation of a property concept belongs.

Quirk and Greenbaum (1973) and Bache (1978) take similar tacks, though their proposals use different property concepts. Overlaps in their typologies, however, produce some interesting results. In English quantities tend to precede value ascriptions, and these tend to precede physical properties, which in turn tend to precede age, and then color: Quantity > Value > Physical Property > Age > Color.

In its general form, this result accords quite well with orderings of modifiers found in languages other than English. For comparison, consider the order of modifiers in Hungarian, Telugu, and Selepet (after Dixon 1982: 26):

Hungarian: Value > Dimension > Age > Physical Property > Color

Telugu: Value > Age > Dimension > Physical Property > Color

Selepet: Dimension > Physical Property > Value/Human Propensity > Age > Color

FIG. 10.7. Comparison of modifier orders from three unrelated languages.

Age tends to precede color and dimensional ascriptions precede physical properties. In two of the three cases, value precedes all else, and in the third, value precedes both age and color. Similar convergences have been noted by Hetzron (1978) with a smaller set of property concepts. English, German, Hungarian, Polish, Turkish, Hindi, Persian, Indonesian, and Basque all order value before size, and those two before color: Value > Size > Color.

Certainly these general convergences between English and other, totally unrelated languages cannot be denied. But what explains these descriptive consistencies? Several explanations have been proposed for these results, all of which rely on stating general conditions on property concept sequencing, without specifying the detail of particular orders within languages. Here we consider two proposals: Seiler's theory of modifier applicability and scope and Hetzron's scale of subjectivity.

10.321. Semantic Applicability and Scope

For Seiler (1978), the order of modifiers is basically an issue of the *scope of the modifiers in relation to the domain modified*. He proposes a kind of *semantic applicability principle* for modifier order: The distance of a modifier from the domain positively correlates with the range of its applicability to the domain.

Those properties serially farther from the domain have wider scope and hence wider applicability to domains. Determiners and quantifiers appear a long distance from their head and have fewer restrictions on cooccurrence. In contrast, properties closer to the domain have narrower scope and narrower applicability. For this reason, material composition, age, and color appear closer to the modified domain, and Seiler argues that they have more restrictions on the domains to which they apply: Material, for example, must be ascribed to a domain that has material properties. Figure 10.8 schematizes Seiler's theory.

←————————————————————— Domain

Wider Application   Narrower Application

(quantities, articles, etc.)   (material, color, etc.)

FIG. 10.8.   Seiler's view of modifier order by applicability.

Though this scope account is proposed to obtain for all languages, it is difficult to see how it applies in certain crucial cases. Color universally appears close to the modified domain, even in languages that have relatively free modifier order, like Chinese (from Hetzron 1978: 173):

43a. yíge hǎukànde dàde húngde chyóu.
     a   pretty   big   red   ball
     a pretty big red ball.
  b. yíge dàde hǎukànde húngde chyóu.
     a   big   pretty   red   ball
     a pretty big red ball.

The expression for 'red,' *húngde,* has a fixed position whereas the other modifiers may be interchanged. Does this mean that color is narrower in applicability than, say, numerical quantification? This is rather difficult to swallow, especially when we consider that languages with binary color term systems must, out of necessity, apply their color terms quite generally.

Conversely, how is logical quantification wider in applicability than, say, material composition? Following Dixon, age is wider in applicability than color, and both are narrower than value. This is a bit hard to comprehend.

The more general principle that seems to underlie Seiler's (1978) observations is one that we have seen elsewhere with respect to scope and negation: The closer an operator is to what it operates on, the more effect the operator has. So, affixal negation has more negative effect than particle negation (see chap. 9). Seiler thus appears to be saying, in logical terms, that modifiers closer to their domains are more intimately connected to their domains. For this reason, material composition appears close to the head, but definiteness, a discourse property, appears some distance away.

10.322.   *Subjectivity and Objectivity*

A different sort of explanation is offered by Hetzron (1978), following arguments made by Quirk and Greenbaum (1973). In this account, modifiers are ordered along a scale of subjectivity and evaluation, such that the closer a modifier is to the domain, the more likely it is to be objectively verifiable as an ascribed property; said otherwise, property concepts in positions near the domain are more impersonal with collective agreement on their applicability. Conversely, the farther the modifier is from the domain, the more likely it is to be subjectively verified as an ascription; property concepts in positions far from the domain are more opinionlike and subject to greater disagreement in applicability. Figure 10.9 schematizes Hetzron's generalization.

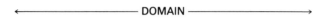

←————————————— DOMAIN —————————————→

Subjective/Opinion Objective/Impersonal Subjective/Opinion

FIG. 10.9.   Hetzron's account of modifier order by subjectivity and objectivity.

Under this view, properties like age, color, shape, material composition, and physical constitution are more likely to appear closer to the domain; indeed, the distributional facts bear this out in a general way, as the comparisons on pp. 483–84 suggest. In contrast, expressions of value and human propensity are more judgmental and hence removed from the domain. Again, the distributional facts fit this characterization. As Hetzron (1978) observes, the overwhelming tendency is for evaluative expressions to precede expressions of size and color. The first is clearly more subjectively determinable than the latter two.

This account of modifier order in terms of a scale of objective or subjective verifiability, attractive as it is, nonetheless raises a number of questions. The observations hold for *clearly* subjective properties, like value, and *clearly* objective ones, like color. But in some languages, like Selepet, value is not positioned very far from the domain. Does this mean that value is objective in this language/culture? What about physical properties? Are they objectively or subjectively measurable? Are human propensity concepts objective or subjective?

In any case, if modifier order does follow a general condition of subjectivity and evaluation, then we might begin to make sense of another interesting correlate of modifier order. Those forms typically found close to the domain of a modifying expression (age and color) are frequently categorematic modifiers. Value, in contrast, is usually a syncategorematic modifier, and, as we know, this property tends to precede age and color. Do subjectively determinable properties tend to appear in syncategorematic modification while objectively determinate properties appear in categorematic form?

In the final sections of this chapter (secs. 10.34 and 10.35), we propose another account of modifier order that begins to get at all these questions. It relies on unifying the formal and typological accounts of modification via intensional and extensional modification. But for this account to make sense, we must first have a fuller description of the formal facts.

10.33. Formal Aspects of Modification

We now know the typological issues surrounding the ordering of modifiers, so we turn to the formal side of modification to see if the logic of modifiers can provide a simple answer to these cross-language regularities in surface expression. Ultimately, we hope to match the descriptive and distributional facts with accounts of modifiers as logical objects to provide a unified explanation of modifier order.

10.331. The Nature of Modifiers:
Predicates, Properties, and Functions

As we noted in Chapter 2, formal analysis of a semantic phenomenon raises the ontological question: What sort of a thing is the phenomenon whose logical form we propose to analyze? What kind of logical type is a modifier? We might say that a modifier is a *predicate,* an attribute or event that must be embodied by an individual (see chap. 5). So the expression *new car* is analyzed formally as new(car): that is, 'newness embodied by the car,' where *new* is a predicate and *car,* the domain modified, is an argument or an individual.

If we analyze *new car* as a predication, we miss an important generalization: Entities, the domains modified, are also predicates. *Car* is really a handy cover term for a *set of characteristics,* like 'vehicular,' 'mobile,' 'constructed,' 'buyable,' and so on, that also have to be embodied by some individual, x. In this view, *car* also denotes a predicate: car(x). If this is true, then the expression *new car* involves *two* predications: new(car(x)): that is, 'newness of the car characteristics embodied by x.'

This notion of generalized predication, given here in only very rudimentary form, is one of the basic insights of modern formal analysis (such as that advocated by Montague 1974). For our purposes here it is important to remember that both modifiers, adjectives in this case, and domains modified, nouns, involve the same logical type in their denotations.

With a little further thought, however, we can see that although both nouns and adjectives involve predication, they markedly diverge in *how the predication is carried out.* A noun denotes a simple predication, but an adjective denotes a complex one. The set of "car properties," which we simply call *the property of being a car,* is embodied by a simple individual, x. But an adjective like *new* does not take a simple individual as an argument; instead, it takes a noun, which is already a predication. So, whereas a noun takes an individual as its argument, an adjective takes a set, the characteristics embodied by x, or *the property of being an x.* Thus the modified expression *new car* is really a complex predication, something like 'the property of being a new property of being a car.'

To put the matter another way, when we think of modification formally, we should not think in the traditional terms of a noun, denoting an object, modified by an adjective, denoting some attribute or ascription. Rather, we should think in terms of entire expressions. What is the relationship between the denotation of the expression *car* and that for the expression *new car?* How does a simple property (a set of characteristics, a predication), denoted by *car* for example, become a complex property, denoted by *new car* for example? Parsons (1980: 37) puts the matter clearly: "The only difference between *brown dog* and *dog* is that the former [is] complex and the latter simple . . . 'brown' stands for a function which maps the property of being a dog onto the property of being a brown dog."

The correct way of viewing modification, then, is as an *operation that constructs complex predications out of simpler ones.* Formally, a modifier does not denote a class of property concepts, as the typological work has it; formally, nouns denote classes of property concepts. A modifier denotes a *function* that associates classes of property concepts. Mathematically, a function is an operation that takes members of a set and uniquely relates them to members of another set. This is exactly what a modifier does. A modifier takes a set as its argument, the property of being a car for example (which is, as we know, a set of characteristics), and produces a more complex set, namely the property of being a new car.[10]

Given all this discussion, we ultimately want to know what value there is in seeing modifiers as functions and not individual properties as such. The view of modifiers as functions provides a straightforward solution to the problem of modifier order. This is because modifying functions have two further formal properties—extensional and intensional modification—and these characteristics unify and simplify all the previously proposed accounts of modifier order.

10.332. *Intensional and Extensional Modification*

An account of modification in terms of functions and logical types yields interesting results for the nature of modification itself. There is an interesting and useful further distinction, based on the way that modifiers as functions map properties onto sets of properties. This is the difference between *extensional* and *intensional* modification (see Kamp 1975; Siegel 1980). A modifier is intensional if, in its modification of a domain, it makes essential reference to the

---

[10]One of the most widely discussed modifying functions is that carried out by determiners. In Barwise and Cooper's (1981) terminology, determiners map simple common nouns—properties— into *generalized quantifiers,* complex quantified noun phrases. For reasons of space, we simply note this influential work. The interested reader should also see Keenan and Stavi (1986) for a thorough analysis of determiner functions.

characteristics that comprise the denotation of the domain modified: that is, its description or *sense*. In contrast, a modifier is extensional if it makes reference to the domain as a whole, whatever its constituent properties: that is, its object or *referent*.

We can see this difference in a comparison of the following two expressions:

44a. long book.
  b. long board.

In both cases, *long* is syncategorematic because, following the set membership test in section 10.14, neither a long book nor a long board is necessarily a long thing. But consider exactly *how long* modifies the domains in each. In (44a), *long* makes reference to a *constituent property* of the denotation of *book*—the page length—and so here *long* modifies intensionally because it selects a descriptive feature of the domain. But in (44b), *long* does not make reference to any constituent property of the domain because a board has no inherent length. In this case, *long* modifies the domain extensionally, by referring to the *domain as a whole*.

Siegel (1980) points out a clear paraphrase difference between intensional and extensional modification in English. Intensional modifiers are paraphrased by *as a*, extensional modifiers by *for a*. Note how this differentiates the examples in (44):

45a. It was long, as a book (is long).
  b. ?? It was long, for a book (as compared to other things).
46. It was long, for a board (as compared to other things).
  b. ?? It was long, as a board (is long).

If a modifier is intensional, as in (45a), in mapping a property onto a set of properties, the function picks out a characteristic that makes up the set called *the property of being X*. Hence, *long,* in its intensional meaning, is sensitive to a "subproperty" of the property it takes as an argument. For this reason, the *as a* paraphrase acceptably continues with a comparison internal to the domain ("as a book is long") (cf. Bolinger's 1967 notion of *reference modification,* whereby individuals are picked out via their properties.)

In contrast, an extensional modifier, as in (46a), maps from a property to a set of properties by picking out the property, a set, as a whole and comparing it to some other property (i.e., a noun) as a whole. Consider how the extensional sense of *long* works in this respect. The *for a* paraphrase of *long board* works because *for a* suggests that there is some *external standard* of comparison against which to judge the length of a board: *long for a board, as compared to other things that could have length* (cf. Bolinger's 1967 notion of *referent modification,* whereby modifiers select entire referents.)

This difference between intensional and extensional modification is related to, but is independent of, categorematic and syncategorematic modification. Syncategorematic modifiers tend to be intensional because both are sensitive to the domain modified; categorematic modifiers tend to be extensional, because both are somehow independent of the domain modified. But these types are not coextensive. Syncategorematic modifiers can be intensional or extensional: *long* is a case in point, having two kinds of mapping. But many other syncategorematic modifiers are extensional: *small, tall,* and *fast,* for example. Others are syncategorematic and intensional: *imitation, alleged, former,* for example. The same division holds for categorematic modifiers, some of which are extensional—like *healthy, alive,* or *asleep*—and some intensional—like *fresh* (Siegel 1980 provides good lists of these).

If there is a clear difference in modification by formal means, intensional mapping versus extensional mapping, then how can we use this difference more broadly in our theoretical pursuits? The intensional/extensional difference appears to offer a formal solution to the problem of the order of modifiers.

10.34. Extensional, Intensional, and the Order of Modifiers

We have found that, all else being equal in the many factors affecting modifier order, the general rule of subjective before objective properties, and wider before narrower applicability, accounts for a large number of cases. At the end of that discussion, we noted that syncategorematic properties tend to precede categorematic properties. Here we pick up these observations and work them in more detail with regard to intensional and extensional modification.

10.341. Intensional > Extensional

When all else is equal in the choice of modifier order, *intensional modifiers precede extensional modifiers.* (This is contrary to what Seiler 1978 proposes.) The tendency for syncategorematic modifiers to precede categorematic modifiers is naturally related to the intensional > extensional ordering. Syncategorematics tend to be intensional and categorematics extensional, so the syncategorematic > categorematic ordering falls out by default. The real issue is how the mapping function is carried out: that is, how the modifying function operates on the set it takes as an argument. It appears that distance from the domain is related to the intensionality of the modification.

Consider the following expression:

47. dark house.

Dark here may mean either 'dark in color' or 'unlighted.' Both senses are categorematic: A dark-colored house is a dark-colored building, and an unlighted house is an unlighted building. But in the sense of 'dark as a color' *dark* is extensional: Note that the paraphrase *dark for a house (as compared to other kinds of buildings with color)* is entirely appropriate here. However in the sense of 'unlighted,' *dark* is intensional: An unlighted house is such by virtue of its constituent features, like lighting, windows, and so on; hence, the paraphrase *dark as a house (is dark)* is appropriate.

Suppose that we add another extensional categorematic adjective to (47), preferably one that matches the ordering claims closely. Age generally precedes color, so let us insert a modifier for age:

48. old dark house.

Old is categorematic: An old house is an old building. It is also extensional: A house is old not from inherent age properties, but from how its age works as a whole. *Old for a house* is the appropriate paraphrase, not ?? *old as a house (is old)*. What are the possible interpretations of (48)? It is ambiguous, meaning either 'aged dark-colored house' or 'aged unlighted house.' That is, the interpretations by function may be either Extensional + Extensional ('aged' + 'dark in color') or Extensional + Intensional ('aged' + 'unlighted').

Consider what happens when we re-order the modifiers:

49. dark old house.

By my intuition, (49) preferentially means 'unlighted aged house,' not 'dark-colored aged house.' When the order of modifiers is inverted, *the intensional sense* of *dark* is salient. It thus appears that if there is a semantic correlate to modifier ordering, then the modifiers farther from the domain are more likely to have intensional meanings. Otherwise, we are hard pressed to explain why *dark,* which has both an extensional and intensional sense, suppresses its extensional meaning when it is moved positionally farther from its domain.

If we look further into English, we can see this principle of Intensional > Extensional in broader operation. Consider (50):

50. plastic man.

Example (50) may mean either 'a man made out of plastic' (i.e., a mannequin) or 'a man whose personality is fake.' In both senses *plastic* is categorematic, but in the former sense, it is extensional (*plastic for a man, as compared to other things*) and in the latter it is intensional (*plastic as a man, as a person, from behavioral attributes*). When we add another extensional categorematic modifier, and invert, as in (49), we get only the intensional reading of *plastic:*

51. plastic young man.

Example (51) may mean only 'youthful man with a fake personality'; it cannot refer to a mannequin. For this later reading, the one that requires the extensional sense, we must leave the modifier in its position nearer to the domain:

52. young plastic man.

Many other examples of this phenomenon can be found. Compare the difference between *reddish old house* and ?? *red old house. Reddish* is arguably an intensional version of *red,* referring as it does not to the house as a whole, but to some characteristic features of the house. For this reason, it can move father from the domain it modifies and otherwise violate the standing rule of English that color follows age.

One might object here and say that the issue at hand is not the intensionality of the modification that licenses removal from the domain, but the change of property class (following Dixon's view of modifier order). Example (51), for example, has only the 'fake' reading because, in this sense, it is no longer a material attribute, but a human property; human properties can precede age, but material attributes cannot, so the 'fake' reading falls out from property class change, not intensionality.

This objection begs the question, however. We have already seen that the classes of property concepts are not theoretically driven, but descriptive heuristics that only organize the data. The classes are admittedly loose, and the criteria for inclusion are often quite doubtful. If the explanation via property class change is correct, then why isn't *plastic* as a material attribute actually a physical property and thus, contrary to the data, required to precede age?

The classes of property concepts make no systematic predictions because the criteria for inclusion in the property concept classes are rules of thumb, not algorithms. On the other hand, the difference between intensional and extensional modification can be systematically determined. Hence the intensional/extensional criterion is a more productive, useful, and theoretically acceptable account.

10.342. *Intensionality and Modifier Order in Spanish and French*

Evidence from other languages supports the view that distance from the domain modified is correlated with the intensionality of the modifying function. In Spanish, a number of modifiers may have either prenominal or postnominal position, and this shift changes the denotation of the form. Consider the difference between the following (after Klein-Andreu 1983):

53a. un triste empleado.
     a   sad   employee
     a lowly employee.
   b. un empleado triste.
      a   employee sad
      a sad employee.

In (53a), where the modifier *triste* precedes the noun, the meaning is 'lowly,' and in (53b), where the modifier follows, the meaning is 'sad.' In the first sense, *triste* is intensional: That is, a lowly employee is lowly *as an* employee. But in the second sense, *triste* is extensional: A sad employee is sad *for an* employee, not sad *as an* employee.

It thus appears that the difference in position correlates with intensional and extensional modification. Interestingly enough, the prenominal modifier is *structurally farther* from the domain because modifiers in Spanish generally follow their domains. *Empleado triste* is a construction where the modifier is closer to the domain, in the normal order; *triste empleado* has the modifier farther away because it is outside of the normal adjective phrase bracketing. As expected, in the latter, where the modifier is removed from the domain, the meaning of the modifier is intensional.

The same facts apparently hold for French, where the analogous distributional patterns appear. Martin (1986) remarks that prenominal modifiers in French specify necessary characteristics of the domain whereas postnominal modifiers simply isolate the class as a whole denoted by the noun modified. *Dangereux terroristes* means 'dangerous terrorists,' where the ascription of 'dangerous' applies to the particular terrorists in question: that is, 'dangerous *as these* terrorists.' On the other hand, *terroristes dangereux* means 'dangerous terrorists' as a specific subset: that is, 'dangerous *for these* particular terrorists,' as compared to other terrorists, where the standard of comparison is external to the domain. Again, it appears that the intensional/extensional distinction underlies the positional difference. Prenominal modifiers in French, as in Spanish, are structurally farther from the domain, and it is these that have the intensional reading.

If it is correct that preposed modifiers in Spanish and French are intensional because they are structurally farther from the domain, while postposed modifiers are extensional because they are closer, then Klein-Andreu's (1983) discourse explanation for this phenomenon comes right into line. She says that nouns with prenominal modification are noncontrastive, whereas those with postnominals are contrastive. By this she means that prenominally modified expressions are not used in discourse to denote differentiated participants, whereas postnominally modified expressions are used in such a fashion. Note how this discourse function follows the semantic facts.

Intensional modification, prenominal in this case, affects the internal structure of the domain, not the referent properties of the domain as a whole. Hence, intensionally modified expressions are really composite, not individuated as a totality. On the other hand, extensional modification, postnominal in this case, modifies the domain, and the property it denotes, as a whole. It seems clear here that extensional modification is much more compatible with discourse contrast because the referent itself is modified.

Another way to put this is to say that extensional modification is more nounlike, which is why extensional modifiers tend to be nearer the noun. Intensional modification is less nounlike, and thus can be removed from the noun as domain. With this kind of explanation, we might say that discourse factors, like informational contrast, are keyed to the extensional/intensional properties of the modifying expressions. Extensional modification is contrastive in Spanish because it is an extension, a total entity, that is being modified.

10.35. Unifying the Formal and Typological Accounts of Modifier Order

To summarize then: The order of modifiers appears to be sensitive not to the property classes that the modifiers themselves denote, but to the *kind of mapping that modifiers as functions execute.* All else being equal, removal from the domain modified correlates with intensional modification; nearness to the domain modified correlates with extensional modification. This more general condition subsumes the categorematic/syncategorematic condition given at the end of section 10.322 because categorematic modifiers tend to be extensional and syncategorematic modifiers intensional.

With a little further thought, however, we can see that the intensional/extensional account subsumes the subjective/objective condition proposed by Hetzron. Objectivity is intuitively related to extensionality because extensional modification applies to the domain as a whole; conversely, intensionality is linked to subjectivity because the modification must make reference to something less than the domain as a whole, and this applicability thus has to be judged in some way. Subjective properties precede objective properties because intensional properties precede extensional properties.

We may also bring into line Seiler's (1978) proposal regarding the logic of modifier order and the scope of modification. Seiler says that modifiers farther from the domain modified have broader applicability and denote fewer properties; those closer to the domain have narrower applicability and denote more properties. All this stands to reason, given the intensional/extensional condition.

Intensional modifiers select a characteristic of the domain. By definition, intensional modification selects a *single* property. In contrast, extensional modification, by definition, selects an *entire domain,* or, in formal terms, a *property* or a *set* of characteristics. So, by definition, extensional modification selects more properties than intensional modification.

We now have accounted for one half of Seiler's theory. How about the claims about the range of applicability? To put it simply, modification via one characteristic (intensional modification) will necessarily have broader applicability than modification by a set of properties (extensional modification) because the former will have fewer restrictions, again by definition. Consider the fact that a set defined by a single criterion admits more members than a set defined by many criteria. Seiler's observations again fall out as a consequence of intensional and extensional modification. Intensional modification gives the impression of broad applicability because, as a function, it maps via a single characteristic of the domain; extensional modification conveys the opposite sense, narrow applicability, because it maps via a set of characteristics, in a formal sense, via a property as a whole.

Formal and typological claims about modification can be unified provided that we have the proper sense of each. A modifier is a particular logical type: a function. As such it can have a number of characteristics. It can map from sets onto sets of sets by making reference to members of the set it takes as its argument: that is, intensionally modify. Or it can map by making reference to its argument set as a whole: that is, extensionally modify. These broad formal differences bring a number of rather difficult and often confusing typological phenomena under one account. Removal from the domain modified, distance from the head noun, is a function of the intensionality of the modification, not a function of the kind of property concept that the modifier denotes.

This result falls out because, from a formal standpoint, modifiers do not denote property concepts at all; they map properties onto other properties and denote functions. It is the finer characteristics of these functions that give rise to typological phenomena. In the case of modification, formal accounts turn out to need typological accounts so that a proper sense of the data is maintained; but typological accounts turn out to require formal accounts for a succinct and complete explanation.

10.36. Summary

In this theoretical section, we have discussed a number of proposals for semantic regularities to modifier order. We have looked at Dixon's description of English adjective order and its applicability to languages other than English (e.g., the universal tendency for value to precede size, and for both to precede color). We have gone through two explanations for these regularities: Seiler's theory of modifier applicability and scope and Hetzron's scale of subjectivity. We postponed our dissatisfaction with these explanations until we considered formal theories of modification. We have seen that modifiers are functions, and come in two types: extensional (or referent-modifying) and intensional (or reference-modifying). Applying this formal distinction to the descriptive regularities, we have seen that, all else being equal, intensional modifiers precede extensional modifiers. This correlation of intensionality and distance underlies Spanish and French pre-/postnominal modifiers and subsumes Seiler's and Hetzron's explanations, thus unifying the formal and typological accounts of modifier order.

SUMMARY OF CHAPTER

We began this chapter by defining modification as the grammatical expression of property concepts. We looked at the organization of modification by domain, property, and delimitation and considered Givón's theory of the temporal stability of properties, Thompson's theory of modifiers as information in discourse, and Wierzbicka's theory of modifiers as single properties. We united these three in picturing modification as the means by which language encodes singular, noncriterial, nonprimitive qualities. We looked at scalar versus absolute properties and categorematic versus syncategorematic modification.

In sections 10.21–10.25, we considered five kinds of property concepts: color, age, value, human propensity, and physical properties. Under color, we discussed basic color terms, Berlin and Kay's hierarchy, and variation in color systems. Under value, we noted the tendency toward overlapping gradients and syncategorematic modification. We defined age as newness and recency rather than as chronological age and saw its scalar and categorematic features. We divided human propensity into three subcategories: mental state, physical state, and behavior. These terms tended to be relative and equipollent. We divided physical properties into seven subcategories: sense, consistency, texture, temperature, edibility, substantiality, and configuration. We saw that many of these denotations were scalar.

We then spent considerable time on quantities. We first considered nonnumerical quantities, more commonly known as quantification. We looked at the inadequacy of universal and existential quantification and recast quantifiers in terms of total (distributive and collective) and partial (maximum and minimum) quantities. We saw how pragmatics and semantics work together closely to determine the ultimate meanings of quantified expressions, especially in the way that implicature picks up where entailment falls off. We closed the discussion of quantifiers by looking at how the denotation of the quantifier and the domain quantified affect scope.

Thereafter, we looked at numerical quantities. We distinguished numbers from numerals and surveyed the atoms, bases, and arithmetical operations that underlie simple and complex numerals. The most common bases were 'ten,' 'twelve,' 'twenty,' and 'four.' Complex numerals derived from the addition, multiplication, subtraction, and division of the atom and base.

We closed the chapter with a discussion of modifier order. We looked at

Dixon's proposal for English modifier order, noting universal tendencies, like the closeness of color ascriptions to the domain. We also considered Seiler's theory of modifier applicability and scope and Hetzron's scale of subjectivity. We then turned to formal theories of modification, where modifiers were functions with extensional and intensional application. We applied these formal facts to the descriptive regularities, and saw that, all else being equal, intensional modifiers preceded extensional modifiers. This connection between intension and distance explained Spanish and French prenominal and postnominal modifiers and unified Seiler's and Hetzron's explanations into a single account of modifier order.

QUESTIONS FOR DISCUSSION

1. Russian appears to have two basic color terms for 'blue': *sinij* 'dark blue' and *goluboj* 'light blue.' How is this a problem for our account of color terms? How would you go about solving this problem? What do the forms denote? Are the forms *basic?* Do Kay and McDaniel's revisions of the hierarchy help here? Hungarian has two terms for 'red': *piros* and *vörös;* Korean has two for 'green': *palahta* and *noksyak.* How do these findings bear on your answer? (You might look at Corbett and Morgan 1988 and Moss 1989 for help.)

2. Listed here are some terms in Wargamay (Dixon 1981) for human propensity and physical properties. Categorize them according to the classes we developed in sections 10.24 and 10.25: *gilbay* 'knowledgeable,' *buŋgul* 'satiated,' *wuɲan* 'promiscuous,' *gawan* 'angry,' *yirgal* 'itchy,' *gagal* 'solid,' *dagardagar* 'prickly,' *ŋugi* 'stinking,' *mada* 'salty,' *dawuɲ* 'hot from a fire,' *baniṭa* 'hot from the sun,' *mulmbiɲ* 'blunt,' *danu* 'broken,' *gunga* 'raw,' *gidul* 'cold.'

3. Turn back to the Yoruba quantifiers on pp. 471–72. Is *òpòlopò* categorematic or syncategorematic? What about English quantifiers? Are they categorematic or syncategorematic? (Consider the difference between *much* and *many* here.) Now consider the scope of *òpò,púpò,* and *òpòlopò.* Though we have not discussed their scope in the chapter, you can make some predictions based on Ioup's revised hierarchy of inherent scope. Which Yoruba quantifier should have the widest inherent scope? Which should have the narrowest? Why? In your answer consider such things as total and partial quantities and the size and individuation of the collection denoted by the forms.

References

Adams, Karen (1986). Numeral classifiers in Austroasiatic. Noun classes and categorization, ed. by C. Craig, 241–62. Amsterdam: Benjamins

Adams, Karen and Nancy Conklin (1973). Toward a theory of natural classification. Chicago Linguistics Society 9.1–10.

Aksu-Koç, Ayhan (1988). The acquisition of aspect and modality. Cambridge: Cambridge University Press.

Aksu-Koç, Ayhan and Dan Slobin (1986). A psychological account of the development and use of evidentials in Turkish. Evidentiality: The Linguistic coding of epistemology, ed. by W. Chafe and J. Nichols, 159–67. Norwood, NJ: Ablex.

Allan, Keith (1977). Classifiers. Language 53.284–310.

Allan, Keith (1980). Nouns and countability. Language 56.541–67.

Allan, Keith (1986). Linguistic meaning (2 vols). London: Routledge.

Allwood, Jens, Lars-Gunnar Andersson, and Östen Dahl (1977). Logic in linguistics. Cambridge: Cambridge University Press.

Anderson, John (1971). The grammar of case: Towards a localistic theory. Cambridge: Cambridge University Press.

Anderson, John (1973). An essay concerning aspect. The Hague: Mouton.

Anderson, John (1984). Objecthood. Objects, ed. by F. Plank, 29–54. New York: Academic Press.

Anderson, Stephen and Edward Keenan (1985). Deixis. Language typology and syntactic description, III: Grammatical categories and the lexicon, ed. by T. Shopen, 259–308. Cambridge: Cambridge University Press.

Aoun, Joseph and Norbert Hornstein (1985). Quantifier types. Linguistic Inquiry 16.623–37.

Ashton, E. M. K., E. G. M. Ndawula, and A. N. Tucker (1954). A Luganda grammar. London: Longman.

Austin, Peter (1982). The deictic system of Diyari. Here and there, ed. by J. Weissenborn and W. Klein, 273–84. Amsterdam: Benjamins.

Bach, Emmon (1980). Tenses and aspects as functions on verb phrases. Time, tense, and quantifiers, ed. by C. Rohrer, 19–37. Tubingen: Niemeyer.

Bach, Emmon (1986). The algebra of events. Linguistics and Philosophy 9.5–16.

Bach, Emmon (1989). Informal lectures on formal semantics. Albany, NY: SUNY Press.

Bache, Carl (1978). The order of pre-modifying adjectives in present-day English. Odense: Odense University Press.

Baek, Eung-Jin (1985). Semantic shifts in Korean honorification. Historical semantics and word formation, ed. by J. Fisiak, 23–31. Berlin: de Gruyter.

Baker, Mark (1988). Incorporation: A theory of grammatical function changing. Chicago: University of Chicago Press.

Barnes, Janet (1984). Evidentials in the Tuyuca verb. International Journal of American Linguistics 50.255–71.

Baron, Robert (1987). The cerebral computer. Hillsdale, NJ: Lawrence Erlbaum Associates.

Barthes, Roland (1967). Elements of semiology. London: Cape.

Barwise, Jon (1988). On the circumstantial relation between meaning and content. Meaning and mental representation, ed. by U. Eco et al., 23–40. Bloomington, IN: Indiana University Press.

Barwise, Jon and Robin Cooper (1981). Generalized quantifiers and natural language. Linguistics and Philosophy 4.159–219.

Batori, Istvan (1982). On verb deixis in Hungarian. Here and there, ed. by J. Weissenborn and W. Klein, 155–65. Amsterdam: Benjamins.

Bennett, David (1975). Spatial and temporal uses of English prepositions. London: Longman.

Berlin, Brent (1968). Tzeltal numeral classifiers. The Hague: Mouton.

Berlin, Brent and Paul Kay (1969). Basic color terms. Berkeley, CA: University of California Press.

Berlin, Brent, Dennis Breedlove, and Peter Raven (1974). Principles of Tzeltal plant classification. New York: Academic Press.

Biber, Douglas and Edward Finegan (1988). Adverbial stance types in English. Discourse Processes 11.1–34.

Bickerton, Derek (1981). Roots of language. Ann Arbor, MI: Karoma.

Bloemen, Johan (1983). Catégorématique vs. syncatégorématique: Essai de définition. Semantikos 6.1–16.

Bloom, Lois (1970). Language development: Form and function in emerging grammars. Cambridge, MA: MIT Press.

Bolinger, Dwight (1967). Adjectives in English: Attribution and predication. Lingua 18.1–34.

Breen, J. G. (1981). Margany and Gunya. Handbook of Australian languages, II, ed. by R. M. W. Dixon and B. Blake, 275–393. Amsterdam: Benjamins.

Brekke, Magnar (1988). The experiencer constraint. Linguistic Inquiry 19.169–80.

Brinton, Laurel (1988). The development of English aspectual systems. Cambridge: Cambridge University Press.

Britto, Francis (1986). Diglossia: A study of the theory with application to Tamil. Washington, DC: Georgetown University Press.

Broadwell, George Aaron (1988). Multiple θ-role assignment in Choctaw. Thematic relations (Syntax and semantics, 21), ed. by Wendy Wilkins, 113–27. New York: Academic Press.

Brown, Penelope and Stephen Levinson (1987). Politeness. Cambridge: Cambridge University Press.

Brown, Roger and Albert Gilman (1960). The pronouns of power and solidarity. Style in language, ed. by T. Sebeok, 253–76. Cambridge, MA: MIT Press.

Brugman, Claudia (1981). The story of over. M.A. thesis, University of California at Berkeley.

Bull, William (1969). Time, tense, and the verb. Berkeley, CA: University of California Press.

Bunt, Harry (1985). Mass terms and model-theoretic semantics. Cambridge: Cambridge University Press.

Burgess, Don (1984). Western Tarahumara. Studies in Uto-Aztecan grammar, 4: Southern Uto-Aztecan grammatical sketches, ed. by R. Langacker, 1–149. Dallas, TX: Summer Institute of Linguistics.

Bybee, Joan (1985). Morphology. Amsterdam: Benjamins.

Bybee, Joan and William Pagliuca (1985). Cross-linguistic comparison and the development of grammatical meaning. Historical semantics and word formation, ed. by J. Fisiak, 59–83. The Hague: Mouton.

Carey, Kathy (1989). Tense as a marker of modal distance in Eastern Neo-Aramaic. Paper presented at the Linguistic Society of America, Washington, DC.

Carlson, Gregory (1977). Reference to kinds in English. Ph. D. Dissertation, University of Massachusetts.

Carlson, Gregory (1979). Generics and atemporal *when*. Linguistics and Philosophy 3.49–98.

Carlson, Gregory (1984). Thematic roles and their semantic interpretation. Linguistics 22.259–79.

Carlson, Lauri (1981). Aspect and quantification. Tense and aspect (Syntax and semantics, 14), ed. by P. Tedeschi and A. Zaenen, 31–64. New York: Academic Press.

Carlson, Robert (1987). Narrative connectives in Supyire. Coherence and grounding in discourse, ed. by R. Tomlin, 1–19. Amsterdam: Benjamins.

Carter, Robin (1976). Chipewyan classificatory verbs. International Journal of American Linguistics 42.24–30.

Chafe, Wallace (1970). Meaning and the structure of language. Chicago: University of Chicago Press.

Chafe, Wallace (1974). Language and consciousness. Language 50.111–33.

Chafe, Wallace and Johanna Nichols, eds. (1986). Evidentiality: The linguistic coding of epistemology. Norwood, NJ: Ablex.

Chierchia, Gennaro and Sally McConnell-Ginet (1990). Meaning and grammar. Cambridge, MA: MIT Press.

Chomsky, Noam (1981). Lectures on government and binding. Dordrecht: Foris.

Chung, Sandra and Alan Timberlake (1985). Tense, aspect, and mood. Language typology and syntactic description, III: Grammatical categories and the lexicon, ed. by T. Shopen, 202–58. Cambridge: Cambridge University Press.

Churchland, Paul (1985). Conceptual progress and word/world relations: In search of the essence of natural kinds. Canadian Journal of Philosophy 15.1–17.

Clark, Herbert (1973). Space, time, semantics, and the child. Cognitive development and the acquisition of language, ed. by T. Moore, 28–64. New York: Academic Press.

Clark, T. W. (1977). Introduction to Nepali. London: University of London.

Coates, Jennifer (1983). The semantics of the modal auxiliaries. London: Croom Helm.

Cole, Peter. (1982). Imbabura Quechua. Amsterdam: North-Holland.

Cole, Peter (1983). The grammatical role of the causee in universal grammar. International Journal of American Linguistics 49.115–33.

Comrie, Bernard (1976a). Linguistic politeness axes: Speaker-addressee, speaker-referent, speaker-bystander. Ms., Cambridge University (Pragmatics microfiche 1.7:A3).

Comrie, Bernard (1976b). Aspect. Cambridge: Cambridge University Press.

Comrie, Bernard (1978). Ergativity. Syntactic typology: Studies in the phenomenology of language, ed. by W. Lehmann, 329–94. Austin, TX: University of Texas Press.

Comrie, Bernard (1981). Language universals and linguistic typology. Chicago: University of Chicago Press.

Comrie, Bernard (1985). Tense. Cambridge: Cambridge University Press.

Corbett, Greville and Gerry Morgan (1988). Colour terms in Russian: Reflections of typological constraints in a single language. Journal of Linguistics 24.31–64.

Cornyn, William and D. Haigh Roop (1968). Beginning Burmese. New Haven, CT: Yale University Press.

Craig, Colette (1977). The structure of Jacaltec. Austin, TX: University of Texas Press.

Crawford, T. D. (1982). Defining basic color terms. Anthropological Linguistics 24.338–43.

Cruse, D. A. (1986). Lexical semantics. Cambridge: Cambridge University Press.

Culicover, Peter and Kenneth Wexler (1980). Formal principles of language acquisition. Cambridge, MA: MIT Press.

Culicover, Peter and Wendy Wilkins (1986). Control, PRO, and the projection principle. Language 62.120–53.

Dahl, Östen (1979). Some notes on indefinites. Language 46.33–41.

Dahl, Östen (1979). Typology of sentence negation. Linguistics 17.79–106.

Dahl, Östen (1981). On the definition of the telic-atelic (bounded-nonbounded) distinction. Tense and aspect (Syntax and semantics, 14), ed. by P. Tedeschi and A. Zaenen, 79–90. New York: Academic Press.

Dahl, Östen (1985). Tense and aspect systems. Oxford: Blackwell.

Dambriunas, Leonardas, Antanas Klimas, and William Schmalstieg (1966). An Introduction to Modern Lithuanian. Brooklyn, NY: Franciscan Fathers Press.

Davidson, Donald (1980). Essays on actions and events. Oxford: Oxford University Press.

Davies, John (1981). Kobon. London: Croom Helm.

Davison, Alice (1978). Negative scope and rules of conversation: Evidence from an OV language. Pragmatics (Syntax and semantics, 9), ed. by P. Cole, 23–45. New York: Academic Press.

de Beaugrande, Robert (1985). Text linguistics in discourse studies. Handbook of discourse analysis, ed. by T. van Dijk, 41–70. New York: Academic Press.

DeClerck, Renaat (1986). The manifold interpretations of generic sentences. Lingua 68.149–88.

DeClerck, Renaat (1988). Restrictive when-cluses. Linguistics and Philosophy 11.131–68.

DeLancey, Scott (1981). An interpretation of split ergativity and related patterns. Language 57.626–57.

DeLancey, Scott (1984). Notes on agentivity and causation. Studies in language 8.181–213.

DeLancey, Scott (1986). Toward a history of Tai classifier systems. Noun classes and categorization, ed. by C. Craig, 437–52. Amsterdam: Benjamins.

Denny, J. Peter (1976). What are noun classifiers good for? Chicago Linguistics Society 12.122–32.

Denny, J. Peter (1978). Locating the universals of space in lexical systems for spatial deixis. Chicago Linguistics Society, Papers from the parasession on the lexicon, 71–84.

Denny, J. Peter (1979). The "extendedness" variable in classifier semantics: Universal features and cultural variation. Ethnolinguistics: Boas, Sapir, and Whorf revisited, ed. by M. Mathiot, 97–119. The Hague: Mouton.

Denny, J. Peter (1986). The semantic role of noun classifiers. Noun classes and categorization, ed. by C. Craig, 297–308. Amsterdam: Benjamins.

Denny, J. Peter and Chet Creider (1986). The semantics of noun classes in Proto-Bantu. Noun classes and categorization, ed. by C. Craig, 217–39. Amsterdam: Benjamins.

Dillon, George (1977). Introduction to contemporary linguistic semantics. Englewood Cliffs, NJ: Prentice-Hall.

Dixon, R. M. W. (1979). Ergativity. Language 55.59–138.

Dixon, R. M. W. (1980). The languages of Australia. Cambridge: Cambridge University Press.

Dixon, R. M. W. (1981). Wargamay. Handbook of Australian languages, II, ed. by R. M. W. Dixon and B. Blake, 1–144. Amsterdam: Benjamins.

Dixon, R. M. W. (1982). Where have all the adjectives gone? The Hague: Mouton.

Doble, Marion (1987). A description of some features of Ekari language structure. Oceanic Linguistics 26.55–113.

Donnellan, Keith (1966). Reference and definite descriptions. Philosophical Review 75.281–304.

Donnellan, Keith (1972). Proper names and identifying descriptions. Semantics of natural language, ed. by D. Davidson and G. Harman, 356–79. Dordrecht: Reidel.

Donnellan, Keith (1978). Speaker reference, descriptions, and anaphora. Pragmatics (Syntax and semantics, 9), ed. by P. Cole, 47–68. New York: Academic Press.

Douglas, Wilfrid (1981). Watjarri. Handbook of Australian languages, II, ed. by R. M. W. Dixon and B. Blake, 197–272. Amsterdam: Benjamins.

Downing, Pamela (1984). Japanese numeral classifiers: A syntactic, semantic, and functional profile. Ph.D. dissertation, University of California, Berkeley.

Downing, Pamela (1986). The anaphoric use of classifiers in Japanese. Noun classes and categorization, ed. by C. Craig, 345–75. Amsterdam: Benjamins.

Dowty, David (1979). Word meaning and Montague grammar. Dordrecht: Reidel.

Dowty, David (1986). Thematic roles and semantics. Berkeley Linguistics Society 12.340–54.

Dowty, David (1989). On the semantic content of the notion of *thematic role*. Properties, types, and meaning, II: Semantic issues, ed. by G. Chierchia, B. Partee, and R. Turner, 69–129. Dordrecht: Reidel.

DuBois, John (1987). The discourse basis of ergativity. Language 63.805–55.

Dugarova, Galina and Natalia Jaxontova (1988). Resultative and perfect in Mongolian. Typology of resultative constructions, ed. by V. Nedjalkov, 209–220. Amsterdam: Benjamins.

Eggers, Ellen (1989). Temporal anaphora and degrees of remoteness. Paper presented at the Linguistic Society of America, Washington, DC.

Enç, Murvet (1986). Tense without scope. Indiana University Linguistics Club.

England, Nora (1983). A Grammar of Mam, a Mayan language. Austin, TX: University of Texas Press.

Ernst, Thomas (1984). Toward an integrated theory of adverb position in English. Indiana University Linguistics Club.

Evens, Martha, et al. (1980). Lexical-semantic relations. Edmonton, Alberta: Linguistic Research.

Farkas, Donka and Yuko Sugioka (1983). Restrictive *if/when* clauses. Linguistics and Philosophy 6.225–58.

Fauconnier, Gilles (1985). Mental spaces. Cambridge, MA: MIT Press.

Ferguson, Charles (1964). Diglossia. Language in culture and society, ed. by D. Hymes, 429–39. New York: Harper and Row.

Fillmore, Charles (1968). The case for case. Universals in linguistic theory, ed. by E. Bach and R. Harms, 1-88. New York: Holt, Rinehart, and Winston.

Fillmore, Charles (1975a). An alternative to checklist theories of meaning. Berkeley Linguistics Society 1.123–31.

Fillmore, Charles (1975b). Santa Cruz lectures on deixis, 1971. Indiana University Linguistics Club.

Fillmore, Charles (1977). The case for case reopened. Grammatical relations (Syntax and semantics, 8), ed. by P. Cole and J. Sadock, 59–81. New York: Academic Press.

Fitch, G. W. (1987). Naming and believing. Dordrecht: Reidel.

Fleischman, Suzanne (1982). The future in thought and language. Cambridge: Cambridge University Press.

Fleischman, Suzanne (1989). Temporal distance: A basic linguistic metaphor. Studies in Language 13.1–50.

Fodor, Janet (1970). The linguistic description of opaque contexts. Ph.D. Dissertation, MIT.

Fodor, Jerry (1970). Three reasons for not deriving *kill* from *cause to die*. Linguistic Inquiry 1.429–38.

Fodor, J., M. Garrett, E. Walker, and C. Parks (1980). Against definitions. Cognition 8.263–367.

Foley, William and Robert van Valin (1984). Functional syntax and universal grammar. Cambridge: Cambridge University Press.

Foley, William and Mike Olson (1985). Clausehood and verb serialization. Grammar inside and outside the clause, ed. by J. Nichols and A. Woodbury, 17–60. Cambridge: Cambridge University Press.

Foley, William and Robert van Valin (1985). Information packaging in the clause. Language typology and syntactic description, I: Clause structure, ed. by T. Shopen, 282–364. Cambridge: Cambridge University Press.

Follesdal, Dagfinn and Risto Hilpinen (1971). Deontic logic: An introduction. Deontic logic: Introductory and systematic readings, ed. by R. Hilpinen, 1–35. Dordrecht: Reidel.

Forrester, James (1989). Why you should: The pragmatics of deontic speech. Hanover, NH: University Press of New England.

Fortescue, Michael (1984). West Greenlandic Eskimo. London: Croom Helm.

Foster, J. F. (1979). Agents, accessories, and owners: The cultural base and the rise of ergative structures, with particular reference to Ozark English. Ergativity, ed. by F. Plank, 489–510. New York: Academic Press.

Frajzyngier, Zygmunt (1985). Truth and the indicative sentence. Studies in Language 9.243–54.

Frajzyngier, Zygmunt (1987). Truth and the compositionality principle: A reply to Palmer. Studies in Language 11.211–17.

Fraser, Bruce (1971). A note on the spray paint cases. Linguistic Inquiry 2.604–7.

Frawley, William (1987). Text and epistemology. Norwood, NJ: Ablex.

Frege, Gottlob (1952). Translations from the philosophical writings of Gottlob Frege. Oxford: Blackwell.

Friedrich, Paul (1970). Shape in grammar. Language 46.379–407.

Friedrich, Paul (1974). On aspect theory and Homeric aspect. Bloomington, IN: Indiana University Press.

Geach, Peter (1962). Reference and generality. Ithaca, NY: Cornell University Press.

Gil, David (1983). Stacked adjectives and configurationality. Linguistic Analysis 12.141–58.

Gil, David (1984). On the notion of "direct object" in patient prominent languages. Objects, ed. by F. Plank, 87–108. New York: Academic Press.

Givón, Talmy (1970). Notes on the semantic structure of English adjectives. Language 46.816–37.

Givón, Talmy (1976). Some constraints on Bantu causativization. The grammar of causative constructions (Syntax and semantics, 6) ed. by M. Shibatani, 325–51. New York: Academic Press.

Givón, Talmy (1979). On understanding grammar. New York: Academic Press.

Givón, Talmy (1982). Evidentiality and epistemic space. Studies in Language 6.23–49.

Givón, Talmy (1984). Syntax: A functional-typological introduction, I. Amsterdam: Benjamins.

Goldsmith, John (1976). Autosegmental phonology. Ph.D. Dissertation, MIT.

Golinkoff, Roberta, et al. (1990). Early object labels: The case for lexical principles. Ms. University of Delaware.

Golovko, Jevgenij (1988). Resultative and passive in Aleut. Typology of resultative constructions, ed. by V. Nedjalkov, 185–98. Amsterdam: Benjamins.

Goodenough, Ward (1956). Componential analysis and the study of meaning. Language 32.195–216.

Greenberg, Joseph (1966). Language universals. The Hague: Mouton.

Greenberg, Joseph (1978a). How do languages acquire gender markers? Universals of human language, 3: Word structure, ed. by J. Greenberg, 48–82. Stanford, CA: Stanford University Press.

Greenberg, Joseph (1978b). Generalizations about numeral systems. Universals of human language, 3: Word structure, ed. by J. Greenberg, 249–95. Stanford, CA: Stanford University Press.

Greenberg, Joseph (1980). Universals of kinship terminology: Their names and the problem of their explanation. On linguistic anthropology: Essays in honor of Harry Hoijer, ed. by J. Maquet, 9–32. Malibu, CA: Undena Publications.

Greenberg, Joseph (1987). The present status of markedness theory: A reply to Scheffler. Journal of Anthropological Research 43.367–74.

Grice, H. Paul (1975). Logic and conversation. Speech acts (Syntax and semantics, 3), ed. by P. Cole and J. Morgan, 41–58. New York: Academic Press.

Grice, H. Paul (1978). Further notes on logic and conversation. Pragmatics (Syntax and semantics, 9), ed. by P. Cole, 113–27. New York: Academic Press.

Gruber, Jeffrey (1967). Look and see. Language 43.937–47.

Gruber, Jeffrey (1976). Lexical structures in syntax and semantics. Amsterdam: North-Holland.

Haiman, John (1980). The iconicity of grammar. Language 56.515–40.

Haiman, John (1983). Iconic and economic motivation. Language 59.781–819.

Haiman, John (ed.) (1985a). Iconicity in syntax. Amsterdam: Benjamins.

Haiman, John (1985b). Natural syntax. Cambridge: Cambridge University Press.

Hale, Kenneth (1973). A note on subject-object inversion in Navajo. Issues in linguistics: Papers in honor of Henry and Renee Kahane, ed. by B. Kachru et al., 300–9. Urbana, IL: University of Illinois Press.

Hall, Barbara (1965). Subject and object in Modern English. Ph.D. dissertation, MIT.

Halliday, M. A. K. (1970). Language structure and language function. New horizons in linguistics, ed. by J. Lyons, 140–65. Harmondsworth: Penguin.

Hand, Michael. (1985). Negation in English: An essay in game-theoretical semantics. Ph.D. Dissertation, Florida State University.

Harada, S. I. (1976). Honorifics. Japanese generative grammar (Syntax and semantics, 5), ed. by M. Shibatani, 499–561. New York: Academic Press.

Heath, Jeffrey (1981). Aspectual "skewing" in two Australian languages: Mara, Nunggubuyu. Tense and aspect (Syntax and semantics, 14), ed. by P. Tedeschi and A. Zaenen, 91–102. New York: Academic Press.

Heeschen, Volker (1982). Some systems of spatial deixis in Papuan languages. Here and there, ed. by J. Weissenborn and W. Klein, 81–109. Amsterdam: Benjamins.

Heim, Irene (1982). The semantics of definite and indefinite noun phrases. Ph.D. dissertation, University of Massachusetts.

Heim, Irene (1987). Where does the definiteness restriction apply? Evidence from the definiteness of variables. The representation of (in)definiteness, ed. by E. Reuland and A. ter Meulen, 21–42. Cambridge, MA: MIT Press.

Hermon, Gabriella (1984). Syntactic modularity. Dordrecht: Foris.

Herskovits, Annette (1986). Language and spatial cognition. Cambridge: Cambridge University Press.

Hetzron, Robert (1976). On the Hungarian causative verb and its syntax. The grammar of causative constructions (Syntax and semantics, 6), ed. by M. Shibatani, 371–98. New York: Academic Press.

Hetzron, Robert (1978). On the relative order of adjectives. Language universals, ed. by H. Seiler, 165–84. Tubingen: Gunter Narr.

Higginbotham, James (1986). On semantics. New directions in semantics, ed. by J. LePore, 1–54. New York: Academic Press.

Higginbotham, James (1988). Contexts, models, and meanings: A note on the data of semantics. Mental representation, ed. by R. Kempson, 29–48. Cambridge: Cambridge University Press.

Hill, Clifford (1974). Spatial perception and linguistic encoding: A case study in Hausa and English. Studies in African Linguistics (Supplement) 5.135–48.

Hill, Clifford (1982). Up/down, front/back, left/right. A contrastive study of Hausa and English. Here and there, ed. by J. Weissenborn and W. Klein, 13–42. Amsterdam: Benjamins.

Hilpinen, Risto, ed. (1981). New studies in deontic logic. Dordrecht: Reidel.

Hintikka, Jaako (1986). The semantics of *a certain*. Linguistic Inquiry 17.331–6.

Hirschfeld, Lawrence (1986). Kinship and cognition: Genealogy and meaning of kinship terms. Current Anthropology 27.217–42.

Hoffman, Carl (1963). A grammar of the Margi language. Oxford: Oxford University Press.

Hopper, Paul (1979). Aspect and foregrounding in discourse. Discourse and syntax (Syntax and semantics, 12), ed. by T. Givón, 213–41. New York: Academic Press.

Hopper, Paul (1982). Aspect between discourse and grammar: An introductory essay for the volume. Tense-aspect: Between semantics and pragmatics, ed. by P. Hopper, 3–18. Amsterdam: Benjamins.

Hopper, Paul (1986). Some discourse functions of classifiers in Malay. Noun classes and categorization, ed. by C. Craig, 309–25. Amsterdam: Benjamins.

Hopper, Paul and Sandra Thompson (1980). Transitivity in grammar and discourse. Language 56.251–99.

Hopper, Paul and Sandra Thompson (1984). The discourse basis for lexical categories in universal grammar. Language 60.703–52.

Hopper, Paul and Sandra Thompson (1985). The iconicity of the universal categories "noun" and "verb." Iconicity in syntax, ed. by J. Haiman, 151–83. Amsterdam: Benjamins.

Horn, Laurence (1989). A natural history of negation. Chicago: University of Chicago Press.

Hornstein, Norbert (1984). Logic as grammar. Cambridge, MA: MIT Press.

Horton, A. E. (1949). A grammar of Luvale. Johannesburg: Witwatersrand University Press.

Huang, C.-T. James (1987). Existential sentences in Chinese and (in)definiteness. The representation of (in)definiteness, ed. by E. Reuland and A. ter Meulen, 226–53. Cambridge, MA: MIT Press.

Hurford, James (1975). The linguistic theory of numerals. Cambridge: Cambridge University Press.

Hurford, James (1987). Language and number: The emergence of a cognitive system. Oxford: Blackwell.

Hyman, Larry (1979). Aghem grammatical structure (Southern California occasional papers in linguistics, 7). Los Angeles: University of Southern California.

Innes, Gordon (1966). An introduction to Grebo. London: University of London.

Ioup, Georgette (1975). Some universals of quantifier scope. Syntax and semantics, 4. ed. by J. Kimball, 37–58. New York: Academic Press.

Ioup, Georgette (1977). Specificity and the interpretation of quantifiers. Linguistics and Philosophy 1.233–45.

Jackendoff, Ray (1971). On some questionable arguments about quantifiers and negation. Language 47.282–97.

Jackendoff, Ray (1972). Semantic interpretation in generative grammar. Cambridge, MA: MIT Press.

Jackendoff, Ray (1983). Semantics and cognition. Cambridge, MA: MIT Press.

Jackendoff, Ray (1985). Multiple subcategorization and the θ criterion: The case of *climb*. Natural Language and Linguistic Theory 3.271–95.

Jackendoff, Ray (1987). The status of thematic relations in linguistic theory. Linguistic Inquiry 18.369–411.

Jackendoff, Ray (1988). Conceptual semantics. Meaning and mental representation, ed. by U. Eco et al., 81–97. Bloomington, IN: Indiana University Press.

Jackendoff, Ray (1990). Semantic structures. Cambridge, MA: MIT Press.

Jacobsen, William (1986). The heterogeneity of evidentials in Makah. Evidentiality: The linguistic coding of epistemology, ed. by W. Chafe and J. Nichols, 3–28. Norwood, NJ: Ablex.

James, Deborah (1982). Past tense and the hypothetical: A cross-linguistic study. Studies in Language 6.375–403.

Jeffries, L. and P. Willis (1984). A return to the spray paint issue. Journal of Pragmatics 8.715–29.

Jensen, John (1977). Yapese reference grammar. Honolulu: University of Hawaii Press.

Johnson-Laird, Philip (1983). Mental models. Cambridge, MA: Harvard University Press.

Kamp, Hans (1981). A theory of truth and semantic representation. Formal methods in the study of language, I, ed. by J. Groenendijk, T. Janssen, and M. Stokhoff, 277–322. Amsterdam: Mathematics Center.

Kamp, J. A. W. (1975). Two theories about adjectives. Formal semantics of natural language, ed. by E. Keenan, 123–55. Cambridge: Cambridge University Press.

Kaplan, David (1978). Dthat. Pragmatics (Syntax and semantics, 9), ed. by P. Cole, 221–43. New York: Academic Press.

Karttunen, Lauri (1968). What do referential indices refer to? Indiana University Linguistics Club.

Katz, Jerrold (1981). Language and other abstract objects. Totowa, NJ: Rowman and Littlefield.

Katz, Jerrold (1986). Common sense in semantics. New directions in semantics, ed. by E. LePore, 159–235. New York: Academic Press.

Kay, Paul (1975). The generative analysis of kinship semantics: A reanalysis of the Seneca data. Foundations of Language 13.201–14.

Kay, Paul and Chad McDaniel (1978). The linguistic significance of the meanings of basic color terms. Language 54.610–46.

Kaye, Alan (1972). Remarks on diglossia in Arabic: Well-defined vs. ill-defined. Linguistics 81.32–48.

Keenan, Edward (1984). Semantic correlates of the ergative/absolutive distinction. Linguistics 22.197–223.

Keenan, Edward and Jonathan Stavi (1986). A semantic characterization of natural language determiners. Linguistics and Philosophy 9.253–326.

Keesing, Roger (1975). Kin groups and social structure. New York: Holt, Rinehart and Winston.

Keil, Frank (1979). Semantic and conceptual development. Cambridge, MA: Harvard University Press.

Keil, Frank (1986). The acquisition of natural kind and artifact terms. Language learning and concept acquisition, ed. by W. Demopoulos and A. Marras, 133–53. Norwood, NJ: Ablex.

Keil, Frank (1988). Commentary: Conceptual heterogeneity vs. developmental homogeneity (on chairs, bears, and other such pairs). Human Development 31.35–43.

Kempson, Ruth (1975). Presupposition and the delimitation of semantics. Cambridge: Cambridge University Press.

Kenney, Anthony (1963). Action, emotion, and will. London: Routledge.

Keyser, S. J. and Thomas Roeper (1984). On the middle and ergative constructions in English. Linguistic Inquiry 15.381–416.

Kiefer, Ferenc (1987). On defining modality. Folia Linguistica 21.67–94.

Kiparsky, Paul and Carol Kiparsky (1970). Fact. Progress in linguistics, ed. by M. Bierwisch and K. Heidolph, 143–73. The Hague: Mouton.

Klein, Harriet (1979). Noun classifiers in Toba. Ethnolinguistics: Boas, Sapir, and Whorf revisited, ed. by M. Mathiot, 85–95. The Hague: Mouton.

Klein, Wolfgang (1980). Deixis and spatial orientation in route directions. Spatial orientation, ed. by H. Pick and L. Acredolo, 283–311. New York: Plenum.

Klein-Andreu, Flora (1983). Grammar in style: Spanish adjective placement. Discourse perspectives on syntax, ed. by F. Klein-Andreu, 143–79. New York: Academic Press.

Klima, Edward (1964). Negation in English. The structure of language, ed. by J. Fodor and J. Katz, 246–323. Englewood Cliffs, NJ: Prentice-Hall.

Koktova, Eva (1986). Sentence adverbials in a functional description. Amsterdam: Benjamins.

Koshal, Sanyukta (1987). Honorific systems of the Ladakhi language. Multilingua 6.149–68.

Kripke, Saul (1972). Naming and necessity. Semantics of natural language, ed. by D. Davidson and G. Harman, 253–355. Dordrecht: Reidel.

Kripke, Saul (1979). Speaker's reference and semantic reference. Contemporary perspectives in the philosophy of language, ed. by P. French, T. Uehling, and H. Wettstein, 6–27. Minneapolis, MN: University of Minnesota Press.

Kronenfeld, David (1974). Sibling typology: Beyond Nerlove and Romney. American Ethnologist 1.489–506.

Kuno, Susumo (1987a). Honorific marking in Japanese and the word formation hypothesis of causatives and passives. Studies in Language 11.99–128.

Kuno, Susumo (1987b). Functional syntax: Anaphora, discourse, and empathy. Chicago: University of Chicago Press.

Ladusaw, William (1979). Polarity sensitivity and inherent scope relations. Ph.D. dissertation, University of Texas.

Ladusaw, William (1988). Semantic theory. Linguistics: The Cambridge survey, I: Linguistic theory: Foundations, ed. by F. Newmeyer, 89–112. Cambridge: Cambridge University Press.

Lakoff, George (1965). On the nature of syntactic irregularity. Ph.D. dissertation, Indiana University.

Lakoff, George (1972). Hedges: A study in meaning criteria and the logic of fuzzy concepts. Chicago Linguistics Society 8.183–228.

Lakoff, George (1987). Women, fire, and dangerous things. Chicago: University of Chicago Press.

Lakoff, George (1988). Cognitive semantics. Meaning and mental representation, ed. by U. Eco et al., 119–54. Bloomington, IN: Indiana University Press.

Lakoff, Robin (1970). Some reasons why there can't be any *some-any* rule. Language 45.608–15.

Landau, Sidney (1984). Dictionaries. New York: Scribners.

Langacker, Ronald (1982). Remarks on English aspect. Tense-aspect: Between semantics and pragmatics, ed. by P. Hopper, 265–304. Amsterdam: Benjamins.

Langacker, Ronald (1987a). Nouns and verbs. Language 63.53–94.

Langacker, Ronald (1987b). Foundations of cognitive grammar, I: Theoretical prerequisites. Stanford, CA: Stanford University Press.

Langendoen, D. Terrence and Thomas Bever (1973). Can a not unhappy person be called a not sad one? Festschrift for Morris Halle, ed. by S. Anderson and P. Kiparsky, 392–409. New York: Holt, Rinehart and Winston.

Lappin, Shalom (1988). The semantics of *many* as a weak determiner. Linguistics 26.977–98.

Lasnik, Howard (1975). On the semantics of negation. Contemporary research in philosophical logic and linguistic semantics, ed. by D. Hockney et al., 279–311. Dordrecht: Reidel.

Lawal, Nike (1986). Some Yoruba quantifier words and semantic interpretation. Studies in African Linguistics 17.95–105.

Lebeaux, David (1988). The feature +affected and the formation of the passive. Thematic relations (Syntax and semantics, 21), ed. by W. Wilkins, 243–61. New York: Academic Press.

Lee, Kee-dong (1975). Kusaiean reference grammar. Honolulu: University of Hawaii Press.

Lehman, F. K. (1979). Aspects of a formal theory of noun classifiers. Studies in Language 3.153–80.

Lehmann, Winfred (1974). Proto-Indo-European syntax. Austin, TX: University of Texas Press.

Lerdahl, Fred and Ray Jackendoff (1983). A generative theory of tonal music. Cambridge, MA: MIT Press.

Levinson, Stephen (1983). Pragmatics. Cambridge: Cambridge University Press.

Lewis, David (1973). Causation. Journal of Philosophy 70.556–67.

Li, Charles and Sandra Thompson (1976). Subject and topic: A new typology of language. Subject and topic, ed. by C. Li, 457–89. New York: Academic Press.

Li, Charles and Sandra Thompson (1981). Mandarin Chinese: A functional reference grammar. Berkeley: University of California Press.

Li, Charles, Sandra Thompson and R. McMillan Thompson (1982). The discourse motivation for the perfect aspect: The Mandarin particle *le*. Tense-aspect: Between semantics and pragmatics, ed. by P. Hopper, 19–44. Amsterdam: Benjamins.

Lichtenberk, Frantisek (1983). A grammar of Manam. Honolulu: University of Hawaii Press.

Lindsey, Geoffrey and Janine Scancarelli (1985). Where have all the adjectives come from? Berkeley Linguistics Society 11.207–15.

Linebarger, Marcia (1981). The grammar of negative polarity. Ph.D. dissertation, MIT.

Lounsbury, Floyd (1956). A semantic analysis of the Pawnee kinship usage. Language 32.158–94.

Lounsbury, Floyd (1964). The structural analysis of kinship semantics. Proceedings of the Ninth International Congress of Linguists, ed. by H. Lunt, 1073–93. The Hague: Mouton.

Lynch, John (1982). Southwest Tanna grammar and vocabulary. Papers in linguistics of Melanesia, 4, ed. by J. Lynch, 1–91. Canberra: Australian National University Press.

Lyons, John (1966). Towards a "notional" theory of the "parts of speech." Journal of Linguistics 2.209–36.

Lyons, John (1968). Introduction to theoretical linguistics. Cambridge: Cambridge University Press.

Lyons, John (1977). Semantics (2 vols.). Cambridge: Cambridge University Press.

Lyons, John (1979). Knowledge and truth: A localistic approach. Function and context in linguistic analysis, ed. by D. Allerton et al., 111–41. Cambridge: Cambridge University Press.

MacDonald, R. Ross (1976). Indonesian reference grammar. Washington, DC: Georgetown University Press.

Machobane, Malillo (1985). Tense and aspect in Sesotho. Indiana University Linguistics Club.

Malone, Terrell (1988). The origin and development of Tuyuca evidentials. International Journal of American Linguistics 54.119–40.

Malotki, Ekkehart (1983). Hopi time. Berlin: Mouton.

Marantz, Alec (1984). On the nature of grammatical relations. Cambridge, MA: MIT Press.

Marchese, Lynell (1986). Tense/aspect and the development of auxiliaries in Kru languages. Dallas, TX: Summer Institute of Linguistics.

Marr, David (1982). Vision. San Francisco: Freeman.

Martin, Robert (1986). Le vague et la sémantique de l'adjectif. Réflexion sur l'adjectif antéposé en français. Quaderni di Semantica 8.246–63.

Maslov, Jurij (1988). Resultative, perfect, and aspect. Typology of resultative constructions, ed. by V. Nedjalkov, 63–85. Amsterdam: Benjamins.

Mathiot, Madeleine (1979). Sex roles as revealed through referential gender in American English. Ethnolinguistics: Boas, Sapir, and Whorf revisited, ed. by M. Mathiot, 1–47. The Hague: Mouton.

McCawley, James (1971). Tense and time reference in English. Studies in linguistic semantics, ed. by C. Fillmore and D. T. Langendoen, 97–114. New York: Holt, Rinehart and Winston.

McCawley, James (1976). Remarks on what can cause what. The grammar of causative constructions (Syntax and semantics, 6), ed. by M. Shibatani, 117–30. New York: Academic Press.

McCawley, James (1977). Lexicographic notes on English quantifiers. Chicago Linguistics Society 13.372–83.

McCawley, James (1978). World-creating predicates. Versus 19/20. 79–93.

McCawley, James (1981). Everything that linguists have always wanted to know about logic. Chicago: University of Chicago Press.

McCawley, James (1988). The syntactic phenomena of English, II. Chicago: University of Chicago Press.

McCloskey, Michael (1983). Naive theories of motion. Mental models, ed. by D. Gentner and A. Stevens, 299–324. Hillsdale, NJ: Lawrence Erlbaum Associates.

McConnell-Ginet, Sally (1979). Prototypes, pronouns, and persons. Ethnolinguistics: Boas, Sapir, and Whorf revisited, ed. by M. Mathiot, 63–83. The Hague: Mouton.

McConnell-Ginet, Sally (1982). Adverbs and logical form: A linguistically realistic theory. Language 58.144–84.

Milsark, Gary (1974). Existential sentences in English. Ph.D. dissertation, MIT.

Miller, George and Philip Johnson-Laird (1976). Language and perception. Cambridge, MA: Harvard University Press.

Mithun, Marianne (1984). The evolution of noun incorporation. Language 60.847–93.

Montague, Richard (1974). Formal philosophy. New Haven, CT: Yale University Press.

Moss, A. E. (1989). Does Russian have a basic term for purple? Linguistics 27.145–55.

Mourelatos, Alexander (1981). Events, processes, and states. Tense and aspect (Syntax and semantics, 14), ed. by P. Tedeschi and A. Zaenen, 191–212. New York: Academic Press.

Mufwene, Salikoko (1980). Number, countability, and markedness in Lingala LI/MA- noun classes. Linguistics 18.1019–52.

Mufwene, Salikoko (1984). Stativity and the progressive. Indiana University Linguistics Club.

Murdock, G. P. (1970). Kin term patterns and their distribution. Ethnology 9.165–207.

Munro, Pamela and Lynn Gordon (1982). Syntactic relations in Western Muskogean: A typological perspective. Language 58.81–115.

Nedjalkov, Vladimir, ed. (1988). Typology of resultative constructions. Amsterdam: Benjamins.

Nedjalkov, Vladimir and Galina Otaina (1988). Resultative and continuative in Nivkh. Typology of resultative constructions, ed. by V. Nedjalkov, 135–51. Amsterdam: Benjamins.

Nedjalkov, Vladimir and Sergeij Jaxontov (1988). The typology of resultative constructions. Typology of resultative constructions, ed. by V. Nedjalkov, 3–62. Amsterdam: Benjamins.

Nerlove, S. and A. K. Romney (1967). Sibling terminology and cross-sex behavior. American Anthropologist 69.179–87.

Newmark, Leonard, Philip Hubbard, and Peter Prifti (1982). Standard Albanian: A reference grammar for students. Stanford, CA: Stanford University Press.

Ney, James (1983). Optionality and choice in the selection of order of adjectives in English. General Linguistics 23.94–128.

Nichols, Johanna (1986). The bottom line: Chinese pidgin Russian. Evidentiality: The linguistic coding of epistemology, ed. by W. Chafe and J. Nichols, 239–57. Norwood, NJ: Ablex.

Nichols, Johanna (1988). On alienable and inalienable possession. In honor of Mary Haas, ed. by W. Shipley, 557–610. Berlin: de Gruyter.

Ogden, C. K. and I. A. Richards (1923). The meaning of meaning. New York: Harcourt, Brace, and Co.

Oh, C. and D. Dinneen (eds.) (1979). Presupposition (Syntax and semantics, 12). New York: Academic Press.

Palmer, F. R. (1976). Semantics: A new outline. Cambridge: Cambridge University Press.

Palmer, F. R. (1986). Mood and modality. Cambridge: Cambridge University Press.

Palmer, F. R. (1987). Truth indicative? Studies in Language 11.206–17.

Parks, Douglas (1976). A grammar of Pawnee. New York: Garland.

Parsons, Terence (1980). Modifiers and quantifiers in natural language. Canadian Journal of Philosophy (supplementary volume) 6.29–60.

Parsons, Terence (1989). The progressive in English: Events, states, and processes. Linguistics and Philosophy 12.213–41.

Partee, Barbara (1973). Some structural analogies between tenses and pronouns in English. Journal of Philosophy 70.601–9.

Partee, Barbara H. (1979). Semantics—mathematics or psychology? Semantics from different points of view, ed. by R. Bauerle, U. Egli, and A. von Stechow, 1–14. Berlin: Springer.

Partee, Barbara (1984). Nominal and temporal anaphora. Linguistics and Philosophy 7.243–86.

Pawley, Andrew (1987). Encoding events in Kalam and English: Different logics for reporting experience. Coherence and grounding in discourse, ed. by R. Tomlin, 329–60. Amsterdam: Benjamins.

Payne, Doris (1986). Noun classification in Yagua. Noun classes and categorization, ed. by C. Craig, 113–31. Amsterdam: Benjamins.

Payne, John (1985) Negation. Language typology and syntactic description, I, ed. by T. Shopen, 197–242. Cambridge: Cambridge University Press.

Pe, Hla (1965). A re-examination of Burmese "classifiers." Lingua 15.163–85.

Pea, Roy (1980). The development of negation in early child language. The social foundations of language and thought, ed. by D. Olson, 156–86. New York: Norton.

Pelletier, Francis, ed. (1979). Mass terms: Some philosophical problems. Dordrecht: Reidel.

Piaget, Jean (1970). The child's construction of time. New York: Basic Books.

Prior, A. N. (1967). Past, present, and future. Oxford: Oxford University Press.

Putnam, Hilary (1975). The meaning of *meaning*. Language, mind, and knowledge, ed. by K. Gunderson, 131–93. Minneapolis, MN: University of Minnesota Press.

Quirk, Randolph and Sidney Greenbaum (1973). A university grammar of English. London: Longman.

Read, Dwight (1984). An algebraic account of the American kinship terminology. Current Anthropology 25.417–49.

Redden, James (1980). A descriptive grammar of Ewondo (Occasional papers in linguistics, 4). Carbondale, IL: Southern Illinois University Dept. of Linguistics.

Reddy, Michael (1973). Formal referential models of poetic structure. Chicago Linguistics Society 9.493–518.

Reddy, Michael (1979). The conduit metaphor: A case of frame conflict in our language about language. Metaphor and thought, ed. by A. Ortony, 284–324. Cambridge: Cambridge University Press.

Reichenbach, Hans (1947). Elements of symbolic logic. Berkeley, CA: University of California Press.

Rescher, Nicholas and Alasdair Urquhart (1971). Temporal logic. New York: Springer.

Reuland, Eric and Alice ter Meulen, eds. (1987). The representation of (in)definiteness. Cambridge, MA: MIT Press.

Rivero, María-Luisa (1975). Referential properties of Spanish noun phrases. Language 51.32–48.

Rivero, María-Luisa (1977). Specificity and existence: A reply. Language 53.70–85.

Rojas, Nelson (1977). Referentiality in Spanish noun phrases. Language 53.61–69.

Rosch, Eleanor (1973). Natural categories. Cognitive Psychology 4.328–50.

Rosch, Eleanor (1975). Cognitive reference points. Cognitive Psychology 7.532–47.

Rosch, Eleanor and Carolyn Mervis (1975). Family resemblances: Studies in the internal structure of categories. Cognitive Psychology 7.573–605.

Rosen, Carol (1984). The interface between semantic roles and initial grammatical relations. Studies in relational grammar, 2, ed. by D. Perlmutter and C. Rosen, 38–77. Chicago: University of Chicago Press.

Ross, John R. (1972). Act. Semantics of natural language, ed. by D. Davidson and G. Harman, 70–126. Dordrecht: Reidel.

Rusiecki, Jan (1985). Adjectives and comparison in English. London: Longman.

Russell, Bertrand (1905). On denoting. Mind 14.479–93.

Russell, Bertrand (1957). Mr. Strawson on referring. Mind 66.385–89.

Ryle, Gilbert (1949). The concept of mind. London: Barnes and Noble.

Sadock, Jerrold (1986). Some notes on noun incorporation. Language 62.19–31.

Safir, Kenneth (1985). Syntactic chains. Cambridge: Cambridge University Press.

Saksena, Anuradha (1982). Contact in causation. Language 58.820–31.

Salkoff, Morris (1983). Bees are swarming in the garden. Language 59.288–346.

Salmon, Wesley (1980). Space, time, and motion. Minneapolis, MN: University of Minnesota Press.

Sapir, Edward (1921). Language. New York: Harcourt.

Sapir, Edward (1944). Grading: A study in semantics. Philosophy of Science 2.93–116.

Sapir, J. David (1965). A grammar of Diola Fogny. Cambridge: Cambridge University Press.

Saul, Janice (1980). Nung grammar. Dallas, TX: Summer Institute of Linguistics.

Saussure, Ferdinand de. (1959). Course in General Linguistics. New York: Philosophical Library.

Schachter, Paul (1976). The subject in Philippine languages: Topic, actor, actor-topic, or none of the above. Subject and topic, ed. by C. Li, 491–518. New York: Academic Press.

Schachter, Paul (1977). Reference-related and role-related properties of subjects. Grammatical relations (Syntax and semantics, 8), ed. by P. Cole and J. Sadock, 279–306. New York: Academic Press.

Schachter, Paul (1985). Parts-of-speech systems. Language typology and syntactic description, I: Clause structure, ed. by T. Shopen, 3–61. Cambridge: Cambridge University Press.

Schaefer, Ronald (1986). Observations on reference object geometry in Emai path expressions. Berkeley Linguistics Society 12.485–96.

Schaefer, Ronald (1989). Property concepts and adjectives in Emai. Paper presented at the Linguistic Society of America, Washington, DC.

Scheffler, Harold (1978). Australian kin classification. Cambridge: Cambridge University Press.

Scheffler, Harold (1984). Kin classification as social structure: The Ambrym case. American Ethnologist 11.791–806.

Scheffler, Harold (1987). Markedness in systems of kin classification. Journal of Anthropological Research 43.203–21.

Schlichter, Alice (1986). The origins and deictic nature of Wintu Evidentials. Evidentiality: The linguistic coding of epistemology, ed. by W. Chafe and J. Nichols, 46–59. Norwood, NJ: Ablex.

Schubert, Lenhart and Francis Pelletier (1986). Problems in the representation of the logical form of generics, plurals, and mass nouns. New directions in semantics, ed. by E. LePore, 387–453. New York: Academic Press.

Schutz, Alfred (1969). Nguna grammar. Honolulu: University of Hawaii Press.

Schwartz, Linda (1988). Thematic relations and case linking in Russian. Thematic relations (Syntax and semantics, 21), ed. by W. Wilkins, 167–89. New York: Academic Press.

Schwartz, Stephen (1979). Natural kind terms. Cognition 7.301–15.

Schwartz, Stephen (1980). Natural kinds and nominal kinds. Mind 89.182–95.

Schwarz, David (1979). Naming and referring. Berlin: de Gruyter.

Searle, John (1969). Speech acts. Cambridge: Cambridge University Press.

Seiler, Hansjakob (1978). Determination: A functional dimension for interlanguage comparison. Language universals, ed. by H. Seiler, 301–28. Tubingen: Gunter Narr.

Seiter, William (1979). Studies in Niuean syntax. Ph.D. dissertation, University of California at San Diego.

Seuren, Pieter (1985). Discourse semantics. Oxford: Blackwell.

Shibatani, Masayoshi (1976). The grammar of causative constructions: A conspectus. The grammar of causative constructions (Syntax and semantics, 6), ed. by M. Shibatani, 1–40. New York: Academic Press.

Shibatani, Masayoshi (1985). Passives and related constructions. Language 61.821–48.

Sichelschmidt, Lorenz (1986). Optionality and choice in the analysis of adjective order: Comments on Ney. Studia Linguistica 40.135–48.

Siegel, Muffy (1980). Capturing the adjective. New York: Garland.

Silverstein, Michael (1976). Hierarchy of features and ergativity. Grammatical categories in Australian languages, ed. by R. Dixon, 112–71. New York: Humanities Press.

Smith, Carlota (1983). A theory of aspectual choice. Language 59.479–501.

Snapp, Allen and John and Joy (sic) Anderson (1982). Northern Paiute. Studies in Uto-Aztecan grammar, 3: Uto-Aztecan grammatical sketches, ed. by R. Langacker, 1–92. Dallas, TX: Summer Institute of Linguistics.

Soga, Matsuo (1983). Tense and aspect in modern colloquial Japanese. Vancouver: University of British Columbia Press.

Sperber, Dan and Deirdre Wilson (1986). Relevance. Oxford: Blackwell.

Stalnaker, Robert (1968). A theory of conditionals. Studies in logical theory, ed. by N. Rescher, 98–112. Oxford: Oxford University Press.

Stampe, David (1976). Cardinal number systems. Chicago Linguistics Society 12.594–609.

Starosta, Stanley (1988). The case for lexicase. Honolulu: University of Hawaii Press.

Strawson, P. F. (1950). On referring. Mind 59.320–44.

Sullivan, Thelma (1988). Compendium of Nahuatl grammar. Salt Lake City, UT: University of Utah Press.

Suppalla, Ted (1986). The classifier system in American Sign Language. Noun classes and categorization, ed. by C. Craig, 181–214. Amsterdam: Benjamins.

Sweetser, Eve (1982). Root and epistemic modals: Causality in two worlds. Berkeley Linguistics Society 8.484–507.

Talmy, Leonard (1975). Semantics and syntax of motion. Syntax and semantics, 4, ed. J. P. Kimball, 181–238. New York: Academic Press.

Talmy, Leonard (1976). Semantic causative types. The grammar of causative constructions (Syntax and semantics, 6), ed. by M. Shibatani, 43–116. New York: Academic Press.

Talmy, Leonard (1983). How language structures space. Spatial orientation, ed. by H. Pick and L. Acredolo, 225–82. New York: Plenum.

Talmy, Leonard (1985). Lexicalization patterns: Semantic structure in lexical forms. Language typology and syntactic description, III, ed. by T. Shopen, 57–149. Cambridge: Cambridge University Press.

Taylor, Barry (1977). Tense and continuity. Linguistics and Philosophy 1.199–220.

Taylor, Charles (1985). Nkore Kiga. London: Croom Helm.

Thomason, Richmond (1972). A semantic theory of sortal incorrectness. Journal of Philosophical Logic 1.209–58.

Thompson, Laurence (1965). A Vietnamese grammar. Seattle, WA: University of Washington Press.

Thompson, Sandra (1988). A discourse approach to the cross-linguistic category "adjective." Explaining language universals, ed. by J. Hawkins, 167–85. Oxford: Blackwell.

Timberlake, Alan (1982). Invariance and the syntax of Russian aspect. Tense-aspect: Between semantics and pragmatics, ed. by P. Hopper, 305–31. Amsterdam: Benjamins.

Topping, Donald (1973). Chamorro reference grammar. Honolulu: University of Hawaii Press.

Trask, R. L. (1979). On the origins of ergativity. Ergativity, ed. by F. Plank, 385–404. New York: Academic Press.

Traugott, Elizabeth (1978). On the expression of spatio-temporal relations in language. Universals of human language, 3: Word structure ed. by J. Greenberg, 369–400. Stanford, CA: Stanford University Press.

Traugott, Elizabeth (1982). From propositional to textual and expressive meanings: Some semantic-pragmatic aspects of grammaticalization. Perspectives on historical linguistics, ed. by W. Lehmann and Y. Malkiel, 245–71. Amsterdam: Benjamins.

Traugott, Elizabeth (1989). On the rise of epistemic meanings in English: An example of subjectification in semantic change. Language 65.31–55.

Ultan, Russell (1978a). The nature of future tenses. Universals of human language, 3: Word structure, ed. by J. Greenberg, 83–123. Stanford, CA: Stanford University Press.

Ultan, Russell (1978b). Toward a typology of substantival possession. Universals of human language, 4: Syntax, ed. by J. Greenberg, 51–84. Stanford, CA: Stanford University Press.

van Bentham, Johan (1986). Essays in logical semantics. Dordrecht: Reidel.

van Riemsdijk, Henk and Edwin Williams (1986). Introduction to the theory of grammar. Cambridge, MA: MIT Press.

van Voorst, Jan (1988). Thematic roles are not semantic roles. Revue québecoise de linguistique 17.245–60.

Vendler, Zeno (1967). Linguistics in philosophy. Ithaca, NY: Cornell University Press.

Verkuyl, H. (1972). On the compositional nature of the aspects. Dordrecht: Reidel.

Verkuyl, H. (1989). Aspectual classes and aspectual composition. Linguistics and Philosophy 12.39–94.

Vet, Co (1983). From tense to modality. Studies in modeltheoretic semantics, ed. by A. ter Meulen, 193–206. Dordrecht: Reidel.

Vlach, Frank (1981). The semantics of the progressive. Tense and aspect (Syntax and semantics, 14), ed. by P. Tedeschi and A. Zaenen, 271–92. New York: Academic Press.

von Wright, Georg (1951). Deontic logic. Mind 60.1–15.

von Wright, Georg (1981). On the logic of norms and actions. New studies in deontic logic, ed. by R. Hilpinen, 3–35. Dordrecht: Reidel.

Weissenborn, Jurgen and Wolfgang Klein (eds.) (1982). Here and there. Amsterdam: Benjamins.

Welsh, Cynthia (1988a). Natural kind terms, lexical semantic competence, and compositionality. Ph.D. Dissertation, University of Chicago.

Welsh, Cynthia (1988b). On the non-existence of natural kind terms as a linguistically relevant category. Paper presented at the Linguistic Society of America, New Orleans, LA.

Whistler, Kenneth (1986). Evidentials in Patwin. Evidentiality: The linguistic coding of epistemology, ed. by W. Chafe and J. Nichols, 60–74. Norwood, NJ: Ablex.

Whorf, Benjamin Lee (1956). Language, thought, and reality. Cambridge, MA: MIT Press.

Wierzbicka, Anna (1980). Lingua mentalis. New York: Academic Press.

Wierzbicka, Anna (1985). Oats and wheat: The fallacy of arbitrariness. Iconicity in syntax, ed. by J. Haiman, 311–42. Amsterdam: Benjamins.

Wierzbicka, Anna (1986). What's in a noun (or: how do nouns differ in meaning from adjectives)? Studies in Language 10.353–89.

Wilkins, David (1988). The semantics and pragmatics of "associated motion" in Mparntwe Arrernte. Paper presented at the Linguistic Society of America, New Orleans, LA.

Wilkins, Wendy (1987). On the linguistic function of event roles. Berkeley Linguistics Society 13.460–72.

Wilkins, Wendy (1988). Thematic structure and reflexivization. Thematic relations (Syntax and semantics, 21), ed. by W. Wilkins, 191–213. New York: Academic Press.

Williams, Edwin (1980). Predication. Linguistic Inquiry 11.203–38.

Williamson, Janet (1987). A indefiniteness restriction on relative clauses in Lakhota. The representation of (in)definiteness, ed. by E. Reuland and A. ter Meulen, 168–90. Cambridge, MA: MIT Press.

Witherspoon, Gary (1980). Language in culture and culture in language. International Journal of American Linguistics 46.1–13.

Wittgenstein, Ludwig (1974 [1918]). Tractatus logico-philosophicus. Atlantic Highlands, NJ: Humanities Press.

Wittgenstein, Ludwig (1953). Philosophical investigations. Oxford: Blackwell.

Wolfart, H. Christoph (1973). Plains Cree: A grammatical study. Philadelphia: American Philosophical Society.

Woodbury, Anthony (1986). The interactions of tense and evidentiality: A study of Sherpa and English. Evidentiality: The linguistic coding of epistemology, ed. by W. Chafe and J. Nichols, 188–202. Norwood, NJ: Ablex.

Woolford, Ellen (1984). Universals and rule options in kinship terminology: A synthesis of three formal approaches. American Ethnologist 11.711–90.

Zalta, Edward (1987). On the structural similarities between worlds and times. Philosophical Studies 51.213–39.

Ziff, Paul (1960). Semantic analysis. Ithaca, NY: Cornell University Press.

Zubin, David and Klaus Köpcke (1986). Gender and folk taxonomy: The indexical relation between grammatical and lexical categorization. Noun classes and categorization, ed. by C. Craig, 139–80. Amsterdam: Benjamins.

Author Index

513

Language Index

Families are listed in parentheses, preceded by further language designation, if necessary. Modern English (Indo-European) is not indexed separately because it appears throughout the book.

Subject Index